Zero to Hero
A Journey to Success

By: Mustafa Nejem

Dedication

This book is an ode to the countless dreamers who dared to defy limits and transform aspirations into global realities. To the resilient souls who navigate uncharted paths and embrace the challenges of entrepreneurship with unwavering determination – this dedication is a tribute to your courage. May the lessons within these pages fuel your journey and inspire the next generation of visionaries. Here's to the dreamers, the doers, and those who believe that from Zero to Hero is not just a destination but a transformative expedition

Foreword

In the following pages, the reader is about to embark on a transformative journey, guided by the profound insights and experiences encapsulated in "Zero to Hero." In this foreword, the narrative unfolds through a lens that observes the intricate tapestry of strategic scaling and entrepreneurial evolution. The reader is invited to explore the triumphs, challenges, and invaluable lessons that lie ahead, as seen from the perspective of those who have witnessed the journey from local to global. This foreword serves as an introduction to the rich narrative that awaits, offering a panoramic view of the resilience of human ambition and the profound impact of visionary leadership. Welcome to a literary expedition that transcends boundaries and charts the course from aspirations to achievements.

Preface

As the pen sets the first strokes on the canvas of "Zero to Hero," a narrative of transformation and triumph begins to unfold. In this preface, the reader is invited to delve into the author's perspective and the journey that led to the creation of this comprehensive guide. Here, the motivations behind distilling the complexities of entrepreneurial evolution into these pages are unveiled. The preface provides a glimpse into the commitment to offering a roadmap for those navigating the exciting yet challenging terrain of global business expansion.

Within these introductory pages, anticipate a fusion of practical strategies, real-world anecdotes, and foundational principles. The prelude sets the tone for an odyssey through the realms of strategic scaling, cultural navigation, and the resilience required to evolve from a local entity to a global force. Each turn of the page beckons the reader into a realm where entrepreneurial dreams meet practical guidance, and aspirations take shape in the crucible of international excellence.

As you embark on this literary journey, consider the preface a compass guiding you through the chapters that follow. It is an invitation to explore the intricacies of market dynamics, the art of adaptation, and the constant pursuit of innovation in a global context. Join the author on a voyage that transcends geographical boundaries and celebrates the spirit of those daring to dream big.

May the pages ahead unfold a tapestry of insights, offering not just a guide but a companion for entrepreneurs, business leaders, and enthusiasts alike. Welcome to the prelude of "Zero to Hero," where the story of scaling and success begins, and every reader is invited to play a vital role in the narrative of their own entrepreneurial journey.

Book Summary

"Zero to Hero" is a captivating journey into the heart of entrepreneurial ambition, unveiling the intricacies of transforming a humble startup into a global powerhouse. This book will walk you through the highs and lows, triumphs and tribulations, of a one-person operation's evolution into a multinational corporation, all while maintaining the agility and innovative spirit reminiscent of a startup.

In the introduction, readers are introduced to the alluring world of international expansion, tantalized by success stories and the promise of going global. From the outset, the narrative emphasizes the dream of a global enterprise, setting the stage for an inspiring narrative that unfolds in the subsequent chapters.

The initial chapters delve into the critical foundations required for global success. The reader is guided through the process of understanding core business values, identifying unique selling propositions, and mastering the local market. This emphasis on laying a robust foundation becomes the bedrock for the strategic scaling that follows.

As the narrative progresses, strategic planning takes center stage. Realistic goal-setting and the creation of a step-by-step expansion roadmap become the guiding lights for the entrepreneurial journey. The book delves deep into market research, emphasizing the importance of cultural intelligence when venturing into international markets. Through engaging anecdotes and practical insights, readers discover the nuances of analyzing target markets and navigating cultural differences.

The financial considerations for scaling up are explored in detail, covering the concept of funding expansion, managing currency risks, and ensuring financial compliance. Legal and regulatory navigation becomes a crucial chapter, tackling issues such as intellectual property rights and international trade laws.

The narrative seamlessly transitions to adapting products and services for global markets. From product localization to building flexibility into offerings, readers gain a comprehensive understanding of the dynamic landscape of international business. Crafting a universal brand identity and executing international marketing strategies take center stage in establishing an international brand.

Building and managing an international team, overcoming language barriers, and optimizing logistics and supply chain management are explored in subsequent chapters. The book expertly navigates the decision-making process between exporting and foreign direct investment, offering strategic insights into forming partnerships and alliances.

As the journey unfolds, the narrative dives into the realm of digital transformation and e-commerce strategies, illuminating the path to leveraging digital platforms for global reach. The importance of global customer service strategies, coupled with insights into technology and tools for international support, adds a layer of practicality to the narrative.

The book anticipates challenges on the global stage, addressing political and economic changes and emphasizing the necessity of maintaining agility and fostering innovation. Sustainability and corporate social responsibility take the spotlight, providing a blueprint for building a responsible multinational company.

Chapters on regulatory compliance and governance, talent acquisition, and data-driven decision-making seamlessly guide the reader through the complexities of a growing global enterprise. The narrative remains current with discussions on innovation and R&D, scalable tech infrastructure, and effective crisis management.

The final chapters culminate in a robust conclusion, recapping the entrepreneurial journey, synthesizing core principles, and underscoring the importance of business scalability and agility. Lessons in adaptability, maintaining a culture of innovation, and customer-centricity as a growth driver are articulated with actionable strategies. The evolution of company culture, adaptive leadership, financial fortitude, and the role of technology are explored, setting the stage for future challenges and opportunities.

In closing, "Zero to Hero" leaves the reader with inspiring words of encouragement and foresight, instilling confidence in the ability to replicate and adapt the success journey. This compelling narrative is not just a guide but a mentor, propelling entrepreneurs toward international excellence with a roadmap that transforms dreams into reality.

Table of Contents

Chapter 1

Introduction:
The Global Dream

At the heart of every innovative venture lies the entrepreneur – a trailblazer, risk-taker, and visionary who navigates uncharted territories in pursuit of success. An entrepreneur is not merely a business owner; rather, they embody the spirit of ingenuity, resilience, and an unyielding desire to create something meaningful. Whether starting a small local business or envisioning global dominance, the entrepreneur is the driving force behind transformative journeys.

Every entrepreneur wants to transcend the confines of their local markets and venture into the global arena. This compelling allure is fueled by a combination of strategic, economic, and aspirational factors, each playing a significant role in shaping the dreams of businesses worldwide.

Strategic Imperatives

Entrepreneurs, akin to modern-day pioneers, embark on a quest for expansion fueled by the vision of carving their niche on a global stage. Recognizing the inherent limitations of local markets, these visionary leaders cast their eyes upon the vast and uncharted potential of global territories. It is here, in the expansive canvas of the international market, that businesses can unfurl their unique value propositions on a scale unimaginable within the constraints of regional boundaries.

The allure of international expansion becomes a strategic imperative to position the business not merely as a local contender but as a formidable global force. This imperative is born out of the realization that growth, in its truest sense, requires breaking free from the confines of familiar landscapes and venturing into the unexplored realms where untapped markets await discovery.

As businesses extend their reach beyond domestic borders, strategic diversification emerges as a cornerstone of resilience in the face of uncertainty. The inherent risks associated with overreliance on a single market become apparent, prompting entrepreneurs to strategically diversify their presence across the global landscape.

The allure lies in creating a robust shield against economic fluctuations and unforeseen challenges that may befall a single market. The international arena becomes a strategic playing field where businesses strategically position themselves to weather storms by spreading their operational footprint. A diversified presence acts as a buffer, allowing businesses to navigate the tumultuous waters of economic uncertainties with greater agility and fortitude.

The strategic imperative for growth is, therefore, a multi-faceted gem that shines with the brilliance of calculated ambition. Entrepreneurs, fueled by the desire for expansion and market dominance, recognize the inherent limitations of local markets. The allure of global expansion is not just about conquering new territories; it is about strategically diversifying the business to withstand the unpredictable tides of the global economic landscape.

Access to Untapped Markets

Embarking on the journey of international expansion unveils a gateway to untapped markets, an opportunity that captivates entrepreneurs with the promise of uncharted possibilities. The allure of accessing previously undiscovered markets stems from the prospect of engaging with a vast pool of potential customers. This expanded reach opens doors to a diverse consumer base, each with its unique needs, preferences, and cultural nuances. The allure lies not only in the potential for increased revenue streams but also in the richness of cultural exchange that inherently accompanies global market penetration.

The core fascination for entrepreneurs lies in the prospect of breaking through geographical boundaries and establishing connections with consumers from different corners of the world. This access to diverse markets becomes a catalyst for fostering cultural exchange within the business ecosystem. Entrepreneurs recognize the invaluable opportunity to gain insights into varying consumer behaviors, cultural intricacies, and market dynamics. This enriching interplay of perspectives goes beyond mere financial gains, shaping the business with a global perspective that transcends regional limitations.

Entrepreneurs are inherently drawn to the idea of tapping into emerging economies, where burgeoning middle classes present unprecedented opportunities for growth. The allure intensifies as these visionary leaders envision themselves as pioneers, navigating uncharted territories and positioning their businesses as trailblazers. In emerging markets, where economic landscapes are evolving, entrepreneurs become architects of change, contributing to the shaping of consumer preferences and market trends. This strategic positioning not only allows for first-mover advantages but also positions the business as an innovative force in the global arena.

The allure of accessing untapped markets is further magnified by the opportunity to introduce novel products or services to regions where they have yet to make their mark. Entrepreneurs find inspiration in the prospect of being trailblazers in markets that may not have experienced their particular offerings before. This pioneering spirit not only fuels the entrepreneur's passion but also positions the business as an innovator on the global stage. The allure becomes a driving force for entrepreneurs to explore and capitalize on markets where their distinct value propositions can make a significant impact.

The access to untapped markets serves as a beacon for entrepreneurs, beckoning them towards a world of possibilities. The allure lies not only in the expansion of revenue streams but also in the cultural exchange that transforms businesses into global entities. Emerging economies present a fertile ground for growth, and the allure intensifies as entrepreneurs envision themselves as pioneers in markets ripe for innovation. The access to untapped markets becomes a transformative journey, where entrepreneurs not only tap into new customer bases but also shape the global landscape with their innovative contributions.

Competitive Edge and Innovation

Stepping onto the global stage is an entrepreneurial quest that places innovation and adaptability at the forefront. The allure of international expansion is intricately woven with the opportunity to not just keep pace with competitors but to surge ahead by introducing cutting-edge products, services, or business models that redefine industries and capture the imagination of consumers worldwide.

In the pursuit of international success, entrepreneurs recognize that standing out in a global marketplace demands a commitment to continuous innovation. The competitive edge lies not only in offering what is currently in demand but in anticipating future needs and trends. The dynamic nature of the global economy necessitates a mindset of perpetual evolution, where entrepreneurs become architects of change rather than passive participants in an ever-shifting landscape.

The allure of innovation in the global arena is underscored by the opportunity to outpace competitors, leaving an indelible mark on industries. Entrepreneurs aspire to be pioneers, introducing groundbreaking solutions that resonate with consumers across borders. The international expansion becomes a canvas for bold ideas, a platform where entrepreneurs can showcase their ability to anticipate market demands and steer their businesses toward the forefront of their respective industries.

Access to diverse talent pools globally amplifies the entrepreneur's aspiration for innovation. The allure lies in building a team that mirrors the global diversity of markets, bringing together individuals with a spectrum of skills, experiences, and perspectives. The infusion of diverse backgrounds and thought processes becomes a catalyst for creativity, propelling the business towards novel solutions and inventive approaches to challenges.

Entrepreneurs are drawn to the prospect of creating a workplace culture that fosters innovation and embraces creativity. The collaborative synergy born from a team with varied viewpoints cultivates an environment where ideas flourish and where every member contributes to the collective creativity of the organization. The competitive edge gained through this diversity is not only a strategic advantage but also a testament to the business's adaptability and resilience in the face of global challenges.

Positioning a business as an industry leader on a global scale requires more than just meeting market demands—it necessitates setting the pace for the industry's evolution. The competitive edge derived from a commitment to innovation becomes a powerful force that propels the business ahead of competitors. Entrepreneurs are not merely participants in the global marketplace; they become visionaries steering their enterprises towards the future.

The allure of international expansion is intricately intertwined with the entrepreneurial pursuit of a competitive edge through innovation. Stepping onto the global stage becomes a commitment to continuous evolution and a declaration that the business is not just a player but a leader in its industry. Access to diverse talent pools globally amplifies this aspiration, transforming the business into a hub of creativity and adaptability. The journey to a competitive edge and innovation in the global arena becomes not just a strategic move but a defining characteristic of the entrepreneurial spirit that propels businesses toward international excellence.

Networking and Collaborative Opportunities

Entrepreneurs, by nature, are adept networkers, weaving intricate webs of connections that propel their ventures forward. However, the allure of international expansion transforms this innate networking ability into a potent force, amplifying the collaborative spirit that defines their character. The global dream becomes a beacon, guiding entrepreneurs towards a world of endless possibilities, where establishing connections with other businesses, industry leaders, and potential partners on a global scale becomes not just an aspiration but a strategic imperative.

At the heart of the allure lies the prospect of delving into a global ecosystem where collaborative opportunities abound. Entrepreneurs recognize that the expansion beyond local boundaries opens doors to a myriad of possibilities for mutually beneficial ventures. The global stage becomes a canvas for fostering innovation and knowledge exchange, where businesses can leverage the collective strengths of diverse partners to achieve shared objectives.

Participating in a global ecosystem propels entrepreneurs into a realm where partnerships and alliances act as powerful catalysts for growth. The allure is not solely about expanding one's reach; it's about tapping into the collective intelligence and resources that a global network can offer. Entrepreneurs envision collaborative ventures that transcend geographical limitations, creating synergies that elevate their businesses to new heights.

The networking allure extends beyond the realm of business, encompassing cultural exchange and a profound understanding of the interconnected world in which their ventures operate. Entrepreneurs are drawn to the idea of breaking cultural barriers and forging connections that transcend borders. These connections not only provide strategic advantages but also enrich the entrepreneurial journey with a deeper appreciation for the diverse perspectives that shape the global business landscape.

In the pursuit of collaborative opportunities, entrepreneurs become architects of a global tapestry where innovative ideas seamlessly intertwine. The global dream becomes a conduit for the exchange of knowledge and expertise, fostering an environment where businesses can thrive through collaborative efforts. The allure of international expansion lies not just in individual success but in the collective achievements that arise from forging meaningful connections across continents.

The collaborative spirit unleashed by international networking becomes a driving force for entrepreneurs to explore uncharted territories. Beyond the allure of economic gains, entrepreneurs are motivated by the potential to contribute to a global community of innovators. Through collaborative ventures, they become agents of change, playing a role in shaping industries, influencing market trends, and contributing to the evolution of the global business landscape.

The allure of international expansion is intricately tied to the networking and collaborative opportunities it presents. Entrepreneurs, with their innate ability to forge connections, find themselves propelled into a global arena where partnerships become the lifeblood of growth. Beyond business gains, the networking allure extends into the cultural fabric of the interconnected world, enriching the entrepreneurial journey with diverse perspectives and collaborative triumphs that transcend geographical boundaries. The global dream, with its promise of expansive connections and shared ventures, beckons entrepreneurs to not only dream big but to collaborate on a scale that transforms their businesses into global entities.

The global entrepreneurial aspiration encapsulates a potent blend of strategic acumen, the quest for untapped opportunities, the drive for innovation, economic efficiency, and the allure of building a global network. As businesses set their sights beyond local borders, entrepreneurs embark on a journey where the pursuit of the global dream becomes a manifestation of their inherent spirit – one marked by resilience, ambition, and the unwavering belief in the transformative power of their ventures on a worldwide stage.

Triumphs: Inspiring Global Success Stories

Here, we will share stories that transcend borders and serve as beacons of inspiration for aspiring entrepreneurs. These businesses not only dared to dream globally but also flourished on the international stage, leaving an indelible mark on the business landscape.

Let's explore a mosaic of success stories that showcase the power of embracing the global dream.

Apple Inc.: A Global Tech Powerhouse

The rise of Apple Inc. from a garage-based startup to a global tech juggernaut represents a quintessential success story in the annals of international business. Established in 1976 by Steve Jobs, Steve Wozniak, and Ronald Wayne, Apple began its journey with a vision to bring cutting-edge computing technology to the masses. The company's evolution into a paragon of international success is a testament to its transformative impact on the tech industry.

Apple's story commenced in a modest garage in Cupertino, California, where the founders, driven by a passion for technology and innovation, assembled the first Apple I computer. This marked the inception of a company that would go on to redefine the consumer electronics landscape. The early years were characterized by the launch of the Apple II, a pioneering personal computer that laid the groundwork for the company's global ambitions.

Apple's triumph lies not only in its ability to create products but in crafting iconic experiences that resonate universally. The iPhone, introduced in 2007, became a game-changer in the mobile industry. Its sleek design, intuitive interface, and the App Store ecosystem redefined what consumers expected from a smartphone. The iPhone, with its continuous iterations, solidified Apple's position as an innovator at the forefront of mobile technology.

The iPad, launched in 2010, further extended Apple's reach by revolutionizing the tablet market. Its intuitive design and seamless integration with the Apple ecosystem contributed to its widespread adoption. Similarly, the Mac lineup, known for its sleek design and powerful performance, gained a dedicated global following, particularly in creative and professional circles.

Apple's success is inseparable from its unwavering commitment to innovation. The company has consistently pushed the boundaries of technology, introducing features and functionalities that set industry standards. The emphasis on design aesthetics, user experience, and seamless integration between hardware and software distinguishes Apple products in a competitive market.

Apple's triumph extends beyond individual product launches; it encompasses the creation of an entire ecosystem. The interconnected nature of Apple devices, coupled with services like iCloud and iTunes, has created a seamless digital experience for users. This holistic approach has contributed to the brand loyalty that Apple enjoys globally.

The global resonance of Apple's products is a testament to their universal appeal. Apple has transcended geographical boundaries, capturing the hearts of consumers across diverse cultures. The sleek and minimalist design philosophy, coupled with a focus on user-friendly interfaces, has made Apple products not just tools but lifestyle statements.

Apple's retail stores, with their distinctive architecture and immersive experiences, further contribute to the brand's global allure. The flagship Apple Store on Fifth Avenue in New York City or the striking Apple Park in Cupertino serves as physical embodiments of the company's commitment to excellence and innovation.

Apple Inc.'s journey from a garage startup to a global tech powerhouse is an inspirational saga of vision, innovation, and international success. The company's ability to create products with universal appeal, coupled with a commitment to pushing the boundaries of technology, has cemented its status as a paragon of excellence in the tech industry. Apple's triumph is not merely in the products it sells but in the transformative impact it has had on how the world interacts with technology.

Alibaba Group: Pioneering Global E-Commerce

In the vast landscape of international business, Alibaba Group emerges as a transformative force, showcasing the immense power of e-commerce on a global scale. Originating in China, Alibaba's ascent from a local e-commerce platform to a global marketplace giant stands as a testament to the vision of its founder, Jack Ma. His foresight and determination propelled Alibaba to become a central player in connecting businesses and consumers across borders, reshaping the landscape of international commerce.

Established in 1999 in Hangzhou, China, Alibaba was initially conceived as a platform to facilitate online trade for small and medium-sized enterprises (SMEs). Jack Ma, a former English teacher, envisioned a digital marketplace that would empower businesses, especially those without significant resources, to engage in global trade. This vision was a response to the challenges faced by Chinese SMEs in accessing international markets, and it marked the beginning of Alibaba's journey toward global prominence.

Alibaba's success story is intricately linked to its pioneering approach to e-commerce, characterized by platforms such as Alibaba.com, Taobao, and Tmall. Alibaba.com, launched in 1999, focused on facilitating global trade for businesses by providing a platform for buying and selling products. Taobao, introduced in 2003, targeted the consumer market, enabling individuals and small businesses to engage in online retail. Tmall, established in 2008, catered to brands and retailers looking to reach Chinese consumers in a growing and dynamic market.

Jack Ma's strategic vision went beyond creating an online marketplace; it aimed to foster an ecosystem where businesses of all sizes could thrive. Alibaba leveraged technological innovations, such as secure payment systems and logistics solutions, to streamline transactions and build trust among users. The introduction of Alipay, an online payment platform, further bolstered Alibaba's standing by providing a secure and efficient payment method for users worldwide.

The transformative power of Alibaba lies in its ability to bridge international commerce through digital platforms. Alibaba.com, in particular, emerged as a global hub for businesses seeking to expand their reach beyond domestic borders. The platform facilitated trade not only between Chinese suppliers and international buyers but also among businesses from various corners of the world. This interconnected marketplace played a pivotal role in democratizing global trade, allowing businesses regardless of size or location to participate in the global economy.

Alibaba's success extends to its foray into cloud computing, digital entertainment, and financial services through subsidiaries like Alibaba Cloud, Alibaba Pictures, and Ant Group, respectively. These diversifications reflect the company's adaptability and commitment to staying at the forefront of technological advancements, further solidifying its global influence.

The global triumph of Alibaba underscores the transformative potential of digital platforms in reshaping traditional models of commerce. The company's journey from a local e-commerce platform to a global powerhouse is a testament to the vision of Jack Ma and the agility of Alibaba Group in navigating the complexities of international business. In essence, Alibaba has not only pioneered global e-commerce but has become a symbol of the interconnected, borderless future of commerce in the digital age.

IKEA: Transforming Homes Globally with Scandinavian Ingenuity

IKEA, the iconic Swedish furniture giant, stands as a global trailblazer that revolutionized the retail landscape by exporting the essence of Scandinavian design principles to homes worldwide. Established in 1943 by Ingvar Kamprad, IKEA's journey from a small mail-order business to an international household name is marked by its distinctive flat-pack, self-assembly model—a model that has become a global phenomenon, making stylish and affordable furniture accessible to diverse markets.

At the core of IKEA's triumph is its unique approach to furniture retail, one that prioritizes simplicity, functionality, and affordability without compromising on aesthetics. The flat-pack model, where furniture is disassembled and packaged efficiently for customers to assemble at home, was a groundbreaking concept. This not only reduced transportation costs but also aligned with the brand's commitment to sustainability by minimizing packaging waste. The ingenious flat-pack design became synonymous with IKEA, shaping the company's identity and transforming the way people furnished their homes.

IKEA's success story extends beyond its innovative packaging concept. The furniture giant's ability to adapt its offerings to resonate with different cultural preferences is a key aspect of its triumph. While rooted in Swedish design principles, IKEA ensures that its products cater to the diverse tastes and needs of global consumers. From minimalist Scandinavian aesthetics to vibrant and eclectic designs, IKEA's product range reflects a cultural sensitivity that transcends borders.

The global appeal of IKEA's offerings is evident in its ability to merge affordability with quality and design. The brand has democratized good design, making it accessible to a wide range of consumers. The affordability of IKEA's products, coupled with a commitment to sustainability, has created a unique value proposition that resonates across diverse markets. Whether it's a small apartment in a bustling city or a suburban home, IKEA's furniture has found its place in households worldwide.

IKEA's global triumph is underpinned by its immersive retail experience. The sprawling blue-and-yellow stores, designed to showcase fully furnished rooms, invite customers to envision how IKEA products can fit seamlessly into their lives. The layout of the stores encourages exploration, turning the shopping experience into a journey of inspiration and creativity. The in-store cafés offering Swedish specialties contribute to the immersive experience, making a visit to IKEA more than just a shopping trip—it becomes an event.

The brand's adaptability is further emphasized by its commitment to sustainability and eco-friendly practices. IKEA has actively sought to reduce its environmental impact by using sustainable materials, investing in renewable energy, and promoting recycling initiatives. This commitment aligns with the values of modern consumers who prioritize ethical and environmentally conscious choices, contributing to IKEA's ongoing success in an evolving retail landscape.

IKEA's triumph on the global stage is a testament to its ability to blend Scandinavian design principles with a keen understanding of diverse cultural preferences. The flat-pack, self-assembly model has not only made stylish and affordable furniture accessible worldwide but has also transformed the way people approach furnishing their homes. By marrying innovation with cultural sensitivity and sustainability, IKEA has become more than a furniture retailer; it's a global influencer shaping the way we live and interact with our living spaces.

Toyota: Driving Global Excellence with Japanese Precision

Toyota, a symbol of Japan's economic prowess, stands as a paradigm of international success that reaches far beyond its origins. The journey of Toyota from a modest beginning to a global automotive giant is not just a testament to the company's prowess but a showcase of how a firm deeply rooted in its national identity can attain international acclaim. Established in 1937 by Kiichiro Toyoda, Toyota's trajectory has been marked by a steadfast commitment to quality, innovation, and pioneering efficient production methods.

At the heart of Toyota's global triumph lies an unwavering dedication to producing high-quality vehicles. The Japanese automaker has long been synonymous with reliability and durability, setting industry standards for manufacturing excellence. The introduction of the Toyota Production System (TPS) revolutionized the automotive industry by pioneering lean manufacturing principles, emphasizing efficiency, minimizing waste, and ensuring continuous improvement. TPS not only streamlined Toyota's operations but became a benchmark for efficiency across industries globally.

Innovation has been a driving force behind Toyota's global leadership in the automotive sector. The introduction of the Toyota Corolla in 1966 marked a milestone, becoming one of the best-selling cars globally and exemplifying the brand's commitment to producing vehicles that cater to diverse consumer needs. Additionally, Toyota's pioneering efforts in hybrid technology with the launch of the Prius in 1997 demonstrated a forward-thinking approach to sustainability, setting the stage for the widespread adoption of hybrid vehicles worldwide.

Efficient production methods, coupled with a dedication to innovation, positioned Toyota as a global leader in the automotive industry. The company's commitment to continuous improvement and adaptability allowed it to navigate through changing market dynamics and consumer preferences. Toyota's success was not confined to its domestic market; it successfully transcended geographical boundaries, becoming a symbol of quality and efficiency in countries across the globe.

Toyota's triumph extends beyond producing vehicles; it encapsulates a profound understanding of the global market and a commitment to localization. The company strategically adapts its products to cater to the diverse needs and preferences of consumers in different regions. This approach has not only contributed to Toyota's global success but has also reinforced the brand's image as a responsive and customer-centric automaker.

The global resonance of Toyota is also mirrored in its extensive network of manufacturing and assembly plants worldwide. By establishing a strong local presence, Toyota has not only streamlined its production processes but has also contributed to the economic development of the regions where it operates. This approach reflects Toyota's commitment to being an integral part of the communities it serves, transcending the boundaries of a traditional automotive manufacturer.

Toyota's journey from a Japanese startup to a global automotive powerhouse is a narrative of quality, innovation, and efficient production methods. The brand's commitment to its national identity, coupled with an open-minded approach to global markets, has allowed Toyota to achieve international acclaim. Toyota's triumph is not just a testament to its manufacturing prowess but also to its ability to navigate the complexities of the global automotive landscape while staying true to its roots. As a symbol of Japanese precision, Toyota continues to drive the future of mobility with a global perspective and unwavering commitment to excellence.

Samsung: A South Korean Conglomerate's Global Odyssey

Emerging from the vibrant landscape of South Korea, Samsung has evolved from a local trading company to a global conglomerate, exemplifying the transformative power of diversification in navigating international markets. Founded in 1938 by Lee Byung-chul, Samsung's journey encompasses diverse sectors, including electronics, shipbuilding, finance, and more. The conglomerate's triumph is rooted in its exceptional agility to adapt to changing global demands and its ability to explore and excel in a spectrum of industries.

Samsung's global ascendancy is most prominently associated with its role in the electronics industry. The company ventured into the world of consumer electronics, beginning with the production of black-and-white televisions in the 1970s. The release of innovative products, such as the Samsung Galaxy smartphones and high-quality LED TVs, solidified Samsung's position as a global technology leader. Its commitment to pushing technological boundaries and investing heavily in research and development allowed Samsung to not only keep pace with the evolving tech landscape but often set new standards.

However, Samsung's triumph goes beyond the realm of electronics. The conglomerate's diversification strategy encompasses a broad spectrum of industries, showcasing its ability to excel in various sectors. From shipbuilding, where Samsung Heavy Industries has been a global player, to finance, with Samsung Life Insurance and Samsung Securities, the conglomerate strategically expanded its portfolio. This diversification not only mitigated risks associated with industry-specific challenges but also positioned Samsung as a multifaceted global player.

The power of Samsung's success lies in its agility to adapt to dynamic global demands. In the rapidly changing landscape of technology and industry, Samsung has consistently demonstrated a forward-thinking approach, anticipating shifts and proactively aligning its strategies. Whether it's embracing new trends in consumer preferences or investing in emerging technologies like artificial intelligence and 5G, Samsung's adaptability has been a key driver of its triumph on the global stage.

Samsung's global journey also highlights the significance of strategic partnerships and collaborations. By forming alliances with other international businesses and forging strategic partnerships, Samsung has strengthened its position in various markets. Collaborations with software developers, telecommunications companies, and content providers have contributed to Samsung's ability to offer comprehensive solutions that resonate with diverse consumer needs.

Furthermore, Samsung's commitment to corporate social responsibility and sustainable practices has reinforced its global standing. Initiatives addressing environmental concerns, labor practices, and community engagement reflect a holistic approach to business that resonates with modern consumers. Samsung's recognition of its responsibility beyond profit margins has contributed to building a positive brand image globally.

Samsung's triumph as a global conglomerate is a testament to its capacity for diversification, adaptability, and strategic foresight. From its origins as a local trading company, Samsung has navigated the complexities of international markets, excelling in diverse industries. The conglomerate's ability to anticipate and respond to changing global demands has not only secured its position as a technology giant but has also shaped its identity as a multifaceted global player. Samsung's journey continues to be a dynamic narrative of innovation, diversification, and global resilience in an ever-evolving business landscape.

Coca-Cola: A Global Icon's Bubbly Triumph

The red-and-white logo of Coca-Cola serves as an emblem recognized in nearly every corner of the globe, encapsulating the success story of a beverage giant that has mastered the art of creating a universally appealing product while adapting marketing strategies to diverse cultural contexts. Established in 1886 by John Stith Pemberton, Coca-Cola's journey is not just about quenching thirst but about crafting a brand that transcends borders, illustrating the potency of building a globally recognized icon.

At the heart of Coca-Cola's global triumph lies the creation of a product with universal appeal. The signature Coca-Cola formula, concocted with a secret blend of flavors, has become more than just a beverage; it's a cultural phenomenon. The distinct taste, effervescence, and iconic contour bottle have made Coca-Cola a symbol of joy, celebration, and refreshment across different continents. The company's commitment to maintaining the consistency and quality of its product has contributed to the enduring loyalty of consumers worldwide.

Coca-Cola's success story is intertwined with its adeptness in adapting marketing strategies to diverse cultural contexts. While the brand's essence remains consistent, Coca-Cola has mastered the art of tailoring its messaging to resonate with local tastes, traditions, and lifestyles. The "Share a Coke" campaign, for instance, involved personalizing Coca-Cola bottles with individual names, connecting the brand to consumers on a personal level and creating a sense of inclusivity.

The company's global marketing efforts extend to sponsorship of major events, such as the FIFA World Cup and the Olympics, reinforcing its presence in diverse cultural landscapes. Coca-Cola's iconic holiday campaigns, featuring the jolly figure of Santa Claus, have become a cultural phenomenon, transcending cultural boundaries and becoming synonymous with festive joy around the world. These strategies reflect Coca-Cola's understanding that while the product itself may be universal, the way it is perceived and embraced is deeply rooted in local cultures.

Coca-Cola's triumph as a globally recognized brand is not solely based on its product and marketing strategies; it is also built on a commitment to social responsibility. The company has undertaken initiatives to address environmental concerns, water conservation, and community development. By aligning itself with societal values and addressing global challenges, Coca-Cola has fostered a positive brand image that resonates with consumers who seek brands with a sense of purpose.

The global resonance of Coca-Cola is also reflected in its distribution and availability. The brand's products can be found in remote villages, bustling metropolises, and nearly every establishment in between. Coca-Cola's ability to establish a ubiquitous presence is a testament to its effective supply chain management and distribution strategies, ensuring accessibility to consumers in diverse geographical locations.

Coca-Cola's triumph on the global stage is a multifaceted narrative that goes beyond the realms of a carbonated beverage. It's a story of crafting a universally appealing product, adapting marketing strategies to diverse cultural contexts, and embracing social responsibility. The iconic red-and-white logo has become more than a symbol of a refreshing drink; it represents a global experience of joy, connection, and celebration. Coca-Cola's journey continues to be a sparkling example of how building a globally recognized brand requires a harmonious blend of consistency, adaptability, and a commitment to shared values.

Amazon: A Digital Disruptor's Global Odyssey

From its humble beginnings as an online bookstore to its current status as an e-commerce juggernaut, Amazon's journey stands as a beacon of the transformative impact of digital disruption on a global scale. Founded in 1994 by Jeff Bezos, Amazon's trajectory epitomizes the evolution of a business model that has reshaped the retail landscape and transcended traditional boundaries. Jeff Bezos's visionary leadership catapulted Amazon into a one-stop-shop for diverse consumer needs, showcasing the potential for disruptive business models to thrive internationally.

At the core of Amazon's global triumph is its ability to leverage digital technologies to redefine the way people shop. The company's pivot from books to a vast array of products, coupled with the introduction of the Kindle e-reader and Amazon Prime, marked strategic steps in expanding its footprint. Amazon's commitment to customer-centricity, convenience, and innovation became the driving forces behind its success, creating a seamless and efficient online shopping experience for millions of consumers.

Amazon's global impact extends beyond e-commerce; it encompasses diverse sectors such as cloud computing, entertainment, and artificial intelligence. Amazon Web Services (AWS), launched in 2006, revolutionized the cloud computing industry, providing scalable and cost-effective solutions to businesses globally. Additionally, ventures like Amazon Prime Video and Amazon Echo demonstrate the company's ability to diversify its offerings, catering to evolving consumer demands and shaping the future of digital services.

The global resonance of Amazon is also attributed to its adaptive approach to diverse markets. The company has expanded its operations internationally, tailoring its strategies to local preferences and regulatory landscapes. Amazon's acquisition of local e-commerce platforms, such as Souq in the Middle East and Flipkart in India, reflects its commitment to understanding and integrating with regional dynamics. This adaptability has enabled Amazon to not only enter but thrive in various markets worldwide.

Amazon's triumph is not only in disrupting traditional retail but also in redefining the logistics and supply chain landscape. The introduction of Amazon Prime with its two-day shipping guarantee set a new standard for delivery speed and efficiency. The company's investment in logistics infrastructure, including fulfillment centers and delivery networks, has not only accelerated shipping times but has also influenced customer expectations globally, shaping the logistics industry at large.

Furthermore, Amazon's foray into artificial intelligence, exemplified by its virtual assistant Alexa, demonstrates its commitment to staying at the forefront of technological advancements. The integration of AI into consumer devices showcases Amazon's vision for a connected and intelligent future, influencing how people interact with technology in their daily lives.

Amazon's success story is also intertwined with its focus on fostering a culture of innovation. The company encourages experimentation and risk-taking, leading to ventures like Amazon Go, a cashier-less retail experience, and initiatives in drone delivery technology. This commitment to innovation has not only kept Amazon ahead of competitors but has also positioned it as a trendsetter, setting industry benchmarks across multiple sectors.

Amazon's journey from an online bookstore to a global e-commerce and technology giant is a testament to the transformative impact of digital disruption. Jeff Bezos's visionary leadership, coupled with the company's commitment to customer-centricity, innovation, and adaptability, has propelled Amazon to the forefront of global commerce. As a disruptive force that reshaped industries and redefined consumer expectations, Amazon's odyssey continues to influence the ever-evolving landscape of business and technology on a global scale.

Zara: Revolutionizing Fashion with Swift Innovation

Originating from Spain, Zara has not just entered but revolutionized the fashion industry by introducing a fast-fashion model that set new standards for agility and responsiveness. Founded in 1974 by Amancio Ortega and Rosalía Mera, Zara's journey exemplifies the transformative impact of a business model centered around swift responses to changing fashion trends, delivering affordable, trendy clothing to a global customer base. Zara's triumph underscores the significance of flexibility and responsiveness in the fast-paced world of international fashion.

At the heart of Zara's global success is its unique approach to fast fashion. Unlike traditional fashion retailers, Zara prioritizes speed and adaptability, enabling the brand to swiftly translate runway trends into accessible, affordable clothing for consumers. The company's vertically integrated supply chain and in-house production capabilities empower Zara to design, produce, and distribute new collections at an unprecedented pace. This model has not only disrupted the traditional fashion calendar but has also set a benchmark for the industry.

Zara's success lies in its ability to anticipate and respond to consumer preferences with remarkable speed. The brand's design and production cycles are incredibly condensed, allowing Zara to bring new styles to stores within weeks. This agility is further enhanced by the incorporation of customer feedback and real-time sales data into the design process. Zara's commitment to understanding and adapting to rapidly changing consumer preferences has contributed to its ability to stay ahead of competitors and cater to a diverse global audience.

The global triumph of Zara is also attributed to its distribution strategy. The brand strategically locates its production facilities close to key markets, enabling faster turnaround times and reducing lead times. Zara's distribution centers act as hubs for shipping products to stores worldwide quickly. This proximity-driven approach not only ensures that Zara can respond swiftly to regional fashion demands but also minimizes excess inventory and waste.

Zara's retail strategy emphasizes the creation of an in-store experience that complements its fast-fashion model. The stores themselves serve as an extension of the brand's commitment to responsiveness. Zara stores are designed to be flexible, allowing for rapid changes to the layout and product displays. Limited quantities of each style are stocked, creating a sense of exclusivity and urgency for consumers. This dynamic retail approach contributes to the overall narrative of Zara as a brand that embraces change and innovation.

Furthermore, Zara's success on the global stage is evident in its international expansion strategy. The brand strategically enters new markets, tailoring its offerings to local tastes and preferences. Zara's ability to cater to a diverse range of consumers globally while maintaining its core identity reflects an understanding of the importance of cultural sensitivity and adaptability in the fashion industry.

In conclusion, Zara's triumph in the fashion industry is a testament to the transformative power of a fast-fashion model centered around flexibility and responsiveness. The brand's ability to swiftly translate runway trends into accessible clothing for a global audience has reshaped industry norms. Zara's success narrative underscores the significance of adaptability, innovation, and a customer-centric approach in navigating the fast-paced and ever-evolving world of international fashion. As a disruptor that has set new benchmarks for the industry, Zara continues to influence how fashion is produced, consumed, and experienced on a global scale.

These exemplary triumphs underline that success on the international stage is not confined by geographical boundaries. Instead, it is rooted in visionary leadership, adaptability, and the ability to create products and strategies that resonate with diverse audiences. Aspiring entrepreneurs can draw inspiration from these global success stories, recognizing that the pursuit of the global dream is not just a possibility but a pathway to transformative achievements.

The Strategic Appeal of Going Global

The decision to go global is not merely a geographical expansion; it's a strategic leap that holds immense promise and potential for businesses seeking to transcend local markets. This strategic appeal is rooted in the recognition that venturing beyond borders offers a multitude of advantages, shaping a company's trajectory towards sustained growth and influence. Let's unravel the strategic allure of going global by investigating five promises and potential inherent in this pivotal decision.

Market Expansion and Diversification

The strategic decision to expand into global markets brings forth a promise of accessing an expansive marketplace that extends beyond the confines of local territories. In the realm of market expansion, the potential for businesses is vast and transformative. The promise lies in the opportunity to tap into new customer bases and demographics, reaching individuals and communities that may have unique needs, preferences, and demands. This expansive reach goes beyond the saturation points of local markets, offering businesses the chance to introduce their products or services to a diverse global audience.

Simultaneously, the potential inherent in market expansion manifests through diversification. Diversifying market presence becomes a strategic move that hedges against economic fluctuations and mitigates risks associated with dependence on specific regions. By entering new markets, businesses create a portfolio of revenue streams that are not singularly tied to the economic conditions of a particular locale. This diversification acts as a risk management strategy, providing a buffer against challenges or downturns in specific regions and enhancing the overall resilience of the business.

The promise of market expansion aligns with the aspiration to grow revenue streams by tapping into the untapped potential of global markets. New customer bases represent fresh opportunities for sales and engagement, and the broader demographic landscape allows businesses to tailor their offerings to different cultural contexts. This promise is particularly attractive to businesses aiming for sustained growth and seeking avenues beyond the limitations of local market saturation.

Additionally, the potential of diversification addresses the strategic need for a well-rounded and resilient business model. Economic fluctuations and regional uncertainties can impact businesses significantly. However, by diversifying market presence across different regions, industries, or consumer segments, companies position themselves to navigate challenges more effectively. The potential for reduced dependence on specific regions is not just a risk management strategy but also a proactive step towards creating a more adaptable and agile business structure.

The strategic appeal of market expansion and diversification extends to various industries and sectors, from retail and technology to manufacturing and services. The promise of accessing new customer bases on a global scale and the potential for diversifying market presence resonate as key drivers for businesses seeking sustained growth and strategic resilience. As companies venture into the intricate landscape of global markets, the synergy of promise and potential in market expansion becomes a dynamic force, propelling businesses towards a future where growth is not confined to local boundaries but spans the diverse horizons of a global marketplace.

Strategic Resource Access

The promise of strategic resource access commences with the prospect of tapping into diverse talent pools. As companies expand their operations globally, they gain the ability to attract and harness the skills and expertise of individuals from different cultural, educational, and professional backgrounds. This promises not only a broader perspective but also a pool of talent that brings varied insights and innovative thinking to the table. The global stage becomes a canvas for assembling a team with a spectrum of skills, fostering a culture of innovation and creativity that is crucial for staying competitive in today's dynamic business landscape.

In addition to talent, the promise extends to accessing innovative technologies that may be at the forefront of development in certain regions. Going global allows companies to integrate groundbreaking technologies into their operations, leveraging advancements that may not be readily available in their domestic markets. This infusion of technology holds the potential to enhance efficiency, streamline processes, and catalyze innovation across various facets of the business.

Moreover, the promise encompasses the availability of raw materials essential for production. Different regions boast different natural resources, and by going global, companies can strategically position themselves to access these resources more efficiently. This not only aids in cost management but also ensures a more stable supply chain, reducing the vulnerability to disruptions caused by regional constraints or fluctuations in resource availability.

The potential inherent in strategic resource access is realized through the enhancement of a company's competitive edge. Accessing resources globally fosters an environment where innovation becomes a cornerstone of sustainable growth. The infusion of diverse perspectives, technologies, and materials sparks creativity and adaptability, enabling companies to stay ahead in rapidly evolving markets. This potential is particularly significant in industries where staying at the forefront of innovation is synonymous with maintaining a competitive advantage.

Furthermore, the global accessibility of resources contributes to more efficient production processes. By strategically sourcing materials and expertise from different regions, companies optimize their supply chains, reduce production costs, and enhance overall operational efficiency. The potential for efficiency gains becomes a driving force behind the decision to go global, aligning with the broader strategic goal of building a resilient and adaptable business model.

The strategic appeal of going global, specifically in terms of resource access, unfolds as a transformative journey. The promise of tapping into diverse talent, innovative technologies, and essential raw materials harmonizes with the potential to elevate a company's competitive edge. As businesses embark on the global stage, the synergy of promise and potential in strategic resource access becomes a dynamic catalyst for growth, innovation, and the creation of a globally competitive and resilient enterprise.

Brand Recognition and Reputation Enhancement

The strategic decision to expand internationally holds the promise of elevating brand recognition to new heights and establishing a positive reputation on a global scale. This promise, coupled with the potential for reputation enhancement, becomes a compelling force, offering businesses the opportunity to not only capture attention but to build lasting credibility and trust among diverse stakeholders on the global stage.

Brand recognition, at its core, is the extent to which a brand's name, logo, or other visual elements are easily identified and associated with the products or services it offers. It transcends mere awareness; it's about creating a distinctive mark in the minds of consumers that goes beyond borders and cultural nuances. Achieving brand recognition on a global scale is a multifaceted endeavor that requires a strategic blend of consistent messaging, impactful visual identity, and an unwavering commitment to delivering value.

One of the primary ways to achieve brand recognition is through a cohesive and consistent brand identity. This involves maintaining uniformity in visual elements such as logos, color schemes, and typography across all communication channels. Consistency breeds familiarity, and as consumers encounter a brand consistently across different regions and platforms, the likelihood of recognition increases. The promise of expanding internationally aligns with the goal of creating a visual identity that transcends linguistic and cultural barriers, resonating with a diverse global audience.

Moreover, achieving brand recognition necessitates strategic marketing efforts that tailor messages to suit different cultural contexts while maintaining core brand values. Understanding the nuances of diverse markets and adapting marketing campaigns accordingly positions the brand as culturally sensitive and relatable. This adaptive approach contributes to the promise of elevating brand recognition by ensuring that the brand's narrative is not only heard but also understood and embraced across the diverse landscapes of an international audience.

The potential for reputation enhancement is intricately linked to the strength of brand recognition. A strong international presence, built on consistent messaging and cultural adaptability, contributes to brand credibility. Consumers worldwide are more likely to trust and engage with a brand that has a recognized and respected identity. A positive reputation becomes a key driver for attracting a more diverse and loyal customer base, fostering brand advocacy, and increasing the likelihood of sustained success in the global market.

Additionally, reputation enhancement extends to stakeholders beyond consumers, including investors, partners, and employees. A brand with a positive global reputation becomes an attractive prospect for collaborations and partnerships, facilitating business growth and market expansion. Furthermore, a positive reputation enhances the brand's ability to attract top talent globally, contributing to the creation of a motivated and skilled workforce that aligns with the brand's values.

The strategic appeal of brand recognition and reputation enhancement in the global arena is not merely about visibility; it's about crafting a global identity that transcends geographical boundaries. Achieving this involves a meticulous blend of consistent brand messaging, cultural adaptability, and a commitment to delivering value that resonates universally. As businesses expand internationally, the promise of elevated brand recognition and the potential for enhanced reputation become integral components of a journey towards building a resilient and revered global brand.

Economies of Scale and Cost Efficiencies

Economies of scale are a fundamental concept in business strategy, representing the cost advantages that a business can achieve when production output increases. This concept is particularly relevant in the context of global operations, where the promise lies in the potential to leverage economies of scale to drive down production costs and enhance overall operational efficiency. The journey towards global expansion holds the commitment to optimizing production processes and realizing cost efficiencies, creating a pathway for businesses to not only compete more effectively but also to generate increased profitability that can fuel further expansion and innovation.

The promise encapsulated in economies of scale emanates from the idea that as a company's production output increases, the average cost per unit of production decreases. This decline in average costs occurs due to the distribution of fixed costs over a larger number of units. Fixed costs, such as machinery, facilities, and technology infrastructure, remain constant regardless of production volume. Therefore, when these fixed costs are spread across a higher number of units, the per-unit fixed cost decreases, contributing to overall cost savings.

Global operations offer a fertile ground for realizing economies of scale on a grand scale. As businesses expand their reach across borders, they often experience an uptick in production volume to meet the demands of diverse markets. This increased production volume becomes a catalyst for achieving economies of scale, driving down costs associated with manufacturing, distribution, and other operational facets. The potential lies in the strategic alignment of production processes with the demands of a global market, ensuring that scale is leveraged effectively to optimize costs.

The potential for cost efficiencies gained through global operations is not confined to the immediate reduction in production costs. Beyond the direct impact on production expenses, achieving economies of scale contributes to increased overall operational efficiency. Streamlining production processes to meet global demands requires a meticulous evaluation and improvement of supply chain logistics, technology infrastructure, and workforce capabilities. This optimization, in turn, enhances the efficiency of the entire business operation, enabling a smoother and more agile global workflow.

Moreover, the promise of economies of scale aligns with the potential for increased profitability. As production costs decrease, the profit margins on each unit sold increase. This enhanced profitability becomes a strategic asset, providing businesses with the financial resources needed for further expansion and innovation. The potential for increased profitability extends beyond immediate gains, creating a cycle where the cost efficiencies realized through global operations serve as a springboard for sustained growth and strategic investments.

Economies of scale and cost efficiencies are integral components of the strategic appeal of global operations. The promise of driving down production costs and enhancing operational efficiency resonates with the potential to not only compete effectively in the global market but also to generate increased profitability. As businesses navigate the complexities of global expansion, the dynamics of economies of scale become a key driver in shaping a resilient and financially robust pathway towards sustained success and innovation.

Strategic Learning and Adaptability

Operating on a global scale exposes companies to a kaleidoscope of consumer behaviors, cultural nuances, and market trends, providing a unique promise—the promise of strategic learning. This promise, coupled with the potential for adaptability, becomes a dynamic force, positioning companies to not only stay ahead of industry trends but also to anticipate changes and respond effectively to the ever-evolving demands of the global market.

Diverse markets are not homogenous landscapes but rather intricate ecosystems shaped by the interplay of cultural, economic, and social factors. The promise of strategic learning emerges as businesses immerse themselves in this diversity, gaining firsthand experience in understanding the distinct behaviors and preferences of consumers in different regions. Learning from these interactions becomes a strategic asset, providing businesses with valuable insights into the intricacies of consumer decision-making, purchasing patterns, and brand perceptions.

Cultural nuances, another facet of the promise of strategic learning, present businesses with the opportunity to adapt their strategies to resonate with local sensibilities. Every market has its unique cultural context, and businesses that embrace and understand these cultural nuances position themselves to forge deeper connections with consumers. This cultural adaptability is not only a demonstration of sensitivity but also a strategic move to align products, services, and marketing messages with the values and expectations of diverse audiences.

The potential inherent in strategic learning extends beyond consumer dynamics to encompass a profound understanding of market trends. As businesses navigate diverse markets, they become attuned to the ever-evolving landscape of global industries. This heightened awareness positions companies to stay ahead of emerging trends, capitalize on new opportunities, and proactively address challenges. The promise of strategic learning, therefore, becomes a compass that guides companies through the intricate maze of industry evolution.

Adaptability, as the potential counterpart to strategic learning, is the application of insights gained from diverse markets to evolve and tailor business strategies. The ability to adapt strategically is crucial in a global context where change is constant. Companies that can seamlessly integrate the lessons learned from diverse markets into their operational frameworks become agile entities capable of responding effectively to shifts in consumer preferences, economic conditions, and industry dynamics.

The strategic positioning that comes with the potential for adaptability is not just reactive but anticipatory. Businesses equipped with strategic adaptability are better prepared to anticipate changes in the global market, enabling them to proactively shape their strategies to align with emerging trends. This foresight becomes a competitive advantage, positioning companies as trendsetters rather than followers in the ever-evolving landscape of the global marketplace.

The strategic appeal of operating in diverse markets lies in the promise of strategic learning and adaptability. The rich insights gained from understanding consumer behaviors, cultural nuances, and market trends become a catalyst for adaptability, positioning companies to stay ahead and respond effectively to the dynamic demands of the global market. As businesses embark on the journey of global expansion, the synergy between the promise of strategic learning and the potential for adaptability becomes a transformative force, shaping a pathway towards sustained success and resilience in the global business arena.

Navigating Challenges

Embarking on the journey of global expansion, while holding the promise of unparalleled growth, innovation, and market reach, is not without its set of intricate challenges. Navigating these challenges becomes an integral aspect of the pursuit of the global dream, requiring businesses to navigate through a landscape fraught with complexities, uncertainties, and diverse hurdles.

One of the foremost challenges lies in understanding and navigating the intricacies of diverse regulatory landscapes. Different countries operate under varied legal frameworks, trade policies, and regulatory standards. For businesses expanding globally, this diversity poses a significant challenge. Navigating the maze of international trade laws, compliance requirements, and intellectual property regulations demands a meticulous approach. Failure to do so can lead to legal complications, financial penalties, and reputational damage. A poignant example is the experience of multinational corporations dealing with data protection regulations, such as the General Data Protection Regulation (GDPR) in the European Union. Ensuring compliance with such regulations while maintaining operational efficiency is a delicate balancing act that requires a deep understanding of international legal nuances.

Currency risk and financial compliance pose additional hurdles. Operating across borders exposes businesses to fluctuations in currency values. These fluctuations can impact the cost of goods, profitability, and overall financial stability. Strategic financial planning becomes imperative to mitigate these risks. Furthermore, adhering to financial compliance standards in different jurisdictions adds complexity. A failure to understand and comply with financial regulations can result in financial losses, legal repercussions, and damage to a company's reputation. For instance, companies engaged in international trade need to navigate complex tax structures and ensure compliance with financial reporting standards in each market they operate, requiring robust financial management strategies.

Language barriers present a multifaceted challenge in global expansion. Effective communication is the cornerstone of successful international operations, but linguistic diversity can impede this. A miscommunication or misunderstanding due to language differences can lead to operational inefficiencies, strained relationships with stakeholders, and even reputational damage. Multinational companies often encounter language challenges in customer support, marketing campaigns, and internal communication. For example, an advertising campaign that fails to accurately translate cultural nuances or language intricacies can result in unintended messages, impacting brand perception negatively.

Cultural differences and consumer behavior add another layer of complexity. Understanding and adapting to diverse cultural contexts is paramount for businesses aiming for international success. Consumer preferences, purchasing behaviors, and societal norms can vary significantly from one market to another. The challenge is not just in recognizing these differences but also in strategically adapting products, services, and marketing approaches to resonate with each unique cultural landscape. McDonald's, a global fast-food giant, provides an illustrative example. The company successfully navigates diverse cultural preferences by adapting its menu to cater to local tastes in various countries. The challenge lies in striking the right balance between global brand consistency and local cultural adaptation.

Logistics and supply chain management become intricate challenges when expanding globally. Streamlining international shipping, managing a global supply chain network, and ensuring timely and efficient distribution demand meticulous planning. Delays, disruptions, or inefficiencies in the supply chain can result in increased costs, dissatisfied customers, and operational setbacks. E-commerce companies, for instance, face challenges in optimizing their supply chain networks to meet the demands of diverse markets with varying infrastructures and regulatory requirements.

Political instability and economic fluctuations present yet another set of challenges. Businesses operating globally must navigate the uncertainties arising from political changes, trade disputes, and economic fluctuations in different regions. A sudden shift in political climate or economic downturn can impact market conditions, consumer spending patterns, and overall business stability. An example is the impact of Brexit on businesses operating in the United Kingdom and the European Union. Companies had to adapt to new trade regulations and economic uncertainties, requiring strategic agility and risk management.

The pursuit of the global dream is a journey rife with challenges and hurdles that demand strategic foresight, adaptability, and resilience. From navigating diverse regulatory landscapes to addressing language barriers, cultural differences, and logistical complexities, businesses expanding globally must confront a myriad of complexities. Successful global expansion requires not only a clear understanding of these challenges but also proactive strategies to overcome them. The ability to navigate these challenges effectively becomes a defining factor in the success of businesses seeking to realize the promise of the global dream.

Chapter **2**

Laying the Foundations

In the pursuit of global expansion, laying a strong foundation becomes the bedrock for sustained success. In this chapter, we will walk you through the crucial phase of establishing the groundwork for international growth. It explores the intricate process of understanding and fortifying core business values, coupled with the identification of a unique selling proposition (USP) that sets a company apart in the global marketplace. This chapter will guide you in laying the foundations that will withstand the complexities of diverse markets and propel them toward the realization of the global dream.

Defining Core Business Values

At the heart of every successful global enterprise lies a set of core business values that serve as the guiding principles shaping its identity and operations. Business values represent the fundamental beliefs that underpin an organization's culture, ethics, and decision-making processes. Defining core business values is a critical step in unraveling the essence of a company's identity, and aligning operations with these values creates a robust foundation for global expansion.

Business values encompass a range of principles that reflect the company's commitment to integrity, innovation, customer satisfaction, social responsibility, and more. These values are not merely a list of abstract concepts; rather, they form the ethical and cultural framework that influences how employees interact, how decisions are made, and how the company is perceived by stakeholders.

The benefits of having well-defined core business values are manifold, especially in the context of global expansion. Firstly, they serve as a compass for decision-making. For instance, if one of the core values is transparency, the company is guided to prioritize openness and honesty in its operations, promoting trust among employees, customers, and partners. This trust becomes a cornerstone for successful global ventures where transparency and integrity are crucial.

For example, the outdoor apparel company Patagonia has defined environmental sustainability as one of its core values. This commitment is reflected not only in its products but also in the company's business practices, including initiatives to reduce its environmental footprint and support environmental causes. The seamless integration of this value has not only contributed to Patagonia's success but also positioned it as a leader in sustainable business practices on a global scale.

Secondly, well-defined values foster a cohesive company culture. When employees share a common set of values, it creates a sense of unity and purpose. This shared culture becomes even more vital in global teams, where diverse backgrounds converge. A company with a strong culture built on common values is better equipped to navigate cultural differences and build a cohesive global workforce.

Furthermore, core business values act as a differentiation factor. In a global market saturated with choices, consumers often gravitate towards companies that align with their own values. For example, a company committed to sustainability and environmental responsibility may attract environmentally conscious consumers worldwide. This alignment becomes a powerful tool for market positioning and attracting a loyal global customer base.

Defining core business values involves a thoughtful and introspective process that goes beyond drafting a list of ideals. It requires a deep exploration of what the company stands for and the principles it holds dear.

Here are key steps in defining core business values:

Reflection on Beliefs

Embarking on the journey to define core business values necessitates a profound reflection on the fundamental beliefs and principles that serve as the compass guiding the company's trajectory. This introspective process is akin to delving into the soul of the organization, unraveling the essence of its existence, and understanding the underlying philosophy that steers its every move. At the heart of this reflection lies a quest to comprehend the company's purpose—its reason for being—and the impact it aspires to create in the world.

Understanding the fundamental beliefs involves peeling back the layers of the company's identity to reveal the core values that shape its culture, drive its decision-making processes, and define its relationships with stakeholders. It goes beyond the surface-level operations and products, seeking to identify the principles that serve as the bedrock of the organization's ethos. For instance, a technology company may reflect on its commitment to innovation, pushing the boundaries of what's possible, and contributing to societal progress through technological advancements.

This introspection delves into the impact the company aims to create. It goes beyond profit margins and market share, reaching into the realm of social and environmental responsibility. Companies are increasingly recognizing the importance of their role in contributing to a positive societal and environmental impact. Reflection on beliefs involves asking questions such as: How does the company envision making a difference? What legacy does it aspire to leave? This aspect of the process aligns with the growing emphasis on corporate social responsibility, where companies actively consider their impact on communities, the environment, and broader global issues.

Ethical considerations form a pivotal component of this reflective journey. Companies are challenged not only to define what they stand for but also to outline the ethical boundaries that guide their actions. It involves contemplating questions of integrity, fairness, and accountability. For instance, a company may reflect on its stance towards fair labor practices, ethical sourcing of materials, and transparency in business operations. This ethical foundation becomes particularly crucial in the global context, where companies must navigate diverse cultural and regulatory landscapes.

The process of reflection on beliefs is not a solitary endeavor confined to the executive suite; it should be inclusive, involving the perspectives of employees, customers, and other stakeholders. This collective reflection helps in shaping values that resonate authentically with the broader community connected to the company. It transforms the definition of core values from a top-down proclamation to a shared commitment, fostering a sense of ownership and unity among those who contribute to the company's success.

The reflection on beliefs is a pivotal phase in defining core business values. It is a journey into the essence of the company, unraveling its purpose, impact goals, and ethical considerations. This introspective process sets the stage for crafting values that transcend rhetoric and become the guiding light steering the company through the complexities of global expansion. As businesses strive to define their core values, this reflective journey becomes a transformative exploration, shaping the very identity that propels them toward sustained success and positive global influence.

Engagement with Stakeholders

The engagement with stakeholders in the process of defining core business values is not merely a procedural step but a profound exploration that taps into the diverse perspectives and expectations of those intricately connected to the company. Stakeholders, including employees, customers, and partners, embody a collective voice that reverberates through the intricate web of the company's ecosystem. This engagement process becomes invaluable, offering a mosaic of insights that shape values resonant with the broader community.

Employees, as internal stakeholders, play a pivotal role in defining core values. They are the heartbeat of the organization, intimately involved in its day-to-day operations. Their perspectives, experiences, and aspirations contribute significantly to the cultural fabric of the company. Engaging with employees involves not only seeking their input but also fostering an environment that encourages open dialogue. Through surveys, focus groups, and interactive sessions, companies can glean valuable insights into the shared beliefs and principles that employees hold dear. This inclusivity not only results in values that authentically reflect the organizational culture but also fosters a sense of ownership and commitment among the workforce.

Customers, as external stakeholders, bring an external perspective that is critical for shaping values aligned with market expectations. Understanding customer expectations, preferences, and ethical considerations provides valuable guidance. Surveys, feedback sessions, and market research become essential tools in this engagement process. For instance, a retail company may engage with customers to understand their values regarding sustainable practices, fair trade, or product quality. Incorporating customer input ensures that the company's values resonate with its target market, enhancing brand loyalty and creating a positive reputation.

Partnerships and collaborations form another dimension of stakeholder engagement. Engaging with partners, suppliers, and other external collaborators offers insights into shared values and ethical considerations. This engagement is crucial, especially for companies operating in global supply chains or complex ecosystems. For example, a technology company collaborating with suppliers worldwide may engage in discussions about ethical sourcing, labor practices, and environmental sustainability. These discussions influence the company's values, ensuring alignment not only within its internal operations but also throughout the extended network of partners.

The engagement process is not a one-time event but an ongoing dialogue that adapts to the evolving needs and expectations of stakeholders. Regular check-ins, forums for discussion, and mechanisms for continuous feedback create a dynamic engagement framework. This ongoing dialogue ensures that core values remain relevant, reflecting the evolving ethos of the organization and its broader community.

The benefits of stakeholder engagement in defining core values are multifaceted. Firstly, it fosters a sense of inclusivity and shared responsibility. When stakeholders are actively involved in the value-defining process, it creates a collective commitment to these values. This collective commitment translates into a more authentic and lived expression of values within the organization.

Secondly, stakeholder engagement enhances transparency and trust. By openly seeking input and considering diverse perspectives, a company demonstrates a commitment to transparency and a willingness to listen. This openness fosters trust among stakeholders, including employees, customers, and partners. In a global context, where diverse cultural and ethical considerations come into play, this trust becomes a foundation for successful international operations.

Moreover, stakeholder engagement mitigates the risk of misalignment between stated values and actual practices. When values are defined in isolation, there is a potential for a misalignment that can lead to reputational damage. Engaging stakeholders acts as a reality check, ensuring that the defined values align with the expectations and perceptions of those directly impacted by the company's actions.

Engagement with stakeholders is a nuanced and comprehensive process that weaves together the varied threads of internal and external perspectives. It is a journey into the collective consciousness of the organization, drawing on the insights of those who contribute to its success. As companies define their core values, this engagement process becomes a transformative exploration, building a values framework that not only reflects the organization's identity but also resonates with the broader community connected to its mission and vision. In the intricate tapestry of global business, stakeholder engagement becomes the brushstroke that colors the canvas of core values with authenticity, relevance, and resonance.

Alignment with Mission and Vision

Defining core values is a nuanced endeavor that gains its true potency when it seamlessly aligns with the company's mission and vision. The mission and vision serve as the north star, guiding the company's journey through the intricate landscape of global business. For core values to be impactful, they must be more than just a set of ideals; they should form an organic extension of the overarching goals and aspirations encapsulated in the mission and vision.

The mission of a company outlines its fundamental purpose, the raison d'être that propels its existence. It encapsulates what the company seeks to achieve, the problems it aims to solve, and the positive impact it aspires to create. As core values are defined, they should be intricately woven into the fabric of this mission. For example, if the company's mission is to empower communities through technological innovation, a core value embracing inclusivity, collaboration, and social responsibility aligns seamlessly. This alignment ensures that the pursuit of global expansion is not just about profit margins but is deeply rooted in a purpose-driven ethos.

Similarly, the vision of a company offers a glimpse into the desired future state it envisions. It articulates the ambitious goals and the transformative impact the company aspires to achieve. Core values, therefore, act as the ethical compass guiding the company toward this envisioned future. If the vision is to be a leader in sustainable practices, the core values should reflect principles of environmental responsibility, ethical sourcing, and a commitment to minimizing ecological impact. This alignment ensures that the journey towards global expansion is not only about reaching new markets but is a conscious effort to shape a sustainable and responsible future.

The process of aligning core values with mission and vision involves a strategic and intentional approach:

- In-depth Analysis: Begin by conducting a comprehensive analysis of the company's mission and vision. Understand the nuances, the overarching themes, and the specific goals outlined in these foundational statements.
- Identify Overarching Themes: Extract the overarching themes and principles embedded in the mission and vision. These could be themes of innovation, social impact, sustainability, customer-centricity, or any other focal points that define the company's aspirations.
- Map Core Values: Map the core values in alignment with these overarching themes. For each value defined, consider how it contributes to the realization of the company's mission and vision. If a core value emphasizes customer satisfaction, it should align with a vision of being a customer-centric industry leader.
- Strategic Integration: Ensure that the integration of core values is not superficial but strategically integrated into various aspects of the company. This includes decision-making processes, employee training programs, and operational practices. For example, if a core value is innovation, implement strategies that foster a culture of continuous improvement and creative thinking.
- Feedback Loop: Establish a feedback loop between the defined core values, mission, and vision. Regularly reassess whether the values align with the evolving mission and vision, especially as the company grows and adapts to changing market dynamics.

The alignment of core values with mission and vision is not just a conceptual exercise but a practical guide that directs the actions and decisions of the company in a global context. When successfully aligned, core values become the ethical underpinning that propels the company's growth while maintaining a principled and purpose-driven approach. In the grand tapestry of global business, this alignment becomes the thread weaving together the past, present, and future of a company's journey towards sustained success and positive impact.

Operational Integration

Defining core values is not an isolated exercise in crafting an inspiring narrative; it's about breathing life into these principles through operational integration. The true measure of a company's commitment to its values lies not in eloquent statements but in the tangible manifestation of these ideals in everyday operations. Operational integration is the bridge that connects the conceptual realm of core values with the practical landscape of the company's day-to-day activities, decision-making processes, and overall business practices.

Decision-making processes are a key arena for the operational integration of core values. Values should not be relegated to a poster on the wall but should actively influence how decisions are made at every level of the organization. For instance, if one of the core values is transparency, decision-making processes should prioritize open communication and honest disclosure. This transparency becomes particularly crucial in the global context, where diverse stakeholders may have varying expectations and cultural interpretations of ethical conduct.

Employee training is another vital dimension of operational integration. Values cannot be merely communicated; they need to be instilled in the organizational culture. This involves incorporating core values into employee training programs, ensuring that new hires understand and embody these principles from day one. Training programs should go beyond theoretical discussions and provide practical examples of how values translate into actions in different global scenarios. This not only facilitates a shared understanding among employees but also fosters a culture where values are actively practiced in their day-to-day work.

Furthermore, overall business practices must be shaped by core values for authenticity and impact. For instance, if a company places a high value on environmental sustainability, its business practices should reflect this commitment. This may involve implementing eco-friendly initiatives in manufacturing, adopting sustainable supply chain practices, and regularly assessing the environmental impact of operations. Such tangible actions align the company's operational reality with its stated values, creating a consistent and trustworthy image in the eyes of stakeholders.

Operational integration requires a strategic and intentional approach:
- Customization to Context: Recognize that operationalizing values may require customization based on the cultural and regulatory context of different markets. What constitutes ethical business conduct may vary across regions, and values must be operationalized with sensitivity to these variations.
- Leadership Example: Leadership sets the tone for operational integration. Executives and managers must exemplify the values in their own actions, serving as role models for employees at all levels. This top-down approach ensures that the commitment to values permeates the entire organizational hierarchy.
- Feedback Mechanisms: Establish feedback mechanisms that allow employees at all levels to provide insights into how well values are being integrated into operations. This feedback loop not only promotes continuous improvement but also empowers employees to actively contribute to the company's ethical foundation.
- Adaptability: Recognize that operational integration is an ongoing process that requires adaptability. As the company evolves and navigates different global landscapes, the integration of values may need adjustments to remain relevant and effective.

Operational integration is the crucible where the ideals of core values are tested, refined, and transformed into actionable principles. It's the tangible embodiment of a company's commitment to ethical conduct and principled decision-making. When core values are seamlessly integrated into day-to-day operations, they become the pulse of the organization, driving its actions, decisions, and interactions in a manner that resonates authentically with stakeholders. In the intricate dance of global business, operational integration ensures that the steps taken align with the ethical rhythm that defines a company's identity and shapes its journey towards global success.

Defining core business values is a strategic endeavor that goes beyond creating a list of ideals; it is about crafting the soul of a global enterprise. Aligning operations and decisions with these values not only forms a robust foundation for global expansion but also fosters trust, unity, and differentiation in a competitive global marketplace. As companies venture into international territories, the essence of their identity, embedded in well-defined core values, becomes a guiding light steering them toward sustainable success and positive global impact.

Crafting a Unique Selling Proposition (USP)

Crafting a Unique Selling Proposition (USP) is a strategic process that goes beyond showcasing what a company offers—it's about identifying what makes it uniquely valuable in the market. In a global context, where competition is fierce and diverse, a compelling USP becomes a beacon that sets a company apart.

Here are the steps in crafting a USP that resonates globally, guiding businesses in defining their distinctive edge:

Market Analysis: Understand Your Landscape

Embarking on the journey to craft a compelling Unique Selling Proposition (USP) necessitates a meticulous exploration of the market landscape. This initial step serves as the compass, guiding businesses through the intricate terrain of competition, trends, and consumer demands. The significance of market analysis lies in its ability to unveil the nuances that shape the industry, providing a comprehensive understanding that forms the foundation for a USP destined to stand out.

The first facet of market analysis involves identifying competitors. Thoroughly examining the playing field allows businesses to discern not only who their direct rivals are but also the strategies these competitors employ. This insight is invaluable, offering a strategic vantage point to position a USP that not only differentiates but strategically outshines others in the field. It's about understanding the strengths, weaknesses, opportunities, and threats posed by competitors, allowing businesses to carve a niche that is uniquely theirs.

Simultaneously, delving into market trends is a crucial dimension of the analysis. Trends are the pulsating heartbeat of any industry, reflecting the evolving preferences and behaviors of consumers. Whether it's a shift towards sustainability, a growing reliance on digital platforms, or changing consumer demographics, these trends present opportunities for businesses to align their USP with the zeitgeist. Crafting a USP that resonates with contemporary market trends positions a business as not just an observer but a proactive participant in the unfolding narrative of the industry.

Equally pivotal is understanding consumer needs. A USP that addresses genuine consumer pain points and aspirations is poised for resonance. Through surveys, focus groups, and data analysis, businesses can gain insights into the desires and expectations of their target audience. This understanding serves as the compass needle pointing towards a USP that is not only distinctive but deeply relevant, meeting the unmet needs of consumers in a way that competitors may overlook.

The synergy of these elements creates a panoramic view of the market landscape, laying the groundwork for a USP that is not conceived in isolation but is a responsive chord struck in harmony with the dynamics of the industry. This strategic approach, informed by comprehensive market analysis, positions businesses to navigate the complexities of global competition with clarity and purpose. Crafting a USP is not just about standing out; it's about standing out with purpose, aligning with the contours of the market landscape to create a unique value proposition that resonates far and wide. In the symphony of global commerce, market analysis serves as the prelude, setting the tone for a USP that echoes with distinction and captures the attention of a discerning global audience.

Define Your Target Audience: Know Who You Serve

When crafting a Unique Selling Proposition (USP), one of the foundational steps is meticulously defining your target audience. This is not merely an exercise in segmentation but a strategic process that involves understanding the nuanced tapestry of demographics, preferences, and pain points that characterize the intended customer base. The success of a USP hinges on its ability to resonate deeply with the specific needs and aspirations of those it aims to serve.

The first aspect of defining your target audience involves delving into demographics. This encompasses a comprehensive understanding of the age, gender, location, income levels, and other defining characteristics of the individuals who form the core consumer base. For example, a luxury fashion brand targeting millennials in urban settings would have vastly different demographics compared to a brand catering to middle-aged suburban homeowners. This demographic insight serves as the cornerstone for tailoring a USP that aligns seamlessly with the characteristics and preferences of the intended audience.

Preferences become the next crucial dimension to explore. What are the lifestyle choices, interests, and purchasing behaviors that define your target audience? This could range from their preferred communication channels and online platforms to the types of products or services they gravitate towards. For instance, a fitness brand targeting health-conscious consumers might find that their audience prefers interactive mobile apps for workout routines and values sustainable packaging. By understanding these preferences, businesses can infuse their USP with elements that deeply resonate with the tastes and preferences of their audience.

Pain points form the third dimension in defining the target audience. What challenges, problems, or unmet needs does your audience face? Identifying these pain points is instrumental in crafting a USP that offers solutions and addresses genuine concerns. A company providing tech solutions to small businesses, for instance, might find that their target audience grapples with the complexity of software integration. A USP emphasizing user-friendly interfaces and seamless integration could directly address this pain point, creating a compelling value proposition.

To execute this process effectively, businesses can employ a variety of methods. Surveys, focus groups, and data analytics are powerful tools for gathering insights into the demographics, preferences, and pain points of the target audience. Social media engagement and online forums can provide real-time interactions with the audience, offering a dynamic understanding of their evolving needs. Additionally, analyzing competitors who successfully cater to a similar audience can offer valuable benchmarks and insights.

Defining your target audience is not a static task but an ongoing exploration. It involves staying attuned to the evolving characteristics and dynamics of the audience, adapting your understanding as market trends and consumer behaviors shift. The success of a USP hinges on this clarity – the ability to resonate authentically with the people it seeks to serve. In the global marketplace, where diversity is a defining feature, defining the target audience becomes the compass, guiding businesses to navigate the varied landscapes with precision and purpose.

Product/Service Differentiation: Uncover Your Unique Offering

At its core, this step involves a meticulous process of uncovering what sets your offering apart from the myriad options in the market. Whether it's a distinctive feature, innovative technology, superior quality, or a novel approach to addressing customer needs, identifying and highlighting this differentiation forms the very essence of a USP that captivates and resonates.

Distinctive features often become the hallmark of a product's identity. Whether it's a unique design element, a proprietary technology, or an exclusive functionality, these features set the product apart in a crowded marketplace. Consider smartphones, where camera capabilities, user interface, or advanced functionalities serve as distinctive features that influence consumer choices. Identifying such features and integrating them into the USP positions the product as not just a choice but a singular and compelling solution.

Innovation is another key dimension of product/service differentiation. Whether through groundbreaking technology, a novel manufacturing process, or an inventive business model, innovation breathes life into a USP. A tech company introducing cutting-edge solutions, for example, emphasizes innovation in its USP, creating a narrative that positions it as a frontrunner in a rapidly evolving landscape.

Superior quality, often synonymous with reliability and durability, can be a powerful differentiator. Consumers gravitate towards products or services that consistently deliver a high level of performance and satisfaction. This quality-centric approach becomes the cornerstone of a USP, signaling reliability and excellence that resonates with discerning consumers.

Taking a novel approach to addressing customer needs is a dynamic facet of product/service differentiation. This could involve reimagining the customer experience, offering customization options, or providing solutions to challenges that competitors overlook. For instance, a subscription-based meal kit service might differentiate itself by not only delivering fresh ingredients but also tailoring recipes to individual dietary preferences, creating a personalized and customer-centric USP.

In essence, product/service differentiation is the art of distilling the unique essence that sets a business apart. It's not just about being different for the sake of standing out; it's about being different in a way that resonates with the specific needs and desires of the target audience. By uncovering and spotlighting these distinctive elements, businesses create a USP that becomes a beacon in the vast sea of consumer choices, attracting and retaining customers through the allure of uniqueness and value.

Benefits Over Features: Focus on Customer Value

It is important to highlight your product features to emphasize the tangible benefits these features bring to the customer. This paradigm shift from features to benefits is not just a semantic tweak but a strategic approach that places the customer at the center of the narrative. By communicating how a product or service directly contributes to improving the customer's life, this customer-centric USP becomes a potent tool for building relevance and impact.

Features, in essence, are the distinctive characteristics or functionalities that a product or service possesses. While these features might be impressive on their own, they gain real value when translated into benefits that address the customer's needs or desires. For example, a smartphone may boast a powerful camera (feature), but the benefit for the customer lies in capturing high-quality memories effortlessly, enhancing their photography experience.

Emphasizing benefits over features is about going beyond the technical specifications and delving into the real-world advantages that customers gain. A laptop with a long-lasting battery life (feature) translates into the benefit of uninterrupted productivity, catering to the customer's need for reliability during long work sessions or travel.

This customer-centric approach is not just about stating the benefits but connecting them to the specific pain points or aspirations of the target audience. For instance, a software solution that offers seamless integration with existing systems (feature) directly addresses the customer's challenge of streamlining operations and reducing workflow disruptions, thus enhancing overall efficiency and productivity (benefit).

Understanding and communicating these benefits require a profound understanding of the target audience. It involves empathizing with their challenges, aspirations, and preferences. By doing so, businesses can craft a USP that not only highlights the unique features of their offering but weaves a narrative around how these features translate into meaningful advantages for the customer.

This shift to benefits in the USP aligns with the broader trend in marketing where the emphasis is on creating value and solving customer problems. It's about moving beyond the 'what' of a product to the 'why'—why does this matter to the customer? By addressing this question, businesses not only communicate the functional advantages of their offering but also tap into the emotional and psychological aspects that drive consumer decision-making.

A customer-centric USP that focuses on benefits over features becomes a persuasive language that speaks directly to the heart of the customer. It's a narrative that goes beyond technical jargon and resonates with the genuine needs and desires of the audience. By making the benefits explicit, businesses create a USP that is not just a statement of uniqueness but a compelling invitation for customers to envision the transformative impact of their product or service in their lives.

Service Excellence: Elevate the Customer Experience

When crafting a compelling Unique Selling Proposition (USP), the spotlight often focuses on product features and benefits. However, for businesses aiming to elevate their USP to a realm of distinction, the integration of exceptional service becomes a potent and transformative element. Whether it's offering unparalleled customer support, hassle-free returns, or personalized interactions, a steadfast commitment to service excellence not only becomes a differentiator but also shapes a unique identity that resonates with customers.

Exceptional service goes beyond the transactional aspects of a business. It embodies a commitment to meeting and exceeding customer expectations at every touchpoint of their journey. A USP that revolves around service excellence positions a business as not just a provider of products or services but as a partner invested in the overall satisfaction and well-being of its customers.

Unparalleled customer support is a prime example of service excellence that can be seamlessly integrated into a USP. Whether it's providing round-the-clock assistance, prompt issue resolution, or personalized guidance, a robust customer support system becomes a testament to a business's dedication to its customers. This commitment transforms a USP from a mere statement of uniqueness into a tangible assurance for customers that they are not alone in their journey with the brand.

Hassle-free returns and a transparent, customer-friendly approach to problem resolution contribute significantly to a USP centered around service excellence. Customers appreciate businesses that prioritize their convenience and satisfaction, and a commitment to seamless experiences in the event of issues or returns becomes a compelling aspect of the overall value proposition.

Personalized interactions add a human touch to the customer experience, another facet of service excellence that can be woven into a USP. Whether it's addressing customers by name, offering tailored recommendations, or remembering their preferences, personalized interactions create a sense of connection and enhance the overall customer journey. This personal touch becomes a defining element of the brand's identity, making it stand out in a sea of impersonal transactions.

Integrating service excellence into the USP requires a holistic approach that permeates every aspect of the business. It involves training and empowering staff to embody a customer-centric mindset, investing in advanced customer support technologies, and continuously seeking feedback to refine and enhance service offerings. By doing so, businesses not only communicate their commitment to service excellence but also build a culture that prioritizes the customer's experience as a cornerstone of their unique identity.

A USP anchored in service excellence is a powerful proposition that resonates with the evolving expectations of modern consumers. In an era where customer loyalty is often forged through exceptional experiences, businesses that elevate service to the forefront of their USP not only differentiate themselves but also create a lasting impression that extends beyond individual transactions. It's not just about what a business offers but how it offers it, fostering a relationship that goes beyond mere transactions and transforms customers into brand advocates.

Sustainability and Social Responsibility: Align with Values

For businesses committed to sustainability or social responsibility, integrating these aspects into the USP becomes not just a strategic move but a reflection of their deeper purpose. In an era where consumers increasingly value businesses that align with their ethical and environmental principles, sustainability and social responsibility in the USP become potent elements that resonate beyond the product or service itself.

Sustainability, in the context of a USP, goes beyond being a buzzword; it becomes a commitment woven into the very fabric of a business's identity. Whether it's through eco-friendly practices, responsible sourcing, or a commitment to reducing environmental impact, a USP anchored in sustainability communicates to consumers that the brand is not only concerned with providing quality products but also prioritizes the well-being of the planet.

Social responsibility, encompassing ethical business practices, community engagement, and philanthropy, is another dimension that can be seamlessly integrated into a USP. Businesses that actively contribute to societal well-being become not just providers of goods or services but contributors to positive change. Highlighting these contributions in the USP positions the brand as a responsible and conscientious entity, fostering a sense of connection with consumers who value businesses that go beyond profit margins.

For businesses embracing sustainability and social responsibility, the integration of these values into the USP requires authenticity and transparency. It's not merely about messaging; it's about demonstrating tangible actions and outcomes that align with these values. Whether it's through fair trade practices, carbon-neutral initiatives, or community outreach programs, businesses need to showcase a genuine commitment to their stated values to resonate with an increasingly discerning consumer base.

The value proposition of sustainability and social responsibility extends beyond the moral high ground. It taps into the growing consumer trend where purchasing decisions are influenced not only by the quality and price of products but also by the broader impact of those choices on the world. Brands that align with the ethical and environmental values of consumers create a sense of shared purpose, fostering loyalty and advocacy.

Integrating sustainability and social responsibility into a USP is not just a strategic choice but a reflection of the evolving expectations of consumers. It's a recognition that values matter in the decision-making process. By aligning the USP with principles that go beyond profit margins, businesses not only differentiate themselves in a competitive market but also contribute to a broader narrative of conscious consumption. In the global landscape where the choices of individual consumers collectively shape industries and influence change, a USP grounded in sustainability and social responsibility becomes a powerful vehicle for businesses to not only thrive but also contribute to a better world.

Clarity and Simplicity: Communicate Effectively

A USP that is clear, concise, and easily understandable possesses a communicative prowess that transcends the complexities often associated with business jargon. By avoiding convoluted language or unnecessary intricacies, a USP becomes a beacon of straightforward communication, ensuring that its unique value proposition is immediately grasped by the target audience.

The essence of a clear and simple USP lies in its ability to convey the distinctive aspects of a product or service without ambiguity. The goal is to make the message accessible to a broad audience, cutting through the noise of information overload. Clear communication ensures that potential customers quickly comprehend the unique benefits and values offered, facilitating a swift and positive response.

Moreover, simplicity in the USP enhances memorability. A straightforward and easy-to-understand statement is more likely to stick in the minds of consumers. In a world where attention spans are fleeting, a USP that can be easily recalled becomes a valuable asset, influencing purchasing decisions and fostering brand recall.

By embracing clarity and simplicity in the USP, businesses cultivate a connection with their audience based on transparency and accessibility. Whether in marketing materials, product packaging, or promotional campaigns, a USP that communicates with simplicity becomes an effective tool in capturing the attention and loyalty of consumers. In essence, clarity and simplicity in the USP reflect a commitment to fostering genuine understanding, resonating with the target audience and paving the way for enduring brand-consumer relationships.

Test and Refine: Iterate for Effectiveness

Before cementing your USP, subject it to scrutiny by presenting it to a sample of your target audience. This iterative process involves gathering feedback and making refinements based on the insights garnered.

Testing a USP provides valuable insights into its resonance with the intended audience. The objective is to assess how well the unique value proposition aligns with the expectations, preferences, and needs of the demographic it targets. By gauging reactions, collecting opinions, and analyzing responses, businesses can refine the USP to ensure that it not only communicates effectively but also strikes a chord with the audience.

This process is a recognition that a USP is not a static entity but an evolving element that should adapt to market dynamics and changing consumer perceptions. Markets are dynamic, and what resonates with consumers today might need adjustment tomorrow. Regularly testing and refining the USP allows businesses to stay attuned to shifts in consumer behavior, emerging trends, and evolving industry landscapes.

Refinement, in this context, involves tweaking the language, emphasizing certain aspects, or even restructuring the entire proposition based on the feedback received. It's about ensuring that the USP remains relevant, impactful, and aligned with the evolving needs of the target audience. This agility in refinement positions businesses to maintain a competitive edge in a landscape where adaptation is key to success.

The journey of crafting a compelling USP doesn't conclude with its creation but extends into the iterative process of testing and refining. This dynamic approach ensures that businesses don't just communicate their unique value proposition but do so in a way that resonates and evolves with the ever-changing dynamics of the market and consumer perceptions.

Global Relevance: Consider Cultural Nuances

To ensure global relevance, it's essential to make the USP culturally sensitive and resonant across diverse markets. This involves a meticulous examination of language, values, and preferences, culminating in a USP that transcends geographical boundaries.

Language plays a crucial role in global communication. A USP should be crafted with an awareness of linguistic subtleties, avoiding expressions or idioms that might be misinterpreted or lost in translation. The goal is to communicate the unique value proposition clearly and effectively in a way that resonates with audiences from different linguistic backgrounds.

Beyond language, understanding cultural values is paramount. What holds significance in one culture might not carry the same weight in another. A culturally sensitive USP considers the diverse values across markets and tailors its messaging to align with the cultural norms and expectations of each audience. This ensures that the value proposition is not only understood but also embraced in different cultural contexts.

Preferences and tastes vary widely across the globe. A successful USP takes into account the nuances in consumer preferences, adapting its messaging to cater to the unique tastes of diverse markets. This involves researching and understanding the specific needs and desires of each target audience, allowing the USP to resonate on a personal level.

Creating a culturally relevant USP is not a one-size-fits-all endeavor. It requires a nuanced approach that involves market research, feedback from diverse audiences, and a commitment to continuous adaptation. By doing so, businesses can foster a sense of connection with consumers worldwide, demonstrating an understanding and respect for the cultural tapestry within which their brand operates.

Global relevance in a USP is intricately tied to cultural sensitivity. By navigating the nuances in language, values, and preferences, businesses can create a value proposition that transcends geographical boundaries, fostering a connection that goes beyond mere transactions. In a world where cultural diversity is celebrated, a culturally relevant USP becomes a bridge that connects businesses with consumers on a global stage.

In the global arena, where businesses compete on an expansive stage, a well-crafted USP serves as a lighthouse, guiding customers to recognize the distinct value a company brings. By following these steps, companies can articulate a USP that not only differentiates them in the market but also resonates with customers on a global scale. Crafting a USP becomes a strategic journey, aligning the company's identity with the aspirations and expectations of a diverse and dynamic audience.

Aligning Values with Market Needs

In the ever-evolving landscape of global business, the intersection between a company's core values and the diverse needs of markets is a pivotal juncture that demands strategic consideration. This crucial alignment ensures a harmonious fit between the business's ethos and the multifaceted expectations of a global customer base. The process of aligning values with market needs involves a strategic journey that requires insight, flexibility, and a deep understanding of both the company's identity and the intricacies of the markets it serves.

At the outset, this alignment process necessitates a comprehensive exploration of a company's core values. These values form the moral compass that guides decision-making, shapes company culture, and defines its overarching purpose. By conducting a thorough introspection into these fundamental beliefs, businesses gain clarity on their identity, fostering a solid foundation upon which market alignment can be built.

Simultaneously, understanding the needs of diverse markets becomes paramount. This involves a nuanced examination of the varying preferences, expectations, and cultural nuances that distinguish one market from another. Market research plays a central role in this phase, providing insights into consumer behaviors, emerging trends, and the specific demands that drive purchasing decisions in each target market.

The next step in the process is to identify the common ground between a company's values and the needs of the markets it serves. This intersection becomes the focal point where the business's ethos aligns strategically with the expectations of its diverse customer base. For instance, if a company values sustainability and environmental responsibility, this alignment might involve adapting products or services to meet the growing demand for eco-friendly solutions in certain markets.

Flexibility emerges as a key characteristic during this alignment process. Recognizing that the needs of markets are dynamic and subject to change, businesses must be agile in adjusting their strategies to maintain resonance with evolving consumer expectations. This may involve tweaking messaging, introducing new features, or even innovating products to align more closely with the shifting demands of the market.

Communication plays a pivotal role in conveying this alignment to the target audience. Articulating how a company's values directly address the needs of the market fosters a connection with consumers. Whether through marketing campaigns, product messaging, or corporate communications, businesses must effectively communicate the strategic harmony between their core values and the solutions they offer to meet market needs.

The success of this alignment is reflected in the positive reception from consumers. When customers perceive a genuine connection between a company's values and the products or services they receive, it fosters brand loyalty and trust. This, in turn, enhances the brand's reputation, positioning it as not just a provider of goods or services but as a conscientious entity that understands and caters to the unique needs of its global clientele.

Aligning values with market needs is a dynamic and ongoing process that demands continuous adaptation and strategic finesse. By navigating the delicate balance between a company's core values and the multifaceted expectations of diverse markets, businesses can create a resonant and lasting connection with their global customer base. This strategic harmony becomes a cornerstone for sustained success, fostering a brand identity that transcends borders and resonates with consumers on a profound level.

Chapter 3
Building a Strong Local Presence

Building a strong local presence transcends mere geographical establishment. It involves ingraining a business into the fabric of the local community, understanding the unique dynamics, preferences, and cultural intricacies that shape the market. This goes beyond transactions, fostering genuine connections and contributing positively to the community. A strong local presence is a strategic investment that lays the groundwork for broader global endeavors.

In this chapter, we shift focus to the foundational steps of mastering the nuances of local markets and strategically leveraging local success as a springboard for broader global strategies. This chapter unfolds the strategic playbook for businesses aiming not just to operate within diverse locales but to become integral, trusted entities in the communities they serve.

Market Mastery: Unveiling Local Dynamics

In the pursuit of global expansion, achieving market mastery involves a deep understanding and strategic navigation of the intricacies inherent to the local market. It encompasses a multifaceted approach that not only involves comprehending the immediate dynamics but also actively engaging with the nuances that shape consumer behaviors and preferences. At its core, market mastery is about unraveling the unique tapestry of each local market, creating a foundation upon which a business can flourish.

Strategies for Market Research

#1. In-Depth Consumer Profiling

Conducting in-depth consumer profiling stands as a fundamental pillar in the strategic endeavor of mastering the local market. This process involves a meticulous exploration of various facets that collectively shape the consumer landscape, allowing businesses to gain profound insights into the demographics, psychographics, and socio-economic factors that intricately influence local buying behavior.

- **Demographic Insights:** The first dimension of consumer profiling focuses on demographics, encompassing variables such as age, gender, education, occupation, and income levels. These foundational factors provide a baseline understanding of the target audience's composition, allowing businesses to tailor their offerings to the specific characteristics of the local population.

- **Psychographic Exploration:** Moving beyond demographics, psychographic factors delve into the intricacies of consumer personalities, lifestyles, values, and interests. This dimension paints a richer picture of the target audience, uncovering motivations, preferences, and the emotional drivers that influence purchasing decisions. By understanding the psychographic makeup of the local market, businesses can craft messages and offerings that resonate on a deeper, more personal level.

- **Socio-Economic Considerations:** Socio-economic factors encompass the broader economic context within which consumers operate. This includes income distribution, employment levels, and overall economic stability. Analyzing these factors aids businesses in gauging the purchasing power of the local market, adjusting pricing strategies accordingly, and ensuring that products and services are accessible to the intended audience.

- **Tailoring Offerings to Local Aspirations:** Consumer profiling goes beyond statistical data; it strives to comprehend the aspirations and desires that drive local buying behavior. Businesses can tailor their products, services, and marketing strategies to align seamlessly with these aspirations. This might involve adapting features, aesthetics, or messaging to resonate with the unique aspirations of the local consumer base.

- **Crafting Targeted Marketing Strategies:** Armed with insights from consumer profiling, businesses can craft targeted and personalized marketing strategies. By understanding the nuances of the target audience, businesses can choose the most effective channels, messages, and promotional activities that resonate with local consumers. This targeted approach enhances the relevance and impact of marketing efforts, fostering a deeper connection with the local market.

- **Competitor Analysis**
  Mastering the local market involves a meticulous exploration of the competitive landscape. Competitor analysis serves as a strategic compass, guiding businesses through the intricacies of local dynamics. This process extends beyond a mere acknowledgment of rival entities; it's a comprehensive examination of their strengths, weaknesses, and the strategies that have proven effective in capturing the attention and loyalty of the local consumer base.

- **Thorough Examination of Competitor Strengths:** Competitor analysis kicks off with a thorough examination of the strengths exhibited by local rivals. This includes an exploration of their product offerings, unique selling propositions (USPs), and the elements that contribute to their market presence. Understanding what makes competitors formidable provides businesses with valuable insights into the expectations and preferences of the local consumer base.

- **Identifying Weaknesses for Strategic Advantage:** Equally important is the identification of weaknesses within the competitive landscape. Pinpointing areas where competitors fall short allows businesses to strategically position themselves to fill these gaps. Whether it's addressing quality concerns, improving customer service, or refining marketing strategies, recognizing and capitalizing on competitor weaknesses becomes a pathway to differentiation and heightened market appeal.

- **Market Gaps: Uncovering Opportunities for Innovation:** Competitor analysis unveils not only the strengths and weaknesses of existing players but also the market gaps—areas where consumer needs are underserved or overlooked. These gaps represent golden opportunities for innovation and strategic positioning. Businesses can leverage these insights to introduce products or services that resonate with unmet needs, establishing themselves as pioneers in addressing specific local market demands.

- **Strategic Positioning:** Crafting Unique Value Propositions: Armed with a nuanced understanding of competitor dynamics, businesses can strategically position themselves by crafting unique value propositions. This involves identifying aspects of the business that set it apart and resonate strongly with the local consumer base. It could be a focus on sustainable practices, superior product quality, or innovative solutions. The goal is to offer something distinctive that not only attracts attention but also fosters loyalty.

- **Discerning Effective Strategies:** Competitor analysis involves discerning the strategies that have proven effective in capturing the local market. This could range from successful marketing campaigns to customer engagement initiatives. By studying these strategies, businesses gain inspiration and insights into what resonates with the local audience. This knowledge becomes a foundation for crafting their own impactful approaches tailored to the nuances of the local market.

Competitor analysis is a dynamic and iterative process that empowers businesses to navigate the local battleground strategically. It's not merely a reconnaissance mission but a proactive endeavor to uncover opportunities, address gaps, and carve a unique niche within the local market. The insights gained from competitor analysis serve as a foundation for businesses to not only compete but to thrive and emerge as key players in the vibrant tapestry of local commerce.

Cultural and Trend Analysis

In the journey to master the local market, businesses embark on a profound exploration of cultural and trend analysis, recognizing that consumer preferences are intricately woven into the fabric of local traditions, values, and contemporary trends. This strategic dive into the local culture is paramount, serving as a compass for businesses seeking to understand, respect, and align with the diverse factors that shape the behavior and choices of the local consumer base.

- **Understanding Cultural Values and Traditions:** Cultural sensitivity begins with a deep understanding of the values and traditions embedded within the local culture. This involves an exploration of belief systems, societal norms, and the rituals that hold significance. By immersing themselves in the cultural tapestry, businesses gain insights into the fundamental principles that influence consumer decisions, allowing them to align products and services with the cultural values held dear by the local community.

- **Adapting Products and Services:** Cultural adaptation is a pivotal aspect of successfully navigating the local market. Businesses must tailor their offerings in a manner that not only respects but celebrates the local culture. This may involve adjustments to product features, aesthetics, or even packaging to ensure a harmonious fit with the preferences of the target market. The goal is not just to sell a product but to integrate seamlessly into the daily lives of local consumers.

- **Analyzing Current Trends:** Trends are dynamic, and staying attuned to current shifts is essential for market mastery. Businesses engage in trend analysis to identify the evolving tastes and preferences of the local consumer base. This could involve tracking fashion trends, lifestyle changes, or shifts in consumer behavior. By embracing current trends, businesses position themselves as dynamic and responsive, ensuring that their offerings remain relevant in the ever-changing landscape of the local market.

- **Staying Relevant and Responsive:** Cultural and trend analysis is an ongoing process that empowers businesses to stay relevant and responsive to the dynamic needs of the local consumer base. This agility is crucial in adapting strategies, products, and marketing approaches to align with shifting preferences. Businesses that integrate cultural and trend insights into their decision-making processes foster a deeper connection with the local market, positioning themselves as not just providers of goods and services but as contributors to the cultural narrative.

Market Segmentation

Market segmentation is a strategic practice that involves dividing a broader market into distinct segments based on various criteria. This process is essential for businesses aiming to implement a targeted approach, tailoring their strategies to meet the specific needs and preferences of different consumer groups within the local market.

One of the primary factors considered in market segmentation is demographics. This involves categorizing consumers based on observable characteristics such as age, gender, income, education, and occupation. For example, a clothing retailer might segment its market by age groups, offering different styles and designs to cater to the preferences of teenagers, young adults, and mature consumers.

Psychographics delve into the psychological and lifestyle attributes of consumers. This includes factors like interests, values, opinions, and activities. By understanding the psychographics of their target audience, businesses can create marketing messages and products that resonate with the beliefs and preferences of specific consumer segments. For instance, a fitness brand might tailor its offerings differently for individuals with an active lifestyle compared to those who prioritize relaxation and leisure.

Purchasing behavior is another crucial criterion for market segmentation. This involves categorizing consumers based on their buying habits, such as frequency of purchases, brand loyalty, and responses to marketing initiatives. Businesses can then design strategies that align with the distinct behaviors of these segments. A company offering skincare products, for example, might customize promotional efforts for consumers who frequently purchase premium skincare items versus those who prefer budget-friendly options.

To execute market segmentation effectively, businesses follow a systematic process:

- **Research and Data Collection:** Gathering relevant data is the foundation of market segmentation. This includes information about the local consumer base, their preferences, behaviors, and any other factors that might influence purchasing decisions.
- **Identifying Segmentation Variables:** Once sufficient data is collected, businesses identify the variables they will use for segmentation. As mentioned, these variables can range from demographics and psychographics to purchasing behavior.
- **Segmentation Analysis:** Using statistical analysis and tools, businesses analyze the collected data to identify distinct segments within the market. This process involves identifying patterns and relationships that exist among different variables.
- **Profile Development:** After identifying segments, businesses create detailed profiles for each. These profiles include a comprehensive understanding of the characteristics, behaviors, and preferences of consumers within each segment.
- **Tailoring Strategies:** With segmented profiles in hand, businesses can then tailor their marketing strategies, product offerings, and communication channels to effectively reach and engage each specific segment. This ensures that the messages resonate with the unique needs and preferences of each target group.
- **Continuous Monitoring and Adjustment:** Markets are dynamic, and consumer behaviors evolve. Continuous monitoring of market segments allows businesses to stay adaptive. Regular assessments and adjustments to strategies ensure that they remain aligned with the shifting landscape of the local market.

Implementing market segmentation provides businesses with a competitive edge by allowing them to focus their resources on the most promising opportunities within the local market. By understanding and responding to the diverse needs of various consumer segments, businesses can create more impactful and personalized strategies that enhance their overall market presence.

Consumer Behavior Analysis

Consumer behavior analysis is a dynamic and sophisticated process that involves dissecting and understanding the various aspects of how individuals interact with products or services. This analytical approach is pivotal for businesses seeking to tailor their strategies to align seamlessly with local preferences, ultimately enhancing their ability to meet the specific needs and expectations of their target audience.

To achieve effective consumer behavior analysis, businesses leverage a variety of tools and methodologies. One critical aspect is the tracking of both online and offline interactions. In today's digital age, online platforms provide a wealth of data on consumer behavior, ranging from website visits and clicks to social media engagement. Businesses employ analytics tools to gather and interpret this data, uncovering insights into how consumers navigate online spaces and interact with their brand.

Purchasing patterns play a crucial role in consumer behavior analysis. Understanding the decision-making processes that lead to a purchase is essential. By analyzing past transactions, businesses can identify patterns such as the frequency of purchases, preferred products or services, and factors influencing buying decisions. This information becomes invaluable for crafting targeted marketing strategies and refining product offerings to better resonate with the preferences of the local market.

Decision-making processes are multifaceted and can be influenced by various factors. Businesses keen on consumer behavior analysis delve into the psychological aspects that drive choices. This involves understanding the cognitive processes, motivations, and emotional triggers that contribute to decision-making. Through surveys, focus groups, and in-depth interviews, businesses gain insights into the underlying factors shaping consumer choices within the local market.

Achieving consumer behavior analysis also involves the integration of data from various touchpoints. The synergy between online and offline data provides a comprehensive view of the customer journey. For instance, understanding how a consumer discovers a product online, conducts research, and eventually makes a purchase offline allows businesses to create holistic strategies that encompass the entire customer experience.

The deployment of artificial intelligence (AI) and machine learning (ML) technologies has become increasingly prevalent in consumer behavior analysis. These technologies can process vast amounts of data in real-time, identifying patterns and predicting future behaviors. From personalized recommendations to predictive modeling, AI and ML tools enable businesses to stay ahead of evolving consumer preferences and anticipate market trends.

In addition to technological tools, businesses engage in direct consumer engagement methods to gain qualitative insights. This includes gathering feedback through surveys, monitoring social media conversations, and conducting focus groups. Direct engagement provides nuanced perspectives on consumer preferences, allowing businesses to refine their strategies with a human-centric approach.

Continuous monitoring and adaptation are key components of successful consumer behavior analysis. Markets evolve, and so do consumer preferences. Regular assessments of data and consumer feedback enable businesses to make informed adjustments to their strategies, ensuring they remain agile and responsive to the ever-changing landscape of the local market.

Consumer behavior analysis empowers businesses to unravel the intricate web of interactions, preferences, and decision-making processes that define the relationship between consumers and products or services. By harnessing these insights, businesses can craft strategies that resonate authentically with the local market, fostering a deeper connection with their target audience.

Adaptation to Regulatory Landscape

Adapting to the regulatory landscape is a critical aspect of global business strategy, requiring diligence and a comprehensive understanding of the local legal environment. The regulatory landscape encompasses a myriad of laws, policies, and governance structures that businesses must navigate to operate ethically and effectively within a specific region or country.

One of the fundamental principles guiding this adaptation is compliance with local laws and regulations. Businesses must not only be aware of the existing legal framework but also ensure that their operations align with these requirements. This involves a meticulous examination of laws related to areas such as corporate governance, labor, taxation, environmental practices, and industry-specific regulations.

Complying with local regulations is not just a legal obligation; it is also a crucial element in building trust and credibility within the local community. By demonstrating a commitment to following the laws of the land, businesses foster positive relationships with stakeholders, including customers, employees, and government authorities. This trust is foundational for long-term success in a foreign market.

Understanding the regulatory landscape is a multifaceted process. It requires thorough research and engagement with legal experts familiar with the intricacies of the local legal environment. This may involve consultations with legal professionals, participation in industry forums, and staying informed about updates and changes in regulations that might impact business operations.

Global businesses often encounter variations in regulatory practices across different regions. The adaptation process involves not only understanding the laws but also developing strategies to navigate these variances effectively. This may include the establishment of robust internal compliance programs, regular audits, and the appointment of legal advisors well-versed in local regulations.

Adapting to the regulatory landscape extends beyond mere compliance—it involves a proactive approach to ethics and corporate responsibility. Businesses must consider not only what is legally required but also what is ethically and socially responsible. This proactive stance can contribute to positive corporate citizenship and enhance the company's reputation in the eyes of consumers and the broader community.

In some instances, businesses may find themselves advocating for changes or improvements in the regulatory environment. This can be done through engagement with policymakers, industry associations, and other stakeholders to address regulatory gaps or inefficiencies that may hinder business operations or hinder industry growth.

The dynamics of the regulatory landscape are continually evolving, influenced by changes in government policies, geopolitical shifts, and global economic trends. As such, adaptation is an ongoing process. Businesses must stay vigilant, regularly reviewing and updating their compliance strategies to ensure alignment with any new or revised regulations.

Adaptation to the regulatory landscape is a fundamental component of successful global business operations. It involves not only complying with local laws but also proactively embracing ethical practices and corporate responsibility. By navigating the legal terrain with diligence, businesses can operate within the framework of local governance, building trust, and credibility while fostering positive relationships with stakeholders in the international market.

Local Triumph, Global Impact: Leveraging Success

Local success stories serve as powerful catalysts for international strategies, demonstrating the viability and appeal of a business within a specific region. These triumphs often originate from a deep understanding of the local market, resonating with the unique needs and preferences of the community. Whether it's gaining a strong foothold in a city, region, or country, local triumphs lay the groundwork for broader expansion.

Seamless Expansion: Leveraging Local Insights

Seamless expansion from local triumph to global prominence is a strategic journey marked by the intelligent utilization of insights gained from initial success. The transition is not merely about replicating success on a broader scale; it's about leveraging the profound understanding acquired in the local market to gain a competitive advantage in the global arena.

Central to this process is a deep comprehension of consumer behavior, an awareness of cultural nuances, and an acute understanding of market dynamics. Businesses that make this transition successfully go beyond the surface level and delve into the intricacies that define their local triumph. They recognize that what resonated with a specific audience in one location may need adjustments to cater to the diverse tastes, preferences, and expectations of global audiences.

The competitive advantage lies in the ability to navigate the complexities of different cultures while maintaining the essence of the brand. Insights derived from local success become invaluable tools for crafting strategies that resonate on an international scale. This involves adapting products, services, and marketing approaches to align seamlessly with the expectations of consumers worldwide.

Consumer behavior, influenced by cultural context, is a critical aspect that savvy businesses take into consideration. By leveraging local insights, companies can tailor their offerings to suit the unique needs of various global audiences. This approach ensures that the transition from local triumph to global prominence is not only seamless but also resonates authentically with customers across different regions.

In essence, businesses that effectively leverage local insights for global expansion recognize the importance of a nuanced and informed approach. The transition becomes a strategic journey that builds upon the foundation of local success, transforming it into a blueprint for international excellence. The ability to navigate the intricacies of diverse markets, fueled by local insights, becomes a cornerstone for businesses aspiring to make a meaningful impact on a global scale.

Case Study: Starbucks

Starbucks, founded in Seattle, Washington, serves as a compelling case study that exemplifies the art of leveraging local triumph for global impact. The coffeehouse chain's journey began in 1971 when three partners opened a single store, initially selling high-quality coffee beans and equipment.

The local triumph of Starbucks in its early years can be attributed to its unique approach in creating a distinct coffee culture. The company's focus extended beyond providing a beverage; it aimed to offer customers an experience, turning coffee consumption into a social and enjoyable activity. This approach resonated profoundly with locals in Seattle, laying the foundation for what would become a global phenomenon.

Starbucks' strategy to transition from a local favorite to a global giant involved a meticulous global expansion plan. As the company ventured into international markets, it recognized the importance of adapting to diverse cultures and tastes. Instead of imposing a standardized menu, Starbucks embraced localization, integrating local flavors and cultural preferences into its offerings.

For instance, in China, Starbucks introduced beverages like the Green Tea Latte and Red Bean Green Tea Frappuccino, catering to local preferences for tea-based drinks. In Italy, the home of espresso, Starbucks respected the local coffee culture and incorporated Italian espresso traditions into its menu.

The company's commitment to maintaining the core essence of the brand while adapting to local contexts was a key factor in its global success. Starbucks created a sense of familiarity for customers worldwide by preserving the distinctive Starbucks experience while making adjustments that respected and embraced cultural diversity.

Today, Starbucks has achieved unparalleled global reach, with thousands of stores in various countries. The brand's logo, with its iconic green siren, is recognized globally, symbolizing a consistent commitment to quality coffee and a unique customer experience.

Starbucks' case study illustrates that the transition from local triumph to global impact requires a delicate balance between maintaining brand identity and adapting to diverse markets. The success lies in understanding that what works in one region may not necessarily apply universally, and the ability to navigate these variations is paramount for sustained global excellence. Starbucks stands as a testament to how a local coffeehouse in Seattle evolved into a worldwide brand, demonstrating the enduring power of leveraging local insights for international success.

Case Study 2 : Alibaba Group

Alibaba Group serves as a remarkable case study showcasing the transformative journey from a local triumph to a global powerhouse. Founded by Jack Ma in 1999, Alibaba started as a platform connecting Chinese businesses with consumers, initially focusing on the domestic market.

The local triumph of Alibaba within China was built on its innovative approach to e-commerce. Jack Ma envisioned a platform that would empower small and medium-sized enterprises, providing them with a digital marketplace to reach a wider audience. This vision resonated strongly with the Chinese business landscape, contributing to Alibaba's rapid growth and success in its early years.

The strategic decision to concentrate on the Chinese market initially allowed Alibaba to establish a robust and trusted brand within its home country. As local businesses and consumers embraced the platform, Alibaba became synonymous with e-commerce in China. The company's success laid a solid foundation for its ambitious global expansion plans.

Alibaba's global impact stems from its ability to leverage the strength of its local triumph. The company gradually expanded its reach beyond China, venturing into international markets with a clear understanding of local business practices, consumer behavior, and regulatory environments. Alibaba's platforms, such as Alibaba.com and Taobao, adapted to suit the needs and preferences of diverse markets while maintaining the core principles that fueled its initial success.

One significant example of Alibaba's global reach is its expansion into Southeast Asia. The company invested in regional e-commerce platforms and logistics companies, recognizing the importance of local partnerships to navigate the complexities of different markets. This approach allowed Alibaba to gain a foothold in regions with distinct cultural and economic landscapes.

Today, Alibaba Group is a global giant, dominating not only the e-commerce sector but also venturing into cloud computing, digital entertainment, and other innovative technologies. Its initial local triumph in China served as a springboard for international success, demonstrating the strategic advantage of building a strong brand foundation at home before expanding globally.

Alibaba's case study highlights the importance of understanding and embracing local dynamics before aiming for global prominence. The company's success narrative underscores the potential for a business to become a global force by meticulously leveraging the insights and recognition gained from a strong local foundation.

Adaptation and Localization: Key Strategies

In the journey from local triumph to global impact, businesses must master the art of adaptation and localization. These key strategies involve recognizing that what resonates well in a local market may require adjustments to align with the diverse preferences of global audiences. The ability to strike a balance between preserving core values and adapting to cultural, linguistic, and consumer behavior differences is a defining characteristic of enterprises that navigate this transition successfully.

- **Maintaining Core Values:** One of the critical aspects of adaptation is the preservation of core values. While expanding globally, businesses must stay true to the fundamental principles and ethos that contributed to their local triumph. This consistency builds trust and ensures a recognizable brand identity across borders. For instance, companies like Starbucks and Alibaba maintained their commitment to quality and empowerment, respectively, while adjusting other aspects to suit diverse markets.
- **Cultural Sensitivity:** Localization goes beyond language translation; it involves a deep understanding of local cultures. Successful businesses invest in understanding the cultural nuances of different regions, incorporating elements that resonate positively with local consumers. For example, fast-food chains like McDonald's adapt their menus to include region-specific items, recognizing the importance of catering to local tastes.
- **Tailoring Marketing Strategies:** Adapting marketing strategies is essential for global success. This includes customizing advertising campaigns, packaging, and promotional materials to align with the cultural and social norms of target markets. Coca-Cola, with its "Share a Coke" campaign, exemplifies how a global brand can tailor its approach by personalizing product labels with popular local names in different countries.
- **Addressing Regulatory Variances:** Navigating diverse regulatory environments is a crucial aspect of adaptation. Local triumphs may involve compliance with specific regulations, and as businesses expand internationally, understanding and adhering to

varied legal frameworks become paramount. Companies like Amazon demonstrate a commitment to navigating regulatory complexities by adjusting their operations to comply with local laws in different regions.

- **Product and Service Customization:** Successful global businesses often customize their products or services to meet the unique needs of different markets. This involves not only language adaptation but also tailoring functionalities, features, or specifications. Technology companies like Apple strategically modify their products to accommodate regional preferences, ensuring global appeal without compromising on innovation.

- **Consumer Behavior Insights:** Adaptation requires a keen understanding of diverse consumer behaviors. Analyzing how consumers engage with products, make purchasing decisions, and respond to marketing efforts helps businesses fine-tune their strategies. E-commerce platforms like Zara excel in adapting to consumer behavior by swiftly responding to fashion trends, ensuring their offerings align with local preferences.

Adaptation and localization are indispensable strategies for businesses transitioning from local success to global prominence. The ability to preserve core values while adjusting to diverse cultural, regulatory, and consumer landscapes is a dynamic skill set that sets apart enterprises capable of thriving on the international stage. Successful global brands master the delicate balance between maintaining their identity and embracing the richness of global diversity.

Case Study 3: McDonald's

McDonald's, originating as a local triumph in the United States, stands as a prime example of successful adaptation and localization in the global market. The company's journey from a humble fast-food chain to a global phenomenon involved a strategic approach to meet the unique demands of diverse international markets.

At the heart of McDonald's success is the preservation of core brand elements that made it a local favorite. The iconic golden arches, efficient service, and a focus on affordability remained consistent across borders. This ensured a sense of familiarity for customers globally, reinforcing the brand's identity while expanding into new territories.

One of McDonald's key strategies for global expansion was the adaptation of its menu to cater to local tastes and cultural preferences. Recognizing that culinary preferences vary significantly, the company introduced region-specific menu items. For instance, in India, McDonald's offers a range of vegetarian options, acknowledging and respecting local dietary norms. In Japan, menu items like the Teriyaki Burger reflect an understanding of the local palate. This flexibility in menu offerings showcases McDonald's commitment to meeting the diverse culinary expectations of its international customer base.

McDonald's excels in tailoring its marketing strategies to resonate with local audiences. Advertising campaigns, promotions, and even the portrayal of its brand in various markets consider cultural nuances and societal norms. The "I'm lovin' it" campaign, for instance, transcends language barriers with its universal appeal but is adapted to suit the cultural context of each region, demonstrating McDonald's adeptness in localized marketing.

Beyond adapting its offerings, McDonald's actively engages with local communities and addresses social responsibility concerns. The company participates in local initiatives, sponsors community events, and often sources ingredients locally, contributing to the economic development of the regions it operates in. This approach not only aligns with McDonald's commitment to being a responsible corporate citizen but also enhances its acceptance in diverse markets.

McDonald's embraces technological innovations to enhance the customer experience, recognizing that preferences for ordering and payment methods can vary globally. The introduction of self-service kiosks, mobile ordering apps, and delivery services in different markets reflects the company's responsiveness to evolving consumer trends. By leveraging technology, McDonald's ensures a seamless and efficient experience tailored to the preferences of local customers.

McDonald's exemplifies how a local triumph can evolve into global success through strategic adaptation and localization. By balancing the preservation of core brand elements with an openness to diversify offerings and strategies, McDonald's has demonstrated the ability to thrive on the international stage while maintaining a strong connection with local communities worldwide.

Local triumphs have the potential to serve as robust catalysts for international strategies. The lessons learned, brand recognition built, and strategies honed in a local market provide a solid foundation for seamless global expansion. Businesses that effectively leverage their local success stories demonstrate a keen understanding of adaptation, localization, and building a brand that resonates globally. The transition from local triumph to global excellence is a testament to the strategic prowess and international vision of businesses that embark on this transformative journey.

Cultural Sensitivity: Navigating Local Values

Cultural sensitivity plays a pivotal role in the establishment of a strong local presence for businesses seeking to expand globally. It involves a nuanced understanding and respect for the values, traditions, and customs of the local population. In a world characterized by diverse cultures and traditions, businesses that prioritize cultural sensitivity demonstrate a commitment to building authentic connections with the communities they serve.

The significance of cultural sensitivity becomes particularly evident when attempting to navigate local values. Every culture has its unique set of norms, beliefs, and customs that shape daily life and consumer behavior. Acknowledging and aligning with these local values is crucial for gaining trust and acceptance within the community. Here are several key aspects that highlight the importance of cultural sensitivity:

Building Trust and Credibility

Cultural sensitivity fosters trust by demonstrating that a business understands and respects the cultural context in which it operates. Trust is the foundation of any successful business relationship, and by aligning with local values, a company can establish credibility and authenticity. This, in turn, contributes to the longevity and success of the business in the local market.

Avoiding Cultural Missteps

Misinterpreting or disregarding local customs can lead to cultural missteps that may harm a brand's reputation. Cultural sensitivity acts as a safeguard against unintentional offenses or inappropriate practices that may arise from a lack of understanding. Businesses that take the time to learn about and embrace local cultures are better equipped to navigate potential pitfalls.

Tailoring Products and Services

Cultural sensitivity extends to product and service offerings. Adapting products and services to align with local preferences and needs demonstrates a genuine interest in meeting the specific requirements of the community. This customization not only enhances the relevance of offerings but also reflects a commitment to providing value that resonates with local consumers.

Effective Communication

Language, communication styles, and symbolism vary across cultures. Cultural sensitivity ensures that communication strategies are tailored to align with local norms. This may involve using appropriate language, considering non-verbal cues, and understanding the significance of certain symbols or colors in the local context. Effective communication enhances engagement and fosters a deeper connection with the target audience.

Social Responsibility and Community Engagement

Cultural sensitivity extends to social responsibility and community engagement. Businesses that are culturally sensitive actively participate in and contribute to local initiatives. This involvement goes beyond philanthropy; it reflects a commitment to understanding and addressing the unique needs and challenges faced by the community. By integrating into the local fabric, businesses can become valuable contributors to the well-being of the community.

Adaptability in Marketing Strategies

Marketing strategies that resonate globally may not necessarily be effective at the local level. Cultural sensitivity involves adapting marketing messages, imagery, and promotional activities to align with the cultural preferences of the target audience. This adaptability ensures that marketing efforts are well-received and positively perceived within the local community.

Fostering Inclusivity and Diversity

Cultural sensitivity promotes inclusivity and diversity within the workforce. Recognizing and embracing diversity not only within the local community but also within the organization itself contributes to a positive corporate culture. Businesses that champion diversity are better equipped to understand and respond to the varied needs and expectations of their diverse customer base.

In conclusion, cultural sensitivity is a dynamic and essential aspect of establishing a strong local presence for businesses operating on a global scale. It goes beyond mere acknowledgment of cultural differences; it involves a genuine effort to understand, respect, and align with local values. By prioritizing cultural sensitivity, businesses can forge meaningful connections, build trust, and cultivate a positive impact within the communities they serve.

Strategic Alliances: Building Local Partnerships

Strategic alliances, characterized by collaborative partnerships between businesses, are instrumental in fostering growth and expanding market reach. In the context of global business expansion, the importance of forging local partnerships cannot be overstated. These alliances go beyond mere transactions; they involve long-term collaborations that leverage the strengths of each partner to achieve mutually beneficial goals. Examining the dynamics of strategic alliances at the local level reveals their pivotal role in laying the foundation for successful global expansion.

Understanding Strategic Alliances

Strategic alliances are collaborative agreements between two or more organizations aimed at achieving common objectives while retaining their independence. These partnerships can take various forms, including joint ventures, licensing agreements, distribution partnerships, or co-marketing initiatives. In the realm of global business, forging alliances at the local level becomes a strategic imperative for several reasons.

Importance of Forging Local Partnerships

Cultural Insight and Market Knowledge

Local partnerships provide invaluable cultural insights and market knowledge. Businesses entering a new market often lack the nuanced understanding of local consumer behavior, preferences, and regulatory nuances. Partnering with a local entity brings in-depth knowledge, ensuring that the strategies implemented align seamlessly with the cultural and market dynamics of the region.

Navigating Regulatory Challenges

Local partners bring familiarity with the regulatory landscape, helping businesses navigate legal and compliance challenges. Regulations vary widely across regions, and having a local partner with established relationships and an understanding of local laws can significantly expedite the entry and operational processes, reducing risks associated with regulatory compliance.

Establishing Credibility and Trust

Building trust with the local audience is essential for successful expansion. Local partnerships enhance credibility by associating the business with a trusted entity in the region. Consumers are more likely to trust brands that collaborate with established local players, facilitating smoother market entry and acceptance.

Access to Established Networks

Local partners often come with established networks of suppliers, distributors, and industry connections. This access accelerates the development of a supply chain and distribution channels, overcoming logistical challenges that businesses might face when entering a new market independently.

Cost Sharing and Risk Mitigation

Global expansion involves substantial investments, and strategic alliances provide a mechanism for cost-sharing. Shared resources, expenses, and risks make the entry into new markets more financially viable. By distributing the financial burden, businesses can allocate resources more efficiently, reducing the overall risk associated with expansion.

Adaptation to Local Trends and Preferences

Local partners contribute to adapting products, services, and marketing strategies to align with local trends and preferences. A collaborative approach ensures that offerings resonate with the specific needs of the local market, increasing the likelihood of acceptance and success.

Cases of Successful Local Partnerships Leading to Global Expansion

IKEA's Localized Approach

IKEA's global success is underpinned by strategic alliances at the local level. Recognizing the importance of understanding local tastes and preferences in the furniture industry, IKEA forms partnerships with local manufacturers. This approach allows IKEA to offer region-specific products while benefiting from the production efficiency of local partners.

Coca-Cola's Bottling Partnerships

Coca-Cola's global presence is partly attributed to its network of local bottling partnerships. By collaborating with local bottling companies, Coca-Cola ensures that its products are not only available globally but also tailored to local tastes. This decentralized production model exemplifies the significance of local partnerships in the beverage industry.

Toyota's Collaborations for Market Entry

Toyota strategically forms alliances when entering new markets. In the Indian market, for instance, Toyota collaborated with Kirloskar Group, leveraging the local partner's understanding of the automotive market. This collaboration facilitated the adaptation of Toyota's offerings to suit local preferences, contributing to the brand's success in India.

Alibaba's Cross-Border Collaborations

Alibaba's global expansion is marked by strategic alliances with local e-commerce platforms. In Southeast Asia, Alibaba invested in Lazada, a leading e-commerce platform, to establish a strong local presence. This partnership enabled Alibaba to navigate the complexities of diverse markets and capitalize on Lazada's established network.

Forging local partnerships is a strategic imperative for businesses aiming at global expansion. These alliances provide a gateway to cultural understanding, regulatory navigation, and access to established networks. Successful cases exemplify how collaborative efforts at the local level not only lay the groundwork for immediate success but also serve as catalysts for sustained global growth. Strategic alliances, built on shared goals and mutual benefits, empower businesses to overcome challenges and capitalize on opportunities in new and diverse markets.

Chapter **4**

Strategic Planning for Global Growth

Strategic planning serves as the compass guiding businesses through the intricate terrain of global expansion. In the dynamic landscape of international business, a well-crafted strategy is not just advantageous; it's imperative for sustainable growth. This chapter explores the essence of strategic planning, emphasizing its pivotal role in setting the foundation for successful global endeavors.

What is Strategic Planning?

Strategic planning is a systematic process that organizations undertake to define their direction, make informed decisions, and align their resources toward achieving specific objectives. In the context of global growth, strategic planning becomes the roadmap that navigates businesses through the complexities of entering new markets, mitigating risks, and capitalizing on opportunities.

Importance of Strategic Planning for Business Growth:

- **Vision and Direction:** Strategic planning provides a clear vision and direction for the business. It helps in articulating long-term goals, defining the company's purpose, and aligning every aspect of operations with these overarching objectives. In the context of global growth, having a defined vision becomes crucial for navigating diverse markets cohesively.

- **Risk Mitigation and Adaptability:** The global landscape is rife with uncertainties and risks. Strategic planning involves thorough risk assessment and mitigation strategies. By anticipating challenges, businesses can proactively adapt to unforeseen circumstances, ensuring a more resilient and flexible approach to international expansion.

- **Resource Allocation and Efficiency:** Efficient allocation of resources is paramount, especially when expanding globally. Strategic planning enables businesses to identify the necessary resources, allocate budgets wisely, and optimize operational efficiency. This ensures that resources are deployed where they will have the most significant impact on achieving international expansion goals.

- **Competitive Advantage:** In the global arena, competition is fierce. Strategic planning allows businesses to identify and leverage their unique strengths, creating a competitive advantage. By understanding how to position themselves in the market, companies can differentiate their offerings and stand out amidst global competitors.

- **Market Entry Strategies:** Developing a comprehensive strategy includes determining the most effective market entry approaches. Whether through partnerships, acquisitions, or organic growth, strategic planning helps businesses choose the entry methods that align with their objectives and the dynamics of the target market.

Setting Realistic Goals for International Expansion

Expanding a business globally requires a meticulous approach to goal setting that goes beyond traditional benchmarks. The process of defining achievable and measurable goals for international expansion involves a strategic blend of foresight, adaptability, and alignment with overarching business objectives.

Understanding the Business Landscape

Embarking on the journey of international expansion demands a meticulous exploration of the global business landscape. This initial step is akin to unfolding a complex tapestry woven with market intricacies, competitive dynamics, and a myriad of challenges and opportunities. At the heart of this exploration lies the imperative to conduct thorough market research. This entails delving into the specifics of each targeted market, unraveling consumer behaviors, economic conditions, and regulatory landscapes.

Market research serves as the compass guiding businesses through the uncharted waters of global markets. It involves a deep dive into the preferences, demands, and expectations of local consumers. Understanding the pulse of the target audience is essential for crafting products, services, and strategies that resonate authentically with diverse markets. Moreover, market research unveils untapped opportunities, allowing businesses to position themselves strategically in areas where demand aligns with their offerings.

In tandem with market research, a comprehensive competitor analysis is indispensable. Recognizing and studying global players in the chosen markets sheds light on industry benchmarks, competitive strategies, and potential gaps to exploit. By understanding the strengths and weaknesses of existing players, businesses can fine-tune their own strategies to stand out and offer unique value propositions.

The global landscape is a terrain of challenges and opportunities, each presenting itself in diverse forms. Identifying potential obstacles, whether they be cultural, regulatory, or logistical, allows businesses to proactively develop mitigation strategies. Simultaneously, recognizing opportunities enables them to leverage favorable conditions for growth. This dual evaluation ensures that goals are set with a realistic understanding of the hurdles to overcome and the pathways to success.

As businesses navigate this landscape, they gain a nuanced understanding of the diverse markets they intend to enter. This insight is pivotal for goal-setting, as it allows companies to tailor their objectives to align with the unique attributes of each region. What works in one market may necessitate adjustments in another due to variations in consumer behavior, cultural nuances, and economic conditions. Thus, a nuanced understanding enables businesses to set goals that are not only ambitious but also contextually relevant.

Understanding the business landscape before setting goals is akin to preparing a detailed map for a grand expedition. It involves deciphering the unique features of each market, learning from global players, anticipating challenges, and embracing opportunities. Armed with this comprehensive understanding, businesses can chart a course for international expansion that is not only informed but also strategically aligned with the global tapestry they seek to navigate.

Aligning with Business Strategy

In the realm of international expansion, the synergy between goal-setting and the overarching business strategy is paramount. Goals should not exist in isolation but rather seamlessly integrate into the fabric of the company's mission, vision, and core values. This alignment establishes a harmonious relationship between the expansion objectives and the fundamental principles guiding the business.

When setting goals that align with the business strategy, companies ensure that their international expansion efforts contribute cohesively to the overarching success of the organization. This holistic approach transcends a mere checklist of objectives and, instead, becomes a strategic roadmap guiding the trajectory of the entire enterprise. The goals set for international expansion, in this context, become integral components in the realization of the company's broader mission and vision.

Moreover, this alignment reinforces the consistency of the brand identity across borders. As businesses venture into new markets, maintaining a unified strategic direction rooted in the company's core values becomes a powerful tool for brand integrity. Consistency in messaging, product offerings, and customer experience not only fosters brand recognition but also instills trust among consumers, regardless of geographical location.

The interplay between international goals and the broader business strategy extends beyond a mere numerical target or market penetration goal. It encompasses a strategic vision that transcends borders, crafting a narrative of growth and success that is universally resonant. This alignment becomes the compass guiding decision-making processes, resource allocation, and adaptation strategies throughout the international expansion journey.

Aligning goals with the business strategy ensures that the pursuit of international expansion is not a detached endeavor but an integral part of the company's holistic growth narrative. It forges a strong link between the micro-level objectives of entering new markets and the macro-level aspirations encapsulated in the company's mission and vision. As businesses set their sights on global horizons, this alignment becomes the linchpin that harmonizes the intricate dance of goals and strategies, ultimately propelling the organization towards enduring success on the international stage.

Defining Measurable Key Performance Indicators (KPIs)

Measurable goals stand as the cornerstone for tracking progress and fostering accountability. To navigate the expansive landscape of international expansion effectively, businesses must articulate clear and precise KPIs that enable them to quantitatively assess their performance on the global stage.

KPIs serve as vital signposts, offering a tangible and quantifiable roadmap for businesses venturing into international markets. These indicators span a spectrum of metrics, encapsulating essential aspects such as market share, revenue growth, and customer acquisition. By establishing these performance metrics, companies gain a robust framework for evaluating their success and efficacy in the complex and diverse markets they engage with. One of the fundamental roles of KPIs is to provide a standardized language for assessing progress. In a global context, where diversity and complexity reign, having a common set of measurable indicators becomes the linchpin for aligning efforts across borders. Market conditions, consumer behaviors, and regulatory landscapes may vary, but a well-defined set of KPIs acts as a universal yardstick, ensuring that all branches of the business move in concert towards overarching goals.

The process of defining KPIs involves a meticulous examination of the specific objectives tied to international expansion. Each KPI should be intricately linked to a strategic goal, creating a direct correlation between the quantitative metric and the broader vision of success. Whether the aim is to establish a foothold in a new market or achieve a specific level of revenue diversification, KPIs provide the necessary granularity to measure progress effectively.

Furthermore, the establishment of KPIs is not a static exercise but an iterative process. As businesses adapt to the nuances of different markets and respond to shifting global dynamics, KPIs must evolve accordingly. Regular reviews and recalibrations ensure that these performance indicators remain relevant and reflective of the ever-changing landscape, allowing businesses to stay agile and responsive.

Ultimately, the prowess of KPIs lies in their ability to transcend the complexity of global expansion, offering clarity and precision in the pursuit of objectives. They become the north star guiding businesses through the vast and diverse oceans of international markets, providing a robust framework for assessment, adaptation, and ultimately, triumph on the global stage.

Adapting to Cultural Nuances

Adapting to cultural nuances stands as a pivotal element in setting and achieving realistic goals. Cultural diversity profoundly influences every facet of global markets, from consumer behaviors to business operations. Recognizing and embracing these cultural differences becomes imperative when formulating and pursuing international expansion goals.

Realistic goals should reflect an astute understanding of the unique cultural landscapes in which a business operates. The intricacies of local customs, values, and communication styles can profoundly impact how products are received, marketing strategies resonate, and overall business operations unfold. By acknowledging and adapting to these nuances, businesses can establish goals that align harmoniously with the cultural fabric of each specific market.

Achieving international success requires a deep appreciation for the diversity of global consumers. Cultural preferences shape purchasing decisions, and market dynamics are often intricately interwoven with local traditions. In this context, realistic goals become those that not only acknowledge these cultural nuances but leverage them as strengths. Whether it's tailoring product offerings, refining marketing messages, or adjusting operational practices, the adaptability of goals ensures that businesses remain attuned to the specific needs and expectations of diverse consumer bases.

Moreover, the ability to adapt goals to cultural nuances fosters a sense of authenticity and relevance. Consumers resonate more profoundly with businesses that understand and respect their cultural context. Realistic goals, therefore, go beyond the numerical targets; they encompass a deeper understanding of how the business can integrate seamlessly into the local environment, becoming a trusted and respected part of the community.

Adaptability also plays a crucial role in responding to unforeseen challenges or opportunities that may arise due to cultural dynamics. Flexibility in goal-setting allows businesses to navigate shifting landscapes, capitalize on emerging trends, and address any cultural sensitivities that may impact their operations. This fluid approach to goal-setting not only enhances the likelihood of success but also positions the business as an agile player in the global arena.

Prioritizing Flexibility

Prioritizing flexibility is not just a practical consideration but a strategic necessity in the realm of global expansion. The international business landscape is inherently dynamic, characterized by constant changes in market conditions, regulatory environments, and consumer behaviors. To navigate this complexity successfully, businesses must engrain flexibility into the very fabric of their goal-setting processes.

One of the key aspects of prioritizing flexibility is acknowledging the inherent uncertainty that accompanies international expansion. Factors such as geopolitical events, economic fluctuations, or sudden shifts in consumer preferences can significantly impact the feasibility of initially set goals. By recognizing these uncertainties, businesses position themselves to adapt swiftly and make informed adjustments when needed.

Furthermore, flexibility in goal-setting is closely tied to the iterative nature of strategic planning. While businesses meticulously plan their international foray, the reality is that some aspects of a new market can only be truly understood once operations are underway. Prioritizing flexibility allows for continuous assessment and refinement of goals based on real-time feedback and insights gathered from the market.

In an ever-evolving global landscape, regulatory changes can also be a significant driver for the need to recalibrate goals. By building flexibility into the goal-setting framework, businesses can respond proactively to shifts in legal and regulatory landscapes across different regions. This adaptability not only ensures compliance but also positions the business to leverage new opportunities that may arise.

Additionally, flexibility is a strategic tool for managing risks effectively. Global expansion often involves navigating diverse cultures, legal systems, and economic environments. Unforeseen challenges are almost inevitable. Businesses that prioritize flexibility can pivot and strategize in response to unexpected hurdles, mitigating potential setbacks and sustaining momentum.

While flexibility is essential, it doesn't imply a lack of direction or strategic focus. Instead, it allows businesses to remain agile without losing sight of their overarching objectives. Goals, even if initially adjusted, should consistently align with the core mission and values of the business. This balance between adaptability and strategic intent is crucial for sustained success in the international arena.

Prioritizing flexibility in goal-setting is not just about being reactive to change; it's about being proactive in the face of uncertainty. Businesses that embrace flexibility as a guiding principle position themselves not only to weather the unpredictable nature of global markets but also to seize unforeseen opportunities. In the intricate dance of international expansion, flexibility is the nimble footwork that allows businesses to navigate the rhythm of change.

Incorporating Risk Mitigation Strategies

Incorporating risk mitigation strategies is an integral aspect of the goal-setting process for businesses venturing into global expansion. The dynamic nature of international markets introduces a myriad of uncertainties, ranging from geopolitical shifts to cultural nuances, making it imperative for companies to adopt a proactive stance in managing risks.

One key element of this strategy involves conducting a thorough risk assessment before finalizing international expansion goals. By identifying potential challenges specific to each target market, businesses can tailor their risk mitigation approaches to address the unique intricacies of diverse regions. This initial analysis lays the foundation for a more resilient and adaptable goal-setting framework.

Diversification is a fundamental risk mitigation strategy that extends beyond investment portfolios. In the context of global expansion, diversifying market presence helps spread risks associated with dependence on a single market. Setting goals that include entering multiple markets simultaneously or consecutively allows businesses to mitigate the impact of unexpected challenges in any particular region.

Cultural risk is a significant factor that businesses must navigate when expanding globally. By incorporating cultural intelligence into their goals, companies can proactively address potential misunderstandings or misalignments that may arise. This includes tailoring marketing strategies, product positioning, and operational approaches to align with the cultural expectations and sensitivities of each market.

Legal and regulatory compliance is another critical area for risk mitigation. Understanding and adhering to the laws of each target market not only ensures a smoother expansion process but also minimizes the risk of legal challenges. Businesses should incorporate specific goals related to legal compliance within their broader international expansion objectives.

Contingency planning is an essential component of risk mitigation. Goals should account for the possibility of unexpected disruptions, whether they be political, economic, or logistical. Establishing clear contingency plans and setting goals that encompass adaptability in the face of unforeseen circumstances provide a safety net for businesses venturing into uncharted territories.

Strategic partnerships and alliances can also serve as effective risk mitigation strategies. By collaborating with local partners who possess a deep understanding of the market, businesses can leverage their insights and networks to navigate potential challenges. Goals that include establishing such partnerships demonstrate a commitment to building a strong foundation for sustainable growth.

Regular monitoring and reassessment of risks should be an ongoing part of the goal-setting process. As global conditions evolve, businesses need to be agile in adjusting their strategies. Goals that include periodic risk reviews and adaptations enable companies to stay ahead of emerging challenges and respond proactively to changes in the international landscape.

Incorporating risk mitigation strategies into the goal-setting process is not merely a precautionary measure; it is a strategic imperative for successful global expansion. By understanding, quantifying, and actively addressing potential risks, businesses position themselves to navigate the complexities of international markets with resilience and foresight. This proactive approach not only safeguards against setbacks but also fosters a culture of adaptability and strategic resilience in the pursuit of global growth.

Establishing Timeframes and Milestones

Establishing timeframes and milestones is a critical component of effective goal-setting for businesses embarking on global expansion. This strategic approach adds a dimension of clarity, structure, and accountability to the overarching objectives.

Here's an exploration of why incorporating timeframes and milestones is crucial for successful international growth:

- **Clarity of Execution:** Timeframes set the pace for execution. By defining specific deadlines for achieving goals, businesses create a sense of urgency and focus. This clarity ensures that the international expansion process moves forward with purpose and avoids potential delays. For instance, if the goal is to enter a new market, having a timeframe for market entry helps allocate resources efficiently and streamlines the decision-making process.

- **Progress Tracking and Adaptability:** Clear milestones facilitate ongoing progress tracking. Breaking down larger goals into smaller, achievable milestones allows businesses to monitor their advancement in real-time. This not only provides a tangible measure of success but also enables prompt identification of any deviations from the planned trajectory. With milestones in place, businesses can adapt their strategies and make necessary adjustments based on the evolving circumstances or unexpected challenges encountered during the global expansion journey.

- **Motivation and Celebration of Success:** Milestones serve as markers of achievement, offering opportunities for businesses to celebrate successes along the way. Celebrating incremental milestones boosts team morale, fostering a positive and motivated work environment. This positive reinforcement is particularly valuable during the complex and demanding process of international expansion, where acknowledging progress contributes to the overall resilience and commitment of the team.

- **Resource Allocation and Efficiency:** Setting timeframes and milestones aids in resource allocation and optimization. Businesses can allocate resources efficiently by aligning them with specific stages of the international expansion process. This strategic resource management ensures that the right resources are deployed at the right time, enhancing overall efficiency. For instance, if the goal is to establish a local presence, having milestones for securing regulatory approvals, hiring local talent, and setting up operations enables a well-coordinated and streamlined approach.

- **Risk Management and Contingency Planning:** Timeframes and milestones play a crucial role in risk management. By establishing milestones that align with potential risk points, businesses can implement proactive contingency plans. This risk-aware approach allows for timely identification and mitigation of challenges, reducing the impact of unforeseen circumstances on the overall timeline.

Establishing clear timeframes and milestones is not just a procedural step in goal-setting; it is a strategic imperative that contributes to the success of international expansion endeavors. It enhances execution clarity, enables efficient progress tracking, motivates teams, optimizes resource allocation, and strengthens risk management. By incorporating these temporal and incremental elements into their goals, businesses create a roadmap that not only guides them through the complexities of global expansion but also positions them for sustained success in diverse markets.

Continuous Evaluation and Adjustment

Continuous evaluation and adjustment form the dynamic core of successful global expansion strategies. Once goals are set, it's imperative to embrace an ongoing process of assessment and adaptation. Regularly evaluating progress involves monitoring key performance indicators (KPIs), comparing actual outcomes with predefined milestones, and soliciting feedback from relevant stakeholders.

Regular feedback loops provide insights into the effectiveness of implemented strategies. This input can come from various sources, including internal teams, local partners, and customer feedback. Analyzing this feedback enables businesses to identify areas of success and areas that may require adjustment. It creates a responsive framework that allows for quick recognition of challenges or opportunities, fostering a proactive approach to international expansion.

The willingness to adjust goals based on evolving circumstances is a hallmark of strategic agility. Global dynamics are subject to change due to factors such as economic shifts, regulatory adjustments, or unforeseen market developments. Businesses must be prepared to pivot when necessary, ensuring that their goals remain relevant and achievable in the ever-changing landscape of international markets.

Continuous evaluation and adjustment also demand a robust system for data collection and analysis. Utilizing technology and data analytics tools enables businesses to gather real-time insights, facilitating informed decision-making. By leveraging data, businesses can identify patterns, trends, and areas for improvement, allowing for a more precise and data-driven approach to goal refinement.

Continuous evaluation and adjustment create a flexible and adaptive framework for global expansion. It's a strategic mindset that values ongoing learning and embraces change as an integral part of the journey. Through this iterative process, businesses not only optimize their goals for success but also build resilience and responsiveness, positioning themselves for sustained growth and prosperity in international markets

Creating a Step-by-Step Expansion Roadmap

Creating a step-by-step expansion roadmap is a meticulous process that involves a comprehensive approach to ensure the success of global expansion endeavors. The roadmap serves as a dynamic guide, offering a structured framework that incorporates crucial elements such as market research, risk assessment, resource allocation, and the strategic implementation of initiatives.

Here is a step-by-step guide to constructing a detailed expansion roadmap:

- **Market Research:** Begin with a thorough analysis of the target markets. Evaluate factors such as market size, consumer behavior, competition, and regulatory landscapes. This foundational step provides essential insights into the viability and challenges of entering specific regions.
- **Risk Assessment:** Identify potential risks associated with global expansion. This involves evaluating geopolitical considerations, cultural differences, legal frameworks, and economic stability in the chosen markets. A comprehensive risk assessment allows businesses to develop mitigation strategies and contingency plans.
- **Resource Allocation:** Determine the resources required for successful expansion. This includes financial investments, human capital, technology, and logistical support. Allocating resources strategically ensures that the business is adequately prepared to navigate the complexities of entering new markets.
- **Strategic Initiatives:** Develop a set of strategic initiatives aligned with the overall business objectives. These initiatives may include marketing campaigns, localization efforts, partnerships, and technology upgrades. Each initiative should be tailored to address specific challenges and leverage opportunities in the target markets.
- **Timeline and Milestones:** Establish a clear timeline with milestones for each phase of the expansion process. This helps in tracking progress, maintaining accountability, and ensuring that the project stays on schedule. Breaking down the expansion into manageable stages enhances efficiency and provides a structured approach to achieving goals.

- **Localization Strategies:** Implement localization strategies that resonate with the cultural and linguistic nuances of the target markets. This may involve adapting marketing messages, product offerings, and customer service to align with local preferences. A well-executed localization strategy enhances brand relevance and fosters acceptance.
- **Regulatory Compliance**: Ensure compliance with local regulations and legal requirements. Understand the nuances of each market's legal framework and adapt business operations accordingly. Compliance not only mitigates risks but also builds trust and credibility within the local communities.
- **Monitoring and Evaluation:** Implement a robust monitoring and evaluation system. Regularly assess key performance indicators (KPIs), gather feedback, and measure the success of implemented strategies. This iterative process allows for continuous improvement and adjustment based on real-time insights
- **Adaptability and Flexibility:** Embed adaptability and flexibility into the roadmap. Recognize that unforeseen challenges may arise, and the ability to pivot and adjust strategies is crucial for navigating the dynamic global landscape effectively.
- **Continuous Improvement:** Conclude the roadmap with a commitment to continuous improvement. Encourage a culture of learning from experiences, both successes and setbacks, to refine future expansion strategies and maintain a competitive edge in the global market.

Constructing a detailed roadmap for global expansion demands a holistic and strategic mindset. By following this step-by-step approach, businesses can navigate the complexities of international markets with clarity, resilience, and a higher likelihood of success.

Adapting Strategies to Cultural Variances

Cultural sensitivity plays a pivotal role in strategic planning for global expansion, requiring businesses to acknowledge and integrate the diverse cultural nuances present in their target markets. Incorporating cultural sensitivity into strategic planning is essential for creating resonance with diverse audiences and ensuring adaptability to the unique attributes of each market.

Understanding Cultural Sensitivity

Cultural sensitivity is a multifaceted concept that transcends mere awareness, delving into the profound recognition and respect for the values, traditions, and behavioral norms that characterize diverse cultures. At its core, cultural sensitivity acknowledges the intricate tapestry of human experience, acknowledging that individuals from various backgrounds bring unique perspectives, beliefs, and practices to the table.

Going beyond surface-level observations, cultural sensitivity necessitates a profound understanding of how cultural factors intricately shape consumer behaviors, preferences, and decision-making processes. This understanding extends to the nuances of communication styles, societal structures, and the implicit cultural cues that influence interactions. Businesses that prioritize cultural sensitivity recognize that each culture possesses its own intricate set of dynamics, and successful engagement requires a willingness to comprehend and appreciate these subtleties.

Respecting the values inherent in different cultures is fundamental to cultural sensitivity. Whether rooted in centuries-old traditions, ethical principles, or social norms, these values serve as guiding forces shaping individuals' choices and perceptions. Cultural sensitivity demands an openness to learning about and respecting these values, avoiding assumptions or stereotypes that might hinder meaningful cross-cultural interactions.

Furthermore, cultural sensitivity recognizes the dynamic nature of cultures, acknowledging that they evolve over time. Embracing this evolution is crucial for businesses seeking to engage with diverse markets effectively. An understanding of cultural shifts allows organizations to adapt their strategies, ensuring they remain aligned with the contemporary values and aspirations of the communities they serve.

In the context of global business, cultural sensitivity becomes a strategic imperative. As companies expand their reach across borders, the ability to navigate the complex interplay of cultural dynamics becomes a competitive advantage. Brands that embody cultural sensitivity in their operations, marketing, and customer interactions position themselves not only as market leaders but also as responsible global citizens.

Ultimately, the essence of cultural sensitivity lies in fostering genuine connections based on mutual respect and understanding. Businesses that cultivate cultural sensitivity create environments where employees, customers, and partners feel valued and heard, transcending geographical and cultural boundaries. This nuanced approach not only enhances business success but also contributes to the broader narrative of fostering harmony and collaboration in an interconnected world.

Incorporating Cultural Nuances

Strategic planning for global expansion demands a nuanced approach that actively integrates cultural nuances into every facet of a business's growth strategies. This comprehensive incorporation extends across various domains, including product adaptation, marketing communication, and customer engagement. Recognizing and responding to the unique aspects of each culture is not just a matter of sensitivity; it's a strategic imperative for sustained success in diverse markets.

One critical aspect of incorporating cultural nuances lies in product adaptation. Beyond the functionality of a product, its features, design, and even packaging can be tailored to align seamlessly with local preferences. This process goes beyond a surface-level adjustment; it requires an in-depth understanding of the cultural context to ensure that the product resonates with the values and aesthetics of the target audience. By customizing products to cater to specific cultural expectations, businesses demonstrate a commitment to meeting the unique needs of each market.

In the realm of marketing communication, cultural sensitivity plays a pivotal role. Language, symbolism, and imagery can vary significantly across cultures, and what may be effective in one region could miss the mark in another. Adapting marketing materials to resonate with the cultural context helps build relatability and trust. This may involve translating content, choosing visuals that align with local sensibilities, and ensuring that messaging is culturally relevant and respectful.

Customer engagement strategies should also reflect cultural understanding. Recognizing the preferred channels of communication, understanding the significance of personal relationships, and adapting customer support practices to align with cultural norms contribute to a positive customer experience. For instance, in some cultures, face-to-face interactions may be highly valued, while in others, efficient digital communication may be the preferred mode.

Moreover, incorporating cultural nuances is not a one-time effort but an ongoing process. Cultures are dynamic, and as they evolve, businesses must adapt their strategies accordingly. Regular assessments and feedback mechanisms can help companies stay attuned to changing cultural dynamics and adjust their approaches proactively.

Successful incorporation of cultural nuances fosters a deeper connection with the local audience. It goes beyond merely avoiding cultural taboos; it involves actively seeking to understand and appreciate the cultural context, thereby building a foundation for meaningful and lasting relationships. Businesses that prioritize cultural integration demonstrate a commitment to the communities they serve, fostering goodwill and establishing themselves as trustworthy partners in global markets.

In summary, incorporating cultural nuances is a strategic imperative that goes hand in hand with effective global expansion. It demands a commitment to understanding and respecting the diversity of the markets a business enters, resulting in products and strategies that resonate authentically with the local audience. In the intricate dance of globalization, businesses that skillfully navigate cultural nuances stand poised for sustained success in the global arena.

Localization Strategies

Going beyond mere adaptation, localization involves tailoring various facets of a business, including products, services, and marketing messages, to align intricately with the cultural expectations and preferences of each target market. This nuanced approach recognizes that a one-size-fits-all model is insufficient in the diverse landscape of global business.

A fundamental aspect of localization is the customization of products to resonate authentically with the local audience. This extends beyond language translation to encompass the features, design, and even packaging of products. By understanding the cultural nuances that influence consumer preferences, businesses can ensure that their offerings not only meet functional needs but also align with the aesthetic and cultural sensibilities of the target market. This attention to detail showcases a commitment to providing a truly relevant and meaningful experience for consumers.

Localization in services is equally crucial. Tailoring services to accommodate local practices, preferences, and expectations enhances the customer experience. Whether it's adjusting service delivery processes or incorporating culturally sensitive customer support practices, a localized approach contributes to building trust and fostering positive relationships with customers. This, in turn, enhances the overall brand perception and increases the likelihood of long-term success in the market.

Marketing communication stands as a central pillar of localization. Crafting messages that resonate with the cultural context requires a deep understanding of local values, symbols, and communication styles. Localization involves adapting not just the language but also the imagery, tone, and overall narrative to align with the cultural nuances of the target audience. By doing so, businesses can create marketing campaigns that feel relatable, authentic, and engaging to the local community.

Moreover, effective localization is not a static process; it necessitates continuous adaptation. As cultures evolve, consumer preferences shift, and market dynamics change, businesses must stay attuned to these developments. Regular assessments, feedback mechanisms, and a commitment to remaining agile allow businesses to refine their localization strategies and ensure ongoing relevance in the face of cultural evolution.

Successful examples of localization abound, where businesses have seamlessly integrated into diverse markets. Whether it's adjusting menu items to cater to local tastes, incorporating cultural symbols in advertising campaigns, or aligning product launches with local festivities, businesses that prioritize localization showcase a deep respect for the diversity of global markets.

Localization strategies play a pivotal role in adapting to cultural variances during global expansion. This comprehensive approach, embracing the entire spectrum of a business's operations, reflects a commitment to understanding and respecting the unique attributes of each market. As businesses navigate the intricate landscape of global markets, effective localization emerges as a powerful tool to build bridges, foster connections, and establish a lasting presence in diverse cultural contexts.

Consumer Behavior Analysis

At the heart of cultural sensitivity in strategic planning lies the imperative of delving into the intricacies of consumer behavior across diverse markets. This entails a comprehensive analysis that recognizes the profound impact of cultural factors on purchasing decisions, brand loyalty, and consumer trust. By understanding the nuanced interplay between culture and consumer behavior, businesses can craft strategies that authentically connect with local audiences and foster meaningful engagements.

An essential aspect of consumer behavior analysis is recognizing the diverse ways in which cultural factors shape the decision-making processes of individuals. Cultural values, social norms, and collective beliefs influence not only what consumers buy but also how they perceive brands, make choices, and build relationships with businesses. For instance, in certain cultures, the emphasis may be on collective decision-making, where opinions of family or community members play a crucial role. In contrast, individualistic cultures may prioritize personal preferences and autonomy in decision-making.

The analysis should extend beyond traditional brick-and-mortar interactions to encompass the digital realm. Online platforms provide valuable insights into how consumers engage with brands, make purchase decisions, and express preferences. Tracking online interactions, social media engagements, and digital reviews can offer a nuanced understanding of the cultural nuances that influence consumer behavior in the digital space.

Brand loyalty, a cornerstone of business success, is intricately linked to cultural sensitivities. Understanding what fosters loyalty within a specific cultural context allows businesses to cultivate lasting relationships with their customer base. Cultural values often play a pivotal role in shaping brand loyalty, with consumers gravitating towards brands that align with their cultural beliefs and resonate with their identity.

Moreover, the establishment of consumer trust is deeply rooted in cultural factors. Trust is not merely transactional; it is built on shared values, ethical considerations, and a sense of authenticity. Cultural sensitivity involves recognizing the elements that contribute to trust-building within a particular cultural setting, whether it's transparency, accountability, or a commitment to social responsibility.

To conduct a meaningful consumer behavior analysis, businesses should employ a mix of qualitative and quantitative research methods. Surveys, focus groups, and in-depth interviews can provide qualitative insights into the cultural nuances shaping consumer behavior. Quantitative data, derived from market research, online analytics, and surveys, adds a layer of statistical validity to the analysis, allowing businesses to identify patterns and trends.

Cultural sensitivity in strategic planning necessitates a profound understanding of consumer behavior across diverse markets. The intricacies of how culture influences purchasing decisions, brand loyalty, and consumer trust form the foundation for crafting strategies that resonate authentically with local audiences. By recognizing and navigating these cultural nuances, businesses can position themselves not just as providers of products or services but as meaningful contributors to the cultural fabric of the communities they serve.

Communication Strategies

Tailoring communication strategies to align with the cultural nuances of each market is imperative, recognizing that how a message is conveyed can profoundly impact its reception. This comprehensive approach involves considering various aspects of communication, including styles, visual elements, and the incorporation of symbols or metaphors that hold cultural significance.

Communication styles vary significantly across cultures, encompassing both verbal and non-verbal aspects. Some cultures may prioritize indirect communication, relying on nuances and context, while others may favor direct and explicit communication. Understanding these preferences helps businesses craft messages that resonate authentically with the local audience. For example, a marketing campaign that emphasizes straightforwardness and clarity might align well with cultures valuing direct communication.

Visual elements play a crucial role in effective communication, and their impact can vary across cultures. Colors, imagery, and design aesthetics carry cultural connotations that may differ significantly from one market to another. For instance, certain colors may evoke positive emotions in one culture but carry different meanings in another. A culturally sensitive approach involves meticulous consideration of these visual elements to ensure they convey the intended message without unintended cultural misinterpretations.

The use of symbols or metaphors with cultural significance can enhance communication by creating a shared understanding with the local audience. However, it requires a nuanced understanding of the cultural context to avoid unintentional misinterpretations. For example, a symbol that represents good luck in one culture may carry a different connotation in another.

An adept communication strategy extends beyond language proficiency, recognizing that cultural nuances influence how messages are perceived and interpreted. It involves actively seeking to understand the cultural context in which communication takes place and adapting strategies accordingly. This approach not only avoids potential misunderstandings but also fosters a positive brand perception within diverse communities.

Moreover, effective communication strategies contribute to building trust, a cornerstone of successful business interactions. Cultural sensitivity in communication goes beyond translating words; it involves understanding the cultural cues that convey authenticity and reliability. Transparent and culturally resonant communication enhances the credibility of a business, fostering positive connections with local communities.

Communication strategies that prioritize cultural sensitivity are integral to successful strategic planning for global expansion. By tailoring communication styles, considering visual elements, and incorporating culturally significant symbols or metaphors, businesses can navigate the complexities of diverse markets with finesse. An adept communication strategy not only enhances brand perception but also cultivates positive relationships with local communities, laying the groundwork for sustainable success in the global arena.

Adapting strategies to cultural variances is a fundamental aspect of successful global expansion. Cultural sensitivity in strategic planning not only mitigates risks but also positions businesses to build authentic connections with diverse audiences. By recognizing and embracing cultural nuances, organizations can foster acceptance, trust, and sustained success in their global growth endeavors.

Chapter **5**

Market Research and
Cultural Intelligence

Market research and cultural intelligence form the bedrock of informed decision-making in the realm of global expansion. Market research involves the systematic gathering, analysis, and interpretation of data related to international markets, providing invaluable insights for strategic planning.

Cultural intelligence, on the other hand, refers to the capability to comprehend and adapt to diverse cultural contexts, enabling businesses to navigate the complexities of consumer behavior and preferences across borders.

Analyzing and selecting target international markets

Selecting the right international markets is a pivotal decision that can significantly impact the success of global expansion. This process involves a careful analysis of various factors to ensure alignment with the company's goals and capabilities.

Market Analysis

Market analysis is a critical component of strategic decision-making when venturing into new international markets. It involves a systematic examination of various factors that can influence the success of a business in a specific region. The process typically begins with a comprehensive evaluation of economic indicators. This includes studying the overall economic health of the potential market, looking at factors such as GDP growth, inflation rates, and employment figures. These indicators provide insights into the market's stability and potential for sustained growth.

Furthermore, assessing the market size is crucial for understanding the scale of opportunities and competition. This involves gauging the number of potential customers, their demographics, and the overall demand for products or services. Starbucks, for instance, meticulously analyzed the market size in each international location it considered. This enabled the company to identify regions where there was a substantial coffee culture and a significant consumer base, aligning with its expansion goals.

Growth potential is another key aspect of market analysis. Businesses need to evaluate whether the target market is poised for expansion and if there are emerging trends that could impact their industry. Identifying these growth opportunities allows companies to position themselves strategically. An illustrative example is Amazon's market analysis before entering the Indian e-commerce space. Recognizing the increasing digital population and a growing middle class, Amazon perceived substantial growth potential in India and strategically entered the market.

Understanding the competitive landscape is equally crucial. Analyzing existing competitors, their market share, and strategies provides valuable insights. This knowledge helps businesses identify areas of opportunity or differentiation. When entering a new market, companies need to be aware of their competitors and devise strategies that set them apart. Uber, for instance, studied the competitive landscape in various countries, adapting its business model to stand out in diverse markets.

Consumer preferences and behavior play a pivotal role in market analysis. Companies need to delve into the tastes, preferences, and buying habits of the local population. This includes understanding cultural nuances that can influence consumer choices. Apple's expansion into China is a testament to understanding consumer behavior. The company tailored its products to cater to Chinese consumers, incorporating features that resonated with local preferences.

Effective market analysis involves a holistic examination of economic conditions, market size, growth potential, competition, and consumer behavior. Successful businesses leverage these insights to make informed decisions on selecting international markets where their products or services align with local needs and preferences. The strategic analysis carried out during this phase sets the foundation for successful market entry and sustained growth on a global scale.

Cultural Considerations

Cultural considerations are paramount when analyzing and selecting target international markets. Each culture holds distinctive values, traditions, and preferences that shape consumer behavior. For businesses aiming to expand globally, recognizing and adapting to these cultural nuances is a key strategic element.

When McDonald's ventured into India, the company encountered a diverse and complex cultural landscape. India has a significant vegetarian population due to cultural and religious beliefs. To align with local preferences, McDonald's had to make substantial adjustments to its menu. The introduction of the McAloo Tikki burger, a vegetarian option, was a strategic move to cater to the predominantly vegetarian consumer base. This exemplifies how cultural considerations directly influence product offerings and business strategies in new markets.

In addition to dietary preferences, cultural considerations extend to factors such as language, communication styles, and societal norms. For example, when entering a market with a different language, businesses often need to localize their marketing materials to ensure effective communication. Cultural differences in communication styles also play a crucial role. Some cultures may value direct and explicit communication, while others may prefer more indirect and implicit forms of expression.

Moreover, societal norms and values impact consumer perceptions and brand acceptance. Companies must navigate these nuances carefully to avoid unintentional cultural insensitivity. For instance, campaigns that may be well-received in one culture might be perceived differently in another due to varying societal norms.

Successful global brands embrace cultural considerations as part of their market entry strategy. They invest in understanding the cultural fabric of the regions they target and tailor their products, services, and marketing strategies accordingly. By doing so, businesses not only demonstrate respect for local cultures but also increase the likelihood of building positive relationships with consumers.

Incorporating cultural considerations into the analysis and selection of international markets is indispensable for successful global expansion. Recognizing and respecting the unique aspects of each culture, whether in terms of dietary preferences, communication styles, or societal norms, allows businesses to connect authentically with consumers. It fosters a sense of cultural sensitivity that goes beyond mere adaptation – it reflects a commitment to understanding and embracing the diversity of global markets.

Regulatory Environment

Analyzing the regulatory environment is a critical step in selecting target international markets. Businesses must carefully examine the legal landscape, trade policies, and any regulatory restrictions that might impact their operations. This thorough understanding not only ensures compliance but also aids in effective risk mitigation.

A notable example of navigating diverse regulatory landscapes is Uber's global expansion. Uber, a ride-sharing platform, faced a myriad of regulatory challenges as it entered different markets. The transportation industry is heavily regulated, and Uber had to adapt its business model to comply with local transportation laws and regulations.

In some regions, Uber encountered resistance and legal barriers from traditional taxi services and regulatory authorities. The company had to engage in extensive dialogues with local governments to address concerns, comply with existing regulations, and, in some cases, advocate for the creation of new regulatory frameworks that accommodated innovative ride-sharing services.

Understanding the regulatory environment is crucial for anticipating potential obstacles and developing strategies to overcome them. It requires a proactive approach to compliance, ensuring that the business adheres to local laws and regulations while navigating any complexities that may arise. Failure to address regulatory considerations can lead to legal challenges, operational disruptions, and damage to a brand's reputation.

Examining the regulatory environment is a fundamental aspect of market analysis when selecting target international markets. Businesses that succeed in global expansion recognize the importance of compliance and risk management. They invest time and resources in understanding the legal intricacies of each market, allowing them to adapt their operations and strategies to align with local regulatory frameworks. This proactive approach not only facilitates smooth market entry but also contributes to building a positive relationship with local authorities and stakeholders.

Consumer Behavior

Understanding consumer behavior is a crucial element in the process of selecting target international markets. Analyzing how potential customers in diverse regions respond to products or services provides valuable insights for businesses seeking global expansion. This involves studying preferences, buying patterns, and overall brand perception within specific cultural contexts.

Apple's strategic entry into the Chinese market serves as an exemplary case of tailoring products based on consumer behavior analysis. Apple recognized the unique preferences and expectations of Chinese consumers and adapted its offerings accordingly. The introduction of features like dual SIM card slots and the incorporation of local apps demonstrated a deep understanding of the Chinese market's distinct demands.

To analyze consumer behavior effectively, businesses employ various research methods, both qualitative and quantitative. Surveys, interviews, focus groups, and observational studies are common techniques used to gather information on how individuals in different markets interact with products and brands. Online analytics tools also play a significant role, providing data on digital interactions, purchase behaviors, and user preferences.

In the case of Apple's expansion into China, the company likely conducted extensive research to comprehend the nuances of Chinese consumer behavior. This involved exploring the preferences of Chinese consumers when it comes to smartphones, understanding their expectations regarding functionality, design, and additional features.

The adaptation of Apple's products to Chinese consumer preferences went beyond just technical specifications. Apple's marketing and communication strategies were also tailored to resonate with the cultural context and values of the Chinese audience. Effective communication, aligned with cultural nuances, contributed to building a positive brand perception among Chinese consumers.

In summary, the analysis of consumer behavior is a multifaceted process that involves understanding the intricate details of how individuals in different markets make decisions and interact with products. It requires a combination of research methods and a keen awareness of cultural factors influencing purchasing behavior. Businesses that excel in global expansion recognize the importance of consumer behavior analysis as a fundamental pillar in the selection of target international markets. It enables them to tailor their offerings to specific preferences and create strategies that resonate with diverse audiences, fostering successful market entry and sustained growth.

Competitive Landscape

In the process of selecting target international markets, a comprehensive analysis of the competitive landscape is essential for businesses aiming to identify opportunities and navigate challenges effectively. Evaluating the existing competitors, understanding market saturation, and recognizing potential gaps in the market provide valuable insights that can shape strategic decisions.

A notable case illustrating the significance of assessing the competitive landscape is Amazon's entry into India. Amazon recognized the potential of the Indian e-commerce market, characterized by a rapidly growing digital population. Before making significant investments, the company conducted a thorough analysis of the competitive environment. This involved studying existing players in the Indian e-commerce space, understanding their market share, and identifying areas where Amazon could offer a unique value proposition.

The competitive analysis enabled Amazon to position itself strategically, identifying opportunities for growth and potential areas where it could differentiate itself from existing competitors. The company's entry into India was marked by innovative strategies tailored to the specific needs of the Indian consumer. This included initiatives such as introducing Amazon Pantry to cater to the grocery segment, implementing localized marketing campaigns, and investing in technology infrastructure to enhance the customer experience.

For businesses engaging in global expansion, a robust competitive landscape analysis involves not only understanding direct competitors but also considering broader market dynamics. Factors such as regulatory environments, cultural preferences, and the level of market saturation contribute to a holistic understanding of the competitive landscape.

In practice, businesses can use various tools and methodologies for competitive analysis. Market research, competitor profiling, and SWOT (Strengths, Weaknesses, Opportunities, Threats) analysis are common approaches. Leveraging data from industry reports, consumer surveys, and market trends enables businesses to make informed decisions regarding their entry strategy into a new market.

By taking a cue from Amazon's approach in India, businesses can learn that a thorough understanding of the competitive landscape is a strategic imperative. This analysis not only helps in identifying growth opportunities but also in formulating strategies that differentiate the business in a crowded marketplace.

The competitive landscape analysis is a vital component of market research when selecting target international markets. It provides businesses with valuable insights into the market dynamics, enabling them to make informed decisions about their entry strategy and positioning within a specific region. Successful global expansion often hinges on the ability to navigate and leverage the competitive environment effectively, ensuring that the chosen markets align with the overall goals and capabilities of the business.

Technological Infrastructure

In the realm of global expansion, businesses must meticulously evaluate the technological infrastructure of target markets, particularly if their operations are intricately tied to digital platforms. This assessment encompasses a thorough understanding of crucial aspects such as internet penetration, mobile usage patterns, and the availability and adoption of digital payment systems.

A prime example highlighting the significance of evaluating technological infrastructure is the global expansion strategy employed by Netflix. As a leading streaming service, Netflix recognized the critical role that technology plays in its business model. Before venturing into new international markets, the company conducted a comprehensive analysis of the technological landscape in each region.

One key factor that Netflix scrutinized was internet penetration. The company needed to ensure that its streaming platform could reach a substantial portion of the population in a given market. Additionally, the analysis involved understanding the prevalent mobile usage patterns since a significant portion of streaming often occurs on mobile devices.

Digital payment systems were another crucial consideration. As Netflix operates on a subscription-based model, having reliable and widely adopted digital payment methods in place was imperative. This included assessing the prevalence of credit cards, digital wallets, and other payment solutions that align with the preferences of the local population.

By considering these technological factors, Netflix aimed to provide a seamless streaming experience for users in each target market. The company strategically adapted its platform to suit the technological readiness of diverse regions, ensuring that potential challenges related to internet connectivity or payment methods were addressed proactively.

For businesses looking to expand globally, the technological infrastructure analysis is a fundamental step in ensuring the success and accessibility of their products or services. It allows companies to tailor their approach to the unique technological characteristics of each market, fostering a more inclusive and user-friendly experience.

The Netflix case exemplifies how a thoughtful evaluation of technological readiness can contribute to a successful international expansion. By aligning its streaming services with the technological capabilities of diverse markets, Netflix not only ensured customer satisfaction but also positioned itself as a global entertainment leader with a presence in numerous countries.

Evaluating technological infrastructure is a pivotal component of market research when selecting target international markets. Businesses that rely on digital platforms, streaming services, or e-commerce must consider factors like internet penetration, mobile usage, and digital payment systems to tailor their offerings effectively. By doing so, companies can navigate the nuances of diverse technological landscapes, providing a foundation for seamless operations and successful expansion.

Analyzing and selecting target international markets is a multifaceted process that involves a comprehensive understanding of economic, cultural, regulatory, and technological aspects. Successful companies strategically leverage market insights to identify markets where their products or services align with local needs and preferences, ultimately fostering sustainable global growth.

Understanding cultural differences and consumer behavior

In the pursuit of global expansion, businesses must delve into the intricate dynamics of cultural differences and consumer behavior to navigate diverse markets successfully. This understanding is fundamental for tailoring products, services, and marketing strategies to resonate authentically with local audiences.

Benefits of Recognizing Cultural Differences

1. Market Relevance

In global markets, the concept of market relevance becomes paramount, particularly when businesses acknowledge and navigate cultural nuances. Understanding the unique needs, values, and preferences of each market is not merely a gesture of cultural sensitivity; it's a strategic imperative for establishing market relevance.

One of the primary benefits of acknowledging cultural nuances is the ability to forge a deeper connection with consumers. Cultures vary significantly in their customs, traditions, and lifestyles. When businesses demonstrate an understanding of these cultural intricacies, consumers are more likely to resonate with the offerings, feeling a sense of familiarity and connection.

Consider, for instance, the global success of technology giant Apple. The company's approach to market relevance involves adapting its products to align with diverse cultural expectations. Whether it's incorporating features specific to certain regions or tailoring marketing campaigns to reflect local values, Apple showcases how acknowledging cultural nuances fosters a deeper connection with consumers worldwide.

Market acceptance is a pivotal factor for the success of any business venturing into international territories. By acknowledging cultural nuances, businesses position themselves to be accepted by the local population. This acceptance is not merely transactional; it extends to the brand being embraced as a part of the local fabric.

An illustrative example is Coca-Cola's global marketing strategy. The beverage giant recognizes the importance of cultural relevance in its campaigns. Coca-Cola's advertisements often reflect local customs, festivities, and traditions. This approach has contributed to the brand being seamlessly integrated into diverse cultures globally, showcasing how market relevance is intricately tied to cultural acknowledgment.

The process of acknowledging cultural nuances goes beyond surface-level gestures; it involves a substantive adaptation of products and services. This adaptation is not about conforming to a set mold but rather about tailoring offerings to meet the specific demands of the local market. IKEA, the Swedish furniture giant, exemplifies this adaptability. Recognizing diverse cultural preferences, IKEA customizes its product offerings to align with the aesthetic and functional needs of different markets. From variations in design to considerations of spatial constraints, IKEA's commitment to market relevance through cultural adaptation has contributed significantly to its global success.

Acknowledging cultural nuances is a strategic imperative for businesses aspiring to establish market relevance on a global scale. It's a nuanced dance that involves not just respecting differences but actively adapting strategies, products, and marketing efforts to align with the specific needs and expectations of diverse consumer bases. The benefits extend beyond immediate market acceptance; they permeate into the realms of brand loyalty, positive perception, and sustained success in the ever-evolving global marketplace.

2. Brand Authenticity

Cultural sensitivity is a cornerstone in cultivating and expressing brand authenticity. In a world where consumers increasingly seek genuine connections with brands, acknowledging and respecting local cultures plays a pivotal role in shaping brand authenticity. This authenticity is not just a marketing strategy; it reflects a commitment to understanding and embracing the diverse tapestry of global communities.

One of the primary ways cultural sensitivity contributes to brand authenticity is through the perception of genuineness. When businesses go beyond surface-level adaptations and demonstrate a sincere understanding of local cultures, consumers are more likely to perceive them as authentic. This authenticity is not just about ticking boxes for diversity; it reflects a deeper commitment to integrating cultural insights into the very fabric of the brand's identity.

The perception of authenticity, in turn, fosters trust. Consumers are more inclined to trust brands that showcase a genuine interest in and respect for local cultures. Trust is a critical factor influencing purchasing decisions and fostering long-term relationships between brands and consumers. For instance, Patagonia, an outdoor apparel company, has built its authenticity by aligning with environmental and social values globally. This authenticity has translated into a dedicated customer base that trusts the brand's commitment to sustainability.

Moreover, brand authenticity contributes to positive brand perception. When consumers perceive a brand as authentic, it creates a positive image that extends beyond the specific products or services offered. This positive perception often results in enhanced brand loyalty, as consumers prefer to align themselves with brands that reflect their values and cultural sensitivities.

Cultural sensitivity, therefore, becomes a powerful tool for brands to differentiate themselves in a crowded marketplace. In an era where consumers are inundated with choices, authenticity becomes a key factor influencing purchasing decisions. Brands that genuinely invest in understanding and respecting local cultures distinguish themselves from those that merely engage in superficial adaptations.

An illustrative example of brand authenticity through cultural sensitivity is Airbnb. The platform recognizes the importance of cultural nuances in the hospitality industry. By encouraging hosts to infuse their listings with local flavors, traditions, and unique experiences, Airbnb taps into the authenticity inherent in diverse cultures. This approach not only sets

Airbnb apart from traditional accommodations but also resonates with travelers seeking authentic and immersive experiences.

Brand authenticity is an invaluable asset in today's competitive global marketplace. Cultural sensitivity acts as the compass guiding businesses towards the authenticity consumers seek. When businesses embrace and respect local cultures, consumers perceive them as genuine, building trust and fostering positive brand perception. This authenticity goes beyond a mere marketing strategy; it becomes a fundamental aspect of a brand's identity, resonating with consumers who increasingly value meaningful connections with the brands they choose to engage with and support.

3. Adaptability

Understanding and embracing cultural differences play a pivotal role in fostering adaptability within businesses. In a globalized marketplace characterized by diverse consumer expectations, dynamic market trends, and evolving societal norms, adaptability becomes a strategic imperative. Businesses that prioritize cultural understanding position themselves to navigate these changes with agility, ensuring relevance and resonance with their target audiences.

One of the key aspects of adaptability facilitated by cultural understanding is the ability to respond swiftly to changes in consumer expectations. Cultures shape consumers' preferences, behaviors, and purchasing patterns. By understanding these nuances, businesses can tailor their products, services, and marketing strategies to align with evolving consumer expectations. This adaptability allows businesses to stay ahead of industry trends and respond effectively to shifts in demand, ensuring that their offerings remain relevant and appealing to their target markets.

Moreover, cultural understanding enables businesses to navigate dynamic market trends successfully. Markets are influenced by cultural shifts, technological advancements, and changing consumer preferences. For instance, the rise of conscious consumerism, driven by cultural values and social awareness, has led to a demand for sustainable and ethical products. Businesses that comprehend these cultural underpinnings can adapt their strategies to meet these trends, ensuring that their products align with the values of contemporary consumers.

Societal shifts also play a crucial role in shaping market dynamics. Understanding the cultural context allows businesses to anticipate and adapt to societal changes, whether they relate to demographics, lifestyles, or cultural movements. For instance, the increasing focus on inclusivity and diversity in many societies has prompted businesses to reevaluate their marketing approaches, product offerings, and corporate values. By being attuned to these cultural shifts, businesses can proactively adapt their strategies, ensuring that they resonate with the evolving expectations of their diverse customer base.

Additionally, cultural understanding enhances adaptability in the face of international expansions. Global markets present a myriad of cultural variations, from communication styles to consumer behaviors. Businesses that comprehend and embrace these differences can tailor their approaches to suit each market. This adaptability is exemplified by multinational companies that successfully localize their products and marketing strategies to align with the unique cultural contexts of different countries.

A noteworthy example of adaptability through cultural understanding is McDonald's. The fast-food giant has demonstrated remarkable adaptability by incorporating local flavors and cultural preferences into its menu in various countries. In India, McDonald's introduced a range of vegetarian options, including the popular McAloo Tikki burger, catering to the dietary preferences of the predominantly vegetarian population. This adaptability not only aligns McDonald's offerings with local culture but also positions the brand as responsive to diverse consumer needs.

Understanding cultural differences is instrumental in fostering adaptability within businesses. This adaptability extends to responding to changes in consumer expectations, navigating dynamic market trends, and successfully expanding into international markets. Businesses that prioritize cultural understanding position themselves as agile and responsive, ensuring that they can effectively navigate the complexities of the globalized marketplace and meet the evolving needs of their diverse consumer base.

Benefits of Analyzing Consumer Behavior

1. Tailored Marketing Strategies

Analyzing consumer behavior is a cornerstone of crafting effective and tailored marketing strategies for businesses. In a landscape where consumer preferences, expectations, and decision-making processes vary significantly, understanding these nuances becomes essential for creating promotional efforts that resonate with the target audience. Tailoring marketing strategies based on consumer behavior not only increases the relevance of the messages but also enhances the overall effectiveness of promotional campaigns.

Consumer behavior analysis provides businesses with insights into the motivations, preferences, and expectations that drive purchasing decisions. By delving into these aspects, businesses can gain a deeper understanding of their target audience, allowing them to create marketing messages that are specifically tailored to meet the needs and aspirations of consumers.

One key advantage of tailored marketing strategies is the ability to craft messages that align with consumer preferences. For instance, if consumer behavior analysis reveals a preference for eco-friendly products, a company can focus its marketing messages on the sustainability features of its offerings. By emphasizing elements that resonate with consumers, businesses can establish a connection that goes beyond product features, creating a more compelling narrative that aligns with the values of their audience.

Furthermore, tailored marketing strategies account for the diverse decision-making processes among consumers. Different individuals may prioritize various factors when making purchasing decisions, such as price, brand reputation, or product features. Consumer behavior analysis helps identify these varying priorities, enabling businesses to customize their marketing messages to address the specific considerations that matter most to their target audience. For example, a tech company may emphasize the innovative features of a product for tech enthusiasts, while highlighting affordability and reliability for budget-conscious consumers.

Personalization is another key aspect of tailored marketing strategies. With insights gained from consumer behavior analysis, businesses can personalize their marketing communications, creating a more individualized experience for consumers. This can involve personalized recommendations, targeted promotions, or customized content that speaks directly to the preferences of each consumer segment. Personalization not only enhances the relevance of marketing messages but also fosters a sense of connection and engagement with the brand.

Effective consumer behavior analysis also aids businesses in identifying the most suitable channels for reaching their target audience. Whether through social media, email marketing, or traditional advertising, understanding how consumers prefer to receive information allows businesses to allocate resources more efficiently. For instance, if a particular consumer segment is more active on social media, businesses can focus their promotional efforts on platforms where they are most likely to capture the attention of their audience.

Analyzing consumer behavior is instrumental in tailoring marketing strategies to the unique preferences and decision-making processes of the target audience. Tailored approaches enhance the effectiveness of promotional efforts by creating messages that resonate with consumers, addressing their specific needs, and fostering a more personalized connection. As businesses navigate the complexities of the modern marketplace, leveraging consumer behavior insights becomes a strategic imperative for staying relevant and impactful in promotional endeavors.

2. Product Development

Consumer behavior insights play a pivotal role in guiding product development for businesses seeking to create offerings that resonate with their target audience. Understanding the factors that drive purchasing decisions provides valuable guidance for refining existing products and introducing new ones that align seamlessly with consumer expectations. This approach not only enhances the relevance of products in the market but also increases the likelihood of success.

One key aspect of leveraging consumer behavior insights in product development is identifying unmet needs and preferences within the target audience. By analyzing consumer behavior, businesses can uncover gaps in the market or areas where existing products may not fully satisfy consumer expectations. For example, a technology company analyzing consumer feedback might discover a desire for more user-friendly interfaces. Armed with this knowledge, the company can focus on developing products that address this specific need, giving them a competitive edge.

Moreover, consumer behavior insights enable businesses to refine existing products to better match the preferences of their audience. Through detailed analysis, companies can gain insights into specific features, functionalities, or design elements that resonate positively with consumers. This information becomes invaluable in product optimization, allowing businesses to make informed adjustments that enhance overall customer satisfaction. For instance, if a cosmetic brand identifies a growing preference for cruelty-free products through consumer behavior analysis, they can adjust their formulations and marketing strategies accordingly.

Consumer behavior insights also play a crucial role in guiding innovation. Businesses can identify emerging trends and changing consumer preferences, providing a foundation for the development of innovative products that capture the evolving demands of the market. For example, the rise of health-conscious consumer behavior has spurred innovations in the food and beverage industry, with companies introducing healthier alternatives to meet this growing demand.

Additionally, understanding the decision-making processes of consumers aids in creating products with the right pricing and packaging strategies. Consumer behavior analysis helps businesses determine the price points that align with perceived value and the packaging that appeals to their target demographic. This strategic approach ensures that products are not only desirable but also positioned effectively in the market to attract and retain customers.

In a rapidly evolving marketplace, consumer behavior insights also assist in predicting future trends and demands. By tracking patterns and shifts in consumer behavior over time, businesses can anticipate changes in preferences or emerging needs, allowing them to proactively adjust their product development strategies. For instance, an electronics company might analyze consumer behavior to identify a growing interest in sustainable technology, prompting them to invest in the development of eco-friendly devices.

Leveraging consumer behavior insights in product development is a strategic imperative for businesses aiming to create offerings that resonate with their target audience. From identifying unmet needs to refining existing products and guiding innovation, consumer behavior analysis provides valuable guidance at every stage of the product development lifecycle. By aligning products with the preferences and expectations of consumers, businesses can enhance their competitive position, foster customer loyalty, and drive success in the dynamic landscape of the modern marketplace.

3. Enhanced Customer Engagement

A profound understanding of consumer behavior serves as a cornerstone for businesses seeking to enhance customer engagement. This deeper insight allows companies to go beyond mere transactions, creating meaningful interactions that foster long-term relationships and cultivate brand loyalty.

Consumer behavior insights offer businesses the ability to tailor their communication strategies to align with the preferences and habits of their target audience. By understanding how consumers prefer to be engaged—whether through social media, email, or other channels—businesses can deliver messages that resonate more effectively. For example, a clothing retailer analyzing consumer behavior may discover that their audience engages more on visual platforms like Instagram. Armed with this knowledge, the company can focus on creating visually appealing content that speaks directly to their audience, resulting in more meaningful and impactful engagement.

Furthermore, understanding the decision-making processes of consumers allows businesses to personalize their interactions. Consumer behavior analysis provides insights into the factors that influence purchasing decisions, such as brand values, product preferences, or pricing considerations. Armed with this information, businesses can tailor their engagement strategies to align with the unique preferences of individual customers. For instance, a subscription service analyzing consumer behavior may discover that certain customers prioritize flexibility over pricing. This knowledge enables the company to offer personalized plans that cater specifically to this segment, enhancing customer satisfaction and loyalty.

Moreover, consumer behavior insights contribute to the development of targeted and relevant marketing campaigns. By identifying the interests, needs, and pain points of their audience, businesses can create messaging that speaks directly to those aspects. This targeted approach increases the likelihood of capturing the attention and interest of consumers, driving more meaningful engagement. For example, a technology company analyzing consumer behavior may uncover a growing interest in sustainability. Incorporating this insight into their marketing campaigns allows the company to resonate with eco-conscious consumers, fostering a stronger connection.

In addition to personalized communication and targeted marketing, consumer behavior insights empower businesses to enhance customer experiences. Understanding the preferences and expectations of consumers allows companies to optimize every touchpoint, from the browsing experience on an e-commerce platform to the post-purchase support. For example, an online retailer analyzing consumer behavior may identify a desire for seamless and hassle-free returns. Responding to this insight, the company can implement a user-friendly return process, elevating the overall customer experience and contributing to brand loyalty.

Ultimately, enhanced customer engagement driven by a profound understanding of consumer behavior is a strategic advantage in a competitive marketplace. Businesses that invest in analyzing and leveraging these insights position themselves to build authentic connections with their audience. By tailoring communication, personalizing interactions, and optimizing experiences, companies can foster long-term relationships, cultivate brand loyalty, and stand out in the hearts and minds of their customers.

Case Study: McDonald's in India

McDonald's entry into the Indian market stands as a captivating case study that underscores the substantial benefits of comprehending cultural differences and consumer behavior. As a global fast-food giant, McDonald's recognized the importance of adapting its strategies to align with the specific needs and preferences of the diverse Indian consumer base.

One of the first and crucial steps taken by McDonald's in India was a deep dive into the cultural fabric of the country. India, with its rich culinary heritage and diverse dietary practices, presented a unique landscape for a fast-food brand. The company meticulously analyzed the cultural nuances that influence Indian consumer behavior, acknowledging the significance of vegetarianism, which is a predominant dietary choice in the country.

Understanding the centrality of vegetarianism in Indian culture, McDonald's made a strategic decision to introduce a range of vegetarian options on its menu. The standout creation was the McAloo Tikki burger, a vegetarian delight that incorporated locally relevant flavors. This move showcased a keen awareness of the dietary preferences of the Indian population and demonstrated McDonald's commitment to providing choices that resonate with local consumers.

The cultural adaptation extended beyond menu modifications. McDonald's in India incorporated elements of Indian festivals and traditions into its marketing strategies. For instance, during festivals like Diwali, the company introduced special festive-themed offerings, tapping into the cultural festivities that hold immense significance for the Indian audience. This approach not only showcased an understanding of cultural values but also allowed McDonald's to actively participate in and celebrate local traditions, fostering a deeper connection with consumers.

Moreover, McDonald's in India embraced the importance of family-centric dining experiences ingrained in Indian culture. The restaurant design and ambiance were tailored to accommodate families and larger groups, aligning with the cultural emphasis on communal dining. This adjustment in the dining experience reflected an astute understanding of the social fabric and lifestyle preferences of the Indian audience.

The success of McDonald's in India is a testament to the positive outcomes that arise from aligning business strategies with cultural insights and consumer behavior. The adaptation of the menu to include vegetarian options not only showcased cultural sensitivity but also addressed a specific consumer need, thereby increasing the brand's relevance in the local market. McDonald's demonstrated that a one-size-fits-all approach does not suffice in diverse markets like India, and businesses need to be attuned to local nuances to succeed.

Furthermore, this case study highlights the broader implication that cultural understanding has on brand perception and acceptance. By demonstrating an authentic appreciation for local culture, McDonald's in India not only gained a competitive edge but also built a positive brand image. The company's commitment to cultural adaptation and consumer-centric strategies resulted in McDonald's becoming a familiar and well-accepted brand in India, reflecting the enduring impact of cultural intelligence on global business success.

McDonald's in India serves as a compelling illustration of how businesses can leverage cultural understanding and consumer behavior analysis to tailor their offerings and strategies. The case study underscores the strategic advantages of aligning with local preferences, showcasing the profound impact that cultural sensitivity can have on a brand's success in a globalized marketplace.

In the global business landscape, recognizing and leveraging cultural differences and consumer behavior is not merely a necessity; it is a strategic advantage. Businesses that invest in understanding diverse cultures and consumer preferences position themselves for market relevance, authenticity, and sustained success. The benefits extend beyond immediate market penetration, contributing to brand loyalty and adaptability in an ever-evolving global marketplace.

Developing effective market entry strategies

Developing effective market entry strategies is a critical aspect of international business expansion, requiring careful planning, analysis, and adaptation to the dynamics of target markets. Below are key steps and considerations to ensure the formulation of successful market entry strategies:

1. Comprehensive Market Research

Before entering a new market, businesses must conduct thorough market research. This involves assessing the economic environment, consumer behavior, regulatory landscape, and identifying potential competitors. Understanding the intricacies of the market provides a solid foundation for strategy development.

2. Target Market Selection

Carefully selecting the target market is crucial. Businesses should evaluate various markets based on factors such as size, growth potential, cultural compatibility, and competition. Consideration of demographics, psychographics, and socio-economic factors is essential to identify the most suitable markets for the product or service.

3. Adaptation to Local Culture

Cultural sensitivity is paramount. Tailoring products, services, and marketing strategies to align with local cultural preferences enhances acceptance and relevance. Successful market entry requires an understanding of local customs, values, and traditions to ensure a seamless integration of the brand.

4. Regulatory Compliance

Navigating the regulatory landscape is fundamental. Businesses must comply with local laws, trade policies, and industry regulations. Ensuring adherence to legal requirements not only avoids potential pitfalls but also builds trust with local stakeholders.

5. Entry Mode Selection

Choosing the right entry mode is critical for success. Options include exporting, licensing, franchising, joint ventures, or establishing wholly-owned subsidiaries. The choice depends on factors like the level of control desired, financial resources, and the nature of the business.

6. Competitive Positioning

Understanding the competitive landscape is essential for effective market entry. Businesses should identify key competitors, assess their strengths and weaknesses, and position themselves strategically. Differentiation strategies should highlight unique value propositions to stand out in the market.

7. Strategic Alliances and Partnerships

Forming strategic alliances with local partners can provide valuable insights, access to distribution networks, and enhance credibility. Partnering with established entities can expedite market entry and mitigate risks associated with unfamiliar markets.

8. Pricing and Distribution Strategies

Developing appropriate pricing strategies and distribution channels is crucial. Understanding local pricing norms and consumer behavior ensures competitive pricing, while optimizing distribution channels ensures efficient product/service delivery.

9. Risk Mitigation

Recognizing and mitigating risks is integral to market entry success. Businesses should conduct risk assessments related to political, economic, social, and technological factors. Developing contingency plans and being adaptable to unforeseen challenges is essential.

10. Marketing and Promotion

Crafting effective marketing and promotional strategies tailored to the target market is vital. This involves localization of marketing materials, advertising campaigns, and utilizing digital platforms effectively. Building brand awareness through culturally resonant messaging enhances market penetration.

Developing effective market entry strategies requires a holistic approach that considers diverse factors impacting the target market. By conducting thorough research, adapting to local cultures, complying with regulations, and strategically positioning the business, companies can enhance their chances of successful international expansion. Each step in the process contributes to building a robust market entry strategy that aligns with the unique dynamics of the chosen market.

Chapter **6**

Financial Considerations
for Scaling Up

Navigating the path of global expansion requires a keen understanding of financial considerations, a facet integral to the success of scaling up operations internationally. Financial planning, investment decisions, and compliance with diverse fiscal landscapes become pivotal elements in determining the trajectory of expansion strategies.

In this chapter, we delve into the crucial financial aspects that businesses must contemplate when embarking on the journey of scaling up globally.

Funding your expansion: Investment and Financial Planning

Embarking on a global expansion journey necessitates a robust financial foundation, requiring careful consideration of investment sources and comprehensive financial planning. Securing the necessary funds is a pivotal step that demands strategic decision-making to ensure sustainable growth in new markets.

Equity Financing

Equity financing stands out as a compelling avenue for businesses seeking funding for their international expansion endeavors. This method involves raising capital by issuing and selling shares of the company to external investors. The investors, often individuals or institutional entities, acquire ownership stakes in the business in return for their financial contributions. This approach is rooted in the principle of shared success—investors become stakeholders in the company, and their interests are inherently tied to the performance and prosperity of the global expansion initiative.

The process of equity financing typically begins with a business assessing its capital needs for international expansion. Once the funding requirements are determined, the company can attract potential investors through various means, such as private offerings, crowdfunding platforms, or engaging with venture capital firms. Investors, attracted by the growth prospects and international market opportunities, buy shares of the company, providing the necessary funds for the expansion.

One of the notable advantages of equity financing lies in its capacity to infuse significant capital into the business without creating debt obligations. Unlike loans, equity investments do not require periodic repayments of principal and interest, offering a degree of financial flexibility for the company. Moreover, the alignment of interests between the business and investors is a key strength. When investors hold ownership stakes, they are inherently motivated to contribute not only capital but also strategic insights and guidance to ensure the success of the international venture.

Equity financing is particularly beneficial for businesses with high growth potential and ambitious global expansion plans. It allows companies to leverage external expertise and networks brought in by the investors, adding substantial value beyond mere financial support. Additionally, the company can benefit from the credibility and validation that come with attracting reputable investors, enhancing its overall market standing.

However, it's crucial to acknowledge that equity financing involves the dilution of ownership for existing shareholders. As new investors acquire shares, the ownership percentage of current stakeholders decreases proportionately. Striking the right balance between securing the necessary funding and preserving the company's overall ownership structure requires careful negotiation and consideration.

Successful examples of equity financing driving international expansion can be observed in the technology and startup sectors. Companies like Uber, Airbnb, and SpaceX have relied on significant rounds of equity financing to fund their global ambitions. These businesses attracted investments from venture capital firms and institutional investors, enabling them to navigate diverse markets, overcome regulatory challenges, and achieve widespread international success.

Equity financing serves as a dynamic mechanism for businesses to fund their international expansion dreams. It not only provides the financial means for venturing into new markets but also establishes a network of committed partners who share in the journey and contribute to the strategic success of the global expansion initiative.

Debt Financing

Debt financing represents a financial strategy in which businesses acquire funds by borrowing from various sources, typically financial institutions such as banks or credit unions. This method involves obtaining loans or credit lines to fulfill diverse financial needs associated with the expansion process, covering aspects such as operational requirements, infrastructure development, or the costs associated with entering new markets. While debt financing introduces the obligation of repayment along with interest, it serves as a practical option for companies that can confidently articulate a well-defined plan for generating returns on their investment.

The process of debt financing initiates with a business identifying its financial requirements for expansion. This could involve estimating the costs associated with international market entry, setting up operations, marketing endeavors, or any other capital-intensive aspects of the expansion plan. Once the financial needs are established, the business can approach lending institutions to secure loans or lines of credit.

One of the key advantages of debt financing lies in its ability to provide businesses with immediate access to substantial capital without diluting ownership. Unlike equity financing, where ownership stakes are traded for funding, debt financing allows companies to maintain control over their operations while utilizing borrowed funds to fuel their expansion ambitions. This financial approach is particularly attractive to businesses with a clear strategy for generating returns on the invested capital.

Debt financing instruments can take various forms, including term loans, revolving credit lines, or even bonds. The terms and conditions of the debt agreement, such as interest rates, repayment schedules, and collateral requirements, are negotiated between the borrowing business and the lending institution. The agreed-upon terms reflect the risk assessment of the lender and the financial capacity and credibility of the borrowing entity.

Businesses opting for debt financing assume the responsibility of repaying the borrowed funds within agreed-upon timeframes. This repayment usually includes both the principal amount and accrued interest. The interest rates associated with debt financing can vary based on prevailing market conditions, the creditworthiness of the borrowing entity, and the specific terms negotiated.

While debt financing provides businesses with the necessary capital for expansion, it's crucial to manage associated risks. The obligation to repay debt, even during challenging economic conditions, introduces financial strain and requires careful cash flow management. Additionally, prudent assessment of the return on investment is essential to ensure that the benefits derived from the expansion outweigh the costs associated with debt financing.

Several successful businesses have utilized debt financing to support their international expansion efforts. For example, multinational corporations often leverage debt to finance the establishment of new facilities, research and development initiatives, or marketing campaigns in diverse global markets. This demonstrates how debt financing can be a strategic tool for businesses seeking to scale up their operations on an international scale.

Venture Capital and Angel Investors

Venture capital and angel investors play pivotal roles in fueling the growth of businesses, particularly those with high-growth potential and innovative concepts. These entities serve as valuable sources of funding for companies seeking to expand internationally, bringing not only financial capital but also strategic guidance and networking opportunities.

Venture capital (VC) firms are professional investment entities that manage pooled funds from various sources, including institutional investors and high-net-worth individuals. These funds are then strategically invested in startups or businesses that exhibit considerable growth potential. Venture capitalists play an active role in the companies they invest in, offering expertise, mentorship, and industry knowledge beyond mere financial backing.

One of the primary functions of venture capitalists is to identify and invest in businesses with promising growth trajectories. They assess the viability and scalability of a business model, its potential market share, and the competence of the management team. For businesses eyeing international expansion, venture capital can be instrumental in providing the necessary funds for market entry, product development, and scaling operations.

Angel investors, on the other hand, are typically affluent individuals who invest their personal funds into early-stage startups or businesses. Unlike venture capital firms, angel investors invest their own money and often have a more hands-on approach in supporting the companies they back. They are often entrepreneurs themselves or retired business professionals with a keen interest in fostering the growth of innovative ventures.

The primary function of angel investors is to provide financial support to startups and emerging businesses, particularly during the critical early stages of development. Angel investors often invest in industries or sectors where they have expertise, allowing them to offer valuable insights, mentorship, and networking opportunities to the companies they support. Their involvement can extend beyond monetary contributions, encompassing strategic advice, introductions to potential partners or clients, and guidance on navigating the complexities of international markets.

For businesses contemplating global expansion, engaging with venture capitalists or angel investors can bring numerous advantages. These investors not only inject capital into the business but also provide access to their extensive networks and industry knowledge. Their experience can be invaluable in navigating the complexities of entering new markets, understanding local business practices, and making strategic decisions for international success.

Additionally, the involvement of venture capitalists or angel investors often serves as a vote of confidence in the business, which can be particularly beneficial when entering unfamiliar markets. The credibility and endorsement from seasoned investors can enhance the business's reputation, making it more attractive to potential clients, partners, and stakeholders in international markets.

Venture capital and angel investors are instrumental in supporting businesses with global ambitions. Their financial contributions, coupled with strategic guidance and industry expertise, can significantly bolster the success of international expansion initiatives. Businesses seeking funding for their global endeavors can benefit from forging partnerships with these investors, leveraging not only their capital but also their wealth of experience in navigating the complexities of the global business landscape.

Government Grants and Subsidies

Government grants and subsidies serve as valuable financial instruments for businesses embarking on international expansion, presenting opportunities to ease financial burdens and promote economic development. Numerous governments around the world extend support to businesses aligning with their economic goals and pursuing cross-border growth initiatives

Governments often allocate funds in the form of grants to support businesses that contribute to specific economic objectives. These grants are typically non-repayable, meaning businesses are not required to return the funds. Governments may offer grants to encourage job creation, stimulate innovation, or enhance global competitiveness. For instance, a country aiming to promote sustainable practices might provide grants to businesses investing in eco-friendly technologies during their international expansion.

Accessing government grants involves a structured application process, where businesses must demonstrate how their expansion aligns with the government's priorities. This could include showcasing job creation plans, detailing investments in research and development, or highlighting contributions to specific industries. Successful grant applications provide businesses with a financial boost for their international endeavors.

Subsidies, on the other hand, are financial support mechanisms where governments cover a portion of specific business costs related to international expansion. These can include subsidies for export activities, trade show participation, or even assistance with market entry expenses. Subsidies aim to make international markets more accessible to businesses by offsetting certain operational costs.

For example, a government might subsidize a company's participation in an international trade fair to promote its products globally. This support encourages businesses to explore new markets and engage with a broader audience, ultimately contributing to economic growth.

Governments may also offer incentives to encourage international expansion. These incentives can take various forms, such as tax breaks, reduced regulatory requirements, or preferential treatment in specific industries. Governments may view certain sectors as strategically important for global competitiveness and provide incentives to businesses operating within these realms.

Understanding and navigating the landscape of government grants and subsidies requires thorough research and engagement with relevant authorities. Businesses should identify programs that align with their expansion plans and fulfill the eligibility criteria outlined by the respective government. Developing a compelling case that demonstrates how the international expansion contributes to local economic objectives is crucial for securing government support.

Engaging with government grants and subsidies necessitates a strategic approach. Businesses should align their expansion initiatives with the priorities outlined by the government offering financial support. This not only enhances the likelihood of securing grants but also positions the company as a contributor to broader economic goals.

Moreover, staying informed about changes in government policies and economic development strategies is essential. Governments may adjust their support programs based on evolving economic priorities, and businesses need to adapt their strategies to align with these shifts.

Government grants, subsidies, and incentives play a crucial role in facilitating international expansion for businesses. By exploring and leveraging these opportunities, companies can benefit from financial support, reduce entry barriers into new markets, and actively contribute to the economic goals of the regions they enter. Thorough research, strategic alignment, and proactive engagement with relevant authorities are key components of a successful approach to accessing government support for global growth.

Strategic Partnerships

Strategic partnerships emerge as a dynamic avenue for businesses seeking funding during international expansion. Forming collaborative alliances with other enterprises, whether on a local or global scale, offers a mutually beneficial strategy for securing financial support. In the realm of international business, joint ventures and partnerships provide access to additional resources, shared risks, and collective successes.

Strategic partnerships enable businesses to pool resources and expertise. By joining forces with another entity, companies can tap into complementary strengths, accessing knowledge, technologies, or market insights that might be crucial for their international endeavors. For example, a technology company expanding globally might form a partnership with a local distributor, leveraging the partner's established market presence.

International expansion often involves inherent risks, whether related to unfamiliar markets, regulatory complexities, or cultural nuances. Strategic partnerships allow businesses to share these risks with their partners. This shared responsibility not only cushions the financial burden but also fosters a collaborative approach to problem-solving. Conversely, successful ventures lead to shared rewards, creating a mutually reinforcing cycle of growth.

Collaborating with strategic partners can streamline market entry. Local partners bring valuable insights into the target market, including consumer behavior, preferences, and regulatory landscapes. This local knowledge is instrumental in navigating complexities that might pose challenges to businesses entering unfamiliar territories. For instance, a fashion brand expanding internationally might form a partnership with a local retailer to navigate regional fashion trends and consumer expectations.

Strategic partnerships provide an avenue for negotiating favorable financial terms. Whether it's sharing investment costs, dividing operational expenses, or jointly funding marketing initiatives, the financial burden becomes more manageable when distributed between partners. This collaborative financial approach enhances the feasibility of international expansion for both entities involved.

Beyond financial considerations, partnerships also offer expanded networks and market access. Collaborating with established local partners provides immediate access to their customer base and networks, accelerating the process of building brand awareness and market share. This interconnectedness opens doors to potential clients, suppliers, and distribution channels, providing a comprehensive foundation for sustained growth.

Strategic partnerships emerge as a dynamic and multifaceted strategy for funding international expansion. By forming alliances with other businesses, companies can access additional resources, share risks and rewards, facilitate market entry, negotiate favorable financial terms, and broaden their networks. The collaborative nature of partnerships aligns well with the complexities of global expansion, enabling businesses to navigate diverse challenges and capitalize on shared successes. Thorough due diligence, clear communication, and alignment of strategic objectives are crucial in establishing and maintaining successful strategic partnerships.

Financial Planning

Budgeting and Cost Estimation

Embarking on the journey of international expansion requires a meticulous approach to financial planning, with budgeting and cost estimation standing as crucial pillars. In this phase, businesses must undertake a comprehensive assessment to estimate the expenses associated with various facets of global growth, including market research, regulatory compliance, marketing efforts, infrastructure setup, and ongoing operational expenses.

Understanding the nuances of target international markets necessitates investment in thorough market research. This includes expenses related to data collection, analysis, and the engagement of professionals who can provide insights into local consumer behavior, competitor landscapes, and market trends. A robust market research budget is pivotal for informed decision-making and setting the stage for a successful entry into new territories.

Navigating diverse regulatory environments demands a financial commitment. Costs associated with legal counsel, compliance professionals, and any fees related to licenses or permits must be factored into the budget. This ensures that the business operates within the legal frameworks of each country, building trust and credibility in the global market.

Establishing a strong presence in new markets requires effective marketing strategies. Businesses should allocate funds for region-specific advertising campaigns, localized content creation, and promotional activities tailored to resonate with diverse audiences. A well-structured marketing budget enhances brand visibility and accelerates the process of capturing the attention of the target market.

Infrastructure Setup and Operational Costs:

Infrastructure setup encompasses expenditures related to establishing physical or digital presence in the target markets. This includes costs for office spaces, technology infrastructure, and distribution networks. Ongoing operational costs such as employee salaries, logistics, and supply chain management should also be included in the budget to ensure seamless day-to-day operations.

In the realm of international expansion, unforeseen challenges can arise. A contingency fund within the budget acts as a safety net, allowing the business to navigate unexpected hurdles without compromising the overall financial health. This proactive approach prepares the company to adapt and respond effectively to changing circumstances.

Budgeting requires a strategic approach to resource allocation. Businesses must prioritize initiatives based on their potential impact on the expansion goals. Allocating resources judiciously ensures that the most critical aspects of the international expansion strategy receive the necessary financial support, optimizing the chances of success.

Rigorous budgeting and cost estimation are integral components of the financial planning process for international expansion. A detailed budget serves as a roadmap, guiding businesses through the complexities of global growth by allocating resources effectively. From market research to regulatory compliance, marketing endeavors to operational costs, a comprehensive budgeting strategy enables businesses to navigate the financial landscape of international expansion with foresight and precision.

Risk Assessment

In international expansion, an integral component of financial planning is the meticulous process of risk assessment. This phase involves a comprehensive evaluation of potential risks inherent in venturing into new markets. Businesses must be vigilant in identifying a spectrum of risks, including but not limited to economic volatility, currency fluctuations, and regulatory changes.

The economic conditions of each target market can be unpredictable, subject to various factors such as geopolitical events, global economic downturns, or regional instability. Businesses must carefully analyze the economic landscape of each country to gauge potential impacts on their operations.

Operating across borders exposes businesses to the risks associated with currency fluctuations. Exchange rate variations can significantly affect the financial health of an international venture. Companies need to implement strategies to hedge against these fluctuations and safeguard their financial interests.

Regulatory environments in different countries can evolve, introducing new laws or altering existing ones. Failure to adapt to these changes may lead to non-compliance and financial repercussions. A thorough understanding of the regulatory frameworks in target markets is crucial for mitigating compliance-related risks.

Identifying risks is only the initial step; devising robust risk mitigation strategies is equally imperative. These strategies may include diversifying investments, using financial instruments to hedge against currency risks, and staying abreast of regulatory developments. Establishing contingency plans ensures a proactive response to unforeseen challenges.

The overarching goal of risk assessment is to fortify the financial plan against potential disruptions. By understanding the intricacies of risks associated with international expansion, businesses can tailor their financial strategies to enhance resilience. Rigorous risk assessment not only safeguards the financial health of the company but also positions it to navigate uncertainties with agility and strategic foresight.

Cash Flow Management

In the dynamic landscape of international expansion, effective cash flow management emerges as a cornerstone of financial planning. Businesses navigating new markets must prioritize the allocation and utilization of working capital to ensure operational continuity and resilience against unforeseen challenges.

Securing adequate working capital is paramount for businesses venturing into international markets. The demands of market entry, regulatory compliance, and infrastructure setup necessitate a robust financial cushion. Ensuring sufficient liquidity enables companies to navigate the initial phases of expansion without succumbing to financial strain.

Vigilant and regular monitoring of cash flow is an indispensable practice. This involves a meticulous examination of inflows and outflows, providing a real-time snapshot of the financial health. Continuous monitoring facilitates proactive decision-making, allowing businesses to identify trends, anticipate challenges, and seize opportunities promptly.

The fluid nature of global business demands an agile response to changing circumstances. Effective cash flow management empowers businesses to make timely adjustments to their financial strategies. Whether it involves reallocating resources, renegotiating contracts, or revisiting investment plans, the ability to adapt based on cash flow insights is crucial for sustained growth.

A well-managed cash flow prevents businesses from encountering financial constraints that could impede their expansion journey. Unforeseen expenses or fluctuations in revenue are inevitable in the international arena. Robust cash flow management serves as a buffer, mitigating the impact of uncertainties and safeguarding the financial stability of the business.

As businesses traverse the complexities of international expansion, they must view cash flow management as more than a financial metric; it is a strategic imperative. The judicious allocation of working capital, coupled with vigilant monitoring and adaptability, ensures that companies not only weather the challenges of global expansion but also seize opportunities for sustainable growth. In essence, effective cash flow management becomes a guiding compass for businesses venturing into new territories, empowering them to navigate financial landscapes with confidence and resilience.

Scenario Planning

Scenario planning is a pivotal component of comprehensive financial planning for businesses venturing into international expansion. It involves the systematic analysis of various potential scenarios, encompassing a spectrum of market outcomes and economic conditions. By considering both best-case and worst-case scenarios, businesses can develop a nuanced understanding of the possible challenges and opportunities that may unfold during their global journey.

In the realm of international expansion, where uncertainties are inherent, scenario planning becomes a strategic tool for proactive decision-making. The process entails mapping out different scenarios that could impact the business, such as changes in consumer behavior, economic downturns, or unexpected regulatory shifts. Each scenario is thoroughly evaluated, with a focus on the potential financial implications and risks associated with the specific circumstances.

Best-case scenarios allow businesses to set aspirational benchmarks and identify opportunities for accelerated growth. This optimistic outlook can inform strategic decisions, such as increasing investment in marketing, expanding product lines, or entering additional markets. Conversely, worst-case scenarios help businesses anticipate potential challenges and develop contingency plans to mitigate risks. These plans may involve adjusting budgets, renegotiating contracts, or exploring alternative funding sources.

Scenario planning goes beyond mere speculation; it involves an in-depth analysis of the factors driving each scenario. This analysis may include macroeconomic indicators, market trends, competitive landscapes, and geopolitical considerations. By delving into the underlying drivers of various scenarios, businesses gain a more nuanced understanding of the dynamics at play, enabling them to tailor their financial strategies accordingly.

The benefits of scenario planning are multifaceted. Firstly, it enhances preparedness by equipping businesses with a roadmap for navigating different potential futures. This foresight allows companies to make informed decisions that align with the evolving circumstances, reducing the likelihood of reactive and unplanned responses. Secondly, scenario planning fosters adaptability, a critical trait in the dynamic landscape of global expansion. Businesses can adjust their financial strategies in real-time based on the unfolding scenario, ensuring a resilient and responsive approach.

Scenario planning is an indispensable tool in the financial toolkit of businesses scaling up internationally. By systematically evaluating diverse scenarios, companies can position themselves to thrive in favorable conditions while being well-prepared to weather challenges. This strategic foresight enhances the robustness of financial planning, making it an integral element of successful global expansion strategies.

Funding global expansion is a multifaceted endeavor that requires a combination of strategic decision-making and meticulous financial planning. By diversifying funding sources and adopting a comprehensive financial strategy, businesses can position themselves for successful entry into new markets and sustained growth on an international scale.

Currency Risk Management

Currency risk, also known as foreign exchange risk or forex risk, is a significant consideration for businesses engaged in international trade or expansion. It arises from the potential impact of fluctuations in exchange rates on the financial performance of a company. Currency risk management is the strategic approach businesses employ to mitigate the adverse effects of these fluctuations and ensure stability in their financial outcomes.

Understanding Currency Risk

Currency risk stems from the fact that exchange rates between different currencies are subject to constant fluctuations influenced by economic, political, and market factors. For businesses operating globally, these fluctuations can have a substantial impact on revenues, costs, and profit margins. Currency risk manifests in various ways, including transaction risk, translation risk, and economic risk.

- **Transaction Risk:** This risk arises from the exposure to unfavorable exchange rate movements during the settlement of financial transactions. For example, if a U.S.-based company sells goods to a European customer and agrees to be paid in euros, the value of those euros in U.S. dollars at the time of payment can be different from the initial transaction.
- **Translation Risk:** Businesses with international operations often consolidate financial statements, which involves translating foreign currency assets and liabilities into the reporting currency. Fluctuations in exchange rates can impact the reported financial position and results of these businesses.
- **Economic Risk**: Also known as operating risk, economic risk refers to the potential impact of exchange rate movements on a company's competitive position and cash flows. Changes in currency values can affect the competitiveness of products or services in foreign markets.

Achieving Currency Risk Management

Effectively managing currency risk involves a combination of understanding exposure, employing risk mitigation strategies, and staying informed about market conditions.

Here are key components of currency risk management:

- **Identify Exposure:** The first step is to identify and quantify exposure to currency risk. This involves assessing all foreign currency transactions, foreign operations, and any other factors that may be affected by exchange rate movements.
- **Use Hedging Instruments:** Hedging is a common strategy to protect against adverse currency movements. Derivative instruments, such as forward contracts, options, and

futures, can be employed to lock in exchange rates for future transactions. For instance, a company expecting payment in a foreign currency in the future can use a forward contract to secure the exchange rate.

- **Diversification:** Diversifying operations and revenue streams across multiple currencies can act as a natural hedge. This strategy can help offset losses in one currency with gains in another, reducing overall exposure to currency risk.
- **Continuous Monitoring:** Given the dynamic nature of currency markets, continuous monitoring is crucial. Keeping abreast of economic indicators, geopolitical events, and market trends helps businesses anticipate potential currency movements and adjust strategies accordingly.
- **Establish Policies and Procedures:** Implementing clear policies and procedures for managing currency risk ensures consistency and discipline in the approach. This includes guidelines on when and how to hedge, risk tolerance levels, and reporting mechanisms.
- **Build Strong Relationships with Financial Institutions:** Working closely with financial institutions that specialize in currency risk management can provide valuable insights and access to sophisticated hedging tools. Collaborative relationships with banks and financial experts can enhance a company's ability to navigate currency risks effectively.

In conclusion, currency risk management is a critical aspect of financial planning for businesses expanding internationally. By proactively identifying, quantifying, and mitigating currency risk, companies can enhance their resilience, protect profitability, and maintain stability in the face of volatile exchange rates. Strategic currency risk management is not merely a defensive measure; it can also be a source of competitive advantage for businesses operating in the global arena.

Financial Compliance in International Markets

Operating in international markets introduces businesses to a myriad of regulatory frameworks and financial compliance requirements. Achieving financial compliance is a multifaceted process that involves adherence to local, regional, and international regulations governing various aspects of financial management. From taxation and reporting standards to anti-money laundering (AML) measures, businesses expanding globally must navigate this complex landscape to ensure legal and ethical financial practices.

Understanding Financial Compliance

Financial compliance refers to the adherence to laws, regulations, and standards related to financial management and reporting. In the context of international markets, financial compliance encompasses a broad spectrum of requirements that vary across jurisdictions.

Key elements of financial compliance in international markets include:

- **Tax Compliance:** Different countries have distinct tax laws, and businesses must comply with local tax regulations. This involves understanding corporate tax rates, filing requirements, and ensuring accurate reporting of income, expenses, and other financial transactions.
- **Financial Reporting Standards:** International Financial Reporting Standards (IFRS) and Generally Accepted Accounting Principles (GAAP) are commonly used frameworks for financial reporting. Businesses operating globally must align their financial statements with the applicable standards in each jurisdiction to ensure transparency and comparability.
- **Anti-Money Laundering (AML) Compliance:** AML regulations are designed to prevent money laundering and the financing of terrorism. Businesses engaging in

international transactions must implement robust AML measures, including customer due diligence and reporting suspicious activities.

- **Transfer Pricing Compliance:** Transfer pricing regulations govern the pricing of transactions between related entities in different tax jurisdictions. Ensuring compliance with these regulations is crucial for businesses with international operations to avoid tax-related challenges.
- **Currency Controls:** Some countries impose restrictions on currency movements to maintain economic stability. Adhering to currency control regulations is essential for businesses engaged in cross-border transactions.
- **Data Privacy and Security Compliance:** International businesses must comply with data protection regulations to safeguard customer information and ensure privacy. Regulations like the General Data Protection Regulation (GDPR) in the European Union set stringent standards for data handling.
- **Customs and Trade Compliance:** For businesses involved in the import and export of goods, compliance with customs and trade regulations is essential. This includes accurate documentation, adherence to tariff schedules, and compliance with import and export restrictions.

Achieving Financial Compliance

Navigating the intricacies of financial compliance in international markets requires a proactive and comprehensive approach.

Here are key strategies for achieving financial compliance:

- **Conduct Thorough Regulatory Research:** Stay informed about the financial regulations in each target market. This involves continuous research to understand updates, changes, and nuances in local financial compliance requirements.
- **Engage Legal and Financial Experts:** Collaborate with legal and financial experts who specialize in international business and compliance. These professionals can provide guidance on specific regulations, interpret complex legal frameworks, and ensure accurate implementation of compliance measures.
- **Establish Robust Internal Controls:** Implementing strong internal controls is essential for ensuring compliance. This includes developing policies, procedures, and monitoring mechanisms to detect and prevent potential compliance issues.
- **Invest in Training and Awareness:** Educate employees and stakeholders about the importance of financial compliance. Training programs can enhance awareness of regulations, instill a culture of compliance, and reduce the risk of inadvertent violations.
- **Utilize Compliance Management Systems:** Implement compliance management systems that facilitate tracking, reporting, and auditing of financial compliance activities. These systems can streamline compliance processes and provide documentation for regulatory authorities.
- **Regular Audits and Assessments:** Conduct regular internal and external audits to assess compliance with financial regulations. This proactive approach helps identify potential issues early and allows for corrective actions to be taken promptly.
- **Stay Adaptable:** Financial compliance requirements can change due to legislative updates or shifts in the global regulatory landscape. Businesses should remain adaptable and be prepared to adjust their compliance strategies in response to evolving regulations.

Financial compliance in international markets is a complex but necessary aspect of conducting global business. Businesses that prioritize compliance not only mitigate legal risks but also enhance their reputation, build trust with stakeholders, and position themselves for sustainable success in the global marketplace. A comprehensive understanding of local regulations, coupled with proactive compliance measures, is instrumental in navigating the intricate financial compliance landscape.

Chapter **7**

Legal and
Regulatory Navigation

Navigating the legal and regulatory landscape is a critical aspect of global business expansion. Understanding and adhering to international laws and regulations is essential for mitigating risks, ensuring compliance, and fostering a conducive environment for sustainable growth.

In this chapter, we delve into the complexities of legal and regulatory considerations, exploring key aspects such as intellectual property rights, international trade laws, and regulations governing cross-border operations.

Intellectual Property Rights Across Borders

Intellectual property (IP) refers to creations of the mind, such as inventions, literary and artistic works, designs, symbols, names, and images used in commerce. Protecting these creations is crucial for businesses operating globally, as it safeguards their innovations, brand identity, and competitive advantages. Navigating intellectual property rights across borders involves understanding the legal frameworks, regulations, and strategies to secure and enforce IP protection in different countries.

One primary aspect of IPR across borders is trademarks, which protect brand names, logos, and symbols. Registering trademarks in each target market helps prevent unauthorized use and strengthens brand recognition. For example, when Apple expanded globally, securing trademarks for its logo and product names in various countries was essential to maintain exclusivity and prevent counterfeit products.

Patents are another critical component of intellectual property, protecting inventions and technological innovations. Navigating international patent laws involves filing applications in multiple jurisdictions to ensure global coverage. Pharmaceutical companies, for instance, often pursue international patent protection to safeguard their research and development investments in new drugs.

Copyrights play a role in protecting original literary, artistic, and musical works. International treaties, such as the Berne Convention, facilitate cross-border recognition of copyrights. Companies involved in content creation, like entertainment and publishing industries, navigate these treaties to ensure the protection of their creative works in diverse markets.

Trade secrets, while not registered, are valuable components of intellectual property. Protecting trade secrets involves implementing robust internal policies, confidentiality agreements, and, when necessary, legal action against unauthorized disclosures. Coca-Cola's secret recipe is a classic example of safeguarding a trade secret over many decades.

Navigating intellectual property rights across borders requires a strategic approach. Here are key considerations:

1. Conduct Comprehensive IP Audits

Conducting comprehensive intellectual property (IP) audits is a fundamental step for businesses contemplating global expansion. An IP audit involves a systematic review and analysis of all intellectual property assets owned or used by a company. This process is essential to identify what requires protection and to assess the current status of trademarks, patents, copyrights, and trade secrets.

- **Identify Intellectual Property Assets:** Begin by creating an inventory of all intellectual property assets within the company. This includes trademarks associated with brand names, logos, and slogans, patents covering inventions and innovations, copyrights for original creative works, and trade secrets such as confidential business information.

- **Assess the Value and Importance:** Evaluate the significance and value of each identified intellectual property asset. Some assets may be critical to the core business, while others may have less strategic importance. This assessment helps prioritize resources and efforts towards protecting the most crucial elements.
- **Verify Ownership and Rights:** Ensure that the company has clear ownership of each intellectual property asset. This verification includes confirming that trademarks and patents are registered in the company's name and that copyrights are appropriately assigned. Understanding the rights associated with each asset is crucial for effective protection.
- **Review Existing Protections:** Examine the current status of registrations and protections for trademarks, patents, and copyrights. Verify that registrations are up to date and in compliance with the laws of the relevant jurisdictions. This review provides insights into the strength and enforceability of existing protections.
- **Assess Trade Secrets Protection:** Evaluate the measures in place to protect trade secrets. This involves examining internal policies, confidentiality agreements, and security protocols. Ensure that employees and relevant stakeholders are aware of the importance of maintaining the confidentiality of trade secrets.
- **Evaluate Licensing Agreements:** If the company licenses its intellectual property to others or obtains licenses from third parties, review these agreements. Confirm that all licensing arrangements are current, valid, and in compliance with legal requirements. Assess the impact of these agreements on the company's ability to expand globally.
- **Identify Potential Risks:** During the audit, identify any potential risks or vulnerabilities associated with intellectual property. This could include pending legal challenges, disputes, or instances of unauthorized use. Understanding these risks is crucial for developing strategies to mitigate or address them.
- **Establish Protocols for Ongoing Audits:** Intellectual property audits should not be a one-time activity. Establish protocols for ongoing audits to ensure that the company's IP portfolio remains aligned with its business objectives. Regular reviews help adapt to changing circumstances and evolving business strategies.

  Conducting comprehensive IP audits serves as a proactive measure to protect and leverage a company's intellectual property assets. By systematically evaluating their IP portfolio, businesses can make informed decisions, strengthen their competitive position, and ensure a solid foundation for successful global expansion.

2. Understand Local Regulations

In the process of expanding globally, understanding and navigating local regulations concerning intellectual property (IP) is paramount. Each country operates under distinct IP laws and regulations, necessitating a comprehensive understanding of the specific requirements and procedures for IP protection in each target market. This understanding encompasses various aspects, including the registration process, the duration of protection, and the enforcement mechanisms in place.

- **Country-Specific Registration Processes:** Intellectual property protection often requires formal registration, and the specific procedures vary across jurisdictions. Companies must be familiar with the registration processes in each target market. For example, the requirements for trademark registration in the United States may differ significantly from those in China or the European Union. Ensuring compliance with these country-specific processes is essential for obtaining legal recognition and protection.
- **Duration of Protection:** The duration of IP protection can vary from country to country. While trademarks and patents generally have a finite term, the length of this term differs globally. Companies must be aware of the specific duration of protection

afforded to their intellectual property in each jurisdiction to plan for renewals or additional filings as necessary.

- **Enforcement Mechanisms:** Knowing how intellectual property rights are enforced in a particular country is critical. Legal systems and enforcement mechanisms differ, impacting the ability to protect IP against infringement. Some countries may have more robust legal frameworks and efficient enforcement agencies, while others may present challenges in pursuing legal actions. This understanding is crucial for developing strategies to safeguard intellectual property effectively.

- **Cultural Considerations:** Cultural nuances can also influence the interpretation and enforcement of intellectual property laws. For instance, attitudes towards counterfeiting or piracy may vary, and local perceptions of what constitutes infringement might differ. Companies need to consider cultural factors in their IP strategies to navigate potential challenges and ensure effective protection.

- **Language and Documentation:** Language plays a pivotal role in complying with local regulations. All documentation related to intellectual property, including applications, legal notices, and contracts, must be accurately translated into the official language(s) of the respective country. Ensuring linguistic accuracy is crucial to avoid misunderstandings and legal complications.

- **Strategic Alignment with Business Goals:** Beyond legal compliance, understanding local IP regulations allows companies to align their strategies with broader business goals. This includes tailoring IP protection strategies to support market entry, brand positioning, and overall business objectives in each specific market.

- **Seek Professional Advice:** Given the complexity and variability of intellectual property regulations worldwide, seeking professional advice is often prudent. Engaging local legal experts or IP professionals with expertise in the target markets can provide invaluable insights. These professionals can guide businesses through the intricacies of local regulations and help tailor strategies for optimal IP protection.

Comprehending and navigating local regulations concerning intellectual property is a multifaceted task that requires meticulous attention to detail. By understanding the specific requirements, duration of protection, enforcement mechanisms, cultural considerations, and language nuances in each target market, companies can formulate robust IP protection strategies that align with their global expansion objectives. This proactive approach not only mitigates risks but also positions businesses for success in diverse international landscapes.

3. Prioritize Timely Filings

In the realm of intellectual property (IP), prioritizing timely filings is a fundamental principle that significantly influences the protection and enforcement of rights globally. The "first-to-file" concept underscores the importance of being the first entity to submit an application for a specific intellectual property right. This principle holds true for various forms of IP, including trademarks, patents, copyrights, and industrial designs.

Trademarks

In the context of trademarks, being the first to file an application with the relevant intellectual property office establishes a party's rights to that mark. This holds irrespective of prior use or common-law rights. Timely filing ensures that a company secures legal recognition and exclusive rights to use its trademark in connection with specific goods or services. Delay in filing may open the door for competitors or malicious actors to register a similar mark, leading to potential conflicts, legal disputes, and the risk of losing the desired brand identity.

Patents

Patents, which grant exclusive rights for an invention, also adhere to the first-to-file principle. In the realm of innovation, the race to secure patent protection is intense. Inventors and companies seeking patent protection must swiftly file their applications to establish priority.

Delays can result in competitors securing patents for similar inventions, restricting the original inventor's ability to capitalize on their innovation. This underscores the importance of a proactive approach to filing patent applications to safeguard inventive concepts and technological advancements.

Copyrights

While copyright protection is generally granted automatically upon creation, timely registration enhances legal advantages. In some jurisdictions, registering copyrights can provide additional benefits, such as the ability to seek statutory damages and attorney's fees in infringement lawsuits. Timely registration is particularly crucial for works with commercial value, such as literary works, artistic creations, or software. Failure to register in a timely manner may limit the remedies available to the copyright owner in case of infringement.

Industrial Designs

Industrial designs, protecting the visual design of objects, also operate under the first-to-file principle. Companies seeking protection for the unique aesthetic aspects of their products must promptly file applications to secure exclusive rights. Delaying the filing of industrial design applications can result in the loss of protection, allowing competitors to replicate or imitate distinctive designs.

Consequences of Delay

The consequences of delayed filings can be severe. In addition to facing legal challenges from competitors, delayed filings may lead to the loss of exclusive rights, hindering a company's ability to leverage its intellectual property assets. Competitors may capitalize on the delay to gain market share, and legal battles over conflicting rights can be costly and time-consuming.

Global Considerations

Timely filings become even more critical in the context of global expansion. Companies venturing into international markets must navigate different intellectual property systems, each with its own rules and timelines. Failing to file in a timely manner in a specific jurisdiction may result in the loss of protection in that market, impacting the overall success of the expansion.

In essence, prioritizing timely filings in intellectual property matters is not merely a procedural formality; it is a strategic imperative. It requires a proactive and vigilant approach to identifying, protecting, and enforcing intellectual property rights. Companies that recognize the significance of being the first to file demonstrate a commitment to securing their innovations, brands, and creative works, thereby fortifying their competitive position in the global marketplace.

4. Monitor and Enforce

In the complex landscape of global business, monitoring and enforcing intellectual property (IP) rights represent integral components of a comprehensive strategy to safeguard creative assets, innovations, and brand identities. This proactive approach involves ongoing vigilance to detect and address potential infringements promptly. Regular and systematic monitoring is crucial to identify any unauthorized use or imitation of protected intellectual property. Companies can employ a variety of tools and services to track trademarks, patents, copyrights, and industrial designs. This constant surveillance helps in promptly identifying potential infringing activities and enables swift responses to protect the integrity of the IP portfolio.

Timely identification of potential infringements necessitates swift and strategic action. Companies need to have well-defined procedures for evaluating potential violations and determining the most appropriate course of action. This may involve sending cease-and-desist letters, initiating negotiations, or pursuing legal action, depending on the severity and circumstances of the infringement.

Utilizing advanced monitoring systems, often aided by technology and specialized software, enhances the efficiency of tracking intellectual property use. Automated monitoring can cover a broader spectrum, enabling companies to cast a wider net in detecting potential infringements across various markets and jurisdictions.

Collaborating with local authorities is a crucial aspect of effective enforcement, especially in the context of international expansion. Establishing partnerships with law enforcement agencies, customs authorities, and relevant regulatory bodies in different jurisdictions strengthens a company's ability to combat intellectual property violations. This collaboration facilitates coordinated efforts to curb counterfeiting, unauthorized copying, and other forms of infringement.

Strategic enforcement involves a judicious choice of actions based on the nature and severity of the infringement. This may include pursuing litigation, filing complaints with relevant intellectual property offices, or engaging in alternative dispute resolution mechanisms. The chosen strategy should align with the company's overall business objectives and risk tolerance.

Beyond the legal ramifications, effective monitoring and enforcement contribute significantly to protecting a company's market reputation. Swift and decisive actions against infringing activities send a clear message about the company's commitment to protecting its intellectual property. This proactive stance resonates with consumers, business partners, and stakeholders, bolstering trust in the brand.

Achieving the right balance between monitoring and enforcement is critical. While proactive monitoring is essential for early detection, the enforcement strategy should be calibrated to avoid unnecessary legal conflicts. A strategic and measured approach ensures that the company focuses resources on addressing genuine threats and mitigates risks associated with aggressive enforcement actions.

The process of monitoring and enforcing intellectual property rights is not a one-time task but an ongoing commitment to safeguarding a company's intangible assets. This commitment is particularly vital in the dynamic landscape of global business, where intellectual property violations can have far-reaching consequences. By integrating effective monitoring systems, collaborating with local authorities, and strategically enforcing rights, companies can fortify their intellectual property protection efforts and uphold the value of their innovations and brands.

Safeguarding intellectual property rights across borders demands a proactive and informed approach. By understanding local regulations, prioritizing protection, and seeking professional guidance, businesses can navigate the complexities of international intellectual property laws and secure their innovative and creative assets globally.

Navigating International Trade Laws and Regulations

International trade brings a myriad of opportunities but is also intricately woven with a complex web of laws and regulations that vary across countries and regions. Effectively navigating this legal landscape is crucial for businesses engaged in cross-border commerce. This involves understanding and adhering to trade laws, import/export regulations, and compliance requirements.

1. Comprehend Trade Laws and Tariffs

Comprehending trade laws and tariffs is a foundational step in navigating international trade successfully. Businesses engaging in cross-border commerce must have a clear understanding of the trade laws governing the countries they operate in. This involves being well-versed in tariffs, import quotas, and trade restrictions that may impact their specific products or industries.

Tariffs, in particular, play a significant role in international trade. They are taxes imposed on imported and, in some cases, exported goods. Being aware of the applicable tariffs is crucial for calculating the cost of importing or exporting goods and ensuring that the business remains economically viable. Import quotas, which limit the quantity of certain goods that can be imported, are another aspect that businesses must navigate to avoid potential penalties or restrictions.

For example, when venturing into the European Union, businesses need to understand the Common Customs Tariff (CCT). The CCT is a comprehensive system that sets the customs duties on various products imported into the EU. This tariff is an essential component of EU trade laws, and businesses must navigate it effectively to ensure compliance. Additionally, businesses operating within the EU need to be aware of other trade regulations and restrictions specific to the region. These may include non-tariff barriers, such as licensing requirements, technical standards, and labeling regulations, which can significantly impact market access.

In the context of understanding trade laws and tariffs, businesses should also consider the broader trade agreements that may influence their operations. For instance, if the country of operation is part of a free trade agreement (FTA), it could provide preferential treatment, such as reduced tariffs or exemptions. Therefore, a thorough comprehension of the applicable trade agreements is essential for optimizing international trade strategies.

Comprehending trade laws and tariffs involves a detailed examination of the legal frameworks governing international trade. This knowledge is vital for calculating costs, ensuring compliance, and strategizing market entry or expansion. Businesses that navigate these aspects effectively position themselves to thrive in the global marketplace by minimizing risks and leveraging opportunities presented by diverse international trade landscapes.

2. Familiarize with Customs Procedures

Navigating customs procedures is a pivotal aspect of international trade. Businesses must comprehend documentation requirements, import and export declarations, and customs valuation methods. Having a robust understanding of customs regulations ensures smooth clearance of goods across borders. As an example, companies engaging in international trade with the United States need to comply with the Customs-Trade Partnership Against Terrorism (C-TPAT) program, which focuses on enhancing border security and trade compliance.

3. Ensure Product Compliance and Standards

Ensuring product compliance and standards is a critical aspect of navigating international trade laws and regulations. Every region has its unique set of product standards and regulations that businesses must navigate to gain market access. Aligning products with the applicable standards of the target market is not only a legal requirement but also essential for building trust with consumers and ensuring the safety and quality of products.

One key consideration in this regard is understanding the technical standards that apply to specific products in the target market. For instance, when exporting electronic devices to Japan, adherence to the country's specific technical standards becomes paramount. The PSE (Product Safety Electrical Appliance & Material) mark is a notable example. This mark signifies compliance with Japan's safety regulations for electrical appliances. Businesses must thoroughly understand these standards, ensuring that their products meet or exceed the required specifications to enter the Japanese market successfully.

Additionally, compliance with product standards extends beyond technical specifications. It often involves adherence to labeling requirements, safety protocols, and environmental regulations. In some cases, businesses may need to undergo certification processes to demonstrate compliance with specific standards. For example, exporting organic products to the European Union requires adherence to the EU's organic farming regulations, and obtaining the EU Organic Certification is crucial for market entry.

The complexity of ensuring product compliance and standards is heightened when dealing with diverse global markets. Each country or region may have its own certification processes, safety requirements, and labeling regulations. Therefore, businesses need to conduct thorough research and engage with local regulatory bodies to understand the specific requirements applicable to their products.

In addition to legal obligations, aligning products with the standards of the target market is a strategic move. It demonstrates a commitment to providing high-quality, safe products tailored to the preferences and expectations of local consumers. Building a positive reputation for product compliance can enhance the brand image and contribute to long-term success in the international marketplace.

Businesses seeking to navigate international trade laws and regulations effectively should integrate product compliance into their overall market entry strategy. This involves conducting comprehensive assessments of the regulatory landscape in each target market, engaging with local authorities, and collaborating with industry associations to stay informed about evolving standards. By prioritizing product compliance, businesses not only fulfill legal requirements but also position themselves as reliable and responsible players in the global marketplace.

4. Embrace Export Controls and Sanctions

Embracing export controls and sanctions is a crucial aspect of navigating international trade, requiring businesses to carefully adhere to regulations imposed by countries for national security and foreign policy reasons. These controls are designed to manage the export of goods and technologies that could have dual-use applications, meaning they may serve both civilian and military purposes. Effectively navigating export controls involves a multifaceted approach, encompassing careful screening of products and business partners to ensure compliance with diverse and often complex regulations.

Countries implement export controls and sanctions as a means of protecting their national security interests and advancing their foreign policy goals. These measures are particularly relevant when dealing with products that have potential military applications or could contribute to activities contrary to international peace and security. To this end, businesses involved in international trade, especially those dealing with dual-use items, must thoroughly understand and comply with the export control regulations of the countries they operate in or trade with.

The screening process is a fundamental component of export control compliance. It involves a meticulous examination of products to determine whether they fall under controlled categories and an assessment of business partners to ensure they are not subject to sanctions or restrictions. For instance, certain goods or technologies may be listed on national control lists, and businesses must ensure that they have the necessary licenses or authorizations before exporting such items.

Dual-use items, which have legitimate civilian applications but can also be used for military purposes, present a particular challenge. Companies dealing with these items must navigate a complex web of regulations to ensure that their products do not end up in the wrong hands. This involves classifying goods accurately, obtaining the required licenses, and establishing robust internal processes to prevent inadvertent violations.

In addition to export controls, sanctions are another dimension that businesses must consider. Sanctions are restrictive measures imposed by one or more countries against another country or specific entities within that country. These measures can include trade restrictions, asset freezes, and financial prohibitions. Businesses engaged in international trade need to be aware of sanctions regimes imposed by various jurisdictions and ensure that they do not engage in prohibited transactions.

An illustrative example is the comprehensive sanctions imposed on certain countries. For instance, businesses operating in sectors such as finance, energy, or technology must be mindful of sanctions targeting specific countries, as engaging in trade with entities from these countries could lead to severe legal consequences.

Embracing export controls and sanctions in the context of international trade necessitates a proactive and diligent approach. Businesses must conduct comprehensive screenings, stay informed about changes in regulations, and establish robust internal processes to ensure compliance. Failure to navigate export controls and sanctions effectively can lead to legal ramifications, reputational damage, and disruption of international business operations. Therefore, a thorough understanding and adherence to these measures are essential for businesses engaged in the complex landscape of global trade.

5. Establish Compliance Management Systems

Establishing compliance management systems is a crucial component of successfully navigating the complexities of international trade laws. In this context, businesses need to implement robust internal policies, conduct regular audits, and stay continuously informed about changes in regulations. These measures are essential for ensuring adherence to the intricate web of international trade laws that govern cross-border commerce.

Internally, businesses must develop clear and comprehensive policies that guide employees and operations to align with relevant trade regulations. These policies should encompass various aspects, including customs documentation, product classification, and adherence to specific trade agreements. By having well-defined internal guidelines, businesses can reduce the risk of inadvertent non-compliance and associated legal consequences.

Regular audits are another integral aspect of compliance management systems. Conducting systematic reviews of trade-related processes and documentation helps identify potential areas of non-compliance or inefficiency. This proactive approach allows businesses to rectify issues promptly, ensuring ongoing adherence to international trade laws. Audits should encompass various facets, such as customs documentation accuracy, adherence to tariff classifications, and compliance with specific regulations governing product standards or safety.

Staying informed about changes in regulations is imperative, given the dynamic nature of international trade laws. The global business environment is subject to frequent regulatory updates, and businesses must remain vigilant to adapt promptly. For instance, the changes brought about by Brexit significantly impacted trade between the United Kingdom and the European Union. Businesses operating in this context needed to adjust their compliance management systems to accommodate new customs procedures, documentation requirements, and trade regulations.

In the European market, businesses faced the challenge of navigating the post-Brexit landscape. The UK's withdrawal from the EU led to changes in customs procedures, VAT regulations, and product conformity assessments. Consequently, businesses needed to update their compliance management systems to align with these alterations, ensuring uninterrupted trade flows and minimizing disruptions.

Effective compliance management is not a one-time endeavor but an ongoing commitment. Businesses engaged in international trade should establish mechanisms to monitor regulatory updates regularly. This can involve subscribing to relevant newsletters, participating in industry forums, or maintaining relationships with legal and trade experts who can provide timely insights. Proactive engagement with regulatory changes allows businesses to stay ahead of compliance requirements and make informed adjustments to their operations.

Establishing compliance management systems is a multifaceted approach that encompasses internal policies, regular audits, and staying informed about regulatory changes. This proactive stance is indispensable for businesses navigating the complexities of international trade laws. By fostering a culture of compliance and adaptability, businesses position themselves to thrive in the global marketplace, mitigating risks and capitalizing on opportunities presented by diverse regulatory landscapes.

6. Engage Legal Experts and Consultants

Engaging legal experts and trade consultants is a strategic move for businesses venturing into international trade, considering the intricate nature of global trade laws. The dynamic and evolving landscape of international regulations necessitates a nuanced understanding, making the expertise of legal professionals invaluable. Seeking their guidance can offer a range of benefits, from ensuring compliance with complex laws to navigating potential legal challenges effectively.

International trade laws encompass a vast array of regulations, including tariffs, customs procedures, and regulatory requirements specific to each country. Legal experts specializing in international trade law can help businesses decipher and navigate these regulations, ensuring that their operations align with the legal frameworks of the countries they operate in. For example, when entering the Chinese market, a country known for its unique trade laws and evolving regulatory environment, businesses can greatly benefit from the insights and guidance of legal experts who understand the nuances of the local legal landscape.

Legal professionals are well-versed in the complexities of trade agreements, tariff structures, and compliance requirements. This expertise is particularly crucial when dealing with intricate legal frameworks such as those found in regional trade blocs like the European Union. Businesses seeking to navigate the EU's trade laws, which involve intricate customs regulations and product standards, can leverage the knowledge of legal experts to ensure seamless market entry and ongoing compliance.

Moreover, engaging legal experts becomes even more critical in situations where businesses face potential legal disputes or challenges. Trade consultants can assist in developing robust strategies to address disputes, mitigate risks, and, when necessary, represent the interests of businesses in legal proceedings. Their expertise extends beyond merely interpreting laws to actively contributing to the strategic decision-making process, enabling businesses to proactively manage legal aspects of international trade.

For businesses considering expansion into new markets, the legal landscape can be a significant factor in decision-making. Legal professionals can provide comprehensive due diligence, helping businesses assess the legal risks and regulatory requirements associated with specific markets. This proactive approach ensures that businesses are well-prepared to navigate potential legal challenges, contributing to a smoother market entry and operational phase.

Engaging legal experts and trade consultants is a proactive and strategic approach for businesses involved in international trade. These professionals bring specialized knowledge and insights into the complex legal frameworks governing cross-border commerce. Whether dealing with tariffs, customs regulations, or dispute resolution, their expertise adds a layer of security and strategic guidance, allowing businesses to navigate the legal intricacies of international trade successfully.

7. Leverage Trade Agreements

Leveraging trade agreements is a strategic imperative for businesses seeking to optimize their international trade endeavors. These agreements, often in the form of free trade agreements (FTAs), play a pivotal role in shaping the conditions under which global commerce operates. A prime example of such an agreement is the Comprehensive and Progressive Agreement for Trans-Pacific Partnership (CPTPP), which stands as a testament to the benefits that businesses can derive from understanding and participating in these arrangements.

Free trade agreements are designed to facilitate trade and commerce between participating countries by eliminating or reducing barriers such as tariffs and quotas. The CPTPP, for instance, involves countries across the Asia-Pacific region, including major economies like Japan, Canada, Australia, and others. Businesses operating within this trade bloc can enjoy preferential treatment, including reduced tariffs and streamlined customs procedures. This provides a competitive advantage, making their products and services more accessible and cost-effective in these markets.

To leverage such trade agreements effectively, businesses must first have a comprehensive understanding of the specific terms and conditions outlined in these agreements. This involves navigating complex legal frameworks that dictate the rules of engagement in cross-border trade. Each agreement has its unique provisions, covering aspects such as tariff schedules, rules of origin, and dispute resolution mechanisms. Therefore, businesses should invest in legal expertise or collaborate with professionals who specialize in international trade law to ensure a nuanced understanding of the opportunities and obligations presented by these agreements.

For businesses operating within the CPTPP, one of the key advantages is the elimination or reduction of tariffs on a wide range of goods and services. This not only makes exports more competitive but also opens up new markets by making imports more affordable. The agreement also incorporates provisions addressing non-tariff barriers, promoting greater regulatory coherence and facilitating smoother cross-border transactions.

Apart from FTAs, businesses should explore and understand other types of trade agreements, such as bilateral agreements and regional partnerships, that may impact their operations. For example, a bilateral trade agreement between two countries may offer specific advantages to businesses engaging in trade between them. By leveraging these agreements, businesses can strategically position themselves in the global marketplace, tapping into opportunities created by collaborative trade frameworks.

Understanding and leveraging trade agreements are essential components of a successful international trade strategy. Businesses that actively engage with these agreements can gain a competitive edge by reducing costs, expanding market access, and navigating the complexities of cross-border trade more effectively. The CPTPP and similar agreements serve as powerful tools for businesses aiming to thrive in the dynamic landscape of international commerce.

Successfully navigating international trade laws and regulations requires a multifaceted approach encompassing legal comprehension, compliance management, and strategic utilization of trade agreements. By staying informed, engaging experts, and adapting to evolving regulatory landscapes, businesses can mitigate risks and capitalize on the vast opportunities offered by the global marketplace.

Cross-Border Compliance: Legal Considerations

Cross-border compliance refers to the adherence to legal and regulatory requirements when conducting business activities that span multiple countries. Navigating the complex landscape of international laws and regulations is a fundamental aspect of operating globally. This discussion delves into the key legal considerations businesses must address to ensure cross-border compliance.

Understanding Cross-Border Compliance

Understanding cross-border compliance is a complex imperative for businesses venturing into international operations. The expansion across borders unravels a tapestry of legal considerations that exhibit considerable diversity across jurisdictions. At its core, cross-border compliance necessitates the harmonization of business operations with the intricate web of laws and regulations prevalent in every country where the company establishes its presence. This sweeping responsibility encompasses various critical domains, encompassing trade regulations, tax laws, employment regulations, data protection, and the nuanced intricacies of industry-specific rules.

The cornerstone of cross-border compliance lies in the recognition of the unique legal frameworks that characterize each jurisdiction. Trade regulations stand as one of the pivotal facets, involving an understanding of tariffs, import/export restrictions, and the labyrinthine customs procedures of each country. Successful navigation of these regulations is vital for facilitating the seamless flow of goods and services across borders. Failure to adhere to these trade regulations can result in disruptions, financial penalties, and, in severe cases, the confiscation of goods.

Tax laws form another integral component of cross-border compliance. Businesses must navigate the intricacies of tax regulations in each jurisdiction to avoid legal ramifications. Transfer pricing, a critical consideration, involves the pricing of goods and services transferred between entities within the same organization. Adherence to country-specific regulations is imperative to prevent legal consequences arising from alleged tax evasion through manipulative transfer pricing practices.

Employment regulations and labor laws constitute a significant area of consideration in cross-border compliance. Managing a global workforce necessitates an in-depth comprehension of the diverse employment regulations governing hiring practices, employment contracts, working hours, and employee benefits in each jurisdiction. Ensuring compliance with these laws is paramount to avoid legal disputes, financial penalties, and reputational damage.

Data protection and privacy laws present a contemporary challenge in cross-border compliance. The burgeoning significance of data has prompted the enactment of stringent regulations worldwide. Compliance entails implementing robust measures to protect customer data and adhering to diverse requirements for collecting, processing, and storing personal information. A breach of data protection laws not only invites legal consequences but also poses a severe threat to the trust and reputation of the business.

Industry-specific regulations further amplify the complexity of cross-border compliance. Each sector, be it pharmaceuticals, finance, or telecommunications, operates within its set of regulations that demand meticulous adherence. Companies expanding globally must navigate these industry-specific rules to ensure legal integrity and operational alignment.

Mitigating risks and seeking legal counsel emerge as pivotal strategies in the pursuit of cross-border compliance. Proactive engagement with legal professionals possessing expertise in international law equips businesses to conduct thorough risk assessments, interpret complex regulations, and structure their operations in a manner that ensures compliance. This approach is particularly vital when confronting challenges such as political instability, where legal experts can offer insights into potential legal pitfalls and guide the development of strategies for risk mitigation.

Understanding cross-border compliance is imperative for businesses venturing into international territories. The multifaceted nature of compliance, spanning trade regulations, tax laws, employment regulations, data protection, and industry-specific rules, demands a nuanced and comprehensive approach. By navigating these legal intricacies adeptly, businesses not only ensure legal integrity but also pave the way for successful and sustainable global operations.

Trade Regulations and Customs Compliance

Trade regulations play a pivotal role in ensuring cross-border compliance for businesses engaged in international operations. These regulations encompass a broad spectrum of rules governing the movement of goods, including tariffs, import/export restrictions, and customs procedures. Businesses operating across borders must meticulously adhere to these trade regulations to facilitate the seamless flow of products while avoiding potential legal pitfalls.

One of the critical aspects of trade regulations is customs compliance. Customs procedures are fundamental for the efficient and timely shipment of goods across international boundaries. Compliance with these procedures involves adherence to specific documentation requirements, accurate classification of goods, and compliance with customs valuation methods. For businesses, ensuring strict adherence to customs compliance is not just a legal necessity but also a means to streamline logistical processes and maintain a positive relationship with customs authorities.

For example, consider a company venturing into global e-commerce. To successfully navigate cross-border shipments, this company needs a profound understanding of the customs regulations in each target country. Import duties, restrictions on certain products, and documentation requirements can vary significantly from one jurisdiction to another. Failing to comply with these regulations could result in delays in product shipments, financial penalties, or even the confiscation of goods, jeopardizing the company's international operations.

In essence, trade regulations and customs compliance act as the gatekeepers of international trade, influencing the speed and efficiency of global supply chains. Businesses must proactively engage with these regulations, keeping abreast of changes, and implementing strategies to ensure compliance.

Beyond the logistical challenges, trade regulations also impact the cost structure of cross-border operations. Tariffs and duties imposed on imported goods can significantly affect the overall expenses for businesses. Therefore, a comprehensive understanding of these trade-related costs is essential for accurate financial planning.

In the context of global e-commerce, the impact of trade regulations is further accentuated. Companies operating online retail platforms need to consider not only the regulatory landscape of their home country but also the regulations governing the markets they intend to enter. Varied import duties, taxes, and restrictions on specific products can influence pricing strategies, supply chain decisions, and overall market competitiveness.

Trade regulations and customs compliance form the bedrock of cross-border business operations. For businesses aiming to expand globally, a thorough understanding of the trade regulations in each target market is non-negotiable. It involves not only compliance with legal requirements but also strategic planning to mitigate potential challenges and optimize the efficiency of international supply chains. As exemplified in the global e-commerce scenario, businesses that master the intricacies of trade regulations position themselves for success in the competitive landscape of international commerce.

Tax Laws and Transfer Pricing

Tax laws play a pivotal role in cross-border compliance for businesses expanding their operations globally. The complexity arises from the need to adhere to the diverse tax regulations of each jurisdiction where a company operates. Complying with tax laws is not just a legal requirement but also a strategic imperative to avoid severe consequences such as fines, legal disputes, and reputational damage. Within the realm of international taxation, a crucial aspect that demands meticulous attention is transfer pricing.

Transfer pricing involves determining the prices at which goods, services, or intellectual property are transferred between entities within the same organization, particularly across different countries. This practice is of paramount importance as it directly influences the allocation of profits among the entities, impacting the overall tax liability. Countries worldwide have established specific regulations to curb potential tax evasion resulting from the manipulation of transfer prices.

In practical terms, consider the example of multinational corporations engaged in intricate cross-border transactions. These transactions often involve the transfer of goods, services, or intellectual property between subsidiaries located in different jurisdictions. To navigate this complexity and ensure compliance with tax laws, businesses must implement robust transfer pricing policies.

Proper documentation is a cornerstone of transfer pricing compliance. Multinational corporations need to maintain comprehensive records that justify the pricing strategies adopted for intra-group transactions. This documentation serves as evidence that transactions are conducted at arm's length, meaning the prices are akin to those that would be agreed upon between unrelated parties.

For example, a technology company with subsidiaries in various countries may transfer the rights to its proprietary software from one entity to another. The pricing of this transaction needs to be in line with what an independent third party would pay for similar intellectual property rights. Failure to adhere to these principles can trigger scrutiny from tax authorities and potentially lead to adjustments in the allocation of profits.

Effective transfer pricing compliance requires businesses to stay abreast of the evolving regulations in each jurisdiction. Countries may have different methodologies for determining arm's length prices, and businesses need to align their practices with these methodologies. This dynamic landscape underscores the importance of proactive engagement with tax professionals and legal counsel specialized in international taxation.

Moreover, businesses must consider the potential for double taxation, wherein the same income is taxed in multiple jurisdictions. To mitigate this risk, many countries have entered into double taxation treaties to provide relief and establish rules for allocating taxing rights.

Tax laws and transfer pricing are critical components of cross-border compliance. Multinational corporations face the intricate challenge of navigating diverse tax regulations, and transfer pricing becomes a strategic tool to manage their tax liabilities. Through meticulous documentation, adherence to arm's length principles, and proactive engagement with tax professionals, businesses can not only ensure compliance with tax laws but also optimize their global tax positions. This approach is fundamental for maintaining financial integrity and mitigating legal risks associated with international expansion.

Employment Regulations and Labor Laws

The realm of cross-border expansion introduces businesses to a complex web of employment regulations and labor laws that vary significantly across jurisdictions. Achieving compliance in this area is paramount, involving a nuanced understanding of hiring practices, employment contracts, working hours, and employee benefits in each targeted region. Failure to adhere to these regulations can result in legal disputes, financial penalties, and reputational damage for the company.

In the context of global expansion, one of the pivotal areas requiring meticulous attention is employment regulations. Different countries may have contrasting frameworks governing how businesses engage with their workforce. From hiring practices to termination procedures, companies must be well-versed in the intricacies of local labor laws to ensure legal integrity.

For instance, consider a tech company seeking to establish offices in multiple countries across Europe and Asia. European countries often prioritize a work-life balance, with regulations stipulating limited working hours and generous vacation entitlements. In contrast, Asian countries may have more flexible working hour norms. Navigating these divergent regulations is crucial for fostering a harmonious work environment and avoiding legal complications.

Hiring Practices and Employment Contracts

Compliance begins at the initial stages of employment, with considerations for hiring practices and employment contracts. Different jurisdictions may have specific requirements for the hiring process, such as equal opportunity regulations and anti-discrimination laws. Crafting employment contracts that align with local laws and clearly outline the terms of employment is essential. Failure to do so can lead to legal challenges and strained employer-employee relationships.

Understanding the legal nuances in hiring practices is exemplified by varying approaches to recruitment in different regions. In some countries, there might be stringent requirements for job advertisements, interview processes, and candidate selection to ensure fair and transparent hiring practices. Companies expanding globally need to adapt their hiring strategies to align with these diverse legal landscapes.

Working Hours and Overtime Regulations

Another crucial aspect of employment regulations is the definition of working hours and rules regarding overtime. European countries, for instance, often emphasize a standard workweek with limited overtime, prioritizing employee well-being. In contrast, certain Asian countries may have more flexible arrangements, allowing for longer working hours.

Compliance with working hour regulations is vital for fostering a healthy work environment and preventing burnout. Implementing systems to track and manage working hours in adherence to local laws ensures that the company remains on the right side of employment regulations.

Employee Benefits and Welfare

Employee benefits and welfare provisions constitute an integral part of labor laws. These encompass health benefits, retirement plans, parental leave, and other perks provided to employees. Variances in these provisions across borders necessitate a careful review and adaptation of benefit packages to meet local legal requirements.

For instance, parental leave policies differ widely between countries, with some regions mandating extended periods of paid leave. A multinational company must align its employee benefits with the legal requirements of each jurisdiction to attract and retain top talent while ensuring compliance with local labor laws.

Employment regulations and labor laws play a pivotal role in the success of cross-border expansion efforts. Businesses must proactively navigate the complexities of hiring practices, employment contracts, working hours, and employee benefits to ensure legal compliance and create a positive workplace environment. By staying abreast of local labor laws and tailoring employment practices accordingly, companies can foster harmonious work environments, mitigate legal risks, and establish a strong foundation for global success.

Data Protection and Privacy Laws

As data becomes a valuable asset for businesses, compliance with data protection and privacy laws is paramount. Different jurisdictions have varying requirements for collecting, processing, and storing personal data. Companies must implement robust data protection measures to safeguard customer information and comply with local regulations.

The General Data Protection Regulation (GDPR) in the European Union imposes strict requirements on how companies handle personal data. Businesses operating in the EU must ensure GDPR compliance to protect individuals' privacy rights.

Industry-Specific Regulations

Certain industries face sector-specific regulations that impact cross-border compliance. Whether it's pharmaceuticals, finance, or telecommunications, businesses must understand and adhere to industry-specific laws in each jurisdiction.

For example, a pharmaceutical company expanding globally must comply with diverse regulations governing drug approvals, clinical trials, and marketing practices in different countries.

Risk Mitigation and Legal Counsel

Navigating cross-border compliance requires a proactive approach to risk mitigation. Engaging legal counsel with expertise in international law is instrumental. Legal professionals can conduct thorough risk assessments, interpret complex regulations, and provide guidance on structuring operations to ensure compliance.

For example, a company considering expansion into a region with political instability should assess the associated risks. Legal counsel can provide insights into potential legal challenges, enabling the company to implement strategies to mitigate those risks.

Cross-border compliance is a multifaceted endeavor that demands a comprehensive understanding of legal considerations in various jurisdictions. Businesses must prioritize compliance with trade regulations, tax laws, employment regulations, data protection, and industry-specific rules. Engaging legal experts and implementing robust compliance strategies are essential for successful cross-border operations, ensuring that businesses navigate the complexities of international laws while maintaining legal integrity.

Chapter **8**

Adapting Your
Product or Service

As businesses embark on global expansion, the need to adapt products or services becomes a strategic imperative. Adapting offerings to resonate with diverse markets involves a thoughtful process of localization and customization.

This chapter delves into the intricacies of tailoring products or services to meet the specific needs and preferences of target audiences. It explores strategies such as product localization, customization, and the importance of building flexibility into offerings for sustained success in an evolving global landscape.

Cultural Considerations in Product Adaptation

In the global marketplace, recognizing and adapting products to cultural nuances is paramount for successful expansion. Cultural considerations encompass a variety of elements, including values, traditions, aesthetics, and preferences. Adapting products to align with these cultural factors not only enhances acceptance in new markets but also fosters positive relationships with local consumers.

Market Research and Cultural Understanding

Market research and cultural understanding serve as foundational pillars for successful product adaptation in the global marketplace. These processes are integral to navigating the intricate tapestry of cultural nuances that influence consumer behavior and shape product preferences. Thorough market research entails delving into the specific cultural elements that might impact the reception and acceptance of a product in a given market.

Colors, symbols, language nuances, and societal norms are among the myriad factors that can significantly influence consumer perceptions. For instance, a color that is associated with prosperity in one culture might carry different connotations in another. A symbol deemed positive in a specific cultural context may have contrasting meanings elsewhere. Understanding these subtleties is crucial for avoiding inadvertent cultural missteps and ensuring that product adaptation aligns with local expectations.

Market research provides a comprehensive understanding of the target audience, allowing businesses to tailor their products effectively. By gauging consumer sentiments, preferences, and behaviors, businesses can anticipate the unique demands of a market and strategically align their products with cultural expectations. This informed approach mitigates the risk of introducing products that may face resistance due to cultural disparities.

Moreover, language plays a pivotal role in cultural understanding. Translating product information accurately is not merely a matter of linguistic conversion; it requires capturing the cultural nuances embedded in language. Idioms, colloquial expressions, and cultural references must be considered to communicate effectively with the local audience. Language localization goes beyond translation; it involves adapting communication to resonate with the cultural context, ensuring clarity and relevance.

Societal norms and values also shape consumer preferences. Conducting market research allows businesses to explore the intricacies of these norms, providing insights into the cultural factors that influence purchasing decisions. For example, consumer behavior in collectivist cultures may differ significantly from that in individualistic cultures. Understanding these cultural dimensions is instrumental in tailoring products that align with the prevailing social dynamics.

A noteworthy illustration of the significance of market research and cultural understanding is the global expansion of technology products. Tech companies conducting extensive research gain insights into the technological preferences, usage patterns, and expectations of diverse cultures. This enables them to adapt their products to suit local technological landscapes, ensuring a seamless integration into the daily lives of consumers.

In the realm of market research, businesses often employ a combination of qualitative and quantitative methodologies. Qualitative research methods, such as interviews and focus groups, provide valuable insights into cultural nuances that may not be immediately apparent through quantitative data alone. Understanding the cultural context through qualitative research enhances the depth of adaptation efforts.

Quantitative research, on the other hand, offers statistical validation and a broader perspective on consumer trends. Surveys, analytics, and data-driven insights contribute to a comprehensive understanding of market dynamics, allowing businesses to identify patterns and correlations that inform product adaptation strategies.

Market research and cultural understanding set the stage for informed decision-making in product adaptation. The knowledge gained from these processes empowers businesses to navigate the diverse landscapes of global markets, ensuring that their products resonate with local consumers on both functional and emotional levels. This strategic approach not only enhances the chances of market success but also fosters cultural sensitivity and positive brand perception in the ever-evolving global marketplace.

Tailoring Features to Local Preferences

Adapting products to local preferences is a nuanced process that involves a deep understanding of cultural expectations and consumer behaviors. One of the key aspects of this adaptation is tailoring specific features to align with the tastes and preferences of the target market. This could encompass various elements, including size, color, packaging, or functionality, depending on the cultural nuances prevalent in the region.

When Coca-Cola expanded its presence into the Chinese market, the beverage giant recognized the significance of adapting its products to cater to local taste preferences. In China, there is a traditional inclination towards beverages with less sweetness. Acknowledging this cultural preference, Coca-Cola adjusted the sweetness level of its beverages to better suit the local palate. This strategic move was a testament to the company's commitment to understanding and respecting the distinct preferences of the Chinese consumers.

Modifying product sizes to align with local expectations is another aspect of tailoring features. In some cultures, smaller or larger packaging may be more suitable based on consumption patterns or cultural norms. This adaptation not only caters to practical considerations but also reflects an awareness of cultural habits and lifestyle choices.

Color plays a significant role in product perception, and cultural associations with colors can vary widely. Adapting the color palette of a product to align with local cultural meanings is a crucial aspect of tailoring features. For example, in some cultures, specific colors may symbolize luck, purity, or prosperity. Understanding and incorporating these cultural connotations into product design contribute to a more positive reception among the local audience.

Packaging adjustments are often necessary to ensure cultural relevance. The visual presentation of a product can carry deep cultural meanings. Companies need to consider the aesthetics, symbols, and imagery that resonate positively with the target market. Packaging that aligns with local cultural expectations not only enhances the product's visual appeal but also communicates an understanding of and respect for the local culture.

Functionality is another key element that may require adaptation. Different cultures may have unique preferences or expectations regarding how a product should function. Adapting the functionality to meet these cultural expectations can significantly impact consumer acceptance. This might involve incorporating features that cater to specific needs or addressing cultural norms related to product usage.

The success of tailoring features to local preferences extends beyond immediate consumer satisfaction. It establishes a deeper connection between the brand and the local community, demonstrating a commitment to meeting their specific needs. This approach goes beyond a one-size-fits-all mentality, acknowledging the diversity of consumer preferences in different markets.

Furthermore, this level of cultural adaptation contributes to brand loyalty and positive word-of-mouth marketing. Consumers are more likely to engage with and remain loyal to brands that demonstrate an understanding of their cultural context. When a product aligns seamlessly with local preferences, it becomes an integral part of the consumer's lifestyle, fostering a sense of resonance and familiarity.

Tailoring product features to local preferences is a critical component of successful international expansion. It requires a deep dive into the cultural intricacies of the target market, acknowledging and respecting the diversity of consumer preferences. Companies that invest in this level of adaptation not only enhance their product's market fit but also build a foundation for long-term success by forging meaningful connections with local consumers.

Language Localization and Packaging

In the realm of cultural adaptation, language localization and packaging play pivotal roles in determining the success of a product in international markets. Accurate translation of product information, labels, and marketing materials is not merely a matter of linguistic conversion; it involves a nuanced understanding of idioms, colloquial expressions, and cultural subtleties. Ensuring effective communication goes beyond literal translation; it requires capturing the essence of the message in a way that resonates with the target audience.

Language localization is a multifaceted process that extends beyond words to include the tone, style, and cultural references in marketing communication. For instance, humor, a powerful tool in marketing, is often culture-dependent. What might be amusing in one culture could fall flat or, worse, be misunderstood in another. Therefore, adapting the language to suit the cultural sense of humor is vital. Companies often employ native speakers or linguistic experts who are familiar with the cultural context to navigate these intricacies.

Moreover, packaging design is an integral part of cultural adaptation. Beyond protecting the product, packaging serves as a visual representation of the brand and communicates its identity. Colors, imagery, and style choices in packaging can convey messages that resonate deeply with the local culture. Understanding the cultural significance of colors is particularly crucial. For instance, in Chinese culture, red is associated with good luck and prosperity, making it a popular choice for festive occasions and packaging. Conversely, in some Western cultures, red may symbolize danger or caution.

Visual elements on packaging, such as images or symbols, also require careful consideration. What may be perceived as positive or neutral in one culture could have different connotations in another. A simple image or symbol that aligns with local customs and beliefs can enhance the appeal of the product. Companies often invest in market research and design expertise to create packaging that not only protects the product but also resonates positively with the local consumer base.

Cultural sensitivity in language and packaging adaptation is not a one-size-fits-all approach. It requires a deep understanding of the target audience, their values, and the cultural context in which the product will be received. This understanding should be dynamic, considering the evolving nature of cultures and consumer preferences. What works in one market today may need adjustments tomorrow.

Furthermore, the adaptation process must be approached with respect and authenticity. Consumers can discern when cultural elements are superficially added for marketing purposes without a genuine understanding of the culture. Authenticity builds trust, and businesses that authentically embrace and reflect the cultural nuances in their language and packaging are more likely to establish lasting connections with consumers.

Language localization and packaging design are integral components of cultural adaptation in the global marketplace. Accurate translation and culturally sensitive communication ensure that the product message is effectively conveyed. Meanwhile, packaging design that aligns with local cultural preferences enhances the visual appeal of the product. Both aspects contribute to creating a positive and meaningful interaction with consumers, fostering brand loyalty and success in diverse international markets.

Adapting Marketing Messages

Cultural adaptation in marketing messages is a pivotal aspect of successfully navigating diverse global markets. Businesses expanding internationally recognize the necessity of aligning their promotional content with the cultural values and communication styles prevalent in the target market. This adaptation extends beyond linguistic translation; it involves a nuanced understanding of humor, storytelling, and the preferred channels for promotion within different cultures.

In the context of global expansion, fast-food chains like KFC provide a compelling example of effective cultural adaptation in marketing. When entering the Indian market, KFC recognized the need to go beyond merely offering a menu that caters to local tastes. They understood the importance of resonating with Indian consumers on a cultural and emotional level. As a result, KFC adjusted its marketing messages to emphasize family values and local traditions.

Family is a significant cultural cornerstone in India, and KFC's marketing strategies reflected this understanding. The advertisements focused on portraying KFC as a place for families to come together and enjoy meals. The marketing content showcased the joy of shared moments, aligning with the cultural emphasis on familial bonds. By doing so, KFC not only adapted its products to suit local tastes but also crafted a marketing narrative that deeply resonated with Indian consumers.

Moreover, storytelling is a powerful tool in marketing, and its effectiveness varies across cultures. Different cultures respond to distinct narrative styles, archetypes, and thematic elements. Businesses must be attuned to these nuances when adapting their marketing messages. For instance, a marketing campaign that employs humor in one culture might not be received similarly in another where cultural sensitivities and preferences differ.

The choice of promotional channels is another critical dimension of cultural adaptation in marketing. Some cultures may favor traditional media, while others might be more receptive to digital platforms. Understanding the media landscape and consumer behaviors in the target market is imperative for crafting effective marketing campaigns. For example, a brand targeting younger demographics may find success with social media platforms in certain regions, while older demographics might still rely on traditional media channels.

Successful examples of cultural adaptation in marketing messages extend beyond the realm of fast food. Global brands like Coca-Cola have demonstrated a keen awareness of cultural nuances in their advertising strategies. In various markets, Coca-Cola has adjusted its campaigns to align with local festivals, traditions, and lifestyle preferences. This approach not only enhances brand relevance but also reflects a genuine effort to connect with consumers on a cultural level.

The importance of cultural adaptation in marketing cannot be overstated, especially in the era of global interconnectedness. Consumers are increasingly drawn to brands that demonstrate an understanding and appreciation of their cultural context. Businesses that fail to adapt their marketing messages risk cultural misalignment, which can lead to misunderstandings or even alienation of potential customers.

Adapting marketing messages to cultural values and communication styles is a strategic imperative for businesses expanding globally. The nuanced approach to humor, storytelling, and promotional channels ensures that marketing resonates authentically with diverse audiences. As demonstrated by brands like KFC and Coca-Cola, cultural adaptation in marketing is not merely a superficial adjustment but a profound acknowledgment of the rich tapestry of global cultures. Embracing and celebrating these cultural diversities can lead to stronger connections with consumers, ultimately contributing to the success of international marketing campaigns.

Sensitivity to Religious and Social Norms

In the realm of cultural adaptation, sensitivity to religious and social norms emerges as a pivotal factor in determining the success of a product or marketing strategy in international markets. Respectful consideration of the diverse customs and beliefs prevalent in different societies is imperative to ensure that businesses not only avoid unintended offense but also establish positive connections with local consumers.

Understanding the unique religious and social landscapes of target markets is the foundation of navigating this facet of cultural adaptation. Different cultures adhere to distinct religious practices, and these practices often extend to various aspects of daily life, including consumption habits. For example, in regions where certain religious guidelines dictate dietary restrictions or ingredient preferences, such as the avoidance of specific animal products, businesses in the food and cosmetic industries need to tailor their offerings accordingly.

Skincare and cosmetic products, in particular, exemplify the necessity for sensitivity to religious norms. In markets with predominant religious influences, such as the Middle East or South Asia, beauty and personal care items may need to comply with Halal or other religious guidelines. This involves ensuring that ingredients are permissible and free from substances that could be deemed inappropriate or non-compliant with religious standards. In some cases, businesses might need to obtain certifications or labels indicating adherence to these religious guidelines to gain trust and acceptance in the local market.

Furthermore, marketing approaches should be carefully crafted to align with local social norms. The portrayal of individuals, relationships, and societal values in advertisements should resonate positively with the cultural fabric of the target audience. Cultural nuances related to family structures, gender roles, and interpersonal relationships must be considered to avoid inadvertently conveying messages that might be perceived as disrespectful or contrary to local values.

For instance, a marketing campaign that emphasizes individualism and independence might resonate well in Western cultures but may not align with the collectivist values prevalent in some Asian societies. Understanding and adapting to these social norms can significantly impact the reception of a product or brand.

Navigating sensitivities to religious and social norms is not just about compliance with local customs; it is about fostering genuine respect and understanding. In cases where businesses inadvertently cross cultural boundaries, it can lead to reputational damage, consumer backlash, and, in extreme cases, legal consequences. Therefore, a proactive approach that involves engaging with local communities, seeking feedback, and being receptive to cultural dialogues is crucial.

Successful businesses recognize the importance of not only avoiding potential pitfalls but actively contributing to the communities they serve. This may involve initiatives that align with local values or address social issues relevant to the region. By doing so, businesses demonstrate a commitment to social responsibility, earning trust and loyalty from consumers who appreciate their cultural sensitivity.

Sensitivity to religious and social norms is an integral aspect of cultural adaptation that goes beyond compliance with rules and regulations. It requires a deep understanding of the values, customs, and beliefs that shape the cultural identity of a target market. Businesses that approach this aspect of adaptation with genuine respect and a commitment to positive engagement are better positioned to create products and marketing strategies that resonate authentically with local consumers. Through such cultural sensitivity, businesses not only avoid potential pitfalls but also contribute positively to the communities they serve, fostering long-term success in diverse international markets.

Technological Adaptation for Cultural Relevance

In the rapidly evolving landscape of global business, technological adaptation plays a pivotal role in ensuring cultural relevance and user engagement. As businesses expand internationally, tailoring technological solutions to align with the preferences and expectations of diverse cultures becomes a strategic imperative. Technological adaptation encompasses a range of considerations, from language preferences to user interface design, and it goes beyond mere functionality to create a seamless and culturally resonant user experience.

- **Language Localization and User Interface Design:** One of the fundamental aspects of technological adaptation is language localization. Adapting software applications, websites, or digital interfaces to accommodate the linguistic diversity of the target market is essential for effective communication. This involves not only translating content but also considering language nuances, idioms, and cultural references. User interface (UI) design is another critical dimension. A culturally adapted UI should be intuitive and align with local design preferences. Icons, color schemes, and navigation elements should resonate positively with the cultural aesthetics of the user.

- **Addressing Cultural Nuances in Features and Functionality:** Technological adaptation goes beyond surface-level changes; it involves understanding and integrating cultural nuances into the features and functionality of digital products. For example, in regions where hierarchical communication is valued, collaborative tools might incorporate features that respect hierarchical structures within organizations. Similarly, e-commerce platforms may need to adapt payment methods to align with local preferences, considering factors like trust levels, banking practices, and preferred payment systems.

- **Navigating Technological Preferences:** Different cultures may have distinct technological preferences or usage patterns. Adapting products to these preferences requires a deep understanding of the local technology landscape. For instance, in regions where mobile devices are the primary means of internet access, ensuring mobile responsiveness and optimizing apps for various devices is crucial. Additionally, adapting to local internet speeds and connectivity challenges is vital for delivering a seamless user experience.

- **Customizing Content and Engagement Strategies:** Technological adaptation involves customizing content and engagement strategies to align with cultural expectations. Social media platforms, for example, may require localization not only in terms of language but also in content creation and engagement styles. Adapting to local norms and trends ensures that digital interactions resonate positively with the target audience, fostering a sense of connection and relevance.

- **Privacy and Data Security:** Cultural attitudes toward privacy and data security vary globally. Adapting technological solutions to align with local expectations regarding data privacy is crucial for building trust. This may involve incorporating robust privacy settings, transparent data usage policies, and compliance with local data protection regulations. Failure to address these concerns can lead to resistance from users and potential legal challenges.

- **Agile Development and Continuous Feedback Loops:** The pace of technological change requires an agile approach to development when adapting products for cultural relevance. Implementing continuous feedback loops that involve local users, stakeholders, and cultural experts is essential. This iterative process allows businesses to respond dynamically to emerging cultural trends, user preferences, and technological advancements, ensuring that their products remain relevant and resonant.

Case Study: WhatsApp

WhatsApp provides a notable example of successful technological adaptation for cultural relevance. Recognizing the importance of diverse languages and communication styles, WhatsApp offers language support for over 60 languages, including those with complex scripts. The app's interface is designed to be user-friendly and intuitive, accommodating a global user base with varying levels of technological familiarity. This adaptability has contributed to WhatsApp's widespread adoption in diverse cultural contexts.

Technological adaptation for cultural relevance is a multifaceted endeavor that requires a holistic understanding of the target market's cultural, linguistic, and technological landscape. By integrating cultural considerations into the design, functionality, and user experience of digital products, businesses can create offerings that resonate with local audiences, foster engagement, and contribute to the success of their international expansion efforts.

Navigating Legal and Regulatory Aspects

Navigating legal and regulatory aspects is an integral part of cultural adaptation when expanding products or services globally. Different countries have diverse legal frameworks, regulatory requirements, and industry-specific restrictions that can significantly impact a business's ability to operate within a new market. Understanding and complying with these regulations are crucial steps for a seamless entry and sustained success.

One of the primary considerations is product compliance with local laws. Some countries have stringent regulations governing certain product categories, such as pharmaceuticals, food and beverages, electronics, or healthcare-related items. Ensuring that products meet the required safety standards, labeling requirements, and any other industry-specific regulations is essential. For example, pharmaceutical companies entering a new market need to navigate complex approval processes to meet regulatory standards, ensuring the safety and efficacy of their products.

Certifications and approvals play a pivotal role in regulatory compliance. Products may need certification from local authorities to be legally sold or distributed. Obtaining these certifications often involves a thorough review of product specifications, testing, and documentation. Failure to secure the necessary certifications can result in legal barriers and product entry restrictions. For instance, electronic devices may need certifications to comply with local safety standards, and obtaining these certifications is critical for market access.

Intellectual property (IP) protection is another vital aspect of legal considerations. Protecting trademarks, patents, and copyrights is essential to safeguard a business's innovations and brand identity. Different countries have varying IP laws and procedures, and navigating the complexities of international IP protection is crucial for preventing unauthorized use or infringement of intellectual property. For example, registering trademarks in each country of operation helps prevent counterfeiting and protects the brand's reputation.

Employment laws and regulations also fall under the umbrella of legal considerations. Each country has its set of rules regarding hiring practices, employment contracts, working hours, and employee benefits. Complying with these regulations is crucial for maintaining a harmonious and legally sound work environment. Non-compliance can lead to legal disputes, fines, and reputational damage. For instance, understanding the intricacies of labor laws is crucial when hiring a local workforce to avoid legal complications related to employment practices.

Trade regulations and tariffs are pivotal components of legal considerations, especially for businesses involved in the import and export of goods. Understanding the specific trade laws of the countries involved is fundamental. This includes being aware of tariffs, import quotas, and trade restrictions that may apply to specific products or industries. For instance, when entering the European Union, businesses need to grasp the Common Customs Tariff and other trade regulations to ensure compliance with EU trade laws.

Environmental regulations are gaining prominence globally, and businesses need to consider their impact. Compliance with environmental standards and regulations is not only a legal obligation but also reflects a commitment to sustainability. Businesses need to assess and adapt their products or services to meet environmental standards and regulations in different markets. Failure to do so may result in legal penalties and damage to the brand's reputation.

Navigating legal and regulatory aspects is a complex and dynamic process that requires ongoing diligence. Staying informed about changes in local laws, industry regulations, and market-specific requirements is crucial for adapting products and services successfully. Establishing relationships with local legal experts or consulting firms can provide valuable insights and assistance in navigating the intricacies of legal and regulatory landscapes. By integrating legal considerations into the broader framework of cultural adaptation, businesses can mitigate risks, ensure compliance, and lay a solid foundation for sustainable growth in new markets.

Feedback Loops and Continuous Improvement

In the realm of global business, cultural adaptation serves as a cornerstone for success, and the process is by no means a one-time endeavor; rather, it is a dynamic and iterative journey. Establishing feedback loops is a pivotal component of cultural adaptation, allowing businesses to create channels of communication with local communities and gain valuable insights. These feedback mechanisms serve as a two-way street, enabling businesses to share their products with the community and, in turn, receive constructive feedback.

Engaging with local communities is essential in building meaningful connections and fostering a sense of inclusion. By actively participating in community events, understanding local traditions, and collaborating with community leaders, businesses can gain deeper insights into cultural nuances. This engagement not only facilitates a better understanding of the community's needs but also establishes trust, an integral element in the success of any international venture.

Actively seeking consumer input is another key aspect of the feedback loop. This involves soliciting opinions and preferences directly from the target audience. Surveys, focus groups, and direct interactions can provide invaluable information about how products are perceived and used in specific cultural contexts. By listening to the voice of the consumer, businesses can identify areas for improvement and tailor their offerings to better align with local expectations.

Moreover, monitoring market trends is indispensable for staying ahead of the curve. Cultural landscapes are dynamic, with preferences and trends evolving over time. Regularly tracking market trends ensures that businesses are not only responsive to current cultural dynamics but also proactive in anticipating future shifts. This proactive stance enables companies to adapt their products in anticipation of changing consumer demands, providing a competitive edge in the ever-evolving global marketplace.

Continuous improvement is the overarching goal of this iterative process. Businesses should view cultural adaptation as a journey of refinement rather than a destination. This involves a commitment to learning and evolving based on feedback and market insights. By embracing a mindset of continuous improvement, companies can foster a culture of innovation that extends beyond product adaptation to encompass all aspects of their operations.

In the realm of technology and globalization, businesses have the means to leverage advanced analytics, machine learning, and artificial intelligence to enhance their feedback loops. Data analytics tools can sift through vast amounts of information, providing valuable patterns and trends. This data-driven approach allows businesses to make informed decisions about cultural adaptation based on quantitative insights. For example, analyzing consumer behavior data can unveil hidden patterns, helping businesses understand how cultural factors influence purchasing decisions.

Machine learning algorithms can play a crucial role in predicting future trends and consumer preferences. By training algorithms on historical data and incorporating real-time feedback, businesses can develop models that anticipate cultural shifts. This predictive capability empowers companies to proactively adapt their products, ensuring they remain culturally relevant and resonate with consumers in the long run.

Artificial intelligence (AI) adds another layer of sophistication to the continuous improvement process. Natural language processing algorithms can analyze consumer sentiments expressed in reviews, social media, and other online platforms. This qualitative data, combined with quantitative insights, offers a holistic view of how products are perceived in different cultural contexts. AI-driven systems can provide actionable recommendations for adapting marketing strategies, product features, or messaging to better align with local cultural expectations.

The establishment of feedback loops and the pursuit of continuous improvement are integral elements of successful cultural adaptation in the global marketplace. Engaging with local communities, actively seeking consumer input, monitoring market trends, and leveraging advanced technologies collectively contribute to a robust and dynamic approach to adapting products for diverse cultural contexts. Embracing this iterative process positions businesses not only to navigate current cultural landscapes effectively but also to anticipate and respond to future changes, ensuring sustained success in the ever-evolving global business environment.

Cultural considerations in product adaptation go beyond surface-level adjustments; they involve a deep understanding of the target market's values and preferences. Successful global expansion requires a commitment to embracing and respecting diverse cultures, ensuring that products not only meet functional needs but also resonate emotionally with consumers. By integrating cultural considerations into the product adaptation process, businesses can build stronger connections with local audiences and position themselves for sustained success in international markets.

Technological Tailoring for Global Markets

In the rapidly evolving landscape of global markets, technological tailoring has emerged as a strategic imperative for businesses seeking to maximize their impact across diverse regions. This involves adapting technological solutions, products, and services to align seamlessly with the unique needs and preferences of various global markets. Achieving technological tailoring for global markets requires a multifaceted approach encompassing customization, localization, and leveraging cutting-edge technologies.

1. Customization for Market Specificity
Understanding Local Needs

Understanding local needs is the cornerstone of successful customization in the global market. It involves a comprehensive exploration of the target market's unique requirements, preferences, and cultural intricacies. To embark on this journey, businesses must conduct thorough market research, delving into the technological landscape, consumer behavior, and the societal fabric of the specific region they aim to penetrate.

In the context of a software company expanding into Southeast Asia, the process begins with a meticulous examination of the technological ecosystem. This includes identifying prevalent software preferences, the adoption rate of emerging technologies, and any gaps that the company's applications could fill. Understanding the technological landscape is vital for tailoring products that seamlessly integrate into the existing infrastructure and cater to the specific needs of the local businesses and users.

Consumer demands form another crucial aspect of customization. Through market research, businesses gain insights into the expectations and requirements of the target audience. This involves understanding not only what features are currently popular but also anticipating emerging trends. For instance, the software company must ascertain whether users in Southeast Asia prioritize certain functionalities, security measures, or user interface designs. This knowledge guides the customization process, ensuring that the final product aligns with consumer expectations and stands out in a competitive market.

Cultural nuances play a pivotal role in customization. Each region has its own cultural identity, which significantly influences consumer behavior and expectations. The software company, therefore, needs to delve into the cultural fabric of Southeast Asia, considering factors such as communication styles, visual preferences, and societal norms. Customizing applications to resonate with the local culture ensures that they are not only functionally effective but also culturally sensitive, fostering a deeper connection with users.

For a software company, tailoring applications to support multiple languages is a tangible example of understanding local needs. Southeast Asia comprises diverse linguistic communities, and offering software in languages such as Malay, Thai, Vietnamese, and others enhances accessibility and user engagement. Additionally, incorporating features that align with regional preferences, perhaps integrating localized payment options or adapting user interfaces to suit specific cultural aesthetics, demonstrates a commitment to meeting the unique needs of the Southeast Asian market.

Understanding local needs goes beyond a surface-level examination. It necessitates an in-depth exploration that takes into account the technological, consumer, and cultural dimensions of the target market. By investing time and resources in comprehensive market research, businesses position themselves to tailor their products effectively, ensuring that they not only meet but exceed the expectations of the local audience. This understanding becomes the foundation upon which businesses can build products that seamlessly integrate into the fabric of the region, setting the stage for successful customization and market penetration.

Flexible Product Architecture

In the realm of technological adaptation for global markets, a flexible product architecture serves as the cornerstone for businesses aiming to customize their offerings to meet diverse market requirements. This foundational concept emphasizes the need for technological solutions that exhibit both modularity and scalability, enabling seamless adjustments and accommodations to cater to the specific needs of various regions.

- **Modularity in Technological Solutions:** Modularity refers to the design principle of breaking down a complex system into smaller, self-contained modules or components. In the context of technological solutions, this means structuring the product in a way that each functional aspect exists as an independent module. These modules can be modified, replaced, or upgraded independently without affecting the entire system. For example, a software application might have modular components for user authentication, payment processing, and content delivery, allowing for targeted modifications based on regional requirements.

- **Scalability for Global Adaptation:** Scalability is the capacity of a system to handle growth, whether it be an increase in users, data volume, or geographical expansion. For businesses seeking global adaptation, scalability ensures that technological solutions can accommodate the complexities and demands associated with diverse markets. This includes the ability to scale up infrastructure to meet increased user loads or scale down in regions with lower demand. Scalability is particularly crucial in cloud-based services, where the flexibility to adjust resources dynamically is paramount for efficient operations across different regions.

Key Components of Flexible Product Architecture

- **API (Application Programming Interface) Integration:** A flexible product architecture often relies on well-designed APIs that enable seamless integration with external systems or services. This allows businesses to incorporate region-specific functionalities or third-party services without disrupting the core architecture. For instance, an e-commerce platform may integrate local payment gateways or shipping services through APIs to adapt to regional preferences.

- **Configurable Settings:** Providing configurable settings within the product allows users to customize certain features based on their preferences or regional requirements. This might include language preferences, currency formats, or other user-specific settings. For example, a global messaging application can allow users to configure language settings to align with their linguistic preferences.

- **Decentralized Data Management:** In the era of data privacy and localization requirements, decentralized data management is vital. Designing the product architecture to store and manage data in a decentralized manner ensures compliance with local data protection regulations. This approach minimizes data transfer across borders and enhances privacy controls, addressing concerns related to varying international data protection laws.

Advantages of Flexible Product Architecture:

- **Agility in Response to Market Changes:** A flexible product architecture empowers businesses with the agility to respond rapidly to changes in market dynamics. Whether it's introducing new features, complying with emerging regulations, or adapting to evolving user preferences, businesses can make adjustments without undergoing extensive overhauls.

- **Reduced Time-to-Market for Regional Features:** Modular and scalable solutions enable faster development and deployment of region-specific features. Businesses can roll out adaptations more efficiently, reducing the time-to-market for innovations tailored to meet the needs of specific global markets.

- **Cost-Efficiency in Maintenance and Updates:** Maintenance and updates become more cost-efficient with a flexible product architecture. Instead of overhauling the entire system, businesses can focus on updating specific modules or components, streamlining the maintenance process and reducing associated costs.

A flexible product architecture stands as a strategic enabler for businesses aiming to navigate the intricacies of global markets. It lays the foundation for adaptive and scalable technological solutions that can seamlessly evolve to meet the unique requirements of diverse regions, contributing to sustained success in an increasingly interconnected world.

Adapting User Interfaces

Tailoring user interfaces (UI) to align with local aesthetics, languages, and user experience expectations is crucial. The way users interact with technology can vary significantly between cultures, and adapting UI elements ensures a more intuitive and user-friendly experience. This includes considerations such as color schemes, iconography, and navigation structures.

2. Localization Strategies

Language Adaptation

One of the primary aspects of technological tailoring is language adaptation. Businesses must not only translate content but also ensure that the language used aligns with local nuances and cultural sensitivities. For example, a global e-commerce platform would need to present product information, reviews, and support in a way that resonates with the linguistic and cultural preferences of each market.

- **Cultural Sensitivity in Design:** Localization goes beyond language and extends to the overall design of technological solutions. Considering cultural sensitivities in design elements, such as imagery, symbols, and layout, is essential. Adapting design to align with local aesthetics fosters a sense of familiarity and comfort for users, contributing to increased acceptance of the technology.

- **Regulatory Compliance:** Localization also involves aligning technological solutions with local regulatory frameworks. Understanding and complying with data protection laws, privacy regulations, and other legal requirements is crucial. For instance, a cloud services provider needs to navigate and adhere to diverse data protection laws when offering services in different regions.

3. Leveraging Cutting-Edge Technologies

- **AI and Machine Learning for Personalization:** In the era of technological tailoring, artificial intelligence (AI) and machine learning play pivotal roles. These technologies enable personalized user experiences by analyzing user behavior, preferences, and patterns. For instance, an e-learning platform can leverage AI to provide customized learning paths based on individual user strengths and weaknesses, enhancing engagement.
- **Predictive Analytics for Market Trends:** Technological tailoring involves staying ahead of market trends. Predictive analytics leverages historical data and real-time insights to forecast future trends in consumer behavior, technological preferences, and market dynamics. This foresight allows businesses to proactively adjust their technological offerings in anticipation of changing market demands.
- **Blockchain for Secure Global Transactions:** Global technological solutions often involve financial transactions across borders. Blockchain technology provides a secure and transparent means of conducting transactions. Implementing blockchain in financial systems ensures the integrity and security of transactions, fostering trust among users in different parts of the world.

4. Continuous Monitoring and Iteration

- **Real-time Feedback Mechanisms:** To ensure the effectiveness of technological tailoring, businesses must establish real-time feedback mechanisms. Monitoring user feedback, analyzing data on user interactions, and actively seeking input from local communities contribute to ongoing refinement. For example, a social media platform can use real-time feedback to adapt content algorithms based on regional preferences.
- **Agile Development Methodologies:** Implementing agile development methodologies is crucial for iterative improvements. Businesses should embrace agile practices, allowing them to respond swiftly to changing market dynamics and user expectations. This iterative approach ensures that technological solutions remain adaptable and responsive to evolving global trends.
- **Cross-Functional Collaboration:** Successful technological tailoring requires collaboration across various functions within the organization. Cross-functional teams, including professionals from product development, marketing, legal, and cultural experts, can collectively contribute to a holistic approach. Regular collaboration ensures that technological solutions are not only functional but also aligned with broader business goals and strategies.

Achieving technological tailoring for global markets is a dynamic and strategic undertaking that demands a nuanced approach. By customizing products to meet market specificity, employing effective localization strategies, leveraging cutting-edge technologies, and embracing continuous monitoring and iteration, businesses can navigate the complexities of diverse global markets. The era of technological tailoring represents a paradigm shift, where businesses move beyond one-size-fits-all solutions to deliver personalized and culturally aligned technological experiences for users around the world.

Strategic Pricing Strategies for International Success

Strategic pricing strategies for international success are a critical component of a company's global market entry and expansion efforts. The essence of these strategies lies in the nuanced approach to pricing that goes beyond a one-size-fits-all model. Achieving success in diverse international markets requires businesses to carefully consider local factors, market dynamics, and consumer behaviors to set prices that are competitive, attractive, and aligned with their overall business objectives.

Understanding Local Market Dynamics

One of the fundamental aspects of strategic pricing for international success involves a deep understanding of local market dynamics. Each market has its unique economic conditions, purchasing power, and consumer behaviors. Conducting thorough market research to comprehend the competitive landscape, price sensitivity, and willingness to pay in each target market is essential. For instance, a pricing strategy that works in a developed Western market may not be suitable for an emerging market with different economic conditions.

Adapting to Cultural Perceptions

Cultural nuances significantly influence how consumers perceive and respond to pricing. Strategic pricing strategies acknowledge and adapt to these cultural variations. This includes considering cultural attitudes towards pricing transparency, perceived value, and negotiation practices. For instance, in some cultures, haggling is a common practice, and businesses may need to incorporate flexibility in their pricing models to accommodate such preferences.

Addressing Currency and Exchange Rate Challenges

International markets often involve transactions in different currencies, and exchange rate fluctuations can impact pricing strategies. Successful strategies consider these challenges and may involve setting prices in local currencies, hedging against currency risks, or adjusting pricing dynamically based on exchange rate movements. This ensures that the pricing remains competitive and stable despite fluctuations in currency values.

Segmented Pricing Strategies

Segmentation is a key element of strategic pricing for international success. Dividing the market into segments based on factors such as demographics, purchasing power, or consumer behavior allows businesses to tailor pricing to specific customer groups. For example, offering different price points for premium and basic product versions enables companies to cater to diverse customer segments with varying preferences and budgets.

Value-Based Pricing Models

Strategic pricing strategies often incorporate value-based pricing models. Instead of solely focusing on production costs, value-based pricing considers the perceived value of the product or service to the customer. This approach aligns pricing with the benefits and solutions offered, allowing businesses to capture the value they provide to customers. Value-based pricing requires a comprehensive understanding of the unique value propositions that resonate with consumers in different markets.

Competitive Pricing and Positioning

Analyzing and positioning prices relative to competitors is crucial for international success. Strategic pricing involves assessing the pricing strategies of key competitors, understanding their positioning, and strategically positioning one's own offerings. This may involve adopting competitive pricing to gain market share or premium pricing to position products as high-quality and exclusive.

Dynamic Pricing and Flexibility

Dynamic pricing is a dynamic and responsive approach to pricing that allows businesses to adjust prices based on real-time market conditions, demand fluctuations, or other variables. This flexibility is particularly valuable in international markets where conditions can change rapidly. Businesses employing dynamic pricing can optimize their pricing strategies to maximize revenue and remain competitive.

Strategic pricing strategies for international success revolve around a holistic understanding of local markets, cultural considerations, and competitive landscapes. These strategies embrace adaptability, segmentation, and value-based approaches to set prices that resonate with consumers, create a competitive advantage, and contribute to sustained success in the global arena. Implementing a well-thought-out pricing strategy enhances a company's ability to navigate the complexities of international markets and capitalize on diverse opportunities.

Chapter **9**

Establishing an International Brand

In the competitive landscape of global business, establishing an international brand is not merely a choice but a strategic imperative. The benefits of a strong international brand extend beyond recognition; they encapsulate consumer trust, loyalty, and the ability to resonate with diverse audiences worldwide.

This chapter delves into the intricacies of crafting and maintaining a robust international brand identity, exploring how businesses can navigate the challenges of global markets while ensuring brand consistency across various cultural landscapes.

Crafting a Universal Brand Identity

Establishing a universal brand identity is a delicate yet crucial process that involves creating a cohesive image that transcends cultural and geographical boundaries. The goal is to develop a brand that resonates with diverse audiences, fostering a sense of familiarity and trust across the global marketplace.

Here's how to craft a universal brand identity:

1. Understand Cultural Nuances

Understanding cultural nuances is the foundational step in crafting a universal brand identity that transcends geographical and cultural boundaries. In the global marketplace, diverse cultures bring different perspectives, values, and expectations. Therefore, businesses must embark on a journey to comprehend and appreciate these nuances to ensure their brand resonates positively worldwide.

Cultural sensitivity involves more than surface-level awareness; it requires a profound understanding of the intricacies that shape consumer behavior, perceptions, and preferences in various regions. This understanding goes beyond stereotypes, delving into the subtle nuances that can significantly impact how a brand is perceived. By acknowledging and respecting these cultural differences, businesses lay the groundwork for a brand that fosters connection rather than causing unintended misunderstandings.

A deep dive into cultural nuances involves studying the customs, traditions, communication styles, and symbolic meanings relevant to each target market. This knowledge forms the basis for developing a brand identity that aligns seamlessly with the local context. For instance, colors may carry different cultural significance, and certain symbols may have diverse interpretations. Without a nuanced understanding of these aspects, a brand risks sending unintended messages or, worse, appearing culturally insensitive.

Moreover, understanding cultural nuances is not a one-time effort but an ongoing process. Cultures evolve, and consumer perceptions change over time. Brands need to stay attuned to these shifts and adapt their strategies accordingly. Regular updates on cultural trends, social changes, and consumer sentiments allow businesses to refine their brand identity to remain relevant and resonant across diverse cultures.

Understanding cultural nuances is the cornerstone of crafting a universal brand identity. It sets the stage for creating a brand that respects and connects with people globally, fostering inclusivity and preventing inadvertent missteps that may alienate potential audiences. This foundational understanding forms the basis for the subsequent steps in developing a brand identity that stands the test of cultural diversity.

2. Emphasize Core Values and Mission

Emphasizing core values and mission is a pivotal step in crafting a universal brand identity that transcends cultural barriers. At the heart of every successful brand lies a set of fundamental principles and a mission that goes beyond product or service offerings. These core elements serve as the compass guiding the brand's journey, and when articulated effectively, they have the potential to resonate universally.

To begin this process, businesses must conduct an introspective examination of their values and mission, seeking to identify those that possess universal appeal. Universal values often revolve around themes such as integrity, authenticity, innovation, sustainability, and inclusivity. By pinpointing values that align with these universal themes, a brand can create a foundation that resonates with people worldwide.

A critical aspect of this emphasis on core values is the articulation of a compelling brand narrative. Narratives have the power to evoke emotions and build connections. Crafting a story around the values and mission of the brand provides a narrative thread that weaves through different cultures, enabling people from diverse backgrounds to relate to and embrace the brand.

Moreover, brands should strive to communicate their positive impact on the world. Consumers, irrespective of their cultural background, are increasingly drawn to brands that contribute to social good, environmental sustainability, or community development. This emphasis on positive impact aligns with a broader societal shift towards conscious consumerism, making it an integral part of a universally appealing brand identity.

By emphasizing core values and mission, a brand becomes more than just a provider of products or services—it becomes a beacon of shared principles. This emphasis goes beyond cultural idiosyncrasies and taps into the common human desire for meaning and purpose. When people can see that a brand is driven by a mission to make a positive impact, it creates a universal resonance that transcends geographical and cultural boundaries.

Emphasizing core values and mission is a strategic move in crafting a universal brand identity. It involves identifying values with global appeal, articulating them through a compelling narrative, and showcasing the positive impact a brand aspires to make. This emphasis establishes a common ground that unites people across cultures and positions the brand as a beacon of shared values and purpose.

3. Create a Consistent Visual Language

Creating a consistent visual language is a pivotal aspect of crafting a universal brand identity that resonates across diverse cultural landscapes. Visual elements play a crucial role in conveying a brand's personality, values, and overall identity. A unified visual language encompasses various components, including color palette, typography, and design elements, working in harmony to create a cohesive and memorable brand image.

A universal brand identity requires a strategic approach to visual consistency. The color palette chosen should not only reflect the brand's aesthetic preferences but also consider cultural associations tied to specific colors in different regions. Colors often carry deep cultural meanings, and understanding these associations is essential to avoid unintended misinterpretations. By selecting a color palette that transcends cultural barriers, a brand can create visuals that evoke positive emotions and resonate universally.

Typography, another crucial element of visual language, demands careful consideration. Different scripts and font styles may be more legible or culturally relevant in specific regions. Adapting typography to suit diverse cultural preferences ensures that the brand's written communication is accessible and visually appealing to a global audience. It's about striking the right balance between maintaining consistency and respecting local nuances.

Design elements, including logos, icons, and imagery, contribute significantly to brand recognition. A well-crafted logo, for example, should be simple, memorable, and versatile enough to maintain its impact across various cultural contexts. Icons and imagery need to be culturally neutral or adapted appropriately to avoid potential misunderstandings. Striking this balance requires a thorough understanding of how different visual elements may be interpreted in diverse cultural settings.

Consistency in visuals goes beyond mere aesthetics; it is a strategic choice to build recognition and ensure that the brand remains easily identifiable regardless of the cultural background of the audience. When consumers encounter consistent visual elements across different touchpoints – be it in advertisements, packaging, or digital platforms – it reinforces the brand's identity and fosters a sense of familiarity and trust.

Moreover, a consistent visual language aids in transcending language barriers. In a globalized world, where brands communicate with audiences from diverse linguistic backgrounds, visuals become a universal language. A well-designed visual identity can convey the essence of the brand without relying heavily on textual elements. This not only enhances accessibility but also contributes to a brand's ability to communicate effectively in multilingual environments.

Creating a consistent visual language is a strategic imperative for crafting a universal brand identity. It involves thoughtful consideration of color choices, typography, and design elements that resonate across different cultural contexts. By maintaining visual consistency, a brand can achieve recognition, foster trust, and communicate its values effectively on a global scale.

4. Adapt Communication Style

Adapting the communication style is a pivotal aspect of crafting a universal brand identity that resonates across diverse cultures. In the global landscape, linguistic nuances, humor, and cultural references significantly influence how messages are received. While maintaining the core messaging consistency, businesses must be attuned to the variations in communication styles that cater to different cultural preferences.

Language, being a potent tool for communication, demands careful consideration. Brands need to ensure that their messaging is not only accurately translated but also culturally relevant. This involves more than a literal translation; it requires an understanding of idioms, colloquialisms, and linguistic subtleties that might carry specific connotations in different regions. For instance, a phrase that is innocuous in one language might have unintended negative implications in another.

Humor, often an integral part of communication, varies widely across cultures. What may be perceived as amusing in one culture might not evoke the same response in another. Brands need to navigate this cultural humor landscape judiciously to strike the right chord. In some cultures, wit may be appreciated, while in others, a more formal and straightforward approach might be preferred. Adapting humor to align with cultural sensibilities ensures that the brand's messaging is not only understood but also positively received.

Cultural references play a significant role in communication, adding layers of meaning that resonate with specific audiences. Incorporating culturally relevant metaphors, symbols, or anecdotes can enhance the relatability of the brand. However, brands must exercise caution to ensure that these references are not exclusive or potentially misunderstood by audiences from different cultural backgrounds.

Maintaining a consistent brand voice while adapting the communication style requires a delicate balance. It involves being flexible enough to accommodate cultural variations without compromising the core identity. Consistency in messaging builds brand recognition and fosters a sense of reliability, while adaptability ensures that the brand remains relatable and engaging across diverse markets.

Adapting the communication style involves navigating linguistic intricacies, understanding cultural humor preferences, and incorporating culturally relevant references. This approach ensures that the brand's message is not lost in translation but resonates authentically with audiences from various cultural backgrounds. Striking the right balance between consistency and adaptability in communication is key to building a universal brand identity that transcends cultural boundaries.

5. Test and Iterate

Testing and iteration are crucial phases in the development of a universal brand identity that transcends cultural boundaries. While a well-researched and culturally sensitive brand identity lays a strong foundation, testing the brand with diverse sample audiences is a strategic move to ensure its resonance and acceptance across different cultures.

Initiating this process involves carefully selecting representative samples from target markets, considering factors such as demographics, socio-economic backgrounds, and cultural nuances. This diversity within the testing pool mirrors the actual global audience the brand aims to engage with. By exposing the brand identity to a varied audience during the testing phase, businesses gain valuable insights into how different cultures interpret and respond to the brand. Feedback becomes a pivotal resource during this testing phase. Soliciting opinions and reactions from individuals representing various cultural perspectives provides nuanced insights. Analyzing this feedback helps identify aspects of the brand that resonate positively and areas that might need refinement. It's essential to remain open to criticism and be willing to make adjustments based on the input received.

The testing phase also allows businesses to gauge the universality of their brand identity. Does it maintain its intended meaning and impact across diverse cultural contexts? Are there elements that may unintentionally clash with certain cultural values or symbols? These questions guide the iterative process, ensuring that the brand identity evolves dynamically based on the feedback received.

Moreover, a universal brand identity is not a static entity but a living concept that should evolve over time. Cultural landscapes shift, societal values transform, and consumer preferences change. Regularly iterating the brand identity in response to these shifts ensures that it remains relevant and resonant across diverse global markets.

Case studies and real-world testing scenarios provide valuable examples of how brands have successfully tested and iterated their universal identities. Companies that have entered new markets or undergone rebranding initiatives often leverage small-scale launches or pilot campaigns to assess audience reactions. Analyzing these cases offers insights into the practical application of testing and iteration strategies, demonstrating their effectiveness in refining brand identities for international appeal.

The testing and iteration phase is a dynamic and integral part of crafting a universal brand identity. By exposing the brand to diverse cultural samples, collecting feedback, and being open to adjustments, businesses ensure that their brand resonates authentically across the globe. This adaptable approach not only fosters inclusivity but also reflects a commitment to continuous improvement and cultural relevance in an ever-evolving global marketplace.

6. Incorporate Local Elements Thoughtfully

In the pursuit of crafting a universal brand identity, businesses should thoughtfully incorporate local elements to enhance resonance with diverse audiences without diluting the core brand identity. The key lies in striking a delicate balance between maintaining a consistent global image and adapting to the unique characteristics of local markets.

Incorporating local elements involves a nuanced approach that goes beyond a one-size-fits-all strategy. It requires a deep understanding of the cultural, social, and linguistic nuances specific to each target market. One way to achieve this is by adapting marketing materials and campaigns to align with local customs and preferences. For instance, the tone and messaging in advertisements might need adjustment to match the communication style prevalent in a particular region. The use of culturally relevant imagery, symbols, or themes can also play a significant role in making the brand feel more connected and relatable to local consumers.

Localization should not be perceived as a mere superficial adjustment but as a strategic decision to authentically connect with the target audience. This could involve collaborating with local artists, influencers, or content creators to infuse authenticity into the brand's representation. By incorporating elements that hold cultural significance, the brand becomes more than a product or service; it becomes a meaningful part of the local narrative.

Furthermore, businesses must approach the incorporation of local elements with a deep sense of cultural sensitivity. What might be perceived positively in one region could have a different impact elsewhere. Therefore, thorough research and understanding are essential to avoid unintentional cultural missteps. It's crucial to engage with local communities, gather feedback, and remain open to adaptation based on the evolving dynamics of each market.

The goal is to create a brand identity that feels both global and locally relevant. The strategic incorporation of local elements demonstrates a brand's commitment to embracing diversity and valuing the distinct characteristics of each market. This approach not only enhances the brand's cultural adaptability but also fosters a sense of belonging among consumers, reinforcing the idea that the brand is not an outsider but an integral part of the local landscape.

Successful examples of incorporating local elements can be found in global brands that have adapted their strategies to align with specific markets. For instance, food and beverage brands often adjust their product offerings to cater to local tastes. A fast-food chain may introduce region-specific menu items, acknowledging and respecting local culinary preferences. This level of customization not only shows adaptability but also communicates a willingness to engage with and understand the local consumer base.

Incorporating local elements thoughtfully is a pivotal aspect of crafting a universal brand identity. It involves a strategic and culturally sensitive approach that acknowledges and respects the uniqueness of each market. By blending global consistency with local relevance, businesses can create a brand that resonates authentically with consumers worldwide, fostering a sense of connection and loyalty.

7. Ensure Accessibility

Ensuring accessibility is a pivotal aspect of crafting a universal brand identity that caters to diverse audiences. In the global landscape, linguistic and literacy differences can present significant barriers to effective communication. Therefore, brands aspiring for international success must prioritize accessibility by adopting strategies that transcend language and literacy constraints.

Multilingual content is a cornerstone of enhancing accessibility. Brands should invest in translating their key messages, marketing materials, and online content into languages relevant to their target markets. This not only facilitates comprehension but also demonstrates a commitment to reaching and engaging with audiences irrespective of their native languages. The use of professional translation services ensures accuracy and cultural appropriateness in conveying brand messages.

In addition to linguistic considerations, the use of symbols or images with universal meanings can bridge communication gaps. Visual elements have the power to convey emotions, concepts, and brand values without relying on language. Icons and symbols that have cross-cultural recognition contribute to a brand's ability to communicate its identity globally. This is particularly crucial in regions with diverse languages and scripts, where visual elements can serve as a unifying language.

Moreover, ensuring a user-friendly online presence is essential for accessibility. The digital era has brought people from different corners of the world closer, and the internet serves as a primary platform for brand interactions. A website that is easy to navigate, irrespective of language proficiency, contributes to a positive user experience. Implementing clear and intuitive design, using standardized icons, and providing straightforward navigation options enhance accessibility for a global audience.

Consideration for accessibility extends beyond the digital realm to encompass physical spaces as well. Brands with a brick-and-mortar presence should ensure that their physical locations are inclusive and accommodating. This may involve incorporating signage in multiple languages, offering multilingual assistance, and providing accessible facilities. Creating an environment where everyone, regardless of linguistic background or literacy level, feels welcome reinforces the brand's commitment to inclusivity.

In the pursuit of international success, brands need to be mindful of the diverse needs and preferences of their target audiences. Accessibility is not just about linguistic inclusivity; it's about creating an environment where everyone can engage with and understand the brand, regardless of their background. By adopting a comprehensive approach that spans linguistic, visual, and physical dimensions, brands can truly embody accessibility in their universal brand identity. This commitment not only expands the reach of the brand but also fosters a sense of connection and inclusivity on a global scale.

8. Align Brand with Global Issues

Aligning a brand with global issues is a strategic move that goes beyond traditional marketing. It involves integrating the brand's identity and messaging with topics of universal significance, creating a meaningful connection with diverse audiences worldwide. This approach acknowledges the interconnected nature of the global community and recognizes that certain issues transcend cultural boundaries.

One powerful way to align a brand with global issues is by embracing sustainability. In an era where environmental concerns are shared globally, consumers across different cultures increasingly prioritize eco-friendly practices. Brands that incorporate sustainable practices into their operations and messaging not only contribute to a healthier planet but also position themselves as socially responsible entities. For instance, a company committed to reducing its carbon footprint, using eco-friendly materials, or supporting environmental initiatives can appeal to consumers who value sustainability, irrespective of their cultural background.

Inclusivity is another global issue that resonates across diverse cultures. Brands that champion diversity and foster inclusivity in their messaging and representation demonstrate an understanding of the varied communities they serve. This can involve showcasing diverse faces in advertisements, promoting gender equality, or supporting initiatives that promote inclusiveness. By embracing inclusivity, brands send a powerful message that goes beyond cultural borders, fostering a sense of belonging and acceptance.

Social responsibility is a broad global issue that encompasses various aspects, including philanthropy, community engagement, and ethical business practices. Brands that actively participate in initiatives addressing social concerns contribute to positive change while enhancing their image. Whether supporting local communities, charitable causes, or humanitarian efforts, aligning with social responsibility demonstrates a commitment to making a positive impact on a global scale. Such brands are likely to be viewed favorably by consumers who value corporate social responsibility, regardless of cultural differences.

Moreover, aligning a brand with global issues can also extend to addressing current events and challenges that affect people globally. Brands that navigate sensitive issues with empathy and authenticity can connect with consumers on a deeper level. For instance, responding to crises or supporting social movements in a thoughtful manner can demonstrate a brand's commitment to being socially aware and responsible.

Aligning a brand with global issues is a strategic decision that requires a genuine commitment to the chosen causes. It's not about superficially jumping on trending topics but about embedding a brand's values into meaningful actions that contribute to positive change. By doing so, brands can transcend cultural boundaries and create a powerful narrative that resonates with a global audience, fostering a sense of shared values and purpose. This alignment not only enhances the brand's image but also positions it as a responsible and influential entity in the global marketplace.

Crafting a universal brand identity involves finding the delicate balance between maintaining a consistent global image and adapting to local contexts. It requires a keen awareness of cultural diversity and a commitment to building a brand that speaks to the shared aspirations and values of people worldwide.

International Marketing and Brand Consistency

International marketing and brand consistency are crucial elements for businesses expanding globally. Achieving a harmonious and consistent brand presence across diverse markets requires a strategic approach that considers cultural nuances while maintaining the core identity of the brand.

Understanding Cultural Nuances

Understanding cultural nuances is a foundational step for businesses engaging in international marketing endeavors. This process involves a deep exploration of the values, customs, and preferences that shape the behavior of consumers in each target market. One notable example of successful cultural adaptation is Coca-Cola, a global brand that has adeptly tailored its marketing strategy to align with diverse cultural contexts while maintaining a cohesive global brand image.

In China, where familial bonds and togetherness hold significant cultural importance, Coca-Cola emphasized these values in its marketing campaigns. The company strategically crafted messages that resonated with the Chinese emphasis on family unity, fostering a positive connection with local consumers. By recognizing and incorporating these cultural nuances, Coca-Cola not only gained acceptance but also strengthened its brand association with positive cultural values.

Similarly, in the Middle East, Coca-Cola showcased its cultural sensitivity by adjusting its marketing approach during Ramadan. Recognizing the religious significance of this period, the company introduced campaigns that resonated with the observances and values associated with Ramadan. This strategic alignment with cultural practices not only demonstrated respect for local customs but also contributed to building positive brand perception among consumers in the Middle East.

Understanding cultural nuances goes beyond surface-level awareness; it requires an in-depth comprehension of how cultural factors influence consumer behavior and decision-making processes. Cultural sensitivity is crucial for avoiding missteps that could lead to misunderstandings or unintentional offense. By investing time and resources in understanding the intricacies of diverse cultural landscapes, businesses can tailor their marketing messages effectively, creating a more meaningful and authentic connection with their target audience.

Cultural adaptation in international marketing is not a one-size-fits-all approach. Each region has its unique cultural tapestry, and recognizing these differences allows businesses to navigate the complexities of global markets successfully. Whether it involves adjusting communication styles, incorporating local traditions, or aligning with specific cultural values, understanding cultural nuances forms the bedrock of building impactful marketing strategies that resonate across borders.

The ability to understand and respect cultural nuances is a strategic imperative for businesses engaged in international marketing. Coca-Cola's success in various markets serves as a testament to the effectiveness of cultural adaptation. As businesses strive for global reach, a nuanced approach that recognizes and integrates diverse cultural influences is key to building authentic connections, fostering positive brand perception, and ultimately achieving success in the competitive landscape of international markets.

Customizing Messaging for Local Relevance

Customizing messaging for local relevance is a fundamental strategy in international marketing, enabling brands to establish authentic connections with diverse audiences. Nike, a global athletic apparel and footwear giant, serves as a compelling example of the effectiveness of tailoring messaging to resonate with different cultures while retaining its overarching brand identity.

Nike's iconic "Just Do It" slogan is a universal message of empowerment and motivation. However, Nike recognizes that achieving resonance in specific markets requires a nuanced understanding of local cultures and values. In China, a market with distinct traditions and consumer behaviors, Nike adopted a localized approach to its messaging.

Understanding that authenticity is crucial, Nike collaborated with local influencers who held sway in the Chinese market. By featuring these influencers in their campaigns, Nike tapped into existing cultural connections, gaining credibility and trust among the audience. This collaboration not only provided an authentic representation of the brand but also showcased a deep understanding of the local landscape.

Moreover, Nike incorporated Chinese traditions and cultural elements into its campaigns, demonstrating a commitment to connecting authentically with the Chinese audience. The brand strategically integrated traditional Chinese symbols, celebrations, and storytelling into its marketing materials. This approach not only resonated with the cultural sensibilities of the target market but also elevated Nike's brand image as one that respects and celebrates diversity.

The success of Nike's localized messaging in China underscores the importance of cultural relevance in international marketing. This strategy goes beyond mere translation of content; it involves a comprehensive understanding of local customs, values, and lifestyle. By acknowledging and incorporating these elements into their campaigns, brands can establish a deeper emotional connection with consumers.

The key takeaway from Nike's approach is the recognition that a one-size-fits-all marketing strategy doesn't suffice in a global context. While maintaining the overarching brand message, adapting the tone, imagery, and cultural references ensures that the brand not only communicates effectively but also resonates emotionally with consumers in different regions.

Nike's success in China is just one example of the broader trend in international marketing, where customization is a vital tool for building relevance. As businesses expand into diverse markets, acknowledging the uniqueness of each audience becomes a strategic imperative. This process involves investing time and resources in understanding local sentiments, preferences, and cultural nuances, and then weaving these insights into the fabric of marketing campaigns.

Customizing messaging for local relevance is not merely an option but a strategic necessity in the realm of international marketing. Brands that invest in understanding and appreciating the diversity of their target markets can create powerful connections that transcend linguistic and cultural barriers. Nike's ability to seamlessly integrate its global message with local nuances in China serves as a testament to the impact of culturally tailored marketing strategies in building a strong and resonant international brand presence.

Consistent Visual Identity

The importance of a consistent visual identity cannot be overstated when building a global brand. Apple, as a prime exemplar, has mastered the art of maintaining visual consistency across a myriad of cultural landscapes. Regardless of the geographical location, Apple's sleek and minimalist design remains a constant thread in its branding strategy. The iconic Apple logo, the minimalistic product design, and the carefully chosen color palette contribute to a visual language that transcends borders.

One of the pivotal aspects of Apple's visual identity is its universally recognizable logo – a simple, bitten apple. This logo has become synonymous with the brand and is instantly associated with Apple's innovative products. Whether displayed on storefronts in bustling cities like New York or Tokyo, the logo serves as a visual anchor, providing a sense of familiarity to consumers globally.

Color schemes play a crucial role in brand recognition, and Apple has strategically adhered to a consistent palette. Predominantly using white in its products and marketing materials, Apple signifies simplicity, sophistication, and modernity. This approach resonates globally, appealing to consumers who appreciate a clean and minimalist aesthetic. The visual simplicity of Apple's products, coupled with a limited color palette, ensures a cohesive and instantly identifiable brand image.

Apple's design elements further enhance its visual identity. The sleek and streamlined product design, characterized by smooth curves and precision, is consistent across its range of devices. From iPhones to MacBooks, the design language remains cohesive, reinforcing the brand's commitment to excellence and innovation. This consistency is crucial when consumers in diverse markets interact with Apple products; they expect and receive a seamless visual experience.

The global impact of Apple's visual consistency becomes evident in its retail spaces. Whether in the avant-garde architectural marvels of its flagship stores or in more conventional mall settings, the visual identity remains unwavering. The minimalist interior design, characterized by open spaces and the use of glass, mirrors the brand's commitment to simplicity and sophistication. This consistency in the retail environment reinforces the brand's image, creating a unified experience for customers worldwide.

Beyond physical spaces, Apple's online presence reflects the same visual identity. The official website, marketing materials, and digital campaigns adhere to the established design principles. This uniformity ensures that consumers navigating Apple's online platforms encounter a seamless and recognizable visual language, regardless of their location. Whether accessing the website in California, Tokyo, or Berlin, the design elements harmonize to create a cohesive brand experience.

Apple's commitment to a consistent visual identity has played a pivotal role in its global success. The sleek logo, carefully chosen color schemes, and design elements contribute to a brand image that transcends cultural boundaries. Apple's visual language is a testament to the power of maintaining consistency in the global marketplace, fostering brand recognition, and creating a sense of unity among consumers worldwide.

Localized Content Strategies

Localized content strategies play a pivotal role in the success of international marketing endeavors, allowing brands to connect with diverse audiences by tailoring their content to match regional preferences and cultural nuances. A prime example of effective localized content strategy is evident in McDonald's approach to adapting its menu and promotional campaigns in different markets.

McDonald's recognizes the importance of aligning its offerings with local tastes and dietary preferences. In India, where a significant portion of the population follows a vegetarian diet due to cultural and religious factors, McDonald's responded with a thoughtful adaptation of its menu. The introduction of a range of vegetarian options, including the popular McAloo Tikki burger, showcased the brand's commitment to catering to local culinary preferences.

This localized content strategy extends beyond menu items to encompass promotional campaigns. McDonald's understands that resonating with consumers in diverse markets requires more than just offering the right products; it involves crafting messages that align with local sensibilities and cultural contexts. In India, where festivals and celebrations hold significant cultural importance, McDonald's has tailored its promotional campaigns to coincide with these events. This not only enhances the brand's relevance but also reflects an understanding and appreciation of the cultural fabric of the local audience.

The success of McDonald's localized content strategies lies in the ability to strike a balance between global brand consistency and regional adaptability. While maintaining core elements of the McDonald's brand, such as the iconic golden arches and the overall dining experience, the brand embraces the diversity of its global audience by making meaningful adjustments to meet local expectations.

Moreover, localized content strategies go beyond language translation; they delve into the cultural context, ensuring that the brand's messaging is culturally sensitive and resonant.

McDonald's doesn't merely replicate its U.S.-centric advertising but invests time and effort to understand the cultural nuances of each market it operates in. This approach enables the brand to create marketing materials that feel authentic to local consumers.

The importance of localized content strategies is further underscored by the dynamic nature of consumer preferences and cultural trends. Markets are not static, and what resonates with consumers today might evolve over time. McDonald's continuous commitment to adapting its content ensures that the brand remains agile and responsive to shifting consumer landscapes.

McDonald's exemplifies how adopting localized content strategies is integral to international marketing success. By tailoring both menu offerings and promotional campaigns to suit local tastes and cultural contexts, McDonald's has created a brand that resonates with consumers worldwide. This approach not only enhances customer satisfaction but also positions the brand as one that understands and embraces the diverse preferences of its global audience.

Social Media Localization

In the realm of international marketing, social media plays a pivotal role in connecting brands with diverse audiences worldwide. Crafting effective strategies that resonate with local cultures and preferences is essential for success. Starbucks stands out as an exemplary model in social media localization, particularly in its approach in Japan.

Japan, with its distinct cultural landscape, poses unique challenges and opportunities for international brands. Starbucks recognizes this and utilizes popular social media platforms, such as Instagram, to engage meaningfully with Japanese consumers. Instagram, known for its visual appeal and interactive features, provides a dynamic space for Starbucks to showcase its products and connect with a broader audience.

Starbucks' approach to social media in Japan involves more than just showcasing products; it incorporates local aesthetics and cultural nuances into its content. Visual elements on Instagram posts often feature traditional Japanese motifs, seasonal themes, and artistic representations that resonate with the local audience. This intentional localization not only adds authenticity to Starbucks' online presence but also creates a sense of familiarity and connection with Japanese consumers.

Cultural resonance is particularly evident in Starbucks' limited-time promotions and campaigns on social media. For instance, during cherry blossom season, Starbucks Japan introduces special sakura-flavored beverages and merchandise. The corresponding social media campaigns leverage imagery and messaging associated with cherry blossoms, aligning the brand with a cherished cultural moment in Japan. This strategy not only attracts attention but also demonstrates Starbucks' commitment to understanding and participating in local traditions.

Additionally, Starbucks ensures that its engagement on social media goes beyond promotional content. The brand actively responds to user-generated content, comments, and questions, fostering a sense of community. By acknowledging and appreciating the content generated by its Japanese customers, Starbucks creates a participatory and inclusive online environment. This personalized approach helps build brand loyalty and strengthens the emotional connection between Starbucks and its Japanese audience.

Localization extends to the language used in social media communication. Starbucks ensures that its content is presented in Japanese, catering to the linguistic preferences of the local audience. This commitment to multilingual communication enhances accessibility and ensures that the brand's messaging is clear and relatable.

The success of Starbucks' social media localization in Japan can be attributed to its meticulous understanding of the cultural context and consumer behaviors. This approach is not a one-size-fits-all strategy but rather a recognition that effective international marketing requires adapting to the unique characteristics of each market.

Social media localization is a dynamic and essential aspect of international marketing. Starbucks' strategy in Japan exemplifies how a brand can leverage popular platforms, incorporate local aesthetics, engage with cultural traditions, and respond to user-generated content to create a meaningful and resonant presence. By embracing social media as a channel for connection and community-building, Starbucks has successfully navigated the nuances of international marketing in Japan, demonstrating the importance of cultural sensitivity in the digital realm.

Unified Brand Guidelines

Unified brand guidelines play a pivotal role in maintaining a consistent and recognizable identity for businesses operating globally. This strategic approach involves standardizing key elements such as typography, imagery, and messaging, ensuring that the brand's core values are upheld across diverse markets. Samsung, a global technology giant, serves as a prime example of the effectiveness of unified brand guidelines in creating a cohesive and enduring international brand image.

Samsung's commitment to a unified brand identity is evident in its consistent visual language, regardless of the geographical location. The company employs a standardized logo, color palette, and design elements that transcend cultural and linguistic differences. This approach enables consumers in South Korea, Samsung's home country, to instantly recognize the brand as well as consumers in the United States or any other part of the world. The power of this visual consistency lies in its ability to foster trust, reliability, and instant recognition among a global audience.

The standardized typography employed by Samsung is another critical aspect of its unified brand guidelines. From marketing materials to product packaging, the use of consistent fonts contributes to a seamless brand experience. Whether a consumer encounters Samsung's products in Seoul or San Francisco, the typography maintains a uniform appearance, reinforcing the brand's identity and creating a sense of familiarity.

Imagery is a potent tool for conveying a brand's identity, and Samsung effectively utilizes a standardized approach across its global markets. From advertising campaigns to product visuals, Samsung ensures that the imagery reflects a cohesive brand narrative. This consistency not only strengthens the brand's visual impact but also reinforces the company's commitment to a unified global presence.

Messaging is an integral part of any brand's communication strategy, and Samsung's approach to unified brand guidelines extends to this critical aspect. The company develops messaging that aligns with its core values and resonates universally. Whether conveying technological innovation, user-centric design, or a commitment to sustainability, Samsung's messaging remains coherent across diverse markets. This approach contributes to building a narrative that transcends cultural barriers, allowing consumers worldwide to connect with the brand on a deeper level.

The benefits of unified brand guidelines extend beyond mere visual consistency. They create a foundation for effective global marketing, enabling businesses to communicate a singular brand identity that resonates with a broad and diverse audience. Samsung's success in maintaining a unified brand identity highlights the importance of this approach in navigating the complexities of international markets.

The implementation of unified brand guidelines is instrumental in ensuring a consistent and recognizable brand identity on a global scale. Businesses that prioritize standardizing elements like typography, imagery, and messaging can build a robust international brand presence. Samsung's example demonstrates that a unified approach not only fosters brand recognition but also instills trust and loyalty among consumers worldwide, ultimately contributing to the sustained success of the brand in the global marketplace.

Multilingual Website and Communication

A pivotal component of successful international marketing is the implementation of a robust multilingual website and communication strategy. Amazon, as a global e-commerce giant, exemplifies the significance of embracing linguistic diversity to enhance user experience and effectively engage with a broad audience.

Amazon's commitment to a multilingual approach is evident through its localized websites tailored to specific regions and markets. These websites feature content translated into the respective languages of the target audience. This linguistic customization extends to product descriptions, user interfaces, and customer support, creating a seamless and inclusive online experience for users worldwide.

The primary advantage of a multilingual website lies in its ability to break down language barriers, allowing consumers from different linguistic backgrounds to navigate and interact with the platform effortlessly. By providing content in the language familiar to the audience, Amazon ensures that users can understand product details, policies, and instructions, fostering a sense of trust and accessibility.

Beyond the practical benefits, a multilingual website is a testament to Amazon's commitment to customer-centricity. It reflects the company's recognition of the diverse linguistic preferences of its global user base. In a digital landscape where personalization is paramount, the ability to access information in one's native language enhances the overall user experience, fostering a positive brand perception.

Moreover, a multilingual communication strategy extends beyond the website, encompassing various channels such as customer support, marketing materials, and promotional content. Amazon's customer support services are often available in multiple languages, ensuring that users can seek assistance and resolve queries in a language comfortable for them. This approach aligns with the brand's dedication to delivering excellent customer service tailored to individual needs.

The commitment to multilingual communication is especially crucial in the context of international marketing, where cultural nuances and language play integral roles. Amazon recognizes that effective communication extends beyond mere translation; it involves cultural sensitivity and an understanding of how language influences consumer perceptions and behaviors.

By implementing a multilingual strategy, Amazon not only addresses linguistic diversity but also taps into the cultural richness of each market. This approach allows the company to resonate with local audiences, demonstrating a nuanced understanding of their preferences and creating a more personalized connection. In essence, a multilingual communication strategy contributes to building a global brand that is not only accessible but also relatable on a cultural level.

Amazon's emphasis on a multilingual website and communication strategy underscores the importance of linguistic diversity in international marketing. By tailoring content to the languages of its diverse customer base, Amazon not only facilitates accessibility but also cultivates a customer-centric image. This strategy aligns with the evolving dynamics of global markets, where brands that embrace linguistic and cultural diversity are better positioned to connect with consumers worldwide.

Global Campaign Adaptations

Global campaign adaptations are integral to the success of international marketing endeavors, demanding a nuanced approach that resonates with diverse cultural sentiments. A notable example illustrating this strategic adaptation is PepsiCo's "Joy of Pepsi" campaign. Recognizing the necessity of tailoring their message to align with local sentiments, PepsiCo executed distinct adaptations in various countries.

In the United States, the campaign leveraged the popularity of American celebrities, tapping into the cultural influence of well-known figures. By featuring familiar faces, PepsiCo aimed to establish a connection with the American audience based on their admiration for local celebrities. This adaptation reflected an understanding of the American entertainment landscape and the preferences of the domestic consumer base.

Conversely, in India, PepsiCo took a different approach by incorporating Bollywood stars into the "Joy of Pepsi" campaign. This adaptation showcased a keen awareness of the cultural significance of Bollywood in India. Bollywood, with its immense popularity, plays a central role in shaping the cultural landscape of the country. By integrating local celebrities from the film industry, PepsiCo aimed to create a more relatable and engaging narrative that would resonate with the Indian audience.

The decision to feature Bollywood stars was strategic, considering the impact of cinema on Indian society and the influence of actors as cultural icons. This adaptation not only aligned the campaign with the cultural preferences of the Indian audience but also contributed to establishing a deeper emotional connection. It demonstrated a thoughtful approach that went beyond a mere translation of the campaign, recognizing the need to authentically embed the brand within the cultural context.

Successful global campaign adaptations require a thorough understanding of the local culture, societal norms, and consumer behavior. PepsiCo's approach exemplifies the importance of embracing the unique characteristics of each market, moving beyond a one-size-fits-all strategy. Rather than imposing a standardized global message, adapting campaigns ensures that the brand remains relevant and resonant within diverse cultural landscapes.

Moreover, this adaptive strategy extends beyond mere celebrity choices. It encompasses considerations of language, imagery, and cultural references, acknowledging that effective communication goes beyond literal translation. PepsiCo's campaign adaptations highlight the brand's commitment to connecting with consumers on a personal and cultural level, fostering a sense of familiarity and shared values.

Global campaign adaptations are a testament to the dynamic nature of international marketing. They embody the principle that successful global brands recognize and embrace the cultural diversity of their audiences. By tailoring campaigns to align with local sentiments, brands can transcend linguistic and cultural barriers, fostering a more meaningful connection with consumers around the world. PepsiCo's "Joy of Pepsi" campaign stands as a compelling illustration of how thoughtful adaptations contribute to a brand's resonance and success in the global market.

International marketing and brand consistency demand a delicate balance between maintaining a global brand identity and adapting to local cultures. Successful brands navigate this challenge by understanding cultural nuances, customizing messaging, ensuring visual consistency, employing localized content strategies, leveraging social media effectively, implementing unified brand guidelines, and embracing multilingual communication. By doing so, businesses can create a strong and consistent international brand presence that resonates with diverse audiences while staying true to their core identity.

Leveraging Cultural Sensitivity in Brand Building

Leveraging Cultural Sensitivity in Brand Building is a strategic approach that recognizes the diverse cultural landscapes within which brands operate. It involves understanding and respecting the values, traditions, and preferences of different cultures to build a brand that resonates authentically with global audiences. This approach brings forth several significant benefits that contribute to the success and sustainability of a brand on the international stage.

1. Establishing Authentic Connections

Cultural sensitivity in brand building facilitates the establishment of authentic connections with consumers. When a brand demonstrates an understanding of and respect for local cultures, it creates a sense of authenticity. Authenticity is a key factor that fosters trust and loyalty among consumers. Brands that genuinely engage with cultural nuances are more likely to be perceived as trustworthy, leading to stronger connections with diverse audiences.

2. Enhancing Brand Relevance

Cultural sensitivity ensures that a brand remains relevant in different markets. Consumer preferences, values, and societal norms vary significantly across cultures. Adapting to these differences allows a brand to stay attuned to the evolving needs and expectations of its target audience. By tailoring messaging and experiences to align with local cultures, brands can maintain relevance and resonate with consumers on a deeper level.

3. Building Positive Brand Perception

A culturally sensitive approach contributes to positive brand perception. Consumers appreciate brands that take the time to understand and integrate cultural nuances into their identity. This not only avoids potential cultural missteps but also positions the brand as socially responsible and considerate. Positive brand perception, in turn, enhances a brand's reputation and can lead to increased consumer loyalty.

4. Overcoming Language and Communication Barriers

Language is a powerful cultural element, and brands need to navigate linguistic diversity effectively. Cultural sensitivity ensures that a brand's communication is not only linguistically accurate but also culturally relevant. This goes beyond mere translation; it involves understanding the cultural connotations of words and expressions. Overcoming language barriers is crucial for effective communication, enabling the brand to convey its message accurately and avoid misunderstandings.

5. Capturing Global Market Share

Brands that leverage cultural sensitivity are better positioned to capture a larger share of the global market. A one-size-fits-all approach often falls short in diverse markets. Adapting to cultural differences enables a brand to connect with a broader range of consumers, breaking into new markets and expanding its global footprint. This adaptability is particularly important in a world where consumers seek personalized and culturally relevant experiences.

6. Mitigating Cultural Risks

Cultural sensitivity acts as a buffer against cultural risks, which can have significant consequences for brands. Cultural missteps or insensitive campaigns can lead to backlash and damage a brand's reputation. Being culturally sensitive minimizes the likelihood of such risks, ensuring that the brand's interactions with consumers are respectful and well-received.

7. Fostering Inclusivity and Diversity

Cultural sensitivity contributes to fostering inclusivity and embracing diversity. Brands that actively incorporate cultural elements from various backgrounds send a message of inclusivity. This not only resonates positively with diverse consumer groups but also aligns with societal values that celebrate diversity. Inclusivity in brand building reflects a commitment to representing and serving a broad spectrum of audiences.

8. Long-Term Sustainability

A culturally sensitive approach lays the foundation for long-term brand sustainability. By adapting to cultural nuances and demonstrating a commitment to diversity and inclusion, brands position themselves for longevity in an ever-changing global marketplace. Sustainability in brand building is not just about short-term gains but about establishing enduring relationships with consumers across different cultures.

In conclusion, leveraging cultural sensitivity in brand building is not merely a trend; it is a strategic imperative for success in the global marketplace. The benefits extend beyond immediate gains, contributing to the establishment of a brand that is authentic, relevant, and resonant across diverse cultural landscapes. Brands that prioritize cultural sensitivity position themselves as global citizens, fostering meaningful connections and contributing positively to the communities they serve.

Chapter **10**

Building an
International Team

In an increasingly interconnected global business landscape, building an international team has become not just a strategic advantage but a necessity for organizations aiming to thrive in diverse markets. An international team comprises individuals from different countries, cultures, and backgrounds working collaboratively towards common organizational goals. This chapter delves into the intricacies of creating and managing such teams, exploring the recruitment, management, cross-cultural communication, and dynamics associated with a global workforce.

Defining an International Team

An international team represents a convergence of talents, expertise, and perspectives from various corners of the world. Unlike traditional teams limited by geographic boundaries, an international team transcends borders, drawing upon the richness of cultural diversity. This diverse composition brings together individuals with distinct skills, experiences, and cultural insights, fostering an environment where creativity and innovation can flourish. In essence, an international team reflects the global nature of contemporary business, where collaboration across cultures is not just an advantage but a fundamental requirement.

Benefits of an International Team

Building an international team offers a myriad of benefits for organizations navigating the complexities of a globalized marketplace. Firstly, diversity within the team brings a variety of perspectives and approaches to problem-solving. This diversity becomes a catalyst for innovation as team members draw from their unique backgrounds to generate creative solutions. Additionally, an international team enhances cultural intelligence within the organization, fostering a deeper understanding of diverse markets and customer needs.

Moreover, an international team can improve a company's ability to navigate global challenges. With members hailing from different regions, the team is inherently equipped to navigate regulatory landscapes, market trends, and consumer behaviors across various countries. This adaptability and local insight contribute to the organization's agility in responding to dynamic global business environments.

Building an International Team

Creating a successful international team involves deliberate efforts in recruitment, management, and communication. The recruitment process should prioritize not only technical skills but also cultural awareness and adaptability. Proactively seeking individuals with cross-cultural experience ensures that the team can effectively navigate the nuances of diverse markets.

Once assembled, effective management of an international team requires a leadership approach that values and leverages diversity. Cultural sensitivity becomes a cornerstone, fostering an inclusive environment where each team member feels valued and understood. Leaders should encourage open communication, actively seeking input from team members with diverse backgrounds and perspectives.

Cross-Cultural Communication and Remote Team Dynamics

Cross-cultural communication is central to the success of an international team. Clear communication channels and protocols must be established, considering language differences and cultural nuances. Emphasizing active listening and providing platforms for open dialogue helps bridge communication gaps and promotes understanding among team members.

Remote team dynamics add an additional layer of complexity. With team members scattered across different time zones, effective collaboration requires robust digital communication tools and strategies. Flexibility in work hours, periodic virtual team-building activities, and fostering a culture of trust become crucial elements in managing a remote international team.

Building an international team is not just about assembling individuals from different countries; it is about harnessing the collective strengths of diversity. Organizations that invest in creating and nurturing such teams position themselves for success in a globalized world. This chapter will delve deeper into the intricacies of recruitment, management, cross-cultural communication, and dynamics associated with building and sustaining effective international teams.

Recruitment and management of a global workforce

Recruiting and managing a global workforce is a multifaceted process that demands a nuanced understanding of cultural, legal, and operational differences across various regions. The intricacies involved in assembling a team with diverse backgrounds require strategic planning, effective communication, and a commitment to fostering an inclusive workplace culture.

1. Cultural Awareness in Recruitment

Cultural awareness is a fundamental consideration when recruiting a global workforce, recognizing that each candidate's background contributes a unique set of skills, experiences, and values to the organization. To effectively navigate this diversity, organizations need to move beyond a one-size-fits-all recruitment approach and tailor strategies to align with the cultural contexts of different regions.

In the realm of cultural awareness, communication styles play a crucial role. A candidate's approach to communication can be deeply rooted in their cultural upbringing. Some cultures may value direct and assertive communication, while others may prioritize a more indirect and nuanced style. Recognizing these variations is essential for recruiters to accurately interpret candidate responses during interviews, ensuring that they are evaluating candidates based on their inherent strengths rather than cultural differences.

Moreover, cultural nuances extend to problem-solving approaches. Different cultures may have distinct ways of approaching challenges, emphasizing collaboration, individual initiative, or a combination of both. Understanding these differences enables recruiters to assess a candidate's problem-solving skills in a context that aligns with their cultural background, providing a more accurate evaluation of their capabilities.

Work ethic, another critical factor, can vary significantly across cultures. Some cultures may place a high value on long working hours, while others prioritize a healthier work-life balance. Recruiters need to consider these cultural perspectives to create work environments that align with diverse expectations, fostering a sense of inclusion and accommodating various work styles.

In practical terms, recognizing cultural diversity in recruitment involves incorporating cultural sensitivity into job descriptions, ensuring that they resonate positively with candidates from different backgrounds. This may include using inclusive language, avoiding cultural biases, and highlighting the organization's commitment to diversity. By presenting an inclusive image from the outset, organizations can attract a more diverse pool of candidates.

Recruitment teams must also be well-versed in cross-cultural interviewing techniques. Creating an interview process that acknowledges and adapts to cultural differences can help candidates feel more comfortable and perform at their best. This may involve providing clear expectations, using culturally neutral language, and assessing candidates based on universal criteria that transcend cultural disparities.

Ultimately, cultural awareness in recruitment goes beyond acknowledging differences; it involves leveraging diversity as a strategic advantage. Organizations that actively seek and embrace diverse talents gain access to a broader range of perspectives, innovative ideas, and problem-solving approaches. By fostering a culture that values and celebrates diversity, organizations not only enhance their global recruitment efforts but also create inclusive environments where employees from diverse backgrounds thrive. In summary, cultural awareness in recruitment is a cornerstone for building a global workforce that brings together the best talents from around the world, contributing to organizational success and resilience in an increasingly interconnected global landscape.

2. Adaptable Recruitment Strategies

Recruiting talent on a global scale is a complex endeavor that demands a keen understanding of the unique dynamics present in each region. One of the core principles underpinning successful global recruitment is the adoption of adaptable strategies. This involves recognizing that what works well in one cultural context may not necessarily yield the same results elsewhere. The essence of adaptable recruitment lies in responsiveness, customization, and a nuanced approach to attract the right talent across diverse international landscapes.

- **Understanding Local Needs:** Adaptable recruitment strategies begin with a thorough understanding of the specific needs and expectations prevalent in each region. This demands more than a superficial awareness; recruiters must delve into the cultural nuances that influence how individuals perceive employment opportunities. For instance, in cultures that prioritize job stability, emphasizing long-term career prospects and organizational commitment in recruitment campaigns can be particularly effective. Conversely, in regions where career growth is highly valued, promotional opportunities and skill development may be more compelling selling points.

- **Leveraging Local Networks:** Successful recruitment often hinges on the strength of local networks. Adaptable strategies involve tapping into these networks, whether they are professional associations, industry groups, or community organizations. This localized approach fosters a more organic connection with potential candidates. In some regions, the influence of personal connections and referrals may outweigh traditional recruitment channels, making it crucial to adapt strategies accordingly. By integrating with local networks, recruiters gain insights into the talent landscape, making it easier to identify and attract qualified individuals.

- **Tailoring Job Descriptions:** Job descriptions play a pivotal role in attracting the right candidates, and tailoring them to align with cultural preferences is a key aspect of adaptability. This customization extends beyond language translation; it involves incorporating elements that resonate with the aspirations and values of the target audience. For example, in cultures where work-life balance is highly prioritized, job descriptions that highlight flexible schedules or remote work options may be more appealing. Understanding regional job market dynamics allows recruiters to craft job descriptions that not only attract candidates but also reflect an awareness of the cultural context.

- **Highlighting Differentiators:** Every region has its unique selling points and attributes that can be leveraged to attract top talent. Adaptable recruitment involves identifying these differentiators and incorporating them into the recruitment strategy. Whether it's showcasing a company's commitment to sustainability, its innovative work culture, or its contributions to the local community, aligning recruitment efforts with what matters most to candidates in a specific region enhances the appeal of the organization. This requires an in-depth understanding of the cultural factors that influence what candidates value in their workplaces.

Adaptable recruitment strategies are the linchpin of successful global talent acquisition. Recognizing and embracing the diversity of cultural expectations, job market dynamics, and networking preferences enables organizations to navigate the intricacies of international recruitment effectively. By tailoring strategies to the specific needs of each region, recruiters can not only attract top talent but also build a workforce that is aligned with the cultural fabric of the organization and the expectations of its global employees.

3. Legal Compliance

Embarking on a global recruitment initiative requires a meticulous understanding and adherence to the intricate web of legal frameworks governing employment in each target country. The importance of legal compliance in this context cannot be overstated, as failure to navigate these laws accurately can lead to significant repercussions for organizations. This aspect of global recruitment encompasses employment laws, visa regulations, and a broader spectrum of compliance requirements that are unique to each jurisdiction.

- **Understanding Local Employment Laws:** One of the first challenges in legal compliance is grappling with the diversity of employment laws across different countries. These laws govern various aspects, including but not limited to, working hours, leave policies, termination procedures, and employee rights. A comprehensive global recruitment strategy necessitates a thorough understanding of these laws to ensure that hiring practices align with the legal landscape of each location. Legal experts or consultants well-versed in international employment law play a pivotal role in providing guidance to organizations navigating this complex terrain.

- **Visa Regulations and Work Permits:** Navigating the intricacies of visa regulations and work permits is a crucial facet of legal compliance in global recruitment. Different countries have distinct visa categories and eligibility criteria, which organizations must navigate to facilitate the legal entry and employment of foreign nationals. Collaborating with immigration specialists or legal professionals versed in visa regulations ensures that the organization adheres to the specific requirements of each jurisdiction, preventing potential legal challenges related to immigration issues.

- **Data Privacy and Confidentiality:** In an era where data privacy is a paramount concern, compliance with data protection laws is a crucial aspect of global recruitment. Organizations must ensure that the collection, processing, and storage of candidate information align with the data protection regulations applicable in each jurisdiction. This is particularly pertinent when conducting background checks, verifying credentials, or sharing candidate information across borders. Adopting robust data privacy practices safeguards organizations from legal pitfalls and upholds the trust of candidates.

- **Anti-Discrimination and Equal Opportunity Laws:** Compliance with anti-discrimination and equal opportunity laws is fundamental to fostering a fair and inclusive recruitment process. Each country has its own set of regulations aimed at preventing discrimination based on factors such as race, gender, age, or disability. Organizations must incorporate these considerations into their hiring practices, from crafting job descriptions to conducting interviews, to ensure alignment with local anti-discrimination laws.

- **Operationalizing Compliance:** Operationalizing legal compliance involves integrating these considerations into the entire recruitment process seamlessly. From the initial stages of posting job openings to the final steps of extending offers, legal compliance should be a guiding principle. This requires creating standardized procedures, checklists, and documentation processes that account for the legal intricacies in each jurisdiction. Regular training for recruiters and hiring managers on the nuances of global employment laws is essential to maintain a consistently compliant approach.

- **Legal Expertise and Partnerships:** Given the complexity of global legal landscapes, organizations often benefit from establishing partnerships with legal experts or consultants specializing in international employment law. These professionals bring a wealth of knowledge and experience, offering guidance on legal compliance, interpreting specific regulations, and helping organizations navigate the complexities of global recruitment. Investing in legal expertise is a proactive measure that mitigates risks, ensures adherence to regulations, and protects the organization from legal challenges that could arise from non-compliance.

In essence, legal compliance in global recruitment is a multifaceted endeavor that demands vigilance, expertise, and a proactive approach. Organizations that prioritize a thorough understanding of the legal frameworks in each target country, collaborate with legal professionals, and operationalize compliance seamlessly position themselves for successful global recruitment initiatives. Legal compliance not only shields organizations from legal ramifications but also reinforces ethical and responsible recruitment practices on a global scale.

4. Language Considerations

Language plays a crucial role in global recruitment, encompassing both written and spoken communication. Organizations need to be mindful of language proficiency requirements based on the locations they are targeting. Job descriptions, interviews, and internal communications should be conducted in a manner that accommodates linguistic diversity. Moreover, embracing multilingualism within the workforce can enhance collaboration and inclusivity. However, it's essential to strike a balance, ensuring that language requirements do not unintentionally become barriers to diversity and inclusion.

5. Inclusive Workplace Culture

Managing a global workforce extends beyond recruitment to cultivating an inclusive workplace culture. This involves fostering an environment where individuals from diverse backgrounds feel valued, respected, and heard. Initiatives such as diversity and inclusion training, cross-cultural awareness programs, and mentorship opportunities contribute to creating a workplace culture that celebrates differences. Leadership should actively champion diversity and ensure that policies and practices promote equality.

6. Remote Team Management

With the rise of remote work, managing a global workforce often includes overseeing teams that span different continents. Effectively managing remote teams demands robust communication tools, well-defined processes, and an emphasis on trust. Regular virtual check-ins, project management software, and virtual team-building activities are essential components of successful remote team dynamics. Leaders need to adapt their management styles to accommodate the challenges and benefits associated with remote work.

The recruitment and management of a global workforce require a strategic and culturally aware approach. Organizations must prioritize adaptability, legal compliance, and the cultivation of an inclusive workplace culture to harness the full potential of a diverse team. By navigating the intricacies involved in recruiting globally, businesses can build resilient, innovative, and high-performing international teams.

Cross-cultural communication and remote team dynamics

Cross-cultural communication in the context of remote team dynamics refers to the ability of team members from diverse cultural backgrounds to effectively exchange information, ideas, and feedback in a virtual or distributed work environment. It encompasses the challenges and opportunities presented by cultural differences, language nuances, and varying communication styles within a team that operates across geographical boundaries.

One of the fundamental aspects of cross-cultural communication is acknowledging and navigating the diverse cultural backgrounds present within the team. This includes recognizing disparities in communication norms, work styles, and the interpretation of professional gestures. For example, a direct communication style valued in one culture might contrast with a more indirect approach preferred in another, necessitating an understanding of these variations to ensure effective collaboration.

Language serves as a powerful tool for communication, but in a cross-cultural remote team, language nuances can pose challenges. Different linguistic backgrounds may lead to misunderstandings, misinterpretations, or the unintentional use of colloquial expressions that don't translate universally. Therefore, a nuanced understanding of the language dynamics is essential to ensure clear and unambiguous communication, reducing the risk of confusion among team members.

Cultural diversity often extends to varying communication styles, encompassing both verbal and non-verbal aspects. Some cultures may value direct and assertive communication, while others might prefer a more indirect and nuanced approach. In a remote team, comprehending these diverse communication styles becomes crucial for fostering an inclusive environment where everyone feels heard and understood.

While challenges abound, cross-cultural communication in remote teams also presents opportunities for growth and enrichment. Exposure to different perspectives, ideas, and communication methods can lead to enhanced creativity and problem-solving. Cultivating an environment that values and appreciates these differences can transform potential hurdles into catalysts for innovation and collaboration.

Understanding cross-cultural communication within the context of remote team dynamics is about recognizing the multifaceted nature of cultural diversity. It involves embracing the challenges posed by linguistic differences and varying communication styles while actively seeking opportunities for learning and collaboration. By fostering a culture of open-mindedness and cultural sensitivity, remote teams can harness the richness that diversity brings to the collaborative process.

Challenges in Cross-Cultural Communication

- **Language Differences:** Varied linguistic backgrounds can lead to misunderstandings and misinterpretations, affecting the clarity of communication.
- **Communication Styles:** Different cultures may have distinct communication norms, such as the degree of directness or formality, impacting how messages are conveyed and received.
- **Time Zone Variances:** Remote teams often span multiple time zones, posing challenges for synchronous communication and real-time collaboration.
- **Cultural Sensitivity:** Awareness and sensitivity to cultural differences are crucial to avoid unintentional conflicts or misunderstandings.

Strategies for Effective Cross-Cultural Communication:

- **Cultural Sensitivity Training:** Providing team members with training on cultural nuances enhances their awareness and ability to navigate cross-cultural interactions with sensitivity.
- **Clear Communication Guidelines:** Establishing clear communication guidelines, including expectations for responsiveness, preferred communication channels, and language considerations, fosters a shared understanding within the team.
- **Regular Check-ins:** Structured and frequent check-ins allow team members to discuss progress, clarify doubts, and build rapport, mitigating communication gaps.
- **Utilizing Diverse Communication Tools:** Leveraging a variety of communication tools, from video conferencing to instant messaging, accommodates different preferences and facilitates richer interactions.
- **Encouraging Open Communication:** Creating a culture that values open communication encourages team members to voice concerns, seek clarification, and share perspectives without fear of judgment.

Remote Team Dynamics

Remote team dynamics are the combination of interactions, collaboration, and the overall functioning of a team operating in a geographically dispersed or remote setting. The landscape of work has transformed significantly, with more organizations embracing remote work options, leading to the evolution of remote team dynamics. This paradigm shift requires intentional efforts to overcome potential challenges while harnessing the unique advantages inherent in diverse, remote work setups.

Challenges in remote team dynamics often stem from the physical separation of team members. Limited face-to-face interactions can result in communication barriers, making it challenging to understand cues, emotions, or non-verbal expressions. Building a sense of camaraderie and team spirit becomes more challenging when team members are scattered across different locations. The coordination of activities and meetings across various time zones can be complex, necessitating strategic scheduling and flexibility. Moreover, remote team members may encounter feelings of isolation and burnout due to the absence of direct social interactions and blurred boundaries between work and personal life.

Addressing these challenges is crucial for fostering effective remote team dynamics. Establishing clear communication protocols is fundamental to overcoming communication barriers. This includes defining expectations for responsiveness, regular updates, and reporting mechanisms. The adoption of virtual team-building activities, such as online games, collaborative projects, or virtual social events, helps create a sense of connection and camaraderie among remote team members. Offering flexibility in work hours accommodates diverse time zones and enables team members to work during their most productive hours, promoting a healthier work-life balance.

Recognition and appreciation play a pivotal role in bolstering remote team dynamics. Regularly acknowledging and appreciating team members' contributions, whether through virtual shout-outs or appreciation emails, enhances morale and motivation. The use of technology is a critical aspect of effective remote team dynamics. Leveraging collaboration tools, project management software, and video conferencing platforms not only facilitates seamless communication but also ensures a smooth flow of information within the team.

Flexibility is a cornerstone of successful remote team dynamics. Organizations must recognize the individual needs and circumstances of their remote team members, fostering an environment that accommodates diverse working styles and preferences. Additionally, cultivating a strong organizational culture that transcends physical boundaries contributes to a sense of belonging among remote team members.

Mastering remote team dynamics involves a multifaceted approach. While challenges exist in the absence of physical proximity, intentional efforts to promote clear communication, virtual team-building, flexibility, and recognition can transform these challenges into opportunities. By navigating these dynamics adeptly, organizations can harness the advantages of remote work and build cohesive, high-performing teams regardless of geographical dispersion.

Challenges in Remote Team Dynamics

- **Communication Barriers:** Limited face-to-face interactions may lead to challenges in understanding team members' cues, emotions, or non-verbal communication.
- **Team Bonding:** Building a sense of camaraderie and team spirit becomes more challenging when team members are physically separated.
- **Time Zone Challenges:** Coordinating activities and meetings across different time zones requires strategic scheduling and flexibility.
- **Isolation and Burnout:** Remote team members may experience feelings of isolation and burnout due to the lack of direct social interactions and clear boundaries between work and personal life.

Strategies for Effective Remote Team Dynamics

- **Clear Communication Protocols:** Establishing clear communication protocols, including expectations for responsiveness, updates, and reporting, enhances coordination and collaboration.
- **Virtual Team Building Activities:** Incorporating virtual team-building activities, such as online games, collaborative projects, or virtual social events, fosters a sense of connection and camaraderie.
- **Flexible Work Hours:** Offering flexibility in work hours accommodates diverse time zones and enables team members to work during their most productive hours.
- **Recognition and Appreciation:** Regularly recognizing and appreciating team members' contributions, whether through virtual shout-outs or appreciation emails, strengthens morale and motivation.
- **Technology Adoption:** Leveraging collaboration tools, project management software, and video conferencing platforms enhances communication and ensures a seamless flow of information within the team.

Navigating cross-cultural communication and remote team dynamics requires a combination of cultural sensitivity, clear communication strategies, and intentional efforts to foster a cohesive remote team environment. Organizations that prioritize understanding and addressing the challenges inherent in these dynamics position themselves for successful collaboration in a global and remote work landscape.

Chapter **11**

Overcoming
Language Barriers

In today's interconnected global landscape, overcoming language barriers is paramount for successful communication and collaboration. Navigating linguistic diversity opens doors to enhanced understanding, improved teamwork, and expanded market reach.

Chapter 11 delves into the challenges posed by language barriers and explores strategies to surmount them, emphasizing the significance of multilingual support and the utilization of language services and technologies.

Embracing Multilingual Support

Multilingual support is a strategic approach that involves providing services and communication in multiple languages to accommodate diverse linguistic preferences and cater to a global audience.

In today's interconnected world, where businesses operate across borders, embracing multilingual support is not just a choice but a necessity for fostering inclusivity, breaking down language barriers, and ensuring effective communication.

Why Multilingual Support Matters

Inclusivity and Market Reach

In today's interconnected global landscape, businesses are increasingly recognizing the strategic importance of multilingual support as a powerful tool for fostering inclusivity and expanding market reach. The concept goes beyond the mere provision of translation services; it involves tailoring communication, products, and services to resonate with diverse linguistic backgrounds. The crux of this approach lies in recognizing that language is not just a means of communication; it is a gateway to diverse markets and an avenue for building connections with a wide range of consumers.

One of the primary advantages of embracing multilingual support is the enhancement of inclusivity. Inclusivity, in this context, refers to the proactive effort to make products, services, and information accessible to individuals from various linguistic backgrounds. This inclusivity fosters a sense of belonging and ensures that language barriers do not impede individuals from engaging with a brand, thus creating a more welcoming and open environment.

A crucial aspect of inclusivity is acknowledging the linguistic diversity present in different regions and markets. Businesses that invest in multilingual support recognize that language is intertwined with culture and identity. By acknowledging and respecting this diversity, companies position themselves as culturally sensitive entities that value the richness of global linguistic landscapes.

Moreover, multilingual support serves as a powerful catalyst for market expansion. When businesses cater to consumers in their native languages, they break down communication barriers, fostering a deeper connection with the target audience. This connection is not solely about understanding the words; it's about grasping the cultural nuances, expressions, and idioms that resonate within specific linguistic communities.

Expanding market reach through multilingual support involves tailoring content, marketing strategies, and user interfaces to align with the preferences and sensibilities of diverse linguistic demographics. For example, an e-commerce platform offering products globally might showcase items with descriptions in multiple languages, ensuring that potential customers can comprehend product details and make informed purchasing decisions.

The significance of multilingual support becomes even more apparent in regions where multiple languages coexist. In countries with linguistic diversity, such as India or Canada, businesses that embrace multilingual strategies are better equipped to navigate complex market landscapes. By acknowledging and addressing the linguistic preferences of different regions within these countries, businesses can forge stronger connections and resonate more profoundly with local consumers.

Multilingual support is not just a practical consideration; it is a strategic imperative for global competitiveness. It enables businesses to go beyond the limitations of a single language, tapping into the vast potential of diverse markets. For instance, a software company providing multilingual interfaces for its applications can attract users from various linguistic backgrounds, leading to increased adoption and user satisfaction.

The integration of multilingual support into business strategies is a forward-thinking approach that goes hand-in-hand with the principles of inclusivity and market expansion. By recognizing the importance of linguistic diversity and actively working to overcome language barriers, businesses position themselves to thrive in a global marketplace where connection and understanding are fundamental to sustained success.

Enhanced Customer Experience

In the realm of global business, where borders are transcended by digital interactions, the concept of enhancing customer experience through multilingual support emerges as a strategic imperative. The essence of this approach lies in recognizing that customer experience extends beyond the quality of products or services; it encompasses the entire journey, from the first point of contact to post-purchase engagement. Multilingual support becomes a pivotal element in crafting a seamless and customer-centric journey.

At its core, providing information and services in the customer's language is not merely a functional necessity; it is a powerful means of fostering a profound connection. The customer experience is significantly enriched when individuals can access information, navigate services, and communicate with a brand in their native language. This linguistic familiarity creates a sense of comfort, breaking down potential barriers that might impede effective communication.

In the context of online interactions, where a significant portion of customer engagement occurs through websites, applications, or digital platforms, multilingual support plays a transformative role. Imagine a scenario where a customer navigates an e-commerce website, finding product details, support information, and FAQs available in their preferred language. This tailored experience not only simplifies the user journey but also communicates a fundamental message – the business values and respects the customer's linguistic background. The enhancement of customer experience through multilingual support goes beyond mere convenience; it is deeply intertwined with building trust. When customers feel that a brand understands and respects their language, they are more likely to trust the information provided, feel confident in their interactions, and perceive the brand as genuinely invested in their needs.

Moreover, language is a conduit for understanding. When customers can express themselves, seek assistance, and receive responses in their language, it fosters a more profound level of understanding. This understanding extends not only to the products or services offered but also to the cultural context in which the customers operate. Businesses that embrace multilingual support showcase an awareness of the diversity of their customer base, reinforcing the notion that they are attuned to the unique needs and preferences of individuals from various linguistic backgrounds.

Positive customer experiences are integral to building brand loyalty. When customers receive a service that caters to their linguistic preferences, it creates a positive association with the brand. This positive association, in turn, contributes to customer satisfaction, increasing the likelihood of repeat business and encouraging customers to become brand advocates.

The significance of multilingual support becomes especially apparent in industries where trust and personalized interactions are paramount. For instance, in sectors like finance, healthcare, or legal services, where sensitive information is exchanged, providing multilingual support is not just a value-added service; it is a fundamental aspect of ensuring clear and secure communication.

The concept of enhancing customer experience through multilingual support transcends the transactional aspects of business. It is about building connections, fostering trust, and acknowledging the diverse linguistic tapestry of the global customer base. Businesses that prioritize and invest in multilingual support are not merely adapting to linguistic diversity; they are actively shaping a customer-centric approach that resonates across borders, ultimately contributing to sustained success in a competitive global landscape.

Global Collaboration

In the contemporary landscape of multinational organizations and globally dispersed teams, the ability to foster effective collaboration is paramount. One of the key pillars supporting this collaboration is the seamless integration of multilingual support. Beyond being a practical necessity, multilingual support becomes a catalyst for unlocking the full potential of global teams, transcending linguistic barriers, and creating an environment where diverse talents can thrive together.

At the heart of global collaboration lies the need for clear and unimpeded communication. When team members communicate in their native languages, it not only enhances comprehension but also facilitates a deeper understanding of nuances and cultural context. This linguistic clarity is particularly critical in collaborative endeavors where precision and shared understanding are vital for successful outcomes.

Imagine a scenario where a multinational team is working on a complex project with members from various regions, each contributing their unique expertise. Without multilingual support, language differences could pose significant challenges, leading to misunderstandings, misinterpretations, and ultimately hindering the collaborative process. Embracing multilingual support helps to bridge these gaps, fostering an environment where diverse perspectives can be expressed and valued.

Moreover, multilingual support promotes inclusivity within global teams. It ensures that all team members, regardless of their native languages, have equal access to information, resources, and opportunities for contribution. Inclusion is not just a matter of policy; it is a lived experience within a team where every member feels heard and valued, irrespective of the language they speak.

Collaboration thrives when individuals can express themselves authentically. Multilingual support empowers team members to communicate in the language they are most comfortable with, eliminating the potential hesitancy or miscommunication that may arise when using a non-native language. This authentic expression enhances the richness of discussions and allows each team member to contribute with confidence.

The global nature of business operations often involves frequent cross-border communication, virtual meetings, and collaborative projects. Multilingual support extends beyond written communication to encompass spoken and visual elements. Video conferences, presentations, and collaborative documents benefit significantly from a multilingual approach, ensuring that participants can fully engage with the content and meaning being conveyed.

Consider a scenario where a multinational corporation is launching a new product globally. The marketing team, comprising members from different regions, collaborates on creating promotional material. Multilingual support ensures that the marketing content is not only translated accurately but also culturally adapted, resonating with the specific audience in each market. This nuanced approach enhances the effectiveness of the campaign and contributes to the overall success of the product launch.

Embracing multilingual support in a global collaboration setting is not just about language translation; it is about creating an inclusive and communicatively rich environment. It is a strategic investment that pays dividends in the form of enhanced teamwork, increased creativity, and improved overall productivity. As organizations continue to navigate the complexities of a globalized world, the role of multilingual support in fostering effective and meaningful collaboration becomes increasingly indispensable.

Achieving Multilingual Support

Implementing effective multilingual support involves a strategic and systematic approach, beginning with a thorough assessment of language proficiency within the target audience or organization. This initial step lays the foundation for a successful multilingual strategy, ensuring that efforts are focused on languages that are most relevant and impactful.

The starting point for any business looking to implement multilingual support is a comprehensive language proficiency assessment. This involves evaluating the linguistic landscape in which the business operates or intends to expand. For businesses already established in specific regions, this assessment is crucial for understanding the linguistic preferences of the local audience. For those planning global expansion, it helps in identifying the primary languages spoken in potential markets.

In conducting a language proficiency assessment, businesses should consider factors such as the linguistic diversity of their target audience, the prevalence of languages in specific regions, and the languages commonly used in business and commerce. Surveys, market research, and data analytics can be valuable tools in gathering insights into the languages that resonate most with the intended audience.

Once the language proficiency assessment is complete, businesses can prioritize languages based on their relevance and impact. Prioritization is a critical step, as it allows organizations to allocate resources effectively and tailor their multilingual support efforts to the languages that will yield the greatest benefits.

Factors influencing the prioritization of languages may include the size of language-speaking populations, the economic significance of certain regions, and the strategic goals of the business. For example, a global tech company planning to expand into Southeast Asia might prioritize languages such as Mandarin, Hindi, and Indonesian, considering the significant user bases in these regions.

In the digital era, technology plays a pivotal role in achieving effective multilingual support. Machine translation, natural language processing, and localization tools have advanced significantly, enabling businesses to automate and streamline the translation process. These technologies not only enhance efficiency but also contribute to maintaining linguistic and cultural nuances, ensuring that translated content resonates authentically with diverse audiences.

When leveraging technology for translation, it's crucial to strike a balance between automation and human touch. While machine translation can handle large volumes of content quickly, human translators bring a depth of understanding and cultural sensitivity that is often essential for accurate and contextually relevant translations.

Multilingual support extends beyond linguistic translation; it encompasses cultural adaptation to ensure that the content aligns with the cultural norms, preferences, and expectations of the target audience. Cultural adaptation involves understanding the context in which language is used, accounting for cultural nuances, and tailoring communication to be culturally appropriate.

For instance, a marketing campaign that uses humor as a persuasive tool may need to be adapted differently for cultures with varying perceptions of humor. Understanding cultural references, idioms, and societal norms is essential for creating content that not only communicates in the audience's language but also resonates with their cultural sensibilities.

Achieving successful multilingual support is an ongoing process that requires continuous monitoring and adaptation. Language preferences and cultural dynamics can evolve over time, and businesses must stay attuned to these changes. Regularly reassessing the linguistic landscape, gathering user feedback, and adapting strategies accordingly contribute to the sustainability and relevance of multilingual support initiatives.

Achieving effective multilingual support involves a strategic approach that begins with a thorough language proficiency assessment, prioritization of languages, and the judicious use of technology for translation and cultural adaptation. It is a dynamic process that requires continuous monitoring and adaptation to stay aligned with evolving linguistic and cultural landscapes. When executed thoughtfully, multilingual support becomes a powerful tool for fostering inclusivity and expanding market reach in a globalized business environment.

Localization of Content

In the realm of global business, localization of content is a strategic imperative that transcends mere translation. It is a nuanced process that involves tailoring content to align seamlessly with the linguistic and cultural preferences of a specific region, ensuring that the message not only communicates in the audience's language but also resonates authentically with their cultural sensibilities.

At its core, localization goes beyond the literal conversion of words from one language to another. While translation is a crucial component, successful localization delves into the intricacies of cultural nuances, imagery, and idiomatic expressions. It is about crafting a message that feels native to the target audience, fostering a sense of connection and relatability.

One fundamental aspect of content localization is linguistic translation. This involves translating written content, such as marketing materials, product descriptions, and user manuals, into the language spoken in the target region. However, linguistic translation alone is not sufficient for effective localization. The process extends to addressing cultural differences that impact how the content is perceived and understood.

Cultural nuances play a pivotal role in localization. Certain words, phrases, or concepts may carry different meanings or connotations in various cultures. For instance, colors, symbols, and even numerical associations can evoke diverse responses. Localization requires a deep understanding of these cultural subtleties to navigate potential pitfalls and ensure that the content aligns with the cultural norms of the target audience.

Imagery is another crucial element in content localization. Visual representations can convey powerful messages, but their impact varies across cultures. Localizing imagery involves selecting visuals that resonate positively with the cultural preferences and sensitivities of the audience. This might entail using region-specific images, adjusting color palettes, or even modifying the composition of visuals to align with cultural norms.

Idiomatic expressions and colloquialisms are linguistic nuances that require careful consideration in localization. Literal translations of idioms may not capture the intended meaning, and in some cases, they could be confusing or even offensive. A successful localization strategy involves identifying these linguistic intricacies and adapting expressions to convey the intended message effectively within the cultural context.

One illustrative example of content localization is the adaptation of marketing slogans or taglines for different markets. A slogan that resonates well in one language may not have the same impact when translated literally. Companies often invest in crafting culturally relevant and impactful taglines that maintain the essence of the brand while appealing to the specific cultural sensibilities of the target audience.

Beyond linguistic and visual aspects, effective content localization also considers the broader cultural context, including societal norms, values, and historical references. This holistic approach ensures that the localized content is not only linguistically accurate but also culturally appropriate, contributing to a deeper connection with the audience.

Technology plays a vital role in streamlining the content localization process. Translation management systems, localization tools, and artificial intelligence-driven solutions enhance efficiency and consistency in delivering localized content. These tools not only expedite the translation process but also facilitate the management of multilingual content across various platforms.

Content localization is a dynamic and multifaceted process that requires a deep understanding of linguistic, visual, and cultural nuances. Successful localization transcends mere translation, embracing the essence of cultural diversity to create content that resonates authentically with diverse audiences. As businesses navigate the global landscape, a thoughtful and strategic approach to content localization becomes a powerful tool for fostering connection, building brand affinity, and driving international success.

Multilingual Customer Support

In the interconnected global marketplace, businesses are increasingly recognizing the significance of multilingual customer support in ensuring a seamless and inclusive customer experience. This strategic approach involves addressing customer queries, concerns, and providing assistance in diverse languages, acknowledging the linguistic diversity of the customer base.

One of the primary components of effective multilingual customer support is the presence of a team of customer support representatives proficient in different languages. This ensures that customers can communicate in their preferred language, breaking down language barriers and creating a more personalized interaction. Having a linguistically diverse support team contributes to customer satisfaction and builds a positive brand image by demonstrating a commitment to catering to the unique needs of a diverse clientele.

Additionally, businesses can leverage language-specific support channels to enhance the accessibility of customer support. This may include dedicated phone lines, email addresses, or chat support in different languages. Implementing these channels not only facilitates smoother communication but also streamlines the resolution process by reducing misunderstandings that can arise due to language differences.

Implementing multilingual customer support goes beyond merely offering translation services. It involves a comprehensive understanding of cultural nuances, communication styles, and customer expectations in different regions. Customer support representatives need to be trained not only in language proficiency but also in cultural sensitivity to effectively address the diverse needs of customers.

For example, a company expanding its operations into European and Asian markets may need to provide customer support in languages such as French, German, Mandarin, and Japanese. Ensuring that customer support representatives are not only fluent in these languages but also understand the cultural context of customer interactions is critical for delivering a service that feels authentic and respectful.

Technology plays a pivotal role in enabling efficient multilingual customer support. Advanced customer relationship management (CRM) systems equipped with multilingual capabilities can help streamline communication and information management across different languages. These systems can store customer data in multiple languages, track interactions, and facilitate a more personalized and efficient customer support experience.

Moreover, artificial intelligence (AI) and chatbot technologies have evolved to offer multilingual support, allowing businesses to automate routine queries and provide instant responses in various languages. While these technologies enhance efficiency, the human touch remains indispensable in complex situations that require empathy, understanding, and cultural sensitivity.

Implementing multilingual customer support is not only a response to linguistic diversity but also a strategic move to gain a competitive edge in global markets. Customers today expect seamless and accessible support in their preferred language, and businesses that can deliver on this expectation stand to strengthen customer loyalty and trust.

Furthermore, multilingual customer support contributes to brand reputation and customer satisfaction, creating positive word-of-mouth marketing within different linguistic communities. Satisfied customers are more likely to become brand advocates, sharing their positive experiences with friends and family, thus contributing to the organic growth of the business.

Multilingual customer support is a vital component of global business strategies, enabling companies to connect with customers across linguistic boundaries. It requires a holistic approach that combines language proficiency, cultural sensitivity, and the judicious use of technology to deliver a customer support experience that is not only multilingual but also responsive and empathetic. As businesses continue to expand their reach into diverse markets, prioritizing multilingual customer support is an investment in customer satisfaction and long-term success.

Technology Integration

In the contemporary global business landscape, technology plays a pivotal role in breaking down language barriers and facilitating effective communication across diverse linguistic backgrounds. Implementing technology solutions for multilingual support is a strategic imperative for businesses seeking to expand their reach and engage with a global audience seamlessly.

A fundamental aspect of technology integration for multilingual support involves leveraging language translation tools across various digital platforms. This includes websites, applications, and communication channels where businesses interact with their audience. Machine translation, chatbots, and other advanced language technologies emerge as powerful assets in streamlining the process of providing information in multiple languages.

Machine translation, a cornerstone of language technology, has witnessed remarkable advancements in recent years. Businesses can deploy machine translation tools to automatically translate content into different languages, offering quick and scalable solutions for multilingual communication. These tools are particularly beneficial for handling large volumes of text, ensuring efficiency and cost-effectiveness in reaching diverse audiences.

Chatbots represent another innovative technology that contributes to multilingual support. These intelligent virtual assistants can engage with users in their preferred language, providing real-time assistance and information. For example, a global e-commerce platform might implement a multilingual chatbot to guide users through product queries, purchase processes, and customer support, tailoring the interaction to the linguistic preferences of each user.

Beyond automated translation tools, businesses can explore content localization platforms that offer comprehensive solutions for adapting content to diverse linguistic and cultural contexts. These platforms go beyond mere translation, incorporating cultural nuances, regional preferences, and contextual relevance into the content adaptation process. By using such platforms, businesses can ensure that their messaging not only speaks the language of the audience but also resonates authentically within the cultural framework.

Additionally, technology facilitates the management of multilingual content through Content Management Systems (CMS) that support multiple languages. A robust CMS allows businesses to organize, update, and publish content in various languages efficiently. This not only streamlines the workflow for content creators but also ensures consistency and accuracy in multilingual communication.

An essential consideration in technology integration for multilingual support is the adaptability of user interfaces and user experiences across languages. Ensuring that digital platforms are user-friendly and intuitive for speakers of different languages is paramount. Businesses should invest in responsive design and user interface adaptations that consider linguistic variations and cultural differences, providing a seamless experience for diverse audiences.

While technology plays a central role, it is crucial to strike a balance with human involvement to achieve nuanced and culturally sensitive communication. While machine translation tools offer speed and scalability, they may not capture the subtleties of certain languages or cultural nuances accurately. Human translators bring a depth of understanding and cultural sensitivity that is essential, especially in contexts where precision and context are critical.

The integration of technology for multilingual support is a dynamic and evolving process. Businesses should continuously explore advancements in language technologies, adopt tools that align with their goals and audience preferences, and strike a balance between automation and human involvement. By embracing technology strategically, businesses can effectively transcend language barriers, enhance global communication, and create a more inclusive and engaging experience for their international audience.

Training and Cultural Sensitivity

In the realm of multilingual support, training becomes a linchpin for fostering cultural sensitivity within the team, particularly for those in customer-facing roles. While language proficiency is a foundational aspect, understanding the cultural nuances that accompany different languages is equally critical for establishing effective communication. Training programs focused on cultural sensitivity not only elevate the quality of interactions but also play a pivotal role in minimizing the risk of misunderstandings in a diverse and globalized business environment.

The essence of training on cultural sensitivity lies in equipping team members with the knowledge and skills to navigate the intricacies of diverse cultures. This extends beyond linguistic nuances and delves into the broader aspects of cultural norms, traditions, communication styles, and societal expectations. The goal is to create a level of awareness and empathy that goes beyond merely understanding words but encompasses the context in which they are used.

One key component of such training is cultural intelligence, often abbreviated as CQ. Cultural intelligence involves an individual's capability to adapt, communicate, and function effectively across different cultures. It emphasizes the ability to comprehend and respect cultural differences, facilitating smoother interactions in a multicultural environment. Through training programs, teams can enhance their cultural intelligence, making them better equipped to engage with diverse audiences.

The training curriculum should address various dimensions of cultural sensitivity, including non-verbal communication, etiquette, gestures, and social norms. For instance, what might be considered a polite gesture in one culture might have a different interpretation in another. Understanding these subtleties helps team members navigate professional and customer interactions with finesse and respect.

Moreover, training should incorporate case studies and practical scenarios that simulate real-world situations. These exercises provide team members with a hands-on experience in applying cultural sensitivity principles. By grappling with hypothetical situations, they develop problem-solving skills that are crucial in dynamic cross-cultural interactions.

Effective training on cultural sensitivity is an ongoing process, reflecting the dynamic nature of global business environments. Regular updates and refresher courses ensure that teams stay attuned to evolving cultural norms and sensitivities. This adaptability is crucial, especially in industries where trends and cultural preferences can change rapidly.

In addition to cultural intelligence, language-specific training is paramount for teams engaged in multilingual support. This includes not only linguistic proficiency but also an understanding of language variations, dialects, and regional differences. For example, Spanish spoken in Spain may differ in certain expressions and vocabulary from Spanish spoken in Latin America. Training programs need to encompass these nuances to provide a comprehensive understanding of the languages used in different markets.

Beyond linguistic and cultural training, emphasizing the importance of empathy is integral to building strong connections with customers from diverse backgrounds. Team members should be encouraged to put themselves in the shoes of customers, considering their cultural perspectives and potential challenges. This empathetic approach fosters a positive and inclusive customer experience, contributing to customer satisfaction and loyalty.

Training on cultural sensitivity is a fundamental pillar for teams engaged in multilingual support. It equips team members with the knowledge and skills to navigate the complex web of diverse cultures, fostering effective communication and minimizing misunderstandings. By embracing cultural intelligence, language-specific training, and an empathetic approach, businesses can elevate their global interactions and create a customer-centric environment that resonates with diverse audiences.

Continuous Improvement

Multilingual support is not a static initiative; it is a dynamic and evolving process that requires a commitment to continuous improvement. To ensure the effectiveness of multilingual support strategies, businesses should embrace a culture of continuous learning, adaptation, and refinement.

One key aspect of continuous improvement in multilingual support is gathering regular feedback from users or team members who engage with the translated content. This feedback can provide valuable insights into the effectiveness of language translations, the cultural relevance of content, and the overall user experience. It opens a channel for understanding how well the multilingual support aligns with the linguistic and cultural expectations of the target audience.

Feedback mechanisms can take various forms, including surveys, user reviews, and direct communication with language users. Actively seek input on the clarity and accuracy of translations, as well as the cultural appropriateness of content. Analyzing this feedback allows businesses to identify areas that may need improvement and address any discrepancies or misunderstandings that users may have encountered.

Additionally, staying informed about linguistic trends and changes in language preferences is crucial for continuous improvement. Languages are living entities that evolve over time, influenced by societal, cultural, and technological shifts. Regularly monitoring linguistic trends helps businesses adapt their multilingual strategies to reflect current linguistic norms and preferences.

For example, the popularity of certain phrases, terminologies, or expressions may change, and staying attuned to these linguistic nuances ensures that translated content remains contemporary and resonates with the audience. It also helps in avoiding outdated or potentially offensive language that might have been acceptable in the past but has evolved in its cultural connotations.

Furthermore, understanding emerging markets and linguistic shifts in those regions is paramount. As businesses explore new markets, they should be proactive in researching the linguistic landscape and cultural nuances specific to those regions. This foresight enables businesses to tailor their multilingual support strategies to meet the linguistic expectations of emerging user bases.

Embracing technological advancements is another facet of continuous improvement in multilingual support. Technology plays a pivotal role in automating translation processes, enhancing efficiency, and ensuring consistency across multilingual content. Regularly assess the latest advancements in language technologies, machine translation, and localization tools to integrate innovations that can optimize the multilingual support workflow.

Incorporating artificial intelligence (AI) and machine learning (ML) into language translation processes can lead to more accurate and contextually relevant translations over time. These technologies learn from user interactions, feedback, and linguistic patterns, contributing to the continuous refinement of multilingual support systems.

Cultivating a cross-functional and collaborative approach within the organization supports continuous improvement in multilingual support. Establish regular communication channels between language specialists, content creators, and technology experts. This collaborative environment encourages the sharing of insights, best practices, and lessons learned, fostering a culture of ongoing improvement.

Continuous improvement in multilingual support requires a multifaceted approach that includes gathering user feedback, staying informed about linguistic trends, understanding emerging markets, embracing technological advancements, and fostering a collaborative organizational culture. By actively seeking ways to enhance language translations, cultural adaptations, and overall multilingual strategies, businesses can ensure that their global audience receives content that is not only linguistically accurate but also culturally resonant and contextually relevant.

Embracing multilingual support is a strategic imperative for businesses aiming to thrive in diverse global markets. It goes beyond mere translation, focusing on creating an inclusive environment where language is not a barrier but a bridge to connect with a broader audience.

Leveraging Language Services

In the interconnected world of global business, leveraging language services is a strategic imperative for organizations seeking to enhance their global communication strategies. Language services encompass a range of solutions designed to facilitate effective communication across linguistic and cultural barriers, ensuring that businesses can engage with diverse audiences and navigate the complexities of multilingual markets.

Understanding Language Services

Going beyond the basic translation of words, these language services form a spectrum of solutions that cater to the diverse communication needs of organizations navigating the complexities of a multilingual world. The crux of language services lies in fostering not just understanding but genuine connection between businesses and their stakeholders, be it customers, partners, or team members spread across the globe.

At the core of language services, translation stands as the bedrock for transforming written content from one language to another. Whether it's documents, marketing collateral, legal texts, or any form of written communication, professional translation ensures accuracy, cultural relevance, and clarity. The goal is not just linguistic fidelity but also the preservation of meaning and context across different languages, allowing businesses to convey their messages with precision and authenticity.

When spoken words take center stage, interpretation services step in to create real-time linguistic bridges. This is particularly crucial in scenarios such as conferences, meetings, or events where participants speak different languages. Simultaneous interpretation, where the interpreter provides translations in real-time, and consecutive interpretation, with pauses for translation, ensure that verbal communication flows seamlessly across language boundaries. This is not just about linguistic accuracy but about capturing the nuances and emotions embedded in spoken language.

While translation addresses the linguistic aspect, localization takes a step further by tailoring content to align with the cultural nuances, preferences, and expectations of specific target markets. Beyond language, localization considers elements like imagery, colors, symbols, and even cultural references to ensure that the content resonates authentically with local audiences. From adapting marketing campaigns to tweaking product designs, localization is the key to making a brand feel native rather than foreign.

Transcreation, a portmanteau of translation and creation, comes into play when the content involves creativity and emotional impact. This is often the case in marketing materials, advertising, or any content where preserving the brand's tone and messaging is as crucial as conveying the information. Transcreation involves more than just linguistic adaptation; it requires a deep understanding of cultural nuances and the ability to infuse creativity while staying true to the brand identity.

In the era of technological advancement, machine translation powered by artificial intelligence has become increasingly sophisticated. While it may not replace the human touch in nuanced or complex content, machine translation serves as a valuable tool for quickly translating vast amounts of information. Businesses can leverage machine translation to enhance efficiency, especially in handling routine or repetitive translation tasks, while still ensuring the quality and accuracy of more nuanced content through human oversight.

Engaging in cultural consultation services provides businesses with valuable insights into the cultural nuances of specific markets. Cultural consultants offer guidance on communication styles, cultural norms, and business etiquette, helping organizations navigate the complexities of diverse cultural landscapes. This form of support goes beyond language to address the broader aspects of cultural intelligence, ensuring that businesses not only speak the language but also understand the cultural context in which they operate.

In the digital realm, UX localization focuses on adapting digital interfaces, websites, and applications to meet the expectations and preferences of users from different linguistic and cultural backgrounds. This goes beyond simple translation of interface elements; it involves considering user behaviors, design preferences, and local usability standards to create a seamless and user-friendly experience for a global audience.

Language services act as a multifaceted toolkit, empowering businesses to navigate the intricacies of a multilingual and multicultural landscape. By understanding and strategically employing these services, organizations can transcend linguistic barriers, foster genuine connections, and build bridges of communication that span the globe.

Translation Services: Bridging Linguistic Gaps

Translation services stand as a foundational pillar in the intricate tapestry of language support, functioning as a dynamic bridge that spans linguistic gaps and facilitates effective communication on a global scale. At its essence, translation involves the meticulous conversion of written content from one language to another, encompassing a wide array of materials such as documents, marketing collateral, websites, and an extensive spectrum of textual communication. The significance of professional translation services lies not merely in rendering words from one language into another but in ensuring linguistic precision, cultural resonance, and a harmonious conveyance of the intended message, irrespective of the linguistic diversity encountered.

The heart of professional translation services lies in linguistic accuracy. The process involves not just the conversion of words but a profound understanding of linguistic nuances, idioms, and the cultural contexts that underpin effective communication. Skilled translators are adept at navigating the intricacies of language, ensuring that the translated content maintains the integrity of the original message while seamlessly adapting to the linguistic and cultural characteristics of the target audience. This precision is paramount, especially in contexts where even the slightest misinterpretation could lead to significant misunderstandings or misrepresentations.

Cultural relevance is another pivotal dimension of translation services. Language is inherently intertwined with culture, and effective translation goes beyond mere linguistic conversion to embrace the cultural nuances embedded in the source material. Professional translators are attuned to the cultural subtleties that influence language usage, idiomatic expressions, and the overall tone of communication. By incorporating these cultural elements, translation services ensure that the message not only reaches the audience in their language but also resonates authentically within their cultural context.

Consistency stands as a hallmark of proficient translation services. Maintaining a consistent voice and style across various translated materials is crucial for building a cohesive brand identity and fostering a seamless user experience. Whether it's technical documents, marketing content, or legal texts, maintaining linguistic consistency ensures that the brand's messaging remains uniform, reinforcing its identity and facilitating a unified communication strategy across diverse linguistic channels.

The scope of translation services extends far beyond the realm of traditional documents. In the digital age, website translation has become a critical component for businesses seeking to expand their reach globally. Websites serve as virtual storefronts, and translating them into multiple languages is a strategic move to engage a diverse audience. A well-translated website not only communicates information effectively but also enhances user experience, making the content accessible and engaging for users who prefer different languages.

Legal translation is a specialized domain within translation services, addressing the unique challenges of legal documents and proceedings. Accuracy in legal translation is paramount, as even minor discrepancies can have profound legal implications. Legal translators possess not only linguistic expertise but also a deep understanding of legal terminology, ensuring that legal documents are faithfully translated while preserving their legal validity.

Technical translation is another specialized facet of translation services, focusing on the translation of technical documents, manuals, and specifications. This requires not only linguistic proficiency but also a solid grasp of technical terminology and concepts. Technical translators play a crucial role in industries such as manufacturing, engineering, and information technology, where precision and clarity are paramount.

The advent of machine translation, powered by artificial intelligence, has introduced new dimensions to translation services. While machine translation serves as a valuable tool for quickly processing vast amounts of information, it is not a panacea. The nuances of human language, especially in contexts requiring cultural sensitivity or dealing with complex subject matter, necessitate the discernment and expertise of human translators who can ensure accuracy and context-awareness.

Translation services embody a multifaceted discipline that goes beyond linguistic conversion. They serve as the vanguards of effective communication, breaking down linguistic barriers and fostering understanding in a globalized world. The interplay of linguistic accuracy, cultural relevance, and consistency within translation services creates a tapestry that not only conveys words but encapsulates the essence and intent of communication across diverse linguistic landscapes.

Interpretation Services: Real-time Language Facilitation

As businesses operate on a global scale, participating in conferences, negotiations, or collaborative events often involves diverse participants speaking different languages. This is where interpretation services take center stage, facilitating communication and ensuring that the essence of conversations transcends linguistic confines.

Simultaneous interpretation stands as a pinnacle of real-time language facilitation. In this mode, interpreters work diligently behind the scenes, translating spoken words into the target language as the speaker talks. This process requires specialized equipment, such as headsets and soundproof booths, allowing participants to receive the interpretation simultaneously. Simultaneous interpretation is the preferred choice for large conferences, international summits, or any event with a diverse audience, as it enables a continuous flow of communication without significant pauses.

On the other hand, consecutive interpretation involves a more intermittent approach. The speaker delivers a segment of their speech, and then the interpreter translates it into the target language during a pause. While this method extends the duration of the conversation, it proves effective in smaller meetings, discussions, or settings where a continuous flow is not as critical.

Consecutive interpretation provides a more relaxed environment, allowing for a nuanced exchange of ideas.

The efficacy of interpretation services extends beyond mere linguistic accuracy; it encompasses cultural sensitivity and an acute understanding of context. Interpreters must not only translate words but also convey the emotions, tone, and cultural nuances embedded in the speaker's message. This dynamic process demands a profound grasp of both source and target languages, coupled with a keen awareness of the cultural intricacies at play.

In international business negotiations, where precision and clarity are paramount, interpretation services act as bridges between diverse stakeholders. Imagine a scenario where a multinational corporation is finalizing a joint venture with a partner from a different linguistic background. In such situations, interpreters play a crucial role in ensuring that every nuance of the negotiation – from contractual terms to subtle cultural considerations – is accurately conveyed, fostering understanding and trust among participants.

Interpretation services extend beyond traditional in-person settings, embracing the digital realm as well. With the rise of virtual meetings and global collaborations, remote interpretation services have gained prominence. Through advanced technology, interpreters can provide their services from a distance, connecting with participants in different locations. This not only enhances accessibility but also allows businesses to seamlessly integrate interpretation services into their digital communication strategies.

One notable example of the transformative power of interpretation services is evident in international conferences, where leaders, diplomats, and experts converge to discuss global issues. The United Nations General Assembly serves as a prime illustration. With representatives from diverse linguistic backgrounds addressing the assembly, interpreters play a pivotal role in ensuring that each speaker's message resonates across languages, fostering a truly inclusive and collaborative environment.

However, the effectiveness of interpretation services hinges not only on the skills of interpreters but also on meticulous planning and coordination. Event organizers must work closely with interpretation service providers to understand the linguistic needs of participants, determine the appropriate interpretation mode, and ensure that the necessary equipment and technology are in place. This collaborative approach guarantees a smooth and successful multilingual event.

Interpretation services emerge as dynamic facilitators of global communication, seamlessly connecting individuals and organizations across linguistic divides. Whether in high-stakes negotiations, international conferences, or virtual collaborations, these services bridge the gap, ensuring that conversations transcend language barriers and cultivate a truly interconnected global landscape.

Transcreation: Balancing Creativity and Cultural Sensitivity

Transcreation is a dynamic approach that goes beyond linguistic precision, aiming to strike a delicate balance between creativity and cultural sensitivity. As a fusion of "translation" and "creation," transcreation stands as the linchpin for businesses seeking to convey their messages authentically in the diverse landscapes of the global market.

At its core, transcreation is not merely about rendering words from one language to another; it's about reimagining the entire message to evoke the same emotional response in a different cultural setting. This process recognizes that certain cultural nuances, idioms, or humor may not seamlessly translate, and attempting a direct conversion risks diluting the impact of the original message. Transcreation, therefore, involves creative adaptation, ensuring that the essence and emotional resonance of the content remain intact across cultural frontiers.

One of the primary virtues of transcreation is its ability to preserve brand consistency while tailoring content for different cultural contexts. Brands are more than just names and logos; they embody a particular personality, voice, and emotional connection with their audience.

Transcreation ensures that these integral elements are not lost in translation but are instead carefully transposed into languages and cultures, maintaining the brand's authenticity and resonance.

The process of transcreation often begins with a thorough understanding of the target audience and their cultural backdrop. Cultural consultants or creative professionals well-versed in the nuances of both the source and target cultures play a pivotal role in guiding this process. This understanding goes beyond language intricacies; it delves into the cultural values, norms, and emotional triggers that shape the audience's responses to content.

Consider a global marketing campaign that employs humor as a central element. A direct translation of the jokes may fall flat or, worse, offend the sensibilities of a different culture. In transcreation, the humor is recalibrated, ensuring it aligns with the cultural context, references, and sensitivities of the target audience. This adaptation not only preserves the intended laughter but also respects the diversity of cultural perceptions.

Transcreation becomes particularly crucial when dealing with slogans, taglines, or creative concepts that heavily rely on wordplay, cultural references, or idiomatic expressions. These linguistic subtleties often defy a straightforward translation, requiring a more nuanced approach. In essence, transcreation becomes a form of linguistic alchemy, where words are transformed to resonate authentically within a new cultural alchemy.

For multinational companies launching products or campaigns across diverse markets, transcreation becomes a strategic imperative. It ensures that the marketing message transcends language barriers, creating emotional connections that resonate universally. Whether it's adapting visuals, modifying slogans, or reworking narratives, the goal is not just linguistic accuracy but emotional impact — an impact that transcends cultural boundaries and speaks directly to the hearts of the audience.

Transcreation emerges as a powerful tool in the arsenal of global businesses seeking to communicate effectively in the complex landscape of diverse cultures. It is the bridge that spans the gap between linguistic precision and cultural nuance, ensuring that the essence of a message remains vibrant and resonant across the vast spectrum of human experiences.

Cultural Consultation: Insights for Strategic Adaptation

In the intricate mosaic of global business, where diverse cultures intersect, cultural consultation emerges as a beacon guiding organizations through the nuanced intricacies of international markets. This service becomes a strategic compass, helping businesses not only understand but effectively navigate the multifaceted dimensions of cultural diversity.

At its core, cultural consultation is a collaborative process where businesses seek expertise from professionals well-versed in the customs, values, and social norms of specific target markets. These consultants, often individuals with deep cultural insights and experiences, act as cultural ambassadors, providing invaluable perspectives that extend beyond mere language translation.

One of the primary roles of cultural consultants is to decode the subtle nuances of communication styles prevalent in a particular culture. Language, while pivotal, is just one layer of the intricate cultural tapestry. Understanding how messages are conveyed, the significance of non-verbal cues, and the role of interpersonal relationships within a specific cultural context is paramount. Cultural consultants delve into these subtleties, offering businesses a roadmap to communicate effectively and authentically.

Cultural norms shape the fabric of societies, influencing behaviors and expectations. Cultural consultants act as cultural interpreters, helping businesses decipher these norms and align their strategies accordingly. Whether it's understanding the hierarchical structures in decision-making, the significance of punctuality, or the etiquette surrounding business meetings, cultural consultation provides businesses with a comprehensive guide to navigate these cultural intricacies successfully.

Business etiquette varies significantly across cultures, and what may be considered polite in one region could be perceived differently in another. Cultural consultants play a pivotal role in advising businesses on the do's and don'ts of professional conduct. From appropriate attire in business settings to the nuances of gift-giving, these consultants ensure that businesses project an image that resonates positively with their target audience, avoiding inadvertent cultural missteps.

In the realm of international negotiations and collaborations, the cultural dimension cannot be overstated. Cultural consultants offer insights into negotiation styles, conflict resolution approaches, and the importance of relationship-building in different cultures. This knowledge is instrumental in fostering positive and productive collaborations, ensuring that businesses navigate the complexities of cross-cultural interactions with finesse.

The ever-evolving nature of global markets requires businesses to adapt their strategies continually. Cultural consultants contribute to this adaptive process by offering insights into market trends, consumer behaviors, and emerging cultural shifts. This foresight allows businesses to stay ahead of the curve, tailoring their products, services, and marketing strategies to align with evolving cultural landscapes.

Beyond avoiding cultural pitfalls, cultural consultation becomes a proactive tool for businesses aiming to thrive in diverse markets. It fosters cultural intelligence within the organization, empowering teams to anticipate and respond effectively to cultural nuances. This not only enhances the organization's external image but also contributes to creating an inclusive and culturally aware internal environment.

Cultural consultation is a linchpin for strategic adaptation in the global business arena. It empowers businesses to move beyond language barriers, tapping into the rich tapestry of cultural diversity. By leveraging the insights provided by cultural consultants, organizations can not only navigate the complexities of international markets but also foster meaningful connections with diverse audiences, laying the foundation for sustained global success.

How to Leverage Language Services Effectively

Here's how to leverage language services:

- **Assess Linguistic Needs: Begin** by conducting a comprehensive assessment of your linguistic needs. Identify target markets, languages spoken by your audience, and the types of content that require translation or adaptation.
- **Select Appropriate Services:** Choose the language services that align with your specific communication goals. Whether you need translation, interpretation, localization, or a combination of these services, tailor your approach to meet the demands of your target audience and the nature of your content.
- **Work with Professional Providers:** Collaborate with reputable language service providers with expertise in your industry and target markets. Professional linguists and cultural experts ensure high-quality and culturally sensitive communication.
- **Integrate Technology Wisely:** Embrace technological advancements, such as machine translation tools, to enhance efficiency. However, balance technological solutions with the expertise of human translators, especially in content that requires cultural nuance and creativity.
- **Cultural Intelligence Training:** Provide cultural intelligence training for your team members who engage in international communication. Understanding cultural nuances is essential for effective communication, and training can enhance cultural sensitivity.
- **Regularly Review and Update:** Continuously review and update your language services strategy. Regular assessments, feedback loops, and staying informed about linguistic and cultural trends contribute to the ongoing effectiveness of your global communication initiatives.

Leveraging language services strategically empowers businesses to break down language barriers, build meaningful connections with diverse audiences, and drive successful global communication strategies. Whether expanding into new markets, engaging with international stakeholders, or fostering global collaboration, effective language services play a pivotal role in facilitating clear and culturally resonant communication.

Integrating Language Technologies

In our interconnected world, where businesses transcend geographical boundaries, effective communication across languages is a prerequisite for success. Integrating language technologies emerges as a transformative strategy, breaking down linguistic barriers and facilitating seamless interactions on a global scale. This process involves the strategic implementation of various tools and technologies designed to enhance language-related aspects within the operational framework of an organization.

Automated Translation Systems: A Cornerstone of Integration

Automated translation systems form a cornerstone of language technology integration. These systems leverage artificial intelligence and machine learning algorithms to translate content from one language to another. By incorporating automated translation tools into daily operations, businesses can facilitate rapid and accurate communication across linguistic divides. These tools are particularly valuable for tasks such as translating documents, emails, or website content, enabling organizations to disseminate information effectively to diverse audiences.

Speech Recognition and Transcription Services

Integrating speech recognition and transcription services further enhances communication channels. These technologies convert spoken language into text, aiding in real-time communication and documentation. For global teams engaged in remote collaboration, speech-to-text capabilities streamline discussions, making it easier to capture, share, and reference information. This ensures that language differences do not impede the flow of ideas and information within a diverse team.

Multilingual Chatbots for Customer Engagement

Customer engagement is a critical aspect of business success, and language technologies play a pivotal role in this domain. Multilingual chatbots equipped with natural language processing capabilities can interact with customers in their preferred language. These intelligent systems provide immediate responses, address inquiries, and offer support, creating a personalized and efficient customer experience. Integrating multilingual chatbots is a proactive step toward enhancing global customer engagement and satisfaction.

Collaborative Translation Platforms for Teamwork

In environments where collaboration is paramount, collaborative translation platforms foster teamwork across language barriers. These platforms enable multiple users to contribute to the translation process collaboratively. Team members can edit, review, and suggest changes, ensuring a collective and accurate translation outcome. Such platforms promote synergy within international teams, allowing individuals to work together seamlessly on multilingual projects.

Localization Management Systems

For businesses with a global footprint, localization management systems are instrumental in tailoring content to specific cultural and linguistic contexts. These systems streamline the localization process by managing translation workflows, maintaining version control, and ensuring consistency across diverse content types. Integrating localization management systems allows organizations to adapt their products, services, and marketing materials effectively to resonate with local audiences.

Implementing Language Technologies: A Strategic Approach

Needs Assessment: Identify Linguistic Requirements

Begin the integration process by conducting a thorough needs assessment. Identify the languages relevant to your business operations, target audience, and internal communication. This assessment forms the foundation for selecting the most appropriate language technologies to meet specific linguistic requirements.

Selecting Appropriate Technologies

Choose language technologies based on the identified needs. Consider factors such as the diversity of languages, the nature of communication (written or spoken), and the context in which these technologies will be applied. Tailor your selection to align with the unique linguistic landscape of your organization.

Integration with Existing Systems

Ensure seamless integration with existing communication and workflow systems. Language technologies should complement rather than disrupt daily operations. Integrate these tools into platforms commonly used by your teams, fostering a user-friendly environment and encouraging widespread adoption.

User Training and Familiarization

Provide comprehensive training to users on the adopted language technologies. Familiarize teams with the functionalities, features, and best practices for effective utilization. User training enhances proficiency, reduces resistance to change, and maximizes the benefits of integrated language technologies.

Continuous Evaluation and Optimization

Implement a continuous evaluation process to assess the effectiveness of integrated language technologies. Gather feedback from users, monitor performance metrics, and identify areas for improvement. Optimize the integration based on evolving linguistic needs, technological advancements, and user experiences.

Benefits of Language Technology Integration

The strategic integration of language technologies yields a spectrum of benefits for organizations operating in diverse linguistic environments:

- **Enhanced Communication Efficiency:** Language technologies streamline communication processes, reducing barriers and enhancing efficiency in global collaboration.
- **Improved Customer Engagement:** Multilingual chatbots and automated translation systems contribute to personalized and responsive customer interactions, fostering enhanced customer engagement.
- **Global Team Collaboration:** Collaborative translation platforms and speech-to-text services empower global teams to collaborate seamlessly, irrespective of linguistic differences.
- **Cultural Sensitivity:** Localization management systems contribute to cultural sensitivity by adapting content to align with local norms, preferences, and nuances.

Integrating language technologies is not merely a functional necessity but a strategic imperative for businesses aiming to thrive in a multilingual world. By embracing these tools thoughtfully and strategically, organizations can unlock new dimensions of global communication, collaboration, and success.

Chapter **12**

Logistics and Supply Chain Management

Logistics and Supply Chain Management (SCM) constitute the lifeblood of global business operations, orchestrating the intricate dance of goods and services across international landscapes. At its core, Logistics and SCM involve the coordination and optimization of processes related to the procurement, production, storage, and transportation of goods.

In this chapter, we delve into the pivotal role of Logistics and SCM in international business, exploring how these strategic disciplines contribute to the seamless flow of products, enhanced efficiency, and ultimately, the success of global enterprises.

Benefits of Logistics and Supply Chain Management:

- **Enhanced Efficiency:** Logistics and SCM streamline processes, minimizing delays and bottlenecks. Efficient supply chain management ensures that goods move swiftly from production to distribution points, reducing lead times and enhancing overall operational efficiency.

- **Cost Optimization:** Effective logistics strategies contribute to cost optimization by minimizing transportation expenses, reducing inventory carrying costs, and optimizing storage and distribution processes. Through strategic planning, businesses can achieve a delicate balance between cost and service levels.

- **Global Market Reach:** Logistics and SCM play a pivotal role in extending a company's market reach. A well-managed supply chain enables businesses to distribute products to diverse geographical locations, reaching a global customer base and capitalizing on new market opportunities.

- **Customer Satisfaction:** Timely delivery, accurate order fulfillment, and responsive supply chain practices contribute to heightened customer satisfaction. Meeting customer expectations in terms of product availability and delivery timelines is a key driver of loyalty and positive brand perception.

- **Risk Mitigation:** Effective supply chain management incorporates risk mitigation strategies. By diversifying suppliers, optimizing inventory levels, and implementing robust contingency plans, businesses can navigate uncertainties such as disruptions in the supply chain or geopolitical challenges.

As we explore the intricacies of Logistics and SCM in the following sections, we will unravel the methodologies and best practices that underpin successful international shipping, distribution, and the overarching management of global supply chain networks.

From optimizing transportation routes to leveraging technology for real-time visibility, the chapters that follow provide a comprehensive guide to mastering the complexities of Logistics and Supply Chain Management in the global arena.

Streamlining international shipping and distribution

Efficient international shipping and distribution are critical components of a well-oiled supply chain, influencing the success and competitiveness of businesses operating on a global scale. The process involves a strategic orchestration of various elements to ensure that products move seamlessly from production facilities to end consumers across international borders.

Here, we delve into the key strategies and considerations for streamlining international shipping and distribution.

1. Strategic Route Planning

The art of strategic route planning is a critical element for businesses seeking to optimize and streamline their logistics operations. At its core, this process involves a meticulous examination and optimization of shipping routes, taking into account a multitude of factors ranging from geographical distances to available transportation modes and potential customs challenges.

Leveraging advanced logistics software and cutting-edge analytical tools, companies can make informed, data-driven decisions. These tools provide invaluable insights into the most efficient routes, ensuring a delicate balance between transit time and cost-effectiveness. For instance, an e-commerce giant with a global footprint can employ data analytics to scrutinize various shipping routes to diverse destinations. This analytical approach enables the identification of the fastest and most cost-effective routes, ensuring that products reach customers in a timely manner while maintaining operational cost efficiency.

However, strategic route planning goes beyond a simplistic quest for the shortest path. It involves a holistic understanding of the entire supply chain network. Companies need to consider variables such as customs requirements, potential delays, and the reliability of transportation modes. The goal is to construct a streamlined and resilient shipping network capable of adapting to the dynamic challenges inherent in global logistics.

Incorporating strategic route planning into logistics operations yields multifaceted advantages. By proactively addressing potential bottlenecks and optimizing routes, businesses enhance their operational agility and responsiveness to market demands. This, in turn, leads to not only timely deliveries but also cost-effectiveness, ultimately fortifying the competitiveness of companies participating in international trade.

For example, in the case of the e-commerce giant, the integration of technology and data analytics in route planning becomes a transformative factor. The company can unveil patterns and insights that might go unnoticed with traditional approaches. Discovering specific transportation modes or corridors that result in significant time and cost savings becomes instrumental in gaining a competitive edge. This level of granularity and precision in route planning is unattainable without the aid of advanced technologies.

Strategic route planning is a proactive strategy that anticipates and mitigates potential challenges in international shipping. By factoring in uncertainties like customs regulations and transportation risks, businesses can enhance the reliability of their shipping networks. The result is not just a cost-effective and efficient shipping process but also an adaptable and resilient supply chain that can navigate the complexities of global trade.

Strategic route planning is not a one-size-fits-all solution; rather, it is a dynamic and adaptive process that empowers businesses to navigate the complexities of international shipping with finesse. Through the integration of technology, data analytics, and a comprehensive understanding of the supply chain, companies can establish a competitive advantage, ensuring that their products reach global markets in a timely, efficient, and cost-effective manner.

2. Efficient Customs Clearance

Efficient customs clearance is great for streamlining the process of international shipping. The intricate web of regulations and procedures associated with customs clearance necessitates a meticulous approach, involving accurate documentation, strict compliance with customs regulations, and the strategic integration of technology to expedite clearance procedures.

In the realm of international trade, businesses encounter a myriad of regulations governing the import and export of goods. Navigating these complexities demands a deep understanding of local customs requirements, tariffs, and trade restrictions. To ensure a seamless customs clearance process, companies often enlist the expertise of customs brokers or leverage electronic customs clearance systems.

Collaborating with experienced customs brokers provides businesses with a strategic advantage. These professionals possess an in-depth knowledge of local customs regulations, documentation requirements, and procedural intricacies. For instance, an electronics manufacturer venturing into international markets may partner with seasoned customs brokers who specialize in managing the unique challenges associated with shipping electronic goods.

The role of technology in efficient customs clearance cannot be overstated. Electronic customs clearance systems, often integrated with advanced logistics platforms, enable businesses to submit accurate and complete documentation electronically. This not only reduces the likelihood of errors or discrepancies but also expedites the clearance process by eliminating manual paperwork and delays associated with traditional methods.

For example, an e-commerce company selling fashion apparel globally may utilize electronic customs clearance systems to submit product information, invoices, and shipping documents electronically. This digital approach not only enhances accuracy but also accelerates the customs clearance process, ensuring that shipments move swiftly through the regulatory checkpoints.

Efficient customs clearance is not merely about adhering to regulatory requirements; it is a strategic imperative for businesses engaged in international shipping. Delays in customs clearance can lead to significant disruptions in the supply chain, impacting delivery timelines and customer satisfaction. Therefore, businesses must adopt a proactive approach to customs compliance, whether through the expertise of customs brokers or the integration of sophisticated electronic systems.

The efficient clearance of goods through customs is a pivotal aspect of streamlined international shipping. By embracing meticulous documentation, compliance measures, and technology-driven solutions, businesses can navigate the intricate customs landscape with agility and precision. This proactive approach not only ensures regulatory compliance but also contributes to the overall efficiency, reliability, and competitiveness of the global supply chain.

3. Technology Integration

The integration of cutting-edge technologies has become a cornerstone in the modernization and efficiency of international shipping and distribution. Among these technologies, the Internet of Things (IoT), Radio-Frequency Identification (RFID) tracking, and real-time monitoring systems have emerged as transformative tools that provide unprecedented visibility and control over the entire supply chain.

Internet of Things (IoT)

The Internet of Things plays a pivotal role in international shipping by connecting physical objects to the internet, enabling them to collect and exchange data. In the context of logistics, IoT devices are embedded in shipments, containers, or even individual products. These devices transmit real-time data throughout the shipping process, offering insights into the location, condition, and status of goods.

Consider a scenario where a pharmaceutical company needs to ship temperature-sensitive vaccines globally. By employing IoT-enabled sensors, the company can continuously monitor the temperature of the vaccines in real-time. This technology ensures that the products remain within the required temperature range throughout the journey, safeguarding their efficacy and compliance with regulatory standards.

RFID Tracking

Radio-Frequency Identification (RFID) is another technology that contributes to the streamlining of international shipping and distribution. RFID tags, affixed to products or packaging, use radio waves to transmit information to RFID readers. This enables automated tracking and identification of goods as they move through the supply chain.

For instance, an apparel retailer managing a diverse range of products can utilize RFID tracking to enhance inventory management and reduce errors. As goods traverse the global supply chain, RFID technology enables real-time tracking, minimizing the risk of lost or misplaced items. The result is improved accuracy, efficiency, and responsiveness to customer demands.

Real-time Monitoring Systems

Real-time monitoring systems provide continuous oversight of shipments, allowing businesses to promptly detect and address any issues that may arise during transit. These systems encompass a variety of sensors and devices that capture data on environmental conditions, security, and handling.

In practice, a consumer electronics company shipping fragile and high-value products globally may deploy real-time monitoring systems. These systems can include impact sensors to detect mishandling, GPS tracking for location monitoring, and security features to prevent tampering. By having instantaneous insights into the status of shipments, businesses can take swift corrective actions, reducing the risk of damage and enhancing overall customer satisfaction.

The integration of technologies such as IoT, RFID tracking, and real-time monitoring systems brings a paradigm shift to international shipping and distribution. These advancements not only provide unprecedented visibility into the supply chain but also empower businesses to proactively manage and optimize their logistics operations. As global trade continues to evolve, leveraging technology becomes imperative for companies aiming to stay competitive, ensuring the seamless movement of goods across borders.

4. Collaborative Partnerships

Establishing alliances with logistics providers, carriers, and third-party logistics (3PL) companies opens avenues for leveraging expertise and infrastructure, ultimately leading to cost efficiencies, enhanced service levels, and expanded distribution networks.

The essence of collaborative partnerships lies in the synergies created through shared resources and capabilities. Businesses can tap into the specialized knowledge and established networks of their logistics partners, gaining a competitive advantage in navigating the complexities of international shipping. This collaborative approach is particularly advantageous for companies looking to expand their global footprint without the need to build and manage an extensive logistics infrastructure from scratch.

For instance, envision a scenario where a fashion retailer forms a collaborative partnership with a globally renowned logistics provider. In this collaboration, the fashion retailer gains access to the logistics provider's well-established network, comprising reliable transportation services, state-of-the-art warehousing solutions, and efficient distribution capabilities. This strategic alliance empowers the fashion retailer to navigate the intricate logistics of international shipping with confidence and efficiency.

Collaborative partnerships extend beyond the physical movement of goods; they encompass a holistic approach to logistics optimization. Logistics providers and 3PL companies often bring advanced technologies and innovative solutions to the table. These can include real-time tracking systems, inventory management tools, and predictive analytics that contribute to the overall efficiency and transparency of the supply chain.

Moreover, the collaborative model facilitates a more agile response to market demands. By outsourcing certain logistics functions to specialized partners, businesses can focus on their core competencies, fostering agility and responsiveness. This is particularly valuable in industries where rapid changes in consumer preferences and market dynamics necessitate swift adjustments in logistics strategies.

However, the success of collaborative partnerships hinges on effective communication, shared goals, and a robust understanding of each partner's role in the supply chain. Clear contractual agreements, defined responsibilities, and mutually beneficial terms are essential elements that contribute to the sustainability and success of such alliances.

Collaborative partnerships play a pivotal role in optimizing international shipping. Businesses that forge strategic alliances with logistics providers and 3PL companies position themselves to thrive in the dynamic and competitive landscape of global trade. By harnessing the collective expertise, infrastructure, and technology of their partners, companies can achieve greater efficiency, cost-effectiveness, and flexibility in their international logistics operations.

5. Inventory Optimization

Effective inventory management is a crucial element for businesses seeking streamlined operations. Striking the right balance between maintaining optimal inventory levels and avoiding excess stock is a delicate art that requires the implementation of advanced tools and strategic approaches.

At the heart of this process lies the utilization of demand forecasting and inventory optimization tools. These technological solutions empower businesses to anticipate market demands, aligning their inventory levels with the ever-changing dynamics of global markets. For example, consider an electronics company that utilizes sophisticated demand forecasting algorithms. By analyzing historical data, market trends, and external factors, these algorithms can predict product demand in different regions with a high degree of accuracy.

Maintaining optimal inventory levels is a strategic imperative. Insufficient stock can result in stockouts, missed sales opportunities, and customer dissatisfaction. On the other hand, excess inventory can lead to increased carrying costs, potential obsolescence, and a strain on financial resources. Therefore, businesses must leverage advanced inventory optimization tools that factor in variables such as lead times, order frequency, and market demand fluctuations.

Furthermore, the integration of technology facilitates real-time visibility into inventory levels across the entire supply chain. Cloud-based inventory management systems, coupled with Internet of Things (IoT) devices and sensors, enable businesses to monitor stock levels, track shipments, and respond swiftly to changes in demand. This level of transparency not only enhances operational efficiency but also mitigates the risks associated with stockouts or overstock situations.

Beyond the technological aspect, inventory optimization also necessitates a strategic mindset. Businesses should establish clear protocols for order fulfillment, warehouse management, and replenishment strategies. This includes identifying key performance indicators (KPIs) related to inventory turnover, carrying costs, and order accuracy.

Moreover, international shipping introduces an additional layer of complexity to inventory management. Businesses operating in multiple regions must consider the nuances of each market, such as varying lead times, customs processes, and transportation costs. This requires a sophisticated approach to inventory optimization that factors in the intricacies of the global supply chain.

Inventory optimization is a linchpin for businesses striving for streamlined international shipping and distribution. By embracing advanced technologies, implementing robust forecasting models, and adopting strategic inventory management practices, companies can navigate the complexities of global trade with agility and efficiency. In the ever-evolving landscape of international commerce, mastering the art of inventory optimization becomes a strategic imperative for sustained success.

6. Customer-Centric Strategies

In the dynamic landscape of e-commerce and heightened global customer expectations, adopting customer-centric shipping strategies has become imperative for businesses seeking to distinguish themselves in the market. A customer-centric approach revolves around placing the customer's needs and preferences at the core of shipping operations, aiming to enhance the overall customer experience from purchase to delivery.

Flexibility in Delivery Options

One pivotal element of a customer-centric shipping strategy involves providing flexible delivery options. Recognizing that customers have diverse schedules and preferences, businesses can offer choices such as standard shipping, express delivery, or even specific time slots for delivery. This flexibility empowers customers to tailor the shipping process according to their convenience, contributing to a positive and personalized experience.

Accurate Shipment Tracking

Accurate and real-time shipment tracking is another cornerstone of customer-centric shipping. In an era where consumers expect transparency and visibility into the status of their orders, businesses can leverage advanced tracking systems. These systems provide customers with real-time updates on the location and estimated delivery time of their shipments. This not only instills confidence but also enables customers to plan accordingly, reducing uncertainties and frustration.

Optimizing Last-Mile Delivery

The last mile of delivery, the final leg of the shipping journey from a distribution center to the customer's doorstep, is a critical focal point in customer-centric strategies. Optimizing last-mile delivery involves efficient route planning, utilizing local delivery partners, and employing innovative technologies. Businesses can explore options like drone deliveries, locker pickup points, or partnerships with local courier services to ensure swift and reliable last-mile delivery. This optimization contributes to timely deliveries, a key factor in customer satisfaction.

Example Illustration

Consider an online retailer implementing a customer portal as part of its customer-centric shipping strategy. Through this portal, customers gain access to a user-friendly interface allowing them to track their shipments in real-time. Additionally, the portal provides various delivery options, empowering customers to choose between standard, expedited, or even scheduled deliveries. Such transparency and flexibility not only meet customer expectations but also contribute to an enhanced shipping experience.

Moreover, the customer-centric approach in global shipping extends beyond the delivery process. It involves actively seeking customer feedback, understanding pain points, and continuously improving shipping processes based on customer insights. By engaging in a continuous feedback loop, businesses can refine their strategies to align with evolving customer expectations, fostering long-term customer loyalty.

Customer-centric shipping strategies are essential for businesses operating in a global and digitally driven marketplace. Offering flexible delivery options, providing accurate shipment tracking, and optimizing last-mile delivery are integral components of this approach. By prioritizing the customer experience throughout the shipping journey, businesses not only meet the demands of the modern consumer but also differentiate themselves in a competitive global landscape.

Streamlining international shipping and distribution requires a holistic approach that encompasses strategic planning, technology integration, collaboration, and customer-centricity. By embracing these principles, businesses can build agile and resilient supply chains that not only meet the challenges of global logistics but also position them for sustained success in the international marketplace.

Managing a global supply chain network

Effectively managing a global supply chain network is a complex undertaking that requires strategic planning, coordination, and adaptability. A global supply chain involves the interconnected flow of goods, information, and finances across international borders. Successful management ensures operational efficiency, risk mitigation, and responsiveness to dynamic market conditions.

Here are key strategies for managing a global supply chain network:

1. Network Visibility and Transparency

Network visibility and transparency are critical components of modern supply chain management, providing organizations with essential insights into the intricate processes of their global supply chains. These aspects play a pivotal role in enhancing operational efficiency, mitigating risks, and fostering agility.

Here's an in-depth exploration of network visibility and transparency in the context of supply chain management.

- **Understanding Network Visibility:** Network visibility refers to the ability of a business to gain real-time and comprehensive insights into various elements of its supply chain. This includes monitoring the flow of goods, information, and finances across the entire network. Achieving visibility involves employing advanced technologies and tools that facilitate the tracking and monitoring of every stage in the supply chain journey.
- **Leveraging Supply Chain Management Software:** Supply chain management software is a cornerstone in achieving network visibility. These sophisticated systems provide a centralized platform for monitoring and managing various supply chain activities. Features often include real-time tracking of inventory levels, order status, and production progress. By leveraging such software, organizations can access a unified view of their supply chain, enabling informed decision-making.
- **Utilizing Analytics Tools for In-Depth Insights:** In addition to management software, analytics tools play a crucial role in extracting valuable insights from the vast amounts of data generated within a supply chain. Predictive analytics, for instance, can forecast demand patterns, allowing organizations to proactively adjust their production schedules and inventory levels. This analytical approach enables businesses to anticipate challenges and opportunities, contributing to a more responsive supply chain.

The Role of Transparency

Transparency in the supply chain context involves openness and accessibility of information related to the movement and status of goods. It extends beyond the internal operations of a company to include the entire network of suppliers, manufacturers, distributors, and other stakeholders. Transparent supply chains foster trust among stakeholders and provide a clear understanding of processes.

Benefits of Network Visibility and Transparency

- **Better Decision-Making:** With real-time insights into inventory levels, production statuses, and shipment movements, organizations can make informed and timely decisions. This is particularly crucial in addressing unexpected disruptions and optimizing various aspects of the supply chain.
- **Identification of Bottlenecks:** Network visibility allows businesses to identify potential bottlenecks or inefficiencies in the supply chain. Whether it's delays in production, issues with suppliers, or challenges in transportation, visibility enables proactive problem-solving.
- **Enhanced Agility:** A transparent supply chain is inherently more agile. When organizations can quickly adapt to changes in demand, market conditions, or disruptions, they gain a competitive edge. This agility is vital in today's dynamic business environment.
- **Improved Collaboration:** Transparency fosters collaboration among different entities within the supply chain. Suppliers, manufacturers, and distributors can share information seamlessly, leading to better coordination and synchronization of activities.
- **Risk Mitigation:** By having visibility into the entire supply chain, organizations can better identify and mitigate risks. Whether it's geopolitical issues, natural disasters, or disruptions in the transportation network, transparency aids in developing effective risk management strategies.

Consider a global electronics manufacturer that utilizes advanced supply chain management software. The software provides real-time visibility into the status of components sourced from various suppliers, production progress at multiple manufacturing sites, and the shipping status of finished products. This visibility enables the company to make quick decisions, adjust production schedules based on demand fluctuations, and maintain optimal inventory levels.

Network visibility and transparency are integral for effective supply chain management in today's interconnected and dynamic business landscape. Leveraging advanced technologies, such as supply chain management software and analytics tools, organizations can achieve real-time insights and foster transparency across their entire supply chain network. This not only enhances operational efficiency but also equips businesses to navigate the complexities and uncertainties inherent in global supply chain operations.

2. Risk Management and Resilience

The complexity and interconnectedness of global supply chains expose businesses to a myriad of risks, ranging from geopolitical uncertainties to natural disasters. Effectively navigating these risks requires a robust risk management strategy and the cultivation of resilience within the supply chain.

Let's delve into the concept of risk management and resilience and explore strategies to achieve them in the context of global supply chains.

Understanding Risk Management

Risk management in the context of global supply chains involves identifying, assessing, and mitigating potential risks that could impact the smooth functioning of the supply chain. These risks can emanate from various sources, including geopolitical events, economic uncertainties, supplier vulnerabilities, and disruptions in transportation networks. The goal of risk management is to proactively address these challenges, ensuring that the supply chain can adapt and continue operations in the face of adversity.

Strategies for Effective Risk Management

- **Comprehensive Risk Identification:** Begin by conducting a comprehensive risk assessment that identifies potential threats to the supply chain. This involves evaluating each stage of the supply chain, from sourcing raw materials to the delivery of finished products. Risks may include geopolitical tensions affecting suppliers, natural disasters impacting manufacturing facilities, or disruptions in transportation routes.
- **Diversification of Suppliers:** Overreliance on a single supplier can intensify risks. Diversifying suppliers across different regions or countries helps spread risk and minimizes the impact of disruptions from a specific source. This approach enhances the supply chain's adaptability and reduces vulnerability to supplier-specific challenges.
- **Contingency Planning:** Develop robust contingency plans that outline specific actions to be taken in the event of identified risks. This may involve establishing alternative suppliers, creating backup inventory, or implementing alternative transportation routes. Contingency plans act as a playbook for responding swiftly and effectively when risks materialize.
- **Monitoring Geopolitical Events:** Geopolitical events, such as trade tensions or political instability, can significantly impact the global supply chain. Establish mechanisms for monitoring geopolitical developments and assessing their potential implications. This proactive approach allows businesses to adjust their strategies in response to evolving geopolitical landscapes.

Building Resilience in the Supply Chain

Resilience goes beyond risk management; it involves the capacity of the supply chain to absorb shocks, adapt to changing conditions, and recover quickly from disruptions. Here are key strategies to foster resilience:

- **Flexibility in Operations:** Design the supply chain with flexibility in mind. This includes the ability to quickly adjust production schedules, reroute shipments, or switch to alternative suppliers. A flexible supply chain is better equipped to respond to unexpected disruptions.

- **Investing in Technology:** Embrace technologies that enhance visibility and transparency across the supply chain. Advanced analytics, real-time tracking, and predictive modeling can provide valuable insights, enabling proactive decision-making and reducing the impact of disruptions.
- **Collaboration with Partners:** Build strong relationships with suppliers, logistics partners, and other stakeholders. Collaborative partnerships foster open communication and information sharing, creating a network that can collectively respond to challenges and disruptions.

Effective risk management and resilience are indispensable for the longevity and success of global supply chains. By identifying, assessing, and mitigating risks, businesses can fortify their supply chains against potential disruptions. Simultaneously, cultivating resilience through flexibility, technology adoption, and collaborative partnerships ensures that the supply chain can adapt and recover swiftly, maintaining continuity even in the face of unforeseen challenges.

3. Supplier Collaboration and Relationship Management

Supplier collaboration and relationship management are pivotal aspects of managing a global supply chain network effectively. In today's interconnected business landscape, forging strong collaborative ties with suppliers across the globe is essential for building a resilient and responsive supply chain. This involves open communication, strategic partnerships, and a shared commitment to mutual success.

Here's an in-depth exploration of the significance of supplier collaboration and relationship management in the context of global supply chains.

- **Open Communication Channels:** Establishing open communication channels with suppliers is the foundation of effective collaboration. Transparent and frequent communication helps in conveying expectations, sharing information, and addressing any challenges promptly. This ensures that both parties are aligned on goals, timelines, and quality standards.
- **Regular Collaboration for Agility:** Regular collaboration goes beyond mere communication; it involves actively working together on various aspects of the supply chain. This could include joint forecasting, demand planning, and even collaborative product development. By engaging in ongoing collaboration, businesses and suppliers can respond swiftly to changes in market demand, supply chain disruptions, and other unforeseen challenges.
- **Developing Strategic Partnerships:** Supplier collaboration evolves into strategic partnerships when there is a shared vision and a commitment to long-term success. Developing these partnerships involves aligning business objectives, fostering mutual understanding, and building trust. A strategic partnership goes beyond transactional relationships, creating a framework for joint decision-making and problem-solving.
- **Mutual Understanding and Trust:** Building a global supply chain network requires a deep level of mutual understanding and trust between businesses and suppliers. This involves understanding each other's capabilities, limitations, and strategic priorities. Trust is especially crucial when navigating uncertainties or disruptions, as there is a foundation of confidence that both parties are committed to finding collaborative solutions.
- **Shared Goals for Resilience:** In times of unforeseen challenges, a well-established relationship with suppliers becomes a strategic asset. Shared goals and a collaborative mindset enable businesses and suppliers to tackle disruptions more effectively. Whether it's adapting to changes in demand, addressing supply chain interruptions, or jointly innovating to overcome obstacles, a collaborative approach enhances the resilience of the entire supply chain network.

Consider a global automotive manufacturer that relies on suppliers from various regions for critical components. Through regular communication and collaboration, the manufacturer and its suppliers jointly monitor market trends and demand forecasts. In a rapidly changing automotive landscape, this collaborative approach allows both parties to adapt quickly to shifts in consumer preferences and emerging technologies.

Supplier collaboration and relationship management are indispensable for the success of global supply chain networks. Open communication channels, regular collaboration, strategic partnerships, and mutual understanding contribute to a more agile, responsive, and resilient supply chain. These elements not only enhance day-to-day operations but also position businesses to navigate the complexities of the global business environment successfully.

4. Demand Planning and Forecasting

In the realm of global supply chain management, demand planning and forecasting emerge as integral components for achieving operational efficiency and maintaining a well-balanced inventory. Accurately predicting demand lays the groundwork for optimizing production, managing inventory levels, and ensuring a streamlined supply chain. Here's a detailed exploration of the significance of demand planning and forecasting in the context of global supply chain networks.

Accurate Demand Planning

Demand planning involves anticipating future market requirements and aligning business operations accordingly. In the context of a global supply chain, where diverse market dynamics come into play, accurate demand planning becomes even more crucial. Businesses need to evaluate various factors, including regional preferences, seasonal fluctuations, and emerging trends, to create a comprehensive demand forecast.

Utilizing Data Analytics and Historical Trends

Harnessing the power of data analytics and analyzing historical trends are essential tools for accurate demand forecasting. Businesses can leverage advanced analytics tools to process large datasets and extract meaningful insights. By examining past sales patterns, market behavior, and other relevant historical data, companies can make informed predictions about future demand, allowing for more proactive and data-driven decision-making.

Collaboration Across Stakeholders

Demand planning is not an isolated activity but a collaborative process that involves input from various stakeholders. Collaborating with sales teams, distributors, and other key partners provides a holistic view of market dynamics. Insights from these collaborations contribute to a more accurate demand forecast, considering factors such as regional variations in consumer behavior and the impact of local events or regulations.

Aligning Production and Inventory Levels

Once the demand forecast is established, the next critical step is aligning production schedules and inventory levels with anticipated demand. Overstocking or shortages can lead to significant challenges in a global supply chain. Striking the right balance ensures that businesses can meet market demand without incurring unnecessary holding costs or facing disruptions due to stockouts.

Preventing Overstocking and Shortages

One of the primary goals of demand planning and forecasting is to prevent both overstocking and shortages. Overstocking ties up valuable resources, increases carrying costs, and may lead to obsolescence. On the other hand, shortages can result in lost sales, customer dissatisfaction, and potential damage to the brand reputation. A well-executed demand planning strategy minimizes these risks and optimizes the utilization of resources.

Example Illustration

Consider a multinational electronics company that operates in diverse markets worldwide. By employing sophisticated data analytics tools, this company analyzes historical sales data, market trends, and regional preferences. Through collaborative efforts with local distributors and sales teams, they gather insights into specific market nuances. This collaborative approach allows the company to align production schedules and inventory levels with anticipated demand, ensuring a responsive and efficient global supply chain.

Demand planning and forecasting are critical elements in the effective management of a global supply chain network. Accurate predictions, facilitated by data analytics and collaboration, enable businesses to optimize production, maintain optimal inventory levels, and respond proactively to market dynamics. This strategic approach not only enhances operational efficiency but also positions businesses to navigate the complexities of the global business landscape successfully.

5. Compliance and Regulatory Adherence

Compliance and regulatory adherence play a pivotal role in ensuring seamless operations and mitigating risks associated with diverse international regulations. Successfully navigating through a myriad of regulations demands continuous vigilance, adaptability, and a comprehensive understanding of the legal frameworks governing the movement of goods across borders.

Navigating Diverse International Regulations

Managing a global supply chain involves dealing with a multitude of regulations that vary across countries and regions. These regulations encompass a spectrum of aspects, including customs procedures, import/export restrictions, and specific industry-related standards. Businesses must stay abreast of these diverse international regulations to facilitate the smooth movement of goods and prevent disruptions in the supply chain.

Staying Informed about Local and International Regulations

Staying informed about local and international regulations is a fundamental step in ensuring compliance. This involves comprehensive research and ongoing monitoring to keep abreast of any changes or updates to existing regulations. Understanding the nuances of each market's regulatory environment enables businesses to proactively address compliance requirements and avoid potential penalties or delays.

Compliance Across All Supply Chain Aspects

Compliance in the global supply chain extends beyond the movement of goods. It encompasses various aspects, including labeling, documentation, and product specifications. Businesses must ensure that every element of the supply chain adheres to relevant regulations specific to each market. This comprehensive approach reduces the risk of non-compliance and enhances the overall reliability of the supply chain.

Regularly Updating Processes

Regulatory landscapes are dynamic, subject to changes influenced by factors such as geopolitical events, economic shifts, or industry developments. To maintain compliance, businesses need to establish a robust system for regularly updating processes. This involves periodic reviews of regulatory requirements and adjusting internal procedures accordingly. Adapting swiftly to changes ensures that the supply chain remains in alignment with the latest regulatory standards.

Example Illustration

Consider a global pharmaceutical company with operations spanning multiple continents. To adhere to diverse regulatory frameworks, the company implements a rigorous compliance strategy. The logistics and transportation teams regularly engage with legal experts to stay informed about changes in international regulations related to pharmaceutical products. This proactive approach ensures that the company's supply chain processes, from labeling medications to documentation for cross-border shipments, align with the regulatory requirements of each market.

Compliance and regulatory adherence form the backbone of a resilient and efficient global supply chain. Businesses that prioritize staying informed, maintain comprehensive compliance across all supply chain aspects, and regularly update their processes are better positioned to navigate the complexities of international regulations successfully. This strategic commitment not only fosters regulatory compliance but also enhances the overall reliability and sustainability of the global supply chain.

6. Technological Integration

Technological integration stands out as a pivotal strategy for optimizing operations and ensuring the seamless flow of information across diverse elements of the supply chain. Leveraging advanced technologies such as Enterprise Resource Planning (ERP) systems, Internet of Things (IoT) devices, and blockchain solutions holds the key to enhancing visibility, traceability, and overall efficiency within the supply chain network.

Enterprise Resource Planning (ERP) Systems

Integrating ERP systems into the supply chain infrastructure enables businesses to consolidate and streamline various functions, from inventory management and order processing to finance and human resources. These systems provide a centralized platform for real-time data access and decision-making, fostering greater coordination and coherence across different operational facets.

Internet of Things (IoT) Devices

The integration of IoT devices offers a transformative impact on supply chain management by enabling the collection and exchange of real-time data from physical objects and devices. Sensors and smart devices embedded in transportation vehicles, warehouses, and even individual products facilitate continuous monitoring. This real-time data exchange enhances visibility into the entire supply chain, allowing businesses to proactively address issues and optimize processes.

Blockchain Technology

Blockchain technology has gained prominence for its ability to provide an immutable and transparent ledger for recording transactions across the supply chain. By implementing blockchain, businesses can achieve enhanced traceability and accountability. Each transaction or movement within the supply chain is securely recorded, creating an unalterable digital trail. This not only reduces the risk of errors but also ensures a higher level of trust among stakeholders.

Enhanced Visibility and Traceability

Technological integration significantly improves visibility and traceability throughout the supply chain. Businesses can track the movement of goods, monitor inventory levels, and access real-time insights into various operational metrics. This enhanced visibility allows for better decision-making, as stakeholders have a comprehensive understanding of the supply chain's current status.

Reduced Manual Errors

Automation and technological integration play a pivotal role in reducing manual errors within the supply chain. By minimizing manual data entry and automating routine tasks, businesses can mitigate the risk of human errors that may lead to inaccuracies in inventory records, order fulfillment, or other critical processes. This, in turn, contributes to operational accuracy and efficiency.

Streamlining Processes

The seamless exchange of real-time data facilitated by technological integration contributes to the overall streamlining of supply chain processes. Timely and accurate information empowers businesses to make informed decisions promptly, respond swiftly to changes in demand or disruptions, and optimize various aspects of the supply chain, from procurement to distribution.

The integration of technology into the global supply chain landscape is not merely a modernization effort but a strategic imperative for businesses aiming to stay competitive and resilient. By adopting ERP systems, IoT devices, blockchain technology, and other advanced solutions, organizations can achieve enhanced visibility, traceability, and efficiency within their supply chain networks. This technological evolution is a cornerstone in navigating the complexities of the global business environment and ensuring a responsive and agile supply chain.

7. Continuous Performance Measurement and Improvement

Continuous performance measurement and improvement play a pivotal role in the ongoing success of a global supply chain network. By establishing Key Performance Indicators (KPIs), businesses can systematically evaluate various aspects of their supply chain performance. Metrics such as order fulfillment time, lead time, and inventory turnover serve as benchmarks for efficiency and effectiveness.

Key Performance Indicators (KPIs)

Setting up KPIs is the foundational step in the continuous performance measurement process. These indicators should align with the strategic goals of the organization and provide meaningful insights into the performance of the global supply chain. For instance, KPIs may include order fulfillment time, indicating how quickly customer orders are processed, or lead time, representing the time taken from order placement to delivery.

Regular Assessment of Performance

Once KPIs are in place, it's crucial to regularly assess the performance of the global supply chain network against these metrics. Regular evaluations help identify patterns, trends, and potential areas for improvement. Businesses can analyze the data to understand where the supply chain is excelling and where there might be challenges or inefficiencies.

Identification of Areas for Improvement

Continuous performance measurement inherently involves identifying areas for improvement. By closely scrutinizing KPIs, businesses can pinpoint specific aspects of the supply chain that may require attention. This could include streamlining certain processes, optimizing inventory management, or addressing bottlenecks in the distribution network.

Implementation of Continuous Improvement Initiatives

Armed with insights from performance assessments, organizations can then implement targeted continuous improvement initiatives. These initiatives are designed to enhance efficiency, reduce costs, and address emerging challenges in the global supply chain. Whether through process optimization, technological enhancements, or strategic realignments, continuous improvement initiatives contribute to the agility and resilience of the supply chain.

Example Illustration

Consider a multinational retail corporation with an extensive global supply chain network. The company establishes KPIs focused on order fulfillment time and inventory turnover. Through regular assessments, they observe that certain regions experience longer lead times, affecting overall customer satisfaction. Recognizing this as an area for improvement, the company implements initiatives such as regional distribution center optimizations and enhanced transportation strategies. These continuous improvement efforts lead to reduced lead times, improved customer satisfaction, and increased overall efficiency in the global supply chain.

Continuous performance measurement and improvement are integral components of effective global supply chain management. Through the establishment of KPIs, regular assessments, identification of improvement areas, and targeted initiatives, businesses can ensure that their supply chain remains adaptive, efficient, and aligned with organizational objectives. This ongoing process not only enhances current performance but also positions the global supply chain for future challenges and opportunities.

Effective management of a global supply chain network requires a holistic and adaptive approach. Visibility, risk management, supplier collaboration, demand planning, compliance adherence, technological integration, and continuous improvement are integral components of successful global supply chain management. By implementing these strategies, businesses can build resilient and efficient supply chains capable of navigating the complexities of the global marketplace.

Chapter **13**

Entering the Market

Entering a new market is a strategic and crucial decision for businesses looking to expand their global footprint. Whether through exporting goods or opting for foreign direct investment, this chapter explores the nuances involved in making this pivotal choice. It delves into the comparative analysis of exporting versus foreign direct investment, emphasizing the strategic decision-making process that underpins successful market entry.

By weighing the pros and cons of each approach, businesses can navigate the complexities of international expansion and make informed decisions aligned with their objectives.

Exporting vs. Foreign Direct Investment

Exporting and Foreign Direct Investment (FDI) represent two distinct approaches to entering foreign markets, each with its own set of advantages and considerations.

Exporting

Exporting is a fundamental international business strategy, allowing companies to expand their reach by selling goods or services produced in one country to customers in another. This versatile approach can be executed through various methods, each offering unique advantages based on business goals and available resources.

One approach to exporting is through direct sales, where companies sell their products or services directly to customers in the target foreign market. This method provides a high degree of control over the sales process, pricing, and branding. For example, a technology company based in the United States might directly sell its software to customers in European countries, leveraging online platforms or establishing a local sales team.

Another common method involves using intermediaries and distributors. In this scenario, a company engages a third party to handle the distribution and sale of its products in the foreign market. This can be advantageous when dealing with complex distribution networks or when a deep understanding of local market dynamics is required. For instance, a Japanese fashion brand might collaborate with local distributors in the United States to ensure effective marketing and distribution.

Partnerships with local businesses represent a collaborative exporting strategy. This could involve forming joint ventures or alliances with companies already established in the foreign market. For instance, an Australian agricultural equipment manufacturer might partner with a local distributor in South America, leveraging their partner's knowledge of the regional market and distribution channels.

The rise of e-commerce has introduced a new avenue for exporting. Many businesses opt to export their products through online platforms, reaching a global audience without extensive physical infrastructure in the target market. An example is a small Italian artisanal food producer selling its products directly to consumers worldwide through an e-commerce website, reaching customers in Asia, North America, and beyond.

Additionally, businesses may engage Export Management Companies (EMCs), which serve as intermediaries specializing in facilitating exports. They handle various roles, including marketing, logistics, and regulatory compliance. An American electronics manufacturer might engage an EMC to navigate the complexities of exporting its products to markets in the Middle East, benefiting from the EMC's expertise in international trade.

Exporting is a dynamic and adaptable strategy that opens avenues for businesses to extend their market presence globally. Whether through direct sales, intermediary partnerships, or digital platforms, exporting allows companies to capitalize on opportunities in diverse international markets, fostering growth and diversification.

Advantages

1. Low Initial Investment

One of the primary advantages of exporting is the relatively low initial investment required compared to other modes of international expansion, such as establishing physical operations in a foreign market. Businesses can leverage existing production capabilities and distribution networks to reach international customers without significant upfront costs. This financial efficiency is particularly beneficial for small and medium-sized enterprises (SMEs) with limited resources.

2. Quick Market Entry

Exporting provides a faster route to entering foreign markets compared to more complex strategies like setting up subsidiaries or joint ventures. Companies can promptly introduce their products or services to a global audience without the lengthy processes associated with establishing a physical presence. This agility is crucial in industries with rapidly changing dynamics or where being an early entrant holds a competitive advantage.

3. Reduced Risk

Exporting allows businesses to test the waters in a new market with a lower level of risk. By avoiding substantial upfront investments, companies can assess market response, consumer preferences, and the competitive landscape before making more significant commitments. This risk mitigation strategy is particularly valuable when entering unfamiliar territories where uncertainties may exist.

4. Diversification of Revenue Streams

Expanding into international markets through exporting enables businesses to diversify their revenue streams. Relying solely on domestic markets can expose companies to economic downturns or fluctuations in local demand. By tapping into global markets, businesses can spread their revenue sources, reducing vulnerability to regional economic challenges.

5. Access to Global Market Trends

Exporting facilitates exposure to global market trends and emerging opportunities. Engaging with diverse markets allows businesses to stay attuned to evolving consumer preferences, technological advancements, and industry trends. This exposure can inspire innovation and strategic adjustments to products or services, keeping the business competitive on a global scale.

6. Economies of Scale

International expansion through exporting provides the potential for economies of scale. Increased production volumes, driven by global demand, can lead to cost efficiencies in manufacturing and distribution. This scalability enhances a company's competitiveness by optimizing operational processes and potentially reducing per-unit production costs.

7. Utilization of Excess Capacity

Exporting allows businesses to utilize excess production capacity. If a company's domestic demand is met with spare production capabilities, exporting becomes an avenue to utilize that surplus capacity. This optimizes production efficiency and enhances overall operational performance.

8. Brand Recognition and Prestige

Global exporting contributes to brand recognition and prestige. A presence in diverse international markets can elevate a company's brand image, signaling to consumers and stakeholders that the business operates on a global scale. This enhanced reputation can positively impact consumer trust and attract potential business partners or investors.

9. Access to Specialized Markets

Certain markets may have specific demands or preferences that align well with a company's products or services. Exporting enables businesses to access these specialized markets where their offerings may be uniquely positioned. For example, a company producing organic skincare products might find niche markets in regions with a strong emphasis on sustainability and natural beauty.

In summary, exporting offers a range of advantages, making it an attractive entry strategy for businesses seeking global expansion. From cost-effectiveness and quick market entry to risk reduction and access to diverse opportunities, exporting provides a versatile pathway for companies to navigate the complexities of international markets.

Considerations

While exporting offers numerous advantages, businesses must carefully navigate certain considerations to ensure a successful and sustainable international expansion. Understanding and addressing these challenges are crucial for companies adopting an exporting strategy.

1. Limited Control

One notable consideration in exporting is the potential limitation of control over distribution and marketing strategies in the foreign market. When relying on local distributors or partners, businesses may face challenges in maintaining consistent branding, messaging, and customer experience. The nuances of cultural differences and market dynamics may impact how products or services are presented and promoted. Companies must strike a balance between granting autonomy to local partners and ensuring that the core brand values are preserved.

Example: A technology company exporting its products to multiple countries might face challenges in controlling the marketing strategies employed by local distributors. Each market may have different promotional approaches, potentially diluting the uniform brand image the company aims to maintain globally.

2. Dependency on Intermediaries

Exporting often involves reliance on intermediaries, such as distributors, agents, or trading companies. While these intermediaries can facilitate market entry, they introduce complexities in managing relationships and ensuring brand consistency. Businesses need to carefully select and manage their intermediaries, ensuring alignment with the company's values, standards, and customer-centric approach. Clear communication, robust contractual agreements, and periodic performance evaluations are essential to maintain a collaborative and effective partnership.

Example: An apparel manufacturer exporting its products may collaborate with local distributors in different countries. The challenge arises in ensuring that these distributors uphold the brand's quality standards, adhere to ethical practices, and align with the company's values.

3. Market Adaptation Challenges

Adapting products or services to local preferences can be challenging when operating primarily through exporting. Without a physical presence in the market, understanding nuanced consumer behaviors, preferences, and cultural influences becomes more complex. Tailoring offerings to resonate with diverse markets requires in-depth market research, strong consumer insights, and strategic partnerships.

Example: A food and beverage company exporting its products might find it challenging to adapt to varied taste preferences without a local presence. Understanding regional culinary traditions and preferences may be more challenging, impacting the company's ability to tailor its offerings effectively.

4. Regulatory Compliance

Navigating diverse international regulations and compliance requirements is a critical consideration in exporting. Different countries have varying standards, certifications, and import/export regulations. Ensuring that products meet the regulatory requirements of each target market is essential to avoid legal complications, delays, or entry barriers.

Example: A pharmaceutical company exporting medications must adhere to stringent regulatory standards in each country. Failure to comply with these standards can lead to regulatory hurdles, fines, or even product recalls.

5. Currency Fluctuations and Payment Risks

Exporting exposes businesses to currency fluctuations, which can impact pricing, profit margins, and overall financial stability. Additionally, dealing with international transactions introduces payment risks, including delayed payments, currency exchange rate fluctuations, and potential non-payment issues. Implementing risk mitigation strategies, such as using forward contracts or collaborating with financial institutions, becomes crucial to manage these financial challenges.

Example: A manufacturing company exporting machinery may face risks related to currency fluctuations, affecting the competitiveness of its pricing. Establishing clear payment terms and utilizing financial instruments can help mitigate these risks.

6. Transportation and Logistics Challenges

The logistics of exporting involve complex transportation, customs procedures, and supply chain coordination. Challenges may arise in terms of shipping costs, delivery times, and potential disruptions in the supply chain. Effective logistics management, including strategic route planning and collaboration with reliable shipping partners, is essential to address these challenges.

Example: An e-commerce company exporting consumer electronics may encounter logistics challenges related to the timely delivery of products. Delays in customs clearance, transportation disruptions, or unforeseen logistical issues can impact customer satisfaction.

7. Intellectual Property Protection

Protecting intellectual property (IP) becomes a significant consideration in exporting, especially in markets with varying levels of IP enforcement. Companies must implement robust strategies to safeguard their trademarks, patents, copyrights, and trade secrets. Understanding the IP landscape in each target market and pursuing legal avenues for protection is essential to prevent infringement and unauthorized use.

Example: A technology company exporting software solutions may need to navigate different IP protection frameworks in various countries. Ensuring proper documentation, patent filings, and legal safeguards are crucial to protecting their intellectual property.

While exporting presents a pathway to global markets, businesses must carefully evaluate and address these considerations to navigate the complexities of international trade successfully. Proactive planning, strategic partnerships, and continuous adaptation are key to overcoming challenges and maximizing the benefits of exporting. By fostering resilience, flexibility, and a deep understanding of global market dynamics, businesses can position themselves for sustained success in their international endeavors.

Foreign Direct Investment (FDI)

Foreign Direct Investment (FDI) represents a more robust and enduring approach to international market entry, requiring businesses to establish a physical presence in a foreign market. Unlike exporting, which involves selling goods or services across borders without a local physical presence, FDI involves significant investments in infrastructure, operations, and local partnerships. This approach comes in various forms, including wholly-owned subsidiaries, joint ventures, or the acquisition of existing businesses.

One common form of FDI is the establishment of wholly-owned subsidiaries. In this scenario, a company sets up a separate entity in a foreign country, fully owned and controlled by the parent company. Wholly-owned subsidiaries provide the parent company with a high degree of control over operations, branding, and strategic decisions. This approach is particularly suitable when the business aims for a comprehensive and independent presence in the foreign market. For example, an automobile manufacturer establishing a wholly-owned subsidiary in a new country would have direct control over manufacturing facilities, distribution networks, and marketing strategies, allowing for a tailored approach to the local market.

Another FDI strategy involves forming joint ventures with local partners. Joint ventures entail collaboration between a foreign business and a local entity, sharing ownership, responsibilities, and risks. This approach allows for leveraging local expertise, navigating cultural nuances, and sharing the financial burdens of market entry. Joint ventures are often chosen when entering markets with complex regulatory landscapes or when local partnerships are essential for success. For instance, a pharmaceutical company entering a market with stringent regulatory requirements might form a joint venture with a local pharmaceutical company, benefiting from their understanding of local regulations and market dynamics.

FDI can also manifest through acquisitions, where a business purchases an existing company in a foreign market. Acquisitions provide a shortcut to establishing a presence, as they involve taking over an established business with its existing customer base, infrastructure, and market share. This approach is strategic when rapid market entry and access to an established customer base are critical. As an example, a technology company looking to expand its global footprint might acquire a local startup with innovative technologies, securing a quick entry into the market and gaining access to local talent.

Advantages

- **Complete Control:** One of the prominent advantages of FDI is the significant level of control it offers to businesses over their operations. Unlike exporting, where products or services are distributed across borders without a local physical presence, FDI allows companies to establish entities that they fully own and control. Whether through wholly-owned subsidiaries, joint ventures, or acquisitions, businesses can shape and implement strategies that align with their global objectives. This complete control extends to decisions related to branding, product positioning, marketing campaigns, and operational processes.

Example: A technology company setting up a wholly-owned subsidiary in a foreign market gains the authority to make decisions on product customization, pricing strategies, and marketing campaigns without being reliant on local partners.

- **Better Understanding of Local Market:** FDI facilitates a deeper understanding of the local market dynamics, customer behavior, and cultural nuances. Having a physical presence allows businesses to engage directly with customers, competitors, and other stakeholders in the local environment. This direct interaction provides valuable insights that may be challenging to obtain solely through exporting. Understanding local preferences, consumer expectations, and market trends becomes more accessible, enabling businesses to tailor their products, services, and marketing strategies to meet specific local needs.

Example: An international food and beverage company establishing a local subsidiary can actively engage with local distributors, retailers, and consumers to understand regional tastes, dietary preferences, and cultural influences that impact purchasing decisions.

- Long-Term Strategic Positioning: FDI is often viewed as a long-term strategic investment that contributes to sustained growth and market presence. By establishing a physical presence in a foreign market, businesses signal a commitment to the region and its customers. This long-term positioning allows companies to build strong relationships with local stakeholders, including customers, suppliers, and regulatory authorities. It also provides stability and consistency, which can be particularly crucial in industries where customer trust and brand reputation play pivotal roles.

Example: An automotive manufacturer investing in a joint venture with a local partner in a growing market signals its commitment to the region. This commitment can enhance brand perception and create a foundation for long-term success.

- Adaptability to Local Conditions: FDI enables businesses to adapt more effectively to local conditions. Whether it's changes in consumer preferences, shifts in market trends, or unexpected challenges, having a physical presence allows companies to respond swiftly and make real-time adjustments. This adaptability is a strategic advantage, especially in dynamic markets where the ability to navigate and capitalize on emerging opportunities is crucial for success.

Example: A multinational fashion retailer, through FDI, can promptly respond to local fashion trends, seasonal preferences, and cultural events, ensuring that its product offerings remain relevant and appealing.

- Technology Transfer and Innovation: FDI often involves the transfer of technology and innovation from the parent company to the foreign subsidiary or partner. This technology transfer can contribute to the advancement of local industries, enhance production processes, and elevate overall industry standards. It creates a mutually beneficial scenario where the foreign market gains access to advanced technologies, and the parent company can leverage local insights and innovations.

Example: A pharmaceutical company establishing a joint venture in a developing market can bring advanced research and development capabilities, contributing to the local healthcare sector's technological advancement.

The advantages of Foreign Direct Investment extend beyond immediate market access. They encompass strategic control, cultural understanding, long-term positioning, adaptability, and the potential for technology transfer. While FDI involves significant commitments and challenges, the enduring benefits in terms of market influence, sustained growth, and innovation make it a compelling choice for businesses with a global outlook.

Considerations

1. **Higher Initial Investment**

Perhaps one of the most notable considerations in opting for Foreign Direct Investment (FDI) is the higher initial investment required. Unlike exporting, where businesses can enter a market with relatively lower upfront costs, FDI involves significant financial commitments. These expenditures encompass setting up facilities, acquiring or leasing real estate, establishing a local workforce, and addressing any infrastructure requirements. The magnitude of this financial investment necessitates a thorough assessment of the potential returns and risks associated with the chosen foreign market.

2. **Complex Regulatory Compliance**

FDI demands a nuanced understanding and compliance with diverse regulatory frameworks in the foreign country. Navigating complex legal and regulatory landscapes can be challenging, requiring businesses to engage with legal experts who specialize in international business laws. Compliance considerations may include industry-specific regulations, labor laws, taxation policies, and other legal requirements. This complexity adds a layer of diligence to the strategic planning process, as overlooking regulatory nuances can result in legal complications and operational disruptions.

3. **Market Entry Timeframe**:

The timeframe for entering a foreign market through FDI is typically longer compared to exporting. The process involves multiple stages, including market research, legal compliance, setting up infrastructure, and obtaining necessary approvals. Delays may arise due to regulatory hurdles, unforeseen challenges, or complexities associated with aligning business practices with local norms. The extended timeline demands careful consideration of the market entry strategy, especially for industries where speed-to-market is critical.

4. **Cultural Adaptation Challenges**

Adapting to local cultures and consumer preferences is a multifaceted challenge in FDI. While having a physical presence facilitates a deeper understanding of the local context, businesses must navigate cultural nuances effectively. This includes tailoring marketing strategies, product offerings, and customer engagement approaches to align with local sensibilities. Failure to adapt to cultural expectations can impede acceptance in the market and limit the success of the FDI venture.

5. **Political and Economic Stability**

Political and economic stability in the foreign countries is a critical consideration. Businesses engaging in FDI must evaluate the geopolitical landscape, economic conditions, and potential risks associated with political instability. Sudden changes in government policies, economic downturns, or geopolitical tensions can impact the viability of the investment. Assessing the stability of the chosen market becomes paramount for long-term success and risk mitigation.

6. **Potential Resistance and Local Competition**

FDI may encounter resistance from local stakeholders or face competition from established local businesses. Cultural, economic, or political factors may contribute to resistance against foreign companies. Additionally, understanding and effectively competing with local businesses that have an established market presence require strategic planning to overcome potential challenges.

While FDI offers significant advantages, businesses must navigate higher initial investment, complex regulatory landscapes, longer market entry timeframes, cultural adaptation challenges, political and economic stability considerations, and potential resistance from local competitors. These considerations underscore the need for meticulous planning, thorough market research, and a comprehensive understanding of the chosen foreign market to ensure the success of the FDI venture.

Decision-Making Process

Choosing between exporting and FDI involves a comprehensive decision-making process. Businesses should consider factors such as:

- **Market Research:** Thoroughly understand the target market, its demand, competition, and regulatory environment.
- **Resource Assessment:** Evaluate the financial resources, capabilities, and risk tolerance of the business.
- **Strategic Objectives:** Align the chosen approach with broader business objectives and long-term strategies.
- **Risk Mitigation:** Assess and mitigate potential risks associated with each approach, considering economic, political, and cultural factors.

Ultimately, the choice between exporting and FDI depends on the specific goals, resources, and risk appetite of the business. Some businesses may start with exporting to test markets and gradually transition to FDI as they gain confidence and experience. Others may opt for FDI from the outset if a deeper market presence is critical to their strategic objectives. A nuanced understanding of the advantages and considerations of each approach is crucial for successful market entry and sustained international growth.

Weighing the pros and cons

Entering a new market is a pivotal decision for businesses, requiring a meticulous evaluation of the pros and cons associated with different strategies. Whether opting for exporting or committing to Foreign Direct Investment (FDI), the decision-making process demands a comprehensive assessment of factors that can significantly impact the success and sustainability of the venture.

Pros of Market Entry

Market Expansion and Revenue Growth

Market expansion through entering new markets is a strategic move that offers businesses significant advantages, primarily in terms of widening their customer base and fostering additional revenue streams. The appeal lies in the opportunity to extend operations into untapped geographic regions, enabling companies to diversify their sources of income.

This diversification is crucial for mitigating risks associated with relying heavily on specific markets. By venturing into new territories, businesses position themselves for overall growth, leveraging the potential of unexplored markets and untapped consumer segments. This advantage becomes particularly impactful in industries where saturation in existing markets prompts the search for new opportunities to sustain and elevate revenue levels.

Entering new markets is a proactive step toward future-proofing a business by reducing its vulnerability to economic fluctuations or unforeseen challenges in established markets. It aligns with the principle of not putting all eggs in one basket, providing a buffer against market-specific downturns. Moreover, it opens avenues for capturing emerging trends, consumer preferences, and market dynamics that may differ from those in existing markets.

Additionally, the pursuit of revenue growth through market expansion aligns with the overarching goal of enhancing the financial health and sustainability of the business. Diversifying revenue streams is a fundamental strategy for ensuring resilience and adaptability in a dynamic business environment. It allows companies to navigate economic uncertainties with greater flexibility and a broader range of opportunities.

The process of entering new markets necessitates a thorough understanding of local conditions, consumer behaviors, and competitive landscapes. This requirement compels businesses to conduct comprehensive market research and adapt their strategies to align with the specific needs and preferences of the target audience in each new market. Such adaptability not only fosters successful market entry but also contributes to building a more resilient and responsive business model.

Furthermore, market expansion can lead to economies of scale, especially in industries where fixed costs play a significant role. As businesses tap into larger markets, they may benefit from spreading fixed costs over a broader production base, potentially reducing per-unit costs and enhancing overall profitability. This efficiency gain is particularly relevant in manufacturing and distribution sectors.

The decision to enter new markets is driven by the prospect of market expansion and revenue growth. By diversifying their customer base and income sources, businesses position themselves strategically to navigate uncertainties, capitalize on emerging opportunities, and strengthen their financial standing. This proactive approach to market expansion not only fosters business growth but also contributes to the long-term sustainability and adaptability of the organization in a dynamic global landscape.

Access to New Customer Segments

Entering a new market presents a myriad of opportunities for businesses, particularly in terms of market expansion and revenue growth. One of the primary advantages is the potential to diversify revenue streams and reduce reliance on specific markets. By expanding into new geographic regions, businesses can tap into previously untapped customer bases, opening avenues for increased sales and profitability. This diversification not only contributes to overall revenue growth but also enhances the resilience of the business by mitigating risks associated with dependence on a single market.

Furthermore, the pursuit of market expansion often results in the discovery of untapped potential within the consumer landscape. Different markets come with their unique characteristics, demands, and preferences. Businesses entering these markets gain valuable insights into diverse customer segments, enabling them to tailor their products and services to meet the specific needs of local consumers. This adaptability is crucial for establishing a strong presence and resonating with the target audience in each new market.

The process of entering a new market is not just about geographical expansion; it's about accessing and understanding varied customer segments with distinct preferences. This access is a strategic advantage that allows companies to fine-tune their offerings, creating a more personalized and targeted approach. By tailoring products and services to suit the specific demands of local markets, businesses can forge stronger connections with consumers. This personalized approach fosters deeper customer loyalty, builds brand recognition, and sets the stage for sustained success in the newly entered territories.

Moreover, market expansion brings the opportunity to explore and capitalize on emerging trends, consumer behaviors, and cultural nuances specific to each region. This exploration enables businesses to stay ahead of the curve, adapting their strategies to align with evolving market dynamics. The adaptability gained through market entry not only contributes to short-term success but also positions the business for long-term growth by remaining attuned to the changing landscape of consumer preferences.

In essence, entering a new market is a strategic move that goes beyond mere geographical reach. It is a multifaceted approach that unlocks potential revenue streams, diversifies customer bases, and positions businesses for sustained growth. The ability to access new customer segments, understand their unique needs, and tailor offerings accordingly provides a competitive edge in the global marketplace. As businesses navigate the complexities of market entry, the rewards of expanded market reach and revenue growth underscore the importance of a well-executed and informed market expansion strategy.

Competitive Advantage

Entering a new market strategically can yield a significant competitive advantage for businesses. This advantage is often associated with being an early mover in the market, allowing companies to establish brand recognition, build robust relationships with local stakeholders, and secure advantageous positions. In industries characterized by intense competition, the ability to enter a market before competitors can be a game-changer.

Brand recognition is a crucial aspect of competitive advantage, and entering a new market provides an opportunity to establish and strengthen the brand's presence. Early movers have the advantage of capturing the attention of consumers in the target market, shaping perceptions, and becoming synonymous with certain products or services. This recognition sets the stage for brand loyalty and preference, making it challenging for later entrants to compete on the same level.

Building strong relationships with local stakeholders, including suppliers, distributors, and regulatory authorities, is another dimension of competitive advantage in a new market. Early entrants can forge partnerships, understand the intricacies of the local business environment, and navigate regulatory landscapes effectively. These relationships contribute to a smoother operational experience and can serve as barriers to entry for competitors trying to establish a foothold in the market.

Securing advantageous positions in the market is often a result of strategic decisions made during the market entry phase. For instance, a company might identify and capture prime locations for retail outlets or distribution centers, securing a competitive edge in terms of accessibility and visibility. The ability to choose the most favorable locations, negotiate favorable terms with suppliers, and optimize the supply chain can significantly contribute to operational efficiency and cost-effectiveness.

In industries where innovation is a key driver of success, being an early mover provides the advantage of setting industry standards. Introducing innovative products or services in a new market not only positions the company as a trendsetter but also allows it to shape consumer expectations. This pioneering role can create a lasting impression and influence the direction of the market, making it challenging for later entrants to catch up.

While the competitive advantage gained through entering a new market is substantial, it is essential for businesses to sustain and leverage this advantage effectively. Continuous innovation, customer engagement strategies, and a commitment to delivering superior value are critical components of maintaining a competitive edge in the long term. However, the initial advantages gained during the market entry phase lay a solid foundation for sustained success and growth in the competitive landscape.

Diversification and Risk Mitigation

Market entry strategies play a pivotal role in diversification, offering businesses the opportunity to spread their operations across different regions. This diversification is a strategic approach that goes beyond geographical expansion; it involves tapping into varied markets, each with its unique economic conditions, regulatory landscapes, and market-specific challenges. The benefits of diversification extend beyond revenue growth, encompassing risk mitigation and overall portfolio resilience.

One of the key advantages of diversification through market entry is the ability to mitigate risks associated with economic downturns. Different markets may respond differently to economic fluctuations, and by having a presence in multiple regions, a business can offset the impact of adverse economic conditions in a particular market. This diversification strategy acts as a risk management tool, providing a buffer against uncertainties that may affect one market while others remain stable or exhibit growth.

Regulatory changes are another factor that can significantly impact businesses. Every region has its own set of rules, regulations, and compliance requirements. By diversifying operations across various markets, businesses can reduce their vulnerability to regulatory changes in any single jurisdiction. This flexibility allows them to adapt to different regulatory environments and navigate compliance challenges more effectively.

Market-specific challenges can also be mitigated through diversification. For instance, a business operating in diverse markets may encounter varying consumer behaviors, competitive landscapes, or cultural nuances. By actively engaging with these differences and tailoring strategies accordingly, companies can adapt to specific challenges in each market. This adaptability is crucial for navigating unforeseen obstacles and ensuring a more robust and resilient business model.

Furthermore, diversification through market entry strategies can enhance overall portfolio resilience. A well-diversified business is less susceptible to the impact of external shocks. Whether it's geopolitical events, currency fluctuations, or industry-specific disruptions, a diversified portfolio provides a level of insulation, allowing a business to absorb shocks in one market while maintaining stability or growth in others.

Diversification through market entry strategies is a strategic tool that goes hand in hand with risk mitigation. By expanding into different regions, businesses can build a diversified portfolio that spreads risk, enhances resilience, and positions them for long-term success. The ability to navigate economic uncertainties, regulatory changes, and market-specific challenges is heightened when operations are strategically diversified across multiple geographic markets. As businesses evaluate market entry opportunities, the inherent benefits of diversification and risk mitigation underscore the strategic importance of a well-considered and diversified global footprint.

Cons of Market Entry

Resource Intensity and Investment Risk

Entering a new market, especially through strategies like Foreign Direct Investment (FDI), entails a notable level of resource intensity and carries inherent investment risks. The resource requirements for market entry are often substantial, encompassing a range of expenditures such as setup costs, marketing expenses, and compliance-related investments. These financial commitments represent a significant upfront investment, which necessitates a thorough assessment to determine whether the potential returns align with the level of financial risk.

The initial investment associated with market entry strategies, particularly those involving FDI, can encompass a spectrum of costs. Setting up a physical presence in a foreign market involves expenditures related to establishing infrastructure, acquiring or leasing facilities, and complying with local regulations. Additionally, marketing expenses are crucial for creating brand awareness and promoting products or services in the new market. Compliance-related expenditures, which include navigating legal and regulatory frameworks, can further contribute to the overall resource intensity of market entry.

The financial risk associated with these resource-intensive endeavors requires a comprehensive evaluation. Businesses must carefully assess whether the potential returns justify the substantial upfront investment. This evaluation involves analyzing market potential, demand projections, and competitive landscapes to gauge the likelihood of achieving the desired financial outcomes. The business case for market entry needs to consider not only the immediate returns but also the long-term strategic positioning and sustained growth prospects.

Moreover, the investment risk extends beyond financial considerations to factors such as market uncertainties, political stability, and economic conditions. Businesses entering new markets must navigate unknown territory, which introduces an element of unpredictability. Political stability, regulatory changes, and economic conditions in the target market can significantly impact the success of the market entry strategy. A thorough risk assessment that encompasses both financial and non-financial dimensions is essential for making informed decisions.

It is crucial for businesses to adopt a nuanced approach in managing resource intensity and investment risks. This involves conducting detailed market research, feasibility studies, and risk assessments to create a comprehensive understanding of the external factors that may influence the success of the market entry strategy. By leveraging robust analytical frameworks and scenario planning, businesses can enhance their ability to navigate uncertainties, make informed investment decisions, and position themselves strategically in new markets.

While the resource intensity of entering a new market poses significant challenges, it also presents opportunities for businesses to tap into untapped potential and diversify their operations. By carefully evaluating the financial and non-financial aspects of market entry, businesses can strike a balance between the resource investments required and the potential returns. A strategic and well-informed approach to managing resource intensity and investment risks is essential for unlocking the growth opportunities that new markets offer.

Complex Regulatory Compliance

Entering new markets introduces businesses to complex regulatory compliance challenges. Each foreign market comes with its own set of legal frameworks, industry-specific regulations, and bureaucratic processes that demand meticulous attention. The complexity of regulatory compliance cannot be overstated, and businesses must navigate this intricate landscape to ensure seamless operations and avoid potential pitfalls.

One of the primary challenges in regulatory compliance is understanding and adhering to diverse legal frameworks. Different countries have unique legal structures, and businesses need to comprehend the intricacies of local laws governing various aspects, including business operations, employment practices, taxation, and intellectual property rights. A failure to grasp and comply with these legal intricacies can lead to legal complications, jeopardizing the business's standing in the foreign market.

Industry-specific regulations further contribute to the complexity of compliance. Various sectors have specific requirements and standards that businesses must adhere to. For example, healthcare, finance, and telecommunications industries often have stringent regulations governing their operations. Businesses entering these markets need to thoroughly understand and comply with sector-specific regulations to ensure lawful operations and maintain the trust of consumers and regulatory authorities.

Bureaucratic processes add another layer of complexity to regulatory compliance. Navigating government agencies, obtaining permits, and meeting documentation requirements can be time-consuming and intricate. Businesses must establish effective processes for dealing with bureaucracy in each foreign market they enter to prevent delays, administrative hurdles, and potential legal consequences.

Failure to comply with local regulations can have severe consequences. Legal complications may result in financial penalties, negatively impacting the bottom line. Operational disruptions, including potential shutdowns or restrictions, can occur if a business is found in violation of regulatory requirements. Beyond financial repercussions, reputational damage can also ensue, eroding trust among consumers, partners, and stakeholders.

To navigate the complexities of regulatory compliance in foreign markets, businesses should adopt a proactive and strategic approach. This involves conducting thorough research on the legal and regulatory landscape of the target market well before market entry. Collaborating with legal experts or local consultants who specialize in international business law is invaluable for gaining insights into local regulations, understanding compliance requirements, and ensuring adherence to legal frameworks.

Establishing robust compliance management systems is another essential step. Businesses should integrate compliance into their operational processes, creating clear protocols and monitoring mechanisms. Regular audits and assessments can help identify potential areas of non-compliance, allowing businesses to take corrective actions promptly.

Moreover, maintaining open lines of communication with local regulatory authorities is crucial. Building positive relationships with relevant government agencies can facilitate smoother compliance processes and provide businesses with insights into changes in regulations. Being proactive and engaged with regulatory bodies demonstrates a commitment to compliance and can contribute to a more favorable regulatory environment for the business.

The complexity of regulatory compliance in foreign markets necessitates a strategic and proactive approach. Businesses should prioritize thorough research, collaborate with legal experts, establish robust compliance management systems, and maintain open communication with regulatory authorities. By addressing regulatory challenges with diligence and foresight, businesses can navigate the intricate regulatory landscape, ensuring lawful and sustainable operations in new markets.

Market Adaptation Challenges

Navigating market adaptation challenges is a crucial aspect of international expansion, as it involves tailoring products or services to align with local preferences. However, this process is not without its complexities, as businesses encounter cultural, linguistic, and consumer behavior nuances unique to each market. Effectively addressing these challenges is essential for ensuring that offerings resonate with the target audience, facilitating successful market entry and sustained growth.

Cultural differences play a pivotal role in shaping consumer preferences, and businesses must navigate this intricate landscape to adapt their offerings appropriately. This involves understanding cultural norms, values, and traditions that influence consumer behavior. For instance, color preferences, symbolism, and even the significance of certain products can vary widely across cultures. Failure to recognize and address these cultural nuances can result in the development of products that may be perceived as inappropriate or irrelevant, hindering market acceptance.

Linguistic considerations are equally vital, especially in regions with diverse languages and dialects. Adapting product names, labels, and marketing materials to resonate with the linguistic nuances of a specific market is essential for effective communication. Mistranslations or cultural insensitivities in language can lead to unintended meanings or even offense, negatively impacting brand perception and consumer trust.

Understanding consumer behavior is at the core of successful market adaptation. Local consumer preferences, buying habits, and decision-making processes vary widely, and businesses must conduct thorough market research to gain insights into these aspects. For example, a product that thrives on impulse purchases in one market may require a more rational and utility-driven marketing approach in another. Failing to align with local consumer behavior can result in products missing the mark and failing to capture the intended audience.

Addressing market adaptation challenges requires a strategic and nuanced approach. Businesses can employ the following strategies to overcome these hurdles effectively:

- **Thorough Market Research:** Conduct comprehensive market research to understand cultural nuances, linguistic preferences, and consumer behavior specific to the target market. This research should delve into the intricacies of local customs, traditions, and lifestyle factors influencing purchasing decisions.
- **Local Partnerships:** Collaborate with local partners or experts who possess in-depth knowledge of the market. Local partners can provide invaluable insights and guide businesses in tailoring their products or services to align with local expectations.
- **Consumer Feedback Loops:** Establish feedback mechanisms to continuously gather insights from the local consumer base. Actively seeking and incorporating feedback allows businesses to adapt their offerings based on real-time information and evolving consumer preferences.
- **Pilot Programs:** Implement pilot programs or soft launches to test the market reception of adapted products or services. This phased approach enables businesses to fine-tune their strategies before full-scale market entry.
- **Flexibility and Iteration:** Maintain a flexible mindset and be prepared to iterate based on market responses. Market adaptation is an ongoing process, and businesses should be responsive to changes in consumer behavior and preferences.

Successfully navigating market adaptation challenges not only enhances the acceptance of products or services but also builds a positive brand image. Businesses that demonstrate cultural sensitivity, linguistic acumen, and a deep understanding of consumer behavior are better positioned to overcome these challenges and establish a meaningful presence in diverse international markets.

Political and Economic Risks

Entering global markets exposes businesses to a spectrum of political and economic risks, necessitating a comprehensive understanding of the intricate dynamics of each region. Political instability, shifts in government policies, and economic downturns are potential challenges that can significantly impact the success of market entry strategies. As businesses navigate these uncertainties, conducting thorough risk assessments becomes imperative to mitigate potential negative impacts.

Political instability is a multifaceted risk that arises from factors such as government changes, civil unrest, or geopolitical tensions. Changes in political leadership or shifts in government policies can lead to unpredictability, affecting business operations and strategies. For example, a sudden change in regulatory frameworks, trade agreements, or tax policies can directly influence the feasibility and profitability of a market entry. Companies must closely monitor political climates in target markets, staying attuned to any indicators of instability that may impact their operations.

Geopolitical considerations are crucial elements in assessing political risks. Regional tensions, trade disputes, or international conflicts can have ripple effects on businesses operating in those regions. Understanding the geopolitical landscape helps businesses anticipate potential disruptions, allowing for strategic adjustments to navigate challenges effectively. A geopolitical risk assessment is, therefore, an integral part of the decision-making process when contemplating market entry.

Economic risks are intertwined with the broader economic conditions of a region. Economic downturns, recessions, or currency fluctuations can pose significant challenges to businesses entering new markets. For instance, a sudden depreciation of the local currency may impact pricing strategies and profitability. Additionally, changes in consumer spending patterns during economic downturns can influence market demand for certain products or services.

Conducting thorough risk assessments involves evaluating the economic health of the target market. This includes analyzing key economic indicators such as GDP growth, inflation rates, and unemployment rates. Businesses must also assess the stability and strength of the local currency, as currency volatility can impact financial performance. By comprehensively understanding the economic landscape, businesses can tailor their market entry strategies to align with prevailing economic conditions.

The strategic consideration of political and economic risks requires a proactive approach. Businesses should incorporate risk management practices into their market entry strategies, developing contingency plans to address potential challenges. Establishing a robust risk management framework involves ongoing monitoring of political and economic developments, regularly updating risk assessments, and adapting strategies to mitigate emerging threats.

While political and economic risks are inherent in global markets, they are not insurmountable obstacles. Instead, they underscore the importance of informed decision-making, strategic planning, and adaptability. Businesses that navigate political and economic uncertainties with a well-informed and proactive approach are better positioned to thrive in diverse and dynamic global markets. Thorough risk assessments serve as a compass, guiding businesses through the complexities of political and economic landscapes, ultimately contributing to the success of their market entry endeavors.

Strategic Decision-Making Process
Market Research and Analysis
The foundation of strategic decision-making in market entry is comprehensive market research. This involves analyzing market size, consumer demographics, competition, regulatory environments, and cultural nuances. Robust market research informs the selection of the most suitable market entry strategy.

Risk Assessment
Conducting a thorough risk assessment is crucial for informed decision-making. Evaluate the potential risks associated with each market entry strategy, considering financial, operational, regulatory, and geopolitical factors. A risk mitigation plan should be developed to address identified challenges.

Cost-Benefit Analysis
Businesses should perform a cost-benefit analysis to weigh the potential returns against the investment required. This analysis includes estimating setup costs, ongoing operational expenses, expected revenue generation, and the timeline for achieving profitability. The goal is to ensure that the chosen strategy aligns with the business's financial objectives.

Evaluation of Resource Capabilities
Assessing the organization's resource capabilities is essential. Consider the financial resources, human capital, and technological infrastructure required for successful market entry. A realistic evaluation of internal capabilities helps in determining the feasibility of the chosen strategy.

Cultural and Consumer Behavior Understanding
Understanding cultural nuances and consumer behavior is critical for market entry success. Businesses should invest in cultural intelligence and consumer research to adapt products, marketing strategies, and communication approaches to local preferences. This understanding enhances the likelihood of positive reception in the target market.

Strategic Flexibility and Adaptability
Given the dynamic nature of global markets, businesses should prioritize strategic flexibility. This involves maintaining adaptability in response to changing market conditions, consumer

trends, and competitive landscapes. A flexible approach allows businesses to adjust strategies based on real-time feedback and evolving market dynamics.

The decision to enter a new market is a complex and strategic process that requires a thorough understanding of market dynamics, careful risk assessment, and alignment with organizational capabilities. By weighing the pros and cons systematically and adopting a strategic decision-making process, businesses can enhance the likelihood of successful market entry and sustainable growth.

The strategic decision-making process

The strategic decision-making process for entering new markets is a multifaceted journey that demands careful planning, analysis, and a keen understanding of both internal and external factors. Navigating global markets requires businesses to make informed choices that align with their overall objectives, risk tolerance, and growth aspirations. The strategic decision-making process involves several key stages, each crucial in shaping the success of market entry initiatives.

1. Market Research and Analysis

The journey begins with thorough market research and analysis. Businesses need to gain a deep understanding of the target market, including its demographics, consumer behavior, competitive landscape, and regulatory environment. This phase involves assessing the market's size, growth potential, and identifying key competitors. Through comprehensive market research, businesses can uncover insights that inform subsequent strategic decisions.

2. Internal Assessment and Capabilities

Before entering a new market, businesses must conduct a thorough internal assessment of their capabilities, resources, and readiness. This involves evaluating whether the organization possesses the necessary expertise, financial strength, and operational flexibility to navigate the complexities of international expansion. Understanding internal strengths and weaknesses informs strategic decisions about the feasibility and timing of market entry.

3. Risk Assessment and Mitigation

Identifying and mitigating risks is a pivotal aspect of strategic decision-making. Businesses need to conduct a comprehensive risk assessment, considering factors such as political, economic, legal, and operational risks. Developing effective risk mitigation strategies ensures that potential challenges are addressed proactively, safeguarding the success of the market entry initiative.

4. Entry Mode Selection

Choosing the right entry mode is a critical decision that depends on factors such as market characteristics, business objectives, and risk tolerance. Common entry modes include exporting, licensing, franchising, joint ventures, and wholly-owned subsidiaries. The selection of the most suitable entry mode aligns with the broader market entry strategy and shapes subsequent operational decisions.

5. Strategic Alliances and Partnerships

Forming strategic alliances and partnerships can be instrumental in the success of market entry strategies. Collaborating with local businesses, distributors, or strategic partners provides access to local expertise, distribution networks, and established customer bases. Choosing the right partners aligns with the overall strategic goals and enhances the effectiveness of market entry initiatives.

6. Localization Strategies

Adapting products, services, and marketing strategies to align with local preferences is a key component of successful market entry. Localization ensures that businesses resonate with the target audience, addressing cultural nuances and consumer expectations. Crafting effective localization strategies enhances market acceptance and fosters positive brand perception.

7. Continuous Monitoring and Adaptation

The strategic decision-making process extends beyond the initial entry phase. Continuous monitoring of market dynamics, consumer behavior, and competitive landscape is essential. Businesses should be prepared to adapt their strategies based on real-time feedback, emerging trends, and changes in the business environment.

The strategic decision-making process for entering new markets is a comprehensive and iterative journey that demands a holistic approach. Successful market entry strategies are built on a foundation of robust research, internal readiness, risk mitigation, and the flexibility to adapt to changing circumstances. By carefully navigating each stage of this process, businesses can position themselves for sustainable growth and success in global markets.

Chapter **14**

Forming Strategic
Partnerships and Alliances

In international business, forming strategic partnerships and alliances is a cornerstone for achieving synergies, fostering growth, and navigating the complexities of global markets. A strategic partnership entails a collaborative alliance between two or more entities, driven by shared objectives, complementary strengths, and mutual benefits.

As we delve into Chapter 14, the focus will be on unraveling the art of finding the right international partners, deciphering various partnership structures, and mastering negotiation tactics to create alliances that propel businesses toward sustained success.

The benefits of strategic partnerships are manifold. They offer avenues for resource sharing, combining expertise, and accessing new markets or technologies. By pooling resources and capabilities, businesses can achieve economies of scale, innovate more effectively, and enhance their competitive positioning.

Additionally, forming strategic partnerships provides a platform for risk mitigation, as entities navigate the challenges of global markets collectively. As we explore the intricacies of finding the right partners and structuring alliances, this chapter will equip businesses with the insights and strategies needed to cultivate impactful partnerships that transcend borders and propel them toward international triumphs.

Finding the right international partners

Finding the right international partners is a nuanced process that demands careful consideration, strategic planning, and a keen understanding of the objectives and dynamics involved. Successful partnerships hinge on aligning with entities that share common goals, values, and a vision for mutual growth.

The following elucidates the multifaceted process of finding the right international partners and highlights key factors to watch out for.

1. Define Objectives and Compatibility

Clearly outlining the objectives of the partnership is essential to align the efforts of both entities toward common goals. Businesses need to identify specific areas where collaboration can bring substantial value, such as leveraging shared resources, gaining access to new markets, or harnessing technological synergies for mutual benefit.

Compatibility assessment is equally crucial, extending beyond mere operational aspects to encompass business culture, values, and long-term goals. By delving into the nuances of each partner's mission, companies can discern whether their strategic visions align harmoniously. A comprehensive understanding of shared values and a congruent commitment to long-term objectives lay the groundwork for a partnership that transcends mere cooperation, evolving into a sustainable and resilient alliance.

The synergy in objectives and compatibility resonates throughout the partnership lifecycle. It serves as a guiding principle, shaping collaborative initiatives and strategic decisions. When partners share a common understanding of their objectives and align their values, the resulting alliance becomes more cohesive, adaptable, and capable of navigating challenges effectively.

Furthermore, defining objectives and ensuring compatibility fosters a sense of trust and commitment between partners. As they embark on collaborative endeavors, a shared vision cultivates an environment where each entity is invested in the success of the other. This commitment extends beyond immediate gains, laying the foundation for enduring relationships built on trust, transparency, and a collective pursuit of excellence.

In practical terms, a partnership founded on clearly defined objectives and compatibility is more likely to weather challenges and capitalize on opportunities. Whether seeking shared resources for cost efficiencies, exploring new markets collaboratively, or harnessing technological synergies to drive innovation, a robust understanding of objectives ensures that collaborative efforts remain focused and purpose-driven.

As businesses increasingly recognize the strategic importance of partnerships in the global landscape, the emphasis on defining clear objectives and assessing compatibility becomes paramount. It acts as a strategic compass, guiding businesses toward alliances that not only achieve short-term objectives but also thrive in the dynamic, ever-evolving terrain of international collaboration. Through this foundational step, companies set the stage for partnerships that transcend transactional arrangements, fostering enduring connections that stand the test of time.

2. Conduct Market Research

Conducting comprehensive market research serves as a foundational step in the process of finding the right international partners. This intricate exploration involves delving into various aspects to identify potential collaborators that not only align with the target market but also fit seamlessly into the industry landscape.

Understanding the Competitive Landscape

An integral part of market research is gaining insights into the competitive landscape. This entails identifying existing players, their market share, and key competitive differentiators. By understanding the competitive dynamics, businesses can pinpoint partners that offer synergies or fill gaps, creating a foundation for mutually beneficial collaboration.

Analyzing Market Trends

Evaluating market trends is crucial to staying ahead in dynamic industries. Potential partners should not only align with current market trends but also demonstrate adaptability to emerging shifts. By assessing how well a partner is positioned within evolving market trends, businesses can ascertain the sustainability and relevance of the collaboration over the long term.

Navigating Regulatory Environments

Different markets come with distinct regulatory environments that can significantly impact business operations. Effective market research involves a thorough examination of regulatory frameworks in the target regions. This ensures that potential partners operate within compliance, minimizing legal risks and enhancing the overall stability of the collaboration.

Pinpointing Complementary Strengths and Weaknesses

The analysis of strengths and weaknesses of potential partners is a critical aspect of market research. It involves a meticulous examination of their capabilities, resources, and areas of expertise. By identifying complementary strengths, businesses can leverage synergies, creating a partnership that enhances overall competitiveness. Simultaneously, understanding weaknesses helps in devising strategies to mitigate potential challenges and establish a balanced collaboration.

Balanced Collaboration for Long-Term Success

Market research aims to facilitate a balanced collaboration where the strengths of each partner offset the weaknesses, fostering a symbiotic relationship. This equilibrium is crucial for the long-term success of the partnership, ensuring that both parties contribute meaningfully to shared objectives and goals.

Conducting comprehensive market research empowers businesses to make informed decisions when selecting international partners. It provides a panoramic view of the competitive landscape, market dynamics, and regulatory intricacies. This meticulous analysis not only enhances the likelihood of finding partners aligned with business goals but also lays the groundwork for robust, enduring collaborations in the global marketplace.

3. Assess Financial Stability

Evaluating the financial stability of potential partners is a pivotal step in the process of forming strategic alliances. Financial health serves as a key indicator of a partner's capacity to fulfill commitments, invest in collaborative initiatives, and weather economic uncertainties. The assessment encompasses various facets that collectively provide insights into the partner's financial robustness.

One fundamental aspect of this evaluation is a meticulous examination of the partner's financial statements, including income statements, balance sheets, and cash flow statements. Analyzing these documents offers a clear picture of the partner's revenue streams, profitability, and overall financial performance over a specific period, aiding in forecasting their ability to contribute meaningfully to the partnership.

Assessing liquidity is crucial to ascertain a partner's short-term financial viability. Liquidity measures the availability of liquid assets to cover immediate financial obligations. A partner with healthy liquidity is better positioned to respond to unforeseen expenses, capitalize on emerging opportunities, and navigate dynamic market conditions, particularly in industries characterized by rapid changes and evolving landscapes.

Examining the debt levels of potential partners provides insights into their financial leverage and risk exposure. Partners with excessive debt may face challenges in meeting repayment obligations, especially during economic downturns. On the other hand, a balanced level of debt indicates prudent financial management, whereas high leverage might signal increased vulnerability to market fluctuations. Understanding the partner's debt structure contributes to a comprehensive assessment of their financial stability.

Effective cash flow management is indicative of a partner's operational efficiency and financial resilience. Positive cash flow ensures the ability to meet day-to-day operational expenses, invest in strategic initiatives, and withstand external economic pressures. Analyzing cash flow patterns, including operating, investing, and financing activities, aids in evaluating the partner's financial discipline and adaptability to market dynamics.

The assessment of financial stability is particularly pertinent in evaluating a partner's resilience to market fluctuations. Industries often experience cyclical changes, external shocks, or economic downturns. Partners with financial stability are better equipped to endure these fluctuations and sustain collaborative efforts. This resilience is essential for maintaining commitment to joint ventures, co-investments, or shared initiatives even during challenging economic climates.

The assessment of financial stability is a comprehensive process that delves into various financial aspects of potential partners. Scrutinizing financial statements, evaluating liquidity, analyzing debt levels, and understanding cash flow dynamics collectively contribute to a robust evaluation. A financially stable partner not only demonstrates a commitment to the alliance but also enhances the overall sustainability and success of the collaborative endeavors.

4. Evaluate Industry Reputation

Evaluating the industry reputation of potential partners is a crucial step in forming strategic alliances, as it directly influences the success and sustainability of the partnership. This multifaceted assessment involves a thorough examination of various factors that collectively contribute to the partner's standing within the industry.

One fundamental aspect of this evaluation is a scrutiny of the partner's track record. Examining their history of engagements, collaborations, and previous partnerships provides valuable insights into their performance and ability to contribute meaningfully to joint ventures. A partner with a positive track record of successful collaborations is likely to bring valuable experience, reliability, and a proven ability to navigate the complexities of cooperative initiatives.

Engaging with industry networks serves as another avenue for gauging the partner's industry reputation. Actively participating in industry events, forums, and associations provides opportunities to interact with peers and gather firsthand information about the potential partner's standing. Networking allows for informal discussions, the exchange of experiences, and the acquisition of valuable insights into the partner's credibility, expertise, and overall industry reputation.

Seeking references from within the industry is an essential component of the evaluation process. Directly contacting current or former collaborators, clients, or partners of the prospective ally offers an unbiased perspective on their performance, reliability, and adherence to ethical business practices. Reference checks provide firsthand accounts of working dynamics, project outcomes, and the partner's contribution to shared initiatives.

In the digital age, online reviews and testimonials play a significant role in shaping perceptions. Evaluating the partner's online presence, including reviews on business platforms, social media, and industry forums, offers additional perspectives on their reputation. Positive reviews highlight strengths, reliability, and successful collaborations, while negative feedback may reveal potential risks or challenges associated with the partner.

Ethical business practices are integral to a partner's industry reputation. Assessing the partner's commitment to ethical conduct, transparency, and corporate responsibility is paramount. Unethical practices can have far-reaching consequences, impacting the reputation of the entire alliance and potentially leading to legal or reputational risks. Evaluating the partner's adherence to industry standards, regulatory compliance, and ethical guidelines is crucial for ensuring alignment with the values and principles of the business seeking collaboration.

The evaluation of industry reputation encompasses a comprehensive analysis of a potential partner's track record, engagement in industry networks, references from collaborators, online reviews, and adherence to ethical business practices. This multifaceted approach provides a holistic view of the partner's standing within the industry, helping businesses make informed decisions about forming strategic alliances.

5. Compatibility in Innovation and Technology

In the ever-evolving landscape of the business world, forming strategic alliances necessitates a thorough evaluation of compatibility in innovation and technology. This facet of partnership assessment acknowledges the pivotal role that technological advancements and innovative strategies play in staying competitive and responsive to market dynamics. Partnerships that align in these areas are better poised to navigate the complexities of the contemporary business environment.

One critical element in evaluating compatibility is an assessment of the technological capabilities of potential partners. This involves scrutinizing the partner's existing technological infrastructure, tools, and systems. A technologically proficient partner possesses the capacity to leverage advanced solutions, streamline operations, and enhance overall efficiency. Assessing the level of technological sophistication enables businesses to gauge the collaborative potential in harnessing shared technological resources.

Furthermore, a comprehensive evaluation of the innovation strategies employed by potential partners is essential. Innovation is a driving force behind sustained growth and relevance in competitive markets. Assessing a partner's commitment to innovation involves scrutinizing their track record of introducing new products, services, or processes. Partners with a proactive approach to innovation contribute to a dynamic alliance that can adapt to changing market demands and capitalize on emerging opportunities.

Willingness to adapt to emerging technological trends is a crucial aspect of compatibility. In an era characterized by rapid technological advancements, businesses must align with partners who demonstrate openness to incorporating cutting-edge technologies. Partnerships that foster a culture of continuous technological evolution are better positioned to seize competitive advantages and respond effectively to industry disruptions.

The agility of a partnership in embracing and integrating emerging technologies is vital for staying competitive in evolving markets. Compatibility in technological innovation ensures that the alliance remains flexible and responsive to industry trends. A collaborative environment that encourages experimentation, prototyping, and implementation of new technologies positions the partnership to capitalize on opportunities and tackle challenges proactively.

Moreover, the compatibility in innovation and technology extends beyond the immediate operational aspects. It influences the strategic direction of the partnership, including joint ventures, research and development initiatives, and shared investments in innovative projects. Partnerships that share a vision for leveraging technology as a strategic enabler can harness synergies that drive long-term success.

Compatibility in innovation and technology is a cornerstone of successful strategic partnerships. Assessing technological capabilities, innovation strategies, and a willingness to embrace emerging trends ensures that the alliance remains dynamic, adaptive, and well-positioned to thrive in the fast-paced and technology-driven business landscape. Partnerships founded on shared values in these areas not only enhance operational efficiency but also contribute to sustained competitiveness and growth.

6. Consider Geopolitical and Cultural Factors

In the intricate landscape of international partnerships, a critical facet that demands thorough consideration is the evaluation of geopolitical and cultural factors. These elements wield substantial influence on the dynamics and success of collaborative ventures, making their comprehensive assessment indispensable.

Geopolitical considerations take center stage, requiring a meticulous evaluation of the political climate in the countries involved. Assessing the stability of these regions is paramount, as political instability can introduce uncertainties that might impact the sustainability of partnerships. Understanding the legal frameworks and trade policies of each country is equally crucial. Variations in regulations and policies can significantly impact the operational landscape, and partners need to align their strategies with the prevailing geopolitical conditions. Moreover, the assessment should extend to the cultural compatibility between potential partners. Cultural alignment fosters effective communication, collaboration, and understanding, forming the bedrock for successful international partnerships. Differences in cultural norms, communication styles, and business practices can pose challenges, potentially leading to misunderstandings or friction within the partnership. Therefore, a nuanced understanding of the cultural fabric of each partner's location is essential to establish a harmonious and productive collaboration.

Within the realm of geopolitics, the stability of a region is a linchpin in determining the feasibility and longevity of a strategic alliance. An evaluation of the political landscape involves an analysis of historical political stability, government structures, and potential risks associated with geopolitical events. Understanding the legal frameworks in each country is imperative to ensure compliance with local regulations and navigate any legal complexities that may arise during the partnership.

Trade policies, tariffs, and regulatory environments also fall under the purview of geopolitical considerations. Changes in these aspects can have a direct impact on the flow of goods and services across borders, influencing the operational efficiency and cost-effectiveness of the partnership. A robust assessment of geopolitical factors enables partners to anticipate and mitigate risks, aligning their strategies with the broader political landscape.

Cultural considerations encompass a nuanced exploration of the values, communication styles, and business practices prevalent in the countries of each partner. This involves delving into cultural nuances such as communication preferences, decision-making processes, and approaches to teamwork. A profound understanding of these aspects is instrumental in fostering effective collaboration and minimizing the potential for misunderstandings or conflicts.

For instance, the hierarchical nature of decision-making in some cultures may contrast with more egalitarian approaches. Recognizing and navigating such differences ensures that the partnership operates smoothly and that each partner's perspective is valued. Additionally, embracing diversity and promoting cultural awareness within the partnership can lead to a richer and more innovative collaboration.

The consideration of geopolitical and cultural factors is integral to the success of international partnerships. Thorough assessments of political stability, legal frameworks, trade policies, and cultural compatibility empower partners to navigate complexities, build strong relationships, and establish collaborations that are resilient in diverse global landscapes.

7. Analyze Legal and Regulatory Compliance

An integral aspect of evaluating potential strategic partners involves a meticulous analysis of their legal and regulatory compliance. This scrutiny is paramount for mitigating risks associated with non-compliance, ensuring that the partnership operates within the bounds of established laws and regulations. The process encompasses a thorough understanding of the legal frameworks in the countries where the potential partner operates, aligning these with the business standards of the evaluating party.

Assessing legal compliance is a proactive measure to minimize the likelihood of future disputes and disruptions that may arise due to regulatory inconsistencies. It involves a comprehensive review of the partner's adherence to local, national, and international laws governing their industry and operations. This scrutiny extends to areas such as labor laws, environmental regulations, intellectual property rights, and other pertinent legal aspects.

Understanding the legal landscape of a potential partner's operating environment is critical. This includes gaining insights into the complexities of local laws, licensing requirements, and any specific regulations that may impact the industry or sector in which the partner operates. For instance, industries such as finance, healthcare, and energy are often subject to stringent regulations, and assessing a partner's compliance with these regulations is crucial for the success and sustainability of the alliance.

Alignment with the legal and regulatory standards of the evaluating party is equally vital. Businesses entering into strategic partnerships should ensure that their potential allies adhere to the same ethical and legal standards, promoting a shared commitment to legal compliance. This alignment reduces the risk of conflicts arising from differing interpretations of legal obligations and expectations.

A comprehensive legal and regulatory analysis involves reviewing the partner's track record of compliance, examining any past legal issues or disputes, and understanding the mechanisms in place for ongoing compliance monitoring. This diligence not only safeguards against potential legal liabilities but also contributes to building a foundation of trust between partners.

Furthermore, the assessment should include an exploration of the partner's approach to risk management and legal due diligence. Partners with robust risk management practices and a proactive approach to legal compliance are better positioned to navigate the evolving legal landscape, adapt to regulatory changes, and proactively address any compliance challenges that may arise during the course of the partnership.

Analyzing the legal and regulatory compliance of potential strategic partners is a crucial step in the due diligence process. It involves understanding the legal frameworks in the partner's operating jurisdictions, assessing alignment with the evaluating party's standards, and delving into the partner's track record of compliance. This comprehensive scrutiny not only mitigates legal risks but also lays the groundwork for a resilient and legally sound strategic partnership.

8. Evaluate Communication and Decision-Making Styles

Effective communication and aligned decision-making processes form the bedrock of successful partnerships. Evaluating the communication styles and decision-making approaches of potential partners is a critical step in establishing a robust and cohesive alliance.

Understanding the communication styles of each partner is essential for fostering transparent and efficient collaboration. Differences in communication preferences, such as the emphasis on formal or informal channels, written or verbal communication, and frequency of updates, can impact the effectiveness of information exchange within the partnership. By assessing these styles, partners can tailor their communication strategies to ensure clarity, avoid misunderstandings, and build a foundation of trust.

Equally important is the alignment of decision-making processes. Different organizations may follow distinct approaches to decision-making, ranging from hierarchical structures to more collaborative and decentralized models. Evaluating these processes helps identify potential synergies or mismatches in decision-making styles. A shared understanding of how decisions will be made, the involvement of key stakeholders, and the speed at which decisions are reached contribute to a smoother and more effective partnership.

In cases where partners have divergent communication and decision-making styles, potential challenges may arise. Miscommunication, delays in decision-making, or conflicting expectations can hinder the progress of collaborative initiatives. Therefore, a thorough evaluation of these aspects early in the partnership exploration phase is essential for mitigating risks and ensuring a strong foundation for cooperation.

Transparent and open communication is crucial throughout the partnership lifecycle. Establishing clear channels for communication, defining roles and responsibilities, and fostering a culture of open dialogue contribute to a healthy and collaborative working relationship. Regular check-ins, status updates, and forums for discussing challenges and opportunities enhance the effectiveness of communication and strengthen the partnership over time.

Decision-making alignment ensures that partners are on the same page when it comes to critical strategic choices. It involves establishing protocols for decision-making, clarifying the roles of key decision-makers, and addressing any potential conflicts in decision authority. By aligning decision-making styles, partners can navigate challenges more efficiently, make informed choices collectively, and adapt to changing circumstances with agility.

Evaluating communication and decision-making styles is a foundational step in forming successful partnerships. It enables potential partners to understand each other's preferences, align expectations, and establish a collaborative framework that promotes effective communication and streamlined decision-making. This alignment lays the groundwork for a resilient and adaptive partnership capable of addressing challenges and leveraging opportunities in a dynamic business environment.

9. Conduct Due Diligence

Conducting due diligence is a crucial step in the partnership formation process, providing a comprehensive validation of the information gathered during the preliminary evaluation. This multifaceted approach involves legal due diligence, financial audits, and an in-depth review of the potential partner's operations, ensuring a thorough understanding of various aspects before finalizing the partnership.

Legal due diligence is imperative to identify any legal risks or issues that might impact the proposed partnership. This involves a meticulous examination of contracts, agreements, intellectual property rights, and compliance with local and international laws. Ensuring that the partner operates within legal frameworks and possesses the necessary permissions and licenses is paramount for avoiding legal complications that could jeopardize the success of the partnership.

Financial audits are an integral part of due diligence, offering a deeper insight into the partner's financial health and operational efficiency. Independent auditors scrutinize financial statements, verifying the accuracy and completeness of financial information provided by the potential partner. This process helps validate the partner's claims, providing assurance to both parties regarding the accuracy of financial data and transparency in reporting.

A comprehensive review of the partner's operations serves to understand the intricacies of their business model, processes, and organizational structure. This involves assessing the efficiency of their supply chain, production capabilities, and overall operational performance. Gaining insights into these operational facets is crucial for aligning expectations, identifying potential areas of collaboration, and ensuring that both parties can effectively integrate their operations for mutual benefit.

Due diligence acts as a safeguard against unforeseen challenges and potential risks that might emerge post-partnership. By systematically verifying information and scrutinizing key aspects, businesses can identify any discrepancies or red flags that could impact the success of the collaboration. This thorough examination helps in making informed decisions, mitigating risks, and building a solid foundation for a resilient and enduring partnership.

Additionally, due diligence contributes to the overall reliability of the partnership by instilling a sense of trust and transparency between the involved parties. A partner who willingly undergoes due diligence demonstrates a commitment to openness and integrity in the collaboration. This transparency fosters a positive working relationship, as both parties can have confidence in the accuracy of the shared information and the viability of the proposed partnership.

Conducting due diligence is a meticulous and necessary process in the formation of strategic partnerships. By delving into legal, financial, and operational aspects, businesses can validate information, mitigate risks, and establish a foundation of trust that is essential for the long-term success of the collaborative venture.

In summary, finding the right international partners requires a meticulous approach encompassing strategic planning, comprehensive research, and a holistic understanding of the prospective collaborators. By emphasizing shared values, assessing compatibility across various dimensions, and conducting rigorous due diligence, businesses can forge partnerships that stand the test of time and contribute to sustainable international success.

Partnership structures and negotiation tactics

Establishing effective partnership structures and employing successful negotiation tactics are pivotal elements in the formation of strategic alliances. These components lay the groundwork for collaborations that are resilient, mutually beneficial, and conducive to long-term success.

Partnership Structures

Partnership structures define the legal and organizational framework within which collaboration takes place. Selecting the most appropriate structure depends on the nature of the partnership, the level of involvement each party desires, and the strategic goals of the collaboration.

Common partnership structures include joint ventures, strategic alliances, and equity partnerships.

Joint Ventures (JVs)

Joint ventures (JVs) represent a collaborative business structure where two or more entities pool their resources and expertise to establish a new entity for a specific project or business endeavor. The core principle behind JVs is to combine the strengths of each partner to achieve mutual benefits and shared objectives.

In the formation of joint ventures, partners embark on a journey of shared control, joint decision-making, and a collaborative approach to realizing common goals. This structure is particularly appealing when a project requires a level of commitment that exceeds the capabilities of a single entity. By creating a separate entity, partners can streamline operations and allocate responsibilities effectively.

One of the distinctive features of joint ventures is the establishment of a new legal entity, separate from the existing businesses of the partners. This new entity operates autonomously, and its structure can vary based on the agreement between the collaborating parties. Typically, partners contribute capital, assets, or intellectual property to the joint venture, and the entity is responsible for managing and executing the agreed-upon project or venture.

The high level of collaboration within joint ventures extends to shared control and decision-making. Partners actively participate in shaping the strategic direction of the joint venture, making key decisions collectively. This collaborative governance model ensures that the interests and perspectives of all partners are considered, fostering a sense of equality and shared responsibility.

However, the benefits of joint ventures come with the requirement for a significant degree of commitment and coordination between partners. Successful joint ventures demand effective communication, aligned objectives, and a commitment to resolving challenges collaboratively. The shared control also implies that decision-making processes may involve negotiations and consensus-building, requiring a level of flexibility and willingness to compromise.

In practice, joint ventures have been utilized across various industries and sectors. For instance, in the technology sector, joint ventures may be formed to collaborate on research and development projects, leveraging the complementary expertise of partner companies. Similarly, joint ventures in the energy sector may involve the joint exploration and development of natural resources.

The success of joint ventures relies heavily on the ability of partners to work cohesively, leveraging their combined strengths for mutual benefit. The coordination of efforts, resource sharing, and effective governance are pivotal aspects that contribute to the achievement of joint venture objectives. Additionally, partners must establish clear agreements detailing the scope of the venture, the allocation of responsibilities, profit-sharing mechanisms, and dispute resolution procedures.

Joint ventures are dynamic collaborations that offer a pathway for entities to combine their resources and expertise to embark on mutually beneficial projects. This business structure emphasizes shared control, collaborative decision-making, and the creation of a separate legal entity. While joint ventures demand a significant commitment from partners, the potential for synergy and achievement of common objectives makes them a compelling option for businesses seeking collaborative growth.

Strategic Alliances

Strategic alliances serve as dynamic and adaptable collaborations designed to achieve specific objectives without necessitating the creation of a new legal entity. Embracing various forms, such as contractual agreements, partnerships, or consortia, these alliances provide a flexible framework for partners to collaboratively address particular projects or initiatives. One notable characteristic of strategic alliances is their versatility, enabling organizations to work together in a targeted manner without the intricate processes involved in establishing a new business entity.

The foundational premise of strategic alliances lies in their ability to pool resources, expertise, and capabilities to pursue common goals. Unlike more formal structures such as joint ventures, strategic alliances allow organizations to maintain distinct legal identities while strategically aligning for specific purposes. This adaptability is particularly advantageous in industries where collaboration on specific projects or initiatives is more beneficial than establishing a comprehensive joint venture or equity partnership.

In strategic alliances, the scope of collaboration is defined by the specific needs of the involved parties. This might involve joint marketing efforts, shared research and development initiatives, or combined efforts to penetrate a new market. The flexible nature of these alliances allows partners to engage in a cooperative venture for a defined period, enabling them to leverage each other's strengths and resources without the enduring commitments associated with more integrated business structures.

One of the primary advantages of strategic alliances is the efficient allocation of resources. Organizations can strategically choose partners based on their expertise and capabilities relevant to a specific project or objective. This targeted collaboration allows each party to contribute its unique strengths, fostering synergy that goes beyond what individual entities might achieve independently. Consequently, organizations can pursue opportunities that align with their strategic objectives without the need for extensive internal investment.

Moreover, strategic alliances contribute to risk mitigation. By sharing responsibilities and leveraging shared expertise, organizations can navigate uncertainties more effectively. In industries marked by rapid changes or evolving market dynamics, strategic alliances offer a mechanism to adapt swiftly to emerging trends without the bureaucratic intricacies often associated with more formal business structures.

Successful strategic alliances hinge on effective communication, mutual trust, and alignment of goals. The collaborative nature of these partnerships requires transparent communication channels and a shared understanding of each party's expectations. Establishing a foundation of trust is paramount to navigate potential challenges and ensure a harmonious collaboration.

Despite their flexibility and advantages, strategic alliances are not without challenges. Managing the complexities of multiple organizations working together, aligning diverse organizational cultures, and ensuring the protection of intellectual property are common hurdles. Effective governance structures, well-defined roles and responsibilities, and clear contractual agreements are essential elements in overcoming these challenges.

Strategic alliances represent a versatile and valuable approach to collaboration in the business landscape. Their ability to provide targeted solutions, efficiently allocate resources, and mitigate risks makes them a strategic choice for organizations seeking collaborative opportunities without the need for more formal and enduring business structures.

Equity Partnerships

Equity partnerships represent a sophisticated form of collaboration where two entities exchange ownership stakes, creating a symbiotic relationship that goes beyond conventional business alliances. In this structure, both partners become shareholders in each other's companies, establishing a mutual interest in the success and growth of their respective ventures.

- **Alignment of Interests:** At the core of equity partnerships is the alignment of interests. By holding ownership stakes, both parties share not only the rewards but also the risks associated with each other's businesses. This shared interest fosters a deeper level of commitment and collaboration, as the success of one partner directly contributes to the prosperity of the other.

- **Deeper Commitment:** Equity partnerships signify a more profound commitment compared to other collaboration structures. The act of becoming shareholders implies a strategic alignment of long-term goals and a willingness to weather challenges together. This depth of commitment often translates into a shared vision for the future and a joint pursuit of sustained success.

- **Mutual Investment in Success:** In equity partnerships, the success of one partner is inherently linked to the success of the other. This interconnectedness creates a unique synergy, encouraging both entities to actively contribute to the growth and well-being of each other's ventures. The mutual investment in success extends beyond financial gains and encompasses shared resources, expertise, and strategic support.

- **Strategic Decision-Making:** Equity partnerships often involve joint decision-making processes. As shareholders, both parties have a say in the strategic direction of the collaborating entities. This shared governance structure promotes open communication, transparency, and a collaborative approach to decision-making, ensuring that major choices are made collectively with the best interests of both partners in mind.

- **Long-Term Collaboration:** While other collaboration structures may be project-specific or limited in duration, equity partnerships are inherently designed for the long term. The shared ownership model encourages partners to view their collaboration as an enduring relationship rather than a short-lived alliance. This long-term perspective fosters stability, continuity, and a commitment to navigating challenges together.
- **Challenges and Considerations:** Despite the advantages, equity partnerships come with their set of challenges. Issues such as differences in corporate culture, divergent growth trajectories, or changes in leadership can impact the dynamics of the partnership. Thorough due diligence, clear legal agreements, and ongoing communication are crucial to addressing and mitigating potential challenges.

Example of Equity Partnership Success

An illustrative example of a successful equity partnership is the collaboration between a technology startup and an established industry leader. The startup, seeking mentorship, resources, and market access, exchanged an equity stake with the industry leader. This collaboration resulted in shared innovation, accelerated market penetration, and the establishment of a strong presence in the technology sector.

Equity partnerships stand as a testament to the depth of collaboration possible in the business landscape. By intertwining ownership stakes, entities forge a connection that transcends conventional business alliances. This structure not only aligns interests but also cements a commitment to shared success, making equity partnerships a powerful model for those seeking enduring and mutually beneficial collaborations.

Setting Up Partnership Structures:

Clearly Define Objectives

Establishing a solid foundation for effective partnerships begins with a clear and articulate definition of objectives. This foundational step is paramount before delving into the complexities of choosing a partnership structure. By clearly defining objectives, organizations set the stage for a collaborative venture that aligns with their strategic goals and maximizes the chances of success.

- **Articulating Purpose:** Defining the purpose of the partnership is the initial step in clearly outlining objectives. Organizations need to ask themselves why they are entering into a collaboration and what they aim to achieve. Whether it's mutual growth, innovation, market expansion, or specific project outcomes, a well-defined purpose forms the basis for selecting a partnership structure that best serves these goals.
- **Setting Concrete Goals:** Objectives should be translated into concrete and measurable goals. These goals act as benchmarks for success and guide the collaborative efforts. Whether it's increasing market share, expanding product lines, or entering new geographical markets, having specific and achievable goals provides a roadmap for both partners to follow.
- **Anticipating Outcomes:** Alongside setting goals, it's essential to anticipate the expected outcomes of the partnership. This includes identifying the tangible and intangible benefits that each partner seeks to gain. Anticipating outcomes helps in aligning expectations, fostering transparency, and ensuring that the selected partnership structure is conducive to achieving these outcomes.
- **Aligning with Strategic Direction:** Objectives should align seamlessly with the overall strategic direction of the organizations involved. A partnership that complements and reinforces the strategic goals of each entity is more likely to be successful. This alignment ensures that the collaboration becomes an integral part of the broader organizational strategy rather than a detached initiative.
- **Avoiding Ambiguity:** Ambiguity in objectives can lead to misunderstandings, misalignment, and potential conflicts during the course of the partnership. Clearly

articulated objectives leave little room for ambiguity, providing both partners with a shared understanding of the collaboration's purpose and intended outcomes.

Example of Objectives in Action

Consider two companies entering a partnership to jointly develop and launch a new line of sustainable products. The clearly defined objectives include reducing the environmental impact, tapping into eco-conscious consumer segments, and driving innovation in sustainable practices. These objectives guide the selection of a partnership structure that allows for shared resources, joint research and development, and a unified marketing strategy.

Clearly defining objectives is a foundational step that organizations cannot afford to overlook when embarking on collaborative ventures. This clarity not only guides the selection of an appropriate partnership structure but also ensures that the collaboration is purposeful, goal-oriented, and strategically aligned. By setting a clear roadmap from the outset, organizations pave the way for successful and mutually beneficial partnerships.

Understand Each Partner's Role

In the intricate landscape of strategic partnerships, the understanding of each partner's role emerges as a cornerstone for fostering effectiveness and synergy. The success of collaborative endeavors hinges on a clear delineation of roles and responsibilities, creating a robust framework that guides contributions, decision-making processes, and the division of responsibilities.

- **Contributions and Commitments:** One fundamental aspect of defining roles is outlining the contributions each partner brings to the table. This spans beyond financial commitments and includes resources, expertise, and any unique value propositions. By understanding the specific strengths and contributions of each partner, organizations can leverage complementary assets to achieve shared objectives.

- **Decision-Making Processes:** Establishing a well-defined decision-making process is crucial to avoid ambiguity and potential conflicts. This involves clarifying how decisions will be made, who holds decision-making authority, and the mechanisms for resolving disagreements. Whether decisions are made collaboratively, through consensus, or based on specific expertise, a transparent process fosters a sense of equality and fairness.

- **Division of Responsibilities:** Clearly outlining the division of responsibilities ensures that each partner understands their role in the partnership's overall success. This extends to operational tasks, project management, and day-to-day activities. A well-structured division of responsibilities prevents duplication of efforts, minimizes gaps, and enhances the efficiency of the partnership.

- **Alignment with Expertise:** Understanding and aligning roles with the expertise of each partner is paramount. This alignment ensures that tasks are delegated to those with the most relevant skills, fostering a collaborative environment where each partner can contribute effectively. It also establishes a foundation for mutual respect and recognition of each other's strengths.

Example of Role Understanding in Action

Imagine a technology company partnering with a marketing agency to launch a new digital product. Clearly defining roles involves acknowledging that the technology company will handle product development and technical aspects, while the marketing agency will lead promotional campaigns and customer engagement. This understanding prevents overlap, ensuring a seamless collaboration where each partner plays to their strengths.

Promoting Harmonious Partnerships

The clarity established in understanding roles serves as a proactive measure against potential misunderstandings. Harmonious partnerships thrive on a shared understanding of who is responsible for what, creating an environment of trust and accountability. When partners are confident in their roles, it contributes to a positive collaborative culture where each party is motivated to contribute its best.

Understanding each partner's role is not merely a procedural step but a fundamental building block for effective and fruitful partnerships. It fosters transparency, minimizes friction, and sets the stage for a collaborative journey where each participant contributes meaningfully to shared goals. As organizations embark on strategic partnerships, investing time and effort in defining and understanding roles is an investment in the partnership's overall success.

Legal Agreements

When engaging in partnerships, particularly in the context of entering a new market, the establishment of comprehensive legal agreements is a crucial step for the success and sustainability of the collaboration. These legal agreements serve as the foundational framework that governs the terms, conditions, and expectations between the partnering entities.

One key aspect that legal agreements should address is the mechanism for profit-sharing. Defining how profits will be distributed among the partners ensures transparency and fairness in the financial aspects of the collaboration. This is especially vital when entering new markets, as different jurisdictions may have varying regulations and tax implications that need to be considered in profit-sharing arrangements.

Another critical component of legal agreements is the inclusion of clear dispute resolution processes. Disputes can arise in any business collaboration, and having predefined mechanisms for resolution helps in mitigating conflicts swiftly and efficiently. This is particularly important when dealing with international partnerships, where legal systems and cultural differences may add complexity to dispute resolution.

Exit strategies should also be carefully outlined in legal agreements. Partners should define the conditions under which either party can exit the partnership and the procedures for doing so. This includes considerations such as the sale of shares, buyout options, or other exit mechanisms. Having a well-defined exit strategy helps manage potential risks and uncertainties, providing a clear path forward for both parties in case the collaboration needs to come to an end.

Confidentiality clauses are integral to protecting sensitive information shared between partners. In the context of entering a new market, partners may exchange proprietary data, trade secrets, or strategic plans. A robust confidentiality clause ensures that such information remains secure and is not misused. This is particularly relevant when dealing with international collaborations, where legal frameworks for intellectual property protection may vary.

To ensure the legal soundness of these agreements, it is advisable to consult legal experts specializing in international business law. Legal professionals can navigate the complexities of cross-border partnerships, ensuring that the agreements comply with local regulations and international standards. This step is crucial for minimizing legal risks and establishing a solid foundation for the partnership.

Drafting comprehensive legal agreements is an essential aspect of entering a new market through partnerships. These agreements provide a structured framework for addressing critical elements such as profit-sharing, dispute resolution, exit strategies, and confidentiality. Seeking the expertise of legal professionals ensures that the agreements are well-crafted, legally sound, and capable of navigating the intricacies of international business collaborations.

Consider Cultural Fit

When embarking on a partnership, one crucial consideration for businesses is the cultural fit between potential collaborators. The success of a partnership is not solely determined by financial agreements or strategic alignment; cultural compatibility plays a pivotal role. Evaluating the cultural fit involves assessing whether there is a shared vision, values, and working culture between the parties involved.

A shared vision sets the foundation for a collaborative relationship. When businesses share common goals and aspirations, it fosters a sense of unity and collective purpose within the partnership. This shared vision aligns the efforts of both parties, driving them toward mutual success. This alignment becomes particularly crucial when navigating challenges or making strategic decisions, as a shared vision provides a cohesive framework for problem-solving and decision-making.

Values form another critical aspect of cultural fit. Businesses with shared values are more likely to navigate challenges and conflicts effectively. These shared values create a common ethical framework, ensuring that both partners operate within similar ethical boundaries. This alignment in values contributes to a sense of trust and integrity within the partnership, fostering a healthy and sustainable collaborative environment.

Understanding and respecting each other's working culture is equally important. Organizational cultures can vary significantly, impacting how teams collaborate, communicate, and approach tasks. When businesses take the time to comprehend and appreciate these cultural nuances, it lays the groundwork for effective communication and collaboration. For example, if one partner values a hierarchical structure while the other promotes a more egalitarian approach, understanding and respecting these differences can prevent misunderstandings and promote a harmonious working relationship.

Harmonious collaboration is not only about avoiding conflicts but also about enhancing the overall effectiveness of the partnership. A culturally compatible partnership often experiences smoother communication, streamlined decision-making processes, and a more synergistic working dynamic. This compatibility extends beyond the initial stages of the partnership, contributing to its long-term success and sustainability.

Considering cultural fit is a strategic imperative when evaluating potential partners. A shared vision, values, and working culture contribute to the foundation of a collaborative relationship. As businesses navigate the complexities of partnerships, understanding and respecting each other's organizational culture enhance the effectiveness and sustainability of the collaboration. This cultural compatibility sets the stage for a partnership that not only achieves strategic objectives but also creates a positive and collaborative environment conducive to mutual growth and success.

Negotiation Tactics

Successful negotiation is fundamental to the formation of strategic partnerships. Employing effective negotiation tactics ensures that both parties feel satisfied with the terms of the collaboration.

Here are key negotiation tactics:

Understand Interests

In the realm of negotiations, understanding the interests, needs, and priorities of all parties involved is fundamental for fostering collaboration and achieving mutually beneficial outcomes. This principle is rooted in the concept of principled negotiation, where the focus is not solely on positions but on the underlying interests that drive those positions. By delving deeper into the core interests of each negotiating party, a more comprehensive understanding emerges, forming the basis for a successful negotiation.

Identifying interests requires a proactive effort to uncover the motivations and desires that fuel the positions taken by each party. This involves open communication, active listening, and a genuine willingness to explore the underlying drivers of their perspectives. For instance, in a business negotiation, understanding the interests of both the buyer and seller could involve exploring factors beyond the financial aspect, such as long-term business relationships, strategic objectives, or specific operational needs.

A collaborative approach is pivotal in negotiations, emphasizing a shared commitment to finding solutions that address the concerns and aspirations of all parties involved. Rather than a competitive mindset where one party's gain is perceived as the other's loss, a collaborative approach seeks to identify areas of common ground and shared interests. This not only paves the way for more creative problem-solving but also fosters a positive and constructive atmosphere for negotiation.

Principled negotiation, as advocated by the Harvard Negotiation Project, encourages negotiators to focus on interests rather than rigid positions. By doing so, negotiators can discover innovative solutions that meet the core needs of all parties, transcending initial stances. For instance, in a negotiation between a company and a labor union, understanding the interests of both parties might reveal shared concerns about employee welfare and organizational sustainability. This shared interest becomes a foundation for collaborative negotiations, fostering a win-win outcome.

Moreover, prioritizing interests over positions allows negotiators to navigate potential roadblocks more effectively. Positions are often fixed and can lead to stalemates, while interests are dynamic and open to creative problem-solving. For instance, a negotiation between a technology company and a regulatory body may involve conflicting positions on data privacy. However, understanding the shared interest in protecting consumer data can lead to collaborative solutions that address regulatory concerns while preserving the company's innovative initiatives.

The emphasis on understanding interests in negotiations underscores the importance of delving beyond surface-level positions. A collaborative approach that seeks to identify and address the core interests of each negotiating party lays the groundwork for more successful and enduring agreements. By embracing principled negotiation principles and fostering open communication, negotiators can create an environment conducive to achieving outcomes that satisfy the needs and priorities of all stakeholders involved.

Build Rapport

Building rapport is a foundational element in any successful negotiation process, especially when entering a new market or forming partnerships. The establishment of a positive and open rapport is crucial for cultivating a relationship built on trust, transparency, and mutual understanding. In the context of international business, where cultural differences and diverse business practices come into play, building rapport becomes even more pivotal.

Trust is the bedrock of successful negotiations, and it is nurtured through consistent and open communication. Businesses should strive to create a collaborative negotiation environment where all parties feel comfortable expressing their needs, concerns, and expectations. This collaborative approach fosters a sense of transparency, allowing each party to understand the motivations and intentions of the other. It also facilitates the exchange of valuable information, leading to a more informed and equitable negotiation process.

Cultivating a relationship of trust involves demonstrating reliability and integrity throughout the negotiation stages. Consistency in actions and communication builds confidence and helps establish a positive rapport. This is particularly important in international negotiations, where partners may be geographically distant and rely heavily on effective communication to bridge the gap.

In a global business landscape, where cultural diversity plays a significant role, understanding the cultural nuances of negotiation styles becomes imperative. Different cultures may have distinct approaches to building relationships, making decisions, and expressing agreement or disagreement. Being culturally sensitive and adapting communication styles accordingly contributes to a harmonious negotiation environment.

Moreover, a positive rapport extends beyond the negotiation table and lays the groundwork for a successful long-term partnership. In many international markets, relationships are not only transactional but are viewed as ongoing collaborations. Building a strong rapport from the outset sets the stage for a lasting and mutually beneficial business relationship.

Building rapport is a strategic component of successful negotiations, especially in the context of entering new markets or establishing partnerships. It involves creating an environment of trust, transparency, and collaboration. Effective communication, cultural sensitivity, and reliability are key elements in cultivating a positive rapport. Businesses that invest time and effort in building strong relationships during the negotiation process are likely to experience smoother collaborations and increased success in their international endeavors.

Seek Win-Win Solutions

Seeking win-win solutions is a fundamental principle in establishing successful collaborations and partnerships. The essence of this approach lies in creating outcomes that are mutually beneficial for all parties involved. By striving for a win-win scenario, businesses can foster positive and enduring partnerships that go beyond immediate gains.

In pursuing win-win solutions, it's crucial to consider the interests, needs, and objectives of each partner. This collaborative mindset emphasizes finding common ground where both parties can derive value from the partnership. This approach is not about one side winning at the expense of the other; instead, it aims to create synergies that enhance the overall success of the collaboration.

Building a foundation for a positive partnership begins with open communication and a willingness to understand the perspectives of all involved parties. This collaborative spirit sets the tone for constructive discussions and negotiations, paving the way for creative problem-solving and innovative solutions. By actively seeking common interests and shared goals, businesses can develop strategies that maximize value for everyone involved.

A win-win outcome is not just about immediate gains; it contributes to the sustainability and longevity of the partnership. When all parties feel that they have gained value and their interests are respected, the foundation for a positive and enduring collaboration is established. This fosters a sense of trust, which is crucial for the success and growth of any partnership over time.

Moreover, the pursuit of win-win solutions reflects a commitment to building relationships based on fairness and mutual respect. In a global business landscape, where partnerships often span cultural and geographical boundaries, this approach becomes even more critical. It transcends short-term transactional benefits and focuses on creating enduring relationships that withstand challenges and uncertainties.

Successful collaborations built on win-win solutions often result in shared successes, as each partner contributes to the growth and achievements of the other. This positive cycle reinforces the collaborative mindset, encouraging continuous cooperation and innovation. Businesses that prioritize win-win outcomes are more likely to establish a positive reputation in the marketplace, attracting like-minded partners and creating a conducive environment for future collaborations.

Seeking win-win solutions is a strategic approach that goes beyond transactional gains. It is a mindset that prioritizes mutual benefits, positive relationships, and long-term success. By embracing this approach, businesses can create enduring partnerships that thrive on shared values, trust, and a commitment to collective growth.

Flexibility and Adaptability

Flexibility and adaptability are paramount attributes when entering a new market. The business landscape is dynamic, and negotiations and market dynamics may require constant adjustments. Maintaining a flexible approach is crucial for navigating the complexities of market entry successfully.

In the context of negotiations, flexibility is a key ingredient for success. Entering a new market often involves dealing with various stakeholders, including local partners, distributors, or regulatory bodies. In these interactions, a rigid stance can hinder progress and compromise the potential for mutually beneficial agreements. Flexibility allows businesses to adapt their strategies, offerings, or terms to align with the evolving needs and expectations of the new market.

Negotiations, by nature, involve give-and-take. Being open to compromise is an integral part of the flexibility required in market entry. Local business practices, cultural norms, and regulatory frameworks may differ significantly from those in the home market. Embracing flexibility in negotiations enables businesses to find common ground, build trust, and foster positive relationships with local partners. This adaptability not only facilitates smoother negotiations but also contributes to the overall success of the market entry strategy.

Moreover, the business environment in a new market can be dynamic and subject to changes. Consumer preferences may evolve, competitors might enter the scene, or regulatory conditions may shift. Being adaptable allows businesses to respond promptly to these changes and adjust their strategies accordingly. This nimbleness is particularly crucial during the early phases of market entry when understanding and acclimating to the local market dynamics are essential.

A flexible approach also extends to the overall market entry strategy. Companies should be prepared to iterate and refine their approach based on real-time feedback and market insights. This iterative process allows businesses to fine-tune their strategies, optimize operations, and enhance their offerings to better resonate with the local audience.

In summary, flexibility and adaptability are indispensable qualities for successful market entry. Whether in negotiations, adjusting strategies, or responding to changes in the market environment, being flexible allows businesses to navigate the complexities of entering a new market with agility and effectiveness. It is a mindset that acknowledges the fluidity of international business and positions companies to seize opportunities and overcome challenges in the ever-evolving global marketplace.

Clearly Communicate

In the realm of international business, effective communication is a cornerstone for successful collaboration. When entering new markets or engaging in foreign direct investment, clear and transparent communication becomes paramount. Articulating expectations, concerns, and requirements helps establish a foundation of mutual understanding, fostering positive working relationships between businesses and their counterparts in the new market.

Open channels of communication are essential to bridge potential language and cultural gaps. When engaging with international partners or stakeholders, conveying messages clearly and precisely ensures that everyone involved is on the same page. This transparency not only minimizes the risk of misunderstandings but also cultivates an environment of trust and cooperation.

Moreover, effective communication extends beyond verbal interactions. Non-verbal cues, body language, and cultural nuances play significant roles in conveying messages accurately. Being aware of these subtleties becomes crucial, especially when dealing with diverse cultures. For instance, what might be considered a positive gesture in one culture might have a different connotation in another. Understanding and respecting these cultural nuances contribute to building rapport and preventing potential misinterpretations.

In the context of market entry or foreign investments, clear communication also involves setting expectations regarding timelines, deliverables, and any potential challenges. Establishing a transparent dialogue about the anticipated milestones and potential hurdles helps align all parties involved. This proactive approach allows for better preparation and, if needed, adjustments to the business strategy.

Additionally, effective communication is a two-way street. Encouraging feedback and actively listening to the concerns and insights of international partners fosters a collaborative environment. This exchange of information not only aids in problem-solving but also provides valuable insights that can enhance the overall success of the venture. By creating a culture of open communication, businesses position themselves to navigate challenges more effectively and capitalize on opportunities that arise in the dynamic landscape of international business.

The importance of clear and effective communication cannot be overstated in the context of international business ventures. Whether entering new markets or engaging in foreign direct investment, the ability to articulate expectations, understand cultural nuances, and foster open dialogue contributes significantly to successful collaborations. Businesses that prioritize transparent communication not only mitigate the risks associated with misunderstandings but also lay the groundwork for mutually beneficial and enduring partnerships in the global marketplace.

Consider the Long-Term Relationship

When venturing into new markets or forming business partnerships, it's paramount to prioritize the establishment of long-term relationships over the pursuit of short-term gains. Sustainable and mutually beneficial partnerships thrive on a foundation of commitment, trust, and shared goals. This approach recognizes the importance of nurturing relationships that extend beyond immediate gains, fostering collaboration and resilience in the face of challenges.

Building a long-term relationship involves more than transactional interactions; it requires a genuine commitment to the success of both parties involved. This commitment translates into a willingness to invest time, effort, and resources into understanding the partner's business, goals, and challenges. It also involves a shared vision for the future, aligning objectives to ensure that the partnership evolves and adapts to changing circumstances.

Moreover, a long-term relationship mindset encourages open communication and transparency. Partnerships built on trust and clear communication weather uncertainties more effectively. This collaborative approach allows for the constructive resolution of issues, continuous improvement, and the ability to seize new opportunities as they arise.

In contrast to short-term, transactional arrangements that may prioritize immediate gains, a long-term relationship perspective emphasizes the value of enduring connections. Businesses that focus on cultivating these relationships position themselves for sustained success and resilience in a dynamic business environment. By emphasizing collaboration, shared objectives, and adaptability, organizations can navigate the complexities of international markets and business partnerships with a strategic eye on long-term prosperity.

Anticipate and Address Concerns

Anticipating and addressing concerns is a critical aspect of successful negotiations and partnerships when entering a new market. Proactively identifying potential challenges and addressing them during the negotiation phase is a strategic approach that contributes to the overall stability and resilience of the collaboration.

By taking a preemptive stance, businesses engaging in market entry negotiations can navigate potential roadblocks before they become significant issues. This not only demonstrates a thorough understanding of the intricacies involved but also showcases a commitment to open communication and problem-solving. Proactively addressing concerns is a demonstration of foresight, signaling to the other party that the business is invested in building a solid foundation for the partnership.

This approach contributes to the establishment of trust between the parties involved. Trust is a fundamental element in any successful partnership, and addressing concerns upfront builds a foundation of transparency and reliability. It sets the tone for a collaborative relationship based on mutual understanding, reducing the likelihood of misunderstandings or conflicts down the line.

In the context of entering a new market, common concerns may include regulatory compliance, cultural differences, or logistical challenges. Proactively addressing these concerns involves conducting thorough market research and due diligence to identify potential pitfalls. Whether it's navigating complex regulatory landscapes or ensuring alignment with local cultural norms, taking preemptive measures to address these concerns fosters a smoother entry into the new market.

Moreover, addressing concerns during negotiations helps align expectations between the parties involved. Clear communication about potential challenges and how they will be managed establishes a framework for collaboration. It allows both parties to make informed decisions and prepares them for the realities of entering a new market.

By anticipating and addressing concerns, businesses set the stage for a more robust and enduring partnership. This proactive approach not only prevents disruptions but also positions the collaboration for success. As businesses venture into new markets, the ability to identify and tackle potential challenges early on is a strategic advantage that contributes to the overall effectiveness of the market entry strategy.

Seek Professional Assistance

Engage negotiation experts or mediators if necessary. Professional assistance can provide an objective perspective, guide the negotiation process, and facilitate constructive discussions.

Strategic partnerships benefit from well-defined structures and effective negotiation tactics. Selecting the appropriate partnership structure and employing collaborative negotiation strategies contribute to the success and sustainability of the collaboration, creating a foundation for mutual growth and achievement of shared objectives.

Chapter **15**

Digital Transformation
and E-commerce Strategies

Chapter 15 will take a look at the transformative realm of digitalization and its profound impact on global commerce. Digital Transformation, a term encompassing the integration of cutting-edge technologies and digital platforms, has become a cornerstone for businesses seeking to expand their global reach and enhance operational efficiency. This chapter explores the strategic deployment of digital tools and the nuanced adaptations within the realm of e-commerce to optimize international sales.

Digital transformation fundamentally reshapes how businesses operate and engage with their audience. It involves harnessing the power of technological advancements to streamline processes, enhance customer experiences, and propel global growth. As companies increasingly navigate a digital-first world, understanding the intricacies of this transformative journey becomes imperative for sustained success.

Within the broader scope of digital transformation, e-commerce strategies take center stage. The chapter delves into how businesses leverage digital platforms to extend their global footprint. From adopting innovative technologies to tailor-made e-commerce adaptations, the strategies discussed aim to navigate the complexities of international markets, offering insights into fostering effective online sales on a global scale.

As we traverse through the nuances of digital transformation and e-commerce strategies in this chapter, the focus remains on providing a comprehensive understanding of how businesses can strategically leverage the digital landscape for unprecedented global reach and navigate the dynamic landscape of international commerce.

Leveraging digital platforms for global reach

In the contemporary business landscape, the strategic utilization of digital platforms stands as a pivotal driver for global expansion and reach. The term 'digital platforms' encompasses a diverse array of online tools, social media channels, and e-commerce platforms that empower businesses to transcend geographical boundaries.

This section explores the profound benefits of harnessing digital platforms for global reach and the transformative impact it has on business dynamics.

Unprecedented Market Access

The digital era has revolutionized the way businesses operate, and one of its standout advantages is the unprecedented market access facilitated by leveraging digital platforms. Unlike the traditional brick-and-mortar model that necessitates a physical presence, digital platforms transcend geographical boundaries, offering businesses the ability to showcase their products or services on a global scale. Through the expansive reach of online channels, companies can connect with potential customers in diverse corners of the world, breaking down barriers that were historically challenging to overcome.

This newfound ability to access global markets without the need for a physical storefront has transformed the landscape for businesses of all sizes. Even small enterprises or startups can now compete on an international stage, reaching audiences that were once considered beyond their grasp. Whether operating from a bustling metropolis or a remote location, businesses can establish a virtual presence that extends far beyond the confines of their immediate surroundings.

The impact of this unparalleled market access extends beyond merely reaching new customers; it fundamentally reshapes the dynamics of global commerce. In the past, expanding into international markets often involved extensive planning, significant investment, and navigating complex logistics. Digital platforms simplify this process, enabling businesses to present their offerings to a worldwide audience with relative ease. This accessibility levels the playing field, allowing companies to compete globally based on the merit of their products or services.

The democratization of market access is particularly evident in the realm of e-commerce. Online marketplaces, social media platforms, and dedicated e-commerce websites serve as gateways to a vast array of consumers, irrespective of their geographic location. A business in a small town can now find customers across borders, and a unique artisanal product can capture the attention of a global audience through the digital marketplace.

Moreover, the flexibility and adaptability inherent in digital platforms further enhance the effectiveness of global market access. Businesses can tailor their online presence to resonate with specific cultural nuances, adjusting content, marketing strategies, and even product offerings to cater to the preferences of diverse international audiences. This adaptability ensures that companies can effectively navigate the nuances of different markets, fostering a more inclusive and resonant engagement with customers worldwide.

For businesses aiming to expand beyond their local or national boundaries, the ability to tap into markets worldwide via digital platforms represents a transformative opportunity. It not only extends the reach but also diversifies revenue streams, reducing dependency on a specific market or region. This diversification contributes to the resilience of businesses, allowing them to weather economic fluctuations or challenges in individual markets.

The unparalleled market access facilitated by digital platforms is a game-changer for businesses operating in the global landscape. It transcends the limitations of traditional business models, offering a transformative means for companies to connect with diverse audiences worldwide. The democratization of global market entry through digital channels empowers businesses to explore new frontiers, fostering growth, innovation, and a more interconnected global marketplace.

Cost-Efficient Marketing and Promotion

In the realm of global business expansion, the cost-efficient nature of marketing and promotion through digital platforms is a transformative advantage. Unlike traditional methods that often involve substantial financial investments, digital avenues provide businesses with a more budget-friendly means to reach a global audience. Social media advertising, an integral component of digital marketing, allows companies to precisely target their desired demographics based on factors such as age, location, interests, and online behavior. This targeted approach ensures that promotional efforts are directed toward individuals who are more likely to be interested in the products or services offered.

Search Engine Optimization (SEO) is another cost-effective strategy within the digital marketing landscape. By optimizing website content for search engines, businesses can enhance their online visibility, making it easier for potential customers to find them organically. This method is particularly beneficial for global reach, as it enables companies to appear in search results relevant to various international markets. The cost savings associated with SEO stem from its ability to attract organic traffic without relying heavily on paid advertising.

Content marketing, a versatile tool in the digital marketing toolkit, allows businesses to create and distribute valuable, relevant, and consistent content to attract and engage a target audience. By crafting content tailored to the preferences and needs of specific global markets, companies can establish themselves as industry authorities and build trust with a diverse customer base. The cost-efficiency of content marketing lies in its long-term impact, as well-crafted content continues to attract and engage audiences over time, reducing the need for constant advertising expenditures.

Furthermore, the inherent flexibility of digital marketing platforms contributes significantly to cost efficiency. Businesses can easily adjust their campaigns, target audiences, and messaging based on real-time data and feedback. This adaptability ensures that marketing budgets are allocated effectively, focusing on strategies that yield the best results in the constantly evolving global market.

In addition to direct cost savings, the cost-efficiency of digital marketing is evident in its measurable impact. Analytics tools associated with digital platforms provide businesses with comprehensive data on the performance of their marketing campaigns. Metrics such as website traffic, conversion rates, and engagement levels are readily available, allowing companies to assess the return on investment (ROI) for each marketing initiative. This data-driven approach empowers businesses to refine their strategies, allocating resources to the most effective channels and optimizing their global marketing efforts.

Ultimately, the cost-efficiency of marketing and promotion through digital platforms extends beyond mere financial savings. It encompasses a strategic and dynamic approach that allows businesses to maximize the impact of their promotional endeavors on a global scale. By harnessing the power of targeted advertising, SEO, content marketing, and adaptable strategies, companies can not only save costs but also enhance the effectiveness of their brand promotion, contributing to sustainable growth in the international marketplace.

Enhanced Customer Engagement and Interaction

In the era of digital transformation, the dynamics of customer engagement and interaction have undergone a profound shift, driven by the capabilities of various digital platforms. The advent of social media, interactive websites, and advanced chat support has redefined how businesses connect with their global audience.

Social media platforms play a pivotal role in fostering direct and immediate communication between businesses and customers worldwide. Companies can leverage these platforms to share updates, promotions, and engage in conversations with their audience in real-time. Customers, in turn, have the opportunity to express their opinions, ask questions, and provide feedback swiftly. This direct line of communication creates a sense of transparency and accessibility, enhancing the overall customer experience.

Interactive websites further contribute to customer engagement by offering dynamic and personalized experiences. Features such as live chat support, product demonstrations, and interactive content keep visitors actively involved. The ability to provide instant assistance through live chat adds a layer of convenience for customers seeking information or assistance. Moreover, interactive elements on websites contribute to a more immersive and memorable user experience, fostering a positive perception of the brand.

The integration of advanced chat support systems represents a significant leap in customer interaction. Chatbots, powered by artificial intelligence, offer instant responses to customer queries, ensuring a timely and efficient resolution of issues. These automated systems operate 24/7, providing customers with support at any time, regardless of their geographical location. The result is not only enhanced customer satisfaction but also increased operational efficiency for businesses handling inquiries on a global scale.

Real-time engagement is particularly crucial in the context of addressing customer queries and concerns promptly. The immediacy of interaction on digital platforms allows businesses to respond swiftly to customer inquiries, building a reputation for reliability and customer-centricity. In the fast-paced global market, where competition is fierce, the ability to offer real-time support can be a decisive factor in winning and retaining customers.

Collecting feedback is an integral part of customer engagement facilitated by digital platforms. Online surveys, feedback forms, and social media polls enable businesses to gather insights directly from their global customer base. This data, in turn, informs product enhancements, service improvements, and overall strategic decision-making. The iterative nature of this feedback loop ensures that businesses remain attuned to customer preferences and can adapt their offerings to evolving market demands.

Building meaningful relationships with customers on a global scale is a multifaceted process enabled by digital platforms. Beyond addressing immediate concerns, businesses can use social media to share behind-the-scenes glimpses, stories, and values. This transparency and authenticity contribute to the humanization of the brand, fostering a sense of connection between customers and the business. Such emotional connections are instrumental in cultivating customer loyalty, as customers are more likely to remain loyal to brands they perceive as genuine and relatable.

Enhanced customer engagement and interaction through digital platforms represent a cornerstone of contemporary business strategies. The ability to connect with a global audience in real-time, provide instant support, and gather feedback is transformative. Businesses that embrace and optimize these digital engagement channels position themselves not only for short-term customer satisfaction but also for the long-term loyalty and advocacy that drive sustained success in the global marketplace.

Data-Driven Decision-Making

In the era of digital transformation, businesses are increasingly relying on data-driven decision-making to navigate the complexities of international markets. Digital platforms serve as powerful data generators, offering a comprehensive view of customer interactions, market trends, and the performance of global outreach initiatives. This wealth of data, when harnessed effectively, becomes a cornerstone for informed decision-making, enabling businesses to tailor their strategies for international expansion.

- **Understanding Customer Behavior**: Digital platforms, particularly e-commerce websites, capture a trove of data related to customer behavior. Analytics tools provide insights into browsing patterns, product preferences, and purchase decisions. By analyzing this data, businesses can discern which products or services resonate most with their international audience, allowing for strategic adjustments to cater to specific market demands. For instance, if certain products gain traction in specific regions, a company can optimize its supply chain to meet the heightened demand in those areas.

- **Tracking Engagement Metrics**: Social media platforms play a crucial role in global outreach, and the engagement metrics derived from these platforms offer valuable insights. Likes, shares, comments, and other interactions provide a real-time gauge of how audiences respond to the brand's messaging and content. Analyzing these metrics enables businesses to understand the effectiveness of their communication strategies in different cultural contexts. For instance, a campaign that resonates well in one country might need adaptation to align with the preferences and sensitivities of audiences in another.

- **Identifying Market Trends**: Digital platforms act as conduits for the rapid dissemination of market trends. Through monitoring online conversations, social media discussions, and tracking emerging patterns, businesses can stay abreast of shifts in consumer preferences and market dynamics. This proactive approach allows companies to anticipate changes in demand or adjust their product offerings accordingly. For instance, an e-commerce retailer can swiftly respond to the popularity of certain product categories in different regions by adjusting marketing campaigns and inventory levels.

- **Consumer Preferences and Personalization**: Data-driven insights empower businesses to understand individual consumer preferences on a global scale. E-commerce platforms often use algorithms to analyze past purchases, search queries, and website interactions to offer personalized recommendations. This level of personalization enhances the customer experience, fostering loyalty and satisfaction. By tailoring marketing messages and product recommendations to suit the diverse preferences of an international customer base, businesses can create more meaningful connections and drive engagement.

- **Effectiveness of Global Outreach Strategies**: Digital platforms provide a measurable framework for assessing the effectiveness of global outreach strategies. Metrics such as website traffic, conversion rates, and customer acquisition costs offer tangible indicators of how well a business is penetrating and resonating in new markets. For example, if a social media campaign aimed at a specific region yields a significant increase in website traffic and conversions, it indicates the success of the strategy in that particular market.
- **Optimizing Marketing ROI:** Informed by data, businesses can optimize their marketing Return on Investment (ROI) by allocating resources where they are most impactful. Through tracking the performance of different marketing channels and campaigns, organizations can identify which avenues deliver the highest returns in specific global markets. This optimization ensures that marketing budgets are strategically allocated to initiatives that generate the most significant impact on brand awareness, customer acquisition, and revenue growth.

The role of data-driven decision-making in international expansion through digital platforms cannot be overstated. By leveraging the insights derived from customer behavior, engagement metrics, market trends, and the effectiveness of outreach strategies, businesses gain a competitive edge in the global marketplace. The ability to make informed decisions not only enhances strategic planning but also positions companies to adapt dynamically to the evolving landscape of international commerce.

Flexibility and Adaptability

In the dynamic landscape of global business, the significance of flexibility and adaptability cannot be overstated, and digital platforms serve as the linchpin for companies seeking to navigate and thrive in this ever-evolving terrain.

- **Real-Time Adjustments and Feedback Utilization:** Digital platforms empower businesses to make real-time adjustments to their strategies. Whether it's refining an online marketing campaign, updating product information on an e-commerce site, or tweaking the messaging on social media, the ability to adapt swiftly is a distinct advantage. This agility is grounded in the capacity to receive immediate feedback from the market. Customer comments, reviews, and analytics data provide invaluable insights that companies can leverage to refine their approach. For instance, if a product receives a sudden surge in interest in a particular region, a business can promptly allocate resources to meet the demand.
- **Market Trend Analysis and Predictive Strategies:** Digital platforms are equipped with sophisticated analytics tools that allow businesses to conduct in-depth market trend analysis. By tracking consumer behavior, preferences, and engagement patterns, companies can discern emerging trends and anticipate shifts in the market. Armed with this data, businesses can proactively adjust their strategies to align with evolving customer expectations. For instance, an e-commerce platform may notice a rising preference for mobile purchases in a specific demographic, prompting the implementation of a mobile-centric marketing strategy.
- **Dynamic Marketing Campaigns:** The adaptability of digital platforms extends to marketing campaigns. Unlike traditional advertising methods that may require significant lead time and resources, digital campaigns can be quickly adjusted to respond to changing circumstances. If a global event or trend becomes prominent, businesses can swiftly integrate these elements into their marketing messages, demonstrating relevance and resonance with the audience. For example, a company leveraging digital advertising can promptly launch a targeted campaign tied to a trending topic, harnessing the immediacy of online platforms.

- **Responsive Online Presence:** Maintaining a dynamic and responsive online presence is fundamental to global success. Digital platforms allow businesses to showcase their brand in a way that resonates with local markets. Whether through localized website content, region-specific social media accounts, or targeted online advertising, companies can tailor their online presence to suit the preferences and cultural nuances of diverse audiences. This adaptability fosters a sense of connection and relatability, crucial elements in building trust and loyalty on a global scale.
- **Product and Service Customization:** The adaptability of digital platforms also extends to product and service offerings. Companies can analyze the performance of products in different markets and tailor their offerings accordingly. This may involve introducing region-specific product variations, adjusting pricing strategies, or even launching exclusive digital promotions for specific regions. By customizing offerings based on the unique demands of each market, businesses can enhance their competitiveness and meet the diverse needs of a global customer base.
- **Crisis Management and Contingency Planning:** In the face of unforeseen challenges, digital platforms provide a lifeline for crisis management and contingency planning. Whether dealing with a global economic downturn, a public relations crisis, or a supply chain disruption, businesses can leverage digital channels to communicate transparently with stakeholders. Social media, in particular, offers a direct line of communication to address concerns, provide updates, and convey the steps being taken to navigate challenges. The ability to swiftly adapt communication strategies is pivotal in maintaining trust and minimizing the impact of crises on a global scale.

The flexibility and adaptability afforded by digital platforms form the cornerstone of successful global business strategies. As markets evolve, consumer behaviors shift, and external factors introduce uncertainties, businesses that can pivot quickly and strategically are positioned not only to survive but to thrive in the dynamic landscape of the global marketplace.

Breaking Down Language Barriers

In the context of global business, overcoming language barriers is facilitated by the transformative capabilities of digital platforms. These platforms, equipped with advanced translation tools and the ability to create multilingual websites, have significantly mitigated challenges posed by linguistic diversity. This transformation broadens business reach and fosters cultural sensitivity, crucial for successful global engagement.

Translation tools play a crucial role in enabling seamless communication across linguistic boundaries. Ranging from machine translation services to sophisticated language processing algorithms, these tools empower businesses to convey accurate messages in multiple languages. For instance, companies launching global marketing campaigns use translation tools to ensure promotional materials resonate effectively with diverse audiences.

Multilingual websites further enhance accessibility for diverse global audiences. Businesses can design websites supporting multiple languages, facilitating an inclusive user experience. This not only broadens the customer base but also demonstrates a commitment to linguistic diversity. An e-commerce platform, for example, can attract a global clientele by offering a multilingual website for a more accessible shopping experience.

Digital platforms also empower businesses to deliver content that is not only translated but localized to suit cultural nuances. This includes adaptations for cultural preferences, idioms, and social norms. By presenting content in a culturally relevant manner, businesses can establish a deeper connection with their audience. A global media streaming service, for instance, can curate content libraries specific to each region, aligning with cultural tastes.

Breaking language barriers through digital platforms inherently broadens the reach of businesses. Companies can confidently target international markets, knowing their digital presence engages audiences in various languages. This aids in reaching new customers and facilitates market penetration by ensuring authentic communication. A technology company, introducing a new software product, can leverage multilingual digital content to penetrate diverse markets effectively.

Beyond practical translation, digital platforms contribute to fostering cultural sensitivity. Businesses can tailor messaging to align with the cultural values of specific regions, demonstrating an understanding of diverse audiences. This enhances the brand's reputation, as customers appreciate efforts to communicate in a way that respects their cultural context. Breaking language barriers through digital platforms becomes foundational for building authentic and culturally aware global relationships.

The capability of digital platforms to break down language barriers represents a transformative force in global communication. Translation tools, multilingual websites, and localized content not only enhance accessibility and reach but also foster cultural sensitivity, crucial for meaningful global engagement. As businesses navigate linguistic diversity through digital innovation, they position themselves to thrive in the rich tapestry of the global marketplace.

24/7 Accessibility

Digital platforms bring a transformative advantage to businesses through their ability to provide 24/7 accessibility. This continuous availability of products and information stands as a significant departure from traditional brick-and-mortar limitations, where operating hours were restricted. In the digital realm, businesses are no longer confined to specific time zones or constrained by conventional working hours. This constant accessibility caters to diverse consumer preferences and varying time zones across the globe.

The unrestricted access to products and information is a fundamental aspect of enhancing the customer experience. Customers, regardless of their geographical location, can engage with a brand, browse products, and seek information at any time. This flexibility aligns with the evolving expectations of modern consumers who value convenience and immediate access. For example, an e-commerce platform allows shoppers from different parts of the world to explore and make purchases whenever it suits them, contributing to a seamless and customer-centric experience.

The significance of 24/7 accessibility extends beyond consumer convenience; it directly impacts a brand's global competitiveness. In the digital landscape, businesses are in perpetual operation, presenting a constant presence to a worldwide audience. This continuous engagement fosters brand visibility and reinforces a company's commitment to serving its customers without temporal constraints. As a result, businesses operating on digital platforms gain a competitive edge by ensuring that potential customers, regardless of their location or the time of day, can interact with the brand.

Moreover, the ability to provide constant accessibility aligns with the expectations of a connected and globalized world. With digital platforms, businesses can establish themselves as responsive and adaptive entities capable of meeting the demands of a diverse and dynamic consumer base. This adaptability not only enhances the brand's reputation but also positions it as a forward-thinking player in the international market.

The 24/7 accessibility facilitated by digital platforms also extends to customer support and service. Businesses can implement chatbots, automated systems, or dedicated support teams that operate around the clock to assist customers, regardless of their location. This proactive approach to customer service contributes to higher satisfaction levels, as consumers appreciate prompt assistance whenever they require it. For instance, an online service provider can utilize automated chat support to address inquiries and provide assistance at any hour, elevating the overall customer experience.

The 24/7 accessibility afforded by digital platforms is a game-changer for businesses operating on a global scale. This continuous availability transcends time zones, caters to diverse consumer preferences, and contributes significantly to the customer experience. Furthermore, it positions businesses as globally competitive entities, capable of meeting the demands of a connected and dynamic international market. As digital platforms continue to evolve, their role in providing uninterrupted access to products, information, and services will remain a cornerstone of success in the modern business landscape.

Elevated Brand Visibility and Recognition

In the realm of global business, a strategically crafted digital presence serves as a powerful tool for elevating brand visibility and recognition. This is particularly evident on various digital platforms, including social media, search engines, and online marketplaces, which collectively amplify a brand's exposure to a global audience. The significance of an enhanced digital presence lies in its ability to set a brand apart in the competitive landscape of the global market, making it more noticeable and memorable.

Social media platforms play a pivotal role in expanding brand visibility. With billions of users worldwide, platforms like Facebook, Instagram, Twitter, and LinkedIn provide businesses with a vast audience to engage with. Through targeted advertising, content sharing, and community building, brands can create a distinctive presence, ensuring their message reaches diverse demographics. For example, a fashion brand can leverage Instagram to showcase its products, connect with a global audience, and build a community around its unique style.

Search engines, as gateways to the vast online landscape, significantly influence brand visibility. A well-optimized online presence ensures that when users search for relevant products or services, a brand appears prominently in search results. Search engine optimization (SEO) strategies, including keyword optimization, content quality, and backlink building, contribute to a brand's visibility and accessibility. For instance, an e-commerce platform specializing in sustainable products can optimize its website to appear prominently in searches related to eco-friendly shopping.

Online marketplaces offer another avenue for brand exposure. Platforms like Amazon, Alibaba, and eBay attract millions of consumers globally. By strategically positioning products on these marketplaces, brands gain access to a massive and diverse customer base. A technology company, for instance, can list its products on multiple online marketplaces to reach consumers worldwide, thereby increasing its brand recognition on a global scale.

The increased recognition resulting from an elevated digital presence is instrumental in attracting both customers and partners. As consumers become more familiar with a brand through repeated exposure online, they are more likely to choose that brand when making purchasing decisions. Similarly, potential business partners are more inclined to collaborate with well-recognized brands, viewing them as reliable and established players in the market.

Moreover, an enhanced digital presence contributes to brand credibility. Consistent and engaging content, positive customer interactions on social media, and a strong online reputation collectively build trust in the brand. Trust is a critical factor in the global market, where customers may be unfamiliar with a brand's history or reputation. A brand known for its reliability and positive online presence stands out as trustworthy in the eyes of consumers.

The benefits of an elevated brand visibility and recognition through a well-executed digital presence are multifaceted. Social media platforms, search engines, and online marketplaces collectively contribute to expanding a brand's reach and making it more noticeable in the competitive global landscape. This heightened visibility not only attracts customers but also builds trust, credibility, and partnerships, positioning the brand for sustained success on the global stage.

In conclusion, the strategic leveraging of digital platforms for global reach opens up a realm of opportunities for businesses. From broadening market access and reducing marketing costs to fostering real-time engagement and breaking down language barriers, the benefits are transformative. In an era where digitalization is a driving force, businesses that effectively harness these platforms position themselves for sustained success in the global marketplace.

E-commerce adaptations and international sales

The adaptation of e-commerce strategies is a pivotal element for businesses seeking to extend their reach across borders. E-commerce adaptations encompass a range of strategies that leverage digital platforms to facilitate international sales, catering to a diverse and geographically dispersed customer base. This multifaceted approach involves considerations related to user experience, payment methods, logistics, and cultural nuances to create a seamless and engaging online shopping environment.

User Experience Optimization

In the dynamic landscape of international e-commerce, crafting a seamless and culturally resonant user experience is a linchpin for success. The process of user experience optimization is a multifaceted strategy that transcends language barriers and aligns digital platforms with the diverse preferences and behaviors of a global clientele.

Central to user experience optimization is the localization of online platforms. This involves translating content into multiple languages to break down linguistic barriers and ensure that users from different regions can access information effortlessly. Imagine a scenario where an e-commerce giant, originating in an English-speaking country, expands its operations to China. By providing a Mandarin language option, the platform caters to the local audience, fostering inclusivity and making the online shopping journey more accessible.

Beyond language translation, user experience optimization delves into the visual and cultural dimensions of a platform. Adapting imagery to align with cultural norms is a crucial step. For example, color preferences, visual aesthetics, and the portrayal of models in promotional images can vary significantly across cultures. A global fashion retailer, venturing into the Middle East, may choose visuals that align with modesty and cultural sensitivities, establishing a deeper connection with the local audience.

Moreover, incorporating region-specific product recommendations enhances personalization. By understanding the unique preferences and trends in specific markets, an e-commerce platform can dynamically showcase products that resonate with local consumers. An electronics retailer, for instance, might highlight smartphones with features popular in Southeast Asia when catering to that market, ensuring that the product assortment aligns with regional preferences.

An illustrative example of user experience optimization can be observed when an e-commerce platform expands into the Japanese market. Here, elements of Japanese design aesthetics could be seamlessly integrated into the platform. From minimalist layouts to the use of symbolic imagery with cultural significance, these adjustments contribute to a user interface that feels familiar and engaging for Japanese consumers. The platform may also consider cultural nuances in product presentation, ensuring that the tone, style, and context align with the expectations of the local audience.

The essence of user experience optimization lies not only in technical adjustments but also in creating an emotional connection with users. A well-crafted online platform goes beyond transactions; it becomes a space where users feel understood, valued, and comfortable. This emotional resonance is particularly crucial in international markets, where cultural sensitivity and a sense of familiarity play pivotal roles in shaping consumer perceptions.

User experience optimization is a strategic imperative for e-commerce adaptations in the realm of international sales. The meticulous localization efforts, spanning language translation, cultural alignment in imagery, and region-specific product recommendations, collectively contribute to a personalized and engaging digital environment. By prioritizing the diverse preferences and behaviors of global audiences, businesses can cultivate a lasting connection with users, fostering loyalty and driving success in the competitive landscape of international e-commerce.

Payment Methods and Currency Considerations

The diversity of global markets extends to payment preferences and currency considerations. E-commerce adaptations involve integrating a variety of payment methods to accommodate the preferences of consumers in different regions. This includes not only major credit cards but also local payment options and digital wallets that are popular in specific markets.

In regions where online payments are commonly made through digital wallets or alternative payment methods, such as Alipay in China or UPI in India, businesses must integrate these options to provide a frictionless checkout experience. Additionally, displaying product prices in local currencies contributes to transparency and helps customers make informed purchase decisions without the need for currency conversions.

Logistics and Supply Chain Optimization

The optimization of logistics and supply chain management plays a pivotal role in shaping the customer experience and overall success of global operations. Efficient logistics practices are instrumental in ensuring timely deliveries, managing customs procedures, and creating a seamless post-purchase journey for customers.

Streamlining the shipping process is a fundamental aspect of logistics optimization. This involves designing a shipping strategy that balances cost-effectiveness with timely deliveries. An e-commerce retailer venturing into international markets may adopt various shipping options based on the preferences and expectations of diverse customer segments. This could include standard shipping, expedited options, or even partnerships with local carriers for last-mile delivery.

Managing customs procedures is another crucial consideration in the international e-commerce landscape. Understanding and navigating the intricacies of customs regulations is essential for preventing delays and ensuring that products reach customers without complications. By staying informed about the specific requirements of each market, businesses can proactively address customs-related challenges and provide customers with a smoother delivery experience.

Transparent tracking mechanisms are integral to customer satisfaction in international e-commerce. Implementing technology that enables real-time tracking allows customers to monitor the progress of their shipments from dispatch to delivery. This transparency not only enhances the customer experience but also builds trust. Customers appreciate visibility into the shipping process, and clear communication about delivery timelines contributes to a positive perception of the brand.

Collaborating with reliable global logistics partners is a strategic approach to overcome the challenges associated with cross-border shipping. Establishing partnerships with logistics providers that have a proven track record in international operations ensures that the e-commerce business can navigate the complexities of different markets effectively. These partners bring expertise in local regulations, customs procedures, and efficient shipping practices, contributing to a smoother and more reliable supply chain.

A practical example of logistics and supply chain optimization in international e-commerce involves the implementation of a strategic fulfillment network. An e-commerce retailer may strategically position fulfillment centers in different regions to reduce shipping times and costs. This approach, known as regional or multi-channel fulfillment, allows businesses to store inventory closer to customers, facilitating quicker deliveries and potentially lowering shipping expenses.

Additionally, leveraging technology is instrumental in enhancing the efficiency of logistics and supply chain operations. Real-time tracking systems, integrated with the e-commerce platform, provide customers with accurate and up-to-date information about their orders. This technology also enables businesses to monitor the movement of goods, identify potential bottlenecks, and proactively address issues that could impact delivery timelines.

Furthermore, technology facilitates real-time updates on customs clearance, a critical aspect of international shipping. Rapid and accurate customs clearance is essential for avoiding delays and ensuring that products reach customers in a timely manner. By leveraging technology solutions that streamline customs procedures, businesses enhance the overall efficiency of their supply chain operations.

Logistics and supply chain optimization form the backbone of successful e-commerce adaptations for international sales. The strategic positioning of fulfillment centers, collaboration with reliable logistics partners, and the integration of technology for real-time tracking contribute to a positive customer experience. As businesses navigate the complexities of cross-border shipping, efficient logistics practices become a key differentiator in fostering customer loyalty and establishing a strong presence in global markets.

Cultural Sensitivity and Marketing Strategies

Cultural sensitivity plays a pivotal role in the success of e-commerce expansions, shaping the way businesses connect with diverse audiences in global markets. Adapting marketing strategies to align with cultural nuances is not merely about language translation; it extends to a deep understanding of local traditions, celebrations, and societal norms. This holistic approach ensures that promotional efforts resonate with the values and preferences of specific target audiences, fostering a sense of connection and trust.

In the realm of e-commerce, tailoring promotional campaigns involves more than just translating written content. It encompasses a visual and emotional alignment with the cultural context of the target audience. Businesses often find success by adjusting marketing visuals to reflect the diversity of their customer base. This inclusivity in imagery not only showcases the brand's commitment to diversity but also helps customers see themselves represented in the products or services offered.

Recognizing local holidays is another key aspect of cultural sensitivity in marketing. Aligning promotional activities with significant cultural or religious events demonstrates a respect for local traditions and enhances the relevance of the marketing message. For example, a global e-commerce platform might tailor its promotions during Chinese New Year to resonate with customers in China, incorporating traditional symbols and themes associated with the celebration.

Incorporating cultural references that resonate with the target audience is a powerful strategy for building a connection. This goes beyond surface-level awareness and delves into understanding the cultural values that matter to the audience. By integrating elements that hold cultural significance, businesses can create campaigns that feel authentic and relatable. Whether it's referencing local folklore, historical events, or cultural symbols, these touches contribute to a deeper connection with the audience.

Beyond the tangible aspects of marketing, businesses also need to be aware of societal norms in different regions. This includes understanding communication styles, appropriate forms of address, and even color symbolism. For instance, colors can carry different meanings in various cultures; adapting to these nuances prevents unintentional cultural missteps that could impact the effectiveness of marketing efforts.

By demonstrating cultural awareness in e-commerce marketing, businesses have the opportunity to go beyond transactional interactions and foster a lasting connection with customers. This connection is not solely about the products or services offered but also about shared values and an understanding of the cultural context in which the business operates. Customers are more likely to engage with brands that acknowledge and respect their cultural identity, contributing to positive brand perception and loyalty.

Cultural sensitivity is a cornerstone of effective e-commerce marketing strategies in global markets. Adapting promotional campaigns to align with cultural nuances involves a thoughtful approach that goes beyond language translation. By reflecting diversity in visuals, recognizing local holidays, incorporating meaningful cultural references, and respecting societal norms, businesses can create a connection that transcends borders. This connection is integral to building a positive brand image, fostering customer trust, and ultimately driving success in the competitive landscape of international e-commerce.

Compliance with Regulatory Requirements

Ensuring compliance with regulatory requirements is a paramount aspect of any successful e-commerce strategy, particularly when venturing into international markets. The intricate web of rules and regulations governing online transactions, data protection, and consumer rights varies significantly from one country to another. Navigating this complex regulatory landscape is not only a legal obligation but also a fundamental strategy for building trust with customers. A noteworthy example of stringent regulatory requirements is found in the European Union with its General Data Protection Regulation (GDPR). The GDPR, implemented to safeguard the privacy and data rights of EU citizens, establishes robust standards for how businesses handle personal data. Adhering to these regulations is imperative for e-commerce businesses seeking to operate in European markets.

Adapting e-commerce practices to align with GDPR involves a multifaceted approach. This includes implementing robust data protection measures, obtaining explicit consent for collecting and processing personal information, and ensuring transparency in data handling practices. Businesses need to provide clear privacy policies, offer options for users to control their data, and promptly address data breach incidents. By doing so, companies not only comply with legal obligations but also convey a commitment to protecting customer privacy.

Building a sense of security and compliance is crucial for fostering trust among European customers. In a landscape where data breaches and privacy concerns make headlines, consumers are increasingly aware of the importance of their data security. Therefore, by proactively aligning with regulatory requirements, e-commerce businesses demonstrate a commitment to safeguarding customer information, which, in turn, enhances their credibility and reputation.

It's important to note that regulatory compliance goes beyond data protection and privacy laws. E-commerce businesses must also consider other aspects, such as consumer protection regulations, taxation rules, and e-commerce-specific laws in each target market. For example, certain countries may require explicit terms and conditions for online transactions, while others may have specific regulations regarding product warranties and returns.

Taking a proactive approach to understand and comply with diverse regulatory frameworks provides e-commerce businesses with a competitive advantage. It ensures smooth operations, minimizes the risk of legal challenges, and establishes a positive relationship with regulatory authorities. Moreover, it enables companies to build a foundation of trust with customers, a critical factor in international markets where consumers may be unfamiliar with the brand or operating in a different legal context.

In conclusion, compliance with regulatory requirements is an integral part of the strategic considerations for e-commerce adaptations in the realm of international sales. From data protection laws like GDPR to country-specific regulations governing online transactions, businesses must navigate a complex web of rules. By diligently adhering to these regulations, companies not only meet legal obligations but also build a foundation of trust, which is indispensable for success in the global e-commerce landscape.

E-commerce adaptations for international sales involve a comprehensive approach that addresses various facets of global market dynamics. Optimizing user experiences, accommodating diverse payment methods, streamlining logistics, demonstrating cultural sensitivity in marketing, and ensuring compliance with regulatory requirements collectively contribute to a successful international e-commerce strategy. By embracing these adaptations, businesses can unlock the vast potential of global markets and establish a strong digital presence that resonates with customers worldwide.

Chapter **16**

Customer Service
Across Borders

Customer service serves as the bridge that connects businesses with their diverse clientele. Customer service refers to the assistance and support provided by a business to its customers before, during, and after a purchase or use of a product or service. It involves addressing customer inquiries, resolving issues, offering guidance, and ensuring a positive and satisfactory experience. Effective customer service is crucial for building and maintaining strong relationships with customers, fostering loyalty, and contributing to a positive brand image. It encompasses various channels such as in-person interactions, phone calls, emails, live chat, and social media interactions, adapting to the diverse preferences of customers.

The significance of customer service extends far beyond resolving issues or answering inquiries; it shapes the very essence of a company's reputation and customer perception. The overarching goal is to create a seamless and positive experience for customers, regardless of their geographical location. A well-crafted global customer service strategy becomes the cornerstone for businesses seeking to navigate cultural nuances, language variations, and diverse expectations in international markets.

Chapter 16 delves into the crucial realm of "Customer Service Across Borders," exploring the profound impact of strategic customer support in fostering lasting relationships and brand loyalty on a global scale.

At its core, this chapter illuminates the art of crafting a global customer service strategy and delves into the technological tools and advancements that propel international support. As businesses transcend borders, the manner in which they address customer needs becomes a pivotal determinant of success. Embracing an inclusive and adaptive approach to customer service not only resolves issues efficiently but also builds trust, enhances brand loyalty, and positions the business for sustained growth in the global arena.

The chapter unfolds with insights into the intricacies of creating a global customer service strategy, emphasizing the need for cultural sensitivity, linguistic versatility, and a deep understanding of international customer expectations. It then navigates through the technological landscape, exploring tools and advancements that empower businesses to provide seamless support across borders. By the end of the chapter, readers will gain a comprehensive understanding of the transformative role customer service plays in international business success and how to leverage technology to ensure unparalleled support on a global scale.

Creating a global customer service strategy

In the interconnected world of business, creating a global customer service strategy is vital for ensuring consistent and high-quality customer experiences across diverse markets. This strategy goes beyond traditional customer service practices, considering cultural nuances, language variations, and the unique expectations of customers worldwide.

Here are essential steps to craft an effective global customer service strategy:

1. Market Research and Cultural Understanding

In the development of a global customer service strategy, the foundational step of market research and cultural understanding plays a pivotal role. This process involves a thorough exploration of the diverse markets a business aims to reach, delving into the intricacies of cultural, social, and economic factors. By gaining insights into the unique characteristics of each market, businesses can tailor their customer service approach to resonate with the specific needs and expectations of local customers.

Understanding customer preferences is a central aspect of this research. Recognizing how customers in different regions prefer to interact, whether through phone calls, emails, live chat, or social media, allows businesses to adapt their communication channels accordingly. This adaptability is essential in meeting customers on platforms they find most comfortable and accessible.

Language considerations are paramount in this context. Identifying the languages spoken in target regions is fundamental for effective customer communication. Multilingual support emerges as a critical component, ensuring that customer service representatives can provide assistance in the languages most relevant to the customer base. This not only facilitates clearer communication but also demonstrates a commitment to inclusivity, making customers feel valued and understood.

Moreover, language considerations extend beyond verbal communication to encompass written content, including website information, product descriptions, and support documentation. Adapting these materials to local languages ensures that customers can engage with the brand in a language they are comfortable with, contributing to a positive and seamless customer experience.

By incorporating market research and cultural understanding into the customer service strategy, businesses set the foundation for customer-centric interactions. This proactive approach positions the business to anticipate and address cultural nuances, resulting in a service that resonates with the diverse backgrounds and expectations of customers across different markets. Through this foundational step, businesses can establish the groundwork for building trust, fostering positive customer relationships, and ultimately enhancing their global reach and competitiveness..

2. Standardized Processes and Protocols

Creating standardized processes and protocols is a foundational element in crafting a robust global customer service strategy. By establishing global standards, businesses aim to provide a consistent and high-quality service experience for customers across diverse geographical locations.

Defining Universal Standards

To initiate this step, companies must meticulously define universal standards that transcend regional disparities. These standards encompass various aspects of customer service, including response times, issue resolution procedures, and communication etiquette. The goal is to create a cohesive framework that ensures a seamless customer experience, irrespective of the specific market dynamics.

Implementing Comprehensive Training Programs

The implementation of comprehensive training programs is pivotal in embedding these global standards within the customer service workforce. Customer service representatives undergo training sessions designed to familiarize them with the standardized processes. This training goes beyond procedural aspects, incorporating elements such as cultural sensitivity and effective communication strategies.

Cultural Sensitivity Training

One critical aspect of the training programs is instilling cultural sensitivity among customer service representatives. Acknowledging and understanding the diverse cultural backgrounds of customers is integral to providing empathetic and relevant support. Representatives learn to adapt their communication styles and problem-solving approaches to align with the cultural nuances of the customers they serve.

Effective Communication Strategies

Training programs emphasize the importance of effective communication strategies in a global context. This involves honing skills in multilingual communication, understanding linguistic subtleties, and employing clarity in written and verbal interactions. By equipping representatives with these skills, businesses enhance their capacity to address customer needs in a manner that resonates across cultural boundaries.

Consistency Across Channels

Standardized processes extend beyond traditional communication channels. Whether customers seek assistance through phone calls, emails, live chats, or social media, a uniform set of procedures ensures consistency in service delivery. This comprehensive approach helps in fostering trust and reliability among customers, reinforcing the brand's commitment to a standardized service experience.

Continuous Evaluation and Improvement

The establishment of standardized processes is not a one-time endeavor; it's an ongoing commitment to excellence. Companies should incorporate mechanisms for continuous evaluation of these processes. Regular assessments, feedback loops, and performance metrics help identify areas for improvement. This iterative approach ensures that global standards remain adaptive and aligned with evolving customer expectations.

Risk Mitigation and Compliance

Standardization plays a crucial role in risk mitigation and compliance. By having consistent processes in place, businesses can navigate legal and regulatory challenges more effectively. Compliance with data protection regulations, for instance, can be standardized across regions, reducing the risk of legal complications and reinforcing trust in customer relationships.

The establishment of standardized processes and protocols is a strategic investment in providing a seamless and uniform customer service experience on a global scale. It empowers customer service teams with the tools and knowledge needed to navigate diverse cultural landscapes while upholding a consistent standard of excellence. This not only contributes to customer satisfaction but also strengthens the brand's reputation as a reliable and customer-focused entity.

3. Technology Integration for Seamless Support

In the contemporary landscape of global customer service, the integration of advanced technologies plays a pivotal role in creating a seamless and efficient support system. This strategic approach not only enhances the overall customer experience but also optimizes the utilization of resources.

Central to this strategy is the integration of a unified customer support platform. This platform serves as a centralized hub that consolidates interactions from diverse channels such as emails, phone calls, live chats, and social media messages. By unifying these communication channels, businesses ensure that customer queries and issues are managed cohesively, irrespective of the channel through which they are initiated.

The advantages of a unified platform extend beyond mere consolidation. It enables customer service representatives to access a comprehensive view of customer interactions and histories, fostering a more informed and personalized support experience. This holistic understanding of customer interactions contributes to quicker issue resolutions and a more responsive service.

The incorporation of artificial intelligence (AI) and automation introduces an additional layer of efficiency into the global customer service strategy. AI-driven technologies, such as chatbots, play a significant role in providing immediate assistance to customers. These intelligent virtual assistants can handle routine inquiries, frequently asked questions, and basic troubleshooting, offering real-time support even outside regular business hours.

The efficiency gains from automation are particularly beneficial in managing high call volumes or surges in customer queries. Automation streamlines repetitive tasks, allowing human resources to focus on more complex and nuanced customer issues that require human intervention. This dual approach enhances the overall responsiveness of the customer service team.

Furthermore, automation contributes to consistency in service delivery. Standardized responses and processes can be programmed into automated systems, ensuring uniformity in addressing common issues. This consistency is vital for maintaining a unified brand image across global markets.

The technological integration doesn't end with implementation; it extends to continuous improvement through data insights. The unified customer support platform and AI-driven systems generate valuable data regarding customer interactions. Analyzing this data provides actionable insights into customer behavior, preferences, and pain points.

Businesses can leverage these insights to refine their support strategies, identify areas for improvement, and anticipate customer needs. For instance, understanding common reasons for customer dissatisfaction allows businesses to proactively address these issues and enhance overall customer satisfaction.

AI technologies also contribute to personalization and predictive support. As the system gathers data on individual customer preferences and behaviors, it can personalize interactions based on historical data. Predictive analytics can anticipate potential issues and provide preemptive solutions, creating a proactive and customer-centric support experience.

The integration of technology for seamless customer support is a transformative approach that aligns with the evolving expectations of global customers. A unified platform, coupled with AI and automation, not only streamlines processes but also elevates the overall quality and efficiency of customer service. This technology-driven strategy positions businesses to provide timely, personalized, and anticipatory support, fostering stronger customer relationships and enhancing their competitive edge in the global marketplace.

4. Multichannel Accessibility

Recognizing the diverse preferences of modern customers, a robust global customer service strategy places significant emphasis on multichannel accessibility. This entails acknowledging that different customers have varying communication preferences and ensuring that support is available through a spectrum of channels.

In implementing multichannel accessibility, businesses need to offer support through a range of communication channels. Traditional avenues such as phone and email coexist with contemporary options like live chat and social media platforms. This diversified approach acknowledges the evolving communication landscape and caters to customers who may have distinct preferences based on the nature of their queries or personal communication habits.

Consistency across all communication channels is paramount. Customers expect a seamless experience, regardless of the channel through which they seek support. This requires uniform responsiveness, standardized processes, and a cohesive approach to issue resolution. Whether a customer initiates contact through email or social media, the quality and efficiency of the support experience should remain consistent.

The global nature of markets introduces the challenge of time zone differences. To address this, a customer-centric strategy strives for 24/7 accessibility. Recognizing that customers may require assistance at any time, businesses implement shifts and support structures that ensure continuous availability. This around-the-clock accessibility not only accommodates customers in different time zones but also caters to those who may have urgent inquiries outside regular business hours.

The advantages of multichannel accessibility extend beyond meeting customer expectations. It contributes to enhanced customer satisfaction, as individuals can choose the channel that aligns with their preferences and urgency of the matter at hand. For instance, a customer with a quick query might prefer the immediacy of live chat, while someone with a more complex issue might opt for email for a detailed and documented interaction.

Moreover, offering diverse communication channels contributes to a more comprehensive understanding of customer needs. Analyzing the usage patterns and preferences across different channels provides valuable insights into customer behavior. Businesses can leverage this data to refine their multichannel strategy, prioritize high-traffic channels, and optimize the allocation of resources for maximum efficiency.

In essence, multichannel accessibility is a customer-centric approach that recognizes the evolving dynamics of communication. By offering diverse channels and ensuring 24/7 availability, businesses not only meet customer expectations but also gain valuable insights, contributing to a more agile and responsive customer service strategy in the global market.

5. Customer Feedback Mechanisms

Feedback Collection: Implement robust mechanisms for collecting customer feedback. Regularly solicit opinions on the quality of service, products, and overall experience.

Based on Feedback: Actively use customer feedback to adapt and improve the customer service strategy. This iterative approach ensures continuous enhancement.

6. Localized Support Teams

In crafting a global customer service strategy, the establishment of localized support teams emerges as a strategic imperative. This approach recognizes the significance of cultural nuances and linguistic diversity in customer interactions, aiming to create a more personalized and effective support experience.

The foundation of localized support teams lies in the formation of regional customer support teams. These teams are strategically composed of individuals familiar with the specific market dynamics, cultural intricacies, and linguistic nuances of the regions they serve. The inclusion of native speakers within these teams ensures a deeper understanding of local languages and dialects, contributing to clearer communication and comprehension.

One of the primary advantages of localized support teams is their ability to resonate with customers on a cultural level. Understanding the cultural context in which customer queries or concerns arise is crucial for providing empathetic and contextually relevant support. This localized approach helps build trust and rapport with customers, as they perceive the support team as not only language-proficient but also culturally attuned.

To further enhance the effectiveness of localized support teams, comprehensive cross-cultural training is imperative. This training equips support representatives with the knowledge and skills necessary to navigate the diverse backgrounds and expectations of customers. It goes beyond language proficiency, delving into cultural norms, communication styles, and sensitivity to cultural differences.

Cross-cultural training aims to bridge potential gaps in understanding that may arise from diverse cultural perspectives. It promotes cultural awareness among support teams, fostering an environment where representatives can adapt their communication and problem-solving approaches to align with the cultural expectations of customers. This adaptability is essential for providing customer service that feels customized and respectful of individual preferences.

Moreover, the cross-cultural training empowers support teams to handle situations where cultural differences may impact customer interactions. It equips them with the tools to navigate misunderstandings, diffuse tensions, and ensure that customers feel heard and valued irrespective of cultural variations.

The localized support team approach is particularly valuable in markets where cultural diversity is pronounced, and customer expectations are shaped by specific cultural norms. It recognizes that effective customer service goes beyond language proficiency to encompass a deep appreciation for the cultural context in which customer interactions unfold.

The integration of localized support teams into a global customer service strategy acknowledges the importance of cultural and linguistic factors in delivering exceptional support. By leveraging regional expertise and investing in cross-cultural training, businesses can create a customer service framework that not only meets the linguistic requirements but also resonates with the diverse cultural backgrounds of their global customer base. This localization strategy contributes to a more personalized and culturally sensitive support experience, fostering stronger customer relationships across varied international markets.

7. Crisis Management and Contingency Planning

The ability to navigate unexpected challenges is integral to maintaining a resilient and reliable customer service strategy. Crisis management and contingency planning form a crucial aspect of this strategy, ensuring businesses are well-prepared to address disruptions effectively.

To initiate a robust response to unforeseen circumstances, it is imperative to develop a comprehensive Global Crisis Response Plan. This plan should encompass a range of potential crises, including but not limited to natural disasters, political unrest, or global events that may impact business operations. The key is to anticipate various scenarios and outline clear protocols for mitigating the impact on customer service.

Contingency planning involves establishing protocols that enable the continuation of customer support during disruptions. These protocols should be designed to ensure minimal disruption to service quality, even in challenging circumstances. The development of such protocols includes identifying alternative communication channels, outlining roles and responsibilities during a crisis, and establishing methods for maintaining transparency and clarity in customer interactions.

Clear communication with customers during times of crisis is paramount. Providing timely and accurate information helps manage customer expectations and builds trust. Businesses should leverage various communication channels, such as email, social media, or a dedicated crisis communication platform, to keep customers informed about the situation, any potential impact on services, and the steps being taken to address the crisis.

Transparency in communication is key. Businesses should openly acknowledge challenges, share their plans for resolution, and provide realistic timelines for the restoration of normal services. This proactive approach demonstrates a commitment to customer satisfaction and helps mitigate potential negative sentiments that may arise during crisis situations.

The global nature of customer service requires businesses to consider regional nuances in their crisis management and contingency planning. Different regions may face distinct challenges, and the response plan should account for these variations. Understanding the local context enables businesses to tailor their communication and support strategies to address the specific concerns of customers in different parts of the world.

Moreover, engaging in scenario planning exercises and regular drills can further refine crisis management strategies. Simulating potential crisis situations allows businesses to assess the effectiveness of their response plans, identify areas for improvement, and ensure that the team is well-prepared to execute the protocols seamlessly.

Incorporating crisis management and contingency planning into the global customer service strategy is not just a precautionary measure; it's a proactive commitment to ensuring customer satisfaction even in the face of unforeseen challenges. By establishing clear response plans, implementing contingency protocols, and maintaining transparent communication, businesses can navigate crises with resilience and uphold their commitment to delivering exceptional customer service on a global scale.

8. Data Security and Privacy Compliance

Ensuring the security of customer data and compliance with privacy regulations is paramount. This strategic imperative not only safeguards sensitive information but also builds trust with customers, reinforcing the credibility of the business on a global scale.

Central to this aspect is the secure handling of customer data. Businesses must implement robust security measures to protect customer information from unauthorized access, breaches, or misuse. Encryption protocols, secure storage solutions, and regular security audits are essential components of a comprehensive data security strategy. Transparent communication about these security measures with customers establishes a sense of trust and confidence, assuring them that their sensitive information is handled with the utmost care.

Compliance with privacy regulations is a multifaceted endeavor, considering the diversity of regulations across different regions. An integral component of this strategy is continuous training for customer service teams on privacy laws and regulations relevant to each market they serve. This ensures that customer interactions align with the specific requirements of the region, mitigating the risk of non-compliance and potential legal repercussions.

Privacy compliance training covers a spectrum of topics, including data collection and storage practices, consent mechanisms, data transfer protocols, and the rights of customers regarding their personal information. This knowledge equips customer service representatives to navigate nuanced privacy landscapes effectively.

A critical element in this training is understanding the nuances of different privacy regulations globally. For example, the European Union's General Data Protection Regulation (GDPR) imposes stringent requirements on businesses handling the data of EU citizens. Training programs need to emphasize the principles of GDPR, such as obtaining explicit consent for data processing, ensuring the right to be forgotten, and implementing data protection impact assessments.

In regions like Asia-Pacific, where privacy laws may vary significantly from one country to another, training becomes even more intricate. Customer service teams must be adept at navigating the specific requirements of each jurisdiction to prevent inadvertent breaches and maintain compliance.

Moreover, businesses should establish clear communication channels with customers regarding data practices. This includes transparent privacy policies, opt-in mechanisms for data processing, and accessible avenues for customers to inquire about or request modifications to their personal information. Transparent communication not only fosters trust but also ensures that customers are well-informed about how their data is handled, aligning with the principles of privacy compliance.

Prioritizing data security and privacy compliance in the global customer service strategy is a foundational element of responsible and ethical business practices. By implementing robust security measures, conducting comprehensive compliance training, and maintaining transparent communication with customers, businesses can navigate the intricate landscape of privacy regulations, build trust, and safeguard the integrity of customer interactions across borders.

Creating a global customer service strategy requires a comprehensive and adaptive approach that aligns with the unique characteristics of each market while maintaining overarching standards for consistency and quality. It's an ongoing process that involves continuous improvement based on customer feedback and evolving market dynamics.

Technology and tools for international support

Leveraging advanced technology and tools is indispensable for providing effective international customer support. These solutions not only enhance operational efficiency but also play a crucial role in meeting the diverse needs of a global customer base.

Here's an exploration of how technology and tools are instrumental in supporting businesses on an international scale:

1. Customer Relationship Management (CRM) Systems

Customer Relationship Management (CRM) Systems play a pivotal role in enhancing international customer support by facilitating personalized interactions and streamlining multichannel support. These systems serve as a centralized repository for comprehensive records of customer interactions, preferences, and feedback. This wealth of data empowers customer service representatives to provide tailored and personalized support, gaining insights into the unique needs and histories of customers from diverse regions. The ability to understand

and cater to individual preferences contributes significantly to customer satisfaction in a global context.

In the realm of multichannel support, CRM systems offer a streamlined approach for businesses serving customers across various platforms. Whether customers choose to engage via email, social media, or live chat, a centralized CRM ensures a cohesive and consistent customer experience. This is particularly crucial for global businesses dealing with customers from different regions, each having its preferred communication channels. By unifying these interactions, CRM systems enable a seamless flow of information, allowing customer service representatives to have a holistic view of customer engagements, regardless of the communication channel used. This not only enhances efficiency but also ensures that customers receive consistent and quality support across diverse platforms.

Moreover, CRM systems contribute to improved customer retention and loyalty by fostering a deeper understanding of customer preferences. By recording and analyzing data related to past interactions and purchase histories, businesses can anticipate customer needs, personalize recommendations, and proactively address concerns. This personalized approach resonates well with customers on a global scale, creating a positive and lasting impression.

The real strength of CRM systems lies in their ability to adapt to the dynamics of international customer support. As businesses expand their global footprint, the need for a unified and standardized approach becomes paramount. CRM systems serve as the linchpin, offering a centralized platform that transcends geographical boundaries. Whether a customer interacts with the business in North America, Europe, or Asia, the CRM system ensures that customer service representatives have access to a consistent set of data, promoting a standardized level of service.

CRM systems serve as a cornerstone for international customer support strategies. By enabling personalized interactions and streamlining multichannel support, these systems empower businesses to navigate the complexities of a global customer base. The seamless integration of data from diverse sources ensures a consistent and tailored approach, contributing to customer satisfaction and loyalty across international markets.

2. Multilingual Chatbots and Automated Systems

In the realm of international customer support, the role of multilingual chatbots and automated systems is paramount, revolutionizing the way businesses interact with a diverse global clientele.

Real-time Assistance in Multiple Languages

One of the key advantages of employing multilingual chatbots and automated systems is their proficiency in delivering real-time assistance in multiple languages. In a globally connected marketplace, where customers may speak different languages, these AI-driven solutions act as linguistic bridge builders. They seamlessly understand inquiries in various languages, process information, and generate instant responses. This capability not only caters to the linguistic diversity of customers but also ensures that language barriers don't hinder efficient communication.

24/7 Availability

Automation technology, embodied in these chatbots and systems, brings the invaluable benefit of 24/7 availability. The global nature of business means that customers might seek assistance at any hour, regardless of time zone differences. Multilingual chatbots, operating round the clock, empower businesses to provide continuous support to customers worldwide. This perpetual availability aligns with the expectations of modern consumers who value instant solutions and ensures that customers from different regions receive assistance whenever they need it. Whether a customer in Asia is facing an issue in the early morning or a customer in Europe needs help late at night, these automated systems ensure that assistance is just a chat away.

Moreover, the 24/7 availability addresses the asynchronous nature of global business operations. With teams and customers distributed across various time zones, having a responsive and multilingual support system becomes not just a convenience but a strategic necessity.

In practical terms, a customer in Japan can interact with a chatbot in Japanese during their daytime, while later in the day, the same chatbot might seamlessly switch to English to assist a customer in a different time zone. This adaptability not only provides efficient support but also enhances the overall customer experience, fostering satisfaction and loyalty.

The integration of multilingual chatbots and automated systems not only breaks down language barriers but also ensures continuous and responsive customer support on a global scale. The combination of linguistic versatility and 24/7 availability positions businesses to meet the diverse needs of their international clientele, contributing to enhanced customer satisfaction and strengthened global relationships.

3. Unified Customer Support Platforms

Unified customer support platforms stand as the cornerstone of modern international customer service strategies, offering a centralized solution for managing diverse customer interactions seamlessly.

Centralized Management of Interactions

In a globalized business landscape where customers engage through various channels, the consolidation of interactions into a single interface is paramount. Unified customer support platforms act as a command center, providing customer service representatives with a comprehensive and holistic view of interactions, irrespective of the communication channel. This holistic approach enables representatives to grasp the complete customer journey, fostering more informed and personalized support.

Efficient Ticketing Systems

Integral to these platforms are efficient ticketing systems designed to organize and prioritize customer queries. These systems categorize inquiries based on urgency, complexity, or other predefined criteria, allowing businesses to address urgent issues promptly and systematically. The structured approach facilitated by efficient ticketing systems ensures that customer support teams can manage their workload effectively, enhancing overall responsiveness and customer satisfaction.

By streamlining the management of diverse customer interactions and introducing efficient ticketing systems, unified customer support platforms not only contribute to operational efficiency but also play a pivotal role in delivering a consistent and high-quality customer experience across global markets. The ability to handle interactions from various channels in a centralized manner aligns with the demands of a global customer base seeking convenience, promptness, and personalized engagement. As businesses continue to expand their reach internationally, the adoption of unified customer support platforms becomes increasingly crucial for maintaining a competitive edge and meeting the expectations of a diverse and geographically dispersed clientele.

Moreover, the centralized nature of these platforms facilitates knowledge sharing among customer support teams, breaking down silos and ensuring a unified approach to addressing customer needs. This collaborative environment enables representatives to access a wealth of information about products, services, and previous interactions, empowering them to provide more informed and efficient support. Consequently, customers benefit from a smoother and more coherent experience, regardless of the geographic location of the support team.

In addition to streamlining customer interactions, unified platforms often include robust reporting and analytics capabilities. These features provide valuable insights into customer behavior, preferences, and emerging trends. Businesses can leverage this data to refine their customer service strategies, identify areas for improvement, and proactively address issues before they escalate. The integration of analytics enhances the adaptability of customer support approaches, allowing businesses to stay agile and responsive in a dynamic international marketplace.

The advantages offered by unified customer support platforms extend beyond operational efficiency and streamlined interactions. They contribute to building a resilient and customer-centric foundation that is essential for success in a globalized business environment. As businesses strive to deliver exceptional customer experiences on an international scale, the adoption of unified customer support platforms emerges as a strategic imperative, empowering organizations to navigate the complexities of diverse markets with agility, consistency, and customer-centricity.

4. Artificial Intelligence (AI) for Sentiment Analysis

In the realm of international customer support, the integration of Artificial Intelligence (AI) for sentiment analysis stands as a transformative force, unraveling valuable insights from customer interactions.

Understanding Customer Sentiments

AI-driven sentiment analysis tools leverage advanced algorithms to assess the sentiments expressed by customers during their interactions. These tools can decipher the emotional tone, attitudes, and opinions embedded in written or verbal communications. This nuanced understanding allows businesses to gauge customer satisfaction levels, identify emerging trends, and gain insights into the overall sentiment surrounding their products or services. By comprehending customer sentiments, businesses can tailor their support strategies to align with the specific needs and expectations of their diverse clientele across global markets.

Proactive Issue Resolution

One of the remarkable advantages of AI-powered sentiment analysis is its ability to enable proactive issue resolution. By identifying negative sentiments early in customer interactions, businesses gain the opportunity to address concerns before they escalate into more significant problems. This proactive approach is particularly crucial in international markets, where addressing issues swiftly and efficiently is paramount for customer satisfaction and retention.

Businesses can leverage the insights gleaned from sentiment analysis to implement targeted improvements, refine products or services, and enhance the overall customer experience. The proactive identification and resolution of issues contribute not only to customer satisfaction but also to the cultivation of a positive brand image, reinforcing the company's commitment to customer-centricity on a global scale.

Furthermore, AI-driven sentiment analysis provides businesses with a real-time pulse on customer perceptions, enabling them to stay agile and responsive to evolving sentiments. This responsiveness is vital in dynamic international markets where customer expectations, preferences, and cultural nuances can vary significantly. By staying attuned to customer sentiments, businesses can adapt their support strategies, communication approaches, and even product offerings to align with the evolving needs of their global customer base.

AI for sentiment analysis serves as a strategic tool that transcends geographical boundaries, offering businesses a deep understanding of their international customer base. By harnessing the power of AI to decipher sentiments, businesses can unlock a wealth of insights that inform decision-making, drive continuous improvement, and foster a customer-centric culture that resonates across diverse markets.

The integration of AI in sentiment analysis represents a forward-looking approach for businesses seeking to elevate their international customer support capabilities, fostering meaningful connections with customers and fortifying their position in the competitive global landscape.

5. Video Conferencing and Virtual Collaboration Tools

The incorporation of video conferencing and virtual collaboration tools serves as a transformative force, enriching communication and fostering collaboration among global teams.

Enhancing Communication

The utilization of video conferencing tools becomes particularly pivotal when addressing complex support issues that benefit from visual explanations or demonstrations. In situations where textual or verbal communication might fall short, the visual element introduced by video conferencing adds a layer of clarity and depth. Customer service representatives can leverage these tools to provide visual walkthroughs, showcase product features, or troubleshoot issues in a more interactive and personalized manner. This visual connectivity not only enhances the quality of support but also contributes to a more engaging and satisfying customer experience.

Facilitating Internal Collaboration

Internally, virtual collaboration tools play a crucial role in ensuring seamless communication among global support teams. In a scenario where teams are dispersed across different geographical locations, the ability to collaborate virtually becomes a cornerstone of efficiency. These tools facilitate real-time information sharing, discussions, and collaborative problem-solving. By breaking down geographical barriers, virtual collaboration ensures that insights and solutions can be rapidly disseminated among team members, leading to faster issue resolution and a consistent support experience across diverse regions.

The integration of video conferencing and virtual collaboration tools into the fabric of international customer support not only addresses the challenges posed by distance but also elevates the overall quality and effectiveness of support interactions. As businesses navigate the intricacies of global markets, the visual connectivity afforded by these tools emerges as a powerful enabler, allowing customer service teams to transcend physical boundaries and deliver a customer experience that is both immersive and responsive. Furthermore, the collaborative aspect extends beyond customer interactions to internal teamwork, fostering a sense of cohesion and shared purpose among support teams irrespective of their geographic dispersion.

6. Data Analytics and Reporting Tools

Data analytics tools play a crucial role in providing businesses with insights into the performance of their customer support operations. These tools enable the tracking of key performance indicators (KPIs) such as response times, resolution rates, and customer satisfaction scores. By meticulously monitoring these metrics, businesses gain a comprehensive understanding of how well their support teams are meeting customer needs and expectations. Performance monitoring not only offers real-time visibility into ongoing operations but also serves as a foundation for informed decision-making and strategic adjustments. For instance, if response times are identified as a critical metric, businesses can implement measures to enhance efficiency and reduce customer wait times, contributing to an improved overall support experience.

Continuous Improvement

The true power of data analytics in customer support lies in its capacity to drive continuous improvement. Through the analysis of customer support data, businesses can identify trends, patterns, and areas for enhancement. By adopting a data-driven approach, organizations gain actionable insights into customer preferences, common pain points, and emerging issues. This information serves as a guide for refining support processes and strategies. For instance, if analytics reveal a recurring challenge faced by customers, businesses can proactively address the root cause, preventing similar issues in the future. Continuous improvement becomes a dynamic and iterative process, fueled by the ongoing analysis of customer support data. By leveraging insights derived from data analytics, businesses can adapt to changing customer expectations, fine-tune their support approaches, and stay ahead of the curve in the competitive landscape.

The integration of data analytics and reporting tools into customer support operations transcends mere performance monitoring; it becomes a catalyst for organizational learning and adaptation. Businesses that harness the potential of these tools not only gain a clearer understanding of their current support landscape but also position themselves to evolve in tandem with the evolving needs and preferences of their global customer base. The iterative nature of continuous improvement, fueled by data-driven insights, ensures that customer support remains a dynamic and responsive function within the broader strategy of international customer engagement.

The integration of technology and tools in international customer support is not merely a convenience but a strategic imperative. These solutions empower businesses to provide personalized, efficient, and proactive support on a global scale. From CRM systems that centralize customer data to AI-driven tools that enhance communication and analysis, the technological arsenal for international support is diverse and essential for thriving in a globally connected business landscape.

Chapter **17**

Navigating Political
and Economic Change

Adeptly navigating political and economic changes is very important in the ever-evolving landscape of international business.

In this chapter, we delve into the benefits of adeptly assessing political risk and stability, as well as the crucial skill of adapting to economic fluctuations. Successful navigation through these dynamic environments is not merely a reactive response; it represents an opportunity for businesses to proactively shape their strategies, fostering resilience, and achieving sustained success amid an ever-changing global landscape.

Assessing political risk and stability

Navigating the complex terrain of international business demands a keen understanding of political risk and stability, as they are pivotal in shaping the success and longevity of ventures in foreign markets. Assessing political risk is not merely a precautionary measure; it is a strategic imperative that empowers businesses to make informed decisions, enhance resilience, and capitalize on opportunities. Here, we unravel the benefits of assessing political risk and stability, shedding light on effective methodologies to undertake this crucial analysis.

Benefits of Assessing Political Risk and Stability:

Informed Decision-Making

The process of assessing political risk plays a pivotal role in fostering informed decision-making within the realm of international business. Businesses that embark on this journey gain valuable insights that contribute to strategic planning and the formulation of effective market entry strategies.

Strategic Planning

Political risk assessment serves as the bedrock for strategic planning in a global landscape. Businesses delve into the intricacies of the political climate to identify potential disruptions and anticipate shifts in government policies. Armed with this foresight, organizations can proactively align their strategies with the prevailing political conditions. Whether navigating changes in regulations or preparing for political unrest, this proactive approach minimizes surprises and fortifies the foundation for smooth business continuity.

Market Entry Strategies

In the realm of international business, the choice of market entry strategy is a critical determinant of success. Political risk assessments become guiding lights in this decision-making process. Businesses carefully analyze the stability and receptivity of the political environment in their target markets. These assessments influence the selection of entry strategies, ensuring they align with the prevailing political conditions.

For instance, a company eyeing a market with political volatility may opt for more cautious market testing initially before committing to extensive investments. On the other hand, in politically stable environments, businesses might confidently pursue direct investments or establish strategic partnerships. The nuances of political risk assessments thus direct businesses towards entry strategies that are not only well-informed but also attuned to the specific challenges and opportunities posed by the political landscape.

Informed decision-making fueled by political risk assessments empowers businesses to navigate the complexities of the international arena with foresight and agility. It transforms uncertainty into strategic advantage, allowing organizations to chart courses that are not just reactive but anticipatory, thereby laying the groundwork for sustainable success on the global stage.

Risk Mitigation

Assessing political risk is not just an exercise in understanding potential challenges; it serves as a foundation for robust risk mitigation strategies. Organizations that delve into political risk assessments often find themselves better equipped to safeguard their interests through insurance, contingency planning, and strategic diversification.

Insurance and Contingency Planning

Understanding political risk prompts businesses to proactively manage potential disruptions through insurance and contingency planning. Political risk insurance becomes a valuable tool to mitigate financial losses resulting from government actions, such as expropriation or regulatory changes. This financial safeguard provides a layer of protection, offering businesses a safety net in volatile political environments.

Contingency plans, tailored to address sudden political changes, further enhance risk mitigation efforts. These plans are designed to ensure operational continuity even in the face of unforeseen political events. By having well-defined procedures in place to respond to political turmoil, businesses can minimize disruptions and maintain a degree of operational stability.

Diversification

Armed with insights from political risk assessments, businesses often leverage diversification as a strategic risk mitigation tactic. Instead of concentrating operations in regions with similar political landscapes, organizations strategically diversify their geographic presence. This diversification is not random but a calculated move to spread operations across countries with varying political conditions.

A diversified portfolio across regions serves as a natural hedge against political uncertainties. If one region faces adverse political events, the impact on the overall operations of the company is mitigated by the stability of operations in other regions. This strategic dispersal ensures that the organization is not overly dependent on the political climate of a single country, reducing the vulnerability to political shocks.

In essence, risk mitigation fueled by political risk assessments is a proactive stance that transforms potential threats into manageable challenges. It reflects a sophisticated understanding of the dynamic interaction between politics and business, allowing organizations to navigate the complexities of the global landscape with resilience and foresight.

Enhanced Stakeholder Confidence:

A robust political risk assessment framework extends its influence to enhance stakeholder confidence, a vital component in the success of any international business. This confidence is particularly critical in the eyes of investors and partners, where a demonstrated understanding of political risk contributes to building trust and credibility.

Investor and Partner Relations

Investors and partners seek assurance that the organizations they engage with are diligent in assessing and managing risks, especially political ones. Regular political risk assessments serve as a testament to an organization's commitment to thorough due diligence. This commitment, in turn, fosters trust among investors and partners who are reassured by the company's proactive stance in understanding and navigating the complexities of the political landscape. As a result, stakeholders are more likely to view the business as a reliable and responsible partner in their ventures.

Supply Chain Management

For businesses with intricate global supply chains, political risk assessments are instrumental in developing a resilient supply chain management strategy. The proactive identification of potential political risks allows organizations to implement contingency plans and mitigation measures. This ensures the reliability and continuity of the supply chain, even in regions where political sensitivities may pose challenges. By demonstrating a thorough understanding of the political dynamics in each region of operation, businesses can build confidence among stakeholders, including suppliers and distributors. This confidence, derived from the organization's ability to navigate political complexities, becomes a cornerstone for sustaining efficient and uninterrupted supply chain operations.

The benefits of enhanced stakeholder confidence extend far beyond immediate interactions. They establish a foundation of trust and reliability that resonates throughout the business ecosystem. Whether in attracting investment, forming strategic partnerships, or ensuring the reliability of the supply chain, political risk assessments become a linchpin in fostering a positive perception among stakeholders, contributing to the overall resilience and success of the international business.

How to Assess Political Risk and Stability

Country Risk Analysis

Conducting a thorough country risk analysis is imperative for businesses venturing into international markets. This multifaceted process involves a comprehensive evaluation of various factors to gauge the overall risk and suitability of a particular country for business operations. Here's an exploration of key elements and considerations in performing country risk analysis:

- **Economic Indicators:** One fundamental aspect of country risk analysis is the evaluation of economic indicators. This involves a meticulous examination of a country's economic landscape, including crucial metrics such as inflation rates, GDP growth, and fiscal policies. Economic stability is intricately linked with political stability, making these indicators essential in assessing the overall risk climate. For instance, a country experiencing high inflation rates and economic volatility might pose challenges for businesses in terms of operational costs and market demand. Conversely, a nation with steady economic growth and sound fiscal policies may offer a more favorable environment for business expansion.

- **Political Landscape:** A detailed examination of the political landscape is paramount in understanding country risk. This encompasses an assessment of political stability, government policies, and the overall political climate. Factors such as political unrest, frequent changes in government, or policies that could adversely impact businesses need to be thoroughly evaluated. For instance, sudden shifts in government policies can lead to regulatory uncertainties, affecting market conditions and business operations. Therefore, a nuanced understanding of the political dynamics is crucial for anticipating potential risks and formulating effective risk mitigation strategies.

- **Legal and Regulatory Framework:** The legal and regulatory framework of a country plays a pivotal role in shaping the risk landscape. Businesses need to analyze the legal systems, regulatory requirements, and compliance standards prevalent in the target country. Understanding the legal framework is essential for ensuring that business operations align with local laws and regulations. Failure to comply with legal requirements can lead to legal disputes, fines, and damage to the company's reputation. A meticulous review of the legal landscape helps businesses navigate complex regulatory environments and establish a solid foundation for their operations.

- **Socio-Cultural Factors:** Socio-cultural factors contribute significantly to country risk analysis. These factors include cultural norms, societal attitudes, and demographic trends. A thorough understanding of the socio-cultural landscape helps businesses tailor their products, services, and marketing strategies to align with local preferences. Ignoring these factors can lead to misalignment with the target market, diminishing the chances of successful market penetration. For instance, a product or advertising approach that is well-received in one culture may not resonate similarly in another, emphasizing the need for cultural sensitivity and adaptation.

- **Market Potential and Competitiveness:** Assessing the market potential and competitiveness within a country is integral to country risk analysis. This involves evaluating the demand for products or services, understanding the competitive landscape, and identifying market trends. An in-depth analysis of market dynamics enables businesses to make informed decisions about market entry and competition strategies. Additionally, understanding the potential for growth and the level of competition aids in setting realistic expectations and formulating effective market entry plans.

Country risk analysis is a multidimensional process that necessitates a holistic examination of economic, political, legal, socio-cultural, and market-related factors. Businesses that invest time and resources in conducting thorough country risk analysis are better equipped to make informed decisions, mitigate potential risks, and establish a solid foundation for successful international ventures.

Political Institutions

Conducting a comprehensive country risk analysis involves a systematic examination of various factors, and the strength and stability of political institutions stand out as a critical dimension. This assessment delves into understanding the structure and functioning of political institutions within a country, with a particular focus on the legal system and regulatory frameworks.

- **Legal System Evaluation:** The legal system forms the backbone of a country's governance, shaping the rules and regulations that govern businesses and individuals. In a country risk analysis, evaluating the legal system involves assessing its fairness, transparency, and efficiency. A robust legal system that upholds the rule of law provides a stable foundation for businesses to operate, ensuring that contracts are enforceable, property rights are protected, and disputes are resolved impartially. Conversely, a weak or unpredictable legal system may pose risks, as businesses could face challenges in navigating legal complexities or may encounter difficulties in seeking legal remedies.

- **Regulatory Frameworks:** Examining the regulatory frameworks is an integral part of assessing country risk. Regulations set the parameters for business operations, covering areas such as taxation, licensing, environmental standards, and labor practices. A conducive regulatory environment fosters a business-friendly atmosphere, encouraging investment and growth. Conversely, excessive bureaucracy, inconsistent regulations, or frequent changes in regulatory policies can introduce uncertainties and challenges for businesses. Through country risk analysis, businesses can gain insights into the predictability and stability of the regulatory landscape, allowing them to adapt strategies accordingly.

- **Indicators of Stability:** Indicators of political stability can also be derived from the strength of political institutions. An analysis might consider the historical stability of government structures, the effectiveness of law enforcement agencies, and the overall level of political cohesion. Countries with well-established and resilient political institutions are often associated with lower political risk, as they provide a reliable and consistent governance framework. Conversely, nations facing frequent changes in leadership, institutional instability, or a lack of adherence to the rule of law may present higher political risks.

In practice, this aspect of country risk analysis involves a combination of desk research and, where possible, on-the-ground assessments. Analysts may study legal frameworks, review historical trends, and engage with local experts to gain a nuanced understanding of the political institutions in a given country. The goal is to gauge the reliability and predictability of the political environment, providing businesses with valuable insights to make informed decisions about entering or operating in a particular market.

Geopolitical Analysis:

Within the realm of assessing political risk, a comprehensive geopolitical analysis is a cornerstone for businesses aiming to navigate the intricate landscape of international operations. This multifaceted approach involves a nuanced examination of regional dynamics and historical relationships between countries.

Regional Dynamics

Understanding the dynamics between nations within a specific region is paramount in geopolitical analysis. Countries often share historical ties, economic dependencies, or geopolitical alliances that influence their interactions. Tensions or collaborations within a region can significantly impact businesses operating within it. For instance, a sudden deterioration in diplomatic relations between two neighboring countries may lead to trade restrictions, affecting the supply chain and market access for businesses. Conversely, positive regional dynamics may present opportunities for collaboration and streamlined operations.

Conflict Analysis

Delving into the history of conflicts and political unrest within a region provides crucial insights for anticipating potential risks. Persistent political instability is a red flag that requires careful consideration. Businesses should analyze the root causes, durations, and resolutions of past conflicts to gauge the likelihood of similar issues arising in the future. This analysis informs decision-making regarding market entry, supply chain management, and overall business strategies.

For example, a company eyeing expansion into a region with a history of prolonged political unrest may need to implement robust risk mitigation strategies. These could include diversified sourcing to minimize supply chain vulnerabilities, close monitoring of local developments, and contingency plans to swiftly respond to any emerging challenges. Conversely, regions with a history of stable political environments may offer a more conducive setting for long-term investments and strategic business expansion.

Geopolitical analysis goes beyond assessing immediate political events; it involves understanding the broader context that shapes political landscapes. By incorporating regional dynamics and conflict analyses into their risk assessment frameworks, businesses can make informed decisions that align with the geopolitical realities of the areas in which they operate. This proactive approach positions companies to navigate political changes more adeptly and seize opportunities even in regions with complex geopolitical dynamics.

Government Stability

A critical facet of assessing political risk involves evaluating the stability of the government, as it significantly influences the overall political environment. To navigate political and economic changes successfully, businesses must focus on key elements related to government stability.

Leadership Changes

Monitoring leadership changes, elections, and potential shifts in government policies is paramount. Sudden leadership changes or policy shifts can introduce uncertainties that may impact businesses. By staying informed about political transitions, organizations can adapt their strategies to align with the priorities and ideologies of the new leadership. Understanding the political landscape allows businesses to anticipate potential challenges and opportunities that may arise with changes in government, enabling them to make informed decisions to safeguard their interests.

Corruption Index

Assessing the level of corruption within the government is a crucial aspect of political risk evaluation. Transparency International's Corruption Perceptions Index offers valuable insights into the perceived levels of corruption in different countries. Businesses can leverage this index to gauge the risk of encountering corrupt practices and assess the potential impact on their operations. High levels of corruption may lead to issues such as bureaucratic hurdles, unethical business practices, or uneven playing fields. Armed with this knowledge, organizations can implement risk mitigation strategies, such as enhanced due diligence and compliance measures, to navigate the challenges associated with corruption and ensure ethical business conduct in their operations.

In scrutinizing government stability provides businesses with a comprehensive understanding of the political landscape in which they operate. By staying attuned to leadership changes and corruption levels, organizations can proactively manage political risks. This proactive approach equips businesses with the foresight needed to adapt swiftly to political changes, fostering resilience in the face of uncertainties and contributing to sustained success in the global arena.

Legal and Regulatory Environment

A vigilant approach to assessing political risk extends to the legal and regulatory landscape, where changes can significantly impact the operational landscape for businesses. The evolving nature of regulations, taxation policies, and industry-specific laws necessitates a constant monitoring mechanism for businesses operating internationally.

Regulatory Changes

Political risk assessments play a crucial role in keeping businesses informed about changes in regulations and laws. Staying abreast of alterations in taxation policies, trade regulations, and industry-specific laws allows organizations to anticipate and adapt to the evolving legal landscape. For instance, a sudden shift in trade regulations may impact the cost structure of imports and exports, influencing pricing strategies and supply chain decisions. By integrating these insights into strategic planning, businesses can proactively navigate the legal complexities, ensuring compliance and mitigating potential risks associated with regulatory changes.

Contractual Protections

Implementing robust contractual protections is a strategic move in response to potential political risks. Contracts that account for unforeseen changes in the political landscape provide businesses with flexibility and adaptability. For example, including clauses that allow renegotiation in the event of regulatory changes or force majeure events related to political instability can safeguard the interests of all parties involved. These contractual safeguards serve as a mechanism for risk-sharing, ensuring that businesses can respond effectively to unforeseen political developments without incurring undue legal or financial consequences.

The legal and regulatory environment is a critical dimension within the realm of political risk. A thorough understanding of the potential impacts of regulatory changes and the implementation of contractual protections positions businesses to navigate the intricacies of the legal landscape confidently. By proactively addressing these considerations, organizations can enhance their ability to respond to political shifts, ensuring legal compliance and minimizing disruptions to operations.

Assessing political risk and stability is a multifaceted endeavor crucial for businesses venturing into international markets. By proactively engaging in comprehensive analyses and leveraging strategic risk management approaches, organizations position themselves not only to weather political uncertainties but also to thrive amid evolving geopolitical landscapes.

Adapting to economic fluctuations and change

Economic fluctuations refer to the periodic variations in economic activity, marked by shifts in factors such as GDP growth, employment rates, inflation, and overall business cycles. These fluctuations are inherent in any economy and can pose challenges for businesses. However, by adopting adaptive strategies, organizations can not only weather economic uncertainties but also position themselves to capitalize on emerging opportunities.

Understanding Economic Fluctuations

Understanding Economic Fluctuations is paramount for businesses seeking to navigate the complexities of dynamic economic environments. Economic fluctuations, often referred to as business cycles, are the natural oscillations in economic activity characterized by alternating periods of expansion and contraction. During expansion, the economy experiences robust growth, increased employment, and rising consumer spending. On the other hand, contractions involve a slowdown in economic activity, higher unemployment rates, and reduced consumer spending.

Recognizing the Signs of Expansion and Contraction is a foundational step for businesses. Various economic indicators serve as barometers for these shifts. For instance, a surge in GDP, increased industrial production, and a decline in unemployment rates are indicative of an expanding economy. Conversely, a contracting economy may exhibit a decline in GDP, reduced manufacturing output, and an uptick in unemployment. By closely monitoring these indicators, businesses gain insights into the broader economic landscape, enabling them to make informed decisions.

Anticipating Changes in Demand is a strategic outcome of understanding economic fluctuations. During periods of economic expansion, consumer confidence is generally high, leading to increased demand for goods and services. Businesses can leverage this opportunity to expand production, invest in new markets, and capitalize on heightened consumer spending. Conversely, in economic contractions, consumers tend to become more cautious, leading to a potential decline in demand. Businesses equipped with a thorough understanding of economic shifts can proactively adjust production levels, manage inventory, and implement targeted marketing strategies.

Adjusting Resource Allocation is a pragmatic response to economic fluctuations. In periods of expansion, businesses may allocate resources toward expansion initiatives, such as hiring additional staff, investing in technology, or launching new product lines. Conversely, during economic contractions, a more conservative approach to resource allocation may involve cost-cutting measures, revisiting expansion plans, and optimizing operational efficiency. Flexibility in resource allocation allows businesses to adapt swiftly to changing economic conditions.

Aligning Strategic Plans is the ultimate goal of understanding economic fluctuations. A business operating in an expanding economy may align its strategic plans with growth objectives, including market penetration, diversification, and innovation. Conversely, in a contracting economy, strategic plans may focus on resilience, cost control, and positioning for recovery. By aligning strategic plans with the prevailing economic conditions, businesses position themselves for sustained success while navigating the intricacies of dynamic economic landscapes.

Understanding economic fluctuations is a strategic imperative for businesses. It empowers organizations to recognize the signs of expansion and contraction, anticipate changes in demand, adjust resource allocation, and align strategic plans accordingly. In a globalized and interconnected world, where economic conditions can impact businesses across borders, a nuanced understanding of economic fluctuations serves as a compass for navigating uncertainties and seizing opportunities.

Build Financial Resilience

Building financial resilience is a fundamental strategy for businesses to navigate the challenges posed by economic fluctuations. This approach involves establishing a strong financial foundation that enables organizations to withstand downturns, capitalize on opportunities, and maintain stability during periods of uncertainty.

- **Prudent Budgeting:** Prudent budgeting is a critical component of financial resilience. Businesses should develop realistic budgets that account for various economic scenarios. By accurately forecasting revenues, expenses, and potential risks, organizations can allocate resources effectively. Prudent budgeting allows businesses to identify areas where cost efficiencies can be achieved and resources redirected to strategic priorities.

- **Cash Flow Monitoring:** Monitoring cash flow is paramount for financial resilience. A comprehensive understanding of cash inflows and outflows allows businesses to identify patterns, anticipate liquidity challenges, and implement timely adjustments. Regular cash flow analysis enables organizations to maintain optimal working capital levels, ensuring operational continuity even in challenging economic conditions.

- **Risk Assessment:** Conducting thorough risk assessments is integral to building financial resilience. Businesses should identify and evaluate potential risks associated with economic fluctuations, market dynamics, and external factors. This includes assessing the impact of currency exchange rate fluctuations, interest rate changes, and geopolitical events. By understanding these risks, organizations can implement risk mitigation strategies and prepare for potential disruptions.

- **Establishing Financial Buffers:** During periods of economic growth, businesses should proactively establish financial buffers. This involves accumulating cash reserves that serve as a financial cushion during downturns. Financial buffers provide the flexibility to continue essential operations, invest in strategic initiatives, and explore growth opportunities when competitors may be constrained by financial challenges.

- **Seizing Investment Opportunities:** Financial resilience not only involves safeguarding against economic downturns but also positioning the organization to seize investment opportunities. During economic contractions, asset prices may experience declines, presenting strategic investment possibilities. Businesses with financial resilience can capitalize on these opportunities, acquiring assets, expanding market presence, or investing in innovation when competitors may face financial constraints.

- **Adaptability in Resource Allocation:** Building financial resilience enables businesses to adapt their resource allocation strategies dynamically. During economic expansions, organizations can allocate resources to growth initiatives, research and development, and market expansion. In contrast, during economic contractions, flexibility in resource allocation allows businesses to prioritize essential functions, streamline operations, and preserve financial stability.

- **Debt Management:** Effective debt management is crucial for financial resilience. Businesses should assess their debt levels, terms, and interest rates, ensuring that debt obligations align with the organization's financial capacity. Managing debt prudently during economic expansions minimizes financial strain during contractions. Businesses can negotiate favorable terms, refinance debt when advantageous, and strategically use debt to fund growth initiatives.

Building financial resilience involves a comprehensive approach encompassing prudent budgeting, cash flow monitoring, risk assessment, establishing financial buffers, seizing investment opportunities, adaptability in resource allocation, and effective debt management. By incorporating these strategies into their financial practices, businesses not only enhance their ability to withstand economic fluctuations but also position themselves for sustainable growth and success in dynamic and uncertain economic environments.

Diversification of Revenue Streams

Diversifying revenue streams is a strategic imperative for businesses aiming to fortify themselves against the impacts of economic fluctuations. The concept revolves around the principle of not putting all proverbial eggs in one basket, thereby reducing vulnerability and enhancing overall resilience in the face of economic uncertainties.

A central motivation behind revenue stream diversification is the reduction of vulnerability during economic downturns. When a business is heavily dependent on a single market or product line, it becomes more susceptible to the specific challenges that may arise in that segment during economic contractions. By diversifying, an enterprise can spread its risks across various sectors, acting as a safeguard when one sector experiences a decline.

One avenue for diversification is entering new markets. Expanding geographic reach allows businesses to tap into different economic climates and consumer behaviors. For example, a technology company experiencing a downturn in one region might find growth opportunities by entering emerging markets where demand for its products or services is on the rise. This strategic move not only provides a buffer against economic volatility but also opens avenues for capturing new market share.

Another facet of revenue stream diversification involves expanding product offerings. Businesses can introduce complementary or entirely new products to cater to different consumer needs or trends. This not only safeguards against fluctuations in demand for specific products but also positions the business to capitalize on emerging market trends. For instance, a clothing retailer diversifying into accessories or athleisure wear can create a more resilient revenue portfolio.

Diversifying revenue streams can also be achieved by targeting different customer segments. Tailoring products or services to meet the needs of distinct demographics or industries provides a hedge against economic downturns that might impact a specific customer base. A technology company, for instance, can diversify its clientele by offering specialized solutions for both businesses and individual consumers.

The essence of revenue stream diversification lies in mitigating risks associated with economic volatility while simultaneously exploring untapped opportunities. By having multiple revenue streams, businesses can offset losses in one area with gains in another. This resilience enables enterprises to weather economic storms more effectively and positions them to capitalize on emerging opportunities that may align with diversified offerings.

Ultimately, revenue stream diversification contributes to enhancing the overall resilience of a business. In a dynamic economic landscape, where fluctuations are inherent, businesses with diversified revenue streams are better equipped to adapt and navigate challenges. Such adaptability not only ensures survival during economic downturns but also positions the business for sustained growth in the long run.

Diversifying revenue streams is not merely a risk mitigation strategy but a proactive approach to navigating the complexities of economic variability. By entering new markets, expanding product offerings, and targeting different customer segments, businesses position themselves as agile entities capable of thriving in diverse economic environments. This strategic diversification is a cornerstone for sustained success in an ever-changing business landscape.

Agile Supply Chain Management

In the dynamic landscape of economic fluctuations, an agile supply chain stands as a cornerstone for businesses seeking resilience and adaptability. The essence of agility in supply chain management lies in the capacity to swiftly respond to changing market dynamics, ensuring operational efficiency, and cost-effectiveness in the face of economic shifts.

Optimizing the supply chain for flexibility and responsiveness is paramount. Businesses can achieve this by leveraging advanced technologies such as predictive analytics and efficient inventory management systems. These tools provide real-time insights into market trends, enabling businesses to make data-driven decisions and adjust their supply chain strategies accordingly.

One key aspect of an agile supply chain is the ability to respond promptly to changes in demand forecasts. During economic upswings, when consumer demand surges, businesses with agile supply chains can scale their operations seamlessly to meet the increased demand. This scalability ensures that products are readily available to meet market demands, contributing to customer satisfaction and capturing opportunities for revenue growth.

Conversely, during economic downturns or periods of reduced demand, an agile supply chain enables businesses to streamline operations effectively. This might involve optimizing inventory levels, implementing cost-saving measures, or adjusting production schedules to align with the prevailing economic conditions. The flexibility to scale down operations efficiently allows businesses to manage costs without compromising on operational efficiency. Predictive analytics plays a crucial role in forecasting demand patterns and identifying potential disruptions in the supply chain. By analyzing historical data, market trends, and external factors, businesses can anticipate fluctuations in demand and proactively adjust their supply chain strategies. This foresight enhances overall supply chain resilience, minimizing the impact of economic uncertainties on operational efficiency.

An agile supply chain is not just about reacting to immediate changes but also about proactively positioning the business for long-term success. It involves cultivating a culture of continuous improvement, where processes are regularly reviewed and refined based on performance data and market insights. This iterative approach ensures that the supply chain remains adaptive and responsive to evolving economic landscapes.

The adoption of an agile supply chain management approach is a strategic response to economic fluctuations. By optimizing for flexibility, responsiveness, and cost efficiency, businesses can navigate the challenges posed by economic shifts. Leveraging technology, predictive analytics, and a commitment to continuous improvement, an agile supply chain becomes a dynamic asset that empowers businesses to thrive in a volatile economic environment.

Strategic Workforce Planning

Adapting to economic fluctuations necessitates strategic workforce planning, a dynamic approach that aligns an organization's human resources with the changing demands of the economic landscape. This strategic adaptation is crucial for businesses aiming to optimize their workforce during both periods of economic expansion and contraction.

In times of economic expansion, businesses often witness an increased demand for skilled talent. Strategic workforce planning involves proactive measures to address this demand, ensuring that the organization is equipped with the right talent to capitalize on growth opportunities. Investment in employee development programs becomes paramount, providing current employees with the skills and knowledge needed to meet the evolving demands of an expanding market. Additionally, robust recruitment strategies come into play, aiming to attract top-tier talent that can contribute to the organization's success during periods of heightened activity.

Conversely, during economic contractions, strategic workforce planning takes a different form. Businesses must navigate leaner periods with a focus on cost-effective measures while preserving the core competencies needed for future growth. Cross-training employees becomes a valuable strategy, allowing for flexibility in task assignments and ensuring that individuals possess a broader skill set. This not only enhances the adaptability of the workforce but also provides a buffer against potential downsizing requirements.

Implementing flexible work arrangements is another element of strategic workforce planning during economic contractions. Businesses can explore options such as reduced work hours, remote work, or alternative work schedules. These approaches help organizations retain valuable talent while adjusting to reduced demand, fostering a more resilient workforce.

Temporary workforce reductions may become necessary during economic contractions, requiring a delicate balance between maintaining operational efficiency and managing costs. Strategic workforce planning involves assessing which areas of the business can sustain temporary reductions without compromising long-term goals. This might include implementing hiring freezes, voluntary leave programs, or temporary layoffs with clear plans for reintegration when economic conditions improve.

Strategic workforce planning is an ongoing process that aligns with the cyclical nature of economic fluctuations. Businesses must be agile in adapting their workforce strategies to meet the unique challenges presented by both expansion and contraction phases. A dynamic and well-thought-out approach to workforce planning positions organizations to optimize their human capital, ensuring that talent is deployed effectively to support the overall goals and resilience of the business.

Market Intelligence and Scenario Planning

In the dynamic realm of business, where economic landscapes are subject to continual shifts, staying ahead of the curve requires a proactive approach centered on market intelligence and scenario planning. These twin strategies empower businesses to navigate economic fluctuations with foresight and strategic acumen.

At the heart of proactive economic adaptation lies market intelligence – the systematic gathering, analysis, and interpretation of information relevant to a business's market. This encompasses a wide spectrum of data, including economic indicators, consumer behavior, industry trends, and competitive landscapes. By investing in robust market intelligence, businesses equip themselves with a comprehensive understanding of the forces shaping their operating environment.

For example, a retail company leveraging market intelligence might track consumer spending patterns, identify emerging trends in the retail sector, and monitor the activities of competitors. This continuous flow of information enables the business to detect shifts in demand, stay attuned to evolving consumer preferences, and strategically position itself within the competitive landscape.

Complementing market intelligence is the practice of scenario planning – a strategic exercise that involves envisioning and preparing for different potential futures. Rather than relying on a single forecast, scenario planning encourages businesses to explore various economic scenarios and craft adaptive strategies for each. This proactive stance allows enterprises to respond swiftly and effectively to unfolding circumstances.

Consider a manufacturing company engaged in scenario planning. In preparation for economic uncertainty, the company may develop scenarios ranging from a robust economic expansion to a downturn. For each scenario, it formulates tailored strategies. In an economic upturn scenario, the company might plan for increased production capacity and expanded market outreach. Conversely, in a downturn scenario, it could implement measures such as cost-cutting, inventory optimization, and diversification of revenue streams.

Armed with market intelligence and scenario planning, businesses are better positioned to execute strategic responses when faced with economic fluctuations. For instance, if market intelligence signals a potential economic downturn, a business might proactively adjust pricing strategies to remain competitive while safeguarding profit margins. Similarly, insights into changing consumer behaviors can inform inventory management strategies, ensuring that product offerings align with evolving demands.

Furthermore, scenario planning allows businesses to explore partnerships and collaborations as a means of enhancing resilience. Recognizing that economic challenges may be mitigated through strategic alliances, companies can initiate discussions with complementary businesses, suppliers, or distributors to share resources and navigate uncertainties collectively.

Market intelligence and scenario planning form a dynamic duo, empowering businesses to proactively adapt to economic variability. The ability to anticipate changes in the economic landscape, coupled with strategic responses tailored to different scenarios, positions businesses not just as reactive entities but as architects of their destinies. In the ever-shifting tapestry of the global economy, those armed with foresight and adaptability are better equipped to thrive.

Governmental and Regulatory Engagement

In business and the economy, governmental and regulatory landscapes play pivotal roles. Adaptation to economic fluctuations demands a nuanced understanding of policies and regulations that can shape the business terrain. Governmental and regulatory engagement emerges as a strategic imperative, offering businesses the means to not only stay informed but actively contribute to the shaping of policies that impact their operations.

Understanding the complex web of regulations and policies requires a proactive stance. Businesses can engage with governmental bodies and regulatory authorities through various channels. One effective avenue is participation in industry associations and forums where discussions on policy matters take center stage. These associations provide a platform for businesses to collectively voice concerns, offer insights, and advocate for policies that foster a conducive business environment.

Through active engagement in industry associations, businesses gain access to valuable information about ongoing and proposed regulatory changes. Regular updates on legislative developments, industry-specific regulations, and potential shifts in economic policies become integral components of a proactive strategy. Armed with this information, businesses can anticipate the impact of regulatory changes on their operations and initiate timely adjustments. Moreover, dialogues with policymakers facilitate a mutual exchange of perspectives. Businesses can share their unique insights into market dynamics, challenges, and opportunities, contributing valuable input to the policymaking process. By actively participating in these conversations, companies position themselves not merely as subjects of regulations but as stakeholders with a voice in shaping the rules that govern their sectors.

Consider a manufacturing company operating in an industry subject to environmental regulations. Through engagement in industry associations, the company becomes aware of impending changes in emission standards. This foresight enables the company to invest in eco-friendly technologies, modify production processes, and align its operations with the forthcoming regulations. Such proactive measures not only ensure compliance but also foster environmental stewardship, aligning the business with evolving societal expectations.

Furthermore, governmental and regulatory engagement allows businesses to play a role in shaping policies that affect their industries. Through constructive dialogue, companies can advocate for regulatory frameworks that strike a balance between fostering economic growth and addressing societal concerns. This involvement positions businesses as responsible corporate citizens actively contributing to the broader socio-economic landscape.

In the realm of international business, the importance of governmental and regulatory engagement is magnified. Operating across borders brings forth a diverse array of regulations, trade policies, and geopolitical considerations. Businesses engaged in global operations must navigate a complex tapestry of international laws and agreements. Engaging with governmental bodies, both domestically and internationally, becomes essential for ensuring compliance, understanding geopolitical risks, and influencing policies that impact cross-border trade.

Governmental and regulatory engagement is not merely a defensive strategy to mitigate risks; it is a proactive approach that empowers businesses to thrive amidst economic fluctuations. By actively participating in policy discussions, staying informed about regulatory changes, and contributing to the formulation of rules that govern their industries, businesses position themselves as architects of their regulatory destiny. In the ever-evolving landscape of economic policies, those who engage wisely stand better equipped to navigate the twists and turns of the regulatory terrain.

Adapting to economic fluctuations requires a multifaceted approach that combines financial resilience, strategic diversification, agile supply chain management, workforce planning, market intelligence, and engagement with regulatory environments. By adopting these adaptive strategies, businesses not only navigate challenges posed by economic uncertainties but also position themselves for sustained growth and resilience in dynamic economic landscapes.

Chapter 18

Maintaining Agility
and Innovation

- Keeping entrepreneurial spirit alive during growth
- Continuous innovation in a multinational context

Chapter **19**

Sustainability and
Corporate Social Responsibility

The notions of sustainability and corporate social responsibility (CSR) have evolved from mere buzzwords to fundamental pillars of organizational success. Sustainability entails mindful practices that consider environmental, social, and economic impacts, while CSR encompasses a company's commitment to ethical behavior and positive contributions to society.

This chapter delves into global sustainability practices and ethics, exploring the ways businesses can build a responsible multinational company. From eco-friendly initiatives to socially responsible endeavors, it explores the transformative power of aligning business strategies with values that benefit both the planet and humanity.

Global sustainability practices and ethics

Sustainability and ethical practices have become integral components of responsible business operations in the global arena. Embracing global sustainability practices requires a comprehensive approach that addresses environmental impact, social responsibility, and ethical considerations.

Here's how businesses can achieve global sustainability practices and ethics:

1. Environmental Stewardship

Environmental stewardship is a fundamental aspect of global sustainability practices, requiring businesses to adopt strategies that mitigate their impact on the environment. Global companies aiming to minimize their ecological footprint employ a range of initiatives.

One critical strategy is the adoption of sustainable and eco-friendly practices within their operations. This includes implementing energy-efficient technologies, which not only reduce carbon emissions but also contribute to cost savings. For instance, investing in renewable energy sources, such as solar or wind power, can power manufacturing processes, offices, and other facilities, showcasing a commitment to environmental responsibility.

Another key aspect of environmental stewardship involves waste reduction. Global businesses actively work to minimize waste generation throughout their operations. This can involve initiatives like optimizing production processes to reduce excess material, implementing recycling programs, and responsibly managing waste disposal. By embracing circular economy principles, businesses can transform waste into resources, contributing to a more sustainable and responsible approach.

Utilizing renewable resources is an integral part of environmental stewardship. Companies are increasingly transitioning from finite resources to renewable alternatives. This might include sourcing raw materials from sustainable suppliers, utilizing recycled materials in production, or exploring innovative materials that have a lower environmental impact. By prioritizing renewable resources, businesses contribute to the preservation of natural ecosystems and biodiversity.

As an illustrative example, a global technology company committed to environmental stewardship might introduce eco-friendly packaging materials. This initiative not only aligns with sustainability goals but also appeals to environmentally conscious consumers. Additionally, incorporating energy-efficient technologies in their manufacturing processes reduces the company's overall carbon footprint, showcasing a dedication to sustainable practices.

Environmental stewardship in global businesses involves a holistic approach, encompassing energy efficiency, waste reduction, and the use of renewable resources. By implementing these strategies, businesses not only contribute to the global sustainability agenda but also demonstrate their commitment to responsible and ethical practices in the pursuit of long-term environmental health.

2. Supply Chain Transparency

Supply chain transparency is a critical component of ethical and sustainable business practices, gaining prominence as consumers and stakeholders demand accountability throughout the production process. This entails businesses adopting a comprehensive approach to ensure visibility and traceability across their supply chains. Ethical considerations encompass fair labor practices, environmental sustainability, and adherence to responsible sourcing principles.

Ethical Labor Practices

Central to supply chain transparency is the commitment to fair and ethical labor practices. This involves scrutinizing suppliers to ensure they provide fair wages, safe working conditions, and respect for workers' rights. Businesses conduct thorough audits and assessments of suppliers' labor practices, aiming to eradicate any form of exploitation, discrimination, or unsafe working conditions. By enforcing strict ethical standards, companies contribute to the well-being of workers along the entire supply chain.

Environmental Standards

Sustainable supply chain practices extend beyond labor considerations to encompass environmental standards. Companies committed to transparency in their supply chains prioritize suppliers that adhere to environmentally responsible practices. This involves assessing the environmental impact of suppliers' operations, evaluating resource management, and promoting initiatives for reduced carbon footprints. By aligning with environmentally conscious suppliers, businesses contribute to the global effort to mitigate climate change and promote sustainable resource management.

Responsible Sourcing Verification

Ensuring the responsible sourcing of materials and components is fundamental to supply chain transparency. Businesses actively collaborate with suppliers who share a commitment to ethical sourcing, avoiding engagement with those associated with practices such as illegal logging, conflict minerals, or environmental degradation. Verification processes, including third-party certifications and audits, play a crucial role in confirming that suppliers adhere to responsible sourcing principles. This scrutiny contributes to the overall integrity of the supply chain.

Audits and Collaboration

Regular audits are integral to maintaining supply chain transparency. Companies conduct comprehensive assessments of their suppliers, evaluating compliance with ethical and sustainability standards. Collaborative efforts involve working closely with suppliers to address any identified issues, implement improvements, and foster a shared commitment to ethical conduct. This collaborative approach is not punitive but rather aims to build long-term partnerships based on shared values and responsibility.

Elimination of Unethical Suppliers

A transparent supply chain necessitates decisive action when unethical practices are identified. Businesses must be willing to sever ties with suppliers engaging in unethical behavior, whether related to labor exploitation, environmental violations, or other unethical practices. Eliminating such suppliers sends a strong message about the company's commitment to ethical conduct and helps maintain the integrity of the supply chain.

Supply chain transparency is a multifaceted commitment that requires ongoing diligence and collaboration. By actively engaging in responsible sourcing, conducting thorough audits, and eliminating unethical suppliers, businesses not only meet consumer expectations but also contribute to building a more ethical and sustainable global supply chain.

3. Social Responsibility

Sustainability practices in the global business landscape extend beyond environmental considerations to embrace social responsibility. A foundational element of this commitment involves establishing ethical labor standards to ensure fair treatment, respect for employee rights, and overall well-being. This encompasses policies prohibiting practices such as child labor, forced labor, and discrimination, while concurrently promoting fair wages, safe working conditions, and opportunities for professional growth.

Diversity and inclusion within the workplace form another critical facet of social responsibility. Companies are urged to create environments valuing individuals from diverse backgrounds, fostering gender equality, cultural diversity, and equal opportunities. This not only aligns with social responsibility principles but also enriches the organizational landscape by bringing in a variety of perspectives that stimulate creativity and innovation.

Community development initiatives stand as a tangible manifestation of a company's social responsibility. These initiatives may include supporting local communities through educational programs, healthcare initiatives, and infrastructure development. For instance, a globally operating company might invest in educational projects, providing scholarships, constructing schools, or offering vocational training. Such endeavors not only enhance the well-being of local communities but also contribute significantly to the overall sustainability of the business. Engaging in projects that support and uplift local communities is a strategic approach to fulfilling social responsibility. This participation could involve collaborating with local businesses, contributing to healthcare clinics, or supporting environmental conservation efforts. By actively addressing the specific needs of the communities in which they operate, companies demonstrate a commitment to social responsibility that goes beyond the boundaries of their business operations.

Fair employment practices represent a cornerstone of social responsibility. Companies should actively work towards ensuring equality in hiring, promotions, and professional development, providing equal opportunities for career advancement irrespective of factors such as gender, race, or background. Creating an inclusive work environment contributes not only to building a socially responsible corporate culture but also to fostering a sense of equity and fairness among employees.

Social responsibility within global sustainability practices involves upholding ethical labor standards, fostering workplace diversity and inclusion, engaging in community development initiatives, supporting local communities, and implementing fair employment practices. By embracing these principles, businesses not only contribute to their own sustainability but also play a crucial role in the well-being and advancement of the broader global community.

4. Ethical Governance and Compliance

Ensuring ethical governance is an integral component of fostering global sustainability within business operations. It involves the meticulous embedding of ethical principles throughout the organizational culture, emphasizing the importance of integrity, transparency, and accountability in decision-making processes. By embracing ethical governance, businesses can not only enhance their own reputation but also contribute to the development of a more responsible and sustainable global business environment.

Compliance with international regulations and industry standards stands as a foundational element of ethical governance. Adhering to established norms not only ensures ethical conduct but also demonstrates a commitment to upholding global expectations. This compliance extends beyond legal requirements to encompass industry-specific standards and ethical benchmarks that resonate with the broader societal values. Businesses operating with a global footprint should stay abreast of evolving international regulations and adapt their practices accordingly to maintain ethical alignment.

A robust code of conduct serves as a guiding framework for ethical governance. It outlines the organization's ethical expectations and provides employees with a clear understanding of the principles that should govern their actions. This code acts as a reference point for decision-making, guiding employees on ethical considerations in various scenarios. Regular communication and reinforcement of the code of conduct contribute to building a strong ethical foundation within the corporate culture.

Ethical training programs for employees play a crucial role in fostering ethical governance. These programs educate employees about the company's values, ethical expectations, and the potential consequences of unethical behavior. Training sessions often include case studies, interactive discussions, and real-world examples to provide practical insights into ethical decision-making. By investing in ongoing ethical education, businesses empower their workforce to navigate complex situations with a keen awareness of ethical considerations.

Conducting regular compliance assessments is another essential practice within ethical governance. These assessments evaluate the organization's adherence to ethical standards, uncovering areas that may require improvement. This process involves internal audits, third-party evaluations, and continuous monitoring to ensure that the company's operations align with ethical principles. Through regular assessments, businesses can identify and address potential ethical challenges before they escalate, fostering a proactive approach to maintaining ethical standards.

Ethical governance and compliance are pivotal elements of global sustainability practices. Businesses that prioritize ethical decision-making, comply with international regulations, establish robust codes of conduct, provide ethical training, and conduct regular compliance assessments contribute not only to their own sustainability but also to the broader ethical framework of the global business landscape.

5. Stakeholder Engagement

Engaging with stakeholders is a vital element for ensuring transparency, inclusivity, and long-term success. Stakeholders include a broad spectrum ranging from customers and employees to local communities, and the degree of engagement with each group significantly influences a company's sustainability efforts.

Customer Engagement

Actively involving customers in sustainability initiatives and decision-making processes is pivotal. Seeking feedback on products, services, and corporate practices helps businesses align their strategies with customer expectations. This can involve conducting surveys on environmental preferences, incorporating sustainable features into products, or providing transparent information about a company's commitment to ethical practices. By engaging customers in these ways, businesses not only meet consumer expectations but also cultivate a loyal customer base that values sustainability.

Employee Involvement

Engaging employees in sustainability initiatives not only boosts morale but also brings diverse perspectives to the table. Inclusivity in decision-making processes and involving employees in corporate sustainability programs create a sense of ownership and shared responsibility. Companies can encourage employees to contribute ideas, participate in volunteering programs, or even initiate their own sustainable projects within the organization. This engagement fosters a culture of sustainability within the workplace and empowers employees to be active participants in the company's ethical journey.

Community Collaboration

Local communities are integral stakeholders, and their engagement is essential for sustainable practices. Collaboration with communities involves understanding their needs, concerns, and expectations. This can take the form of supporting local businesses, implementing environmental conservation projects, or addressing community-specific challenges. By actively engaging with local communities, businesses not only contribute to the well-being of those they impact but also build a foundation of trust and positive relationships.

Transparent Communication

Transparency is a fundamental aspect of stakeholder engagement. Clear and honest communication about corporate practices, sustainability goals, and any challenges faced is crucial for building and maintaining trust. This transparency extends to addressing concerns raised by stakeholders promptly and effectively. Whether it's responding to customer inquiries, sharing updates with employees, or collaborating with local communities, open communication establishes a foundation of trust that is essential for the success of sustainable and ethical business practices.

Stakeholder engagement in sustainable practices involves actively involving customers, employees, and local communities in decision-making processes, seeking their input and feedback, and ensuring transparent communication. By fostering a culture of inclusivity and collaboration, businesses not only enhance their sustainability efforts but also create a positive impact on the diverse stakeholders they engage with.

6. Innovation for Sustainability

Encouraging and fostering innovation is a pivotal strategy in achieving global sustainability practices for businesses. By investing in research and development initiatives that prioritize sustainability goals, companies can contribute significantly to the broader environmental and societal well-being. This commitment to innovation is not only forward-thinking but also aligns with the imperative to address global challenges.

One avenue for innovation in sustainability involves research and development efforts aimed at creating sustainable technologies, products, and services. For instance, businesses can focus on developing energy-efficient products that minimize environmental impact during manufacturing, usage, and disposal phases. By embracing innovation in this realm, companies contribute to the larger goal of reducing energy consumption and mitigating the ecological footprint associated with traditional manufacturing processes.

Exploring and investing in renewable energy solutions is another facet of innovation that aligns with sustainability goals. Transitioning towards renewable energy sources not only reduces a company's carbon footprint but also supports the global shift towards cleaner, more sustainable energy practices. This innovative approach is increasingly critical as businesses strive to meet their energy needs while simultaneously minimizing their impact on the environment.

Incorporating circular economy principles into product design represents a paradigm shift that emphasizes sustainability throughout the entire product lifecycle. Instead of adhering to a linear model of production and consumption, where products are made, used, and discarded, a circular economy promotes designing products with an emphasis on reusability, recycling, and minimizing waste. Companies embracing this innovative approach contribute to reducing the strain on natural resources, lowering waste generation, and fostering a more sustainable approach to consumption.

Moreover, innovation for sustainability extends beyond products to encompass service-oriented solutions. Businesses can explore innovative service models that promote resource efficiency, such as sharing or subscription services. By encouraging a shift from ownership to access, companies contribute to a more sustainable consumption pattern, reducing the overall demand for new products and minimizing the environmental impact associated with manufacturing and disposal.

Innovation for sustainability in global business involves strategic investments in research and development, focusing on sustainable technologies, renewable energy solutions, and embracing circular economy principles. By prioritizing innovation aligned with sustainability goals, businesses not only position themselves as leaders in environmental responsibility but also contribute to a more resilient and sustainable global future.

7. Measurement and Reporting

In the realm of global sustainability practices, the establishment of robust measurement and reporting mechanisms is paramount. Businesses committed to sustainability often define key performance indicators (KPIs) to assess their environmental impact, social responsibility initiatives, and adherence to ethical standards. This meticulous tracking not only provides an accurate snapshot of the company's sustainability performance but also enables the identification of areas for improvement and strategic adjustments.

Environmental metrics represent a critical aspect of sustainability measurement. This involves quantifying a company's carbon footprint, energy consumption, water usage, and waste generation. Establishing benchmarks and KPIs for these metrics allows businesses to set specific targets, monitor progress, and implement strategies to minimize environmental impact. Regularly assessing and reporting on these metrics not only demonstrates transparency but also reflects a commitment to mitigating the environmental consequences of business operations.

Social impact measurement is equally essential in the context of global sustainability practices. Companies engaged in social responsibility initiatives should evaluate the effectiveness of their programs by assessing their impact on local communities, employee well-being, and societal inclusivity. Metrics related to community engagement, diversity and inclusion, and employee satisfaction contribute to a comprehensive understanding of the company's social impact.

Adherence to ethical standards is a fundamental element of sustainability measurement. Companies need to track their compliance with established ethical guidelines, ensuring that their operations align with principles such as fair labor practices, human rights protection, and anti-corruption measures. Monitoring ethical standards involves internal assessments, third-party audits, and transparent reporting on the company's commitment to upholding ethical business practices.

Regular reporting on sustainability metrics is typically done through sustainability reports. These documents serve as a communication tool, allowing businesses to share their achievements, challenges, and future sustainability goals with stakeholders. Sustainability reports often include a detailed breakdown of environmental, social, and governance (ESG) metrics, providing a comprehensive overview of the company's commitment to global sustainability.

The act of reporting on sustainability metrics contributes to the accountability and transparency of a business. Stakeholders, including investors, customers, and employees, can evaluate the company's sustainability performance and make informed decisions based on this information. Transparency in reporting not only builds trust but also fosters a culture of continuous improvement as companies strive to meet and exceed their sustainability goals.

Measurement and reporting in global sustainability practices involve the establishment of key performance indicators, tracking environmental metrics, assessing social impact, monitoring adherence to ethical standards, and communicating these efforts through sustainability reports. This systematic approach not only allows businesses to gauge their sustainability performance but also reinforces their commitment to responsible and ethical business practices on a global scale.

8. Collaboration and Partnerships

In the pursuit of global sustainability practices, collaboration and partnerships play a pivotal role in fostering collective efforts towards shared environmental and social goals. Businesses, industry peers, non-governmental organizations (NGOs), and governmental bodies can collaborate to leverage collective knowledge, expertise, and resources, amplifying the impact of sustainability initiatives.

Forming partnerships with industry peers who share a commitment to sustainability allows businesses to pool resources and engage in joint initiatives. For example, companies within a particular sector may collaborate on research and development projects focused on eco-friendly technologies or collectively work towards reducing their carbon footprint. By sharing best practices and insights, these collaborations enhance the overall effectiveness of sustainability efforts.

NGOs are key allies in driving global sustainability practices. Collaborating with environmental and social-focused NGOs provides businesses with valuable insights, expertise, and access to networks dedicated to sustainability causes. Joint initiatives may include supporting conservation projects, implementing responsible sourcing practices, or participating in advocacy campaigns. Such collaborations not only contribute to environmental and social causes but also enhance a company's credibility and reputation.

Engaging with governmental bodies is essential for aligning sustainability practices with regulatory frameworks and policy initiatives. Businesses can collaborate with governments on sustainability policies, participate in industry consultations, and provide input on environmental and social legislation. By actively participating in the regulatory process, companies can help shape policies that promote sustainability while ensuring compliance with legal requirements.

Collaborative initiatives go beyond individual business interests and can address systemic challenges on a global scale. Issues such as climate change, human rights, and poverty require collective efforts for meaningful impact. Collaborating with a diverse range of stakeholders allows businesses to contribute to addressing these complex challenges, whether through supporting global initiatives like the United Nations Sustainable Development Goals or participating in industry-wide sustainability frameworks.

Partnerships also play a crucial role in driving innovation for sustainability. Collaborating with research institutions, academic organizations, and startups can lead to the development of innovative solutions to environmental and social challenges. For example, a technology company might collaborate with a university on research projects focused on sustainable practices within the tech industry.

Collaboration and partnerships are integral components of achieving global sustainability practices. Whether working with industry peers, NGOs, or governmental bodies, businesses can leverage collective expertise and resources to address environmental and social challenges. By forming alliances and actively participating in collaborative initiatives, companies contribute to the development of a more sustainable and ethical global business environment.

In conclusion, global sustainability practices and ethics are multifaceted, requiring a holistic and integrated approach. Businesses that prioritize environmental stewardship, supply chain transparency, social responsibility, ethical governance, stakeholder engagement, innovation, measurement, and collaboration are better positioned to navigate the complex landscape of global sustainability and corporate social responsibility.

Building a responsible multinational company

Establishing a responsible multinational company involves integrating sustainability and corporate social responsibility (CSR) into the core fabric of business operations. This not only aligns with ethical principles but also addresses the growing expectation from stakeholders for businesses to contribute positively to society and the environment.

Here are key strategies to achieve a responsible multinational company:

1. Define Clear Sustainability Goals

Defining clear sustainability goals is the foundational step for any responsible multinational company. These goals serve as a guiding compass, aligning the company's actions with its values and societal expectations. By setting measurable objectives, businesses can articulate their commitment to environmental and social responsibility. For instance, a company might establish goals to reduce carbon emissions, signaling a dedication to mitigating its environmental impact. Simultaneously, goals related to supply chain transparency underscore a commitment to ethical sourcing, ensuring that the entire value chain adheres to fair labor practices and environmental standards. Promoting social inclusion and supporting community development may represent additional goals, demonstrating a commitment to broader societal welfare.

Clear sustainability goals act as a roadmap, providing a structured framework for integrating sustainability into the core fabric of the organization. These goals not only guide decision-making at various levels but also set the tone for how the company aims to contribute positively to the world. For example, a multinational company with a goal to enhance supply chain transparency might implement initiatives such as regular supplier audits, ethical sourcing practices, and partnerships with suppliers who align with their sustainability objectives.

Moreover, the definition of these goals involves a thoughtful examination of the company's values and the expectations of the broader society it serves. By considering these factors, businesses can identify areas where their actions can make a meaningful impact, fostering a sense of purpose and responsibility. This process of goal-setting is not just about compliance but reflects a proactive stance toward making a positive contribution to environmental, social, and community welfare.

In practice, a multinational company setting sustainability goals might commit to a percentage reduction in carbon emissions over a specific timeframe. This could involve investing in renewable energy sources, improving energy efficiency in operations, or adopting eco-friendly practices. Similarly, goals related to supply chain transparency might include implementing traceability systems, ensuring fair labor practices, and reducing the environmental footprint of the supply chain. Social inclusion goals could involve diversity and inclusion programs within the workforce, aiming to create a more representative and equitable organizational culture.

Ultimately, these goals are not static; they should evolve with the changing landscape of societal expectations and environmental challenges. The iterative nature of goal-setting allows companies to continuously reassess their impact and adapt their strategies to remain at the forefront of sustainability practices. Through clear sustainability goals, companies signal their commitment to responsible business practices, providing a solid foundation for the integration of sustainability into the very essence of their multinational operations.

2. Integrate Sustainability into Corporate Strategy

Integrating sustainability into the corporate strategy is a fundamental step for companies aspiring to be responsible and contribute positively to the environment and society. Sustainability should not be a standalone initiative but seamlessly woven into the fabric of the organization's overall strategy.

Aligning sustainability goals with business objectives is crucial for fostering a synergy that benefits both the company and its stakeholders. For instance, if a business objective is to increase operational efficiency, a corresponding sustainability goal could involve reducing energy consumption or waste production. This alignment ensures that sustainability is not perceived as a parallel effort but is directly connected to the company's core mission and values.

By embedding sustainability into corporate strategy, organizations can weave eco-friendly and socially responsible practices into their day-to-day operations. This integration encompasses various aspects, including product development, supply chain management, and market expansion strategies. For instance, when developing new products, companies can prioritize eco-friendly materials, production processes with lower environmental impact, and consider the product's entire life cycle.

In supply chain management, integrating sustainability means working closely with suppliers to ensure they adhere to ethical and environmental standards. Companies can implement criteria that suppliers must meet regarding fair labor practices, reduced carbon footprint, and responsible resource usage. This integration fosters a sustainable supply chain that aligns with the company's overall strategic objectives.

Moreover, when expanding into new markets, businesses can consider sustainability factors in their market entry strategies. This involves assessing the environmental and social impact of their operations in the new market, adapting products or services to local sustainability expectations, and aligning with the values of the local community. By doing so, companies not only respect the cultural and environmental nuances of different regions but also enhance their reputation as responsible global citizens.

The integration of sustainability into corporate strategy also promotes long-term resilience. As businesses face increasingly complex and interconnected global challenges, having sustainability ingrained in their strategic decision-making processes enables them to navigate uncertainties more effectively. Whether responding to regulatory changes, shifting consumer preferences, or addressing environmental concerns, a company with sustainability at its strategic core is better positioned to adapt and thrive.

Furthermore, integration fosters a culture of responsibility throughout the organization. When sustainability is part of the corporate strategy, employees at all levels become more conscious of their environmental and social impact. This awareness can lead to innovative solutions, increased efficiency, and a shared commitment to the company's broader mission.

The integration of sustainability into corporate strategy is not just a trend; it's a strategic imperative for responsible businesses. It goes beyond meeting compliance requirements or gaining positive PR; it becomes a guiding principle that influences every decision and action. This holistic approach ensures that sustainability is not an isolated effort but an integral part of the organization's DNA, driving positive change both internally and in the broader global context.

3. Implement Ethical Supply Chain Practices

Integrating sustainability into the corporate strategy is a fundamental step for companies aspiring to be responsible and contribute positively to the environment and society. Sustainability should not be a standalone initiative but seamlessly woven into the fabric of the organization's overall strategy.

Aligning sustainability goals with business objectives is crucial for fostering a synergy that benefits both the company and its stakeholders. For instance, if a business objective is to increase operational efficiency, a corresponding sustainability goal could involve reducing energy consumption or waste production. This alignment ensures that sustainability is not perceived as a parallel effort but is directly connected to the company's core mission and values.

By embedding sustainability into corporate strategy, organizations can weave eco-friendly and socially responsible practices into their day-to-day operations. This integration encompasses various aspects, including product development, supply chain management, and market expansion strategies. For instance, when developing new products, companies can prioritize eco-friendly materials, production processes with lower environmental impact, and consider the product's entire life cycle.

In supply chain management, integrating sustainability means working closely with suppliers to ensure they adhere to ethical and environmental standards. Companies can implement criteria that suppliers must meet regarding fair labor practices, reduced carbon footprint, and responsible resource usage. This integration fosters a sustainable supply chain that aligns with the company's overall strategic objectives.

Moreover, when expanding into new markets, businesses can consider sustainability factors in their market entry strategies. This involves assessing the environmental and social impact of their operations in the new market, adapting products or services to local sustainability expectations, and aligning with the values of the local community. By doing so, companies not only respect the cultural and environmental nuances of different regions but also enhance their reputation as responsible global citizens.

The integration of sustainability into corporate strategy also promotes long-term resilience. As businesses face increasingly complex and interconnected global challenges, having sustainability ingrained in their strategic decision-making processes enables them to navigate uncertainties more effectively. Whether responding to regulatory changes, shifting consumer preferences, or addressing environmental concerns, a company with sustainability at its strategic core is better positioned to adapt and thrive.

Furthermore, integration fosters a culture of responsibility throughout the organization. When sustainability is part of the corporate strategy, employees at all levels become more conscious of their environmental and social impact. This awareness can lead to innovative solutions, increased efficiency, and a shared commitment to the company's broader mission.

The integration of sustainability into corporate strategy is not just a trend; it's a strategic imperative for responsible businesses. It goes beyond meeting compliance requirements or gaining positive PR; it becomes a guiding principle that influences every decision and action. This holistic approach ensures that sustainability is not an isolated effort but an integral part of the organization's DNA, driving positive change both internally and in the broader global context.

4. Foster Diversity and Inclusion

Promoting diversity and inclusion is a crucial pillar in building a responsible multinational company. Acknowledging and embracing diverse perspectives not only contributes to a more vibrant and dynamic workplace but also aligns with ethical principles and societal expectations. Here's an in-depth exploration of fostering diversity and inclusion within an organization:

Equal Opportunities for All

A responsible multinational company understands the significance of providing equal opportunities for all employees, irrespective of their backgrounds. This involves creating a level playing field where individuals are assessed based on their skills, capabilities, and potential, rather than factors such as gender, ethnicity, or cultural background. By ensuring equal opportunities, the company contributes to a fair and meritocratic work environment.

Addressing Unconscious Biases

Unconscious biases can inadvertently influence decision-making processes within an organization. Recognizing and addressing these biases is fundamental to fostering diversity and inclusion. Companies can implement training programs to raise awareness about unconscious biases, enabling employees to make more informed and unbiased decisions in recruitment, promotions, and other aspects of talent management.

Inclusive Workplace Policies

Establishing inclusive workplace policies is essential for creating an environment where every employee feels valued and included. This includes policies that address issues like discrimination, harassment, and unequal treatment. Clearly defined policies set the tone for an inclusive culture and provide a framework for addressing any instances of non-compliance.

Diversity at All Levels

A responsible multinational company ensures that diversity is not confined to specific roles or levels within the organization. Diversity initiatives should span across all levels, from entry-level positions to leadership roles. This holistic approach ensures that diverse perspectives are represented at every decision-making level, contributing to a more comprehensive and well-rounded organizational strategy.

Cultural Competency Training

To foster inclusion, organizations can provide cultural competency training to employees. This training enhances awareness and understanding of different cultures, traditions, and communication styles. It encourages employees to appreciate diversity and work collaboratively, breaking down cultural barriers and promoting a harmonious work environment.

Employee Resource Groups

Establishing Employee Resource Groups (ERGs) is an effective strategy for promoting diversity and inclusion. These groups provide a platform for employees with shared characteristics or experiences to connect, support one another, and contribute to organizational initiatives. ERGs can focus on various aspects of diversity, such as gender, ethnicity, LGBTQ+ inclusion, and more.

Mentorship and Sponsorship Programs

Mentorship and sponsorship programs play a pivotal role in fostering diversity by providing guidance and support to underrepresented groups. Mentorship connects employees with experienced professionals who can offer advice and insights, while sponsorship involves influential individuals advocating for the career advancement of their protégés. These programs help break down barriers and create pathways for diverse talent to excel.

Metrics and Accountability

To ensure progress, a responsible multinational company establishes metrics to measure diversity and inclusion efforts. Regularly tracking these metrics provides insights into the effectiveness of diversity initiatives and areas that may need improvement. Accountability mechanisms, such as tying diversity goals to performance evaluations, further emphasize the organization's commitment to fostering an inclusive workplace.

Fostering diversity and inclusion is not just an ethical imperative but a strategic advantage for a responsible multinational company. By promoting equal opportunities, addressing biases, implementing inclusive policies, and supporting initiatives that span all levels of the organization, companies can create a workplace where diversity is celebrated, and inclusion is embedded in the organizational culture. This, in turn, contributes to a more innovative, resilient, and socially responsible business.

5. Engage Stakeholders Effectively

Engaging stakeholders effectively is a pivotal aspect of building a responsible multinational company with a strong commitment to sustainability and corporate social responsibility (CSR). Stakeholders encompass a broad spectrum, including customers, employees, local communities, and investors. Establishing transparent and open communication channels is crucial to foster a two-way dialogue that ensures diverse perspectives are heard and considered.

Transparency and Open Communication

Transparent communication is the foundation of effective stakeholder engagement. Companies should proactively disclose information about their sustainability efforts, goals, and performance. Transparency builds trust among stakeholders and demonstrates the company's commitment to openness and accountability. Clear communication channels can include regular sustainability reports, public disclosures, and accessible platforms for stakeholders to raise concerns or provide feedback.

Listening to Stakeholder Concerns

Engaging stakeholders means actively listening to their concerns and understanding their expectations. This involves conducting regular surveys, hosting focus groups, and creating forums for open discussions. By understanding stakeholder perspectives, companies can tailor their sustainability initiatives to address specific concerns and align with the values of different groups.

Community Involvement and Collaboration

For multinational companies, engaging with local communities is particularly significant. Establishing meaningful relationships with communities where the company operates is crucial for understanding their unique needs and challenges. Collaborative initiatives, such as community development projects or partnerships with local organizations, demonstrate a commitment to being a responsible corporate citizen.

Employee Participation

Employees are key stakeholders whose engagement is critical for the success of sustainability initiatives. Actively involve employees in decision-making processes related to CSR and sustainability. This can include setting up employee-led sustainability committees, providing training on sustainable practices, and encouraging employees to contribute ideas for improvement. Engaged employees are more likely to embrace and champion sustainability within the organization.

Inclusive Decision-Making

Inclusive decision-making processes involve stakeholders in key choices related to sustainability initiatives. This ensures that diverse perspectives are considered, and decisions reflect the concerns and expectations of various stakeholder groups. Inclusive decision-making can be facilitated through advisory boards, consultation sessions, or collaborative workshops that bring together representatives from different stakeholder categories.

Measuring and Reporting Impact

Effectively engaging stakeholders requires a commitment to measuring and reporting the impact of sustainability efforts. Companies should communicate not only their goals and intentions but also the actual outcomes of their initiatives. This includes reporting on key performance indicators (KPIs) related to sustainability and CSR, showcasing progress made, and being transparent about challenges faced.

Adapting Strategies Based on Feedback

Stakeholder engagement is an ongoing process that requires adaptability. Companies should be receptive to feedback from stakeholders and be willing to adjust their strategies based on this input. This iterative approach ensures that sustainability initiatives remain relevant and responsive to evolving stakeholder expectations.

Effective stakeholder engagement is integral to the success of a responsible multinational company's sustainability efforts. By establishing transparent communication channels, actively listening to concerns, involving communities and employees, embracing inclusive decision-making, measuring impact, and adapting strategies based on feedback, companies can build lasting relationships with stakeholders and contribute positively to the global business landscape.

6. Invest in Employee Education and Training

A fundamental element in constructing a responsible multinational company lies in recognizing the pivotal role that employees play in driving sustainability initiatives. Investing in employee education and training becomes a strategic imperative, fostering awareness, ethical practices, and a deep understanding of social responsibility within the workforce. This involves creating awareness of sustainability issues, promoting ethical business practices, and fostering a culture of social responsibility. Aligning employees with corporate sustainability goals, encouraging innovative thinking, and enhancing engagement and retention are outcomes of this investment. Additionally, it ensures the workforce adapts to evolving sustainability standards, positioning the company as a leader in corporate responsibility. Ultimately, by building a culture of responsibility within the organization, organizations can harness the collective power of their workforce to drive positive change and contribute to a more sustainable and socially responsible business environment.

7. Embrace Innovation for Sustainability

In the realm of sustainability, innovation stands as a powerful catalyst, driving positive change and creating a pathway towards a more responsible business model. Encouraging a culture of innovation within a company is not just a strategic choice but a necessity in addressing environmental challenges and contributing to sustainable development.

Adopting Renewable Energy Sources

One impactful way for a company to innovate for sustainability is by adopting renewable energy sources. This involves transitioning towards clean and renewable sources of energy such as solar, wind, or hydropower. By reducing reliance on fossil fuels, businesses can lower their carbon footprint, decrease greenhouse gas emissions, and contribute to the global effort to combat climate change. Implementing energy-efficient technologies and practices also aligns with the overarching goal of achieving a more sustainable energy landscape.

Improving Resource Efficiency

Innovation can lead to significant improvements in resource efficiency, a key component of sustainable business practices. This includes optimizing production processes, reducing waste generation, and utilizing resources more judiciously. Technologies like smart sensors, data analytics, and automation can be leveraged to monitor and enhance resource utilization throughout the value chain. By minimizing resource consumption, companies not only contribute to environmental preservation but also often realize cost savings and increased operational efficiency.

Developing Sustainable Products

The development of sustainable products is a direct outcome of innovative thinking. Companies can explore alternative materials, design processes, and manufacturing techniques that prioritize environmental and social considerations. This may involve creating products with longer lifecycles, utilizing recycled or biodegradable materials, or ensuring ethical sourcing throughout the supply chain. Innovative product design contributes to a circular economy where products are designed to be reused, refurbished, remanufactured, and recycled, minimizing waste and environmental impact.

Cultivating a Culture of Innovation

To truly embrace innovation for sustainability, companies must cultivate a culture that fosters creativity, experimentation, and a willingness to challenge traditional norms. This involves encouraging employees at all levels to contribute ideas, providing platforms for cross-functional collaboration, and recognizing and rewarding innovative initiatives. By instilling a culture of innovation, businesses can tap into the collective intelligence of their workforce, unlocking solutions that may have far-reaching positive effects on sustainability.

Investing in Research and Development

Dedicated investments in research and development (R&D) are instrumental in driving sustainability through innovation. Companies can allocate resources to explore new technologies, methodologies, and solutions that align with their sustainability objectives. Collaborating with external research institutions, startups, or industry partners can bring diverse perspectives and expertise, accelerating the pace of innovation. R&D efforts can lead to breakthroughs that not only benefit the company but also contribute valuable insights and solutions to broader sustainability challenges.

Adapting to Technological Advancements

The rapid pace of technological advancements provides an ever-expanding toolkit for companies aiming to innovate sustainably. Embracing advancements in areas such as artificial intelligence, the Internet of Things (IoT), and green technologies enables businesses to optimize processes, enhance efficiency, and reduce environmental impact. Staying abreast of technological trends and integrating relevant innovations into business practices is essential for remaining at the forefront of sustainable innovation.

Embracing innovation for sustainability is not merely a strategic choice; it is a commitment to shaping a responsible and resilient future. By integrating renewable energy sources, improving resource efficiency, developing sustainable products, fostering a culture of innovation, investing in research and development, and adapting to technological advancements, businesses can position themselves as leaders in the pursuit of sustainable and responsible business practices. Innovation becomes the driving force that propels companies towards a harmonious balance between economic prosperity, environmental stewardship, and social well-being.

8. Establish Robust Reporting Mechanisms

Establishing robust reporting mechanisms is a critical component of building a responsible multinational company committed to sustainability and corporate social responsibility (CSR). Transparency serves as a cornerstone in fostering trust among stakeholders, including customers, investors, employees, and the broader community. By implementing effective reporting practices, companies can not only track their sustainability performance but also communicate their achievements, challenges, and future aspirations in a transparent manner.

Transparency as a Foundation

Transparent reporting forms the foundation of responsible business practices. It involves openly sharing information about a company's environmental, social, and governance (ESG) performance. This transparency extends beyond financial metrics, encompassing a broader spectrum of metrics that reflect the company's impact on the environment, its social responsibility initiatives, and its commitment to ethical governance.

Implementing Effective Reporting Mechanisms

To ensure transparency, responsible multinational companies must implement effective reporting mechanisms. This involves the creation and dissemination of sustainability reports that provide a comprehensive overview of the company's initiatives and performance in the realm of sustainability. These reports typically include key indicators, progress toward sustainability goals, and details about ongoing initiatives.

Tracking Sustainability Performance

One of the primary purposes of robust reporting mechanisms is to track and measure sustainability performance accurately. This entails monitoring key performance indicators (KPIs) related to environmental impact, social responsibility, and governance. For instance, tracking carbon emissions, waste reduction efforts, diversity and inclusion metrics, and adherence to ethical business practices allows companies to assess their progress over time.

Highlighting Achievements

Sustainability reports serve as a platform to showcase the company's achievements in the realm of responsible business practices. Whether it's achieving carbon neutrality, implementing renewable energy sources, or contributing to community development projects, these reports offer a space to highlight positive outcomes. This not only acknowledges the company's commitment to sustainability but also reinforces its positive impact on the environment and society.

Addressing Challenges Transparently

In addition to highlighting achievements, responsible reporting involves addressing challenges transparently. Companies are expected to candidly discuss hurdles faced in their sustainability journey and the strategies employed to overcome them. This openness acknowledges the complexities of sustainable business practices and demonstrates a commitment to continuous improvement.

Future Goals and Aspirations

Sustainability reports also provide a platform for companies to outline their future goals and aspirations. This forward-looking approach demonstrates a commitment to ongoing improvement and sets the stage for the company's trajectory in the realm of sustainability. Whether it's setting ambitious targets for reducing environmental impact or enhancing social initiatives, articulating future goals provides a roadmap for stakeholders.

Building Trust Among Stakeholders

Transparency in reporting is instrumental in building trust among stakeholders. Stakeholders, including consumers, investors, and employees, increasingly value companies that are open about their sustainability practices. By regularly sharing comprehensive information through sustainability reports, companies can foster a sense of trust and credibility, aligning themselves with the expectations of an informed and socially conscious audience.

Demonstrating Commitment to Accountability

Robust reporting mechanisms are a tangible demonstration of a company's commitment to accountability. When companies willingly share information about their sustainability practices, it signals a dedication to being held accountable for their impact on the environment, society, and governance. This accountability is a fundamental aspect of responsible business practices that resonates positively with stakeholders.

The establishment of robust reporting mechanisms is not just a compliance requirement; it is a strategic imperative for responsible multinational companies. Transparent reporting not only allows companies to track and communicate their sustainability performance but also builds trust, showcases achievements, addresses challenges openly, outlines future aspirations, and underscores a commitment to accountability in the pursuit of responsible business practices.

9. Collaborate with External Organizations

Building a responsible multinational company is a complex endeavor that often requires collaboration with external organizations. Engaging with non-governmental organizations (NGOs), industry associations, and sustainability-focused initiatives can significantly amplify the impact of a company's sustainability efforts. This collaborative approach fosters a collective commitment to addressing global challenges and advancing sustainability goals on a broader scale.

One effective way for a multinational company to enhance its sustainability impact is by actively participating in collaborative projects. Joining forces with other businesses, NGOs, and research institutions in joint initiatives allows for shared resources, knowledge exchange, and a pooling of efforts. These projects can tackle specific sustainability challenges, such as environmental conservation, social development, or ethical business practices, fostering innovation and creating a more profound impact than individual efforts.

Transparency and openness are key elements of responsible business practices. Collaborating with external organizations provides a platform for sharing best practices. Companies can learn from each other's successes and challenges, gaining valuable insights that can inform their own sustainability strategies. This knowledge exchange not only contributes to the continuous improvement of individual companies but also accelerates the adoption of sustainable practices across industries.

Active participation in industry associations and initiatives is crucial for contributing to larger, sector-wide sustainability goals. By joining industry-wide efforts, companies can collectively address common challenges, set industry benchmarks, and advocate for sustainable practices. This collaborative approach strengthens the influence of the business sector in shaping policies and standards that promote sustainability.

NGOs and advocacy groups play a pivotal role in driving sustainability agendas. Multinational companies can collaborate with these organizations to leverage their expertise, networks, and grassroots influence. Partnerships with NGOs can extend a company's reach into local communities, enhance social responsibility initiatives, and ensure that sustainability efforts align with the needs and aspirations of diverse stakeholders.

External organizations often oversee certification and standards initiatives that validate sustainable practices. Collaboration with these entities allows companies to align their operations with globally recognized benchmarks. Seeking certifications, such as those related to environmental management, fair trade, or ethical sourcing, not only demonstrates a commitment to sustainability but also builds credibility and trust with consumers, investors, and other stakeholders.

Collaborative efforts can extend beyond project-based initiatives to include collective advocacy for policy changes and systemic improvements. By uniting with other organizations, multinational companies can amplify their voice and influence policymakers to enact regulations that promote sustainability. This joint advocacy can contribute to creating a more supportive regulatory environment for responsible business practices.

In a world characterized by interconnected challenges, ranging from climate change to social inequality, collaboration becomes an essential strategy for navigating global complexities. Collaborative efforts enable companies to address challenges that transcend borders, leveraging a collective approach to finding innovative solutions and driving positive change.

Collaborating with external organizations is a cornerstone of building a responsible multinational company. Through participation in collaborative projects, sharing best practices, contributing to industry-wide efforts, engaging with NGOs, leveraging certification initiatives, and harnessing collective advocacy, companies can magnify their impact and contribute meaningfully to global sustainability objectives. This collaborative ethos not only strengthens the fabric of responsible business practices but also reinforces the interconnected nature of the global business community in addressing pressing environmental and social challenges.

10. Continuous Improvement and Adaptation:

Embracing a mindset of continuous improvement and adaptation is paramount for building a responsible multinational company committed to sustainability. Sustainability is an ongoing journey rather than a static destination, and companies must integrate this philosophy into their organizational DNA.

Regular reassessment of sustainability goals is a fundamental aspect of this approach. As societal expectations, environmental conditions, and economic landscapes evolve, it's crucial for companies to evaluate the relevance and effectiveness of their sustainability objectives. Periodic reviews enable organizations to identify areas for improvement, realign strategies with emerging challenges, and ensure that sustainability efforts remain aligned with the evolving global context.

Updating sustainability strategies based on evolving challenges and opportunities is a proactive measure that enables companies to stay ahead of the curve. This adaptability is essential in navigating dynamic environments, where unforeseen circumstances or emerging issues may require a shift in approach. For instance, advancements in sustainable technologies or changes in regulatory frameworks may present new opportunities that companies can leverage to enhance their sustainability impact.

Remaining agile in responding to changing societal expectations is a key component of continuous improvement. As awareness and consciousness around sustainability grow, so do societal expectations regarding corporate responsibility. Companies need to actively engage with their stakeholders, including customers, employees, investors, and the wider community, to understand evolving expectations. By staying attuned to these expectations, organizations can adjust their sustainability strategies to meet the ever-changing demands of a socially conscious global audience.

A commitment to continuous improvement and adaptation also involves fostering a culture of innovation within the organization. Encouraging employees to contribute ideas, explore new technologies, and propose sustainable solutions fosters a dynamic environment that thrives on creativity. This innovative spirit is essential for identifying novel approaches to sustainability challenges and capitalizing on emerging opportunities.

Moreover, integrating sustainability considerations into the decision-making processes of the organization contributes to continuous improvement. From product development to supply chain management, companies should embed sustainability criteria into their decision frameworks. This ensures that sustainability is not treated as a separate function but rather as an integral aspect influencing every facet of the business.

Adopting a mindset of continuous improvement and adaptation is crucial for companies aspiring to be responsible multinational entities. By regularly reassessing sustainability goals, updating strategies based on changing circumstances, and remaining agile in response to societal expectations, organizations can build resilience, foster innovation, and contribute meaningfully to global sustainability efforts. This commitment to continuous improvement positions companies as dynamic leaders in the journey towards a more sustainable and responsible business future.

Building a responsible multinational company requires a holistic and integrated approach that permeates the entire organizational culture. By setting clear goals, aligning sustainability with core business strategies, engaging stakeholders, and fostering a culture of responsibility and innovation, companies can contribute meaningfully to a sustainable and socially responsible global business landscape.

Chapter **21**

Navigating Regulatory
Compliance and Governance

In this chapter, we will take a look at the concept of regulatory compliance and governance for growing companies, unraveling the complexities of legal frameworks across diverse regions. Navigating through this landscape is essential to ensure your company not only meets various regulatory standards but also upholds good governance practices. This chapter provides insights into the strategies and approaches necessary for maintaining compliance while fostering effective governance in an evolving global business environment.

Establishing Robust Compliance Frameworks

In today's global business landscape, companies encounter a myriad of regulatory requirements and legal standards across different jurisdictions. Navigating this complex terrain requires the establishment of robust compliance frameworks. Such frameworks not only mitigate legal risks but also contribute to building a culture of integrity, trust, and sustainability within the organization.

Benefits of Establishing Robust Compliance Frameworks
Risk Mitigation

In the dynamic landscape of global business, risk mitigation is a paramount objective for companies seeking sustainable growth and resilience. A robust compliance framework serves as a strategic shield against potential pitfalls, offering multifaceted advantages in the realm of risk management.

The initial step in leveraging compliance for risk mitigation involves a meticulous identification of potential compliance risks. This encompasses a comprehensive assessment of internal processes, external market dynamics, and regulatory landscapes. By conducting thorough risk assessments, companies gain insights into areas where compliance vulnerabilities may arise.

One of the core benefits of a robust compliance framework is its capacity to prevent legal complications. Legal entanglements can arise from a variety of sources, including regulatory violations, contractual breaches, or non-compliance with industry standards. A well-structured compliance program anticipates and addresses these issues before they escalate into legal disputes, safeguarding the company from costly litigation and associated damages.

Non-compliance with regulatory standards often leads to financial penalties, which can significantly impact a company's bottom line. By proactively identifying and rectifying compliance risks, organizations can avoid these penalties. The financial resources that would otherwise be allocated to addressing legal issues can be redirected toward strategic investments and business development initiatives.

Reputation is a priceless asset in the business world, and a robust compliance framework plays a pivotal role in preserving a company's reputational integrity. By adhering to ethical and legal standards, organizations demonstrate their commitment to responsible business practices. This commitment resonates positively with stakeholders, including customers, investors, and partners, fostering trust and confidence in the brand.

A proactive approach to compliance not only mitigates risks in the present but also contributes to building a resilient business environment for the future. Companies that prioritize compliance are better equipped to navigate uncertainties, adapt to changing regulatory landscapes, and withstand external shocks. This resilience positions them as trustworthy entities capable of weathering challenges and sustaining long-term success.

Beyond the tangible benefits of risk mitigation, a robust compliance framework instills a culture of proactive compliance within the organization. Employees become aware of the importance of adhering to rules and regulations, leading to a collective effort in identifying and addressing potential risks. This cultural shift creates an environment where compliance becomes an integral part of day-to-day operations rather than a reactive measure.

The effective mitigation of risks is a fundamental advantage derived from a robust compliance framework. The identification and proactive addressing of compliance risks enable companies to navigate the complexities of the business landscape with confidence. By avoiding legal complications, financial penalties, and reputational damage, organizations can foster a resilient business environment conducive to sustained growth and success.

Enhanced Corporate Reputation

The commitment to compliance not only serves as a shield against legal risks but also significantly contributes to enhancing a company's corporate reputation. In the contemporary business landscape, where transparency and ethical conduct are highly valued, a strong reputation is a strategic asset that can positively impact various stakeholders.

Customers, as discerning consumers, increasingly prioritize companies that align with their values and exhibit a sense of corporate responsibility. A company known for its commitment to legal and ethical standards stands out in the market, attracting customers who seek trustworthy and responsible partners. This positive association fosters a sense of loyalty among consumers, who are more likely to choose products and services from a reputable and socially responsible organization.

Investors, too, place significant emphasis on corporate reputation when making investment decisions. A company with a strong commitment to compliance signals a well-managed and responsible business, mitigating investment risks associated with legal complications and ethical concerns. Investors are more likely to be attracted to organizations that prioritize compliance, as this reflects a commitment to sustainable and long-term success.

Partnerships and collaborations in the business world thrive on trust and credibility. Companies with enhanced corporate reputations through a commitment to compliance are viewed as reliable and ethical partners. Potential collaborators, suppliers, and distributors are more inclined to engage with organizations that prioritize legal and ethical standards, as this ensures a stable and trustworthy business relationship.

The positive impact of an enhanced corporate reputation extends beyond external stakeholders to include employees. A company known for its commitment to compliance creates a positive and ethical work environment. This, in turn, attracts and retains top talent, as employees are drawn to organizations that prioritize ethical conduct. A strong corporate reputation contributes to employee satisfaction, engagement, and pride in being associated with a socially responsible company.

An enhanced corporate reputation is a consequential outcome of a steadfast commitment to compliance. The positive image created by adherence to legal and ethical standards attracts customers, investors, and partners, fostering trust and credibility in the business community. This virtuous cycle of enhanced reputation not only benefits external stakeholders but also contributes to a positive work culture, making compliance a cornerstone of sustainable and responsible business practices.

Operational Efficiency

Operational efficiency stands as a cornerstone benefit of a well-defined compliance framework within a company. By establishing clear rules, processes, and procedures, compliance frameworks provide employees with a structured guide to navigate their roles. This clarity minimizes the likelihood of errors, ensuring that operations run smoothly and efficiently. In the context of international business, where diverse regulatory requirements may exist across different regions, a standardized compliance framework becomes especially invaluable.

In a global business environment, companies often operate in multiple jurisdictions, each with its own set of rules and regulations. Without a well-defined compliance framework, employees may encounter confusion and uncertainty about how to conduct their tasks within the bounds of the law. This lack of clarity can lead to inefficiencies, mistakes, and potential legal complications. However, a robust compliance framework acts as a guiding compass, providing employees with the necessary information and guidelines to ensure that their operations align with the relevant regulatory requirements.

Furthermore, the implementation of compliance frameworks fosters a culture of accountability and responsibility among employees. When rules and expectations are clearly communicated, employees are more likely to adhere to them, understanding the importance of their role in maintaining compliance. This sense of accountability contributes to a more disciplined and efficient workforce.

Efficiency gains extend beyond individual tasks to the broader organizational structure. A well-defined compliance framework enables companies to streamline their processes, eliminating redundant or unnecessary steps that might hinder productivity. This optimization becomes particularly crucial in international operations, where coordination across different regions demands a cohesive and efficient organizational structure.

Standardization through compliance frameworks also facilitates scalability. As businesses grow and expand globally, having consistent processes and procedures becomes essential for maintaining operational efficiency. A compliance framework ensures that as operations scale, they do so in a structured and controlled manner, reducing the risk of inefficiencies that can arise from ad-hoc or inconsistent practices.

Moreover, operational efficiency contributes to cost-effectiveness. By minimizing errors and streamlining processes, companies can allocate resources more effectively. This efficiency is not only conducive to the bottom line but also positions the organization for sustainable growth in the long term.

Operational efficiency is a pivotal advantage derived from a well-defined compliance framework. By providing clarity, accountability, and standardization, these frameworks empower employees to navigate their tasks seamlessly, reducing errors and fostering a more efficient and productive organizational environment. This efficiency is particularly vital in the complex landscape of international business, where adherence to diverse regulatory requirements is paramount for sustained success.

Access to Global Markets

Access to global markets is a pivotal advantage that stems from compliance with international standards. In an interconnected world where borders are no longer barriers to trade, adherence to stringent regulatory requirements becomes a gateway to unlocking opportunities in diverse markets. Many countries and trading blocs impose specific standards and regulations that businesses must meet to operate within their borders.

By establishing a robust compliance framework that guarantees adherence to these international standards, companies position themselves favorably for market access and international expansion. This compliance not only satisfies legal requirements but also aligns businesses with the expectations and norms of the global marketplace. It is particularly crucial in industries where strict quality, safety, or ethical standards are prerequisites for market entry.

For instance, the European Union (EU) imposes stringent regulations on various industries, including product safety, environmental sustainability, and data protection. Companies looking to tap into the vast European market must ensure that their products and operations comply with these regulations. Achieving and maintaining compliance with EU standards not only facilitates access to this lucrative market but also enhances the credibility of the business in the eyes of European consumers.

Similarly, trading blocs like the North American Free Trade Agreement (NAFTA), now succeeded by the United States-Mexico-Canada Agreement (USMCA), have specific compliance requirements that businesses must meet to benefit from the trade advantages within the bloc. Ensuring alignment with these standards not only streamlines cross-border trade but also positions companies to leverage the economic benefits of regional cooperation.

In the realm of international trade, compliance extends beyond product standards to encompass customs regulations, import/export requirements, and ethical business practices. A comprehensive compliance framework addresses these multifaceted aspects, ensuring that businesses not only meet the minimum legal requirements but also adhere to ethical and responsible business conduct. This commitment to responsible practices resonates positively in global markets, enhancing the brand image and fostering trust among international consumers.

Moreover, compliance with international standards is often a prerequisite for participating in global supply chains. Many multinational corporations have stringent criteria for selecting suppliers and partners, and adherence to recognized standards is a common criterion. By aligning with these standards, businesses position themselves as reliable and responsible partners in the global supply network.

In essence, access to global markets is a compelling benefit that emerges from a commitment to compliance with international standards. Beyond the legal obligations, this adherence signals a company's dedication to responsible business practices, quality assurance, and ethical conduct – qualities highly valued in the international arena. As businesses navigate the complexities of global trade, a robust compliance framework becomes a strategic enabler for reaching new markets, fostering international growth, and building a resilient global presence.

Financial Stability

Financial stability is a cornerstone of a company's success, and compliance frameworks play a crucial role in maintaining this stability. One significant contribution comes in the prevention of legal entanglements that could otherwise lead to substantial financial setbacks. By adhering to established compliance standards, organizations proactively shield themselves from the financial burdens associated with regulatory violations, fines, or potential litigation costs.

In the absence of a robust compliance framework, companies may find themselves entangled in legal disputes that can drain financial resources. Regulatory violations often incur hefty fines imposed by governing bodies, diverting funds that could otherwise be allocated to strategic business initiatives. Moreover, the costs associated with legal proceedings, including attorney fees and settlement amounts, pose additional financial risks. By implementing and maintaining an effective compliance program, organizations create a protective barrier against these financial pitfalls.

A proactive approach to compliance not only prevents financial losses from legal complications but also ensures the efficient allocation of resources for sustained growth. Companies can redirect the financial resources that would have been consumed by legal battles towards critical areas such as research and development, market expansion, or talent acquisition. This strategic allocation of resources enhances the overall financial stability of the organization, fostering an environment conducive to long-term success.

Financial stability is intricately linked to investor confidence and stakeholder trust. Companies with a robust compliance framework send a strong signal to investors that they prioritize ethical business practices and risk management. This commitment to compliance builds trust among stakeholders, including shareholders, customers, and partners, contributing to the overall financial health of the organization.

Furthermore, financial stability is closely tied to a company's creditworthiness and borrowing capacity. Organizations with a history of regulatory compliance are viewed favorably by financial institutions, making it easier to secure loans or access capital when needed. This improved financial standing provides companies with the flexibility to invest in growth opportunities, navigate economic fluctuations, and withstand unforeseen challenges.

Financial stability is a multifaceted benefit derived from effective compliance frameworks. By preventing legal entanglements, avoiding financial penalties, and strategically allocating resources, organizations create a solid financial foundation for sustained growth. This stability not only safeguards against potential financial setbacks but also enhances investor confidence, stakeholder trust, and overall creditworthiness, positioning the company for long-term financial success.

How to Establish Robust Compliance Frameworks

Conduct a Comprehensive Risk Assessment:

Begin by conducting a thorough risk assessment to identify potential areas of compliance vulnerability. Assess both internal and external factors that could impact the organization's compliance landscape.

Understand Applicable Laws and Regulations

Invest time in understanding the specific laws and regulations relevant to the industry and regions where the company operates. This includes employment laws, data protection regulations, environmental standards, and industry-specific compliance requirements.

Create Policies and Procedures

Develop clear and comprehensive policies and procedures based on the identified legal requirements. These documents should outline the expected behavior of employees, detailing the steps they need to take to ensure compliance with relevant laws and regulations.

Implement Regular Training Programs

Educate employees on compliance standards through regular training programs. This not only enhances their understanding of legal requirements but also instills a culture of compliance within the organization. Training should cover topics such as anti-corruption measures, data privacy, and industry-specific regulations.

Establish Monitoring and Reporting Mechanisms

Implement robust monitoring and reporting mechanisms to track compliance. Regular audits, internal controls, and reporting channels for potential violations are essential components of an effective compliance framework.

Appoint a Compliance Officer

Designate a Compliance Officer or Compliance Team responsible for overseeing and managing the compliance program. This role involves staying updated on regulatory changes, addressing compliance concerns, and ensuring the organization's ongoing adherence to standards.

Engage in Continuous Improvement

Regularly review and update the compliance framework to adapt to changing regulatory landscapes and evolving business needs. Engage in continuous improvement by incorporating lessons learned from incidents, feedback, and emerging compliance trends.

Establishing robust compliance frameworks is a strategic imperative for companies operating in diverse regulatory environments. The benefits extend beyond mere legal adherence, encompassing risk mitigation, enhanced reputation, operational efficiency, market access, and financial stability. By following a systematic approach and fostering a culture of compliance, organizations can navigate the complexities of regulatory compliance and governance with confidence.

Implementing Effective Corporate Governance

Effective corporate governance is paramount for the sustained success and ethical operation of any organization. It encompasses the practices, policies, and structures that guide decision-making, ensure accountability, and protect the interests of stakeholders. Implementing effective corporate governance involves a comprehensive approach that aligns organizational strategies with ethical standards, transparency, and regulatory compliance.

1. Board Composition and Independence
Definition
A fundamental aspect of effective corporate governance is ensuring the composition of the board of directors reflects a balance of skills, experience, and independence.

Implementation
Achieving effective corporate governance involves implementing key strategies to ensure a well-rounded and unbiased decision-making process. One crucial aspect is fostering diverse expertise within the board. This entails selecting members with a broad range of skills, backgrounds, and industry knowledge. The goal is to assemble a board that collectively possesses a diverse spectrum of insights.

Another vital component is the appointment of independent directors. These individuals bring an impartial perspective to decision-making, mitigating conflicts of interest and ensuring that the board's choices align with the best interests of the company and its stakeholders.

The emphasis on diverse expertise directly contributes to well-informed decision-making within the organization. A board with varied skills and backgrounds is better equipped to analyze complex situations from different angles, leading to comprehensive and thoughtful decisions.

Independent directors play a crucial role in enhancing ethical oversight within the company. Their impartial stance promotes transparency and accountability. By providing an external perspective, they contribute to maintaining high ethical standards, which is vital for the trust and confidence of stakeholders.

The synergy of these implementation strategies results in a board that not only reflects a mosaic of skills but also upholds the principles of impartiality and ethical governance. Through diverse expertise and independent oversight, organizations can navigate challenges with a comprehensive understanding, fostering a governance environment that is both inclusive and ethically sound.

2. Transparency and Disclosure
Transparency involves providing clear, accurate, and timely information about the company's financial and operational performance, as well as potential risks.

Implementation
Effective implementation of corporate governance involves key practices to enhance transparency, communication, and ethical disclosure. Robust reporting is a fundamental aspect, entailing the development of comprehensive and easily understandable financial reports. These reports serve as vital tools for stakeholders to assess the company's financial health and future prospects.

Establishing regular communication mechanisms is equally important. This involves creating channels for consistent interaction with stakeholders, including shareholders, employees, and customers. Timely and transparent communication fosters an environment of openness and trust.

Ethical disclosure is another critical component of implementation. Companies should be committed to disclosing potential risks and uncertainties openly. This commitment fosters a culture of transparency and demonstrates the organization's dedication to ethical business practices.

The implementation of robust reporting, regular communication, and ethical disclosure contributes to several significant benefits for the organization. One key advantage is the enhancement of stakeholder confidence. Transparent practices, including comprehensive reporting and regular communication, build trust among stakeholders. This trust, in turn, boosts confidence in the company's operations and decisions.

Risk mitigation is another notable benefit. Ethical disclosure of potential risks and uncertainties allows stakeholders to make informed decisions. By providing a clear understanding of the challenges and uncertainties the company faces, organizations enable stakeholders to assess and mitigate potential negative impacts. This proactive approach contributes to a more resilient and adaptive business environment.

3. Code of Ethics and Conduct

A code of ethics outlines the principles and values that guide ethical behavior within the organization, setting expectations for employees and leadership.

Implementation

Implementing effective corporate governance involves specific measures to ensure ethical behavior and compliance. Clear and concise policies are paramount in this regard. Companies should develop policies that explicitly outline expected ethical behavior, covering areas such as conflicts of interest, confidentiality, and fair treatment. These policies serve as a guide for employees, setting clear expectations for ethical conduct.

Regular training programs complement clear policies. Conducting these programs ensures that all employees understand and adhere to the established code of ethics. Training sessions help instill ethical principles, providing employees with the knowledge and tools to make ethical decisions in their roles.

An essential component of implementation is the establishment of a confidential whistleblower mechanism. This mechanism allows employees to report unethical behavior without fear of retaliation. Creating a safe and confidential channel for reporting unethical conduct promotes transparency and accountability within the organization.

The implementation of clear policies, training programs, and a whistleblower mechanism brings forth several benefits for the organization. One significant advantage is the cultural alignment toward integrity. A well-defined code of ethics fosters a culture where integrity and ethical decision-making are not just encouraged but embedded into the organization's DNA. This cultural alignment creates an ethical work environment where employees are more likely to make decisions based on ethical considerations.

Legal compliance is another key benefit. Clear policies, coupled with comprehensive training programs, contribute to legal compliance. By aligning operations with ethical standards and legal requirements, companies reduce the risk of ethical lapses and potential legal complications. This proactive approach safeguards the organization's reputation and ensures adherence to legal frameworks.

4. Shareholder Rights and Engagement

Ensuring the protection of shareholder rights and facilitating engagement with shareholders are integral to effective corporate governance.

Implementation

Implementing effective corporate governance involves specific actions to ensure transparency, shareholder participation, and informed decision-making. Proxy voting is a crucial aspect of this implementation. By enabling shareholders to exercise their voting rights through proxy voting, companies empower shareholders to have a say in key matters without the need to attend physical meetings. This mechanism promotes inclusivity and allows shareholders to actively participate in decision-making processes.

Regular annual meetings are another essential element of implementation. These meetings provide a structured platform for shareholders to express concerns, ask questions, and engage with the company's leadership. Conducting annual meetings ensures open communication channels between the company and its shareholders, fostering a sense of transparency and accountability.

Transparent communication is fundamental throughout the implementation process. Companies should communicate clearly about their performance, strategies, and future plans. Transparent communication builds trust among shareholders, demonstrating a commitment to openness and honesty. Providing shareholders with comprehensive and understandable information contributes to a positive perception of the company's operations.

The benefits of these implementation measures are significant for the organization and its stakeholders. One key advantage is enhanced investor confidence. By protecting shareholder rights and facilitating their active participation through proxy voting and annual meetings, companies demonstrate a commitment to fair and equitable treatment. This commitment enhances investor confidence in the company's governance practices, fostering trust and positive relationships with shareholders.

Informed decision-making is another crucial benefit. Engaging shareholders in the decision-making process fosters a sense of inclusion. Shareholders who are well-informed about the company's strategies and plans are better equipped to make decisions aligned with their interests. This level of engagement contributes to a more informed and empowered shareholder community.

5. Risk Management and Internal Controls

Risk management involves identifying, assessing, and mitigating potential risks to the organization, while internal controls ensure the integrity of financial and operational processes.

Implementation

Implementing a strong risk management and internal control framework is crucial for organizational resilience and financial integrity. Regular risk assessment is a foundational step, involving the systematic identification and documentation of potential risks. This process should encompass both internal factors, such as operational vulnerabilities, and external factors, such as changes in the regulatory environment or market conditions.

Establishing robust internal controls is another key element of implementation. These controls serve to safeguard assets, prevent fraud, and ensure the accuracy of financial reporting. Internal controls create a structured environment that minimizes the likelihood of errors or intentional mismanagement, contributing to the overall stability of the organization.

Conducting periodic audits is a complementary measure in the implementation process. Audits serve to verify the effectiveness of risk management and internal control mechanisms. These assessments provide an independent and objective evaluation of the organization's processes, offering insights into areas of improvement and ensuring compliance with established standards.

The benefits of implementing a comprehensive risk management and internal control framework are substantial for the organization:

Operational resilience is a key advantage. Effective risk management enhances the organization's ability to navigate challenges and uncertainties. By identifying and mitigating potential risks, companies can build resilience, ensuring continuity and stability in their operations even in the face of unexpected events.

Financial integrity is a crucial outcome of robust internal controls. These controls contribute to the accuracy and reliability of financial reporting. Stakeholders, including investors and regulatory bodies, rely on accurate financial information to make informed decisions. Maintaining financial integrity builds trust with stakeholders, enhancing the organization's reputation and credibility.

The implementation of a structured risk management and internal control framework not only mitigates potential risks but also strengthens the overall operational and financial foundation of the organization.

6. Long-Term Strategy and Sustainability

Corporate governance extends to the formulation and execution of a long-term strategy that aligns with the organization's values and contributes to sustainability.

Implementation

Implementing sustainable practices involves the integration of environmental, social, and governance (ESG) considerations into the organization's long-term strategy. This requires a holistic approach that goes beyond short-term gains and considers the broader impact on the environment, society, and corporate governance.

Stakeholder involvement is a critical component of the implementation process. Engaging with stakeholders, including employees, customers, and communities, ensures that their perspectives are considered in the strategic planning process. This inclusivity not only aligns the organization with the values and expectations of its stakeholders but also enhances the legitimacy and acceptance of strategic decisions.

Fostering a culture of innovation is another key element of implementation. Innovation is essential for adapting to evolving market conditions, technological advancements, and changing consumer preferences. By encouraging a mindset of continuous improvement and creativity, organizations can stay ahead of the curve and remain competitive in a dynamic business landscape.

The benefits of implementing sustainable practices, stakeholder involvement, and innovation are substantial for the organization:

Responsible growth is a primary advantage. A sustainable strategy promotes growth that is not only profitable but also responsible and ethical. Considering the long-term impact on society and the environment ensures that the organization contributes positively to the communities it operates in and minimizes adverse effects on the planet.

Adaptability is another significant benefit. Incorporating stakeholder perspectives and fostering innovation enhances the organization's adaptability. In a rapidly changing business landscape, the ability to adapt to new challenges, technologies, and market dynamics is crucial for long-term success.

The implementation of sustainable practices, stakeholder involvement, and innovation contributes to responsible growth and enhances the organization's adaptability. These elements are integral for building a resilient and forward-thinking company in today's complex business environment.

Implementing effective corporate governance involves a holistic approach that considers various facets of organizational structure, behavior, and strategy. By focusing on board composition, transparency, ethical conduct, shareholder engagement, risk management, and long-term sustainability, organizations can cultivate a governance framework that not only complies with regulatory standards but also fosters ethical decision-making, stakeholder trust, and long-term success.

Chapter **22**

Talent Acquisition
and Retention Strategies

In the ever-evolving landscape of global business, attracting and retaining top talent is a mission-critical aspect for sustained success. Chapter 22 will take a look into the world of Talent Acquisition and Retention Strategies. From navigating the challenges of global competition to fostering a company culture that resonates across diverse geographies, this chapter explores the nuanced approaches needed to build and maintain a workforce that propels your organization forward.

In the global marketplace, where talent knows no borders, understanding how to strategically attract, hire, and retain the best individuals is essential. This chapter will guide you through the intricacies of talent management, from identifying key skills and competencies to creating an inclusive company culture that transcends geographical boundaries.

Strategic Talent Acquisition

Talent acquisition is more than just filling job vacancies; it's a strategic approach to identifying, attracting, and onboarding the right individuals to drive an organization's success. In a global context, this process becomes even more intricate, requiring a nuanced understanding of diverse markets, cultures, and skill landscapes.

Methodologies for Global Talent Acquisition

1. Comprehensive Workforce Planning

Comprehensive workforce planning serves as the foundation for effective talent acquisition on a global scale. It involves a meticulous assessment of an organization's long-term goals, aligning talent needs with strategic objectives. This strategic alignment is crucial in ensuring that the workforce possesses the necessary skills and competencies to drive the organization's success in a rapidly evolving global landscape.

By conducting comprehensive workforce planning, organizations can strategically identify critical roles essential for achieving their objectives. This process goes beyond merely filling existing vacancies; it anticipates the future needs of the organization, accounting for emerging challenges and opportunities on a global scale. Through a systematic approach, organizations can identify key skill sets and competencies required to navigate the complexities of diverse markets and industry landscapes.

The process involves collaboration between HR professionals, department heads, and key stakeholders to define the organization's strategic direction. This collaboration ensures that talent acquisition efforts are tightly aligned with the overarching goals of the organization. By mapping out the critical roles and skills needed, organizations can proactively address potential talent gaps and create a roadmap for attracting and retaining top talent globally.

Comprehensive workforce planning also considers the dynamic nature of the global business environment. It involves forecasting changes in market trends, technological advancements, and shifts in consumer behavior that may impact talent requirements. This forward-thinking approach allows organizations to be agile in responding to evolving industry demands and maintaining a competitive edge in the global marketplace.

Moreover, by understanding the intricacies of global challenges, such as economic fluctuations, political changes, and cultural shifts, organizations can tailor their talent acquisition strategies to meet specific demands. This strategic alignment ensures that the workforce possesses the adaptability and resilience required to thrive in diverse and often unpredictable global contexts. Comprehensive workforce planning is a strategic exercise that enables organizations to proactively shape their talent acquisition strategies. It empowers them to anticipate future needs, align talent with strategic objectives, and foster a workforce capable of navigating the intricacies of a global business landscape. Through this holistic approach, organizations lay the groundwork for effective and sustainable talent acquisition on a global scale.

2. Global Talent Mapping

In the dynamic realm of talent acquisition, global talent mapping emerges as a strategic cornerstone, guiding organizations in identifying and attracting top talent on a global scale. This multifaceted process involves the systematic identification, analysis, and visualization of talent pools, encompassing both internal and external spheres.

Talent mapping commences by meticulously identifying key individuals within the organization, recognizing high-performing employees whose skills and expertise contribute significantly to the company's success. Simultaneously, the process extends its purview to industry leaders, analyzing their profiles to understand the skills and attributes that contribute to their achievements. By delving into competitor insights, talent mapping provides a comprehensive view of the talent landscape, discerning the strengths of rival organizations and identifying potential candidates who can contribute uniquely to the company.

Moreover, talent mapping goes beyond the known landscape and explores emerging professionals, recognizing rising stars and recent graduates who exhibit promising potential. This forward-looking approach ensures that organizations stay ahead of industry trends and are well-prepared for future skill requirements.

A critical aspect of global talent mapping is its emphasis on regional talent pools. Understanding the unique strengths, cultural nuances, and skill concentrations in different regions allows organizations to strategically position talent. This regional perspective is particularly valuable in global operations, where diverse skill sets and cultural understanding are essential.

The advantages of talent mapping are manifold. Firstly, it empowers organizations with informed decision-making. By having a comprehensive understanding of the talent landscape, organizations can make strategic decisions about talent acquisition, placement, and development. This knowledge is especially valuable in a global context where the dynamics of talent vary across regions.

Secondly, talent mapping provides a competitive advantage. By understanding the strengths and weaknesses of competitors and identifying high-potential candidates, organizations can position themselves as industry leaders. This proactive approach to talent acquisition enhances the overall competitiveness of the organization.

Thirdly, talent mapping contributes to proactive talent management. Rather than reacting to immediate talent needs, organizations can forecast future requirements and develop a pipeline of skilled professionals. This strategic foresight ensures that organizations are well-equipped with the right talent to meet evolving business demands.

Global talent mapping is an indispensable asset in the complex landscape of global talent acquisition. It goes beyond traditional approaches by offering a holistic view of talent pools, encompassing internal, external, and global perspectives. The strategic insights derived from talent mapping empower organizations to make informed decisions, gain a competitive edge, and proactively manage their talent resources in the ever-evolving global business environment.

3. Cultivating Employer Branding

In the contemporary landscape of talent acquisition, the concept of employer branding has risen to prominence as a powerful tool for attracting top talent globally. An organization's reputation as an employer, encapsulated in its employer brand, holds substantial sway over the decisions of prospective candidates. Crafting and cultivating a strong employer brand is a strategic imperative, and the process involves showcasing the company's values, culture, and commitment to employee development.

Central to the cultivation of employer branding is the articulation of a compelling narrative that resonates with global professionals. This narrative extends beyond the traditional dimensions of job descriptions and salary packages; it delves into the essence of the organization, encapsulating its core values, vision, and the unique employee experience it offers. Through this storytelling, organizations can create an emotional connection with potential candidates, fostering a sense of alignment between their aspirations and the company's ethos.

One of the primary channels for disseminating this narrative is social media. With its pervasive reach and influence, social media platforms serve as dynamic arenas for organizations to present their employer brand to a global audience. Engaging content, such as employee testimonials, behind-the-scenes glimpses of workplace culture, and updates on corporate social responsibility initiatives, can be shared across platforms like LinkedIn, Twitter, and Instagram. This not only provides a window into the organization's internal dynamics but also contributes to building a community of engaged professionals who are drawn to the company's values.

Moreover, employer branding is not a one-time effort but an ongoing process of cultivation. Consistency in messaging is key, and organizations should regularly reinforce their brand narrative through various touchpoints. This could involve integrating the employer brand into recruitment materials, updating the company's careers webpage, and incorporating it into internal communications.

A strong employer brand offers several strategic advantages. Firstly, it acts as a magnet for top talent. In a competitive global job market, where professionals have the flexibility to choose their employers, a compelling employer brand becomes a distinguishing factor. Talented individuals are drawn to organizations that align with their values, provide a positive work culture, and offer opportunities for growth and development.

Secondly, a robust employer brand contributes to employee retention. Once top talent is attracted, maintaining a positive employee experience becomes crucial. Organizations with a well-defined and positive employer brand often experience higher levels of employee satisfaction and engagement. This, in turn, fosters a sense of loyalty and reduces turnover.

Cultivating employer branding is not merely a marketing endeavor; it is a strategic imperative in the talent acquisition landscape. By weaving a compelling narrative that reflects the organization's values and culture, leveraging social media for global visibility, and ensuring consistency in messaging, organizations can position themselves as employers of choice. A strong employer brand not only attracts top talent but also fosters employee retention, contributing to a dynamic and resilient workforce in the ever-evolving global business environment.

4. Leveraging Technology and Analytics

In the contemporary landscape of talent acquisition, leveraging cutting-edge technology and analytics is not just an option; it's a strategic imperative. Organizations embracing advanced tools like Applicant Tracking Systems (ATS), data analytics, and artificial intelligence (AI) are poised to revolutionize the talent acquisition process on a global scale.

Applicant Tracking Systems serve as the backbone of a modern talent acquisition strategy. These systems streamline the recruitment process by automating various tasks, from posting job openings to managing candidate applications. The efficiency gained through ATS allows recruiters to focus on more strategic aspects of talent acquisition, such as building relationships and assessing cultural fit.

Data analytics plays a pivotal role in enhancing the effectiveness of talent acquisition. By harnessing the power of data, organizations can gain valuable insights into their recruitment processes. Analyzing historical data helps in identifying patterns related to successful hires, understanding the sources of top talent, and recognizing areas for improvement. These insights enable data-driven decision-making, allowing organizations to refine their recruitment strategies based on empirical evidence.

Artificial intelligence introduces a transformative dimension to talent acquisition. AI algorithms can analyze vast datasets to identify correlations and predict future talent needs. This predictive capability is particularly valuable in a global context, where talent requirements may vary across regions and industries. AI can assist in forecasting trends, helping organizations stay ahead of the curve in talent acquisition.

Moreover, technology facilitates a more inclusive and diverse talent acquisition process. AI-driven tools can eliminate biases from job descriptions, ensuring that they appeal to a diverse audience. This inclusivity is crucial for attracting a wide range of candidates, fostering a culture of diversity within the organization.

The benefits of leveraging technology and analytics in talent acquisition are manifold. Firstly, it significantly reduces time-to-hire. Automated processes and predictive analytics enable recruiters to identify and connect with top talent swiftly, ensuring that critical positions are filled promptly.

Secondly, it enhances the quality of hires. By leveraging analytics, organizations can assess the effectiveness of their recruitment channels, focusing on sources that consistently yield high-quality candidates. This data-driven approach contributes to building a workforce with the right skills and cultural fit.

Thirdly, technology-driven talent acquisition is cost-effective. By automating repetitive tasks, organizations can allocate resources more efficiently. This efficiency not only reduces recruitment costs but also allows recruiters to concentrate on strategic activities that add substantial value to the organization.

The integration of technology and analytics in talent acquisition is a transformative journey for organizations aiming to attract top talent globally. The synergy of advanced tools, data analytics, and artificial intelligence not only streamlines the recruitment process but also empowers organizations to make informed, data-driven decisions. As the global talent landscape evolves, those who embrace these technological advancements are poised to lead the way in acquiring and retaining the best talent.

5. Global Talent Networks and Partnerships

In the pursuit of top-tier talent on a global scale, organizations are increasingly turning to the strategic establishment of relationships with global talent networks, universities, and industry organizations. This proactive approach not only broadens the scope of potential candidates but also lays the foundation for long-term collaborations that contribute to organizational growth.

Building strategic relationships with global talent networks entails engaging with platforms that connect professionals worldwide. By leveraging these networks, organizations gain access to a diverse pool of candidates with varied skill sets, cultural backgrounds, and industry experiences. This diversity is a valuable asset, enriching the organizational landscape with fresh perspectives and innovative thinking. Moreover, these networks often serve as hubs for industry-specific talent, allowing organizations to tap into a wealth of expertise aligned with their sector.

Universities stand as fertile grounds for nurturing emerging talent. Establishing partnerships with academic institutions globally provides organizations with a direct channel to engage with students and recent graduates. By collaborating on internship programs, research initiatives, or industry-specific projects, organizations not only identify promising individuals but also contribute to the development of future leaders in the field. This symbiotic relationship ensures a steady influx of skilled professionals who are well-acquainted with the latest industry trends and possess a solid academic foundation.

Industry organizations play a pivotal role in connecting professionals within specific sectors. Collaborating with these entities allows organizations to participate in events, conferences, and networking opportunities tailored to their industry. These engagements facilitate direct interactions with professionals who have a profound understanding of the industry landscape, making them valuable additions to the talent pool. Furthermore, industry partnerships can foster knowledge exchange, providing organizations with insights into emerging trends and best practices.

Creating a pipeline of skilled individuals aligned with organizational needs is a key outcome of these global partnerships. By actively participating in the talent development process, organizations ensure that they are well-positioned to identify and attract individuals who possess the right skills and cultural fit. This strategic alignment is crucial for organizational success, as it ensures that talent acquisition efforts are directed towards individuals who not only meet current needs but are also poised to contribute significantly to future growth.

The establishment of global talent networks and partnerships is a proactive strategy that enhances an organization's ability to attract top talent on a global scale. By connecting with diverse talent pools, engaging with universities, and collaborating with industry organizations, organizations not only broaden their talent landscape but also contribute to the development of skilled professionals. This strategic approach not only meets immediate talent acquisition needs but lays the groundwork for sustained organizational excellence in the dynamic global business environment.

6. Diversity and Inclusion Initiatives

Recognizing the pivotal role of diversity and inclusion in talent acquisition is not merely a nod to societal expectations but an integral strategic imperative for organizations operating on a global scale. In an interconnected world, where markets are diverse and dynamic, fostering a workplace that mirrors this diversity is not just a moral stance; it's a pragmatic business approach.

Diversity, spanning dimensions such as gender, ethnicity, age, and cultural backgrounds, enriches the talent pool by introducing a plethora of perspectives and skills. In the global talent acquisition landscape, where businesses navigate complex markets with varying cultural contexts, embracing diversity becomes a catalyst for innovation and adaptability. A diverse workforce isn't just a checkbox; it's a wellspring of creativity and resilience, positioning organizations to navigate the intricate challenges of a globalized business environment.

To actively champion diversity and inclusion, organizations need to implement initiatives that go beyond superficial commitments. A fundamental shift in the mindset is required to create an inclusive hiring process that transcends geographical boundaries and reflects a global perspective. This shift is rooted in the understanding that a homogenous workforce lacks the richness necessary to navigate the multifaceted challenges posed by a global market.

Initiatives should be designed to attract talent from different backgrounds, ensuring that the recruitment process is accessible, unbiased, and open to individuals with varied experiences. Outreach programs, partnerships with diverse professional networks, and targeted recruitment strategies are instrumental in broadening the talent pool and reaching individuals who might otherwise be overlooked.

Inclusive hiring goes beyond recruitment practices; it extends to creating a workplace culture that celebrates differences. Organizations must foster an environment where every employee feels valued and has equal opportunities for growth. This involves developing policies that address unconscious biases, providing diversity training for employees, and establishing mentorship programs that support the professional development of underrepresented groups.

The benefits of robust diversity and inclusion initiatives in global talent acquisition are profound. Beyond the ethical imperative, organizations that prioritize diversity and inclusion are better equipped to understand and navigate diverse markets. This cultural intelligence becomes a strategic advantage, enabling businesses to connect with customers, partners, and stakeholders on a deeper level.

Moreover, a diverse workforce enhances creativity and problem-solving. The interplay of varied perspectives sparks innovation, driving organizations to find unique solutions to complex challenges. In a global context, where markets are characterized by rapid change and unpredictability, this innovative capacity is a competitive differentiator.

The acknowledgment of diversity and inclusion as integral components of talent acquisition is a strategic imperative for organizations with global aspirations. It goes beyond compliance and moral responsibility; it's a recognition that a diverse workforce isn't just a reflection of societal values but a critical asset for navigating the complexities of a globalized business landscape. Organizations that champion diversity and inclusion in talent acquisition position themselves not only as ethical leaders but as agile and innovative contenders in the global marketplace.

7. Cross-Border Recruitment Events

In the pursuit of top-tier global talent, organizations are increasingly turning to cross-border recruitment events as a strategic avenue for identifying and engaging with prospective candidates. These events, ranging from traditional job fairs and industry conferences to modern virtual meetups, serve as dynamic platforms that transcend geographical boundaries, fostering connections in the pursuit of exceptional talent.

Participation in cross-border recruitment events offers organizations a unique opportunity to engage with a diverse pool of candidates. Whether attending a physical job fair or participating in a virtual meetup, these events facilitate direct interactions, allowing recruiters to gauge the skills, experiences, and cultural fit of potential candidates. This hands-on approach is invaluable in assessing talent beyond the confines of resumes and interviews, providing a more holistic understanding of candidates' suitability for global roles.

Moreover, these events offer a firsthand exploration of regional nuances. In a globalized workforce, understanding the specific dynamics and expectations of different regions is crucial. Cross-border recruitment events enable organizations to immerse themselves in local cultures, gaining insights into the professional landscape, employment preferences, and industry trends. This understanding is foundational for tailoring recruitment strategies to align with the unique attributes of each region.

Hosting recruitment events also serves as a powerful tool for organizations looking to showcase their commitment to global talent acquisition. Whether as an exhibitor at a physical job fair or a featured participant in a virtual meetup, organizations can leverage these platforms to communicate their values, work culture, and dedication to fostering a diverse and inclusive workforce. This not only attracts potential candidates but also contributes to building a positive employer brand on an international scale.

Virtual meetups, in particular, have emerged as a convenient and effective channel for cross-border recruitment. With the advent of advanced communication technologies, organizations can connect with candidates from around the world without the constraints of physical proximity. Virtual events allow for real-time engagement, enabling recruiters to conduct interviews, presentations, and networking sessions seamlessly. This flexibility not only accommodates the preferences of global candidates but also aligns with the evolving landscape of remote work and digital connectivity.

Cross-border recruitment events represent a strategic linchpin in the global talent acquisition toolkit. Whether through traditional job fairs, industry conferences, or virtual meetups, these events provide a dynamic platform for organizations to connect with diverse talent, understand regional intricacies, and underscore their commitment to global workforce diversity. As organizations navigate the intricacies of cross-border recruitment, active participation in these events emerges as a powerful strategy to not only identify top talent but also cultivate a robust and globally aware recruitment approach.

8. Localized Recruitment Strategies

In the pursuit of global talent acquisition, the significance of localized recruitment strategies cannot be overstated. These strategies go beyond the one-size-fits-all approach and recognize the diverse cultural, regulatory, and employment landscapes that characterize different regions.

By tailoring recruitment efforts to local contexts, organizations can not only attract top talent but also foster a workplace culture that resonates with individuals from varied backgrounds. Understanding the cultural nuances of a specific region is a fundamental aspect of localized recruitment. It involves recognizing the social norms, communication styles, and work preferences that shape the local workforce. For instance, in some cultures, a strong emphasis on teamwork may be prevalent, while in others, individual achievements might be more highly valued. Tailoring recruitment messages and processes to align with these cultural nuances demonstrates cultural sensitivity and a genuine interest in integrating with local values.

Moreover, localized recruitment strategies delve into the regulatory landscapes of different regions. Employment laws and regulations vary widely across countries, impacting aspects such as hiring processes, employment contracts, and benefits. By adapting recruitment strategies to comply with local regulations, organizations not only ensure legal compliance but also showcase a commitment to ethical and responsible business practices.

Localized recruitment is a testament to an organization's commitment to diversity and inclusion. Recognizing and respecting the diversity of talent across the globe is not only ethically sound but also strategically advantageous. A diverse workforce brings varied perspectives, fosters creativity, and enhances problem-solving capabilities. By tailoring recruitment efforts to local contexts, organizations actively promote inclusivity and create an environment where individuals from diverse backgrounds feel valued and appreciated.

The appeal of localized recruitment is further amplified by its potential to mitigate challenges associated with talent retention. When candidates see that an organization invests time and effort in understanding and adapting to local contexts, they are more likely to feel a sense of belonging. This, in turn, contributes to higher job satisfaction and retention rates. Individuals are more likely to stay with an organization that recognizes and appreciates their unique contributions and cultural backgrounds.

Localized recruitment strategies form a crucial pillar in the architecture of global talent acquisition. They embody a nuanced understanding of cultural diversity, regulatory landscapes, and employment preferences across different regions. By embracing localized approaches, organizations not only attract top talent but also build a workplace culture that values and integrates the richness of global perspectives. In the intricate tapestry of global talent acquisition, localized recruitment strategies emerge as a powerful tool for creating a diverse, inclusive, and dynamic organizational ecosystem.

9. Agile Talent Pipelining

In the dynamic landscape of talent acquisition, where the demand for specialized skills and expertise is ever-evolving, the concept of Agile Talent Pipelining emerges as a strategic imperative. This approach transcends traditional recruitment models by proactively anticipating future talent needs and cultivating a responsive and versatile talent pipeline.

The foundation of Agile Talent Pipelining lies in its forward-looking approach. Organizations keen on staying ahead of the curve delve into identifying potential future roles within the company. This involves a meticulous analysis of the evolving needs of the organization, considering factors such as business expansion, technological advancements, and industry trends. By having a clear vision of the roles that might be crucial in the future, organizations can strategically align their talent acquisition efforts with their long-term objectives.

Furthermore, Agile Talent Pipelining doesn't merely stop at internal considerations; it extends its reach to comprehend broader industry trends. Understanding the trajectory of the industry helps organizations identify emerging skill sets and competencies that will be in demand. This industry foresight is pivotal in sculpting a talent pipeline that not only meets the current needs but is also equipped to address the future requirements of the rapidly changing business landscape.

Proactive engagement is another hallmark of Agile Talent Pipelining. Rather than adopting a reactive stance when a specific role needs to be filled, organizations actively nurture relationships with potential candidates over time. This involves continuous communication, networking, and providing valuable insights into the organization's culture and vision. By fostering these relationships, organizations ensure that when the need arises, they have a pool of engaged and interested candidates ready to step into key roles.

The agility of the talent pipeline becomes particularly crucial in swiftly responding to evolving talent demands. In today's fast-paced business environment, where market conditions can change rapidly, having a pipeline that can adapt to unforeseen circumstances is a strategic advantage. Whether it's a sudden expansion, a shift in business focus, or the emergence of a new skill set, an agile talent pipeline positions the organization to respond swiftly and effectively.

Agile Talent Pipelining represents a paradigm shift in talent acquisition – a shift from reactive recruitment to proactive talent management. By anticipating future needs, aligning with industry trends, and proactively engaging with potential candidates, organizations embracing this approach ensure that they are not merely filling positions but strategically building a reservoir of talent that aligns seamlessly with their evolving business goals.

10. Continuous Learning and Adaptation

Fostering a culture of continuous learning and adaptation stands as a fundamental principle. The landscape of global talent acquisition is shaped by a myriad of factors, including technological advancements, shifts in industry trends, and transformations in global employment patterns. As such, recruitment teams must embrace a proactive approach that goes beyond conventional methodologies.

Continuous learning within the recruitment team involves staying abreast of industry trends and emerging technologies. The rapid evolution of job markets and skill requirements necessitates a keen awareness of the latest developments. By staying informed about industry-specific advancements, the recruitment team can tailor their strategies to align with the current demands of the global workforce.

Furthermore, the dynamic nature of global employment patterns calls for regular assessments and refinements of talent acquisition strategies. Adopting a proactive stance involves evaluating the effectiveness of existing practices and adapting them to the evolving needs of the organization. This process is not a one-time endeavor but rather a continuous cycle of learning, implementation, and refinement.

The integration of adaptive strategies is crucial in addressing the changing expectations of candidates. With a growing emphasis on workplace flexibility, remote work, and diverse skill sets, talent acquisition strategies must align with these evolving preferences. Incorporating innovative approaches to candidate engagement, such as virtual recruitment events and interactive assessments, reflects a commitment to staying ahead in the competitive talent acquisition landscape.

Moreover, the globalization of talent acquisition introduces unique challenges that necessitate adaptability. Cross-cultural considerations, diverse employment laws, and varying candidate expectations across regions demand a nuanced approach. Continuous learning involves understanding these intricacies and tailoring recruitment strategies to each geographic context.

Adopting a culture of continuous learning and adaptation not only ensures relevance in the face of change but also cultivates a dynamic and resilient recruitment team. Team members become adept at navigating uncertainties, embracing new technologies, and proactively addressing emerging challenges. This adaptability becomes a cornerstone in building a talent acquisition strategy that not only meets the immediate needs of the organization but also positions it strategically for the future.

In conclusion, continuous learning and adaptation are not mere strategies but foundational principles for success in global talent acquisition. By embracing a culture of perpetual learning, recruitment teams equip themselves with the agility and insight required to navigate the dynamic terrain of the global workforce. This commitment to staying ahead of industry trends and proactively adapting strategies is a key driver in building a resilient and effective talent acquisition framework.

Strategic talent acquisition on a global scale demands a proactive and dynamic approach. By combining comprehensive workforce planning, leveraging technology, fostering diversity and inclusion, and embracing localized strategies, organizations can position themselves to attract and retain top talent, ensuring sustained success in the global marketplace.

Cultivating a Diverse Company Culture

Company culture is the collective personality of an organization, encompassing its values, beliefs, behaviors, and the overall environment in which employees operate. It is the glue that binds individuals together, shaping their experiences and influencing their engagement, productivity, and satisfaction within the workplace. Cultivating a diverse company culture is not only a strategic imperative but a transformative journey that contributes to the success and sustainability of a global organization.

Defining Company Culture

At its core, company culture reflects the shared values and principles that guide how employees interact, collaborate, and contribute to the organization's objectives. It goes beyond the tangible aspects of the workplace, extending to the intangible aspects that define the organization's character. A robust company culture aligns the workforce with the organization's mission and vision, fostering a sense of belonging and shared purpose.

Creating a Diverse Company Culture

Inclusive Leadership

Inclusive leadership goes beyond mere rhetoric; it involves tangible actions and a commitment to embodying the principles of diversity and inclusion. Inclusive leadership is a transformative force that sets the tone for an organization's culture, influencing behaviors, and promoting an environment where individuals feel a sense of belonging and authenticity.

Inclusive leadership begins with leading by example. Executives and leaders serve as role models whose behaviors shape the collective identity of the organization. When leaders exemplify inclusive practices, such as recognizing and respecting diverse perspectives, it sends a powerful message throughout the entire workforce. Leading by example means actively engaging with employees from different backgrounds, appreciating their unique contributions, and creating an atmosphere that values differences as strengths rather than challenges.

Actively promoting diversity at the leadership level is not just a commitment to fairness; it's a strategic move that enriches decision-making processes. A diverse leadership team brings a spectrum of perspectives, experiences, and approaches to the table. This diversity is a wellspring of creativity and innovation, fostering a culture where robust discussions and critical thinking are the norm. By having leaders with varied backgrounds, organizations gain insights into different markets, customer segments, and global trends, enabling more informed and strategic decision-making.

Moreover, diverse leadership teams act as visible proof of an organization's commitment to inclusivity. It serves as a beacon that attracts top talent from diverse backgrounds, reinforcing the idea that everyone has an opportunity to rise based on merit, skills, and leadership capabilities. This not only contributes to a healthier workplace culture but also positions the organization as a magnet for diverse talents seeking environments where their perspectives are not only tolerated but celebrated.

Inclusive leadership creates an environment where employees feel acknowledged and heard, fostering a sense of belonging and commitment. It breaks down barriers and ensures that the organization benefits from the collective wisdom of a workforce that reflects the rich tapestry of the global community. As organizations continue to navigate the complexities of a diverse and interconnected world, inclusive leadership remains a linchpin for sustained success and resilience.

Clear Values and Communication

At the heart of cultivating a company culture that resonates with a diverse workforce lies the establishment of clear values and transparent communication. These elements serve as foundational pillars, guiding the organization's identity and reinforcing its commitment to fostering an inclusive environment where diversity, equity, and inclusion are not just buzzwords but integral components of the organizational DNA.

Defining core values that explicitly emphasize diversity, equity, and inclusion is the initial step toward creating an inclusive company culture. These values should be more than mere statements; they should reflect a genuine commitment to embracing differences and promoting a workplace where every individual is valued for their unique contributions. When diversity is entrenched in the core values, it becomes a guiding principle that shapes decision-making, policies, and interactions throughout the organization.

For instance, a technology company might include values such as "Innovation through Diversity" or "Equity in Every Code" to signify its commitment to harnessing diverse perspectives for creative problem-solving and ensuring fairness in all aspects of its operations. Transparent communication serves as the bedrock upon which an inclusive culture is built. Establishing open channels for communication ensures that employees are not only aware of the organization's commitment to diversity but also feel empowered to engage in dialogue about its importance. Regular communication about the significance of diversity, equity, and inclusion reinforces the message that these principles are not just organizational policies but shared beliefs that drive the company's ethos.

This communication should be a two-way street, encouraging feedback and fostering a culture where employees feel heard. Transparency extends to explaining the organization's strategies for promoting diversity and inclusion, celebrating achievements, and addressing challenges. It also involves acknowledging areas for improvement and demonstrating a commitment to continuous growth in fostering an inclusive workplace.

For example, a manufacturing company might use regular town hall meetings, newsletters, and dedicated online platforms to communicate its diversity initiatives, share success stories, and provide resources for employees to engage in educational opportunities about inclusivity.

Establishing clear values and transparent communication is pivotal for creating an inclusive company culture. By embedding diversity, equity, and inclusion in the organization's core values and fostering open communication channels, companies set the stage for a workplace where individuals from diverse backgrounds thrive, collaborate, and contribute to the collective success of the organization.

Employee Resource Groups (ERGs)

Employee Resource Groups (ERGs) stand as vibrant communities within an organization, fostering a sense of belonging and connection among employees who share common characteristics or experiences. These groups, often formed around factors like ethnicity, gender, or other affinity ties, play a crucial role in creating an inclusive workplace where individuals feel seen, heard, and valued.

One of the primary functions of ERGs is to provide a dedicated space for employees to connect and find support within the organization. By bringing together individuals who share commonalities, ERGs act as support networks where members can share experiences, insights, and advice. This sense of community is particularly powerful in addressing the unique challenges that certain groups may face in the workplace, whether related to cultural identity, gender dynamics, or other shared experiences.

These groups not only provide a sense of belonging but also contribute to the broader company culture by promoting understanding and empathy among all employees. ERGs become a cornerstone in weaving a fabric of inclusivity that extends beyond the individual groups, creating a workplace where everyone feels a part of something greater.

Beyond fostering connections, ERGs contribute significantly to organizational diversity and inclusion through collaborative initiatives. Encouraging ERGs to join forces on projects and activities amplifies their impact. This collaboration can take various forms, from organizing events that celebrate cultural diversity to conducting training sessions that enhance awareness and sensitivity across the workforce.

Mentorship programs within ERGs, for instance, create pathways for professional development while establishing strong networks of support. These initiatives not only benefit the members directly involved but also ripple through the organization, promoting a culture of understanding and unity.

Moreover, ERGs often play a pivotal role in educating the broader workforce about diverse perspectives and experiences. Through their initiatives, employees gain insights into the richness of diversity, challenging stereotypes and fostering a workplace culture that values differences. As a result, ERGs become instrumental in driving cultural change within the organization, helping to break down barriers and build bridges of understanding.

ERGs emerge as dynamic entities that transcend their initial purpose of providing support to specific groups. They become catalysts for positive change, actively contributing to the creation of an inclusive, empathetic, and culturally aware workplace where diversity is not just acknowledged but celebrated. As organizations increasingly recognize the benefits of diverse and inclusive environments, ERGs stand as powerful tools for building bridges across differences and driving lasting cultural transformation.

Inclusive Policies and Practices

In the pursuit of a truly inclusive company culture, the formulation and implementation of inclusive policies and practices are pivotal. These strategies not only shape the internal dynamics of an organization but also broadcast a commitment to diversity and equity, influencing the perception of the company in the broader community.

A key aspect of fostering inclusivity is transforming the recruitment process to be genuinely diverse and inclusive. This goes beyond slogans; it involves implementing tangible practices that actively seek out and welcome individuals from a variety of backgrounds. Establishing partnerships with educational institutions, community organizations, and professional networks allows organizations to tap into diverse talent pools. By participating in initiatives that target underrepresented groups, companies can broaden their reach and actively engage with individuals who might bring unique perspectives and skills to the table.

Moreover, an inclusive recruitment strategy involves reevaluating job descriptions and requirements to ensure they are free from bias and do not inadvertently discourage candidates from underrepresented groups. The goal is to create an environment where all individuals, regardless of their background, feel encouraged to apply, knowing that their skills and potential are valued.

Equitable policies form the backbone of an inclusive organizational culture. This encompasses a spectrum of practices, from ensuring fair compensation structures to providing flexible work arrangements that accommodate diverse needs. Transparent and unbiased promotion processes are also integral components, ensuring that career progression is based on merit and skills rather than favoritism or preconceived notions.

Fair compensation practices involve conducting regular pay equity assessments to identify and rectify any gender or diversity-related gaps. Beyond salaries, organizations need to assess and address disparities in benefits, bonuses, and other forms of compensation. This commitment to fairness not only adheres to ethical standards but also enhances employee satisfaction and loyalty.

Flexible work arrangements are another critical element of inclusive policies. Recognizing that individuals have diverse needs and responsibilities outside of work, offering flexibility in terms of working hours, remote work options, or compressed workweeks contributes to a culture that values work-life balance and understands the unique circumstances of each employee.

Inclusive policies and practices go beyond compliance; they are the embodiment of an organization's commitment to fostering an environment where everyone feels seen, heard, and valued. These policies not only attract a diverse workforce but also create conditions for their success and advancement within the organization. As companies navigate the complexities of a global and interconnected workforce, the adoption of inclusive policies becomes not just a strategic imperative but a moral and ethical obligation.

Continuous Learning and Development

Continuous learning and development is an essential pillar that fortify the foundation of an organization. These initiatives go beyond the traditional scope of skill enhancement; they become powerful tools for instilling a mindset of diversity, equity, and inclusion across all levels of the workforce.

An integral aspect of continuous learning within a diverse company culture is the provision of ongoing diversity and inclusion training for all employees. These programs serve as immersive experiences, shedding light on the nuances of diversity and challenging biases that may exist. Through interactive workshops, educational sessions, and awareness campaigns, employees gain insights into the importance of embracing differences and fostering a culture of respect. Continuous exposure to diversity training not only equips individuals with the knowledge to navigate various cultural landscapes but also plays a pivotal role in dismantling stereotypes and fostering a more inclusive mindset.

Encouraging continuous learning and skill development is not just about staying competitive in a rapidly evolving market; it's also about empowering employees to navigate diverse and multicultural environments effectively. In a globalized workforce, where interactions span across geographical boundaries, possessing skills related to cross-cultural communication, adaptability, and cultural intelligence becomes paramount. Organizations can facilitate this by offering workshops and training sessions that focus on developing these crucial skills.

By providing resources for skill development, organizations enable employees to grow both professionally and personally. Skill enhancement programs might encompass language training, cultural sensitivity workshops, and leadership development initiatives that emphasize inclusive leadership styles. These initiatives not only contribute to personal growth but also foster an environment where employees are better equipped to collaborate seamlessly in a diverse and globalized workplace.

Continuous learning and development initiatives contribute to the creation of a dynamic and adaptive workforce that embraces diversity as a strength rather than a challenge. As employees become more adept at navigating differences and fostering inclusion, the organization, in turn, reaps the benefits of a creative, innovative, and resilient team prepared for the challenges of a diverse and interconnected world.

Recognition and Celebration

In the mosaic of a diverse workforce, recognition and celebration serve as vital threads that weave together an inclusive company culture. Acknowledging diversity goes beyond mere tolerance; it involves actively appreciating and valuing the unique contributions that individuals from various backgrounds bring to the collective tapestry of the organization.

Acknowledging Diversity: A Cornerstone of Inclusivity

Recognition programs play a pivotal role in fostering a culture where diversity is not just acknowledged but celebrated. By acknowledging the diverse talents, skills, and perspectives of employees, organizations communicate a clear message of inclusivity. This recognition goes beyond mere individual achievements; it embraces the richness that stems from having a workforce with diverse experiences, cultures, and viewpoints.

In an environment where individuals feel seen and valued, employees are more likely to be engaged, motivated, and committed to their work. Recognition becomes a powerful tool for reinforcing the organization's commitment to diversity and creating a positive and inclusive atmosphere.

Global Celebrations: A Tapestry of Cultural Understanding

Celebrating global observances and cultural festivities is a tangible way to demonstrate an inclusive approach that transcends geographical boundaries. By recognizing and participating in global celebrations, organizations send a message that they honor the diverse cultural backgrounds of their employees.

Participating in global celebrations provides an opportunity for cultural exchange within the workplace. It fosters an environment where employees learn about and appreciate different traditions, customs, and holidays. This not only promotes cultural understanding but also contributes to the creation of a more harmonious and inclusive workplace.

Moreover, celebrating global observances can be a source of unity within the workforce. It builds a sense of community as employees come together to share in the festivities, irrespective of their individual cultural backgrounds. This shared experience helps break down barriers, fostering a collaborative and supportive atmosphere where individuals from diverse backgrounds feel a sense of belonging.

Recognition and celebration form the bedrock of an inclusive company culture. By actively acknowledging diversity through recognition programs and participating in global celebrations, organizations create an environment where each employee feels valued and appreciated. This commitment to inclusivity not only enhances employee morale and engagement but also contributes to the establishment of a workplace that reflects the vibrancy of a global community.

Benefits of a Diverse Company Culture:

- **Enhanced Innovation and Creativity:** Diverse teams bring a variety of perspectives and ideas, fostering creativity and innovation. A culture that values diversity stimulates out-of-the-box thinking, driving organizational innovation.
- **Improved Employee Engagement:** An inclusive culture promotes a sense of belonging among employees. When individuals feel heard, respected, and valued, their engagement and commitment to the organization increase.
- **Broader Market Appeal:** A diverse company culture resonates with a broad audience. It enhances the organization's reputation, making it an attractive employer for individuals from different backgrounds.
- **Adaptability to Global Markets:** In a globalized business landscape, a diverse company culture positions the organization to understand and adapt to various markets, customer preferences, and cultural nuances.

In conclusion, cultivating a diverse company culture is an ongoing and multifaceted journey. It requires intentional efforts from leadership, clear communication, inclusive policies, and a commitment to continuous learning. A strong and diverse company culture not only attracts and retains top talent but also serves as a catalyst for innovation, employee engagement, and sustained success in the global marketplace.

Chapter **23**

Data-Driven
Decision Making

For modern businesses, the ability to turn data into actionable insights is a cornerstone for success. In this chapter, we will unravel the intricacies of data-driven decision making, a strategic approach that empowers businesses to glean valuable insights from big data analytics. As organizations navigate the vast realms of market trends, customer behaviors, and operational intricacies, leveraging data becomes not just advantageous but imperative for informed decision-making.

We delve into the methodologies of extracting meaningful patterns and correlations from data, illuminating how businesses can translate this information into strategic choices.

From understanding market dynamics to tailoring personalized customer experiences, this chapter explores the multifaceted impact of data analytics on growth and innovation.

In an era where information reigns supreme, the chapter unfolds the narrative of how businesses can harness the power of data to steer their course, foster innovation, and drive sustainable expansion.

Implementing Effective Data Analytics Strategies

In the contemporary business landscape, effective data analytics is not merely a competitive advantage; it is a fundamental necessity for strategic decision-making. Implementing robust data analytics strategies requires a holistic approach that encompasses technology, talent, and a keen understanding of business objectives.

1. Define Clear Objectives

Establishing clear and precise objectives is a foundational step that shapes the trajectory of the entire analytical journey. As organizations delve into data analytics endeavors, their objectives vary widely, encompassing goals such as enhancing operational efficiency, understanding customer behavior, or predicting market trends. The clarity and specificity of these objectives are paramount, acting as the guiding compass for data analytics teams.

For organizations aiming to bolster operational efficiency through data-driven insights, clear objectives might involve optimizing processes, identifying bottlenecks, or streamlining workflows. These could include reducing production costs by a certain percentage, minimizing turnaround times, or improving resource allocation. Similarly, for businesses focused on understanding customer behavior, objectives might revolve around creating personalized experiences, improving customer satisfaction, or boosting customer retention rates. Clear goals in this context could include achieving a specific Net Promoter Score (NPS), understanding the customer journey across various touchpoints, or predicting purchasing patterns.

In the dynamic realm of predicting market trends, strategic objectives may involve accurately forecasting demand for products or services, identifying emerging market trends ahead of competitors, or adapting marketing strategies based on predictive analytics. These objectives serve as a roadmap for the data analytics journey, providing a structured path for teams to follow. The roadmap helps streamline the analytical process and facilitates effective resource allocation.

Crucially, the effectiveness of data analytics objectives is intertwined with their measurability and attainability. Objectives should be framed in a way that allows for quantitative measurement, enabling organizations to assess the success of their analytics initiatives. Moreover, these goals should be realistic and achievable within a defined timeframe, avoiding overly ambitious or vague aspirations.

Clear objectives are not isolated entities; they must align seamlessly with overarching organizational goals. Whether an organization aims for revenue growth, cost reduction, or market expansion, data analytics objectives should directly contribute to these broader aspirations. This alignment ensures that data analytics efforts are purposeful and contribute meaningfully to the organization's success.

Throughout the data analytics journey, well-defined objectives serve as a compass guiding decision-making processes. These objectives influence decisions related to data sources, analytical methods, and result interpretation. Every decision made within the data analytics framework should be aligned with the ultimate objectives to ensure coherence and relevance.

While clear objectives provide direction, they should also allow for flexibility and iterative refinement. The iterative nature of data analytics means that objectives may evolve as insights are gained and organizational priorities shift. A flexible approach allows teams to adapt their strategies based on emerging findings and changing business dynamics.

Defining clear objectives in data analytics is not a mere formality but a strategic imperative. It is the compass that ensures organizations embark on a purposeful and effective journey, leveraging data to achieve tangible outcomes that align with overarching business goals. Whether seeking operational efficiency, understanding customer behavior, or predicting market trends, the clarity of objectives shapes the entire trajectory of data analytics strategies.

2. Build a Robust Data Infrastructure

Building a robust data infrastructure is fundamental to the success of any data analytics initiative. Organizations must invest in systems that can adeptly handle the three Vs of data – volume, velocity, and variety. This involves selecting and implementing appropriate storage solutions capable of accommodating large volumes of data, managing the speed at which data is generated and processed (velocity), and handling diverse data types and sources (variety). A key aspect of this infrastructure is ensuring data quality, encompassing accuracy, completeness, consistency, and timeliness.

Efficient data governance practices play a pivotal role in maintaining the integrity and reliability of the data infrastructure. This involves establishing policies and procedures for data management, defining roles and responsibilities, and ensuring compliance with regulatory requirements. A well-architected data governance framework provides a structured approach to data handling, reducing the risk of errors, inaccuracies, and security breaches.

Moreover, organizations need to consider scalability and flexibility when building their data infrastructure. As data volumes grow and new sources are integrated, the infrastructure should have the capacity to scale seamlessly. This scalability ensures that the analytics platform can evolve alongside the organization's expanding data needs. Additionally, flexibility in the data infrastructure allows for the incorporation of emerging technologies and methodologies, ensuring adaptability to the evolving landscape of data analytics.

Ultimately, a robust data infrastructure serves as the bedrock upon which meaningful analytics are built. It facilitates the storage, processing, and retrieval of data in a manner that is efficient, reliable, and aligned with organizational goals. By investing in the right technologies and governance practices, organizations lay the foundation for extracting valuable insights from their data, contributing to informed decision-making and strategic advancements.

3. Leverage Advanced Analytics Tools

The choice of tools plays a pivotal role in determining the success and depth of insights derived from analytical endeavors. As organizations navigate the intricate web of data complexity and analytical sophistication, leveraging advanced analytics tools emerges as a strategic imperative. The selection process involves identifying tools that seamlessly align with the intricacies of the available data and the sophistication of the analytical goals.

Various categories of advanced analytics tools are at organizations' disposal, ranging from robust business intelligence platforms to cutting-edge machine learning algorithms. Business intelligence platforms, equipped with intuitive dashboards and visualization capabilities, serve well for organizations seeking to gain quick and accessible insights from their data. These platforms offer a user-friendly interface that enables non-technical users to explore and comprehend complex datasets.

On the other end of the spectrum, machine learning algorithms are instrumental for organizations with more intricate analytical objectives. These algorithms, powered by artificial intelligence, possess the capability to discern patterns, predict trends, and uncover latent insights within vast datasets. Machine learning tools thrive in scenarios where the analytical goals demand a deeper understanding of data relationships, predictive modeling, and complex pattern recognition.

The effectiveness of these tools is not solely determined by their standalone capabilities but by their seamless integration into existing workflows. Integration ensures that the tools become an intrinsic part of the organization's analytical ecosystem, promoting a cohesive and streamlined approach to data-driven decision-making. Seamless integration enables teams to extract actionable insights more efficiently, eliminating silos and fostering a collaborative environment.

As organizations delve into the realm of advanced analytics, the choice of tools should be guided by a comprehensive understanding of the specific analytical goals and the nature of the available data. The intricacies of the organization's objectives should align harmoniously with the functionalities of the selected tools, creating a symbiotic relationship that amplifies the impact of data analytics efforts.

Furthermore, the selection process should consider factors such as scalability, user-friendliness, and the potential for customization. Scalability ensures that the chosen tools can grow in tandem with the organization's expanding data needs. User-friendliness is paramount, especially in environments where a diverse range of users, including non-technical stakeholders, interact with the analytics tools. Customization capabilities cater to the unique requirements and nuances of the organization's analytical goals.

The strategic deployment of advanced analytics tools is a cornerstone of successful data-driven decision-making. The journey involves careful consideration of the organization's analytical objectives, the nature of the available data, and the specific functionalities offered by different tools. The harmonious integration of these tools into existing workflows enhances their efficacy, fostering a data-driven culture that thrives on actionable insights.

4. Cultivate Analytical Talent

Cultivating analytical talent stands as a pivotal aspect of fostering a data-driven culture within an organization. Building a proficient team that encompasses diverse analytical skills is crucial for unlocking the full potential of data. This team typically comprises individuals with expertise in data science, analytics, and domain-specific knowledge. The synergy among these professionals allows for a holistic approach to data analysis, ensuring that insights derived are not only statistically significant but also contextually relevant to the specific industry or business domain.

Investing in continuous training and development is paramount to keeping the analytical team at the forefront of evolving analytics techniques and technologies. The field of data analytics is dynamic, with constant advancements and innovations. Providing ongoing opportunities for training and skill development ensures that the team remains well-equipped to navigate the changing landscape. This investment not only enhances the individual capabilities of team members but also contributes to the overall analytical prowess of the organization.

Data scientists play a key role in this analytical ensemble. Their expertise in advanced statistical methods, machine learning algorithms, and data modeling is instrumental in extracting meaningful insights from complex datasets. Analysts complement this skill set by bringing a proficiency in data visualization, interpretation, and communication. Additionally, domain experts contribute valuable industry-specific knowledge, allowing for a deeper understanding of the nuances within the data.

Collaboration is the cornerstone of a successful analytical team. By bringing together individuals with varied skills and perspectives, organizations can create a symbiotic environment where each team member's strengths compensate for the others' areas of expertise. This collaborative approach enhances the quality and depth of insights derived from data, making them more actionable and aligned with the organization's strategic goals.

Furthermore, cultivating analytical talent goes beyond recruiting individuals with existing skills. It involves fostering a culture of continuous learning and knowledge sharing within the team. Encouraging the exchange of ideas, best practices, and lessons learned contributes to a dynamic and innovative analytical environment. This collaborative culture not only enhances individual skills but also elevates the collective intelligence of the team.

Cultivating analytical talent is an ongoing commitment to building a high-performing team that can navigate the complexities of data analytics. By bringing together data scientists, analysts, and domain experts, organizations can harness the power of diverse skills to extract meaningful insights. Continuous investment in training and development ensures that the team remains agile and adaptive in the ever-evolving field of data analytics. Ultimately, a well-cultivated analytical team becomes a strategic asset, driving informed decision-making and contributing to the organization's overall success.

5. Establish a Data-Driven Culture

Building a data-driven culture within an organization is a transformative journey that goes beyond the adoption of tools and technologies. It requires fostering a mindset that values and prioritizes data in decision-making processes. Central to this endeavor is the promotion of data literacy across all levels of the organization. From leadership to front-line employees, everyone should be equipped with the skills to understand, interpret, and leverage data effectively.

Encouraging employees to integrate data into their decision processes is a pivotal step in establishing a data-driven culture. This involves providing training and resources to enhance data literacy, ensuring that employees feel confident in working with data. It's not solely about creating a cadre of data specialists but empowering all members of the organization to harness the insights derived from data in their respective roles.

Recognition and rewards play a crucial role in reinforcing the importance of data-driven achievements. Acknowledging individuals or teams that exemplify effective use of data creates positive reinforcement. This recognition serves as a powerful motivator, inspiring others to follow suit and contributing to the cultural shift toward embracing the power of data.

In a culture that values data-driven decision-making, innovation becomes a natural byproduct. Teams are empowered to explore new ideas, experiment with data-driven solutions, and adapt strategies based on insights. The agility fostered by a data-driven culture positions the organization to respond proactively to changes in the business landscape, customer preferences, and market dynamics.

Furthermore, communication is key in embedding a data-driven culture. Leadership should consistently communicate the importance of data in decision-making and its alignment with the organization's strategic objectives. Clear communication helps demystify the use of data and underscores its relevance in achieving business goals.

Establishing a data-driven culture is not a one-time initiative but an ongoing commitment. Regular training programs, workshops, and forums for sharing success stories can help reinforce the importance of data across the organization. Additionally, leadership plays a pivotal role in championing a data-driven mindset by exemplifying its value in their decision-making processes.

Ultimately, a data-driven culture is a transformative force that propels organizations toward greater efficiency, innovation, and resilience. It instills a collective understanding that data is not merely a resource but a strategic asset that fuels informed decision-making and drives organizational success. Through the establishment of this culture, organizations can navigate the complexities of the modern business landscape with agility and confidence.

6. Ensure Data Security and Compliance

Ensuring data security and compliance is a non-negotiable pillar essential for the success and integrity of any analytics initiative. This imperative involves a multifaceted approach, encompassing stringent cybersecurity measures, encryption protocols, and meticulous access controls to fortify the protection of sensitive information.

Robust cybersecurity measures form the first line of defense against potential threats. These measures may include firewalls, intrusion detection systems, and regular security audits to identify and rectify vulnerabilities. By implementing a comprehensive cybersecurity infrastructure, organizations bolster their resilience against external threats, safeguarding data from unauthorized access or malicious activities.

Encryption protocols play a pivotal role in securing data during storage, transmission, and processing. Employing state-of-the-art encryption algorithms ensures that even if unauthorized access occurs, the intercepted data remains indecipherable and unusable. This layer of protection adds an additional barrier against potential breaches, reinforcing the confidentiality and integrity of the data.

Equally critical are access controls that regulate who can access specific datasets and what actions they can perform. By implementing granular access permissions, organizations can restrict data access to only those individuals or roles that legitimately require it. This not only minimizes the risk of data misuse but also aligns with the principle of least privilege, enhancing overall security.

In the landscape of data analytics, compliance with relevant regulations is paramount. Depending on the industry and geographic location, organizations must adhere to specific data protection laws, such as GDPR, HIPAA, or other regional regulations. This entails understanding the legal frameworks that govern data privacy, ensuring that data analytics practices align with these regulations. Non-compliance not only poses legal risks but can also result in severe financial penalties and reputational damage.

Beyond the risk mitigation aspect, ensuring data security and compliance plays a pivotal role in building trust with stakeholders. In an era where data breaches and privacy concerns are at the forefront of public discourse, organizations that prioritize and demonstrate a commitment to data security are better positioned to earn the trust of customers, partners, and investors.

Transparency in data practices, clear communication regarding security measures, and adherence to established regulations send a powerful message to stakeholders about an organization's commitment to ethical data handling. This trust, once established, becomes a valuable asset that can enhance the organization's reputation, foster customer loyalty, and attract partners who prioritize data security in their collaborations.

Ensuring data security and compliance is not just a technical necessity; it is a strategic imperative that underpins the ethical and responsible use of data in analytics. By prioritizing robust cybersecurity measures, encryption protocols, and compliance with regulations, organizations fortify their data against potential threats, build stakeholder trust, and create a foundation for successful and ethical data analytics initiatives.

7. Integrate Data Across Departments

Breaking down data silos is a crucial step in unleashing the full potential of data analytics within an organization. The integration of data across different departments signifies a departure from isolated, compartmentalized datasets toward a more interconnected and comprehensive view of organizational performance. In many organizations, various departments maintain their datasets independently, leading to data silos that hinder the ability to derive holistic insights.

Integrating data across departments involves creating a unified framework where data from different functional areas seamlessly coexists and interacts. This integration can encompass data related to sales, marketing, finance, operations, and more. By adopting an integrated approach, organizations foster a collaborative environment where cross-functional teams can leverage shared data resources to gain a holistic understanding of the company's dynamics.

The pitfalls of data silos become apparent when insights are fragmented, and departments operate with partial information. For instance, marketing teams may be working with data that lacks insights from customer support, hindering their ability to tailor campaigns to address specific customer needs. Similarly, operations may miss out on valuable insights from sales data, impacting their ability to optimize processes based on market demand.

Data integration transcends the mere aggregation of datasets; it involves creating connections and relationships between different data points. This interconnectedness is pivotal for uncovering correlations, identifying patterns, and extracting meaningful insights that can guide strategic decision-making across the organization.

Furthermore, integrated data facilitates a more efficient and streamlined workflow. When different departments share a common data infrastructure, it eliminates redundancies, reduces the risk of errors, and promotes consistency in reporting. This, in turn, enhances the overall efficiency of data-driven processes and contributes to a more agile and responsive organizational structure.

Cross-functional collaboration is a natural byproduct of integrated data. Teams can collectively analyze and interpret data, drawing from diverse perspectives to arrive at well-rounded insights. For example, sales teams can align their strategies with marketing initiatives, and finance teams can better understand the impact of operational decisions. This collaborative approach is instrumental in addressing complex business challenges that require insights from multiple angles.

Integrating data across departments marks a transformative shift from fragmented information to a unified, interconnected data landscape. This holistic view not only improves the quality of insights but also fosters a collaborative culture where cross-functional teams can work cohesively toward common objectives. As organizations strive for data-driven excellence, the dismantling of data silos emerges as a strategic imperative to unlock the true potential of their data assets.

8. Continuous Monitoring and Optimization

The implementation of a robust data analytics strategy doesn't end with the initial deployment; rather, it requires a commitment to continuous monitoring and optimization to ensure ongoing relevance and effectiveness. Establishing a systematic approach for continuous monitoring is imperative to gauge the performance of data analytics processes over time. This involves regular assessments of the algorithms employed, the validity and significance of chosen metrics, and the overall alignment of analytics strategies with evolving business dynamics.

Continuous monitoring serves as a proactive mechanism to identify potential issues, bottlenecks, or shifts in data patterns. By regularly evaluating the performance of algorithms, organizations can ensure that these analytical tools remain accurate and reliable. It allows for the detection of anomalies or changes in data patterns that might impact the validity of analytical models.

Furthermore, the assessment of chosen metrics is crucial for maintaining relevance. Business priorities may shift, market dynamics could change, and customer preferences might evolve. Regularly evaluating the significance of chosen metrics ensures that the analytics efforts remain aligned with the most pertinent indicators of organizational success. It enables organizations to adapt their analytics strategies in response to emerging trends or shifts in the competitive landscape.

The optimization of data analytics strategies is a natural outcome of the continuous monitoring process. As insights are gained from ongoing assessments, organizations can refine and enhance their analytical approaches. Optimization might involve tweaking algorithms for better accuracy, adjusting the focus of metrics to better align with current business priorities, or incorporating new data sources for a more comprehensive view.

The iterative nature of continuous monitoring and optimization is particularly critical in the fast-paced and dynamic world of data analytics. Business environments are subject to constant change, influenced by factors such as market trends, technological advancements, or shifts in consumer behavior. Therefore, the ability to adapt analytics strategies through continuous monitoring and optimization is paramount for maintaining the effectiveness and relevance of data-driven decision-making.

The journey of data analytics extends beyond the initial implementation phase. Continuous monitoring and optimization represent a commitment to keeping analytics efforts aligned with organizational goals in the face of ever-evolving business landscapes. This iterative approach ensures that data analytics processes remain accurate, relevant, and capable of providing actionable insights to drive informed decision-making within the organization.

9. Collaborate with External Experts

Collaborating with external experts in the field of data analytics emerges as a strategic initiative that organizations can adopt to enhance the depth and breadth of their analytical capabilities. In the dynamic landscape of data-driven decision-making, external perspectives contribute valuable insights and bring a fresh outlook to the analytical table. Leveraging the expertise of consultants or specialists in data analytics can be particularly beneficial when organizations encounter specific challenges or aim to identify untapped opportunities.

External collaborations in data analytics serve as a symbiotic relationship where the organization benefits from the specialized knowledge and experience of external experts, while the experts gain a deeper understanding of the organization's unique challenges and objectives. This exchange of insights and perspectives can lead to innovative solutions and approaches that may not have been apparent within the confines of the organization's internal dynamics.

When facing intricate challenges in the data analytics realm, external experts can offer tailored solutions, drawing from their experiences with diverse clients and industries. This external input becomes invaluable in overcoming obstacles and refining analytical strategies. Moreover, external collaborators can contribute to the continuous learning culture within the organization, introducing the latest industry trends, emerging technologies, and best practices.

External collaborations also play a pivotal role in identifying untapped opportunities within an organization's data landscape. The fresh set of eyes from external experts can uncover novel patterns, correlations, or predictive insights that might have gone unnoticed. This proactive approach to exploring uncharted territories fosters a culture of innovation and keeps the organization at the forefront of data analytics advancements.

The collaboration with external experts is not limited to addressing immediate challenges; it extends to capacity building within the organization. By working alongside external specialists, internal teams have the opportunity to learn from their expertise, gaining new skills and perspectives. This knowledge transfer strengthens the organization's internal capabilities and empowers teams to independently navigate future data analytics endeavors.

Furthermore, external collaborations inject diversity into the analytical process. The varied backgrounds, experiences, and approaches of external experts contribute to a richer analytical ecosystem. This diversity promotes creativity and ensures a well-rounded assessment of data-related issues and opportunities. It also aligns with the broader trend of inclusivity in decision-making, ensuring that a multitude of perspectives is considered in shaping data-driven strategies.

The decision to collaborate with external experts in data analytics is a strategic move that amplifies the capabilities of organizations in navigating the complexities of data-driven decision-making. This collaboration introduces fresh perspectives, innovative solutions, and a continuous learning culture that propels the organization towards greater efficiency and effectiveness in leveraging data for strategic outcomes.

10. Stay Agile and Adaptive

The ability to stay agile and adaptive is a fundamental principle that ensures organizations can navigate the ever-evolving terrain of technologies and methodologies. The field of data analytics is marked by continuous advancements, with new tools, techniques, and approaches emerging regularly. Organizations committed to leveraging data for strategic decision-making must cultivate an environment of agility, remaining receptive to changes that can enhance their analytics capabilities.

Being agile in the context of data analytics involves a proactive approach to embracing innovations and incorporating new methodologies into existing frameworks. This adaptability is crucial for organizations aiming not only to keep pace with industry advancements but also to stay ahead of the curve. It requires a mindset that encourages exploration and experimentation with emerging technologies, ensuring that analytics processes are aligned with the latest industry standards and best practices.

One aspect of staying agile in data analytics is the willingness to explore and adopt new tools and technologies that can augment analytical capabilities. Whether it's integrating advanced machine learning algorithms, adopting more efficient data visualization tools, or leveraging cloud-based analytics platforms, organizations must be open to incorporating innovations that can enhance their analytical workflows. This proactive approach enables them to harness the full potential of evolving data landscapes.

Adaptability, in the context of data analytics, extends beyond technology to encompass methodologies and strategies. It involves reassessing existing analytical frameworks and methodologies regularly to ensure they remain effective and aligned with organizational objectives. This might involve revisiting data collection and processing approaches, refining analytical models, or exploring novel techniques to extract meaningful insights from data.

The pace of change in the data analytics field also underscores the importance of fostering a culture that values continuous learning and skill development. Teams involved in data analytics must be encouraged to stay updated on industry trends, attend training programs, and engage in professional development activities. This commitment to ongoing learning ensures that organizations have the expertise needed to leverage the latest advancements in data analytics effectively.

Moreover, staying agile and adaptive in data analytics is not just about responding to external changes but also about actively seeking opportunities for improvement. Organizations should foster an environment that encourages feedback and collaboration, allowing teams to share insights and collectively identify areas for enhancement. This collaborative approach promotes a culture of innovation, where teams work together to refine analytical processes and uncover new ways to derive value from data.

Staying agile and adaptive is a cornerstone of effective data analytics strategies. Embracing change, being open to innovation, and fostering a culture of continuous learning position organizations to not only navigate the complexities of the dynamic data landscape but also to capitalize on emerging opportunities. By remaining agile, organizations can harness the full potential of data analytics, making informed and strategic decisions that drive business success.

In summary, effective data analytics strategies are not a one-size-fits-all solution but a tailored approach that aligns with organizational goals, embraces technological advancements, and nurtures a culture that values the transformative power of data-driven decision-making. As businesses traverse the data-driven journey, the key lies in the continuous refinement of strategies to extract actionable insights and drive sustained growth.

Utilizing Customer Data for Personalized Experiences

In the contemporary business landscape, leveraging customer data for personalized experiences has become a cornerstone of successful marketing and customer relationship management. Customer data comprises a wealth of information gathered from various interactions and transactions between customers and a business. It encompasses both personal and behavioral data, providing insights into individual preferences, purchase history, demographics, and engagement patterns.

Components of Customer Data

Personal Information

This category of customer data delves into the foundational aspects of an individual's identity, offering businesses key insights into their customer base. Beyond the basic details such as name, age, gender, location, and contact information, personal information forms the cornerstone of a comprehensive customer profile. By understanding these foundational elements, businesses can create a more nuanced understanding of their clientele, allowing for tailored interactions and personalized experiences.

Transactional Data

Within the realm of customer data, transactional data stands as a rich reservoir of information, capturing the dynamic interactions between customers and a business. It spans the entire history of a customer's engagements, including intricate details of purchase records, order history, and specifics regarding products or services bought. This multifaceted dataset serves as a vital resource for deciphering intricate buying patterns and discerning individual preferences. Transactional data provides a panoramic view of a customer's journey with a business, enabling strategic decision-making, targeted marketing efforts, and the optimization of products or services to align with customer expectations. As a fundamental element in the realm of customer analytics, transactional data plays a pivotal role in shaping customer-centric strategies and fostering long-term relationships between businesses and their clientele.

Behavioral Data

Behavioral data is an indispensable aspect of customer insights, providing a comprehensive understanding of how customers interact with a company's digital platforms. This multifaceted data encompasses various online behaviors, such as website visits, clicks, the amount of time spent on specific pages, and interactions with diverse online content. By delving into behavioral data, businesses gain profound insights into user preferences, engagement patterns, and the effectiveness of their online presence. Analyzing this data not only aids in refining digital strategies but also allows for the creation of personalized and intuitive online experiences that resonate with individual users.

Communication Preferences

Communication preferences form another crucial dimension of customer data, shedding light on how customers wish to be contacted by businesses. This information extends beyond merely choosing between email, SMS, or other communication channels—it delves into the nuanced preferences of each customer. Whether a customer favors regular email updates, prefers receiving exclusive offers via SMS, or engages better with personalized communication through specific channels, understanding these preferences is paramount. Businesses can leverage this data to tailor their communication strategies, ensuring that interactions align with the customer's preferred mode and frequency. This personalized approach not only strengthens customer engagement but also contributes significantly to an enhanced overall customer experience.

Customer Feedback and Reviews

In the ever-evolving landscape of customer-centric business strategies, customer feedback and reviews play a pivotal role. These testimonials provide qualitative insights into customer satisfaction, preferences, and pain points. By actively collecting and analyzing this valuable data, businesses gain a profound understanding of their customers' experiences. Such insights become a compass for organizations, guiding them toward addressing concerns, enhancing products or services, and crafting tailored experiences that align with the sentiments of their customer base.

Utilizing Customer Data for Personalized Experiences

Segmentation

Segmentation, a cornerstone of personalized marketing, is a strategic application of customer data that goes beyond surface-level categorization. By harnessing the power of data analytics, businesses can delve into intricate details, allowing for the identification of shared characteristics, behaviors, and preferences within their customer base. This segmentation serves as the bedrock for delivering not just targeted but hyper-personalized content to specific groups. Whether through tailored marketing campaigns, customized product recommendations, or personalized communications, this strategic use of customer data cultivates a deeper connection between the business and its audience. This approach ensures that every interaction resonates with the unique needs and preferences of distinct customer segments, fostering engagement, loyalty, and ultimately contributing to the overall success of the business. In the digital era, where personalization is a driving force in customer experience, leveraging customer data for segmentation is an indispensable strategy for businesses aiming to stay competitive and relevant.

Personalized Marketing Campaigns

Armed with deep insights gleaned from comprehensive customer data, businesses can strategically craft personalized marketing campaigns that resonate on a profound level. Through channels like email marketing, precisely targeted advertisements, or enticing promotions, these campaigns go beyond generic messages. Instead, they speak directly to individual preferences, creating a sense of personal connection. In doing so, businesses not only capture attention but also drive higher engagement and significantly boost conversion rates. This tailored approach acknowledges the uniqueness of each customer, fostering a more meaningful and impactful interaction.

Tailored Product Recommendations

Delving into the intricate details of a customer's purchase history and preferences provides businesses with the power to deliver highly tailored product recommendations. By leveraging this wealth of data, companies enhance the overall shopping experience, presenting customers with items meticulously selected to align seamlessly with their tastes and needs. This level of personalization not only makes the shopping journey more enjoyable but also increases the likelihood of customer satisfaction and loyalty. The ability to anticipate and cater to individual preferences sets businesses apart, transforming routine transactions into curated and delightful encounters that leave a lasting positive impression.

Enhanced Customer Service

The access to comprehensive customer data not only allows businesses to offer more personalized and efficient customer service but also revolutionizes the entire customer support ecosystem. Armed with a nuanced understanding of individual preferences, purchase history, and communication preferences, customer service agents can proactively anticipate customer needs. This predictive approach empowers agents to resolve issues promptly and provide tailored recommendations or solutions, elevating the overall customer experience.

Predictive Analytics

In the realm of predictive analytics, businesses harness the power of advanced statistical algorithms and machine learning models to analyze vast sets of historical customer data. This sophisticated analysis goes beyond merely understanding past behaviors; it becomes a strategic tool for foreseeing future customer behavior. By identifying patterns, trends, and correlations within the data, companies gain predictive insights that enable proactive decision-making. This foresight becomes particularly invaluable in staying ahead of market trends and anticipating the evolving needs and preferences of customers.

Predictive analytics serves as a strategic compass for businesses, guiding them in making informed decisions that align with the trajectory of customer behavior. It transforms data into actionable intelligence, allowing companies not only to react swiftly to current trends but also to position themselves strategically for future market shifts. This forward-thinking approach, driven by predictive analytics, empowers businesses to tailor their offerings, marketing strategies, and overall business operations to meet the evolving demands of their customer base.

Optimized User Experience

Customer data serves as a guiding force for optimizing user experiences on websites and applications. This process involves tailoring every aspect of the online journey to align with the preferences, behaviors, and needs of individual users. One significant application of customer data in optimizing the user experience is through personalized landing pages. By analyzing data such as browsing history, purchase patterns, and demographic information, businesses can dynamically adjust the content, layout, and offers on landing pages. This personalized approach significantly enhances engagement, as users are greeted with content that resonates with their interests and intentions.

Moreover, customer data plays a pivotal role in shaping product recommendations within the user interface. By understanding what products or services a customer has previously interacted with or purchased, businesses can strategically present recommendations that align with the individual's preferences. This not only streamlines the decision-making process for the user but also contributes to increased satisfaction and the likelihood of making additional purchases.

Cross-Channel Consistency

Customers interact with brands across multiple channels, including websites, social media, and physical stores. Customer data serves as the common thread that weaves together a consistent and personalized experience across these diverse touchpoints. With a comprehensive view of customer data, businesses can ensure that the messaging, branding, and interactions remain cohesive, regardless of the channel through which a customer engages with the brand.

For instance, if a customer explores certain products on a company's website, this information can be seamlessly integrated into social media advertising. The customer may encounter targeted ads showcasing the products they previously viewed, creating a consistent and personalized narrative. This cross-channel consistency is essential for building a unified brand identity and reinforcing the customer's perception of the brand.

Furthermore, businesses can leverage customer data to understand the customer's preferred channels of interaction. Some customers may prefer to research products online but make purchases in-store, while others might engage primarily through social media. By respecting these preferences and tailoring the experience accordingly, businesses can strengthen customer relationships and optimize their overall cross-channel strategy.

Customer Loyalty Programs

The strategic utilization of customer data becomes particularly evident in the design and implementation of loyalty programs. These programs, powered by the insights derived from customer data, are instrumental in building enduring relationships and fostering brand loyalty. By tapping into customer data, businesses can tailor loyalty programs to offer personalized rewards that resonate with individual preferences and purchase histories. This level of customization goes beyond the one-size-fits-all approach, ensuring that the rewards are not only relevant but also enticing for each customer. Whether it's exclusive discounts on frequently purchased items, personalized recommendations, or early access to new products, these tailored incentives create a sense of value and appreciation for the customer.

Moreover, businesses can leverage customer data to track and analyze individual engagement patterns. By understanding the specific behaviors that contribute to loyalty, such as frequent purchases, brand advocacy, or consistent interaction with promotions, businesses can fine-tune their loyalty programs. This iterative optimization, based on real-time data analysis, ensures that loyalty initiatives remain aligned with evolving customer expectations and market trends.

In addition to personalized rewards, loyalty programs often incorporate exclusive perks that cater to the unique preferences of each customer segment. This might include early access to sales, members-only events, or personalized communication that enhances the overall customer experience. Such exclusive offerings, driven by a nuanced understanding of customer data, not only strengthen loyalty but also contribute to a sense of belonging and exclusivity.

Furthermore, the strategic use of customer data in loyalty programs extends beyond immediate rewards. It enables businesses to craft long-term engagement strategies by predicting and responding to changing customer needs. For example, if data analysis reveals a shift in a customer's preferences or purchasing behavior, businesses can proactively adjust loyalty program offerings to align with these changes, ensuring sustained relevance.

Customer loyalty programs fueled by comprehensive data insights represent a dynamic and personalized approach to cultivating customer allegiance. By tailoring rewards, analyzing engagement patterns, and offering exclusive perks, businesses can create loyalty programs that not only retain existing customers but also attract new ones. In this way, the marriage of customer data and loyalty initiatives becomes a powerful driver of sustained customer satisfaction and brand affinity.

The effective utilization of customer data for personalized experiences is a strategic imperative in today's competitive landscape. By harnessing the insights derived from various facets of customer data, businesses can not only meet but exceed customer expectations, fostering stronger relationships and driving long-term success.

Chapter 24

Sustaining
Innovation and R&D

Sustaining the spirit of innovation is imperative for long-term success. In chapter 24, we will take a look at the intricacies of maintaining this innovative ethos during and after expansion, emphasizing the crucial role of Research and Development (R&D) in staying at the forefront of industry advancements.

Innovation, the lifeblood of entrepreneurial endeavors, is explored as an ongoing process that transcends the startup phase, guiding businesses through the challenges of growth and global expansion.

Innovation Culture

Innovation culture is not just a buzzword; it is the heartbeat of organizations aiming for sustained growth and relevance in a rapidly changing business landscape. This aspect of corporate culture revolves around creating an environment that not only encourages but also celebrates innovation at every level of the organization. Fostering such a culture is essential for nurturing creativity, adaptability, and a continuous drive for improvement.

At its core, an innovation culture is characterized by an openness to new ideas, a willingness to take risks, and a recognition that failure is often a stepping stone to success. To embed innovation into the organizational DNA, leaders must champion a mindset that values creativity as a strategic asset rather than a sporadic occurrence.

Here are key strategies to cultivate and sustain an innovation culture within a company:

1. Leadership Commitment

In fostering an innovation culture, leadership commitment stands as the cornerstone, shaping the organization's ethos and inspiring a collective drive for creativity. Leaders, by leading by example, play a pivotal role in creating an environment where exploring new ideas is not only encouraged but embraced.

Lead by Example

Leaders must embody the values they wish to instill in the organization. By actively participating in the exploration of new ideas and showing a willingness to embrace change, leaders send a clear message that innovation is not just a slogan but a way of operating. When leaders engage in experimentation and showcase a tolerance for calculated risks, they foster a culture where employees feel empowered to do the same. This not only breaks down barriers but also encourages a sense of shared ownership over the innovation process.

Communication of Vision

Effectively communicating the vision for innovation is a critical step in gaining the commitment of the entire organization. Leaders should articulate a clear and compelling narrative that defines the role of innovation within the broader context of the company's mission and goals. When every member understands how their contributions align with the vision, a sense of purpose emerges, fostering a shared commitment to innovation.

The vision for innovation should go beyond mere words on a mission statement; it should be woven into the fabric of daily operations. Leaders can illustrate this vision through storytelling, providing real-world examples that showcase the transformative power of innovation. By creating a narrative that employees can connect with emotionally, leaders strengthen the ties between the organizational vision and the day-to-day activities of every team member.

Empowering Through Purpose

A shared sense of purpose is a powerful motivator. When employees understand that their work contributes to a larger vision of innovation, they become more engaged and invested in the success of the organization. Leaders, by consistently reinforcing the connection between individual contributions and the overarching vision, help establish a culture where innovation is not an isolated endeavor but an integral part of everyone's role.

Creating a Learning Organization

Leadership commitment to innovation also involves fostering a learning organization. Leaders should actively encourage a mindset of continuous learning and improvement. This includes acknowledging that failures are part of the innovation journey and using them as opportunities for growth. When leaders openly communicate about lessons learned from both successes and setbacks, it creates a culture that values adaptation and resilience.

Leadership commitment is not a passive endorsement of innovation; it is an active, dynamic force that shapes the culture and mindset of the entire organization. By leading by example, effectively communicating the vision, and empowering employees through a shared sense of purpose, leaders lay the groundwork for a thriving innovation culture. This commitment transforms innovation from a lofty goal into a lived experience, driving sustained creativity and growth.

2. Encouraging Creativity at All Levels

At the heart of an innovation culture is the commitment to encouraging creativity across all levels of the organization. This involves breaking down traditional silos and fostering a collaborative ecosystem where diverse perspectives intersect and give rise to groundbreaking ideas.

Cross-Functional Collaboration

A key strategy in fostering creativity is breaking down departmental silos and encouraging collaboration across different functions. Innovation often thrives at the convergence of diverse viewpoints and skill sets. By fostering cross-functional teams, leaders can create an environment where employees with varied expertise collaborate to tackle challenges and generate novel ideas. This collaborative approach not only enriches the creative process but also leads to innovative solutions that draw on a spectrum of knowledge and experiences.

Idea Generation Platforms

Establishing platforms for idea generation is crucial in unleashing the creative potential of every employee. This can take various forms, from traditional suggestion boxes and innovation workshops to modern digital platforms designed for idea sharing. By providing accessible avenues for employees at all levels to contribute their ideas, organizations empower their workforce to actively participate in the innovation process. This inclusivity not only taps into the diverse perspectives within the organization but also communicates a message that every individual's input is valued.

Innovation should not be confined to a specific team or department; it should be a pervasive force that permeates the entire organizational structure. Cross-functional collaboration and idea generation platforms democratize innovation, turning it into a collective effort where creativity can emerge from unexpected sources. This approach fosters a sense of ownership and belonging among employees, creating an environment where everyone feels invested in the innovation journey.

Moreover, these initiatives contribute to a culture of continuous improvement. Idea generation platforms, whether physical or digital, serve as dynamic channels for ongoing dialogue. They allow employees to continuously contribute insights, suggestions, and feedback, creating a feedback loop that keeps the innovation process alive and adaptive. This iterative approach aligns with the dynamic nature of the business landscape, ensuring that the organization remains responsive to changing trends and challenges.

Encouraging creativity at all levels is about creating a collaborative innovation ecosystem where every employee feels empowered to contribute their unique insights. By fostering cross-functional collaboration and establishing accessible idea generation platforms, organizations not only tap into the collective intelligence of their workforce but also build a resilient foundation for sustained innovation and growth.

3. Risk Tolerance and Learning from Failure

In the pursuit of an innovation culture, fostering a climate that embraces risk and views failure as a stepping stone rather than a stumbling block is paramount. Creating a safe-to-fail environment is a fundamental aspect of this approach, and it requires a deliberate commitment to encouraging calculated risks.

Safe-to-Fail Environment

An innovation culture thrives when employees feel empowered to take calculated risks without the fear of severe consequences. Leaders should actively cultivate an environment that supports experimentation, where teams can test ideas and approaches without the looming threat of punitive measures. This doesn't mean endorsing recklessness but rather creating a framework that allows for thoughtful risk-taking. Establishing guidelines and boundaries ensures that risks are taken within a strategic context, aligning with the overall goals of the organization.

Failure as a Learning Opportunity

Shifting the perspective on failure is crucial in fostering innovation. Rather than viewing failure as a setback, promote it as a valuable learning opportunity. Encourage teams to see mistakes not as endpoints but as stepping stones toward improvement. When failures occur, leaders should champion a post-mortem culture, where teams systematically analyze what went wrong, extract meaningful lessons, and apply those insights to future endeavors. This iterative process turns setbacks into valuable experiences that contribute to the organization's overall learning curve.

Leadership plays a pivotal role in setting the tone for risk tolerance and learning from failure. When leaders openly communicate their support for experimentation and acknowledge that not every venture will succeed, it creates a culture where employees are more likely to push boundaries and think innovatively. By normalizing the idea that setbacks are inherent in the innovation journey, leaders create an atmosphere where employees are not afraid to take risks, knowing that even failures contribute to the collective knowledge and growth of the organization.

Embracing risk and learning from failure are integral components of an innovation culture. Establishing a safe-to-fail environment allows teams to explore uncharted territories, knowing that their contributions are valued. Moreover, seeing failure as a learning opportunity transforms setbacks into stepping stones for continuous improvement, fostering a culture of resilience and adaptability.

4. Recognition and Rewards

In cultivating an innovation culture, recognizing and rewarding contributions to creative endeavors becomes a pivotal strategy. Acknowledging and celebrating the innovators within an organization not only validates their efforts but also signals to the entire workforce that innovation is a valued and integral part of the company's identity.

Celebrating Innovators

An essential aspect of fostering an innovation culture is the public acknowledgment of individuals or teams that contribute innovative solutions. This celebration goes beyond merely highlighting successes; it reinforces the idea that innovation is a core value of the organization. By shining a spotlight on those who bring inventive ideas to fruition, leaders create role models within the organization. This public recognition not only boosts the morale of the innovators but also serves as inspiration for others, encouraging a collective mindset that embraces and seeks out opportunities for creative thinking.

Incentives for Innovation

Beyond celebrations, organizations can incorporate innovation metrics into performance evaluations, linking individual achievements to the broader innovation agenda. By making innovation a measurable component of performance assessments, employees are encouraged to actively contribute to the organization's creative objectives. Moreover, providing tangible incentives for those who significantly contribute to the innovation agenda aligns individual goals with the broader organizational vision. Whether through financial rewards, career development opportunities, or other forms of recognition, these incentives create a culture where innovation is not only valued but also actively pursued.

Strategic Alignment

Recognition and rewards should be strategically aligned with the organization's overall goals and values. By tying innovative contributions to the company's mission and objectives, leaders ensure that the recognized efforts contribute directly to the organization's success. This strategic alignment not only reinforces the importance of innovation but also channels creative energy toward areas that align with the company's strategic priorities.

Continuous Feedback Loop

Establishing a continuous feedback loop is essential in the realm of recognition and rewards for innovation. Regularly communicating the impact of innovative contributions, whether through team meetings, newsletters, or other channels, provides a constant stream of positive reinforcement. This ongoing feedback loop not only recognizes past achievements but also serves as a catalyst for continuous improvement. It fosters a culture where individuals feel valued for their creative contributions and are motivated to explore new possibilities.

Flexibility in Recognition

Recognizing that innovation takes various forms and occurs at different levels within the organization is crucial. While high-impact, groundbreaking innovations deserve special acknowledgment, fostering a culture of innovation also involves recognizing incremental contributions and efforts to improve existing processes. This flexibility in recognition ensures that every individual, regardless of their role or level within the organization, feels valued for their unique contributions to the innovation journey.

Recognition and rewards are not just gestures of appreciation; they are powerful tools in shaping the culture of an organization. By celebrating innovators, providing incentives for innovation, strategically aligning recognition efforts, establishing a continuous feedback loop, and maintaining flexibility in acknowledgment, leaders contribute significantly to the development and sustenance of a vibrant innovation culture within their organizations.

5. Continuous Learning and Skill Development

In cultivating an innovation culture, the emphasis on continuous learning and skill development becomes paramount. This involves strategic investments in training programs designed to instill and enhance the skills crucial for fostering creative thinking and effective problem-solving.

Training Programs

Organizations committed to innovation should invest in comprehensive training programs that go beyond traditional skill sets. These programs should focus on cultivating a mindset of creative thinking and provide practical tools to enhance problem-solving skills. Techniques such as design thinking or agile methodologies can be integrated into training, offering employees structured approaches to innovation. By equipping the workforce with these methodologies, organizations empower individuals to navigate challenges with a dynamic and inventive mindset.

Continuous Feedback

Establishing a culture of continuous improvement requires ongoing feedback mechanisms. Regular check-ins with employees serve as a valuable means to gauge the pulse of the innovation process. These interactions provide an opportunity to understand the challenges employees are facing, offer timely support, and identify areas for improvement. In a continuously evolving landscape, feedback serves as a compass, guiding the organization toward effective strategies that align with the dynamic needs of the innovation journey.

Moreover, these feedback loops contribute to a sense of inclusivity and collaboration. When employees know that their insights and challenges are valued, it fosters a culture of openness where ideas can be freely exchanged. This not only accelerates the innovation process but also strengthens the bonds of teamwork and collective problem-solving.

By integrating continuous learning initiatives and feedback mechanisms into the fabric of the organization, companies ensure that innovation is not merely a one-time effort but an ongoing, adaptive process. In this dynamic environment, employees evolve alongside the organization, equipped with the skills and insights needed to navigate the complexities of the innovation landscape. This commitment to continuous learning propels the workforce forward, ensuring that the organization remains at the forefront of innovative practices and industry advancements.

6. Agility and Adaptability:

In the pursuit of fostering an innovation culture, the principles of agility and adaptability emerge as crucial components that enable organizations to navigate the dynamic and ever-evolving landscape of innovation.

Embracing Change

A fundamental aspect of fostering innovation is instilling a mindset that embraces change. Leaders should communicate that innovation is not a linear path but a journey filled with twists and turns. By emphasizing the value of adaptability, organizations encourage employees to view change not as a disruptor but as an inherent part of the innovation process. This mindset shift is pivotal in preparing teams to respond effectively to shifting market dynamics, emerging technologies, or unforeseen opportunities.

Iterative Processes

Central to fostering an innovation culture is the encouragement of iterative processes. This involves breaking down larger innovation projects into smaller, more manageable components. By adopting an iterative approach, organizations can facilitate frequent feedback loops, enabling teams to make adjustments based on real-time insights. This iterative methodology not only accelerates the pace of innovation but also minimizes the risks associated with pursuing large, untested ideas. Through incremental progress and continuous refinement, organizations can fine-tune their innovations, ensuring they align closely with market needs and evolving expectations.

Embracing agility and adaptability is akin to providing organizations with the flexibility to navigate uncharted territories. The dynamic nature of the innovation landscape demands an approach that can pivot swiftly in response to emerging challenges and opportunities. By fostering a culture that values change, embraces iterative processes, and views adaptation as a strength, organizations position themselves to thrive in the unpredictable and exciting realm of innovation.

7. Strategic Alignment

In the dynamic landscape of business, fostering innovation requires a deliberate focus on strategic alignment. This alignment ensures that innovation efforts are not isolated endeavors but integral components of the organization's broader goals and aspirations.

Alignment with Business Goals

The foundation of strategic alignment lies in ensuring that innovation efforts are intricately linked with the overarching business objectives. For innovation to be truly impactful, it must be directed toward areas that align with the company's growth trajectory, market positioning, and long-term strategy. Leaders need to communicate a clear vision of how innovation contributes to achieving these goals, illustrating the integral role it plays in shaping the future of the organization. This alignment ensures that innovation is not pursued for its own sake but as a strategic driver of the company's success.

Regular Assessment

The landscape of business is ever-evolving, and so too should be the approach to innovation. Regular assessments of the effectiveness of innovation initiatives are essential for maintaining strategic alignment. Periodic reviews provide an opportunity to evaluate the impact of ongoing innovation efforts, identify areas of success, and pinpoint areas that may require adjustment. This dynamic feedback loop allows the organization to adapt its innovation strategies in response to changing market dynamics, emerging trends, and the evolving needs of the business.

Continuous evaluation is not solely about measuring the success or failure of specific projects but understanding how well these projects align with the organization's strategic trajectory. It involves gauging whether the innovation initiatives contribute to the desired outcomes, whether they are in sync with market demands, and whether they position the organization advantageously within its competitive landscape.

Moreover, the assessment process should go beyond quantitative metrics to include qualitative insights. Understanding the narrative behind the data helps in capturing the nuances of innovation impact. This holistic evaluation allows leaders to make informed decisions about the continuation, refinement, or redirection of innovation initiatives.

Strategic alignment in innovation is not a static achievement but an ongoing process. It requires a continuous loop of setting clear directions aligned with business goals, executing innovation initiatives with precision, and regularly evaluating the outcomes. This iterative approach ensures that innovation remains a dynamic force that propels the organization toward its strategic objectives, contributing to sustained growth and competitiveness.

Building and sustaining an innovation culture is an ongoing process that requires commitment, adaptability, and a genuine belief in the transformative power of innovation. By weaving these strategies into the fabric of the organization, businesses can create an environment where innovation becomes not just a goal but an integral part of the organizational identity.

Strategic R&D Investments

In the fast-paced realms of business, staying competitive necessitates a proactive stance towards innovation, and at the forefront of this endeavor lies the strategic allocation of resources for Research and Development (R&D). Strategic R&D investments are not merely financial allocations; they are pivotal decisions that shape the trajectory of a company's innovation journey, influencing its competitive edge, market positioning, and long-term sustainability.

Importance of R&D in Staying Competitive

At its core, Research and Development (R&D) is the heartbeat of innovation within a company. It involves the systematic exploration of new ideas, technologies, and processes with the aim of driving progress and maintaining a competitive advantage. The landscape of business is marked by continuous evolution, and those companies that actively engage in R&D are better positioned to navigate the complexities of change.

1. Technological Advancements

Strategic Research and Development (R&D) investments stand as the linchpin for companies aiming to harness and capitalize on technological advancements, propelling them to the forefront of innovation. A stellar example of this strategic approach can be witnessed in the journey of tech behemoth Apple. Renowned for its unswerving commitment to R&D, Apple's strategic investments have been instrumental in bringing about groundbreaking technological advancements, epitomized by the transformative iPhone.

Apple's continuous dedication to R&D is not merely a financial allocation but a deliberate strategy to drive innovation in the fiercely competitive technology landscape. The creation of the iPhone, one of the most iconic and influential consumer electronics devices of the 21st century, is a testament to the success of Apple's strategic R&D investments. The iPhone not only revolutionized the smartphone industry but also redefined the way people communicate, work, and consume information.

The strategic integration of technological advancements through R&D investments allowed Apple to secure and consolidate its position as a market leader. The company's relentless pursuit of innovation, evidenced by regular product releases and technological updates, has not only sustained its market relevance but has propelled it to the pinnacle of the tech industry.

Moreover, Apple's strategic R&D investments have had a profound impact on the entire smartphone industry. The introduction of touchscreens, app ecosystems, and sleek design aesthetics by Apple set new industry standards and spurred a wave of innovation across competitors. As a result, the smartphone market witnessed a paradigm shift, with companies globally recalibrating their R&D strategies to keep pace with the technological benchmarks set by Apple.

Strategic R&D investments enable companies not only to stay abreast of technological advancements but also to pioneer transformative innovations that redefine markets. It is this forward-looking approach that differentiates industry leaders from followers, allowing them to shape and influence the trajectory of technology landscapes. As technology continues to evolve at an unprecedented pace, companies that strategically invest in R&D position themselves not just as market participants but as architects of the digital future. Apple's strategic R&D journey stands as a beacon, illustrating how the marriage of vision, investment, and innovation can propel a company to the forefront of technological advancements, leaving an indelible mark on the industry it serves.

2. Market Adaptation

Research and Development (R&D) plays a pivotal role in helping companies adapt to the ever-changing dynamics of the market. Nowhere is this more evident than in the pharmaceutical industry, where companies invest substantial resources in R&D to discover novel drugs and therapeutic solutions. This commitment to research not only addresses critical healthcare needs but also positions these companies to remain at the forefront of an industry where breakthroughs are paramount.

In the pharmaceutical sector, where advancements can directly impact human health and well-being, R&D serves as the cornerstone of innovation. Companies engage in extensive research to identify new molecules, understand disease pathways, and develop effective treatments. This continuous pursuit of knowledge and innovation not only leads to the creation of life-saving medications but also ensures that companies are equipped to navigate the complexities of a highly regulated and dynamic market.

The pharmaceutical R&D process involves a series of rigorous stages, from early discovery to clinical trials and eventual regulatory approval. Each phase demands substantial investments in terms of finances, talent, and infrastructure. These investments are not only a commitment to scientific advancement but also a strategic move to adapt to market demands and maintain a competitive edge.

Furthermore, R&D in pharmaceuticals is not confined to the creation of new drugs alone; it extends to improving existing medications, optimizing formulations, and exploring innovative delivery methods. This adaptability in response to market needs is particularly crucial in an environment where regulatory requirements, patient preferences, and emerging healthcare challenges are in constant flux.

The competitive landscape of the pharmaceutical industry necessitates a forward-thinking approach, and companies that invest strategically in R&D position themselves as industry leaders. Breakthrough discoveries not only provide a competitive advantage but also open up new avenues for market expansion and revenue generation.

In addition to the scientific aspects, R&D investments in pharmaceuticals contribute to building intellectual property portfolios. Patents resulting from innovative research protect the company's discoveries, creating barriers to entry for competitors and securing market exclusivity. This strategic positioning, facilitated by R&D initiatives, strengthens a company's market adaptation capabilities by establishing a foundation for long-term success.

Moreover, the ability to adapt to changing market dynamics through R&D is not limited to the pharmaceutical sector. It serves as a broader principle applicable across industries. Companies that leverage R&D as a tool for market adaptation are better equipped to anticipate trends, meet evolving consumer demands, and navigate competitive landscapes. In essence, R&D becomes a strategic enabler, allowing companies not just to respond to change but to proactively shape the future of their markets.

3. Product Differentiation

In the realm of business, product differentiation serves as a powerful strategy for companies aiming to carve a unique identity in competitive markets. Strategic Research and Development (R&D) investments play a pivotal role in enabling this differentiation by fostering innovation and groundbreaking advancements. A notable exemplar of R&D-led product differentiation is Tesla, the electric vehicle and renewable energy solutions company, which has disrupted traditional industries through its pioneering approach.

Tesla's strategic focus on R&D has propelled the company to the forefront of the automotive and energy sectors. The differentiation begins with the core of Tesla's identity – electric vehicles. By investing significantly in battery technology, Tesla has overcome one of the primary challenges in the adoption of electric cars: limited range and long charging times. The development of high-performance batteries, such as the lithium-ion batteries used in Tesla vehicles, has extended the driving range and reduced charging times, addressing key barriers to widespread electric vehicle adoption.

Moreover, Tesla's emphasis on autonomous driving technology sets it apart in the automotive landscape. Through continuous R&D efforts, Tesla has integrated advanced driver-assistance systems and machine learning algorithms, gradually moving towards achieving fully autonomous driving capabilities. This not only enhances the driving experience for Tesla owners but also positions the company at the forefront of the autonomous vehicle revolution.

In the realm of renewable energy solutions, Tesla's strategic R&D investments extend beyond automobiles. The company has diversified its portfolio to include solar energy products and energy storage solutions. Through innovations such as the Tesla Solar Roof, which seamlessly integrates solar cells into roofing materials, and the Powerwall energy storage system, Tesla has created a comprehensive ecosystem. This approach not only differentiates Tesla in the market but also aligns with broader sustainability goals, appealing to environmentally conscious consumers.

The success of Tesla's product differentiation strategy is evident not only in its market position but also in its impact on the entire automotive industry. Other automakers are compelled to accelerate their own R&D efforts to catch up with, and potentially surpass, Tesla's advancements. This competitive dynamic driven by R&D investments not only benefits consumers by fostering innovation but also stimulates broader industry transformation towards cleaner and more sustainable technologies.

In conclusion, strategic R&D investments serve as the engine of product differentiation, allowing companies like Tesla to redefine industries and set new benchmarks. By pushing the boundaries of technology and continuously innovating, companies can position themselves as trailblazers, disruptors, and leaders in their respective markets. Tesla's journey exemplifies how R&D-led differentiation can revolutionize traditional sectors, shape consumer preferences, and contribute to the broader societal shift towards sustainable and cutting-edge solutions.

Allocating Resources Strategically for Effective R&D Outcomes:
Strategic R&D investments go beyond financial commitments; they encompass a holistic approach to resource allocation, ensuring that every aspect of the R&D process is aligned with the company's overall objectives.

Talent Acquisition

In the realm of Research and Development (R&D), the heartbeat of innovation is inseparable from the caliber of talent steering the process. Talent acquisition stands as a linchpin, a critical component that can elevate R&D from a mere endeavor to a strategic powerhouse. In the pursuit of breakthroughs and advancements, companies strategically invest in acquiring skilled researchers, scientists, and engineers, recognizing that the right talent is the catalyst for transformative innovation.

Central to the success of R&D is the ability to assemble a team with diverse and complementary expertise. Companies embark on strategic talent acquisition initiatives to ensure that their R&D teams possess a spectrum of skills, perspectives, and capabilities. This diversity not only enriches the ideation and development processes but also fosters an environment of collaborative creativity.

A poignant example of strategic talent acquisition in the R&D domain is Google's acquisition of DeepMind. In 2014, Google strategically acquired this London-based artificial intelligence research lab, recognizing the immense potential it held for advancing machine learning and AI technologies. DeepMind's expertise, coupled with Google's resources, propelled the tech giant into the forefront of AI research. This move showcased how a targeted acquisition could be a masterstroke in strengthening R&D capabilities and securing a competitive edge.

Talent acquisition in R&D goes beyond merely filling positions; it involves identifying individuals with a track record of innovation, a passion for exploration, and the ability to envision the future. Skilled researchers bring not only technical prowess but also a mindset that embraces challenges and sees them as opportunities for discovery. Companies invest in attracting such talent, knowing that these individuals can be the driving force behind groundbreaking advancements.

Furthermore, strategic talent acquisition in R&D is not confined to hiring for immediate needs; it involves forward-thinking. Companies scout for individuals who not only fit the current requirements but also have the potential to grow and adapt in tandem with the evolving landscape of innovation. This forward-looking approach ensures that the acquired talent remains a valuable asset, contributing to the company's long-term R&D goals.

The synergy between strategic talent acquisition and R&D excellence is evident in the outcomes it produces. It empowers companies to tackle complex challenges, explore uncharted territories, and innovate in ways that redefine industries. By strategically investing in acquiring the right talent, organizations position themselves not only to keep pace with technological advancements but also to pioneer transformative discoveries that shape the future. In the intricate dance of R&D, talent acquisition emerges as the choreographer, orchestrating the movements that lead to a symphony of innovation.

Infrastructure and Technology

The significance of infrastructure and technology cannot be overstated. It forms the backbone of effective R&D outcomes, influencing the depth and scope of scientific exploration. Pharmaceutical companies, as exemplary entities in this context, undertake strategic investments to establish robust infrastructure and gain access to cutting-edge technologies. This strategic allocation serves as the cornerstone for pushing the boundaries of scientific discovery.

- **Robust Laboratories and Equipment:** One key facet of infrastructure investment is the establishment of state-of-the-art laboratories. These laboratories are purposefully equipped with advanced instruments and technologies, providing R&D teams with an optimal environment for conducting intricate research. For pharmaceutical companies engaged in drug discovery, these laboratories become the epicenter of innovation, facilitating experiments, analyses, and the development of novel therapeutic solutions.

- **Cutting-Edge Technologies:** Access to cutting-edge technologies is paramount in the dynamic landscape of R&D. Pharmaceutical R&D, for instance, relies on sophisticated technologies such as high-throughput screening, genomics, and bioinformatics. These technologies enable researchers to analyze vast datasets, conduct complex experiments, and accelerate the drug discovery process. By strategically investing in these technologies, pharmaceutical companies position themselves at the forefront of scientific advancements.

- **Accelerating Drug Discovery:** The strategic allocation of resources to infrastructure and technology expedites the drug discovery journey. In an industry where time-to-market is critical, having advanced laboratories and technologies significantly accelerates the research and development phases. This acceleration is vital not only for gaining a competitive edge but also for addressing urgent healthcare needs, as seen in the quest for innovative treatments and vaccines.

- **Enabling Innovation and Collaboration:** Robust infrastructure and cutting-edge technologies not only propel internal innovation but also foster collaboration. Research institutions, academia, and even cross-industry partnerships benefit from the infrastructure provided by pharmaceutical companies. This collaborative ecosystem becomes a melting pot of ideas, expertise, and resources, amplifying the potential for groundbreaking discoveries and advancements.

- **Quality and Compliance:** In highly regulated industries like pharmaceuticals, infrastructure investments ensure adherence to stringent quality and compliance standards. State-of-the-art laboratories are designed to meet regulatory requirements, contributing to the credibility and reliability of R&D outcomes. This strategic focus on quality not only aligns with industry standards but also enhances the trust placed in the research findings.

- **Long-Term Strategic Vision:** The investment in infrastructure and technology reflects a company's long-term strategic vision. It is a commitment to staying ahead in a rapidly evolving landscape. As technologies evolve, companies that continually invest in upgrading their infrastructure demonstrate adaptability and resilience. This strategic foresight positions organizations to navigate challenges, embrace emerging methodologies, and sustain a culture of innovation over time.

The strategic allocation of resources to establish robust infrastructure and gain access to cutting-edge technologies is pivotal for effective R&D outcomes, particularly in industries where innovation is synonymous with progress. Pharmaceutical companies, through these strategic investments, not only enhance their internal capabilities but also contribute to the broader scientific community, advancing our understanding of health and medicine.

Collaboration and Partnerships

Strategic Research and Development (R&D) thrive on collaborative efforts, and partnerships stand out as pivotal in amplifying innovation potential and addressing complex challenges. R&D extends beyond the boundaries of a single company, prompting strategic collaborations with external entities such as research institutions, startups, and industry partners. A prime example of this collaborative approach is the partnership between IBM and the Massachusetts Institute of Technology (MIT) in advancing Artificial Intelligence (AI) research.

In this strategic alliance, both IBM and MIT bring unique strengths to the table, combining resources, expertise, and perspectives. IBM, as a technology giant, contributes its vast technological infrastructure, industry experience, and global reach, while MIT, a renowned academic institution, brings cutting-edge research capabilities, a pool of talented minds, and an environment conducive to innovation.

The focus of the IBM-MIT collaboration is on advancing AI research, a field characterized by its dynamic and rapidly evolving nature. Collaborative projects involve exploring novel algorithms, developing innovative applications, and addressing challenges that require interdisciplinary expertise. This shared commitment to AI research underscores the strategic intent to stay at the forefront of technological innovation.

Strategic R&D collaborations optimize resources, allowing entities to achieve more collectively than they could individually. By pooling resources – whether financial, human, or technological – collaborators create a more formidable force in tackling intricate problems. This resource optimization is particularly crucial in R&D, where the scale and complexity of projects often demand diverse skill sets, specialized equipment, and significant investments.

Collaborations open doors to diverse expertise and perspectives. In the IBM-MIT partnership, the collaboration enables the integration of academic research insights with practical industry applications. This fusion of knowledge from academia and industry enriches the research outcomes, ensuring a holistic approach to AI advancements. Access to diverse expertise accelerates the pace of innovation by bringing together individuals with varied backgrounds, experiences, and skills.

Strategic R&D collaborations are often forged with the intent to address complex challenges that transcend the capabilities of individual entities. AI research, being inherently intricate, benefits significantly from collaborative efforts. Challenges such as developing ethical AI frameworks, enhancing machine learning algorithms, and ensuring the responsible deployment of AI technologies require multifaceted solutions. Through strategic partnerships, entities like IBM and MIT position themselves to collectively navigate and overcome these challenges.

Ultimately, collaborations in strategic R&D are drivers of innovation. The IBM-MIT partnership, as an exemplar, is not just about advancing AI research; it is a testament to the commitment to driving innovation forward. Through shared goals, mutual trust, and collaborative endeavors, entities participating in such partnerships contribute not only to their own advancements but also to the broader landscape of technological innovation.

Risk Management

Effective risk management is integral to strategic Research and Development (R&D) investments, acknowledging the inherent uncertainties and challenges associated with innovation. Companies engaging in innovative endeavors, such as pharmaceutical firms focusing on drug development, recognize the need for a robust risk management strategy. In the realm of pharmaceutical R&D, where the journey from initial research to regulatory approvals and clinical trials is fraught with uncertainties, companies strategically allocate resources to mitigate potential risks.

Anticipating challenges is a fundamental aspect of risk management in R&D. In drug development, for instance, companies navigate the intricate process of clinical trials and regulatory approvals, recognizing the multifaceted nature of risks involved. These risks can range from unexpected side effects in clinical trials to regulatory hurdles that may delay or impact market entry.

Strategic R&D investments involve a proactive approach to identifying, assessing, and mitigating risks. This anticipatory stance allows companies to allocate resources judiciously, ensuring that potential challenges do not derail the overall R&D objectives. In the pharmaceutical sector, this might involve implementing risk mitigation strategies such as diversifying the drug pipeline, collaborating with regulatory bodies early in the process, and staying informed about evolving industry standards.

The high stakes and lengthy timelines associated with drug development underscore the importance of a comprehensive risk management strategy. Companies invest strategically in mechanisms to monitor and address risks throughout the R&D lifecycle. This includes continuous evaluation of clinical trial data, proactive engagement with regulatory agencies to address potential concerns, and the development of contingency plans to navigate unforeseen challenges.

Strategic R&D investments demand a delicate balance between innovation and risk mitigation. While innovation propels companies forward, the risks associated with R&D can be substantial. Companies operating in sectors with prolonged R&D timelines, such as pharmaceuticals, acknowledge that the dynamic nature of the industry necessitates an adaptive and comprehensive risk management framework.

Moreover, the strategic allocation of resources for risk management in R&D reflects a commitment to responsible innovation. Companies recognize that embracing innovation goes hand in hand with acknowledging and addressing potential risks. This approach not only safeguards the company's interests but also aligns with ethical considerations by prioritizing the safety and well-being of end-users, especially in industries where the outcomes of R&D directly impact human health and well-being.

What's more? Strategic R&D investments go beyond the pursuit of innovation; they encompass a thorough risk management strategy. By anticipating, assessing, and mitigating potential challenges, companies ensure that their innovative endeavors are not derailed by unforeseen obstacles. In sectors like pharmaceuticals, where the stakes are high and uncertainties are inherent, a strategic approach to risk management is a cornerstone of successful and responsible R&D initiatives.

Strategic R&D investments are a dynamic interplay of financial commitments, talent acquisition, infrastructure development, and collaborative initiatives. By aligning these elements with the company's broader objectives, organizations can navigate the innovation landscape successfully. Companies that strategically invest in R&D not only stay competitive in their respective industries but also contribute to shaping the future of markets and technologies.

Chapter 25

Building a Scalable
Tech Infrastructure

As businesses evolve and expand, the need for a robust and adaptable technological foundation becomes paramount. This chapter explores the intricacies of designing and managing technical systems capable of seamlessly growing with your company. From harnessing the power of cloud computing to implementing comprehensive Enterprise Resource Planning (ERP) systems, we unravel the key components and strategies that underpin a scalable tech infrastructure.

Cloud Computing Strategies

Cloud computing is a transformative force, offering organizations the agility and scalability needed to navigate the complexities of a rapidly evolving technological environment. Cloud computing, at its core, refers to the delivery of computing services—including storage, processing power, and applications—over the internet. This paradigm shift from traditional on-premises infrastructure to the cloud has revolutionized the way businesses approach IT strategies, providing unparalleled flexibility and scalability.

What is Cloud Computing?

At its most fundamental level, cloud computing involves the delivery of computing services over the internet, eliminating the need for organizations to invest in and maintain extensive physical infrastructure. These services are typically categorized into three main models:

Infrastructure as a Service (IaaS)

In the realm of cloud computing, Infrastructure as a Service (IaaS) stands as a foundational pillar, revolutionizing how businesses manage their IT infrastructure. IaaS provides virtualized computing resources accessible over the internet, encompassing essential components like virtual machines, storage, and networking capabilities. At its core, this model liberates organizations from the traditional constraints of physical hardware, introducing a new era of flexibility and efficiency in IT operations.

Central to IaaS is the concept of virtual machines (VMs), serving as the fundamental building blocks of the computing environment. These VMs emulate the functionality of physical computers but exist in a virtualized space, enabling businesses to deploy diverse operating systems and applications without the limitations of physical hardware.

IaaS extends its scope to scalable storage solutions, allowing organizations to leverage resilient storage options without concerns about on-premises limitations. The pay-as-you-go model ensures a cost-effective approach to managing data, adapting storage capacity based on evolving requirements.

Networking components play a pivotal role in IaaS, facilitating seamless connectivity and communication within the virtualized environment. With services like virtual private networks (VPNs), load balancers, and firewalls, businesses can design sophisticated network architectures tailored to their needs.

One of the primary advantages of IaaS is its ability to empower businesses to construct and manage their IT infrastructure with unprecedented ease. Without substantial physical hardware investments, organizations can swiftly provision and configure virtualized resources through intuitive interfaces provided by IaaS platforms. This agility expedites the deployment of applications and services, enabling rapid adaptation to changing business requirements.

The key benefits of IaaS include cost efficiency, scalability, flexibility, global reach, and resilience. The pay-as-you-go model optimizes expenditure, scalability aligns with dynamic business conditions, flexibility fosters innovation, global reach supports seamless expansion, and built-in resilience ensures high availability of services.

In essence, Infrastructure as a Service redefines IT infrastructure management, offering businesses the flexibility and efficiency needed to navigate the complexities of the modern digital landscape.

Platform as a Service (PaaS)

Platform as a Service (PaaS) emerges as a game-changing paradigm within the realm of cloud computing, presenting organizations with a comprehensive solution to streamline application development. At its core, PaaS provides a platform that empowers businesses to develop, run, and manage applications without grappling with the intricacies of maintaining the underlying infrastructure.

The essence of PaaS lies in simplifying the entire application development lifecycle. By abstracting the complexities associated with infrastructure management, PaaS enables developers to focus solely on the creation and enhancement of applications. This streamlined development process translates into faster time-to-market for applications, a critical advantage in today's dynamic business landscape.

With PaaS, developers gain access to a cohesive environment that includes tools, libraries, and services, fostering an environment conducive to efficient collaboration and innovation. This comprehensive platform offers a standardized framework for coding, testing, and deploying applications, reducing the need for developers to delve into the intricacies of infrastructure provisioning and configuration.

One of the hallmark features of PaaS is its ability to provide scalability and flexibility in application development. Organizations can easily scale their applications based on demand, ensuring optimal performance even during peak usage periods. This adaptability aligns with the fluctuating needs of businesses, allowing them to respond swiftly to changing market dynamics.

PaaS also facilitates enhanced collaboration among development teams, as they can work seamlessly within a shared environment. This collaborative approach fosters innovation by promoting the exchange of ideas and the integration of diverse skill sets. Moreover, PaaS often includes built-in features for version control, automated testing, and continuous integration, further enhancing the overall efficiency of the development process.

Platform as a Service (PaaS) stands as a catalyst for revolutionizing application development, offering a cohesive and simplified platform that accelerates time-to-market, encourages collaboration, and provides the flexibility needed to meet the demands of a rapidly evolving business landscape.

Software as a Service (SaaS)

Software as a Service (SaaS) epitomizes a transformative approach to software distribution, revolutionizing how users access, manage, and interact with applications. This cloud computing model delivers software applications over the internet, eliminating the traditional requirement for users to install, maintain, or update software on their local devices. In the SaaS paradigm, applications are hosted and maintained by a third-party provider, and users can access them through web browsers, fostering a new era of convenience and collaboration.

One of the hallmark features of SaaS is its ability to eradicate the burdens associated with software installation and maintenance. Users no longer need to grapple with the intricacies of installation processes or concern themselves with software updates. Instead, the responsibility for these aspects rests with the SaaS provider, who manages the software centrally in a secure and scalable environment.

Examples of SaaS applications span a diverse range of functionalities, including cloud-based email services like Gmail, customer relationship management (CRM) systems such as Salesforce, and collaborative tools like Google Workspace. These applications serve as exemplars of the versatility and accessibility that SaaS brings to the software landscape.

The advantages of SaaS extend beyond simplified software management. The subscription-based model, characteristic of SaaS offerings, ensures cost predictability for users. Instead of upfront capital expenses, users typically pay a recurring fee, which covers not only software usage but also ongoing maintenance, updates, and support. This predictability is particularly advantageous for businesses seeking to optimize their budgeting processes.

Moreover, the accessibility of SaaS applications from any device with an internet connection facilitates enhanced collaboration and productivity. Whether teams are geographically dispersed or working remotely, the centralized nature of SaaS applications ensures that all users, regardless of location, operate on the same version of the software in real-time.

Software as a Service represents a paradigm shift in software delivery, prioritizing accessibility, cost-effectiveness, and streamlined management. As businesses increasingly embrace cloud-based solutions, SaaS stands as a cornerstone in reshaping how organizations leverage and interact with software applications.

Strategies for Harnessing Cloud Computing

Scalability and Flexibility

The scalability and flexibility inherent in cloud computing form a dynamic duo, providing businesses with the agility needed to respond to the unpredictable nature of the digital landscape. Elasticity, a hallmark of cloud solutions, allows organizations to scale computing resources seamlessly in response to fluctuating demand. This ensures optimal performance during peak periods when resources are required to handle increased workloads, while simultaneously enabling cost savings during lulls in demand by automatically scaling down resources.

Auto-scaling, a strategic component of cloud architecture, takes this adaptability a step further by introducing automated responses to changing conditions. By defining predefined criteria or conditions, organizations can implement auto-scaling mechanisms that dynamically adjust computing resources. For instance, if an application experiences a sudden surge in user activity, auto-scaling can trigger the provisioning of additional computing power to maintain responsiveness. Conversely, during periods of reduced demand, the system can automatically scale down resources, minimizing costs while ensuring operational efficiency.

The combined power of elasticity and auto-scaling not only optimizes resource utilization but also enhances the overall efficiency of cloud-based operations. Businesses can confidently navigate scenarios with variable workloads, secure in the knowledge that their IT infrastructure aligns precisely with the demands of the moment.

This adaptability ensures a cost-effective approach to resource management, preventing overprovisioning during quiet periods and guaranteeing optimal performance during surges in activity. As organizations strive for operational excellence, the scalability and flexibility provided by cloud computing emerge as indispensable tools, enabling them to thrive in the face of ever-changing demands.

Cost Optimization

Efficiently managing costs is a paramount consideration for organizations leveraging cloud computing services, and two strategic approaches within the Infrastructure as a Service (IaaS) framework stand out for optimal financial control.

- **Pay-as-You-Go Model:** A cornerstone of cost optimization, the pay-as-you-go pricing model aligns cloud expenses directly with resource utilization. This flexible approach ensures that organizations only pay for the computing resources consumed, mitigating the risk of overprovisioning and eliminating costs associated with idle resources. As demand fluctuates, the pay-as-you-go model accommodates variations in resource usage, providing a cost-effective solution for dynamic workloads. This financial flexibility is particularly advantageous for businesses with variable computing needs, allowing them to scale resources up or down in response to real-time requirements.

- **Reserved Instances:** For workloads characterized by stability and predictability, the utilization of reserved instances presents a compelling strategy. In this approach, organizations commit to a specific amount of computing resources for a predetermined term, typically one to three years. By doing so, businesses secure a significant reduction in costs compared to on-demand pricing. Reserved instances provide a level of predictability in cloud expenditure, making them suitable for steady-state workloads with consistent resource requirements. While this commitment offers substantial cost savings, it is essential for organizations to carefully assess their long-term resource needs before opting for reserved instances to ensure maximum financial benefit.

Together, the pay-as-you-go model and reserved instances empower organizations to navigate the financial landscape of cloud computing strategically. By aligning costs with actual resource consumption and leveraging reserved instances for stability, businesses can optimize their cloud expenditures, unlocking the full potential of cost-effective and scalable infrastructure.

Security and Compliance

Ensuring the security and compliance of data within cloud computing environments is paramount for businesses entrusting their operations to these platforms. One fundamental aspect of this assurance is the implementation of robust data encryption practices. Businesses should prioritize data encryption both during transit and when at rest. By employing advanced encryption protocols, sensitive information is shielded from unauthorized access, bolstering the overall security posture of the cloud infrastructure.

Moreover, maintaining compliance with industry-specific standards and regulations is imperative, especially for sectors like healthcare, finance, and government that have stringent data protection requirements. Cloud deployments must align with these standards, ensuring that the handling, storage, and transmission of data adhere to the specific guidelines set forth by regulatory bodies. This not only mitigates the risk of legal repercussions but also fosters trust among clients and stakeholders who rely on the organization's commitment to data protection and privacy.

In the healthcare industry, for instance, complying with the Health Insurance Portability and Accountability Act (HIPAA) is non-negotiable. Cloud solutions handling patient data need to implement stringent security measures and controls to meet HIPAA requirements. Similarly, financial institutions must adhere to regulations like the Payment Card Industry Data Security Standard (PCI DSS) when utilizing cloud services for processing and storing sensitive financial information.

By integrating data encryption and compliance adherence into their cloud computing strategies, businesses can navigate the intricate landscape of digital security with confidence. This proactive approach not only fortifies the resilience of cloud-based systems but also instills a sense of reliability and trust among users and stakeholders. As the digital realm continues to evolve, prioritizing security and compliance remains a foundational principle for any organization harnessing the power of cloud computing.

Hybrid and Multi-Cloud Approaches

In the dynamic landscape of cloud computing, organizations are increasingly turning to hybrid and multi-cloud approaches to optimize their IT architectures. These strategies offer nuanced solutions, addressing diverse needs ranging from data security to service flexibility.

- **Hybrid Cloud Strategy:** Organizations often find themselves grappling with the challenge of balancing the advantages of cloud scalability with the need to secure sensitive data on-premises. A solution to this dilemma is the implementation of a hybrid cloud strategy. This approach seamlessly blends on-premises infrastructure with cloud services, allowing businesses to harness the scalability of the cloud for certain workloads while maintaining control over sensitive data within their physical premises.

By striking this delicate balance, organizations can optimize the benefits of cloud computing without compromising on data security and compliance requirements.

- **Multi-Cloud Architecture:** Embracing a multi-cloud approach involves distributing workloads across multiple cloud service providers. This strategy introduces a layer of resilience, as organizations are not solely dependent on a single cloud provider. In a multi-cloud setup, if one provider faces downtime or service interruptions, other providers can seamlessly shoulder the load, ensuring uninterrupted service delivery. Beyond resilience, a multi-cloud approach mitigates the risks associated with vendor lock-in. Organizations can cherry-pick services from different cloud providers based on specific needs, fostering a best-of-breed ecosystem that aligns precisely with their requirements. This flexibility empowers organizations to adapt to changing technological landscapes, leverage specialized services, and optimize costs.

The hybrid and multi-cloud approaches represent strategic responses to the evolving demands of modern businesses. They offer a nuanced orchestration of on-premises infrastructure and cloud services, ensuring that organizations can navigate the complex terrain of digital transformation with resilience, security, and flexibility at the forefront.

Disaster Recovery and Business Continuity

Within the realm of cloud computing, the critical aspects of disaster recovery and business continuity are addressed with a strategic focus on ensuring data availability and minimizing downtime. The implementation of robust measures revolves around the principles of data replication and automated backup and recovery mechanisms.

- **Data Replication:** A fundamental strategy in disaster recovery involves the implementation of data replication across multiple geographic regions. This strategic approach aims to create redundancy by duplicating critical data and applications across disparate locations. In the unfortunate event of a regional outage or a disaster affecting one location, the replicated data in alternative regions remains accessible. This not only enhances business continuity by ensuring continuous access to vital information but also acts as a preventive measure to minimize the impact of localized disruptions.

- **Automated Backup and Recovery:** The adoption of automated backup and recovery mechanisms represents a pivotal component in fortifying disaster recovery strategies. Automation streamlines the process of backing up essential data and applications at regular intervals. In the event of a disruption or outage, this automation accelerates the recovery process by swiftly restoring the backed-up data and applications. The automated nature of these processes minimizes the reliance on manual intervention, reducing the time required to resume normal operations. This efficiency is paramount in mitigating the potential consequences of downtime, ensuring that businesses can recover swiftly and resume their operations with minimal disruption.

By combining data replication strategies for geographic redundancy with automated backup and recovery mechanisms, organizations bolster their resilience in the face of unforeseen events. These measures not only safeguard against data loss but also contribute to maintaining operational continuity, underscoring the integral role of cloud computing in fortifying disaster recovery and business continuity strategies.

Cloud computing strategies are integral to unlocking the full potential of scalable and flexible IT architectures. Embracing the principles of scalability, cost optimization, security, hybrid and multi-cloud approaches, and disaster recovery positions organizations to harness the transformative power of the cloud, driving innovation and resilience in the digital era.

Optimizing ERP Systems

Enterprise Resource Planning (ERP) systems stand as the backbone of modern businesses, orchestrating a symphony of interconnected processes and data to streamline operations. The strategic optimization of ERP systems is not merely a technical endeavor but a pivotal business imperative. It involves aligning these systems with organizational goals, ensuring efficiency, and harnessing the full potential of data-driven insights. In the quest for effective utilization and optimization of ERP systems to support business growth, several key strategies come to the forefront.

1. Comprehensive System Assessment

The journey to optimize an ERP system commences with a comprehensive assessment of the existing infrastructure. This involves scrutinizing each module, functionality, and integration point within the ERP ecosystem. Identifying inefficiencies, redundancies, or areas where the system falls short of meeting business needs is crucial. This assessment serves as the foundation upon which targeted optimization strategies can be crafted.

2. Customization for Strategic Alignment

ERP systems, by their nature, often require customization to align with specific business processes and industry requirements. Customization, when judiciously applied, can enhance the system's effectiveness. However, a delicate balance must be maintained to avoid over-customization, which may lead to increased complexity and challenges during system upgrades. Strategic customization involves tailoring the ERP to meet specific organizational needs, ensuring that it becomes an enabler rather than a constraint on business processes.

3. Data Accuracy and Governance

The reliability and accuracy of data within an ERP system are paramount. Inaccurate or inconsistent data can lead to flawed insights and decision-making. Establishing robust data governance practices ensures the quality and integrity of information. This involves defining data ownership, implementing validation rules, and employing regular data cleansing procedures. A well-governed data environment not only enhances the accuracy of ERP-generated insights but also instills confidence in the decision-making processes relying on this data.

4. Integration Excellence

The optimization journey includes a focus on seamless integration, connecting the ERP system with other business applications and third-party solutions. This integration streamlines data flow across the organization, fostering a unified view of operations. For instance, integrating ERP with Customer Relationship Management (CRM) systems ensures that sales, marketing, and customer service teams have a consolidated view of customer interactions. Integration excellence enhances collaboration, reduces manual data entry, and accelerates decision-making processes.

5. Performance Monitoring and Analytics

Continuous improvement is the essence of ERP optimization. Implementing performance monitoring tools and analytics within the ERP environment allows organizations to track system performance, user behavior, and overall efficiency. These insights provide a basis for identifying areas of improvement and fine-tuning the system to align with evolving business needs. Analytics-driven optimization ensures that ERP systems remain adaptive, responsive, and capable of supporting dynamic business requirements.

6. User Training and Adoption

The effectiveness of an ERP system is intricately tied to the proficiency of its users. Investing in comprehensive user training programs ensures that employees can leverage the full capabilities of the ERP system. Empowering users with the skills to navigate the system, input accurate data, and extract meaningful insights contributes to overall optimization. Additionally, fostering a culture of continuous learning encourages users to stay abreast of system updates and advancements, maximizing the long-term value of the ERP investment.

7. Scalability and Flexibility

Optimizing ERP systems involves anticipating future business growth and ensuring the scalability and flexibility of the system architecture. This requires an assessment of the ERP's ability to accommodate increased data volumes, user numbers, and evolving business processes. Scalability ensures that the ERP system remains a reliable companion on the journey of organizational expansion, accommodating increased complexities without sacrificing performance.

In the fast-paced landscape of business evolution, the optimization of ERP systems emerges as a strategic imperative. It is a dynamic process that requires a holistic approach, encompassing technical, operational, and strategic dimensions. By aligning ERP systems with organizational goals, harnessing the power of accurate data, and fostering a culture of continuous improvement, businesses can navigate the path to ERP optimization. The result is a robust and responsive ERP ecosystem that acts as a catalyst for sustained business growth and competitiveness.

Chapter **26**

Effective Crisis Management

In the business world, unforeseen challenges and crises are inevitable. Whether triggered by external forces or internal factors, crises can test the resilience and adaptability of an organization. Effective crisis management is not merely about reacting when adversity strikes but also involves proactive anticipation, strategic planning, and the establishment of robust structures to navigate through turbulent times.

Anticipating Potential Crises

Anticipation, as a strategic imperative in crisis management, constitutes the initial layer of defense against the unpredictable and disruptive nature of crises. It involves developing a forward-looking, proactive mindset within an organization, instilling a culture that not only reacts to challenges but actively seeks to foresee and prepare for potential threats. Here, we explore the multifaceted dimensions of anticipating crises, emphasizing the strategic importance of this proactive stance.

Environmental Awareness and Emerging Trends

To anticipate potential crises, organizations must cultivate a keen awareness of their business environment. This involves monitoring industry trends, technological advancements, and socio-economic factors that could impact operations. An organization attuned to emerging trends can spot potential disruptions early on. For instance, a retail company anticipating shifts in consumer preferences toward online shopping might proactively invest in e-commerce capabilities to stay ahead of the curve.

Scenario Planning as a Strategic Tool

Scenario planning is a pivotal element in the anticipation toolkit. It involves creating hypothetical scenarios that explore different futures and potential challenges. By envisioning various crisis scenarios, organizations can strategize and prepare for a range of outcomes. For instance, a manufacturing company might conduct scenario planning to anticipate supply chain disruptions due to geopolitical tensions, enabling them to implement contingency plans and build resilience into their operations.

Risk Assessments for Proactive Mitigation

Conducting thorough risk assessments is another crucial aspect of anticipation. Organizations need to systematically identify, evaluate, and prioritize potential risks. This involves examining internal processes, external relationships, market dynamics, and regulatory landscapes. By understanding vulnerabilities, organizations can implement risk mitigation strategies. For example, a financial institution conducting a risk assessment may identify cybersecurity threats and proactively invest in advanced security measures to safeguard customer data.

Staying Attuned to Internal and External Indicators

Effective anticipation requires a constant vigilance for both internal and external indicators of potential crises. Internally, organizations should monitor key performance indicators (KPIs), employee morale, and operational metrics. Externally, staying abreast of market fluctuations, geopolitical events, and changes in consumer behavior is crucial. By establishing a robust monitoring system, organizations can detect early warning signs and respond swiftly. For instance, a global supply chain anticipating disruptions might closely monitor geopolitical tensions, allowing them to reroute shipments or secure alternative suppliers in advance.

Fostering a Proactive Mindset

Cultivating a proactive mindset within the organizational culture is the linchpin of effective anticipation. This involves fostering a mindset where employees at all levels are encouraged to be vigilant, challenge assumptions, and contribute to identifying potential risks. Leadership plays a pivotal role in instilling this mindset by promoting open communication, rewarding foresight, and demonstrating a commitment to proactive risk management. An organization with a proactive mindset is better equipped to foresee potential challenges and adapt swiftly, turning potential crises into opportunities for growth.

Anticipating potential crises is a holistic approach that involves environmental awareness, scenario planning, risk assessments, and a proactive organizational mindset. Organizations that embrace anticipation as a strategic imperative position themselves not only to navigate through uncertainties but to emerge stronger and more resilient in the face of evolving challenges.

Managing Crises Effectively

When a crisis unfolds in the business world, effective management becomes the linchpin that determines an organization's ability to weather the storm and emerge resilient. Crisis management transcends reactive measures; it involves a strategic, coordinated response to mitigate the impact of the crisis and guide the organization back to stability.

Here, we take a look at the methodologies for managing crises with composure, highlighting the crucial elements of crisis communication, stakeholder engagement, and adaptive leadership.

Real-world case studies serve as beacons, illuminating the intricate terrain of crisis management and extracting invaluable lessons from those who have successfully navigated through turbulent times.

Swift Decision-Making

In the tumultuous landscape of a crisis, the ability to make swift and informed decisions becomes the cornerstone of effective crisis management. Time, often a luxury in such situations, transforms into a critical resource that can either amplify or mitigate the impact of the crisis.

Strategies for cultivating a decision-making environment that strikes the delicate balance between speed and precision are explored. This involves creating frameworks that guide decision-makers, ensuring that actions align with organizational goals and values. The chapter underscores the importance of pre-established protocols and well-defined roles, enabling key stakeholders to act decisively without sacrificing the quality of their decisions.

Drawing insights from real-world scenarios where swift decisions played a pivotal role in crisis resolution, the chapter highlights the attributes that contribute to effective decision-making under pressure. It showcases instances where organizations successfully managed crises by making timely and well-calibrated decisions. These examples serve as lessons in understanding the dynamics of decision-making in high-pressure situations and provide a basis for developing strategies that can be applied across various crisis scenarios.

Empowerment of key stakeholders emerges as a key theme, as the chapter advocates for a culture that fosters decisive action at all levels of the organization. This involves not only providing the necessary tools and information but also instilling a mindset that values agility and quick thinking. By empowering individuals throughout the organization to make informed decisions in alignment with the overarching crisis management strategy, organizations can enhance their ability to navigate crises with agility and effectiveness.

The chapter also delves into the potential challenges and pitfalls associated with swift decision-making during a crisis. It addresses the need for a balance between urgency and thoughtful consideration, cautioning against impulsive actions that may exacerbate the situation. Strategies for mitigating the risks associated with rapid decision-making are explored, ensuring that organizations can harness the benefits of speed without compromising on the quality and effectiveness of their responses.

Swift decision-making is not merely a reaction to the immediacy of a crisis; it is a proactive and strategic approach that requires preparation, empowerment, and a clear understanding of the organization's goals.

Clear Communication

Effective crisis communication stands as a beacon in the storm, guiding an organization through tumultuous times. The chapter delves into communication strategies that transcend chaos and instill confidence. It explores the role of transparency, accuracy, and empathy in conveying information to internal and external stakeholders. Real-world examples illustrate how organizations that prioritize clear communication not only manage crises more effectively but also emerge with enhanced reputations and strengthened relationships with stakeholders.

Stakeholder Engagement

Engaging with stakeholders is a strategic pillar in crisis management, fostering resilience through collaboration. The chapter examines methodologies for identifying, prioritizing, and engaging with diverse stakeholders during a crisis. It underscores the significance of building relationships before a crisis occurs, allowing for more effective collaboration when it is needed most. Case studies demonstrate how organizations that prioritize stakeholder engagement navigate crises with a collective strength that surpasses individual efforts.

Adaptive Leadership: Steering through Uncertainty

In the face of a crisis, adaptive leadership emerges as a guiding force, steering organizations through uncertainty. The chapter explores the attributes of adaptive leaders – those who can pivot, innovate, and inspire confidence amid chaos. Drawing insights from leaders who successfully navigated crises, it delves into the skills and mindset required to lead effectively in turbulent times. Adaptive leadership is presented as a dynamic force that not only guides organizations through crises but positions them for post-crisis growth and resilience.

Effective crisis management is a multifaceted endeavor that requires swift decision-making, clear communication, stakeholder engagement, and adaptive leadership. By exploring these methodologies and drawing lessons from real-world cases, this chapter aims to equip organizations with the knowledge and tools to navigate crises with composure, resilience, and a strategic eye toward the future.

Structures for Resilience

The importance of building structures that enhance organizational resilience cannot be overstated in the dynamic landscape of today's business environment. These structures serve as a proactive shield, fortifying companies to withstand and recover from crises effectively. In this chapter, we delve into the significance of various structures, ranging from crisis response teams to communication protocols and robust business continuity plans, outlining a comprehensive blueprint for organizations to navigate and emerge stronger from unexpected disruptions.

At the core of resilient organizations lies the establishment of crisis response teams. These teams are strategically composed of individuals from diverse functions within the company, bringing together a spectrum of skills and expertise. The chapter explores the critical components of a well-rounded crisis response team, emphasizing the need for clear roles, defined responsibilities, and efficient coordination mechanisms. Through real-world examples, it illustrates how these teams act as the first line of defense during crises, making swift and informed decisions to guide the organization through turbulent times.

Communication protocols emerge as another integral facet of resilient structures. Timely and transparent communication is paramount in crisis situations, shaping perceptions and guiding stakeholder expectations. The chapter outlines strategies for developing communication plans that ensure a seamless flow of information internally and externally. It highlights the role of technology in facilitating communication during crises, emphasizing the need for agile and adaptable communication channels that can evolve with the nature of the crisis.

The concept of robust business continuity plans takes center stage in the chapter's exploration of resilient structures. These plans provide a roadmap for organizations to sustain critical functions during and after a crisis, minimizing disruptions to operations. The chapter delves into the key elements of effective business continuity planning, including risk assessments, resource identification, and scenario-based simulations. It emphasizes the iterative nature of these plans, encouraging organizations to regularly review and update them to align with evolving risks and challenges.

Practical guidance for implementing crisis simulations into regular training programs is a key feature of the chapter. Simulations serve as invaluable tools for stress-testing organizational resilience, allowing teams to rehearse their responses and identify areas for improvement. By incorporating real-world scenarios into training exercises, organizations can enhance the preparedness of their teams, fostering a culture of continuous learning and adaptation.

Building resilient structures necessitates a holistic approach that integrates various elements seamlessly. The chapter underscores the interconnectedness of crisis response teams, communication protocols, and business continuity plans, emphasizing the need for a cohesive and well-coordinated framework. It showcases successful examples of organizations that have navigated crises by leveraging resilient structures, drawing lessons from their experiences.

The section serves as a comprehensive guide for organizations aspiring to fortify themselves against unforeseen disruptions. It provides actionable insights into the design and implementation of structures that enhance organizational resilience, empowering companies to not only weather crises but emerge from them with newfound strength and adaptability.

In summary, Effective Crisis Management is a comprehensive exploration of the strategies, tools, and mindsets necessary for anticipating, managing, and recovering from crises. By delving into the core principles of crisis anticipation, effective management techniques, and the establishment of resilient structures, you will be equipped on how to navigate through turbulent waters with confidence and strategic acumen.

Chapter **27**

Mastering the
Art of Delegation

Delegation is a cornerstone of effective leadership, especially as companies expand and face the complexities of scaling operations. This chapter delves into the nuanced art of delegation, offering insights into recognizing opportune moments for delegation and mastering the strategies to maintain operational effectiveness without succumbing to the pitfalls of micromanagement. As organizations grow, the ability to delegate becomes not just a managerial skill but a crucial element in sustaining a healthy and dynamic workplace.

Delegation also fosters professional development by providing team members with opportunities to take ownership of tasks, enhancing their skills and confidence. For leaders, effective delegation is a catalyst for focusing on strategic priorities and preventing burnout. As the company scales, the ability to delegate becomes an indispensable skill for leaders navigating the challenges of increased responsibilities and a growing team.

Strategic Delegation Techniques

Delegation, when approached strategically, transforms from a mere distribution of tasks to a potent tool for organizational growth. In the dynamic landscape of scaling businesses, mastering the art of strategic delegation is imperative.

Here, we take a look at the various methodologies that not only align with organizational goals but also capitalize on individual team members' strengths, fostering a culture of empowerment, efficiency, and professional development.

1. Understanding Organizational Objectives

At the core of strategic delegation lies a fundamental principle: a profound understanding of organizational objectives. Leaders navigating the intricate landscape of a scaling business must have a clear grasp of the broader mission and goals. This understanding serves as the guiding compass, directing leaders to strategically delegate tasks that harmonize with the overarching strategy.

The delineation of organizational objectives provides leaders with a comprehensive roadmap. It enables them to discern the critical tasks and functions that are integral to achieving the company's success. When delegation is anchored in these strategic objectives, every assigned responsibility becomes a contributory force, propelling the organization forward.

Strategic alignment with organizational objectives is more than a tactical maneuver; it's a symbiotic relationship between delegated tasks and the company's overarching vision. For instance, if a primary objective is to expand market reach, leaders may strategically delegate responsibilities related to market research, product positioning, or customer engagement. By doing so, they ensure that every task aligns with the strategic compass, collectively propelling the company toward its growth targets.

Moreover, this alignment instills a sense of purpose among the team. Team members become cognizant of how their delegated responsibilities fit into the larger picture, fostering a collective understanding of the company's mission. This shared understanding not only cultivates a more engaged workforce but also propels the organization toward its goals with a unified and purposeful momentum.

Understanding organizational objectives serves as the cornerstone of effective strategic delegation. It transforms delegation from a routine assignment of tasks to a purpose-driven strategy. Leaders armed with a profound awareness of the company's goals can strategically navigate the intricacies of delegation, ensuring that every delegated responsibility becomes a catalyst for achieving organizational success.

2. Skill Assessment and Matching

Strategic delegation hinges on the careful evaluation of team members' skills and competencies, recognizing the unique strengths that each individual brings to the table. In this process, leaders embark on a journey of skill assessment to gain an in-depth understanding of the capabilities within their team. This involves a comprehensive analysis of technical proficiencies, soft skills, and specialized knowledge that team members possess.

Leaders can employ various methods for skill assessment, including performance reviews, self-assessment tools, and feedback from colleagues. The goal is to create a nuanced understanding of the diverse talents within the team. Once these skills are identified, leaders can strategically match tasks and responsibilities with individuals whose strengths align with the demands of the assignments.

This matching process goes beyond a mere task distribution; it's a nuanced art of aligning the right person with the right job. By capitalizing on team members' strengths, leaders ensure that tasks are not only completed proficiently but also with a heightened sense of purpose. Individuals feel a stronger connection to their work when it resonates with their competencies, fostering a positive and empowering work environment.

Moreover, the strategic matching of skills contributes to a more cohesive and collaborative team. When each team member is assigned tasks that align with their expertise, it creates a harmonious dynamic where individuals complement each other's strengths. This collaborative synergy not only enhances task execution but also fosters a sense of mutual support and camaraderie among team members.

The process of skill assessment and matching in strategic delegation isn't a one-time endeavor; it's an ongoing, dynamic process. As teams evolve, and as individuals develop new skills or refine existing ones, leaders must continuously reassess the skill landscape within the team. Regular evaluations and open communication channels ensure that the delegation process remains responsive to changes in team dynamics and organizational needs.

Strategic delegation based on skill assessment and matching is a proactive approach that transforms a team from a collection of individuals into a harmonized force. It maximizes the potential of each team member, enhances task efficiency, and contributes to a workplace culture where individuals are not just assigned tasks but are strategically positioned to thrive based on their unique strengths and competencies.

3. Balancing Challenge and Competence

In the realm of strategic delegation, achieving a delicate equilibrium between challenge and competence is paramount for optimizing team performance and fostering a positive work environment. This balance requires leaders to carefully gauge the competencies of their team members, ensuring that delegated tasks are challenging enough to engage and stimulate professional growth, yet not so overwhelming that they lead to frustration or burnout.

One key aspect of this balancing act is understanding the skill set and capacity of each team member. Leaders should conduct thorough assessments to identify individual strengths, weaknesses, and areas for growth. By gaining insights into the competencies of their team, leaders can strategically select tasks that align with each member's current skill set while introducing an element of challenge.

Tasks that are too easy may result in complacency and underutilization of skills, leading to a lack of engagement and motivation. On the other hand, tasks that are excessively challenging without aligning with the team member's current skill set can lead to frustration, stress, and potential burnout. Therefore, leaders must carefully match tasks to the capabilities of their team members, creating an environment that encourages continuous learning and skill enhancement.

This balance contributes significantly to a positive work environment. Team members who feel appropriately challenged are more likely to be engaged and motivated in their roles. The sense of accomplishment derived from overcoming challenging tasks fosters a positive attitude and a commitment to professional growth. Additionally, a positive work environment promotes collaboration, creativity, and a collective sense of achievement within the team.

Moreover, by aligning tasks with the competence level of team members, leaders demonstrate a keen understanding of their workforce. This understanding builds trust and confidence among team members, as they feel that their leaders are making thoughtful decisions about task assignments based on their individual strengths and capabilities. The result is a harmonious work environment where individuals are empowered to thrive, knowing that their leaders value their contributions and are invested in their professional development.

Achieving a balance between challenge and competence in strategic delegation is a nuanced art. Leaders who can accurately assess the competencies of their team members and align tasks accordingly create an environment that not only maximizes individual potential but also contributes to a positive, collaborative, and growth-oriented workplace. This delicate equilibrium ensures that team members are appropriately challenged, engaged, and motivated, laying the foundation for sustained success and professional fulfillment.

4. Clear Communication of Expectations

Effective delegation hinges on clear and transparent communication of expectations, forming the bedrock of a successful workflow. Leaders undertaking strategic delegation must articulate their expectations with precision, leaving no room for ambiguity. This entails outlining the desired outcomes, setting clear deadlines, and establishing any specific parameters relevant to the delegated task. By doing so, leaders provide a comprehensive roadmap for their team members, guiding them toward successful task completion.

Clarity in communication is pivotal for several reasons. Firstly, it minimizes the risk of misunderstandings or misinterpretations that can derail the delegated task. Ambiguity often leads to confusion, inefficiencies, and, in some cases, errors that could have been avoided with explicit communication. When team members have a precise understanding of what is expected of them, they are better equipped to meet those expectations.

Furthermore, transparent communication ensures alignment with organizational goals. By clearly conveying how the delegated task contributes to the broader mission and objectives of the company, leaders foster a sense of purpose among team members. Understanding the significance of their contributions, individuals are more likely to engage wholeheartedly in their delegated responsibilities, contributing meaningfully to the overall success of the organization.

Empowering team members to take ownership of their delegated responsibilities is another critical aspect of clear communication. When expectations are articulated transparently, individuals feel a greater sense of autonomy and responsibility. They understand the boundaries of their delegated task and can navigate it with confidence. This empowerment not only enhances job satisfaction but also cultivates a culture of accountability within the team.

Moreover, clear communication of expectations serves as a mechanism for feedback and evaluation. When leaders express their expectations explicitly, it becomes easier to assess the progress of delegated tasks. Regular check-ins and updates can be framed around these expectations, allowing leaders to gauge whether the task is on track, identify any challenges, and offer guidance or support as needed. This iterative feedback loop contributes to the overall success of the delegation process.

Clear communication of expectations is the linchpin that holds together the various elements of effective delegation. It acts as a guiding light for team members, ensuring they comprehend the task at hand, its significance in the larger organizational context, and the specific criteria for success. This clarity not only minimizes the likelihood of errors but also empowers individuals to take ownership and contribute meaningfully to the collective success of the team and the organization.

5. Encouraging Autonomy and Decision-Making

Encouraging autonomy and decision-making stands as a pivotal principle, transforming the dynamics of task execution. Beyond the mere assignment of responsibilities, this facet emphasizes creating an environment where team members are not only entrusted with tasks but are also empowered to make decisions within the purview of their delegated domains.

Encouraging autonomy is a catalyst for expeditious task execution. When team members are empowered to make decisions autonomously, it eliminates bottlenecks and bureaucratic delays. Decisions can be made promptly, and tasks progress at a swifter pace. This acceleration is particularly crucial in the context of dynamic business environments, enabling the organization to respond nimbly to challenges and opportunities.

Autonomy fosters a profound sense of ownership among team members. When individuals are entrusted with decision-making authority, they feel a heightened responsibility for the outcomes of their actions. This sense of ownership cultivates a deeper connection to the work they do, instilling a commitment to delivering high-quality results. Team members become personally invested in the success of their delegated tasks, leading to increased dedication and accountability.

Fostering autonomy contributes to the development of a responsibility culture within the organization. As team members exercise autonomy in decision-making, it creates a culture where individuals take responsibility for their actions and decisions. This cultural shift is fundamental for building a workforce that operates with a proactive and accountable mindset. It aligns with the principles of strategic delegation, where tasks are not merely assigned but are seen as opportunities for individuals to contribute meaningfully to the organization's success.

Encouraging autonomy is a powerful confidence-building mechanism. When team members are trusted to make decisions, it enhances their self-esteem and confidence in their capabilities. Knowing that leaders have confidence in their judgment boosts morale and motivates individuals to approach tasks with a sense of empowerment. This confidence becomes a driving force that propels team members to take on challenges and tackle complex problems with resilience and enthusiasm.

At the core of encouraging autonomy is the establishment of trust within the team. Leaders who foster an environment where autonomy is valued demonstrate a profound trust in their team members' abilities. This trust is reciprocal, as team members feel a heightened sense of trust in their leaders. A trusting environment is essential for effective collaboration, open communication, and the cultivation of strong working relationships within the organization.

Encouraging autonomy and decision-making is a cornerstone of strategic delegation. It not only accelerates task execution and cultivates a sense of ownership but also contributes to building a culture of responsibility, fostering confidence, and nurturing an environment of trust. When autonomy is embraced as a guiding principle, it becomes a catalyst for unleashing the full potential of individuals and teams, propelling the organization toward sustained growth and success.

6. Continuous Feedback Loop

The establishment of a continuous feedback loop is a recipe for success. This practice involves creating a dynamic and ongoing mechanism for communication and evaluation, ensuring that the delegated tasks align with organizational goals and individual capabilities.

A continuous feedback loop is an instrumental component because it enables leaders to keep a pulse on the progress of delegated tasks. Regular check-ins serve as touchpoints to assess the status of ongoing projects, identify any potential roadblocks, and gauge the overall trajectory. This proactive approach empowers leaders to intervene promptly if adjustments are required, preventing tasks from veering off course and ensuring that they remain aligned with strategic objectives.

The iterative nature of a continuous feedback loop contributes to agility in task management. As tasks unfold, circumstances may evolve, and new insights may emerge. Through regular check-ins, leaders can stay attuned to these changes, allowing for real-time adjustments. This adaptability is crucial in dynamic business environments, where flexibility and responsiveness are paramount for effective task execution.

Furthermore, a continuous feedback loop enhances communication channels within the team. It creates an open and collaborative environment where team members feel comfortable sharing updates, expressing concerns, and seeking guidance. This transparency is foundational for building a culture of trust and cooperation, as it fosters a sense of mutual understanding between leaders and their teams.

The feedback loop serves as an avenue for addressing challenges and offering guidance. If team members encounter obstacles or uncertainties during the execution of delegated tasks, the continuous feedback loop provides a structured platform for seeking assistance. Leaders can offer insights, share best practices, and provide the necessary support, ensuring that challenges are met with solutions and opportunities for skill development.

Moreover, the continuous feedback loop contributes to professional development. Through constructive feedback, team members gain valuable insights into their performance, strengths, and areas for improvement. This ongoing dialogue supports the growth and skill enhancement of individuals, aligning with the principles of strategic delegation where tasks are not only about achieving outcomes but also about fostering the development of team members.

The establishment of a continuous feedback loop is a cornerstone of strategic delegation. It not only facilitates real-time adjustments and ensures task alignment with organizational goals but also enhances communication, fosters transparency, and contributes to the professional growth of team members. Through this iterative process, leaders and their teams navigate the complexities of delegated tasks with agility, collaboration, and a shared commitment to achieving success.

7. Professional Development Opportunities

Strategic leaders recognize that delegation extends beyond the mere assignment of tasks; it is a strategic tool for nurturing the professional growth of individuals within the organization.

Leadership that embraces strategic delegation views each task as a potential avenue for professional development. Tasks are not merely distributed based on workload; rather, they are intentionally aligned with the career aspirations and developmental goals of team members. By thoughtfully delegating tasks that resonate with individual career paths, leaders create opportunities for their team members to enhance their skills, acquire new knowledge, and broaden their expertise.

This approach to strategic delegation has a dual benefit. On one hand, it propels individual growth by exposing team members to challenges that align with their career aspirations. Individuals find themselves engaged in tasks that require them to stretch beyond their current capabilities, fostering a continuous learning mindset. As team members tackle new responsibilities, they acquire valuable experiences that contribute to their professional development.

On the other hand, strategic delegation fortifies the organization with a skilled and motivated workforce. By aligning tasks with individuals' career aspirations, leaders ensure that team members are intrinsically motivated to excel in their delegated responsibilities. This intrinsic motivation, fueled by the connection between tasks and career goals, drives a higher level of commitment and enthusiasm. Team members are more likely to invest additional effort, go the extra mile, and demonstrate a proactive approach when they see the direct correlation between their tasks and their long-term career trajectory.

Professional development opportunities through strategic delegation contribute to the cultivation of a talent-rich environment within the organization. As team members engage in tasks that align with their career aspirations, they become a reservoir of diverse skills and expertise. This reservoir not only enhances the organization's overall capability but also creates a collaborative ecosystem where individuals can leverage their unique strengths for collective success.

Strategic leaders recognize that investing in professional development through strategic delegation is an investment in the organization's future. By facilitating the growth of individual team members, leaders create a pipeline of skilled professionals who are not only adept at their current responsibilities but are also prepared for future leadership roles. This approach ensures that the organization remains agile, adaptive, and well-equipped to navigate the complexities of an evolving business landscape.

Professional development opportunities are a key facet of strategic delegation. This approach transcends the traditional view of delegation as task assignment; instead, it becomes a deliberate strategy for empowering individuals, fostering continuous learning, and fortifying the organization with a highly skilled and motivated workforce. When professional development becomes intertwined with strategic delegation, it becomes a powerful catalyst for individual growth and organizational success.

In essence, strategic delegation is a multifaceted approach that requires a keen understanding of organizational dynamics, individual strengths, and the delicate balance between challenge and competence. By adopting these methodologies, leaders can leverage delegation as a catalyst for growth, empowerment, and sustained success in the ever-evolving landscape of scaling businesses.

Mitigating Delegation Challenges

Delegation, while a powerful tool for effective leadership and team efficiency, comes with its set of challenges. Recognizing and mitigating these challenges is crucial to ensure smooth and productive delegation. In this section, we will delve into the common challenges associated with delegation and provides strategies for addressing them, creating a roadmap for leaders to navigate the delicate balance between oversight and autonomy.

1. Maintaining Accountability

One of the primary challenges in delegation is ensuring accountability. Leaders may worry about tasks slipping through the cracks or team members not taking ownership of their responsibilities.

To strategically address this challenge, it is crucial to establish clear expectations right from the outset. This involves precisely defining tasks, setting explicit deadlines, and articulating expected outcomes. Implementing regular check-ins and feedback sessions is instrumental in tracking progress, identifying potential roadblocks, and offering timely support. Additionally, fostering a culture of responsibility is paramount. Leaders should instill a sense of ownership within each team member, emphasizing the profound impact of their contributions on the overall success of the project or the organization as a whole.

By creating a framework of clear expectations, consistent communication, and a shared sense of responsibility, leaders can effectively tackle the accountability challenge associated with delegation. This strategic approach not only mitigates the risk of tasks falling through the cracks but also instills a proactive mindset within the team, aligning individual efforts with overarching organizational goals.

2. Balancing Oversight and Autonomy

Achieving the delicate balance between oversight and autonomy is a critical aspect of effective leadership and delegation. The challenge lies in avoiding micromanagement, which can hinder creativity and motivation, while still providing enough guidance to prevent misunderstandings or deviations from the intended path. Strategic leaders tackle this challenge by recognizing the unique strengths and working styles of their team members.

Understanding the diverse strengths within the team enables leaders to tailor their oversight to individual preferences and the specific requirements of each task. Some team members may thrive with a more hands-on approach, benefiting from detailed guidance and regular check-ins. Others may excel when given the autonomy to explore their own solutions and strategies. By acknowledging these differences, leaders can create a customized approach to oversight that caters to the varied needs of their team.

Open communication is a linchpin in finding this equilibrium. Strategic leaders foster an environment where team members feel comfortable expressing their preferences and concerns. Regular communication channels, such as team meetings and one-on-one check-ins, become forums for understanding the progress of tasks, addressing challenges, and offering support. This not only ensures that team members feel supported but also allows them the freedom to showcase their skills and initiative without the fear of being micromanaged.

The nature of the task at hand also plays a pivotal role in determining the appropriate balance between oversight and autonomy. Tasks with clear guidelines or routine processes may require less direct supervision, allowing team members the freedom to execute with minimal intervention. On the other hand, projects with high complexity or ambiguity may benefit from more hands-on guidance to navigate uncertainties effectively.

Strategic leaders navigate the challenge of balancing oversight and autonomy by embracing flexibility. They recognize that the optimal level of supervision may evolve based on the task, the team members involved, and the project's stage. This adaptive approach ensures that the team receives the necessary support while maintaining the freedom to leverage their skills and creativity. In essence, strategic delegation involves tailoring leadership styles to the unique needs of both the team and the tasks at hand, fostering an environment that maximizes productivity, innovation, and job satisfaction.

3. Effective Communication

Communication breakdowns are a common challenge in delegation, leading to misunderstandings, missed deadlines, and suboptimal outcomes. Strategic leaders prioritize effective communication by establishing clear channels for information flow. Regular team meetings, concise task briefings, and the use of collaboration tools can enhance communication. Encourage an open-door policy where team members feel comfortable seeking clarification or raising concerns. Additionally, consider the diverse communication preferences within the team and adapt your approach accordingly.

4. Developing Trust

Leaders often encounter challenges when it comes to placing confidence in their team members for crucial tasks and decision-making. Building trust is a gradual process that involves a strategic and intentional approach. To initiate this trust-building journey, leaders can begin by assigning small, manageable tasks that allow team members to showcase their capabilities. These initial assignments serve as opportunities for leaders to observe performance, gauge reliability, and understand individual strengths.

As positive outcomes unfold, leaders can incrementally increase the complexity of delegated tasks, matching the team's evolving capabilities. Simultaneously, providing constructive feedback becomes an essential component of building trust. Acknowledging and reinforcing successful outcomes through timely and specific feedback not only fosters a positive work environment but also instills confidence in team members.

Transparency is a cornerstone of trust-building. Leaders should openly communicate their expectations, making sure team members have a clear understanding of their roles and responsibilities. This transparency extends to expressing any concerns or uncertainties promptly. Addressing challenges head-on and offering guidance when needed creates an environment where trust can flourish.

Trust is a two-way street, requiring leaders to reciprocate the faith placed in their team. This involves providing the necessary support, resources, and guidance to empower team members in their delegated roles. Open lines of communication further enhance the trust dynamic, allowing team members to voice concerns, seek clarification, and actively participate in decision-making processes.

Developing trust in the context of delegation is a deliberate process that involves gradual task escalation, constructive feedback, transparency, and reciprocal support. As trust becomes ingrained in the team's interactions, leaders can confidently delegate more significant responsibilities, knowing that their team is not only capable but also invested in the shared success of the organization.

5. Skill and Task Matching

In dynamic work environments, aligning team members' skills with delegated tasks can be a complex undertaking. A strategic approach to this challenge begins with the implementation of regular skill assessments within the team. These assessments aim to comprehensively understand each team member's strengths, weaknesses, and areas for development. By gaining insights into the unique skill set of each individual, leaders can strategically match tasks to align with their expertise.

Understanding the strengths of team members is not only about recognizing their current capabilities but also about identifying opportunities for growth. A strategic leader goes beyond merely assigning tasks based on existing skills; they look to foster continuous development. This involves creating a culture of learning and improvement within the team.

Once the skill landscape is mapped, leaders can tailor their delegation strategy to capitalize on the strengths of each team member. Tasks that align with their expertise become more manageable and are likely to yield better results. Simultaneously, identifying areas for development allows leaders to offer tasks that provide growth opportunities, challenging individuals to enhance their skills and broaden their professional repertoire.

In addition to matching skills with tasks, a strategic approach involves implementing cross-training initiatives. Cross-training enhances the versatility of the team, ensuring that members are equipped to handle diverse tasks effectively. This approach not only prepares individuals for a broader range of responsibilities but also creates a collaborative environment where team members can support each other when facing challenges.

Ultimately, strategic skill and task matching contribute to the overall effectiveness of delegation by aligning the right people with the right tasks. This not only optimizes performance but also fosters a sense of purpose and satisfaction among team members, as they are engaged in work that both leverages their strengths and provides opportunities for continuous improvement. Through this strategic alignment, leaders set the stage for a dynamic and resilient team capable of navigating the challenges of a rapidly evolving work landscape.

6. Feedback and Recognition

In the realm of leadership and team dynamics, the effective delivery of feedback and recognition is a cornerstone for fostering growth and maintaining motivation among team members. Striking the right balance between constructive criticism and positive reinforcement is an art that strategic leaders master to address this particular challenge.

Strategic leaders recognize that feedback should not only pinpoint areas for improvement but also celebrate successes. Regular acknowledgment of the efforts and achievements of team members builds a positive and encouraging work environment. By consistently recognizing hard work, dedication, and accomplishments, leaders contribute to the development of a culture that values and appreciates the contributions of each team member.

When providing feedback, a strategic approach involves focusing on specific actions and their impact rather than making it a personal critique. This nuanced feedback helps team members understand the areas in which they excel and the aspects that require refinement. Constructive criticism is framed in a way that encourages improvement without demotivating individuals, emphasizing a commitment to continuous learning and development.

Moreover, strategic leaders ensure that feedback is not a one-way street. They create an environment where team members feel comfortable providing input and suggestions. This two-way communication fosters a collaborative atmosphere, promoting open dialogue and enhancing the overall feedback culture within the team.

The strategic handling of feedback and recognition transforms these elements from mere managerial duties into powerful tools for individual and collective growth. By nurturing a culture that values both positive achievements and areas for improvement, strategic leaders contribute to a motivated, engaged, and continuously improving team.

By addressing these common challenges through a strategic lens, leaders can navigate the intricacies of delegation effectively. This approach not only mitigates potential pitfalls but also transforms delegation into a catalyst for individual and team success.

Chapter 28

Financing Growth

Chapter 28 delves into the critical aspect of financing growth, exploring the various avenues available to companies seeking to expand their operations. Financing growth is a strategic imperative for businesses aiming to scale up, enter new markets, or invest in innovative initiatives. This chapter navigates through the intricacies of funding expansion, offering insights into diverse financial instruments, from venture capital to initial public offerings (IPOs).

Understanding how to secure the necessary capital for growth is fundamental for businesses at different stages of development. Whether considering external investment, debt financing, or exploring public markets, the chapter provides guidance on the factors to consider when choosing the right financing path tailored to the unique needs and ambitions of your company. Explore the dynamic landscape of financing growth and gain valuable insights to fuel your company's journey toward sustainable expansion.

Venture Capital: Unlocking Investment for Innovation

Venture capital (VC) stands out as a dynamic and pivotal avenue for funding expansion, particularly for businesses with innovative and high-growth potential. This form of financing involves investment from venture capital firms, which pool funds from various sources to support startups and emerging companies. Venture capital plays a crucial role in driving innovation, fostering entrepreneurship, and fueling the growth of companies in their early stages.

One of the distinctive features of venture capital is the willingness of investors to take on higher risks in exchange for potential high returns. VC firms provide funding to startups and growth-stage companies in exchange for equity or ownership stakes. This strategic alignment of interests motivates both the entrepreneurs and investors to work collaboratively toward achieving success.

1. Early-Stage Funding

In the realm of business development, the early stages are often the most challenging for startups, marked by financial uncertainties and the need for substantial capital. Venture capital emerges as a critical and transformative force during this phase, addressing a key challenge faced by startups – obtaining funding when traditional bank loans might be inaccessible. Given the absence of a well-established financial track record, startups may struggle to secure loans from conventional sources. Venture capitalists step into this void by providing capital injections to promising ventures in their nascent stages.

The significance of venture capital in early-stage funding lies in its ability to catalyze crucial aspects of a startup's journey. These funds empower startups to embark on essential activities such as product development, market validation, and initial business operations. This financial backing is pivotal for transforming innovative ideas into tangible, market-ready products or services. It not only fuels the development of groundbreaking concepts but also provides the necessary resources for startups to validate their market potential, laying the foundation for future growth.

Moreover, early-stage venture capital funding goes beyond just financial support. Successful venture capitalists often bring valuable expertise, industry knowledge, and strategic insights to the table. The collaborative nature of the relationship between venture capitalists and startups ensures that entrepreneurs receive not only the necessary capital but also guidance from seasoned professionals who have navigated similar challenges. This mentorship component enhances the chances of success for startups, offering them a unique opportunity to learn and iterate based on the experiences of those who have successfully scaled their businesses.

Early-stage funding through venture capital is a linchpin for the growth and development of startups. By filling the funding gap left by traditional financing options, venture capitalists play a pivotal role in shaping the trajectory of emerging businesses. The injection of capital at this critical juncture empowers startups to embark on their entrepreneurial journey, validating their ideas, creating viable products, and setting the stage for future expansion. The combination of financial support and strategic guidance makes venture capital a catalyst for innovation, propelling early-stage companies toward sustainable growth and success.

2. Scaling Operations

In the dynamic journey of a company's growth, the transition from the startup phase to scaling operations is a critical juncture, and venture capital emerges as a strategic ally during this transformative stage. Scaling operations involves expanding various facets of the business, including the team, marketing initiatives, and overall infrastructure. This expansion requires a substantial infusion of capital, and venture capital provides the necessary financial backing.

One of the primary challenges during the scaling phase is managing the increased demand for products or services. Venture capital funding allows companies to build and strengthen their teams, hiring skilled professionals across various departments. Whether it's bolstering the sales team to capitalize on market opportunities or bringing in experts to enhance operational efficiency, the financial support from venture capitalists facilitates the strategic expansion of the workforce.

Marketing efforts are another crucial aspect of scaling operations, as companies seek to broaden their market reach and establish a more significant presence. Venture capital funding offers the financial leverage needed to invest in comprehensive marketing strategies, from digital campaigns to traditional advertising. This increased visibility not only helps in attracting a larger customer base but also solidifies the company's position in the competitive landscape.

Infrastructure enhancement is often a priority during the scaling phase, as companies need to ensure that their systems, technologies, and operational capabilities can seamlessly accommodate the growing demands. Venture capital provides the capital required to invest in advanced technologies, upgrade existing systems, and build a robust infrastructure that can support the increased scale of operations. This may involve expanding production facilities, upgrading IT infrastructure, or investing in logistics and supply chain optimization.

Moreover, venture capitalists bring more than just financial resources to the table during the scaling phase. Successful VC firms often have a network of industry experts and seasoned professionals who can provide strategic guidance. This mentorship aspect becomes particularly valuable as companies navigate the complexities of rapid growth, offering insights into scaling strategies, market dynamics, and operational efficiency.

Scaling operations with the support of venture capital is about strategically leveraging financial resources to propel the company forward. The infusion of capital not only addresses immediate financial needs but positions the company for sustainable growth by enhancing its capabilities, expanding its reach, and preparing it to seize emerging market opportunities. Through this collaborative partnership, companies can navigate the challenges associated with rapid growth and establish a solid foundation for long-term success.

3. Expertise and Mentorship

One of the distinctive advantages of engaging with venture capitalists is the multifaceted support they provide beyond mere financial investment. Successful VC firms typically house seasoned professionals with substantial industry experience and a proven track record in nurturing startups. This wealth of knowledge extends far beyond the boardroom, as entrepreneurs gain access to invaluable expertise, mentorship, and strategic guidance.

Venture capitalists, often referred to as smart money, bring a deep understanding of the challenges and opportunities specific to the industry in which they invest. Their hands-on involvement in the growth and development of startups goes beyond the traditional role of financial backers. By tapping into this reservoir of experience, entrepreneurs benefit from insights that can shape their strategic decision-making, product development, and overall business operations.

The mentorship aspect of venture capital is particularly transformative for emerging business leaders. Seasoned professionals affiliated with VC firms frequently take on advisory roles, providing direct guidance to entrepreneurs navigating the complexities of scaling their businesses. This mentorship extends not only to the technical aspects of running a company but also encompasses crucial soft skills, leadership development, and strategic thinking.

The collaborative approach between venture capitalists and entrepreneurs goes beyond a transactional relationship. It evolves into a partnership where shared goals and interests drive mutual success. Entrepreneurs gain a mentorship network that understands the intricacies of their industry, and VC firms benefit from actively contributing to the success of the startups in which they invest.

This collaborative dynamic accelerates the learning curve for emerging business leaders. Instead of relying solely on trial and error, entrepreneurs can draw upon the experiences and insights of their venture capital partners. This accelerated learning process is invaluable in fast-paced industries, providing entrepreneurs with a strategic advantage as they navigate the challenges and uncertainties of scaling their ventures.

The expertise and mentorship offered by venture capitalists are integral components of the value proposition they bring to the table. Beyond financial investment, the infusion of industry knowledge, strategic guidance, and mentorship creates a synergistic relationship that significantly enhances the chances of success for startups and emerging businesses. The collaborative approach fosters a learning environment where entrepreneurs can tap into the collective wisdom of seasoned professionals, positioning them for accelerated growth and sustained success.

4. Innovation and Disruption

Venture capital's close association with fostering innovation and driving disruptive technologies makes it a catalyst for reshaping industries. The injection of funds into companies pursuing groundbreaking ideas facilitates the development of new products, services, and technologies. This focus on innovation aligns seamlessly with the risk-taking nature of venture capital, where the pursuit of transformative ideas inherently comes with uncertainties.

In the realm of venture capital, disruptive technologies are often groundbreaking solutions that challenge traditional norms and redefine market landscapes. Startups that receive venture capital funding are frequently engaged in developing and implementing technologies that have the potential to revolutionize industries. This might involve introducing novel approaches, methodologies, or products that fundamentally alter the way businesses operate or how consumers experience certain services.

The venture capital ecosystem thrives on identifying and supporting these disruptive innovations. Investors in the venture capital space understand that by backing companies at the forefront of technological advancements, they not only contribute to these innovations but also position themselves for potentially significant returns on investment. This symbiotic relationship between venture capital and disruptive innovation reflects the dynamic nature of the industry, where risk and reward are intricately linked.

Moreover, venture capital's emphasis on disruptive technologies extends beyond financial considerations. It actively contributes to the evolution of industries by supporting ventures that challenge the status quo and push the boundaries of what is possible. The infusion of capital, coupled with the strategic guidance provided by venture capitalists, empowers entrepreneurs to take calculated risks, experiment with groundbreaking concepts, and pioneer changes that reverberate throughout their respective sectors.

Venture capital's role in fostering innovation and driving disruptive technologies is a key element in the success of startups and emerging companies. By injecting funds into ventures pursuing groundbreaking ideas, venture capital not only fuels innovation but also contributes to the transformative changes that shape industries. This alignment of venture capital with the pursuit of transformative ideas underscores its crucial role in pushing the boundaries of what is achievable in the dynamic landscape of business and technology.

5. Portfolio Approach

The portfolio approach is a fundamental strategy employed by venture capital (VC) firms to navigate the inherent uncertainties and risks associated with investing in early-stage companies. Recognizing that not every startup will achieve a successful outcome, VC firms diversify their investments across a range of startups, forming a portfolio. This deliberate diversification serves as a risk-mitigation tactic, acknowledging that some ventures may face challenges or even fail, while others may achieve remarkable success.

By managing a diverse portfolio, venture capitalists aim to balance the potential upsides and downsides of their investments. The expectation is that the successes of a few standout companies within the portfolio will outweigh any failures, resulting in a net positive return on investment. This approach aligns with the unpredictable nature of startups and acknowledges that predicting which ventures will thrive can be challenging.

Diversification within the portfolio provides a level of insulation against the uncertainties and risks associated with individual startup performance. The rationale is that even if some investments face challenges or do not meet anticipated milestones, the overall performance of the portfolio can remain positive due to the successes of other ventures.

Moreover, the portfolio approach reflects the understanding that innovation and entrepreneurship inherently involve experimentation and risk-taking. Not all groundbreaking ideas will achieve widespread market adoption, and some may encounter unforeseen challenges. The portfolio strategy allows venture capitalists to cast a wide net, supporting a variety of ventures pursuing diverse market opportunities and technological advancements.

This approach is rooted in the belief that successful startups have the potential to deliver substantial returns on investment, compensating for any losses incurred by less successful ventures. It also aligns with the long-term perspective of venture capital, recognizing that the journey of a startup involves multiple stages, and outcomes may evolve over time.

The portfolio approach in venture capital is a strategic response to the unpredictable nature of startup investments. By managing a diverse range of investments, VC firms aim to balance risks and rewards, acknowledging that not every venture will achieve success. This risk-mitigation strategy allows venture capitalists to support innovation and entrepreneurship while optimizing the potential for overall positive returns within their investment portfolios.

In conclusion, venture capital serves as a catalyst for innovation and growth, particularly for startups and companies with disruptive potential. By providing not just financial resources but also expertise and mentorship, venture capital plays a vital role in nurturing and propelling emerging businesses toward success. Entrepreneurs seeking to finance expansion and navigate the challenges of early-stage development often find in venture capital a strategic partner that aligns with their ambitions for innovation and growth.

Initial Public Offerings (IPOs): Going Public to Fuel Expansion

An Initial Public Offering (IPO) marks a significant milestone for companies seeking to fuel expansion by going public and offering their shares to the broader investment market. The process of going public through an IPO involves several key stages, each contributing to the company's transition from a private entity to a publicly traded one.

1. Preparation and Due Diligence

Before initiating the IPO process, a company must thoroughly prepare by conducting extensive due diligence. The first crucial step involves a thorough examination of various facets of the company's operations, financial health, and overall business strategy. Financial advisors, legal experts, and underwriters are instrumental during this preparatory phase, guiding the company through the intricacies of the IPO process.

Financial due diligence is paramount, requiring a detailed analysis of the company's financial statements, historical performance, and future projections. This scrutiny aims to provide potential investors with a clear understanding of the company's financial health and growth prospects. Legal due diligence delves into the company's compliance with regulatory requirements, potential legal liabilities, and the resolution of any outstanding legal matters. This phase helps ensure that the company is well-positioned to meet the stringent regulatory standards associated with being a publicly traded entity.

Operational due diligence examines the efficiency and sustainability of the company's operational processes. Identifying areas for improvement and optimization is crucial to enhance operational resilience in the dynamic public market environment. Additionally, a thorough review of the overall business strategy, market positioning, and competitive landscape is conducted to align the company's narrative with the expectations of potential investors.

This preparation phase is not merely a procedural requirement but a strategic initiative to instill confidence in investors, regulators, and the broader financial market. Companies must present a transparent and compelling picture of their business, addressing any potential concerns or uncertainties that may arise during the IPO process. By investing time and resources in thorough preparation and due diligence, companies set the stage for a smoother transition to public ownership, fostering trust and credibility in the eyes of stakeholders.

2. Selection of Underwriters

The selection of underwriters is a critical step in the Initial Public Offering (IPO) process, as these financial institutions play a pivotal role in guiding the company through the complexities of going public. Underwriters, often investment banks with extensive experience in managing IPOs, collaborate closely with the company to determine the optimal offering price for its shares. This involves a thorough assessment of the company's financial health, market conditions, and industry benchmarks.

The chosen underwriters aid in structuring the offering to ensure it aligns with the company's strategic goals and market dynamics. Their expertise becomes particularly valuable during the pricing phase, where they contribute insights into demand forecasts and investor sentiment. By leveraging their market knowledge, underwriters help strike a balance between setting an attractive offering price that appeals to investors and achieving a valuation that aligns with the company's worth.

Moreover, underwriters act as intermediaries between the company and potential investors, facilitating the sale of shares across both institutional and retail markets. Their role extends to managing the allocation of shares to different investor groups based on demand, ensuring a fair distribution process. This allocation strategy aims to optimize the overall success of the IPO and support a stable initial trading performance once the shares are listed on the stock exchange. The selection of underwriters is a strategic decision that goes beyond mere transaction facilitation. Companies consider factors such as the underwriters' track record in successfully managing IPOs, industry expertise, and the strength of their investor relationships. A collaborative and effective partnership with underwriters can significantly contribute to the success of the IPO, from the initial stages of due diligence to the exciting moment when the company's shares become publicly tradable.

3. SEC Registration

SEC registration is a critical step in the process of taking a company public through an Initial Public Offering (IPO). This involves submitting a comprehensive registration statement, commonly known as the prospectus, to the U.S. Securities and Exchange Commission (SEC) or relevant regulatory authorities in other jurisdictions where the company plans to offer its securities. The prospectus serves as a detailed document offering transparency into various aspects of the company's financial health, operational activities, associated risks, and the intended utilization of the funds raised through the IPO.

The prospectus is a comprehensive disclosure document, providing potential investors with the information necessary to make informed investment decisions. It includes detailed financial statements, management discussions and analysis, and a thorough examination of the company's business model. Importantly, it outlines the specific ways in which the company intends to use the capital raised during the IPO.

Once the prospectus is submitted, the SEC reviews its contents to ensure compliance with regulatory disclosure requirements. This scrutiny is a fundamental aspect of the IPO process, aiming to safeguard the interests of investors by promoting transparency and accurate representation of the company's financial standing. The SEC's review involves assessing the completeness and accuracy of the disclosed information, confirming that all pertinent details are provided, and verifying that there is no misleading or inadequate information that could compromise investor understanding.

Successful SEC registration signifies regulatory approval for the company to proceed with its IPO. It provides the green light for the company's shares to be offered to the public and traded on the stock exchange. The SEC's role in this process is pivotal, as it contributes to establishing confidence among potential investors and maintaining the integrity of the financial markets.

Navigating the SEC registration process requires collaboration between the company and its legal and financial advisors to ensure the accuracy and completeness of the prospectus. The company must adhere to regulatory guidelines and address any queries or feedback from the SEC promptly. Ultimately, the SEC registration sets the stage for the company's debut on the public markets, marking a transformative moment in its financial journey.

4. Marketing and Roadshow

The marketing and roadshow phase is a pivotal component of the Initial Public Offering (IPO) process, marking the company's proactive engagement with potential institutional investors and the broader market. Following the approval of the registration statement by regulatory authorities, such as the U.S. Securities and Exchange Commission (SEC), the company, alongside its underwriters, initiates a comprehensive marketing and promotional campaign known as the roadshow.

During the roadshow, key executives and representatives from the company, often accompanied by underwriters, embark on a series of meetings with institutional investors. These encounters provide a strategic platform to present the investment case, showcase the company's financial health, discuss its business strategy, and highlight future growth prospects. The roadshow serves as an opportunity to foster direct communication between the company's leadership and potential investors, allowing them to address queries, provide additional insights, and build confidence in the IPO.

Crucially, the roadshow plays a decisive role in gauging investor interest and sentiment, which, in turn, informs the final offering price for the IPO. Through these interactions, the company gains valuable feedback on how the market perceives its valuation, helping to strike a delicate balance between achieving a fair valuation and satisfying demand.

The effectiveness of the roadshow hinges on the ability of the company's executives to articulate a compelling narrative that resonates with investors. Transparency, clarity in financial disclosures, and a persuasive depiction of the company's growth potential are essential elements during these presentations. The success of the roadshow not only impacts the pricing of the IPO but also sets the tone for the company's initial trading days on the stock exchange.

The marketing and roadshow phase is a dynamic and interactive process that positions the company to make a strong market debut. It is a strategic opportunity to build confidence, generate enthusiasm among potential investors, and ultimately contribute to the success of the IPO.

5. Pricing and Allotment

The crucial stage of an Initial Public Offering (IPO) involves determining the offering price and allocating shares to investors. Following the comprehensive roadshow, during which the company and underwriters engage with potential investors, the pricing and allotment process commences. This phase relies on the feedback gathered from institutional and retail investors to establish the final offering price.

The determination of the offering price is a delicate balance, taking into account the perceived value of the company, market conditions, and investor demand. The underwriters play a pivotal role in advising the company on setting a price that reflects the company's true worth as it transitions into the public market. This price essentially becomes the valuation of the company as it begins trading on the stock exchange.

Once the offering price is established, the allotment process begins. Shares are allocated to both institutional and retail investors based on their demand and the overall supply of shares available. Striking a balance in this allocation is crucial to meet investor demand while ensuring a fair valuation for the company. Institutional investors often receive larger allocations, but the goal is to allocate shares in a manner that maximizes participation and interest from a diverse range of investors.

The pricing and allotment phase is a critical moment in the IPO journey, impacting the initial trading performance of the stock. If the offering price is set too high, it may deter investor interest, while setting it too low could undervalue the company. Achieving a fair valuation and ensuring a balanced allotment process contribute to a successful market debut and sets the stage for the stock's performance in the public market. It is a complex decision-making process that requires careful consideration of various factors to align the interests of the company, underwriters, and investors.

6. Debut on the Stock Exchange

The culmination of an Initial Public Offering (IPO) is the company's debut on the stock exchange, a momentous event that signifies its transition from a privately held entity to a publicly traded one. This moment is punctuated by the opening bell ceremony, a symbolic gesture marking the company's official entry into the public markets. The ringing of the opening bell is often accompanied by celebrations and media coverage, highlighting the significance of the company's newfound status.

The first day of trading following the IPO is a critical juncture, attracting substantial attention from investors, analysts, and the financial community. The stock's performance on this inaugural day is meticulously scrutinized, as it sets an initial valuation benchmark and can significantly influence future investor sentiment. Positive performance, such as a strong opening price and robust demand for shares, can bolster confidence in the company's prospects, potentially attracting more investors. Conversely, a lackluster debut may raise questions and impact the stock's perceived value.

Investors closely analyze the opening day's trading activity to gauge market sentiment and the level of enthusiasm for the newly public company. Factors influencing the stock's performance on debut include the pricing strategy, demand during the roadshow, prevailing market conditions, and broader economic trends. It is not uncommon for the stock to experience volatility during its initial trading sessions as the market absorbs new information and adjusts to the company's public status.

Beyond the immediate market response, a successful debut contributes to the company's overall reputation and visibility. A positive first impression can enhance the company's standing within the investment community, potentially attracting institutional investors and increasing liquidity in the stock. However, the company's leadership must remain vigilant and focused on executing its strategic plans to sustain long-term investor confidence and deliver value to shareholders. The debut on the stock exchange is a pivotal moment that encapsulates the outcome of extensive preparations, from the IPO planning stages to the roadshow. It signals the beginning of a new chapter for the company, characterized by increased transparency, market scrutiny, and the opportunities and challenges that come with being a publicly traded entity.

Benefits of Going Public

- **Access to Capital:** One of the primary reasons companies go public is to raise capital for expansion, acquisitions, or debt repayment. Going public provides access to a broader investor base and larger funding opportunities.

- **Liquidity for Shareholders:** Going public allows existing shareholders, including founders and early investors, to sell their shares and realize liquidity. This liquidity can be used for personal financial goals or reinvested in the company.

- **Enhanced Visibility and Prestige:** A public listing increases a company's visibility and credibility in the business world. It can attract attention from customers, partners, and potential employees, contributing to the company's overall prestige.

- **Stock-Based Acquisitions:** Publicly traded companies can use their stock as a valuable currency for acquisitions. Stock-based acquisitions offer an alternative to cash transactions, enabling companies to expand their operations through strategic purchases.

- **Employee Stock Options:** Going public can enhance the company's ability to attract and retain top talent by offering stock-based compensation, such as employee stock options. This aligns employees' interests with the company's long-term success.

While going public offers numerous advantages, it also comes with increased regulatory requirements, scrutiny from investors and analysts, and the need for transparent and timely financial reporting. Companies must carefully weigh the benefits and challenges to determine if an IPO aligns with their strategic objectives and growth plans.

Chapter 29

Corporate Social Responsibility and Sustainability

This chapter will take a look into the realm of Corporate Social Responsibility (CSR) and Sustainability, exploring how businesses can integrate these principles into their core operations. Corporate Social Responsibility involves a commitment to ethical practices, sustainable initiatives, and responsible business conduct, transcending mere profit-making objectives. As companies recognize their broader impact on society and the environment, CSR becomes an integral part of their business model, influencing decision-making and fostering a more sustainable approach to growth.

Understanding the symbiotic relationship between business success and social responsibility is crucial in today's conscientious consumer landscape. This chapter explores the dynamics of aligning growth with ethical practices and sustainability, emphasizing the positive impact on brand reputation and the cultivation of a loyal customer base. By adopting CSR principles, businesses not only contribute to the betterment of communities and environmental conservation but also enhance their own resilience and long-term viability.

In the pursuit of corporate social responsibility, companies embark on a journey to integrate ethical, social, and environmental considerations into their daily operations. This chapter elucidates the key tenets of CSR, examining how it works as a transformative force within organizations. From embracing sustainable practices to engaging with local communities, the chapter unravels the multifaceted aspects of CSR and sustainability.

Sustainable Business Practices

Sustainable business practices form the bedrock of Corporate Social Responsibility (CSR) and are integral to fostering a harmonious relationship between business operations and environmental stewardship. This section delves into the intricacies of sustainable business practices, elucidating how companies can weave ethical and environmentally conscious strategies into their operational fabric.

At its core, sustainable business practices revolve around the idea of conducting operations in a manner that meets the present needs of the business without compromising the ability of future generations to meet their own needs. This entails considering the environmental, social, and economic impact of business decisions.

One fundamental aspect of sustainable business practices is the adoption of eco-friendly initiatives. This includes implementing measures to reduce carbon emissions, minimize waste, and conserve resources. For example, companies may invest in renewable energy sources, adopt energy-efficient technologies, and implement waste reduction programs. These initiatives not only contribute to a healthier planet but also often result in cost savings and increased operational efficiency.

Another key facet is ethical sourcing and responsible supply chain management. Companies are increasingly scrutinizing their supply chains to ensure that products are sourced ethically, with attention to fair labor practices, human rights, and environmental considerations. For instance, a fashion brand may opt for sustainably sourced materials, ensuring that the production process does not exploit workers or harm ecosystems.

Beyond environmental considerations, sustainable business practices extend to fostering a positive social impact. This involves actively contributing to the well-being of communities in which a business operates. Companies may engage in philanthropic activities, support local education initiatives, or contribute to healthcare programs. By aligning with social causes, businesses not only fulfill their ethical obligations but also build stronger connections with communities, enhancing their brand reputation.

Additionally, sustainable business practices involve cultivating a corporate culture that prioritizes diversity and inclusion. Companies can implement policies that promote equal opportunities, fair wages, and a supportive work environment. This not only contributes to social equity but also enhances employee morale and productivity.

Measurement and reporting play a crucial role in the implementation of sustainable business practices. Companies often develop Key Performance Indicators (KPIs) to track their environmental and social impact. Regular sustainability reports communicate these metrics transparently to stakeholders, showcasing the company's commitment to responsible business practices.

Moreover, embracing sustainable business practices is increasingly becoming a market differentiator. Consumers are more inclined to support brands that align with their values, and businesses that prioritize sustainability often enjoy a competitive advantage. This section explores the strategies for communicating sustainability efforts to consumers, emphasizing the importance of authenticity and transparency in building trust.

In conclusion, sustainable business practices encompass a holistic approach to corporate responsibility. By integrating ethical, environmental, and social considerations into daily operations, businesses not only contribute to a better world but also position themselves for long-term success in an evolving market landscape. This section provides insights into the multifaceted nature of sustainable business practices, offering a roadmap for companies seeking to harmonize growth with a conscience.

Community Engagement and Social Impact

Community engagement and social impact are pillars of Corporate Social Responsibility (CSR) that extend beyond business operations, emphasizing a commitment to the well-being of communities and society at large. This section delves into the intricate dynamics of community engagement and social impact, elucidating the benefits, strategies, and the transformative potential they hold for businesses and the communities they serve.

Community Engagement

Community engagement is a collaborative and participatory process through which businesses establish meaningful connections with the communities in which they operate. It involves two-way communication, active involvement, and mutual understanding between the company and its stakeholders, including local residents, non-profit organizations, and governmental bodies.

Benefits of Community Engagement

1. Enhanced Corporate Reputation

Actively participating in community engagement initiatives provides businesses with a unique opportunity to enhance their corporate reputation. When companies align their interests with the well-being of the community, they cultivate a positive image that extends beyond the products or services they offer. This positive perception is particularly crucial in today's socially conscious landscape, where consumers increasingly value businesses that actively contribute to societal welfare. A robust corporate reputation, built on a foundation of community engagement, can become a competitive advantage, attracting customers who prioritize socially responsible businesses.

2. Stakeholder Trust and Support

Community engagement serves as a catalyst for strengthening relationships with key stakeholders, fostering a sense of trust and support. Key stakeholders, including customers, employees, and investors, often view businesses more favorably when they observe a genuine commitment to community well-being. Customers are inclined to support companies that actively contribute to the communities they serve, establishing a sense of loyalty and advocacy. This strengthened bond extends to employees, who find pride and purpose in working for an organization that prioritizes its social responsibilities. Investors, too, may view community engagement as a positive indicator of long-term sustainability and responsible business practices, influencing their decisions and support for the company.

3. Risk Mitigation

Engaging with communities can also act as a risk mitigation strategy for businesses. By proactively involving themselves in local issues and concerns, companies gain insights into potential challenges or conflicts that might arise. Addressing these issues early on can prevent them from escalating into larger problems that could negatively impact the business. Through community engagement, businesses can navigate potential pitfalls, anticipate concerns, and build a reservoir of goodwill that may serve as a protective shield during challenging times.

4. Brand Differentiation

Beyond enhancing reputation and building trust, community engagement contributes to brand differentiation. In a crowded marketplace where products and services can be similar, businesses that stand out by actively engaging with and supporting local communities create a distinct identity. This differentiation becomes a valuable asset, influencing consumer choices and driving brand preference. A brand associated with positive community impact not only captures attention but also establishes an emotional connection with customers, further solidifying the brand's position in the market.

5. Public Positive Relations

Community engagement initiatives often garner media attention, leading to positive public relations. When a company is actively involved in initiatives that contribute positively to the community, it creates compelling narratives that resonate with the public. Media coverage of such efforts not only amplifies the impact of the initiatives but also positions the business as a socially responsible entity. This positive publicity extends the reach of the company's message, influencing public perception and further reinforcing its commitment to corporate social responsibility.

6. Innovation and Local Insight

Engaging with local communities provides businesses with valuable insights. Local residents often have a deep understanding of the unique challenges and opportunities in their area. This local knowledge can drive innovation and help businesses tailor their strategies to meet specific community needs.

Strategies for Effective Community Engagement

- **Open and Transparent Communication:** Establish clear channels of communication with the community. Regularly communicate business activities, initiatives, and changes, and actively seek input and feedback.
- **Partnerships with Local Organizations:** Collaborate with local non-profits, community groups, and governmental organizations. Partnering with established entities ensures that initiatives are aligned with genuine community needs and priorities.
- **Inclusive Decision-Making:** Involve community members in decision-making processes. Solicit input on projects, policies, and initiatives that may impact the community. This inclusive approach empowers residents and strengthens the sense of ownership.

Social Impact

Social impact refers to the positive change that an organization's activities, initiatives, or investments bring about in society. It goes beyond philanthropy, focusing on sustainable and measurable outcomes that contribute to the well-being of individuals, communities, and broader societal goals.

Benefits of Social Impact Initiatives:
- **Fulfillment of Corporate Purpose:** Social impact initiatives allow businesses to align their activities with a higher purpose. Contributing to social well-being gives employees a sense of fulfillment and purpose, fostering a positive workplace culture.
- **Brand Differentiation:** Businesses that prioritize social impact often stand out in the market. Consumers increasingly prefer brands that are socially responsible, and showcasing meaningful contributions can differentiate a company in a competitive landscape.
- **Talent Attraction and Retention:** Employees, especially the younger generation, are drawn to employers with a strong commitment to social impact. Engaging in initiatives that contribute to a better world enhances a company's ability to attract and retain top talent.
- **Long-Term Business Sustainability:** Social impact initiatives are aligned with sustainable business practices. By investing in initiatives that address social and environmental challenges, businesses contribute to long-term sustainability, mitigating risks associated with societal issues.

Strategies for Driving Social Impact:
- **Identifying Key Social Issues:** Understand the pressing social issues relevant to the business and the communities it serves. This involves conducting thorough assessments to identify areas where the company can make a meaningful difference.
- **Measurable Goals and Metrics:** Establish clear and measurable goals for social impact initiatives. Define key performance indicators (KPIs) to track progress and assess the effectiveness of the initiatives over time.
- **Collaboration with Stakeholders:** Collaborate with various stakeholders, including NGOs, governmental bodies, and other businesses. Partnerships amplify the impact of social initiatives and create a collective effort toward positive change.
- **Education and Awareness:** Social impact often involves addressing societal challenges through education and awareness. Companies can play a role in promoting awareness, education, and behavioral change that contribute to societal well-being.

Community engagement and social impact are integral components of responsible corporate citizenship. By actively engaging with communities and driving positive change, businesses not only fulfill their ethical obligations but also position themselves as contributors to societal progress. This section serves as a comprehensive guide to navigating the complexities of community engagement and leveraging social impact initiatives for lasting positive change.

Chapter 30

Preparing for a
Merger or Acquisition

Embarking on a merger or acquisition is a strategic move that demands careful planning, astute decision-making, and meticulous execution. Whether your company is considering merging with another entity or acquiring a business, the process involves multifaceted considerations, from financial evaluations to cultural integrations. This chapter delves into the intricacies of preparing for a merger or acquisition, guiding business leaders through the essential steps to position their companies for success in the complex landscape of corporate consolidation.

Valuation Methods

Valuation is a fundamental component of the merger and acquisition (M&A) process, playing a pivotal role in determining the worth of a target company. It involves assessing the financial health, assets, liabilities, and future earning potential to arrive at a fair market value. Accurate valuation is crucial for both the acquiring and target companies, as it influences deal pricing, negotiation strategies, and overall success in achieving strategic objectives.

Several valuation methods exist, each with its strengths, limitations, and suitability for different scenarios. The choice of method often depends on the nature of the industry, the financial structure of the companies involved, and the specific goals of the M&A transaction.

Here are some key valuation methods frequently employed in the M&A landscape:

1. Comparable Company Analysis (CCA)

Comparable Company Analysis (CCA) is a valuation method that evaluates the worth of a target company by comparing it to similar publicly traded companies. This approach relies on analyzing various financial metrics, ratios, and performance indicators of comparable firms in the same industry or sector. The underlying principle is that the market's valuation of similar companies can serve as a benchmark for determining the target company's relative value. Key metrics considered in CCA include price-to-earnings (P/E) ratios, enterprise value multiples, and other relevant financial benchmarks.

Application

CCA proves effective when there is a substantial pool of comparable companies with readily available financial data in the public domain. The method is particularly advantageous in industries where multiple companies share comparable characteristics, allowing for meaningful comparisons. CCA provides a market-driven perspective on valuation, leveraging the collective wisdom of investors and market participants. This approach assumes that companies with similar risk profiles, growth prospects, and operational metrics should command similar valuations in the market.

To conduct a CCA, analysts typically identify a group of comparable companies, known as a peer group or set, that share similarities with the target company. Parameters for selection may include industry, size, growth trajectory, and business model. The financial metrics of the target company are then benchmarked against those of the selected peers. This comparative analysis helps in determining whether the target company is overvalued or undervalued relative to its industry counterparts.

An important aspect of CCA is the consideration of multiples, which are ratios derived from the market value or enterprise value of a comparable company divided by a financial metric such as earnings, revenue, or book value. These multiples provide a quantitative basis for assessing the target company's valuation. For example, if the average P/E ratio of the peer group is higher than that of the target company, it may indicate that the market values the target company less favorably.

While CCA offers valuable insights into market sentiment and comparable valuations, it is essential to recognize its limitations. Market dynamics, investor perceptions, and short-term fluctuations can influence stock prices and, consequently, the multiples used in the analysis. Additionally, the method assumes that the selected peers accurately reflect the target company's operational and financial characteristics.

Comparable Company Analysis is a powerful tool in the valuation toolkit, providing a market-driven perspective that aligns with investor sentiments. It offers a comprehensive view of a company's relative value within its industry context, aiding decision-makers in M&A transactions, investment assessments, and strategic planning. However, like any valuation method, CCA should be applied judiciously, considering its assumptions and potential limitations in capturing the full complexity of a company's unique attributes and market dynamics.

2. **Comparable Transaction Analysis (CTA)**:

Comparable Transaction Analysis (CTA) stands as a robust and insightful method in the arsenal of valuation techniques used in the context of mergers and acquisitions (M&A). Its fundamental premise revolves around assessing the value of a target company by drawing parallels with the prices paid for similar entities in recent M&A transactions. This approach goes beyond merely looking at financial ratios; it delves into the transaction-specific details, including deal multiples, transaction structures, and the broader strategic context surrounding those transactions.

The application of CTA becomes particularly valuable when confronted with a scenario where there is a limited number of comparable public companies. In industries or sectors where publicly available financial data is scarce, relying solely on Comparable Company Analysis (CCA) might be challenging. CTA, in such instances, steps in as a practical alternative. It essentially offers a lens into understanding how the market values entities that share similarities in terms of industry, size, and business characteristics, especially in the context of M&A transactions.

The process of conducting a Comparable Transaction Analysis involves meticulous examination of recent transactions in the relevant market or industry. Analysts identify deals that share similarities with the target company in terms of size, market position, growth prospects, and other relevant factors. Once these comparable transactions are identified, the analysis considers the multiples at which those deals were executed. Deal multiples, such as the enterprise value to EBITDA ratio, are crucial metrics as they provide a measure of the company's value relative to its earnings or other financial metrics.

Furthermore, CTA takes into account the transaction structures employed in these comparable deals. Whether a transaction involved a stock purchase, asset purchase, or other structures can significantly impact the valuation and terms of the deal. Understanding these intricacies is crucial for accurately assessing the value of the target company in the context of a potential acquisition.

The strategic context surrounding the comparable transactions is another critical dimension considered in CTA. It goes beyond the numerical aspects of valuation and looks at the motivations, synergies, and strategic rationale behind each deal. For instance, if a similar company was acquired for strategic reasons, such as gaining access to a new market or complementary technology, it provides valuable insights into the strategic importance of similar targets.

In summary, Comparable Transaction Analysis serves as a dynamic and context-rich approach to valuing a target company in the realm of M&A. Its strength lies in its ability to offer nuanced insights into the transactional aspects and strategic underpinnings of comparable deals. By focusing on the real-world context of M&A transactions, CTA contributes valuable information to the decision-making process, helping acquirers make informed and strategic choices in the pursuit of growth and expansion.

3. Discounted Cash Flow (DCF) Analysis

Discounted Cash Flow (DCF) analysis is a widely used valuation method that provides a comprehensive perspective on the intrinsic value of a company. This approach revolves around assessing the present value of a company's projected future cash flows. The primary goal is to determine the fair market value of the business by discounting anticipated cash inflows and outflows to their present values. The fundamental principle behind DCF is rooted in the concept of the time value of money, acknowledging that a dollar today is worth more than a dollar in the future.

To execute a DCF analysis, the first step involves forecasting the free cash flows the company is expected to generate over a specified period. These cash flows encompass the funds available to the company after covering operational expenses and capital expenditures. The forecast period usually extends into the future, capturing a horizon that aligns with the strategic goals and industry dynamics.

Once the cash flows are projected, the next critical element is the application of a discount rate. This rate serves to reflect the opportunity cost of investing in the business and considers the risk associated with future cash flows. A higher risk profile typically warrants a higher discount rate. Commonly, the Weighted Average Cost of Capital (WACC) is used as the discount rate, incorporating the cost of equity and debt in proportion to their contribution to the capital structure.

Following the determination of the discount rate, the forecasted cash flows are discounted back to their present value. The summation of these present values results in the Net Present Value (NPV), representing the intrinsic value of the company. If the NPV is positive, it suggests that the company's projected cash flows exceed the cost of capital, indicating a potentially sound investment. Conversely, a negative NPV may signal a less favorable investment opportunity.

Application

DCF is particularly valuable when assessing companies with predictable cash flow patterns and stable growth trajectories. This method is commonly employed in industries where future cash flows are a crucial indicator of value, such as technology, manufacturing, and service-oriented sectors. Additionally, DCF is well-suited for companies operating in dynamic environments where their strategic decisions significantly impact future performance.

While DCF offers a robust approach to valuation, it comes with its challenges. Forecasts are inherently uncertain, and small changes in assumptions can yield substantial variations in outcomes. Sensitivity analysis, scenario planning, and a meticulous examination of key assumptions are crucial steps in mitigating the risks associated with DCF analysis.

DCF analysis is a powerful tool for estimating the intrinsic value of a company by evaluating its future cash flows in the context of the time value of money. The application of DCF requires a careful examination of the company's financials, industry dynamics, and a thoughtful consideration of risk factors. When executed diligently, DCF provides a comprehensive and nuanced perspective that aids in strategic decision-making during mergers, acquisitions, and other significant financial transactions.

4. Asset-Based Valuation

Asset-Based Valuation stands as a robust method for determining a company's worth by examining its net asset value. This valuation approach takes into account tangible assets, encompassing real estate, equipment, and inventory, and subtracts liabilities. Unlike other methods that predominantly focus on future earnings or market comparables, asset-based valuation provides a snapshot of a company's intrinsic value based on its tangible resources and financial obligations. This makes it particularly relevant for industries where the book value of assets significantly contributes to overall value, such as manufacturing or real estate.

Application

In industries characterized by substantial tangible assets, the Asset-Based Valuation method shines in capturing the essence of a company's value. Manufacturing companies, for instance, often possess considerable machinery, inventory, and property. Asset-based valuation is instrumental in providing a clear understanding of the company's net worth based on these tangible resources. Similarly, real estate firms, where property holdings form a substantial portion of their value, find asset-based valuation particularly pertinent. This method's application extends beyond these industries to any business where a significant portion of its value is tied to tangible assets.

Benefits and Considerations

The asset-based approach offers several benefits. Firstly, it provides a straightforward and tangible measure of a company's worth, making it accessible and easily understandable. For industries where the value lies in physical assets rather than intangibles like brand reputation or intellectual property, asset-based valuation offers a practical lens for assessment. It also serves as a useful method when companies are undergoing liquidation or facing financial distress, as it helps determine the residual value of assets.

However, it's essential to acknowledge certain considerations when employing this method. Asset-based valuation might undervalue companies with substantial intangible assets, such as technology or service-oriented firms, where intellectual property and brand recognition play a significant role in overall value. Additionally, the method assumes that the recorded book value of assets reflects their fair market value, which might not always be the case, especially if assets have appreciated over time.

Implementation

Implementing asset-based valuation involves a detailed examination of a company's balance sheet. Tangible assets like property, equipment, and inventory are identified, and their book values are recorded. Liabilities, including debts and obligations, are then subtracted from the total value of these assets to arrive at the net asset value. This approach can be complemented by considering the fair market value of assets, especially if there are indications that book values might not accurately reflect their current worth.

Asset-Based Valuation provides a grounded and tangible perspective on a company's worth, particularly in industries where tangible assets significantly contribute to value. As one of the multiple methods available for valuing companies, it offers a distinctive lens that complements other approaches, providing a more comprehensive understanding during mergers and acquisitions, financial transactions, or strategic decision-making.

5. Depreciation, and Amortization (EBITDA) Multiple

EBITDA (Earnings Before Interest, Taxes, Depreciation, and Amortization) multiples represent a key valuation method utilized in mergers and acquisitions (M&A). EBITDA is a financial metric that offers insights into a company's operational performance by excluding non-operating expenses, providing a clearer picture of its core profitability. The EBITDA multiple involves applying a factor to a company's EBITDA to determine its overall value. This multiple is particularly valuable because it focuses on the operating aspects of a business, excluding certain financial elements that might obscure its fundamental profitability.

The formula for calculating the EBITDA multiple is straightforward. It involves dividing the enterprise value (EV) by the EBITDA. The resulting multiple indicates how many times the EBITDA a buyer is willing to pay for the acquisition. This method helps in standardizing the valuation process, especially when comparing companies of different sizes, capital structures, or tax situations.

Application

EBITDA multiples find widespread application across various industries, and their popularity is especially notable in sectors such as technology, healthcare, and service-oriented businesses.

The rationale behind this broad usage lies in the suitability of EBITDA for assessing the operational performance and profitability of companies, particularly those in high-growth or capital-intensive industries.

Technology Industry

In the technology sector, where companies often focus on innovation and rapid growth, EBITDA multiples offer a useful metric for valuation. Investors and acquirers may prioritize EBITDA over net income as a measure of a tech company's financial health. This is because technology firms may incur significant depreciation and amortization charges related to intellectual property and research and development, which can distort traditional earnings metrics.

Healthcare Sector

In healthcare, where capital expenditures and amortization of intangible assets are common, EBITDA multiples provide a clearer picture of a company's core profitability. Pharmaceutical companies, for example, might have substantial amortization related to drug development. By utilizing EBITDA multiples, potential acquirers can focus on the operational aspects of these businesses without being overly influenced by non-operating expenses.

Service-Oriented Businesses

Service-oriented industries, such as consulting or professional services, often prioritize EBITDA multiples in valuation. These companies typically have lower capital expenditures and depreciation, making EBITDA a more meaningful measure of their operational success. Moreover, the EBITDA multiple simplifies comparisons between companies in this sector, helping investors and buyers assess their relative value.

Considerations

While EBITDA multiples offer valuable insights, it's essential to recognize their limitations. Critics argue that relying solely on EBITDA multiples can overlook important aspects of a company's financial health, such as capital expenditures and changes in working capital. Therefore, it is often recommended to use EBITDA multiples in conjunction with other valuation methods to form a comprehensive understanding of a company's value.

The EBITDA multiple stands as a versatile and widely employed valuation approach in the M&A landscape. Its application across diverse industries attests to its effectiveness in capturing the core operational performance of companies, making it a valuable metric in negotiations and strategic decision-making during mergers and acquisitions.

Choosing the appropriate valuation method or a combination of methods requires a deep understanding of the target company, the industry landscape, and the specific goals of the M&A transaction. In many cases, a comprehensive approach that incorporates multiple valuation methods provides a more holistic view of a company's worth, aiding in informed decision-making during negotiations and due diligence.

Negotiation Tactics

Negotiation is a pivotal aspect of the mergers and acquisitions (M&A) process, influencing the terms, conditions, and overall success of the deal. Mastering negotiation tactics is essential for aligning interests, resolving differences, and ultimately creating a mutually beneficial agreement. Here, we explore key negotiation strategies, from fostering open communication to addressing potential challenges, with the aim of guiding M&A professionals through the intricate process of deal-making.

1. Building Strong Relationships

In the realm of mergers and acquisitions (M&A), the ability to cultivate strong relationships is a foundational element that significantly influences the trajectory of deal-making. Successful M&A negotiations go beyond the exchange of terms and conditions; they hinge on the establishment of robust relationships with key stakeholders.

Establishing strong relationships begins with a deep understanding of the motivations driving each party involved. Stakeholders enter negotiations with diverse interests, whether financial, strategic, or cultural. By investing time in comprehending these motivations, negotiators can tailor their approaches to align with the underlying drivers, fostering a more collaborative and mutually beneficial negotiation environment.

Trust is the bedrock of successful negotiations. Cultivating trust involves consistent and transparent communication, demonstrating integrity, and delivering on commitments. Trust-building extends beyond the negotiation table and encompasses various interactions, from formal meetings to informal engagements. A reputation for reliability and honesty enhances the level of trust among negotiating parties, creating an atmosphere where genuine collaboration can flourish.

Successful deal-making is not solely about adversaries reaching an agreement; it's about partners aligning their interests for shared success. Building strong relationships involves creating an environment that reflects a sense of partnership rather than opposition. This shift in perspective sets the tone for collaborative problem-solving, where parties work together to overcome challenges and optimize the value of the impending deal.

The scope of relationship-building extends beyond the negotiation table. Informal settings, such as social events or team-building activities, provide valuable opportunities for stakeholders to interact on a personal level. These moments foster a more profound understanding of individuals, their values, and the dynamics that shape their decision-making. Building rapport beyond the confines of formal negotiations contributes to a richer and more nuanced relationship landscape.

In an increasingly globalized business landscape, M&A negotiations often involve entities with diverse cultural backgrounds. Understanding and respecting cultural nuances is an integral aspect of relationship-building. Sensitivity to cultural differences, whether in communication styles or business etiquettes, demonstrates a commitment to fostering an inclusive and respectful negotiation environment.

Tensions and conflicts can arise during negotiations, and how they are handled influences the strength of relationships. Skilled negotiators understand the importance of addressing tensions constructively. Open communication, active listening, and a collaborative mindset are tools that can be employed to mitigate tensions, fostering an environment where relationships can weather challenges and continue to thrive.

Building strong relationships in M&A negotiations is an investment that pays dividends throughout the deal-making process and beyond. Stakeholders who engage in genuine relationship-building lay the groundwork for collaborative decision-making, effective problem-solving, and successful long-term partnerships. As negotiations unfold, the relationships established early on become the bedrock upon which the success of the M&A deal is built.

2. Clearly Defined Objectives:

Effective negotiation in the realm of mergers and acquisitions (M&A) demands a fundamental prerequisite: clearly defined objectives. Clarity regarding objectives serves as the compass guiding negotiators through the intricate terrain of deal-making. Both parties engaged in negotiations must articulate their goals, priorities, and non-negotiable red lines. This process establishes a shared understanding of each party's expectations, fostering an environment of transparency and collaboration.

Transparent communication regarding objectives is pivotal in minimizing misunderstandings that could impede the negotiation process. When each party is explicit about its aspirations and limitations, negotiators can navigate discussions with a clear understanding of the parameters within which they operate. This level of clarity sets the stage for collaborative problem-solving, where parties work together to find creative solutions that address the needs and priorities of all involved.

Clearly defined objectives operate as a roadmap during negotiations, offering a structured path toward mutually beneficial outcomes. This roadmap helps negotiators remain focused on key priorities and avoid veering off course. In the dynamic landscape of M&A negotiations, where various interests intersect, having a clear roadmap becomes especially crucial in steering discussions toward resolutions that align with the overarching goals of both parties.

The articulation of objectives serves not only as a communication tool but also as a foundation for building trust. When negotiators are forthright about their goals, it fosters an atmosphere of honesty and integrity. This transparency contributes to the development of a more open and collaborative negotiation environment, where trust becomes a guiding force.

Negotiators should consider objectives not only as static endpoints but as dynamic elements that can evolve during the negotiation process. As discussions unfold and new information surfaces, the ability to adapt and refine objectives becomes essential. Negotiators should remain agile, ready to adjust their goals based on emerging insights and changing circumstances, ensuring that the negotiation remains responsive to the evolving needs of both parties.

In summary, clearly defined objectives in M&A negotiations are foundational to the success of the deal-making process. They provide a shared understanding, minimize misunderstandings, and act as a roadmap for negotiators. This clarity not only facilitates effective collaboration but also contributes to the establishment of trust, fostering an environment conducive to successful negotiations and, ultimately, a mutually beneficial outcome.

3. Flexibility and Adaptability

Negotiation is dynamic, and unforeseen challenges often arise. Maintaining flexibility and adaptability is crucial for navigating unexpected turns and finding creative solutions.

The dynamic nature of negotiations means that unforeseen challenges are virtually inevitable. In this context, negotiators must embody a mindset of flexibility, allowing them to navigate unexpected turns and devise creative solutions in response to evolving circumstances.

The fluidity of negotiation scenarios demands an agile approach. Rigidity, often counterproductive, can act as a barrier to progress. Negotiators who cling to fixed strategies may find themselves ill-equipped to deal with the twists and turns inherent in the M&A landscape. On the other hand, those who embrace flexibility can adjust their tactics in real-time, effectively responding to challenges and capitalizing on emerging opportunities.

Maintaining flexibility encompasses a willingness to reassess and adapt strategies based on the evolving dynamics of the negotiation process. This adaptability is particularly crucial when faced with unexpected hurdles or when new information surfaces. Instead of adhering rigidly to preconceived plans, negotiators should be ready to pivot and explore alternative pathways that better align with the shifting landscape of the negotiation table.

The ability to adapt is not synonymous with compromise; rather, it's a strategic maneuver to navigate complexities while staying true to overarching objectives. A flexible negotiator can explore innovative solutions, adjusting the course without sacrificing the core goals of the negotiation. This nuanced approach allows negotiators to overcome challenges creatively and enhance the likelihood of arriving at a mutually satisfying agreement.

In essence, flexibility and adaptability act as the dynamic undercurrents that propel successful negotiations forward. They empower negotiators to respond effectively to unforeseen challenges, seize opportunities, and maintain momentum. In the unpredictable terrain of M&A negotiations, where variables are in constant flux, negotiators who embody flexibility not only weather uncertainties but also position themselves to steer the negotiation towards a successful and mutually beneficial outcome.

4. Effective Communication

Clear communication begins with the articulate expression of each party's positions, concerns, and expectations. Precision in conveying these elements is paramount, as it establishes a shared understanding and serves as the foundation for constructive dialogue. The art of effective communication, therefore, involves not just expressing one's stance but doing so with clarity and precision, leaving minimal room for interpretation.

Equally significant in the communication process is the practice of active listening. Negotiators must go beyond the surface of statements to comprehend the nuanced perspectives embedded in their counterparts' words. Active listening not only captures the explicit content of the communication but also grasps the subtle undertones, allowing negotiators to gain insight into the motivations and priorities of the other party.

Transparency, a direct outcome of effective communication, plays a crucial role in mitigating ambiguity. By laying bare the intentions, expectations, and concerns of each party, negotiators create a more predictable environment. This transparency, in turn, cultivates an atmosphere of collaboration, where both parties feel informed and engaged in the negotiation process.

In the context of M&A negotiations, where intricate details and potential complexities abound, effective communication becomes a linchpin. The stakes are high, and misinterpretations can lead to misunderstandings that may have significant consequences. Thus, a commitment to clear and open communication serves not only to convey information but also to build a bridge of understanding between negotiating parties.

Beyond its functional aspects, effective communication fosters a cooperative atmosphere. When negotiators communicate openly and transparently, it encourages a sense of collaboration rather than contention. This collaborative spirit lays the groundwork for finding common ground and working towards solutions that accommodate the interests of all involved parties.

Effective communication is not merely a tool in negotiations; it is the medium through which negotiations unfold. It is the conduit through which ideas, concerns, and expectations traverse, and when navigated skillfully, it paves the way for negotiations to progress smoothly towards mutually agreeable outcomes.

5. Win-Win Solutions

The essence of a win-win approach lies in the pursuit of outcomes where both negotiating entities perceive substantial value and benefits. While the negotiation process often involves compromises, the overarching focus remains on identifying solutions that not only address the needs and interests of each party but also harness the combined strengths of the entities involved.

In the context of M&A negotiations, where the complexity and multifaceted nature of the deal demand careful consideration, the win-win principle becomes a guiding beacon. Rather than viewing negotiation as a zero-sum game, where one party's gain is offset by another's loss, the emphasis is on crafting agreements that elevate the overall value proposition.

Compromises are inevitable in any negotiation, and the win-win approach acknowledges this reality. However, it reframes the concept of compromise from a concession to a strategic move aimed at optimizing the collective advantages that both parties bring to the table. This shift in perspective transforms negotiations into collaborative endeavors rather than adversarial contests.

A win-win strategy extends beyond the negotiation table, influencing the post-deal landscape. By prioritizing solutions that genuinely meet the needs of both parties, negotiators lay the foundation for enduring partnerships and positive relationships after the deal is finalized. This forward-looking approach recognizes that the success of a negotiation is not solely measured by the signed agreement but also by the sustainability and synergy it fosters in the aftermath.

The win-win principle aligns with the ethos of strategic collaboration—a cornerstone of successful M&A endeavors. It encourages negotiators to think beyond immediate gains and consider the long-term implications of the deal. This perspective, rooted in mutual benefit, not only fosters goodwill but also contributes to the establishment of partnerships built on trust and shared success.

The pursuit of win-win solutions in M&A negotiations is not just a strategy; it is a mindset that shapes the trajectory of the deal and its aftermath. By prioritizing outcomes where both parties emerge as winners, negotiators elevate the discourse from a transactional exchange to a collaborative journey toward mutual success.

6. Thorough Due Diligence

At the heart of thorough due diligence is the commitment to acquiring comprehensive knowledge about the target company. This encompasses a deep dive into various facets, including the financial, legal, and operational dimensions. The objective is to unearth critical insights that go beyond surface-level evaluations, providing negotiators with a nuanced understanding of the target's strengths, weaknesses, opportunities, and potential risks.

Financial due diligence, a key component of the process, involves meticulous scrutiny of the target company's financial health. This includes a detailed analysis of financial statements, cash flow projections, and an assessment of any existing or potential financial liabilities. By gaining a clear understanding of the target's financial landscape, negotiators are equipped to navigate discussions related to valuation, funding, and financial structuring with precision.

Legal due diligence is equally pivotal, aiming to uncover any legal obligations, pending litigations, or regulatory challenges associated with the target. This information is crucial for evaluating potential legal risks and liabilities, enabling negotiators to factor these considerations into the overall deal structure and terms.

Operational due diligence rounds out the triad, focusing on the day-to-day functioning of the target company. This involves an examination of operational processes, supply chain dynamics, and the identification of any operational bottlenecks. Armed with insights into the operational intricacies of the target, negotiators can anticipate challenges that may impact post-merger integration, ensuring a smoother transition.

The knowledge amassed through thorough due diligence becomes a strategic asset during negotiations. It not only bolsters negotiators' understanding of the target's current state but also positions them to anticipate potential challenges and opportunities. This proactive approach transforms negotiations from reactive exchanges to informed decision-making processes.

Moreover, the insights garnered from thorough due diligence empower negotiators to negotiate from a position of strength. Armed with a comprehensive understanding of the target's intricacies, negotiators can assertively address issues, propose well-informed solutions, and navigate the negotiation landscape with a heightened level of confidence.

In the context of M&A, where uncertainty and complexity abound, thorough due diligence serves as a compass, guiding negotiators through uncharted territories. It aligns with the ethos of strategic preparation, ensuring that negotiators are well-equipped to make decisions that align with the broader objectives of the deal.

Thorough due diligence emerges not only as a negotiation tactic but as a strategic imperative. It is the linchpin that transforms negotiations from speculative endeavors into well-informed, proactive processes. By investing in a meticulous examination of the target company, negotiators pave the way for negotiations that are grounded in knowledge, foresight, and strategic acumen.

7. Contingency Planning

At its core, contingency planning involves a forward-looking assessment of potential hurdles that may arise during negotiations. This strategic foresight is instrumental in preventing negotiations from faltering when confronted with unexpected obstacles. By identifying these challenges in advance, negotiators can proactively devise alternative solutions, ensuring that the negotiation process maintains momentum even in the face of adversity.

The proactive nature of contingency planning aligns seamlessly with the dynamic and uncertain nature of M&A transactions. These strategic endeavors involve a myriad of variables, from regulatory considerations to cultural integration challenges. Contingency planning acknowledges the inherent unpredictability of such complex negotiations and positions negotiators to respond effectively to various scenarios.

One key aspect of contingency planning is the identification of potential roadblocks. This encompasses a thorough analysis of conceivable challenges, ranging from legal and regulatory hurdles to cultural misalignments between merging entities. Anticipating these roadblocks enables negotiators to approach the negotiation table with a heightened awareness of potential pitfalls, paving the way for agile decision-making.

The formulation of alternative solutions is another critical facet of contingency planning. Instead of being caught off guard when faced with challenges, negotiators armed with contingency plans can seamlessly pivot to alternative approaches. This agility not only prevents negotiations from stalling but also showcases negotiators' adaptability and strategic acumen.

Contingency planning serves as a tangible manifestation of negotiators' preparedness. It sends a clear signal that negotiators are not only focused on the current state of affairs but are actively considering the "what ifs" that may arise. This preparedness enhances negotiators' credibility and positions them as strategic partners capable of steering negotiations through various twists and turns.

Moreover, contingency planning contributes to maintaining a positive negotiation atmosphere. When negotiators are equipped with alternative solutions, the emphasis shifts from dwelling on challenges to collaboratively finding solutions. This constructive approach fosters a sense of partnership between the involved entities, laying the groundwork for smoother negotiations and post-deal integration.

Contingency planning is not merely a precautionary measure; it is a strategic imperative in the realm of negotiations. By anticipating potential roadblocks, formulating alternative solutions, and demonstrating proactive preparedness, negotiators enhance their ability to navigate the complexities of M&A transactions. In a landscape where adaptability is key, contingency planning stands as a beacon, guiding negotiators through the unpredictable terrain of high-stakes negotiations.

8. Emotional Intelligence

Emotional intelligence encompasses the ability to recognize, understand, and manage one's own emotions, as well as being attuned to the emotions of others. In the context of negotiations, this skill set becomes invaluable, influencing the tone, tenor, and ultimately, the outcome of the discussions.

Understanding the emotional landscape is a fundamental aspect of emotional intelligence in negotiations. Negotiators with a high level of emotional intelligence can discern not only their own emotional states but also the emotions of their counterparts. This awareness allows for a nuanced understanding of the underlying dynamics, enabling negotiators to tailor their approach to the prevailing emotional context.

Moreover, emotional intelligence equips negotiators with the capacity to manage emotions effectively. In negotiations, where stakes are high and pressures can escalate, the ability to remain composed and focused is paramount. Emotional intelligence enables negotiators to navigate sensitive issues without succumbing to emotional triggers, fostering an environment where rational decision-making prevails.

Building empathy is another cornerstone of emotional intelligence in negotiations. Empathy involves understanding and sharing the feelings of others, a skill that can significantly impact the negotiation process. Negotiators who cultivate empathy can connect with counterparts on a human level, transcending transactional interactions and creating a sense of mutual understanding.

The establishment of a cooperative atmosphere is a direct outcome of emotional intelligence. Negotiations often involve multifaceted discussions where parties may have divergent interests and priorities. Emotional intelligence allows negotiators to navigate these differences with finesse, fostering an atmosphere where collaboration is prioritized over confrontation.

Emotional intelligence is particularly crucial when addressing sensitive issues or potential conflicts during negotiations. Negotiators who possess this skill set can approach such discussions with a heightened level of tact and diplomacy, minimizing the risk of escalations and working towards mutually agreeable solutions.

Emotional intelligence stands as a linchpin in the realm of negotiations, influencing the overall dynamics and outcomes of high-stakes discussions. From understanding and managing emotions to building empathy and fostering cooperation, negotiators equipped with emotional intelligence navigate negotiations with finesse, contributing to positive interactions and successful deal-making.

9. Legal Expertise

Legal expertise within the negotiation team serves as a safeguard, providing a comprehensive understanding of the intricate legal landscape that underpins any agreement. Legal professionals bring a wealth of knowledge in interpreting and deciphering complex contractual language, ensuring that the terms and conditions are precisely articulated and leave no room for ambiguity.

One of the primary contributions of legal expertise is the identification and mitigation of potential legal risks. In the ever-evolving legal environment, negotiations may traverse a terrain fraught with intricacies and potential legal challenges. Legal professionals within the negotiation team are adept at identifying these risks, offering insights that enable negotiators to proactively address and navigate them.

Furthermore, the integration of legal expertise serves to align agreements with regulatory requirements. As businesses operate within a framework of laws and regulations, ensuring that negotiated agreements adhere to these legal parameters is paramount. Legal professionals bring a nuanced understanding of regulatory landscapes, contributing to the creation of agreements that not only meet the needs of the involved parties but also comply with the legal frameworks governing the business environment.

The strategic advantage of legal expertise extends beyond risk identification to the overall structuring of agreements. Legal professionals contribute to the formulation of contracts that are not only legally sound but also strategically aligned with the objectives of the negotiation. This integration ensures that the agreement serves the interests of both parties and stands up to scrutiny in legal contexts.

Moreover, having legal expertise in negotiations contributes to transparency and trust. Parties involved in negotiations can have confidence that the terms are legally robust, reducing the likelihood of disputes arising from unclear or contested contractual language. This transparency fosters an environment of trust, essential for building positive post-deal relationships.

Negotiation in mergers and acquisitions is an intricate dance that requires a blend of strategic thinking, effective communication, and adaptability. Successful negotiators understand that the process is not solely about reaching an agreement but also about laying the groundwork for a collaborative and fruitful post-deal relationship. By employing these negotiation tactics, M&A professionals can navigate the complexities of deal-making, fostering agreements that contribute to the long-term success of the involved entities.

Conclusion
The Global Business

In the expansive journey from a local entrepreneurial endeavor to a global force, our exploration covered crucial milestones, core principles, and strategies for success. Reflecting on this odyssey underscores the transformative power of adaptation, scalability, and a relentless commitment to innovation. As we conclude this guide on future-proofing your global enterprise, let's revisit the key insights and consider the ongoing commitment to international excellence.

Recap of the Entrepreneurial Journey

The entrepreneurial journey we embarked on began with the lone entrepreneur navigating local markets and gradually unfolded into a global enterprise navigating the complexities of a dynamic international landscape. From establishing a local presence to strategically expanding operations, the narrative unfolded chapter by chapter, revealing the evolution of strategies, mindset, and the very fabric of the organization.

Synthesis of Core Principles

Throughout the journey, we emphasized core principles that resonate across diverse industries and geographical boundaries. The interplay of these principles, including adaptability, customer-centricity, and financial fortitude, forms the bedrock of sustained success. Their integration into the business model ensures a holistic approach to navigating challenges and leveraging opportunities.

The Importance of Business Scalability and Agility

A central theme emerged: the delicate balance between scaling the business and maintaining the agility inherent in a startup. We stressed the necessity of managing growth without compromising adaptability, allowing organizations to navigate the intricate pathways of global expansion while remaining responsive to market shifts.

Lessons in Adaptability

Adaptability emerged as a linchpin for success in the dynamic global market. The ability to pivot, innovate, and embrace change positions businesses not just as survivors but as leaders in their respective industries. The lessons in adaptability extended beyond immediate challenges to the cultivation of a flexible business model that can withstand the test of time.

Maintaining a Culture of Innovation

Innovation, a recurrent theme, was not confined to a specific phase but was highlighted as a continuous imperative. Fostering a culture of innovation at all stages, from inception to global expansion, emerged as a key driver for sustainable growth. Strategies for cultivating an environment that encourages creativity were explored, emphasizing the role of leadership in nurturing innovative thinking.

Customer-Centricity as a Growth Driver

Placing the customer at the forefront of business decisions was underscored as a growth driver. Understanding evolving customer needs and expectations and aligning business strategies accordingly became a compass guiding enterprises through the intricacies of a global market.

The Evolution of Company Culture

As businesses grow, the evolution of company culture becomes both inevitable and crucial. Preserving core values during expansion emerged as a strategic imperative. Strategies were provided to ensure that the cultural fabric of the organization remains resilient even as it extends its reach globally.

Adaptive Leadership for a Multinational Entity

Leadership styles were explored in the context of a growing multinational entity. The transformational journey from entrepreneurial leadership to managing complex, large-scale operations necessitated adaptive leadership qualities. Effectiveness in this arena requires a blend of strategic vision, emotional intelligence, and the ability to inspire and guide teams across diverse cultural landscapes.

Financial Fortitude and Risk Management

Sound financial management was highlighted as the bedrock of sustaining growth. The exploration extended to understanding and approaching risks in a larger corporate context. The importance of foresight, strategic planning, and risk mitigation strategies became clear as organizations expand their global footprint.

Technology: A Tool for Efficiency and Market Edge

Harnessing technology for operational efficiency and market competitiveness was acknowledged as a strategic imperative. The impact of data-driven decision-making emerged as a game-changer, empowering organizations to stay ahead in a digitally transformed business landscape.

Strategies for Future Challenges and Opportunities

Anticipating and preparing for future challenges was woven into the fabric of our exploration. Identifying potential disruptors and applying the lessons learned from the book was discussed as a proactive approach. Navigating future opportunities was framed as an extension of the strategies employed throughout the journey, ensuring continued competitiveness and growth.

Closing Remarks

In closing, this guide serves as a compass for entrepreneurs and business leaders navigating the complexities of a global business landscape. The insights shared, strategies discussed, and principles emphasized are not static; they are adaptable and applicable to the evolving dynamics of the business world. As you venture forth, remember that your journey is unique, and the challenges you encounter are opportunities for growth. Embrace change, stay innovative, and lead with resilience. The commitment to international excellence is not just a goal; it is a continuous journey, and your ability to adapt and innovate will determine the trajectory of your global enterprise. Best of luck on your ongoing pursuit of success.